residential creations home plans

Photos (top to bottom):

Plan #582-016D-0029 (p. 347)

Plan #582-026D-0161 (p. 376)

Plan #582-055D-0046 (p. 178)

Plan #582-026D-0162 (p. 247)

COVER HOME The home featured on the cover is Plan #582-016D-0029 featured on page 347. Photo courtesy of Axelrod Home Plans, Hal Lyman; Photographer

Current Printing 5 4 3 2 1

Selecting the Perfect Home for Your Lot

Top: Home Plan #582-007D-0038, for more information see page 472.
Above: Home Plan #582-026D-0161, for more information see page 376.

Tackling narrow lots

Building a home on a narrow lot often presumes physical limitations. There are many options to choose from to overcome the setbacks.

Narrow lots are generally those that are 50 feet wide or less. A simple way of increasing living space is to choose a plan that rises up instead of spreading out. Many two-story homes are perfect for narrow lots. In addition to fitting into the space you have, two-story homes are often less expensive to build because of less foundation and roof area.

Another option is to choose a plan that is wide but not very deep and turn it to the side. This will work exceptionally well if the home has decorative windows on the side and an appealing roofline to add curb appeal.

A main challenge with narrow lots is the garage placement. Ideally, you will be able to place the garage at the rear of the home, as is done in the home pictured to the left. If the garage must be placed to the front of the home, pay close attention to the design of the doors. Consider adding an extended roofline to soften the look and offer a warmer appearance. A porch also adds to a home's inviting appeal, as in the photo at top left.

With any home plan you can extend the boundaries by creating a visual connection between the home and surrounding environment. A good landscape design will add dimension to a small area.

Narrow lots should not be seen as a problem. There are many exciting home plans to choose from. Take a look at pages 337-474 for our home plans specially designed to tackle those narrow lots.

Building beautiful scenery with a sloping lot

Available, affordable land today often means a less-than-perfect building site. Sloping lots can offer many design opportunities. These lots generally offer spectacular views that will inspire you to choose a plan that includes panoramic windows and roomy outdoor living spaces.

Sloping lots are often designed as beach houses, vacation homes or cottages. Even if you're not building on the beach, these homes look charming anywhere.

Many sloping lot homes have walk-out basements to take advantage of the space. Some provide private living quarters or exceptional entertaining spaces in the lower level. Many windows will flood this space with warm natural light.

By choosing a plan that places the garage on the high side of the slope, you will minimize foundation costs and eliminate stairs to the garage. Alternatively, you can pick a plan with a drive under garage that makes perfect use of a sloping lot such as in the home shown to the right.

Sloping lots can lend space for the most beautiful homes. Browse through our plan pages to find your perfect home.

Above: Home Plan #582-052-0031, for more information see page 189.

About this book - *Residential Creations Home Plans* is a collection of best-selling small and narrow lot style homes for family living. These plans cover a broad range of architectural styles for a wide variety of lifestyles and budgets. Each design page features floor plans, a front view of the house, interior square footage of the home, number of bedrooms, baths, garage size and foundation types. All floor plans show room and exterior dimensions.

Blueprint Ordering - Fast and easy - Your ordering is made simple by following the instructions on page 480. See page 479 for more information on which types of blueprint packages are available and how many plan sets to order.

Quick & Easy Customizing

Make Changes To Your Home Plan In 4 Steps

Here's an affordable and efficient way to make changes to your plan.

1. Select the house plan that most closely meets your needs. Purchase of a reproducible master is necessary in order to make changes to a plan.

2. Call 1-800-373-2646 or e-mail customize@hdainc.com to place your order. Tell the sales representative you're interested in customizing a plan. A $50 nonrefundable consultation fee will be charged. You will then be instructed to complete a customization checklist indicating all the changes you wish to make to your plan. You may attach sketches if necessary. <u>If you proceed with the custom changes the $50 will be credited to the total amount charged.</u>

3. FAX the completed customization checklist to our design consultant. Within 24-48* business hours you will be provided with a written cost estimate to modify your plan. Our design consultant will contact you by phone if you wish to discuss any of your changes in greater detail.

4. Once you approve the estimate, a 75% retainer fee is collected and customization work gets underway. Preliminary drawings can usually be completed within 5-10* business days. Following approval of the preliminary drawings your design changes are completed within 5-10* business days. Your remaining 25% balance due is collected prior to shipment of your completed drawings. You will be shipped five sets of revised blueprints or a reproducible master, plus a customized materials list if required.

Sample Modification Pricing Guide

The average prices specified below are provided as examples only. They refer to the most commonly requested changes, and are subject to change without notice. Prices for changes will vary or differ, from the prices below, depending on the number of modifications requested, the plan size, style, quality of original plan, format provided to us (originally drawn by hand or computer), and method of design used by the original designer. To obtain a detailed cost estimate or to get more information, please contact us.

Categories	Average Cost*
Adding or removing living space	Quote required
Adding or removing a garage	Starting at $400
Garage: Front entry to side load or vice versa	Starting at $300
Adding a screened porch	Starting at $280
Adding a bonus room in the attic	Starting at $450
Changing full basement to crawl space or vice versa	Starting at $495
Changing full basement to slab or vice versa	Starting at $495
Changing exterior building material	Starting at $200
Changing roof lines	Starting at $360
Adjusting ceiling height	Starting at $280
Adding, moving or removing an exterior opening	$65 per opening
Adding or removing a fireplace	Starting at $90
Modifying a non-bearing wall or room	$65 per room
Changing exterior walls from 2"x4" to 2"x6"	Starting at $200
Redesigning a bathroom or a kitchen	Starting at $120
Reverse plan right reading	Quote required
Adapting plans for local building code requirements	Quote required
Engineering and Architectural stamping and services	Quote required
Adjust plan for handicapped accessibility	Quote required
Interactive Illustrations (choices of exterior materials)	Quote required
Metric conversion of home plan	Starting at $400

*Prices and Terms are subject to change without notice.

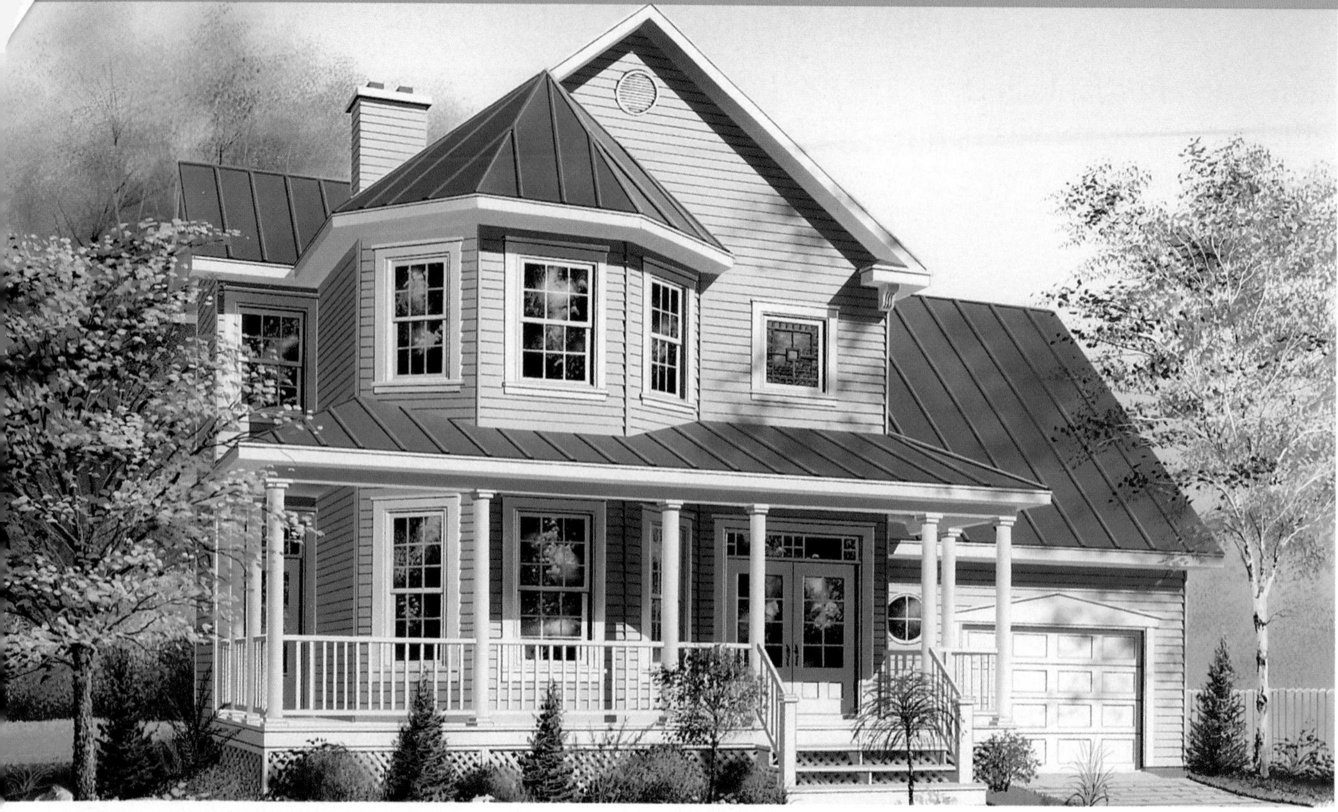

Plan #582-032D-0022

Price Code B

Special Features • 1,760 total square feet of living area • Second floor master bedroom is large enough for a sitting area and features a luxury bath • 9' ceilings on first floor • Energy efficient home with 2" x 6" exterior walls • Bonus room on the second floor has an additional 256 square feet of living area • 3 bedrooms, 2 1/2 baths, 1-car garage • Basement foundation

Second Floor
880 sq. ft.

First Floor
880 sq. ft.

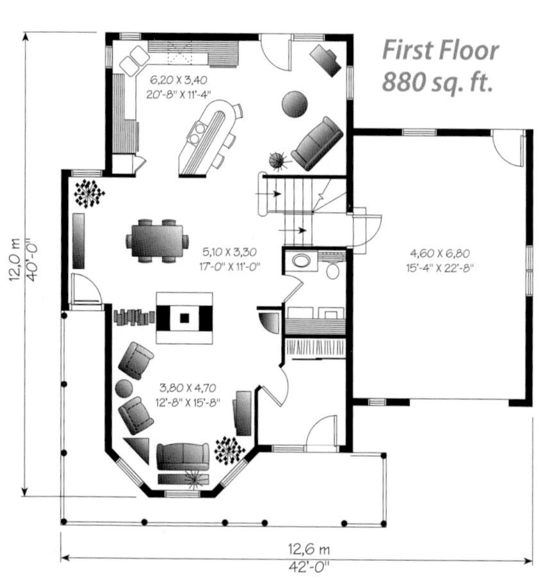

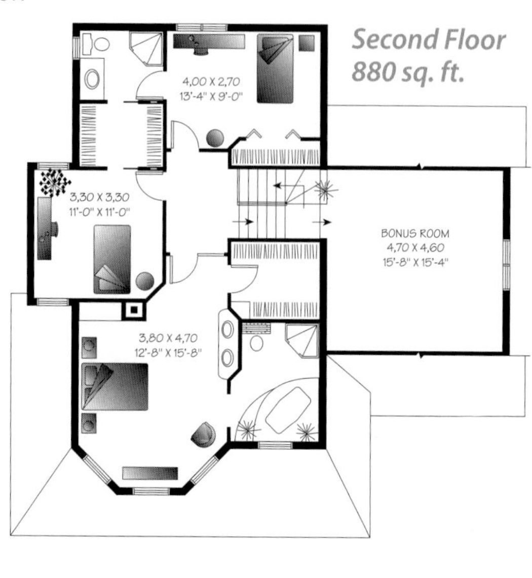

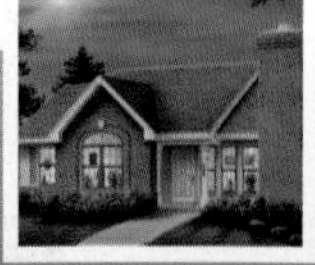

Vaulted Ceilings And Light Add Dimension

Plan #582-003D-0002

Price Code B

Special Features • 1,676 total square feet of living area • The living area skylights and large breakfast room with bay window provide plenty of sunlight • The master bedroom has a walk-in closet and both the secondary bedrooms have large closets • Vaulted ceilings, plant shelving and a fireplace provide a quality living area • 3 bedrooms, 2 baths, 2-car garage • Basement foundation, drawings also include crawl space and slab foundations

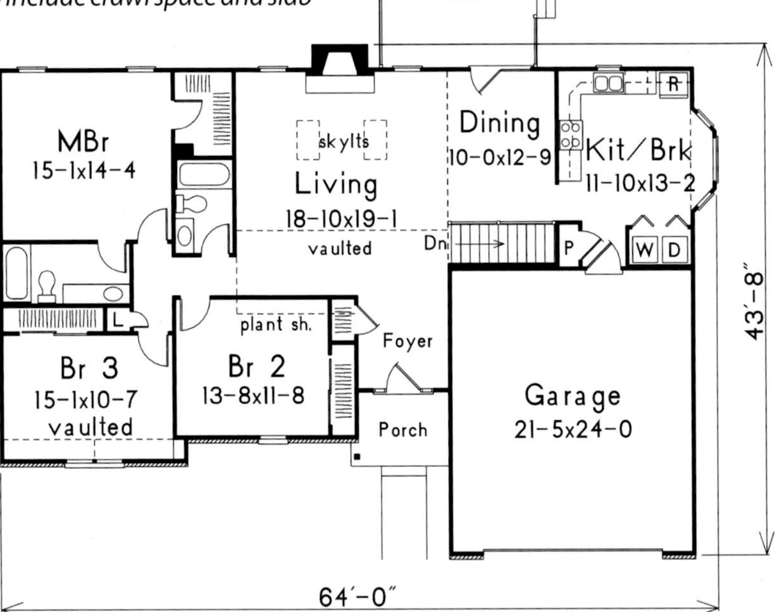

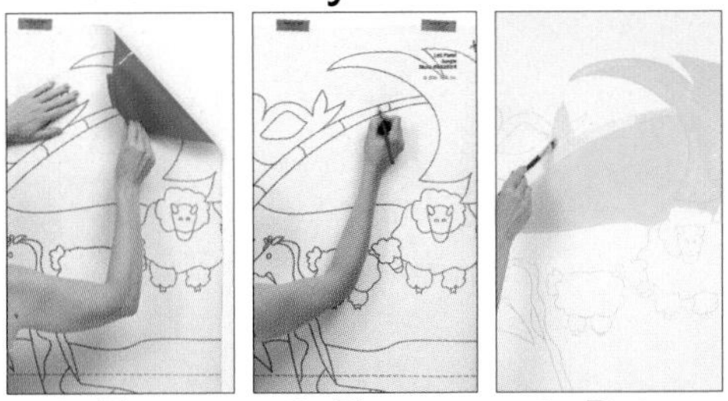

Plan #582-011D-0004

Price Code D

Special Features • 1,997 total square feet of living area • Corner fireplace warms the vaulted family room located near the kitchen • A spa tub and shower enhance the master bath • Plenty of closet space throughout • 4 bedrooms, 2 1/2 baths, 3-car garage • Crawl space foundation

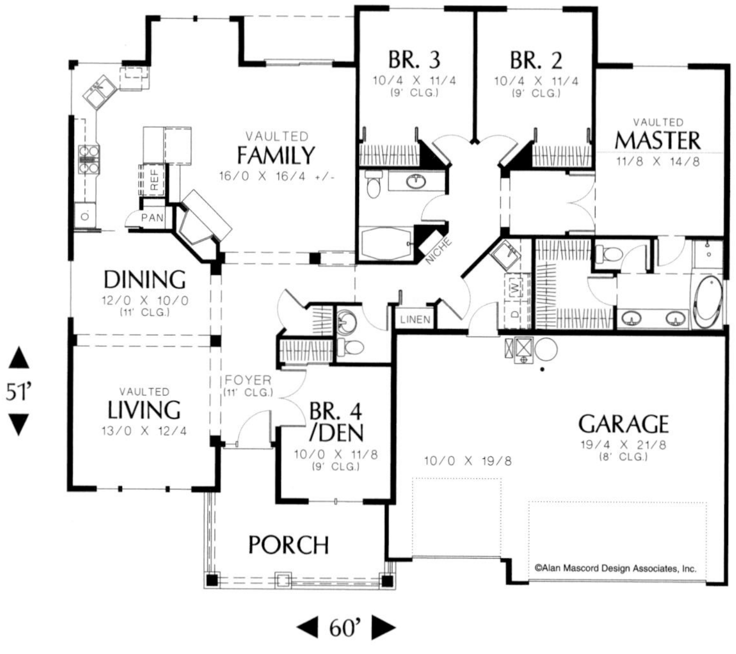

1-800-DREAM HOME (373-2646)

Great Room Window Adds Character Inside And Out

Plan #582-022D-0018

Price Code A

Special Features • 1,368 total square feet of living area • Entry foyer steps down to open living area which combines great room and formal dining area • Vaulted master bedroom includes a box-bay window, large vanity, separate tub and shower • Cozy breakfast area features direct access to the patio and pass-through kitchen • Handy linen closet is located in the hall • 3 bedrooms, 2 baths, 2-car garage • Basement foundation

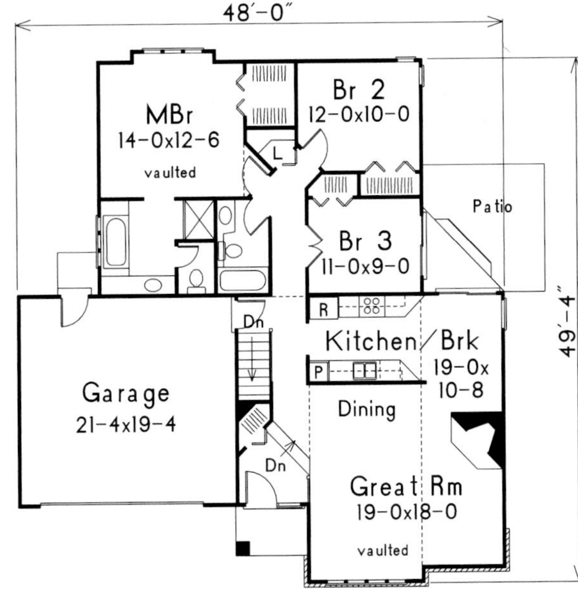

www.houseplansandmore.com

Cozy Front Porch Welcomes Guests

Plan #582-040D-0026

Price Code B

Special Features • *1,393 total square feet of living area* • *L-shaped kitchen features walk-in pantry, island cooktop and is convenient to the laundry room and dining area* • *Master bedroom features a large walk-in closet and private bath* • *Convenient storage/coat closet in hall* • *View to the patio from the dining area* • *3 bedrooms, 2 baths, 2-car detached garage* • *Crawl space foundation, drawings also include slab foundation*

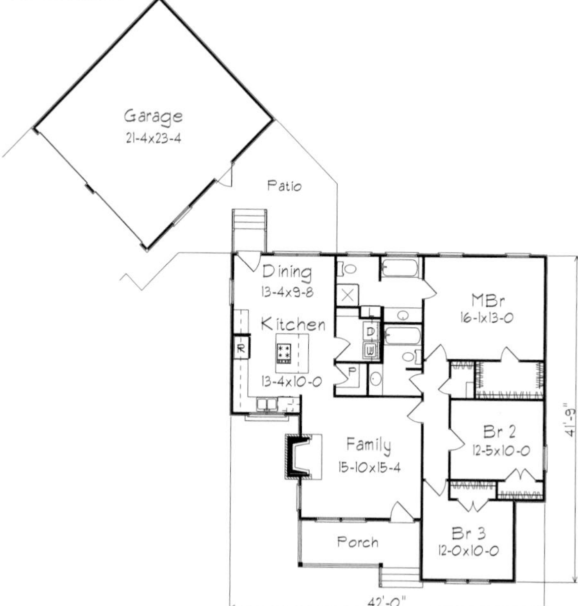

1-800-DREAM HOME (373-2646)

Brick And Siding Enhance This Traditional Home

Plan #582-010D-0006 — Price Code AA

Special Features • 1,170 total square feet of living area • Master bedroom enjoys privacy at the rear of this home • Kitchen has an angled bar that overlooks great room and breakfast area • Living areas combine to create a greater sense of spaciousness • Great room has a cozy fireplace • 3 bedrooms, 2 baths, 2-car garage • Slab foundation

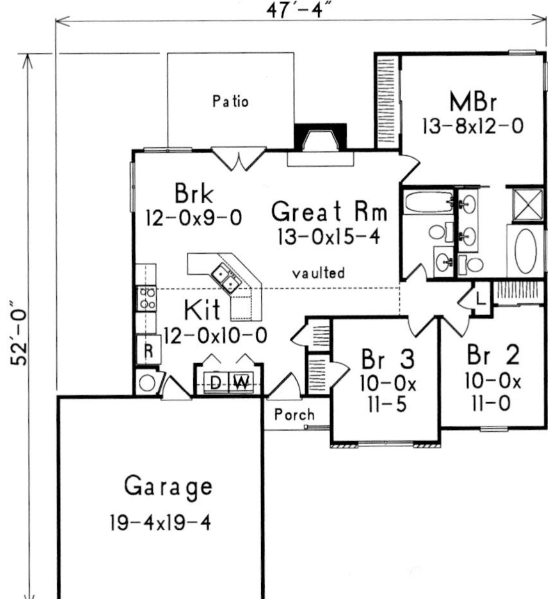

Organized Kitchen, Center Of Activity

Plan #582-007D-0017

Price Code C

Special Features • 1,882 total square feet of living area • Handsome brick facade • Spacious great room and dining room combination is brightened by unique corner windows and patio access • Well-designed kitchen incorporates breakfast bar peninsula, sweeping casement window above sink and walk-in pantry island • Master bedroom features large walk-in closet and private bath with bay window • 4 bedrooms, 2 baths, 2-car side entry garage • Basement foundation

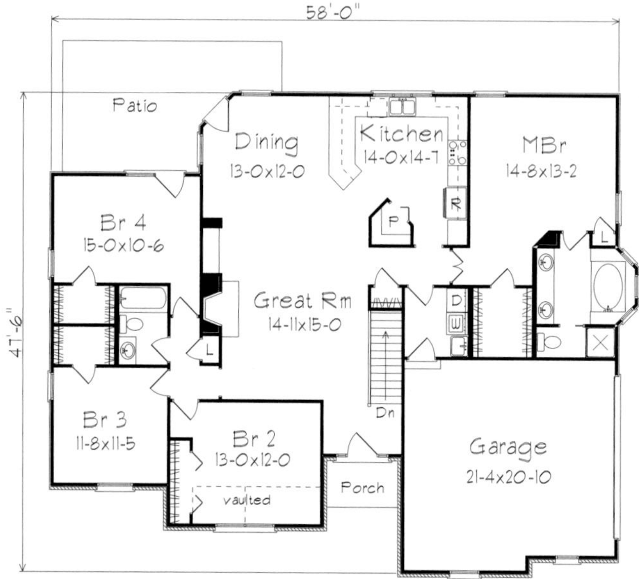

Country-Style Porch Adds Charm

Plan #582-029D-0002

Price Code B

Special Features • 1,619 total square feet of living area • Private second floor bedroom and bath • Kitchen features a snack bar and adjacent dining area • Master bedroom has a private bath • Centrally located washer and dryer • 3 bedrooms, 3 baths • Basement foundation, drawings also include crawl space and slab foundations

First Floor
1,259 sq. ft.

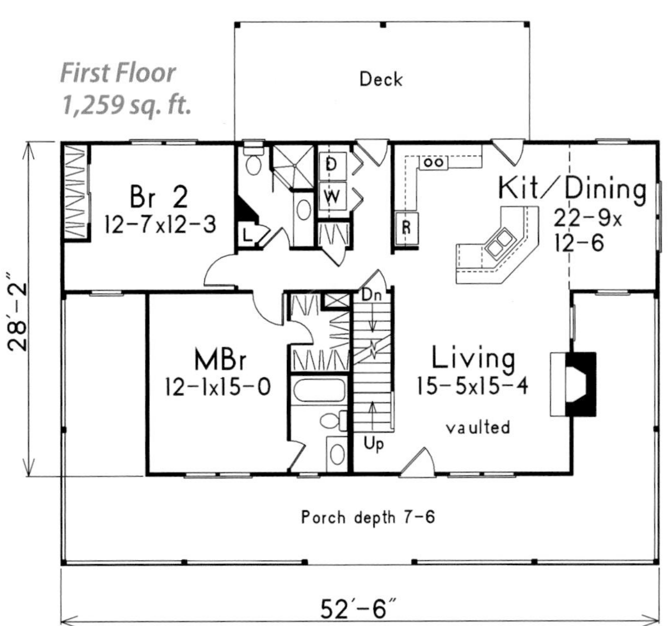

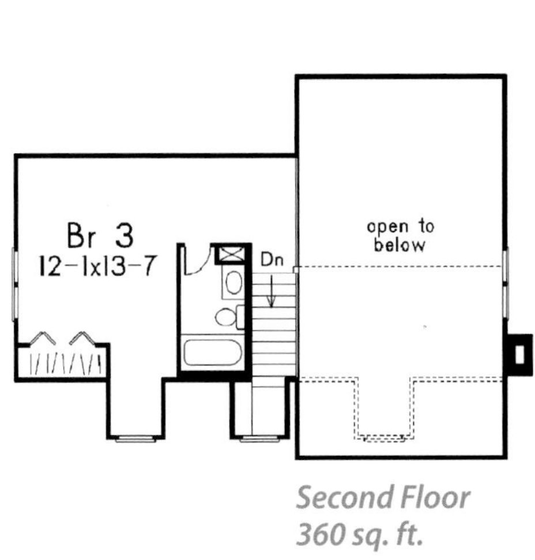

Second Floor
360 sq. ft.

Pillared Front Porch Generates Charm And Warmth

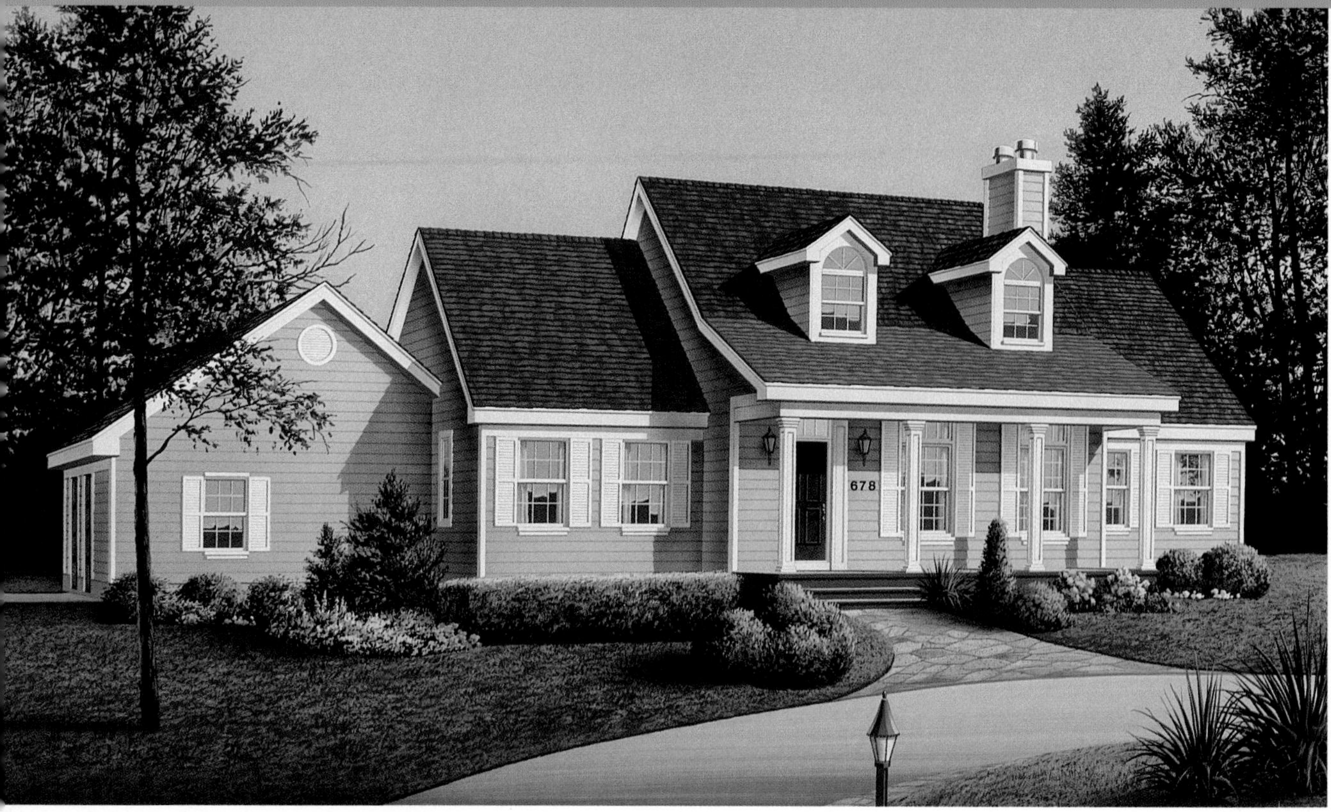

Plan #582-017D-0007

Price Code C

Special Features • 1,567 total square feet of living area • Living room flows into dining room shaped by an angled pass-through into the kitchen • Cheerful, windowed dining area • Future area available on the second floor has an additional 338 square feet of living area • Master bedroom is separated from other bedrooms for privacy • 3 bedrooms, 2 baths, 2-car side entry garage • Basement foundation, drawings also include slab foundation

First Floor
1,567 sq. ft.

Optional Second Floor

1-800-DREAM HOME (373-2646)

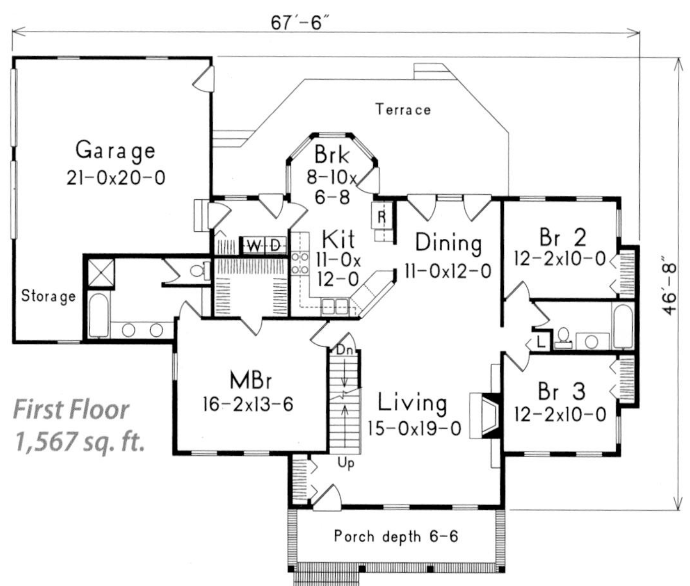

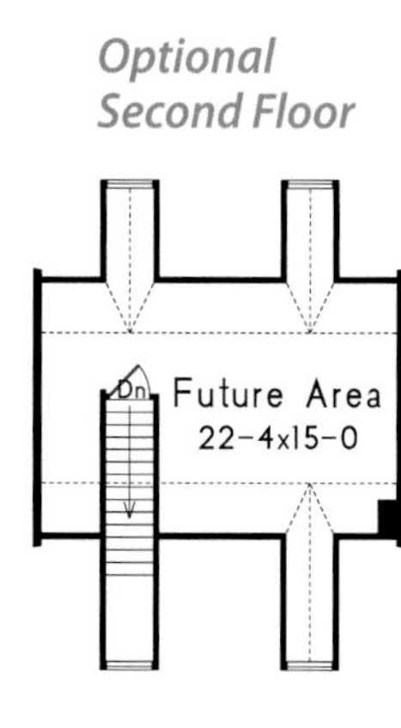

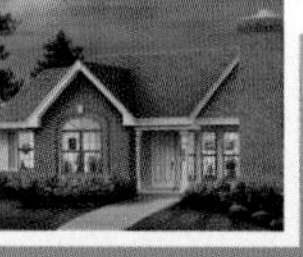

Plan #582-052D-0002

Price Code A

Special Features • *1,208 total square feet of living area* • *Master bath is graced with an oversized tub, plant shelf and double vanity* • *A U-shaped kitchen promotes organization while easily accessing the dining area* • *Hall bath includes a laundry closet for convenience* • *3 bedrooms, 2 baths, 2-car drive under garage* • *Basement foundation*

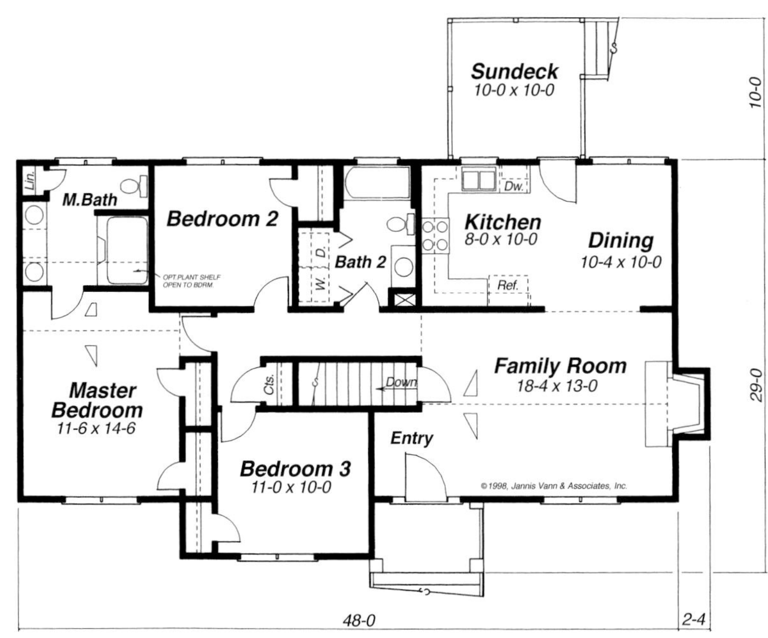

Country Colonial Feel To This Home

Plan #582-028D-0002

Price Code A

Special Features • *1,377 total square feet of living area* • *Master bedroom has double-door access onto screened porch* • *Cozy dining area is adjacent to kitchen for convenience* • *Great room includes fireplace* • *Optional second floor has an additional 349 square feet of living area* • *3 bedrooms, 1 bath* • *Crawl space or slab foundation, please specify when ordering*

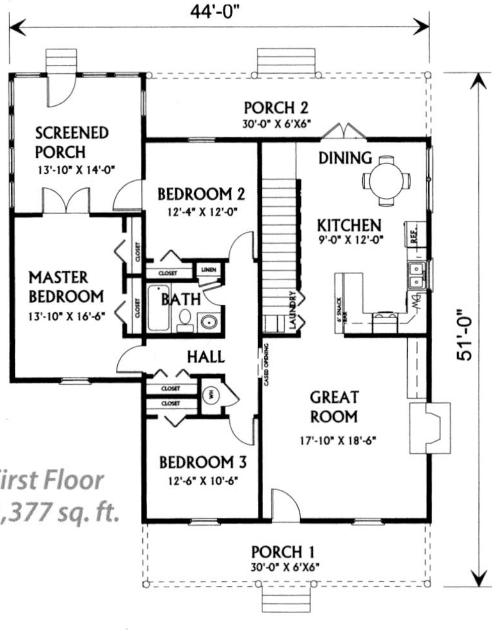

44'-0"

PORCH 2
30'-0" X 6'X6"

SCREENED PORCH
13'-10" X 14'-0"

DINING

BEDROOM 2
12'-4" X 12'-0"

KITCHEN
9'-0" X 12'-0"

MASTER BEDROOM
13'-10" X 16'-6"

BATH

HALL

GREAT ROOM
17'-10" X 18'-6"

BEDROOM 3
12'-6" X 10'-6"

PORCH 1
30'-0" X 6'X6"

51'-0"

First Floor
1,377 sq. ft.

Optional Second Floor

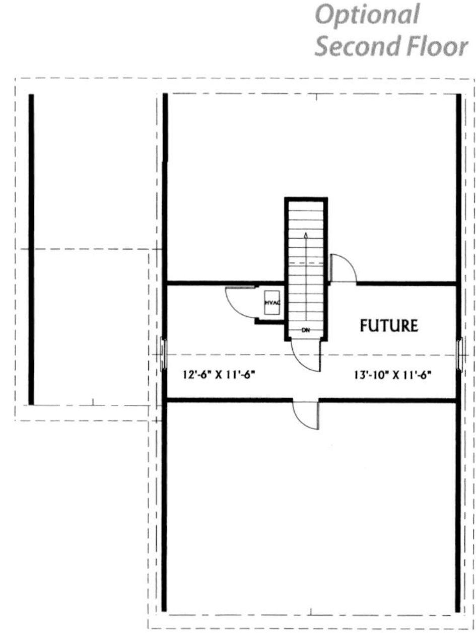

1-800-DREAM HOME (373-2646)

© 2003, Garrell Associates, Inc.

Plan #582-056D-0007

Price Code G

Special Features • 1,985 total square feet of living area • 9' ceilings throughout home • Master suite has direct access into sunroom • Sunny breakfast room features bay window • Bonus room on the second floor has an additional 191 square feet of living area • 3 bedrooms, 3 baths, 2-car side entry garage • Slab foundation

First Floor
1,985 sq. ft.

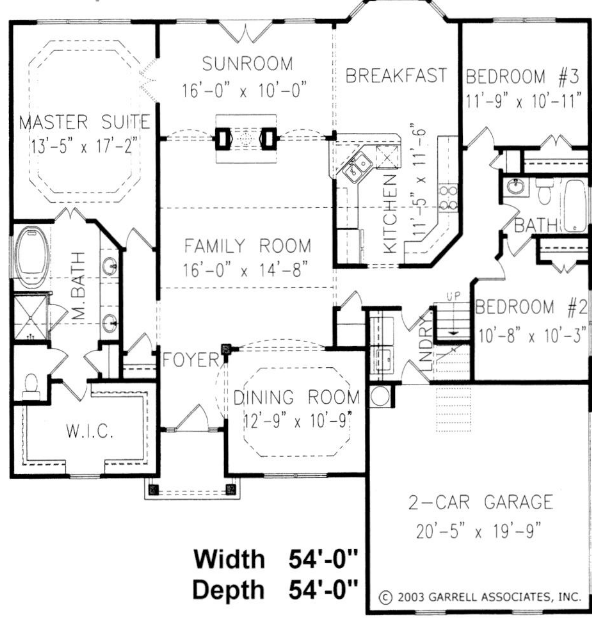

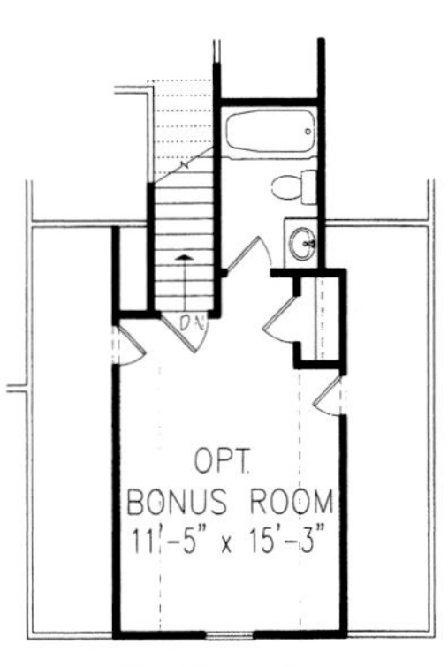

Optional
Second Floor

Inviting Covered Porch

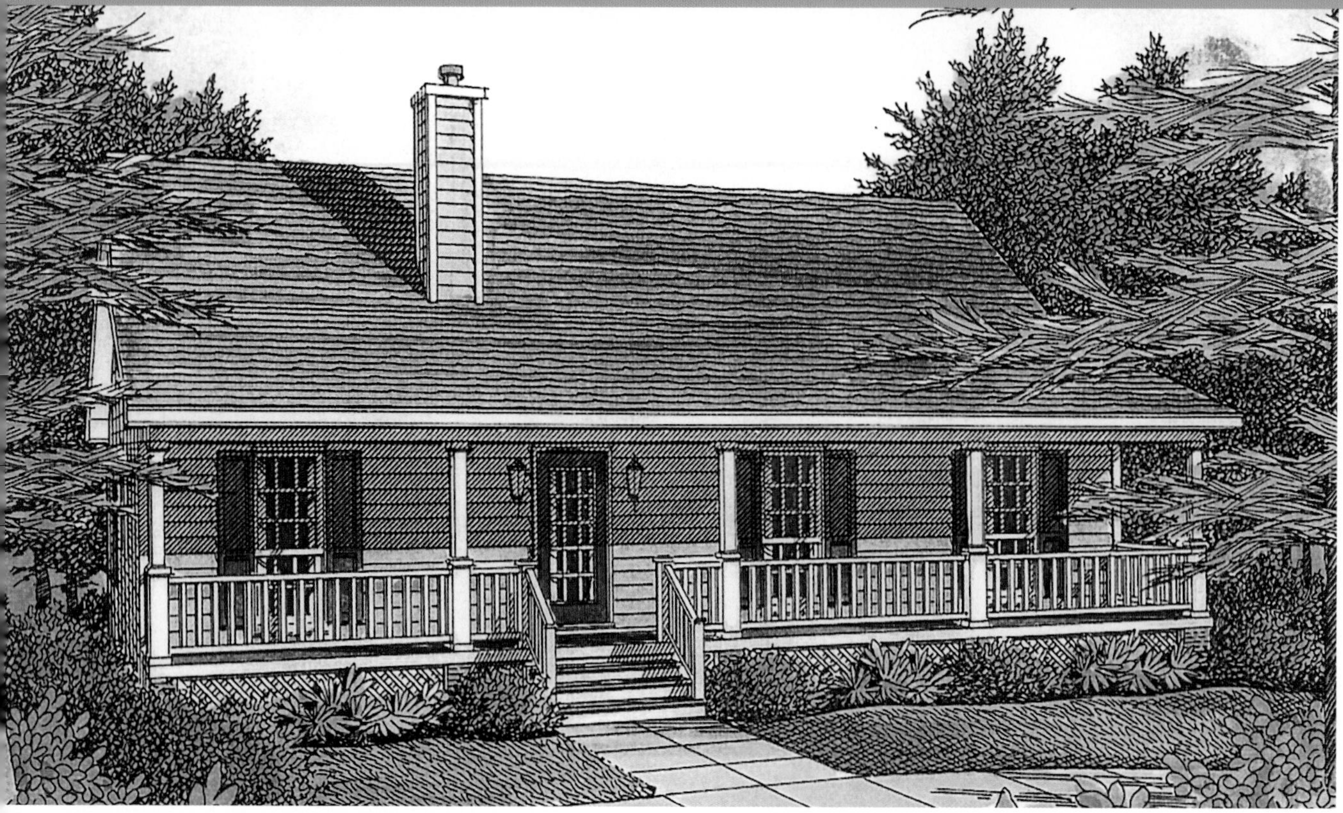

Plan #582-069D-0006 — *Price Code A*

Special Features • *1,277 total square feet of living area* • *Expansive great room features an 11' vaulted ceiling, cozy fireplace and coat closet* • *Utility room, kitchen and dining area combine for an open atmosphere* • *Master bedroom is located away from secondary bedrooms for privacy* • *3 bedrooms, 2 baths* • *Slab or crawl space foundation, please specify when ordering*

1-800-DREAM HOME (373-2646)

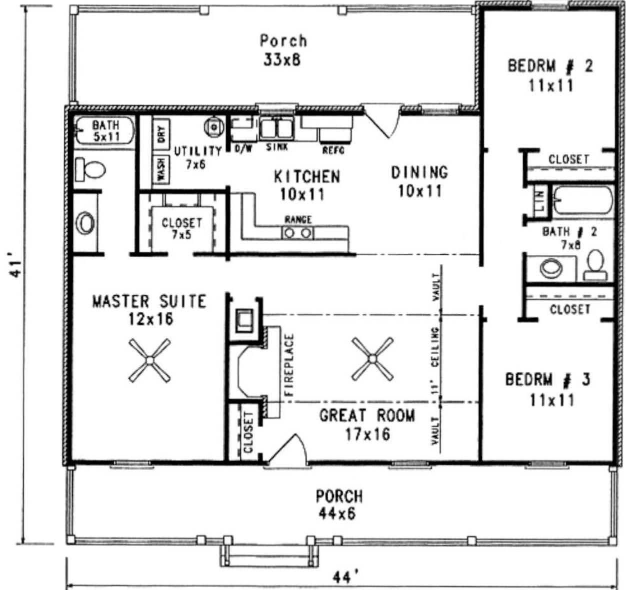

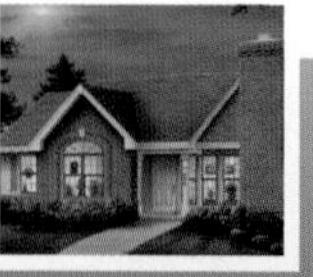

Plan #582-025D-0013

Price Code B

Special Features • 1,686 total square feet of living area • Secondary bedrooms are separate from master suite maintaining privacy • Island in kitchen is ideal for food preparation • Dramatic foyer leads to great room • Covered side porch has direct access into great room • 3 bedrooms, 2 baths, 2-car side entry garage • Slab foundation

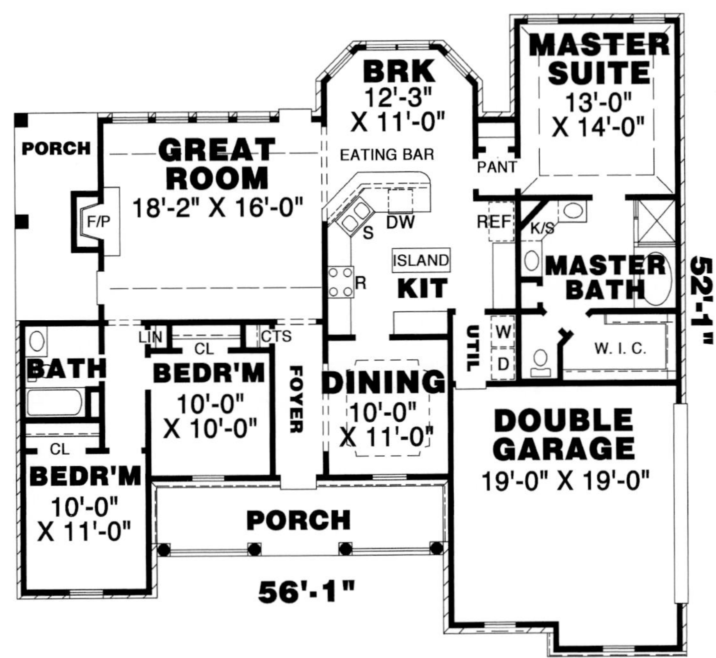

Plan #582-062D-0050

Price Code A

Special Features • 1,408 total square feet of living area • A bright country kitchen boasts an abundance of counterspace and cupboards • The front entry is sheltered by a broad verandah • A spa tub is brightened by a box bay window in the master bath • 3 bedrooms, 2 baths, 2-car side entry garage • Basement or crawl space foundation, please specify when ordering

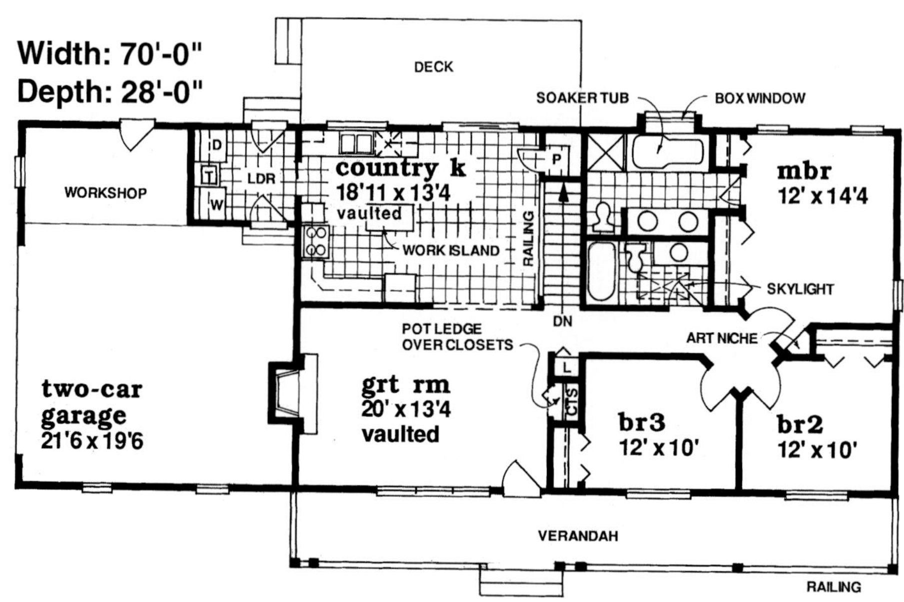

Plan #582-001D-0031 **Price Code B**

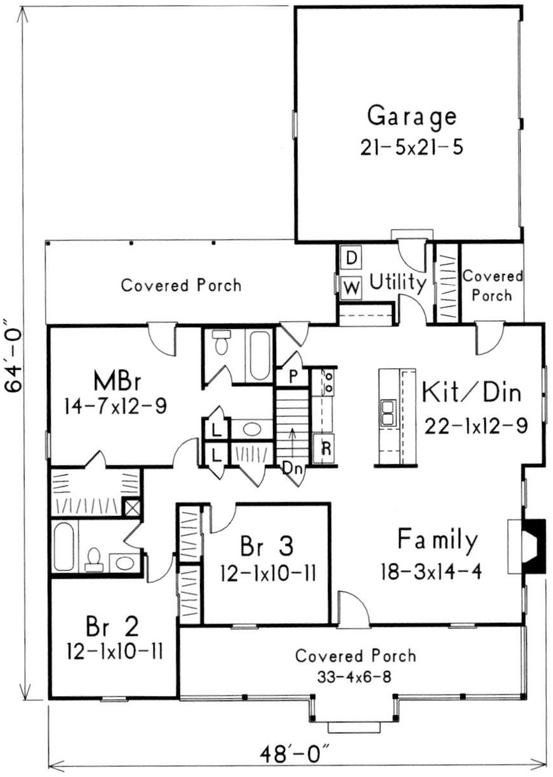

64'-0"

Garage
21-5x21-5

Covered Porch

D

W

Utility

Covered Porch

MBr
14-7x12-9

P

Kit/Din
22-1x12-9

L

L

R

Dn

Br 3
12-1x10-11

Family
18-3x14-4

Br 2
12-1x10-11

Covered Porch
33-4x6-8

48'-0"

Special Features • *1,501 total square feet of living area* • *Spacious kitchen with dining area is open to the outdoors* • *Convenient utility room is adjacent to garage* • *Master bedroom features a private bath, dressing area and access to the large covered porch* • *Large family room creates openness* • *3 bedrooms, 2 baths, 2-car side entry garage* • *Basement foundation, drawings also include crawl space and slab foundations*

Plan #582-055D-0067

Price Code A

Special Features • *1,472 total square feet of living area* • *8' wrap-around porch entry is inviting and creates an outdoor living area* • *Great room has a rock hearth fireplace and is open to the second floor above* • *Side grilling porch has a cleaning sink for fish or game* • *Optional bonus room on the second floor has an additional 199 square feet of living area* • *4 bedrooms, 2 baths* • *Crawl space or slab foundation, please specify when ordering*

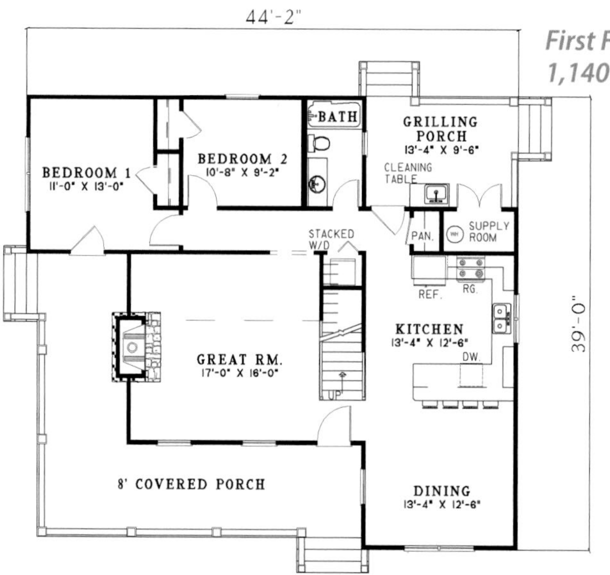

First Floor
1,140 sq. ft.

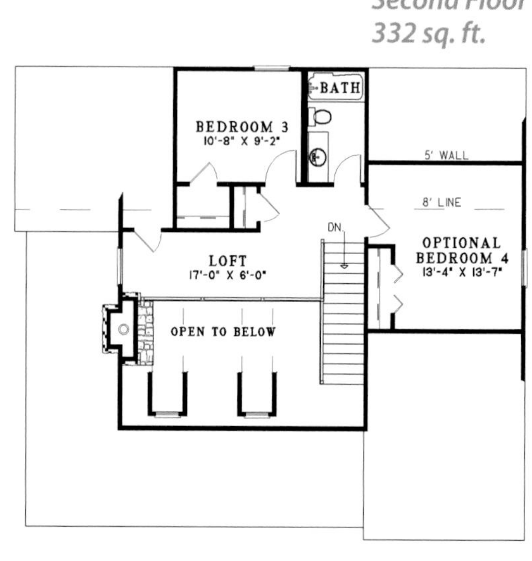

Second Floor
332 sq. ft.

Atrium's Dramatic Ambiance, Compliments Of Windows

Rear View

Plan #582-007D-0010

Price Code C

Special Features • *1,721 total square feet of living area* • *Roof dormers add great curb appeal* • *Vaulted dining and great rooms are immersed in light from atrium window wall* • *Breakfast room opens onto covered porch* • *Functionally designed kitchen* • *3 bedrooms, 2 baths, 3-car garage* • *Walk-out basement foundation, drawings also include crawl space and slab foundations* • *1,604 square feet on the first floor and 117 square feet on the lower level*

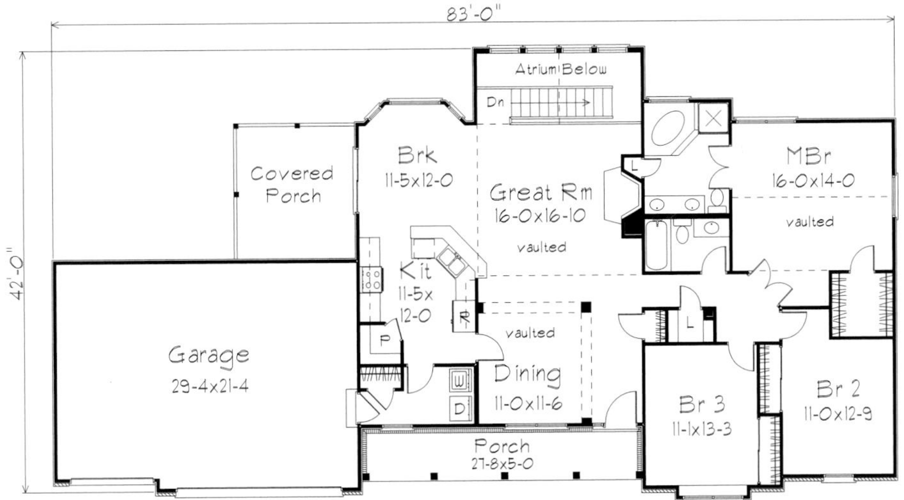

Transom Windows Create Impressive Front Entry

Plan #582-021D-0011 — Price Code D

Special Features • 1,800 total square feet of living area • Energy efficient home with 2" x 6" exterior walls • Covered front and rear porches add outdoor living area • 12' ceilings in the kitchen, breakfast area, dining and living rooms • Private master bedroom features an expansive bath • Side entry garage has two storage areas • Pillared styling with brick and stucco exterior finish • 3 bedrooms, 2 baths, 2-car side entry garage • Crawl space foundation, drawings also include slab foundation

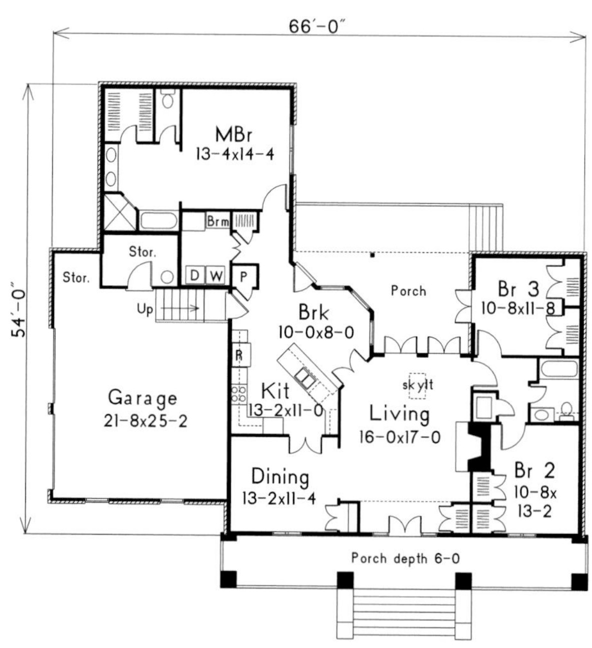

Lovely, Spacious Floor Plan

Plan #582-058D-0016

Price Code B

Special Features • 1,558 total square feet of living area • Spacious utility room is located conveniently between the garage and kitchen/dining area • Bedrooms are separated from the living area by hallway • Enormous living area with fireplace and vaulted ceiling opens to the kitchen and dining area • Master bedroom is enhanced with a large bay window, walk-in closet and private bath • 3 bedrooms, 2 baths, 2-car garage • Basement foundation

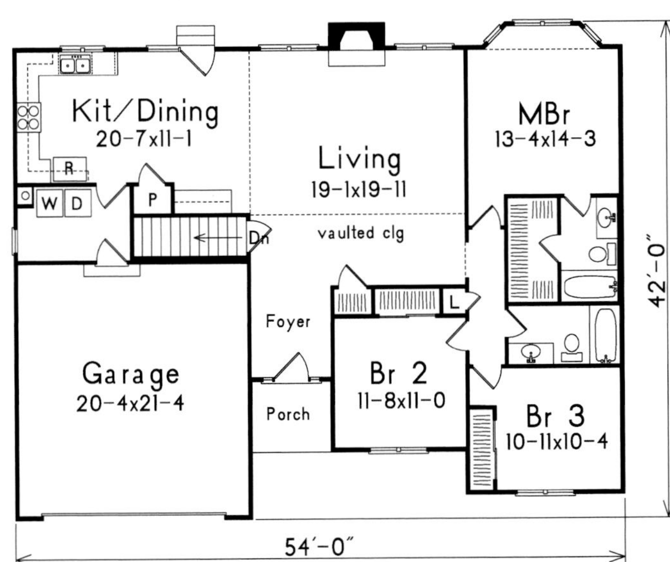

Country Classic With Modern Floor Plan

Plan #582-014D-0014

Price Code D

Special Features • *1,921 total square feet of living area* • *Energy efficient home with 2" x 6" exterior walls* • *Sunken family room includes a built-in entertainment center and coffered ceiling* • *Sunken formal living room features a coffered ceiling* • *Master bedroom dressing area has double sinks, spa tub, shower and French door to private deck* • *Large front porch adds to home's appeal* • *3 bedrooms, 2 1/2 baths, 2-car garage* • *Basement foundation*

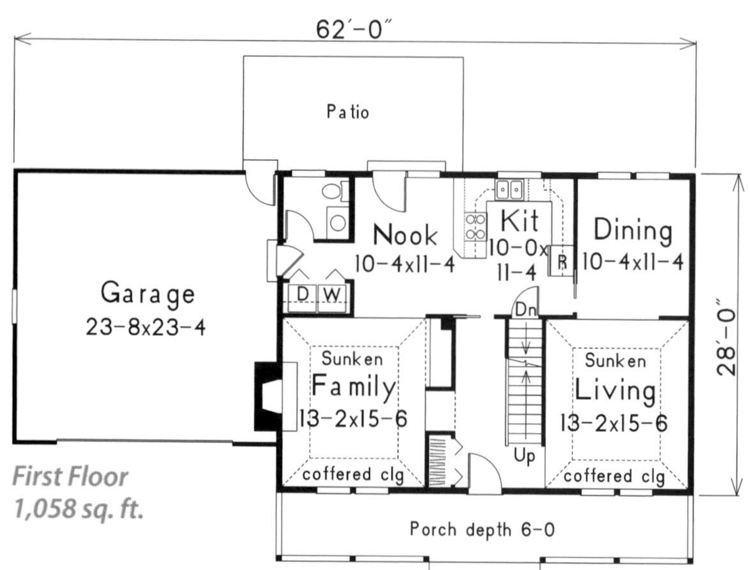

First Floor
1,058 sq. ft.

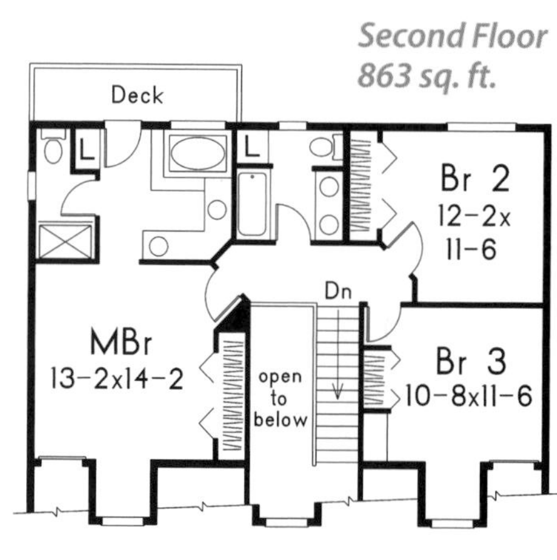

Second Floor
863 sq. ft.

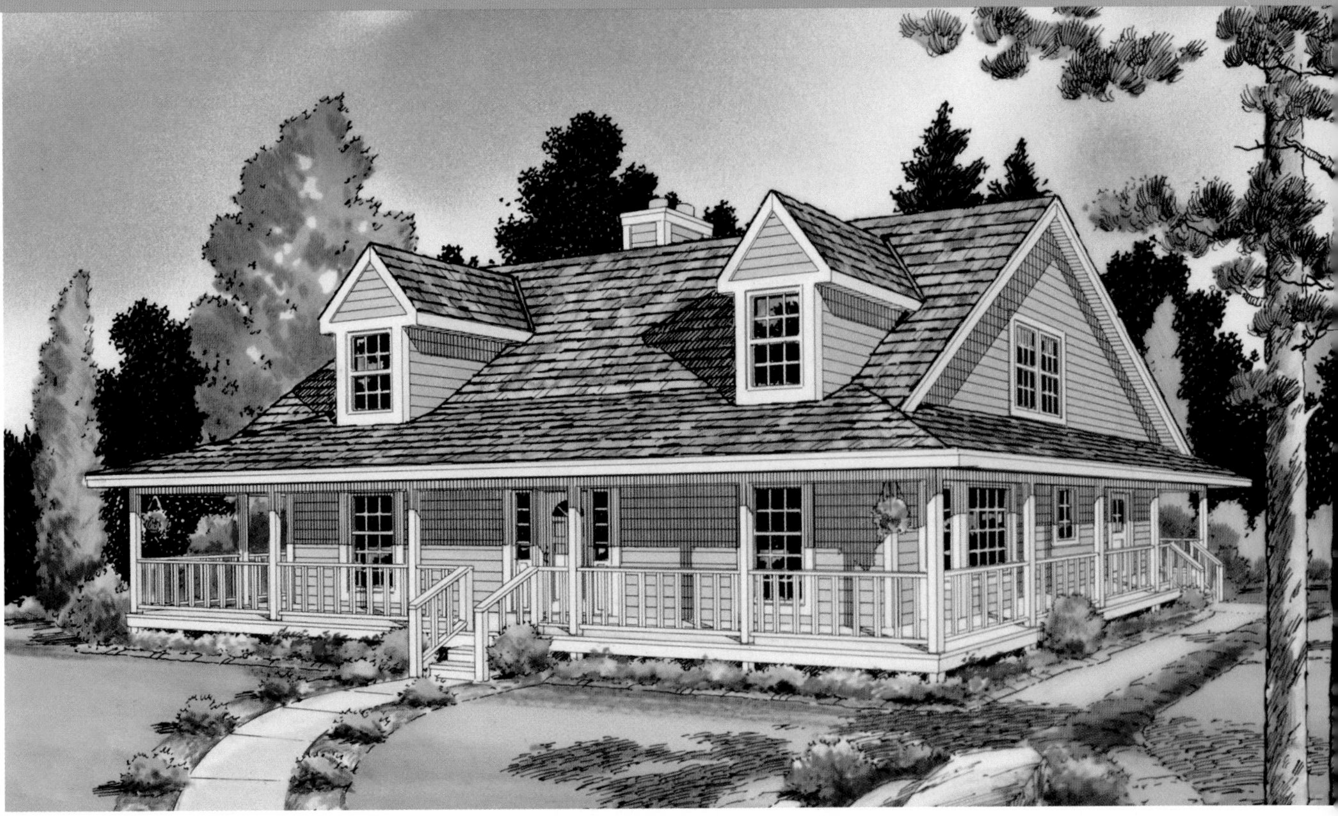

Plan #582-038D-0007

Price Code C

Special Features • 1,907 total square feet of living area • Two-story living room is a surprise with skylight and balcony above • Master bedroom is positioned on the first floor for convenience • All bedrooms have walk-in closets • 3 bedrooms, 2 1/2 baths • Basement, crawl space or slab foundation, please specify when ordering

slope
skylight
open to below
Balcony
Br 2
10-4 x 14
DN
lin.
Br 3
11 x 14
plant ledge
slope

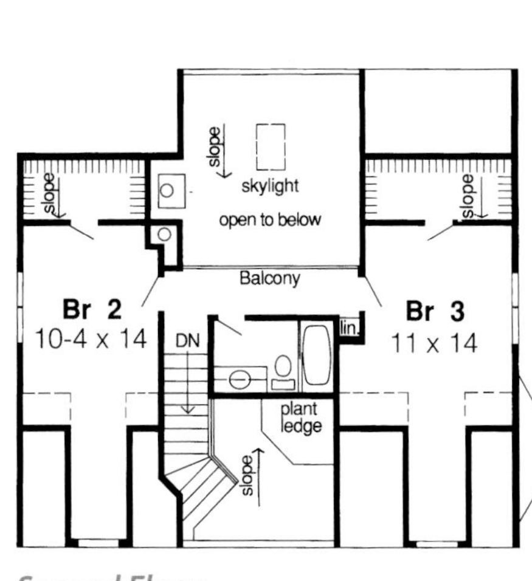

Second Floor
638 sq. ft.

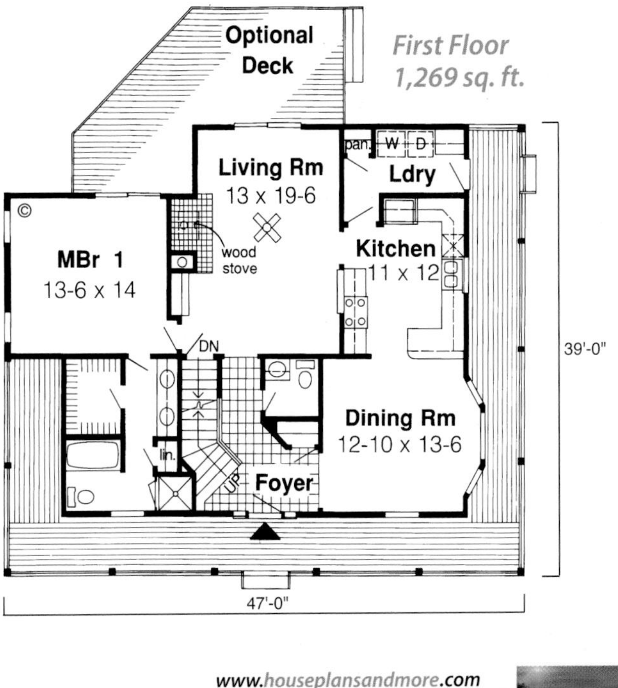

Optional Deck
Living Rm
13 x 19-6
wood stove
pan.
W
D
Ldry
Kitchen
11 x 12
MBr 1
13-6 x 14
DN
lin.
UP
Foyer
Dining Rm
12-10 x 13-6
39'-0"
47'-0"

First Floor
1,269 sq. ft.

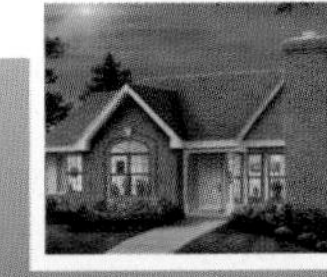

Central Living Area Keeps Bedrooms Private

Plan #582-033D-0012

Price Code C

Special Features • *1,546 total square feet of living area* • *Spacious, open rooms create a casual atmosphere* • *Master bedroom is secluded for privacy* • *Dining room features a large bay window* • *Kitchen and dinette combine for added space and include access to the outdoors* • *Large laundry room includes convenient sink* • *3 bedrooms, 2 baths, 2-car garage* • *Basement foundation*

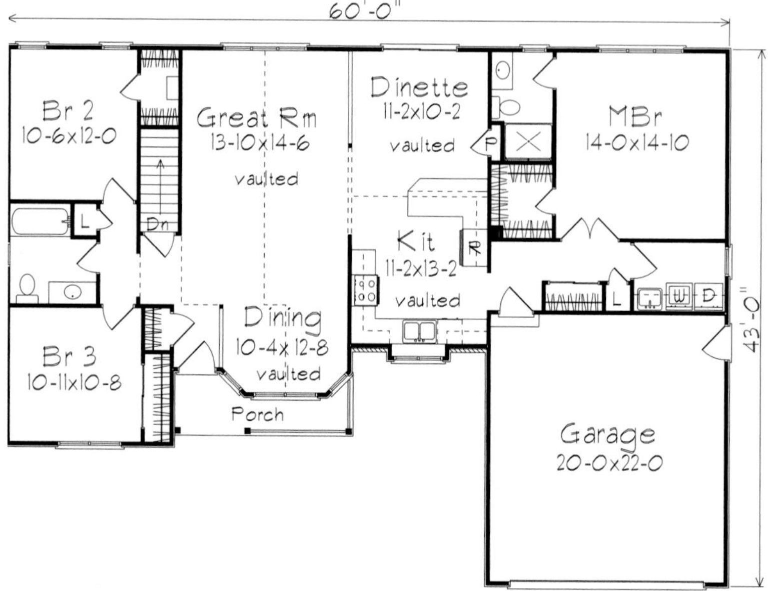

Plan #582-026D-0123

Price Code C

Special Features • 1,998 total square feet of living area • Lovely designed family room offers double-door entrance into living area • Roomy kitchen with breakfast area is a natural gathering place • 10' ceiling in master bedroom • 3 bedrooms, 2 1/2 baths, 2-car garage • Basement foundation

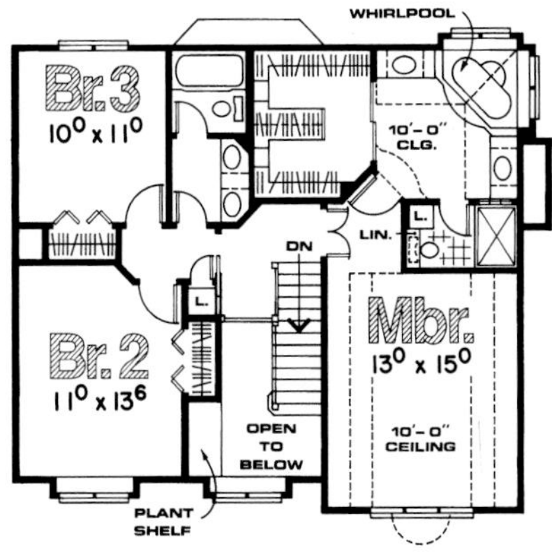

Second Floor
905 sq. ft.

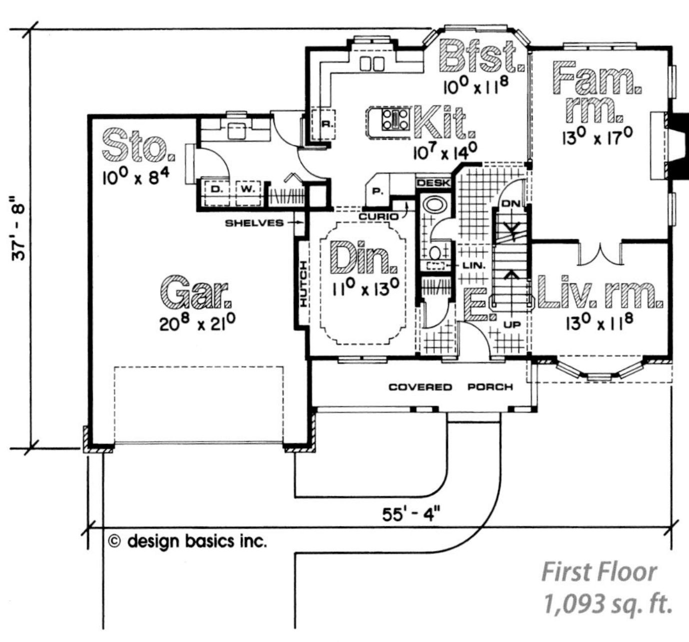

First Floor
1,093 sq. ft.

Classic Ranch Has Grand Appeal With Expansive Porch

Plan #582-005D-0001

Price Code B

Special Features • 1,400 total square feet of living area • Master bedroom is secluded for privacy • Large utility room has additional cabinet space • Covered porch provides an outdoor seating area • Roof dormers add great curb appeal • Living room and master bedroom feature vaulted ceilings • Oversized two-car garage has storage space • 3 bedrooms, 2 baths, 2-car garage • Basement foundation, drawings also include crawl space foundation

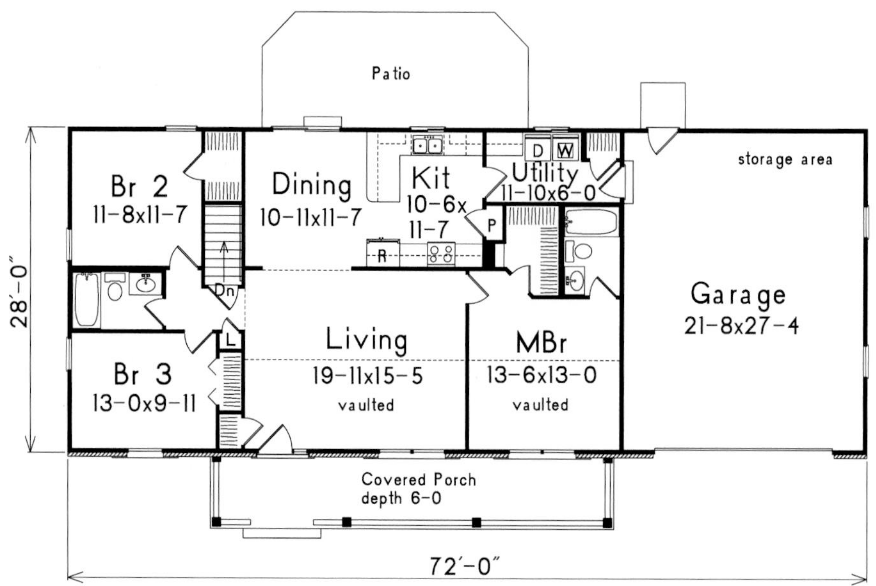

Full-Length Front Porch

Plan #582-024D-0004

Price Code B

Special Features • 1,500 total square feet of living area • Living room features corner fireplace adding warmth • Master bedroom has all the amenities including a walk-in closet, private bath and porch access • Sunny bayed breakfast room is cheerful and bright • 3 bedrooms, 2 baths, 2-car garage • Slab foundation

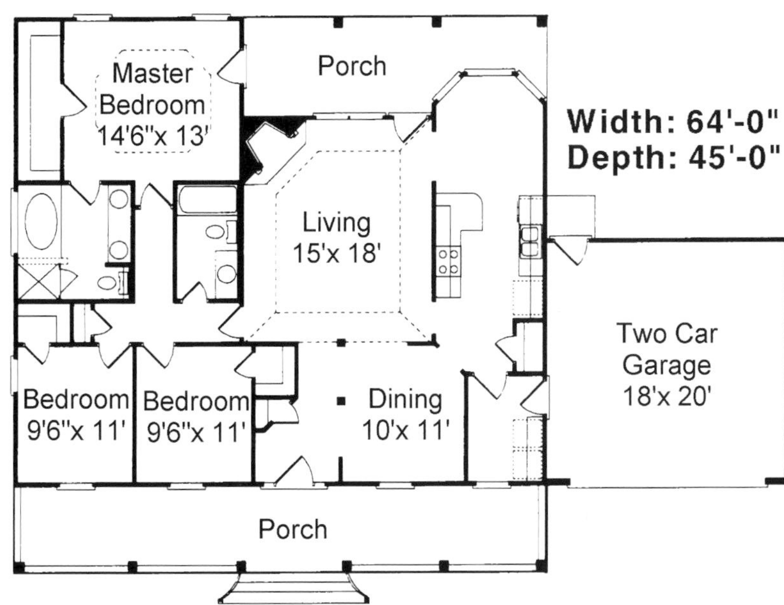

www.houseplansandmore.com

Plan #582-076D-0013

Price Code B

Special Features • *1,177 total square feet of living area* • *The vaulted master bedroom enjoys two walk-in closets, whirlpool tub and a double vanity* • *A grand fireplace flanked by windows graces the spacious family room* • *Kitchen and breakfast area combine for a relaxing atmosphere and feature access onto the rear patio* • *3 bedrooms, 2 baths, 2-car side entry garage* • *Slab foundation*

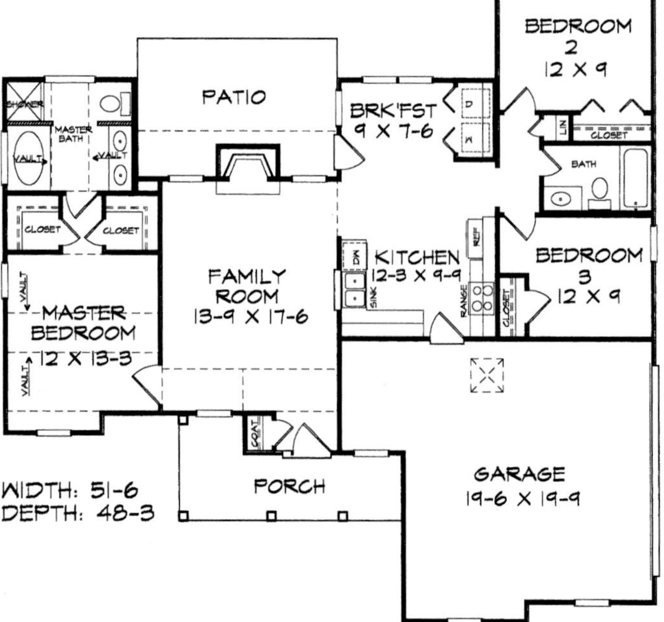

Compact Home For Functional Living

Plan #582-053D-0029

Price Code A

Special Features • 1,220 total square feet of living area • Vaulted ceilings add luxury to the living room and master bedroom • Spacious living room is accented with a large fireplace and hearth • Gracious dining area is adjacent to the convenient wrap-around kitchen • Washer and dryer are handy to the bedrooms • Covered porch entry adds appeal • Rear deck adjoins dining area • 3 bedrooms, 2 baths, 2-car drive under garage • Basement foundation

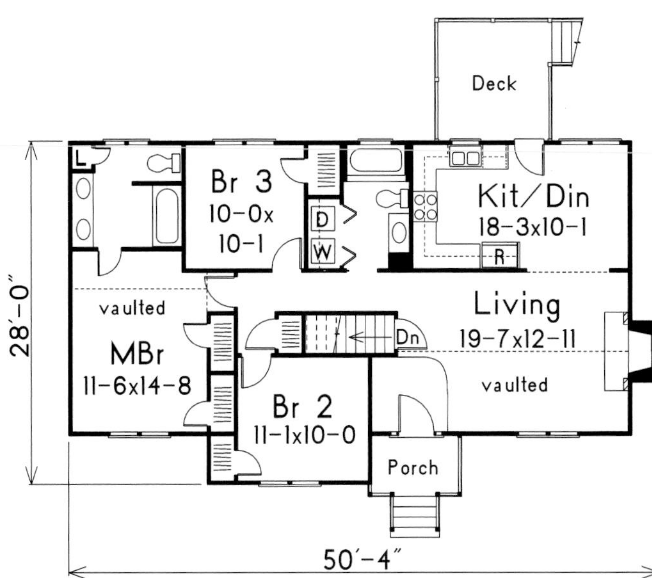

Covered Porch Adds Charm

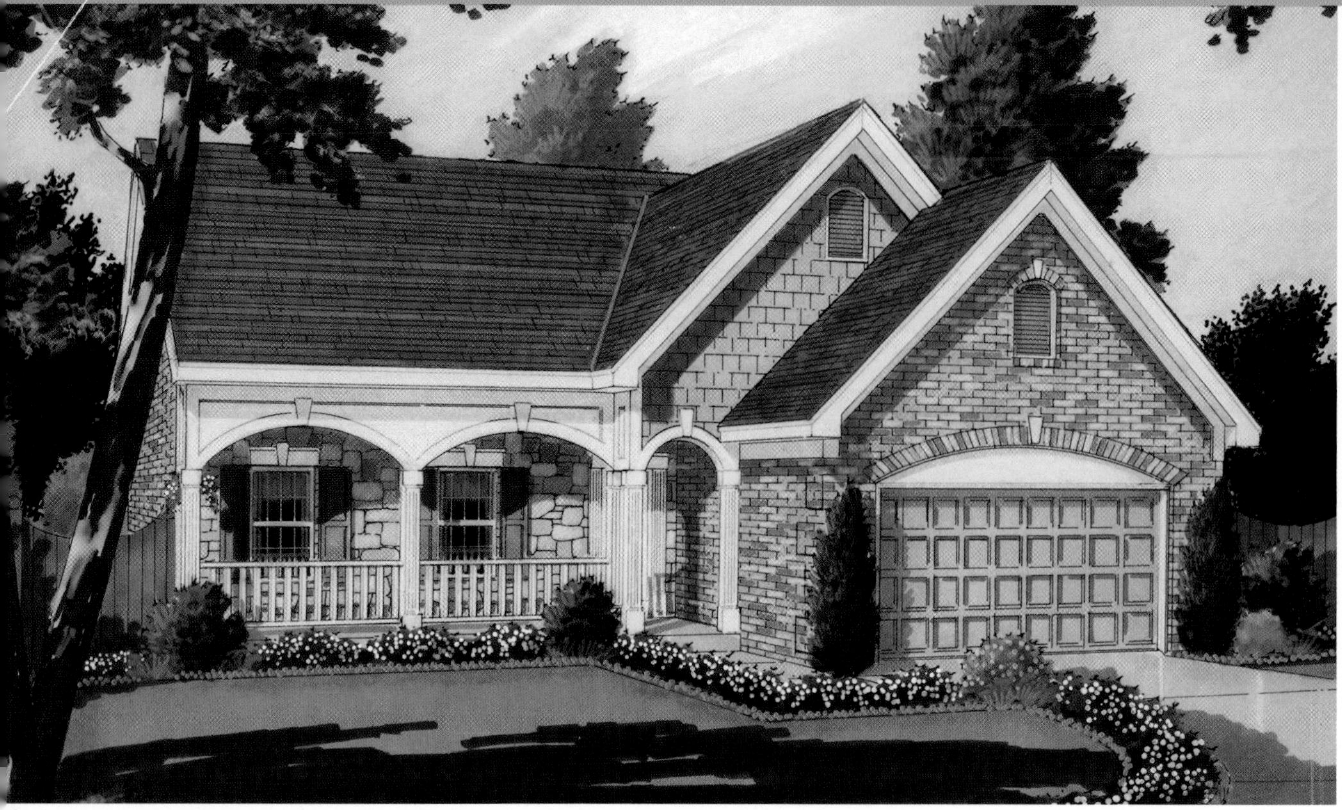

Plan #582-065D-0027

Price Code B

Special Features • 1,595 total square feet of living area • The front secondary bedroom could easily convert to a library or home office especially with its convenient double-door entry • An expansive deck is enjoyed by the open great room and bayed dining area • A walk-in closet organizes the master bedroom • 3 bedrooms, 2 baths, 2-car garage • Basement foundation

Plan #582-008D-0013

Price Code A

Special Features • 1,345 total square feet of living area • Brick front details add a touch of elegance • Master bedroom has a private full bath • Great room combined with dining area adds spaciousness • Garage includes handy storage area which could easily convert to a workshop space • 3 bedrooms, 2 baths, 2-car side entry garage • Basement foundation, drawings also include crawl space and slab foundations

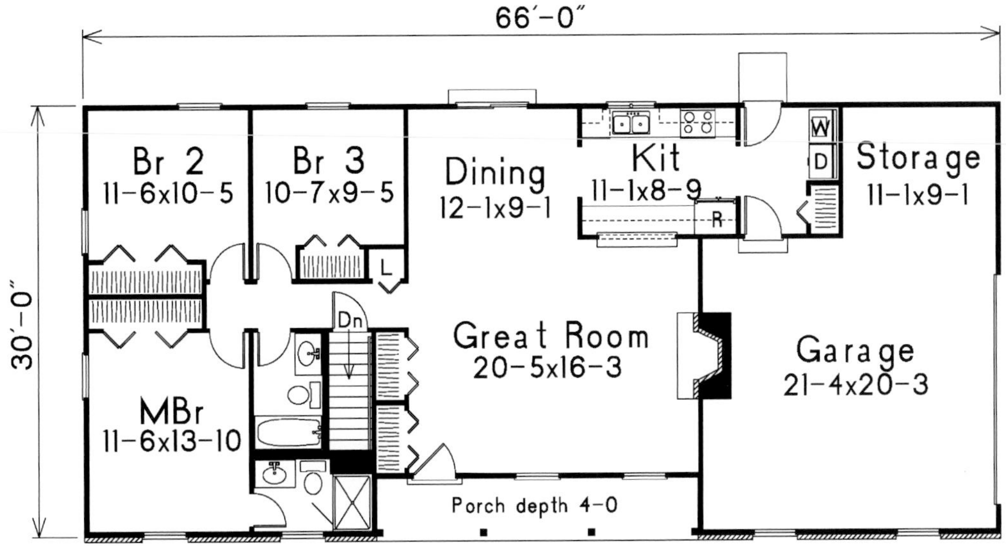

Surrounding Porch For Country Living

Plan #582-058D-0020

Price Code A

Special Features • *1,428 total square feet of living area* • *Large vaulted family room opens to the dining area and kitchen with breakfast bar* • *First floor master bedroom offers a large bath, walk-in closet and nearby laundry facilities* • *A spacious loft/bedroom #3 overlooking the family room and an additional bedroom and bath complement the second floor* • *3 bedrooms, 2 baths* • *Basement foundation*

Second Floor
415 sq. ft.

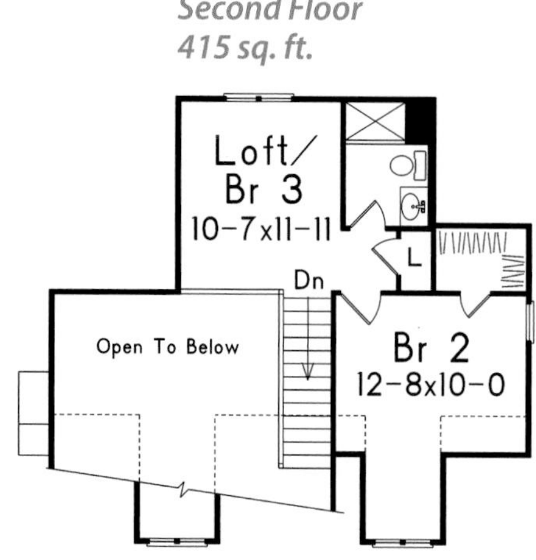

First Floor
1,013 sq. ft.

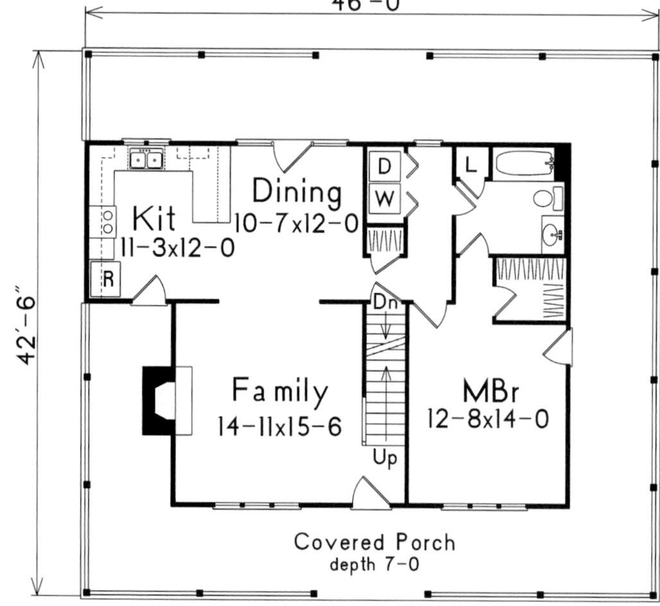

Rear View

Plan #582-007D-0075

Price Code B

Special Features • 1,684 total square feet of living area • Delightful wrap-around porch anchored by full masonry fireplace • The vaulted great room includes a large bay window, fireplace, dining balcony and atrium window wall • Double walk-in closets, large luxury bath and sliding doors to exterior balcony are a few fantastic features of the master bedroom • Atrium opens to 611 square feet of optional living area on the lower level • 3 bedrooms, 2 baths, 2-car drive under garage • Walk-out basement foundation

Optional Lower Level

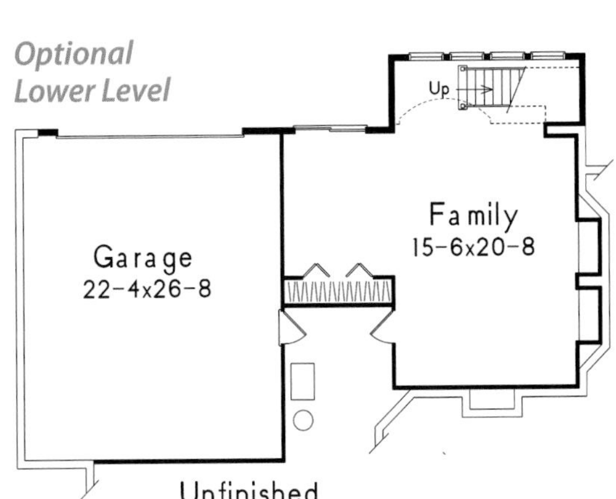

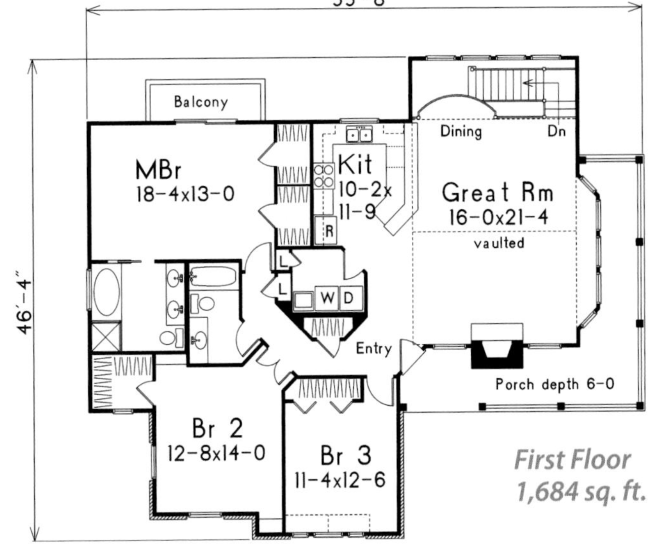

First Floor
1,684 sq. ft.

Wrap-Around Porch Adds Curb Appeal

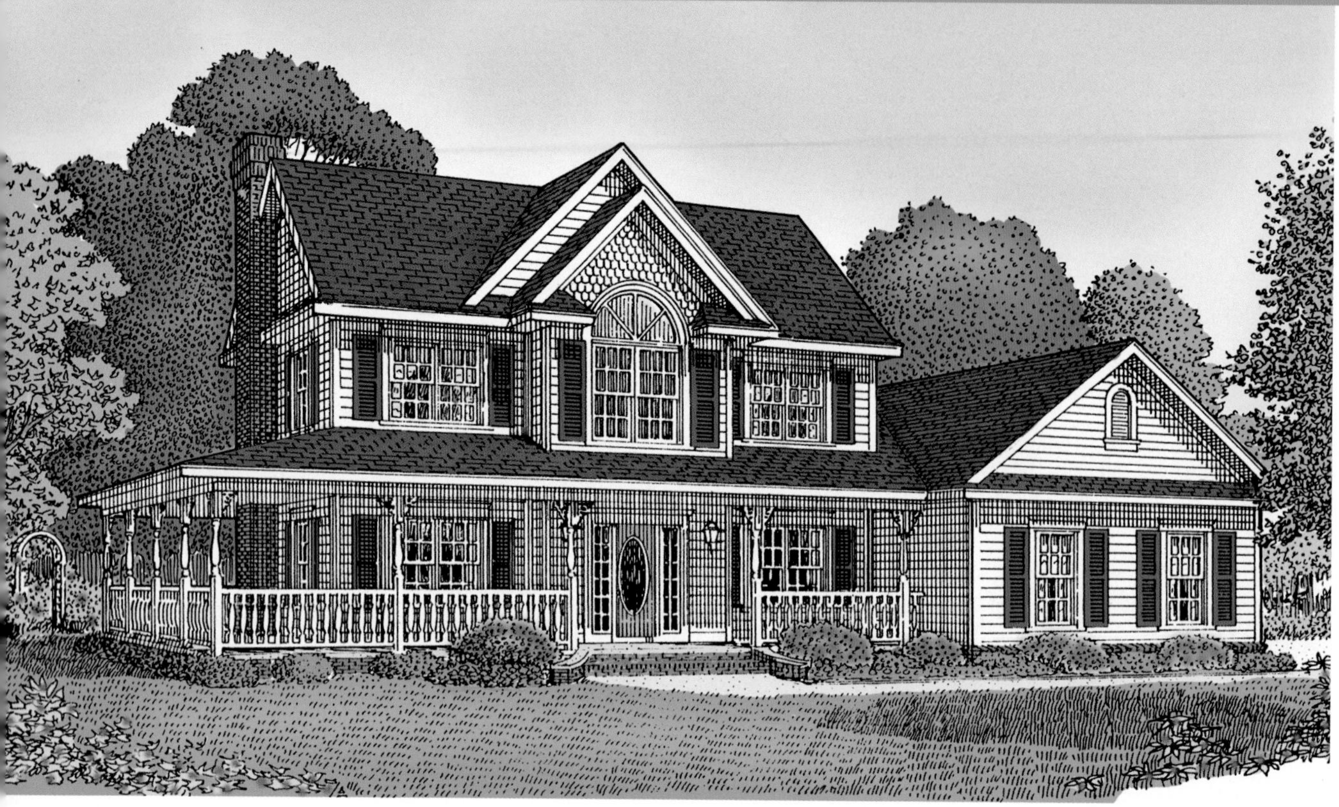

Plan #582-067D-0006

Price Code C

Special Features • 1,840 total square feet of living area • All bedrooms are located on the second floor for privacy • Counter dining space is provided in the kitchen • Formal dining room connects to the kitchen through French doors • 4 bedrooms, 2 1/2 baths, 2-car side entry garage with shop/storage • Basement, crawl space or slab foundation, please specify when ordering

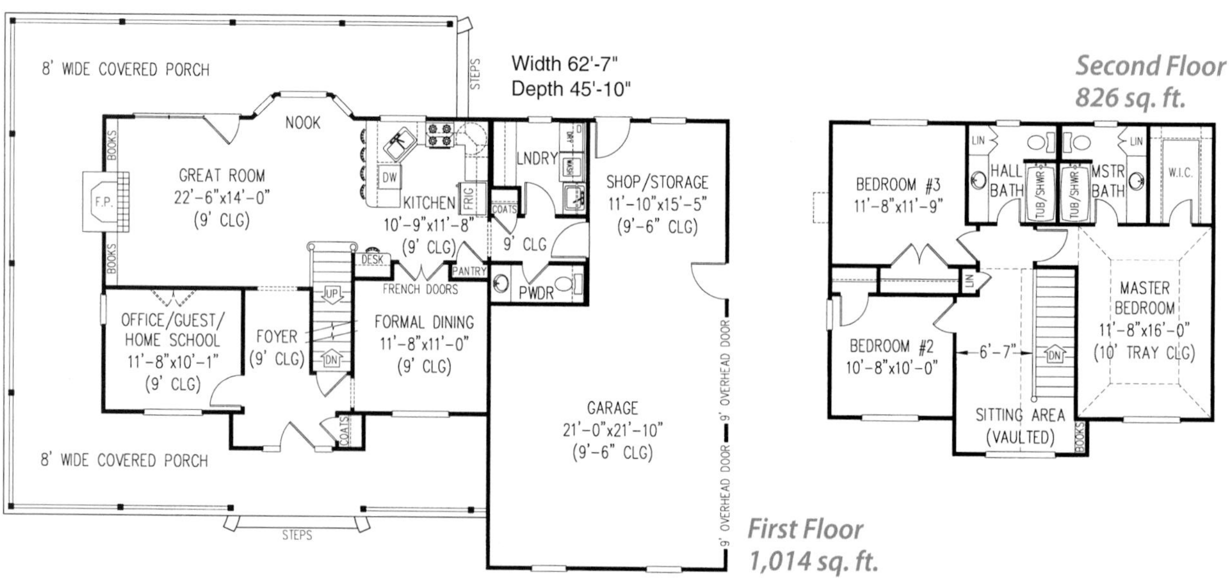

Plan #582-070D-0007

Price Code B

Special Features • 1,974 total square feet of living area • Bayed study has a double-door entry • Large mud room and laundry closet are perfect for family living • Kitchen island has sink and space for dining • 3 bedrooms, 2 1/2 baths, 2-car side entry garage • Basement foundation

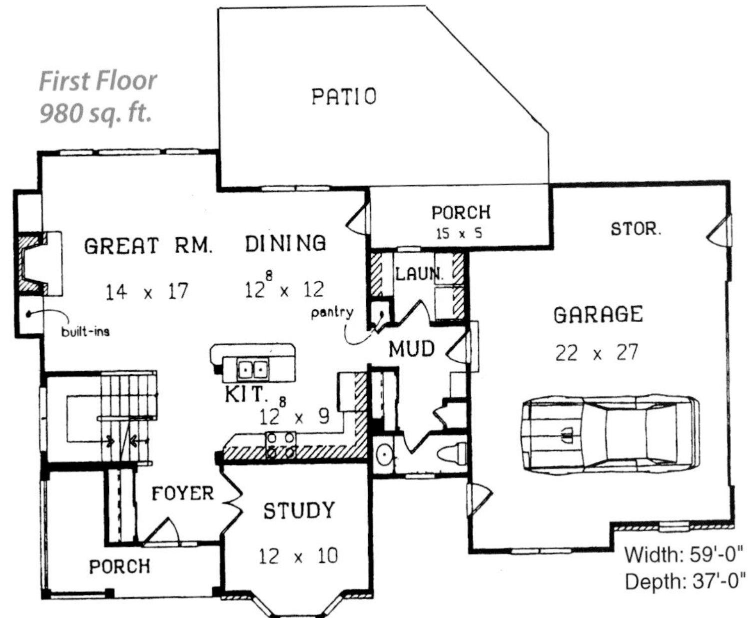

First Floor
980 sq. ft.

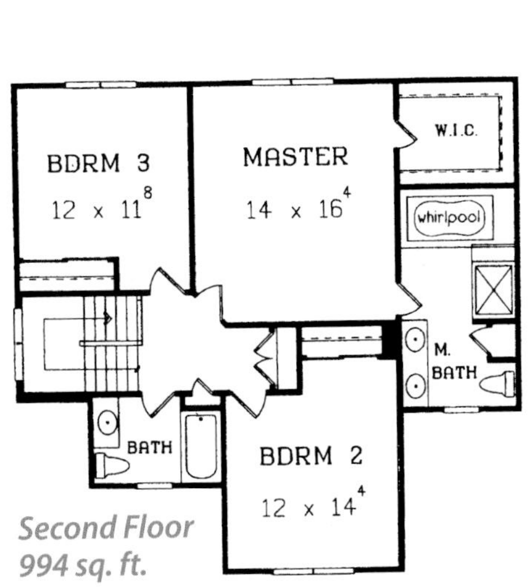

Second Floor
994 sq. ft.

www.houseplansandmore.com

Bayed Great Room Brightens This Ranch

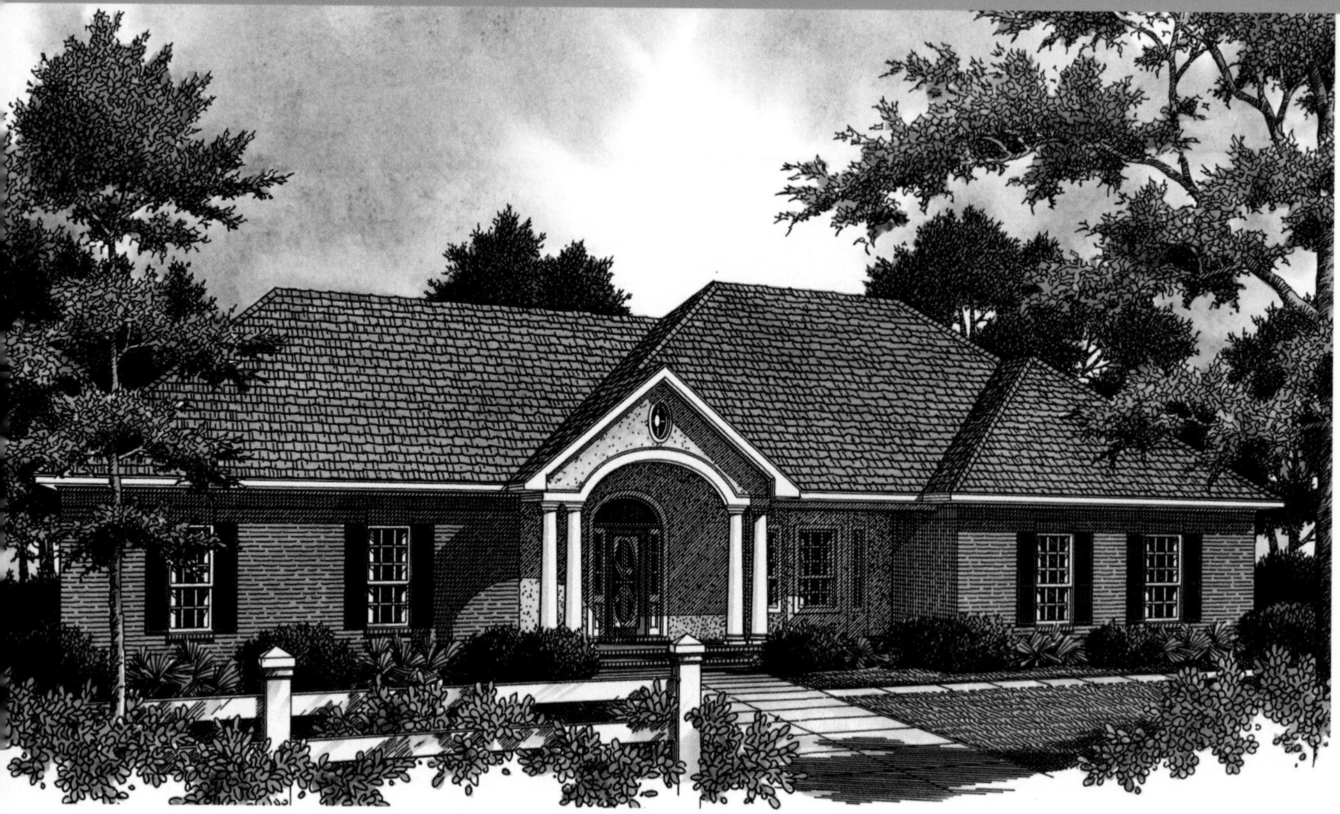

Plan #582-077D-0003

Price Code D

Special Features • *1,896 total square feet of living area* • *The vaulted great room features a grand fireplace flanked by built-in bookshelves* • *U-shaped kitchen opens to dining area which enjoys access onto the covered porch* • *The large utility room includes a sink and walk-in pantry* • *Plenty of storage throughout with a walk-in closet in each bedroom* • *3 bedrooms, 2 1/2 baths, 2-car side entry garage* • *Basement, crawl space or slab foundation, please specify when ordering*

1-800-DREAM HOME (373-2646)

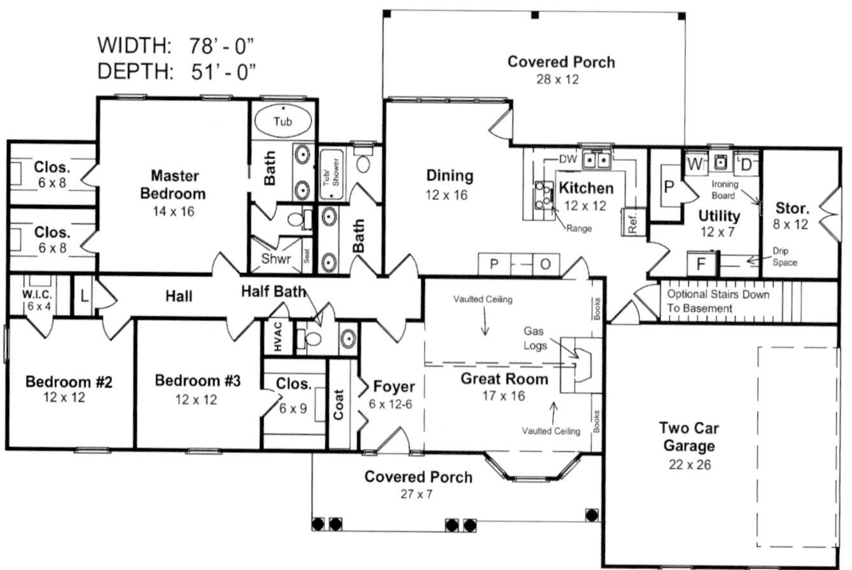

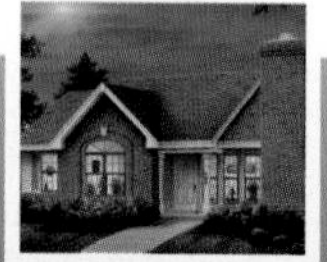

Warm And Inviting Home

Plan #582-016D-0028

Price Code C

Special Features • 1,667 total square feet of living area • The centrally located fireplace lends warmth to the surrounding rooms • Vaulted ceilings and skylights add elegance • The foyer opens into the dining and living rooms with 12' ceilings and a wall of windows for an open and spacious feel • The large laundry room offers an abundance of storage space • 3 bedrooms, 2 baths, 2-car side entry garage • Basement, crawl space or slab foundation, please specify when ordering

Basement Stair Location

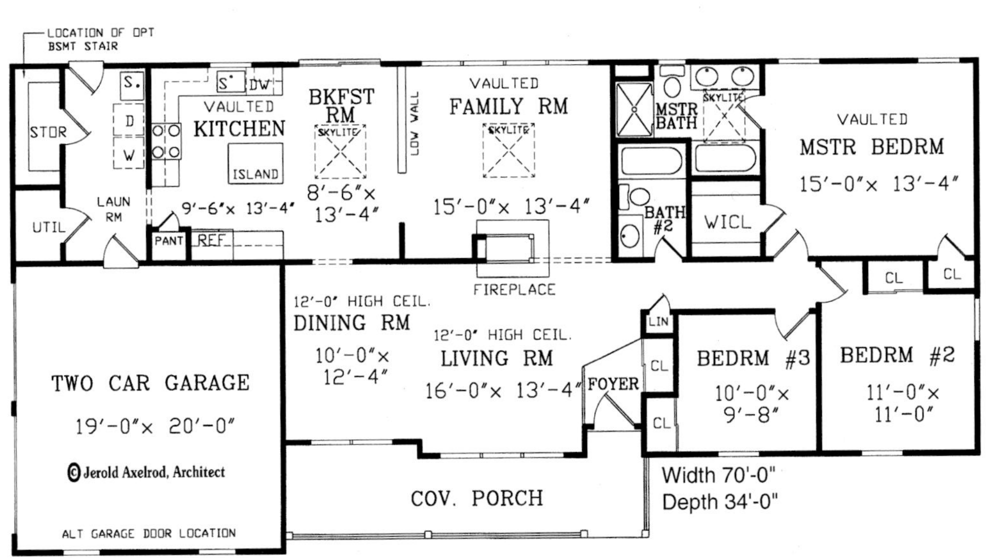

Plan #582-038D-0039

Price Code B

Special Features • *1,771 total square feet of living area* • *Den has a sloped ceiling and charming window seat* • *Private master bedroom has access to the outdoors* • *Central kitchen allows for convenient access when entertaining* • *2 bedrooms, 2 baths, 2-car garage* • *Basement, crawl space or slab foundation, please specify when ordering*

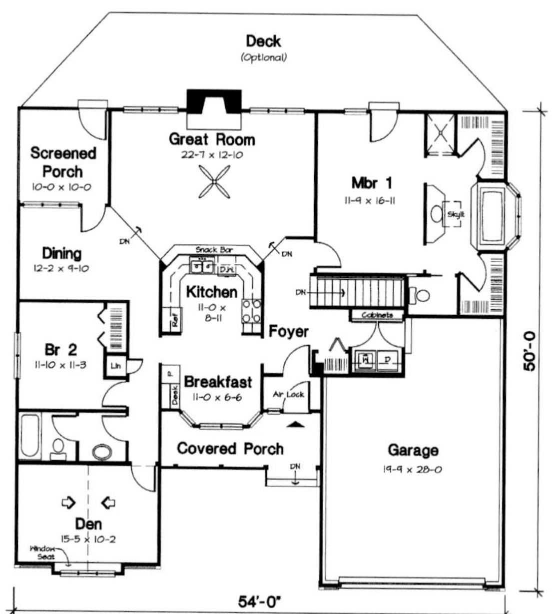

Plan #582-025D-0005

Price Code A

Special Features • *1,429 total square feet of living area* • *Master bedroom features a spacious private bath and double walk-in closets* • *Formal dining room has convenient access to the kitchen which is perfect for entertaining* • *Additional storage can be found in the garage* • *3 bedrooms, 2 baths, 2-car garage* • *Slab foundation*

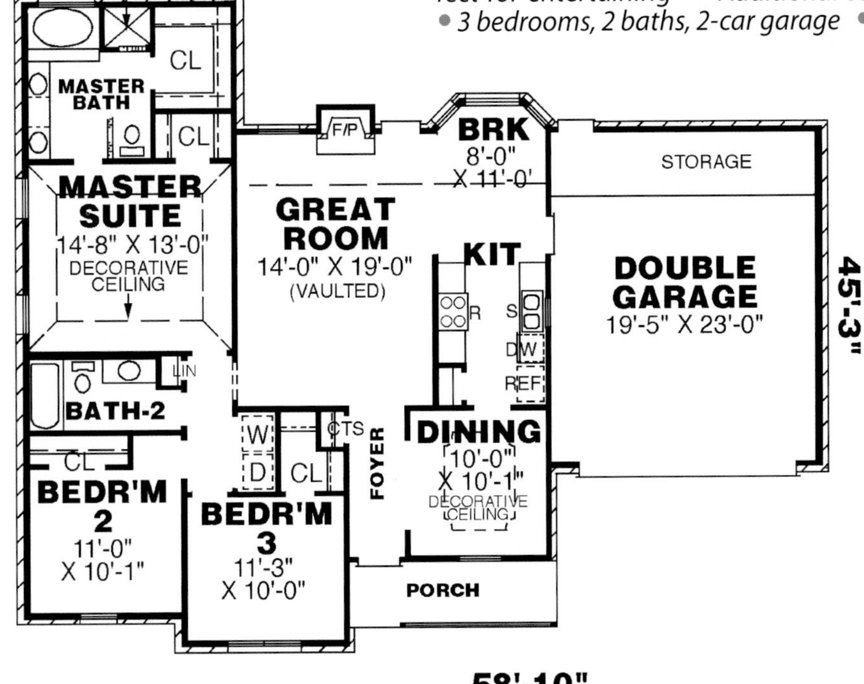

Corner Fireplace Adds Warmth

Plan #582-020D-0016

Price Code C

Special Features • 1,984 total square feet of living area • Living room has sloped ceiling and corner fireplace • Kitchen has breakfast bar overlooking dining room • Master suite is separate from other bedrooms for privacy • Large utility/storage area • 3 bedrooms, 2 baths, 2-car side entry garage • Slab foundation, drawings also include crawl space foundation

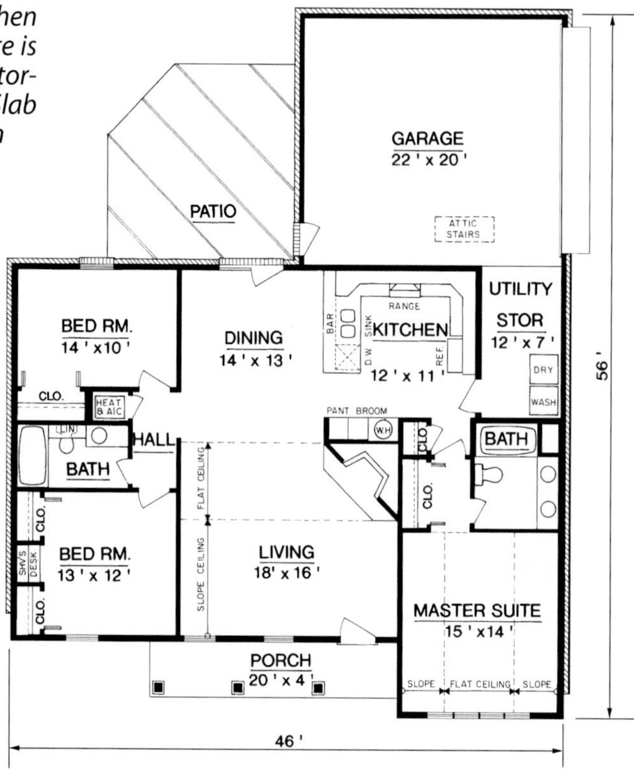

Layout Creates Large Open Living Area

Plan #582-001D-0067

Price Code B

Special Features • 1,285 total square feet of living area • Accommodating home with ranch-style porch • Large storage area on back of home • Master bedroom includes dressing area, private bath and built-in bookcase • Kitchen features pantry, breakfast bar and complete view to dining room • 3 bedrooms, 2 baths • Crawl space foundation, drawings also include basement and slab foundations

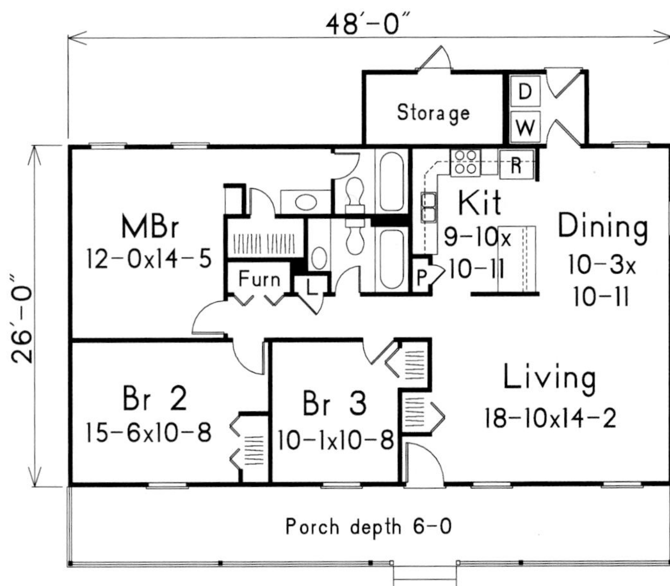

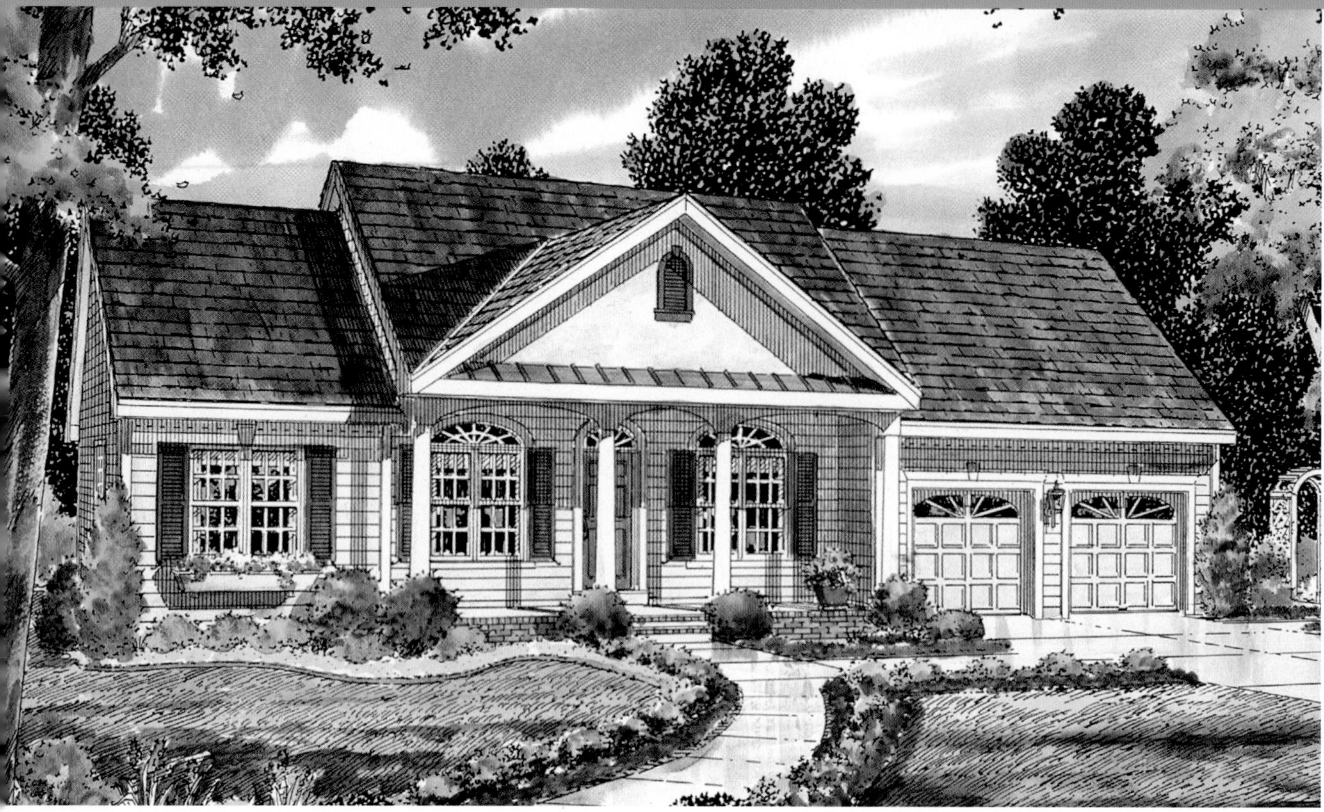

Plan #582-038D-0040

Price Code B

Special Features • *1,642 total square feet of living area* • *Built-in cabinet in dining room adds a custom feel* • *Secondary bedrooms share an oversized bath* • *Master bedroom includes private bath with dressing table* • *3 bedrooms, 2 baths, 2-car garage* • *Crawl space foundation*

First Floor
1,642 sq. ft.

Optional Basement Stairs

1-800-DREAM HOME (373-2646)

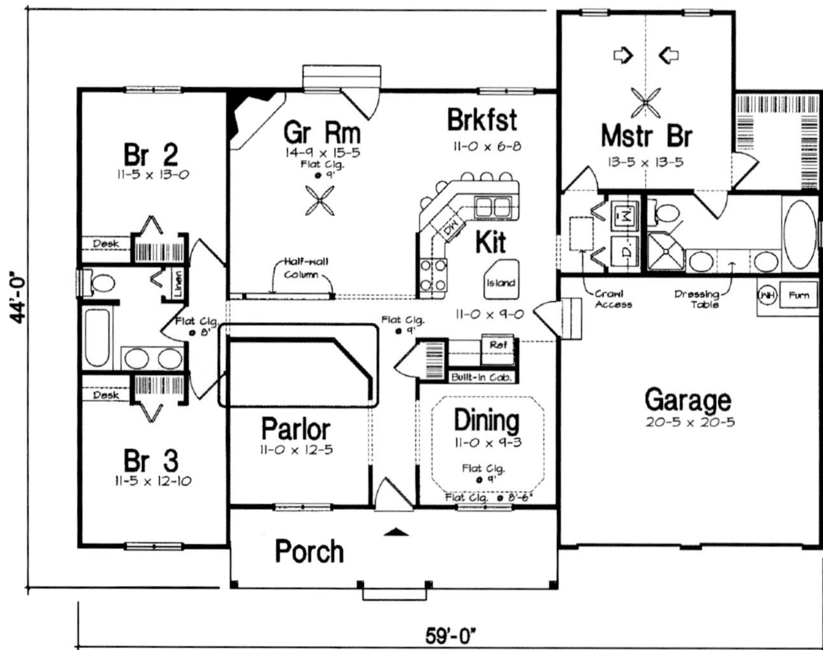

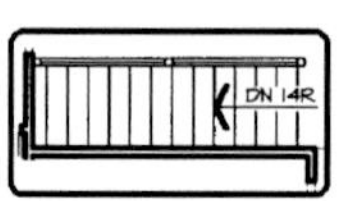

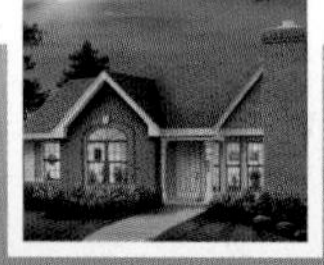

Classic Exterior Employs Innovative Planning

Plan #582-007D-0049

Price Code C

Special Features • 1,791 total square feet of living area • Vaulted great room and octagon-shaped dining area enjoy views of covered patio • Kitchen features a pass-through to dining area, center island, large walk-in pantry and breakfast room with large bay window • Master bedroom is vaulted with sitting area • 4 bedrooms, 2 baths, 2-car garage with storage • Basement foundation, drawings also include crawl space and slab foundations

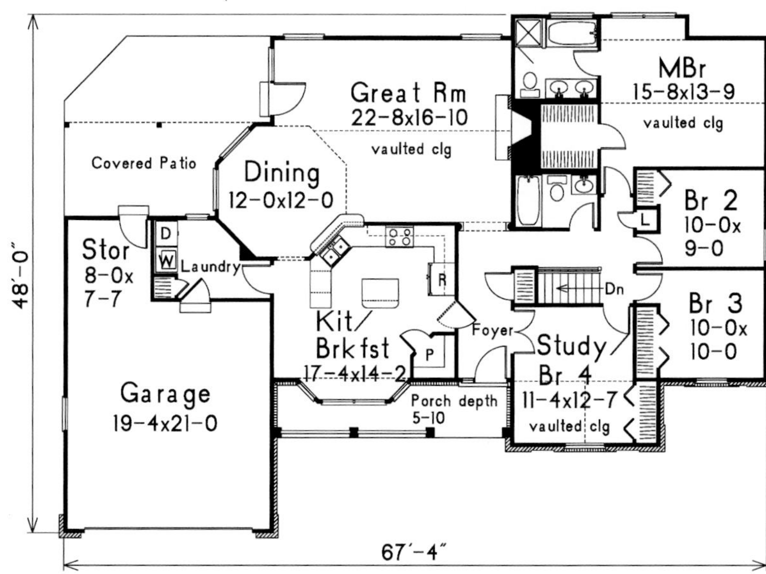

www.houseplansandmore.com

Plan #582-078D-0008 Price Code D

Special Features • 1,450 total square feet of living area • The floor plan centers around an open living/dining area that features a vaulted, beamed ceiling and a large fireplace flanked by built-in bookcases • A comfortable open kitchen enjoys a cooking island, generous pantry and plenty of counterspace • An expansive rear deck provides ample room for indoor/outdoor dining and entertaining • The spacious master suite boasts a cozy wood-stove and a spiral staircase ascending to a large loft • 2 bedrooms, 2 baths, 2-car side entry garage • Crawl space foundation

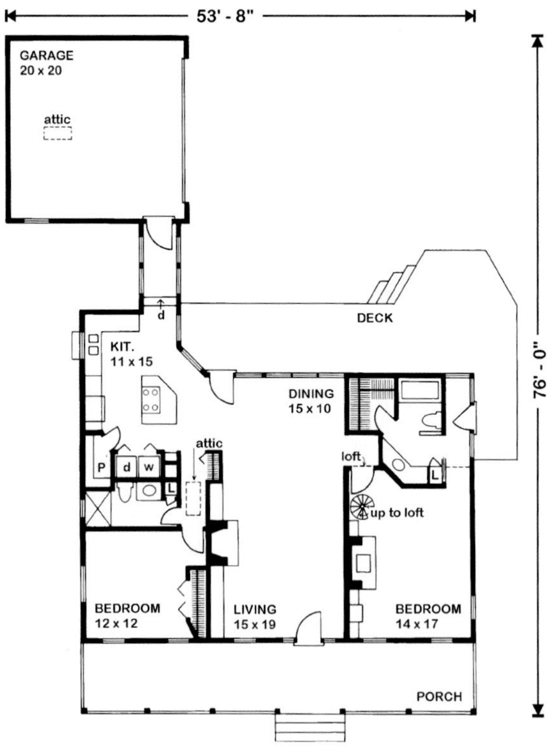

Simple And Cozy

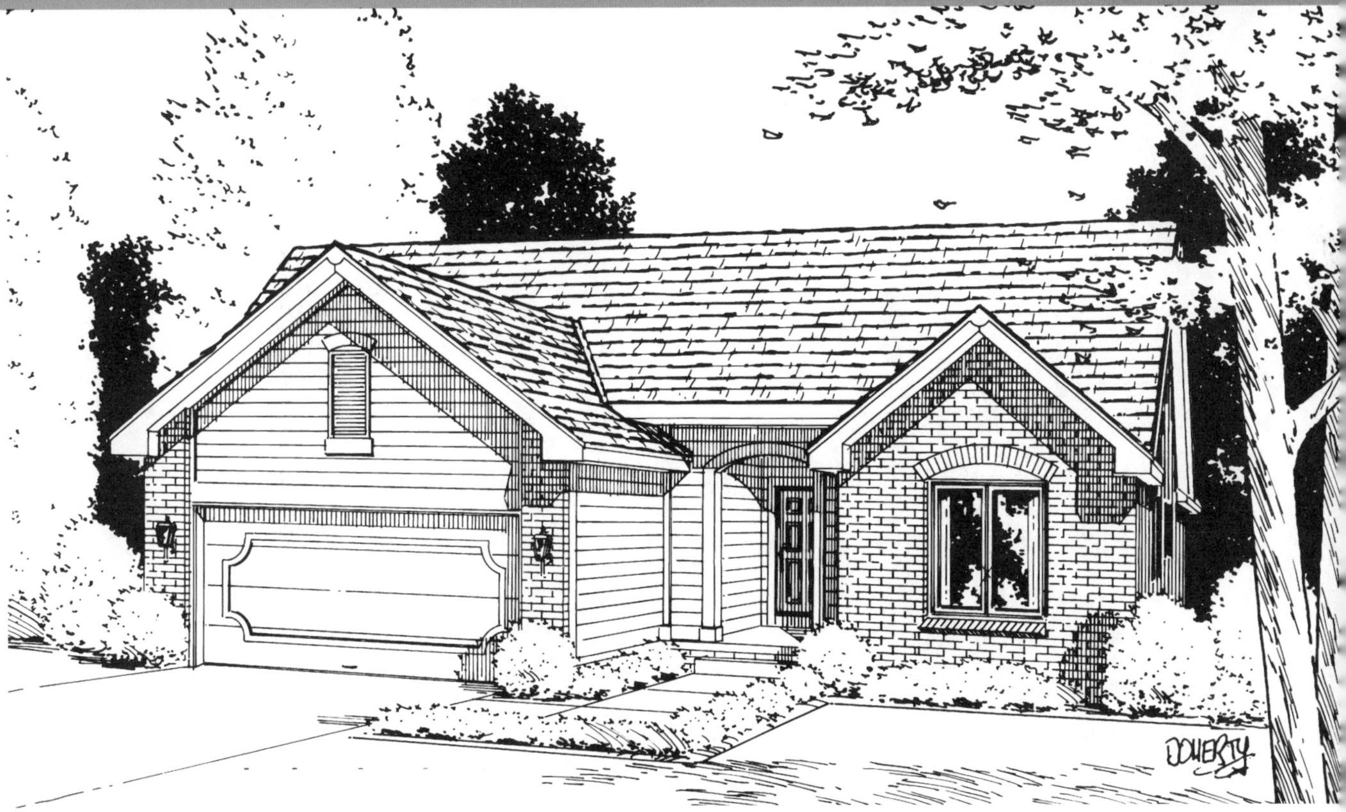

Plan #582-026D-0154 Price Code A

Special Features • 1,392 total square feet of living area • Centralized great room welcomes guests with a warm fireplace • Master bedroom has a separate entrance for added privacy • Kitchen includes breakfast room, snack counter and laundry area • 3 bedrooms, 2 baths, 2-car garage • Basement foundation

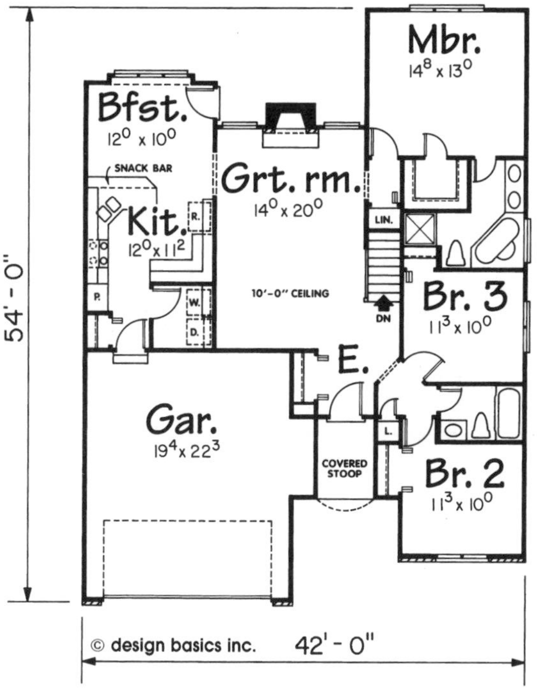
Mbr.
14⁸ x 13⁰
Bfst.
12⁰ x 10⁰
SNACK BAR
Grt. rm.
14⁰ x 20⁰
Kit.
12⁰ x 11²
R.
LIN.
10'-0" CEILING
P.
W.
D.
DN
Br. 3
11³ x 10⁰
E.
Gar.
19⁴ x 22³
L.
COVERED STOOP
Br. 2
11³ x 10⁰
54' - 0"
© design basics inc.
42' - 0"

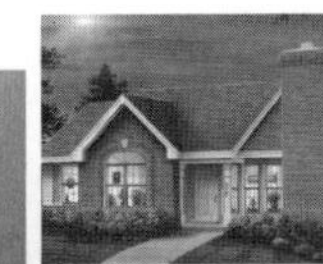

Plan #582-007D-0018

Price Code C

Special Features • 1,941 total square feet of living area • Dramatic, exciting and spacious interior • Vaulted great room is brightened by sunken atrium window wall and skylights • Vaulted U-shaped gourmet kitchen with plant shelf opens to dining room • First floor half bath features space for stackable washer and dryer • 4 bedrooms, 2 1/2 baths, 2-car garage • Walk-out basement foundation

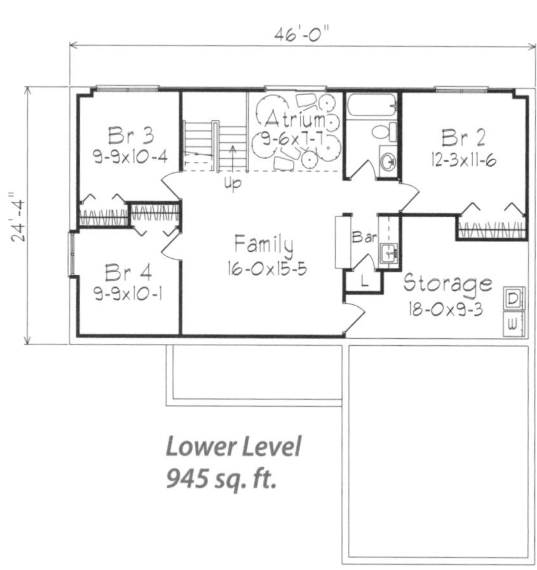

Lower Level 945 sq. ft.

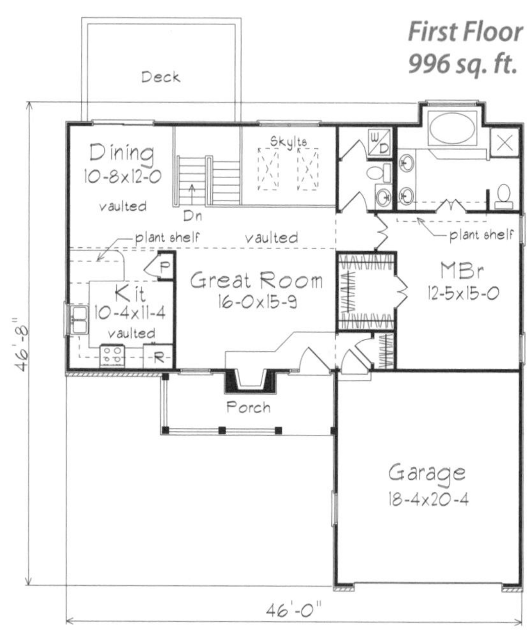

First Floor 996 sq. ft.

1-800-DREAM HOME (373-2646)

Plan #582-001D-0050

Price Code C

Special Features • *1,827 total square feet of living area* • *Two large bedrooms are located on the second floor for extra privacy, plus two bedrooms on the first floor* • *L-shaped kitchen is adjacent to the family room* • *Ample closet space in all bedrooms* • *4 bedrooms, 2 baths, 2-car garage* • *Crawl space foundation, drawings also include basement and slab foundations*

Br 3
13-7x18-5
Dn
L
Br 4
13-2x18-5
sloped clg

Second Floor
651 sq. ft.

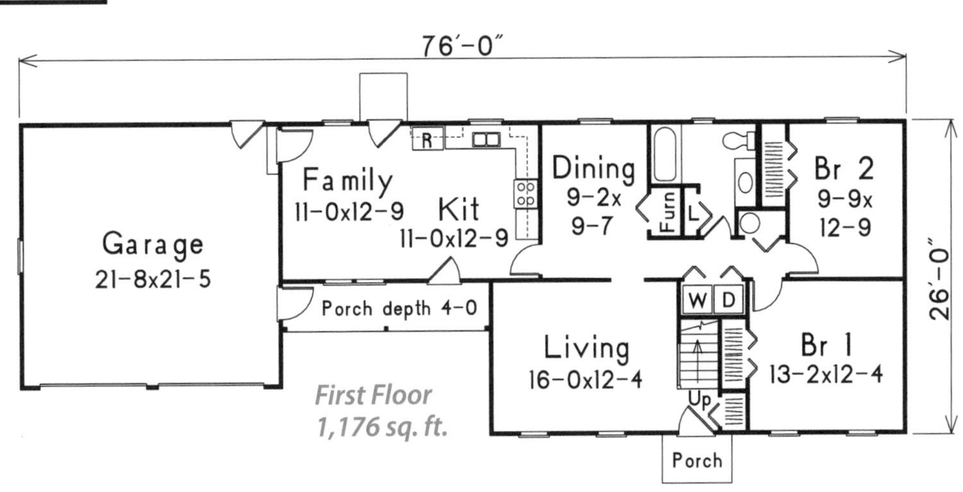

First Floor
1,176 sq. ft.

www.houseplansandmore.com

Covered Porch Adds Charm To Entrance

Plan #582-040D-0015

Price Code B

Special Features • *1,655 total square feet of living area • Master bedroom features a 9' ceiling, walk-in closet and bath with dressing area • Oversized family room includes 10' ceiling and masonry see-through fireplace • Island kitchen with convenient access to laundry room • Handy covered walkway from garage to kitchen and dining area • 3 bedrooms, 2 baths, 2-car garage • Crawl space foundation*

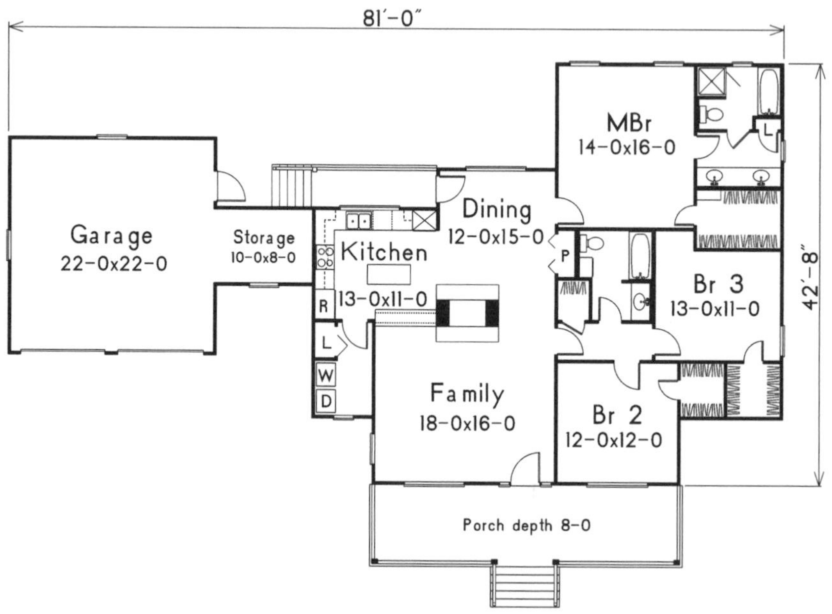

Beauty And Practicality Designed As One

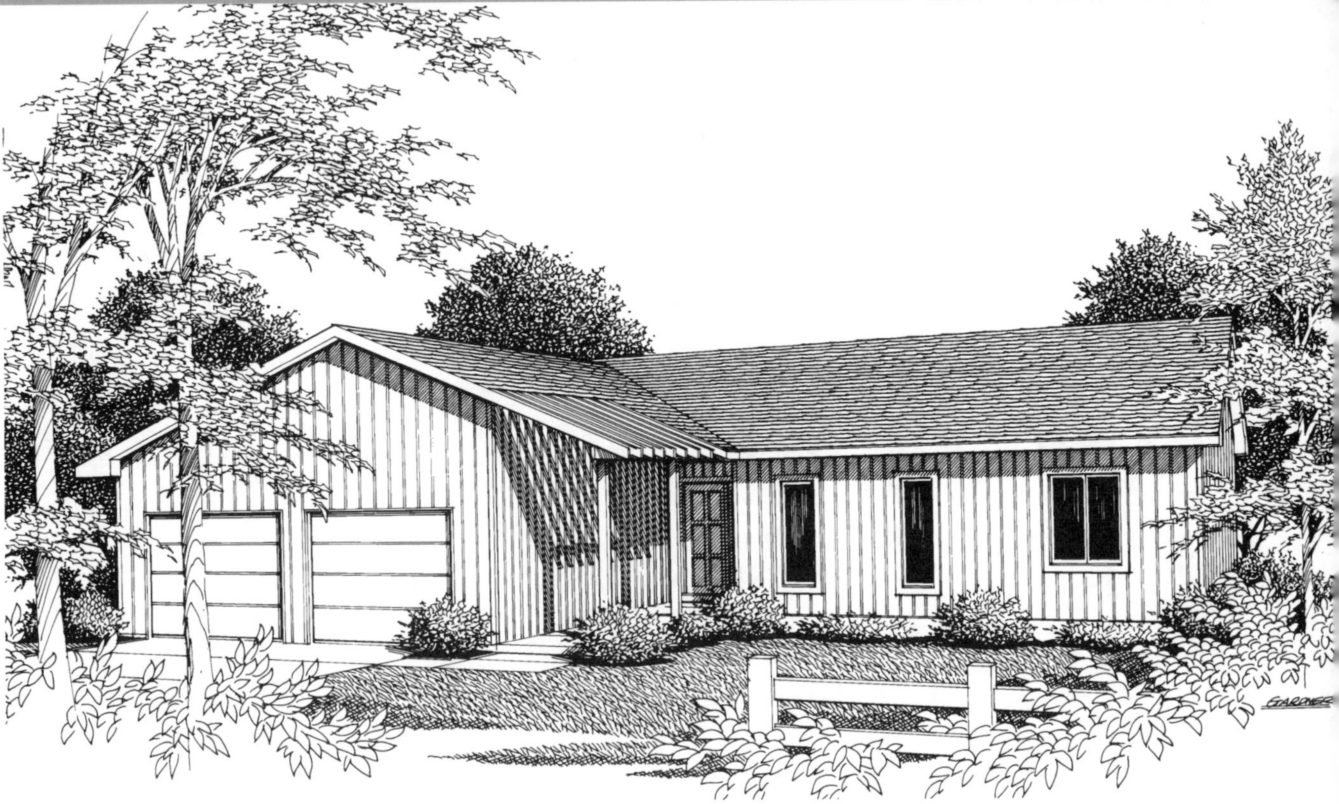

Plan #582-001D-0069

Price Code B

Special Features *• 1,504 total square feet of living area • Private master bedroom features double walk-in closets, linen closet and bath • Laundry room is conveniently located near garage • Open great room and dining area create a spacious living atmosphere • Generous closet space in secondary bedrooms • Kitchen features breakfast bar, pantry and storage closet • 3 bedrooms, 2 baths, 2-car garage • Crawl space foundation, drawings also include basement and slab foundation*

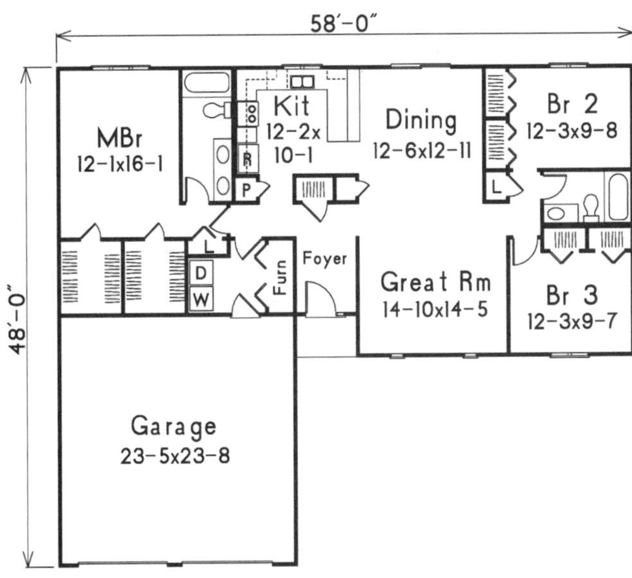

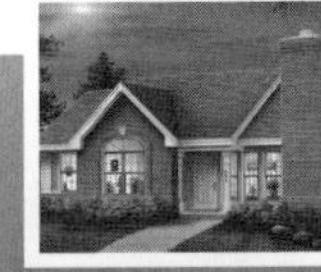

Double Gable With Dramatic Arched Window

Plan #582-052D-0007

Price Code A

Special Features • 1,273 total square feet of living area • 10' ceilings in the living and dining areas add spaciousness • Master bedroom is a private retreat from the rest of this home • Kitchen has lots of counter-space and cabinetry • 3 bedrooms, 2 baths, 2-car drive under garage • Basement foundation

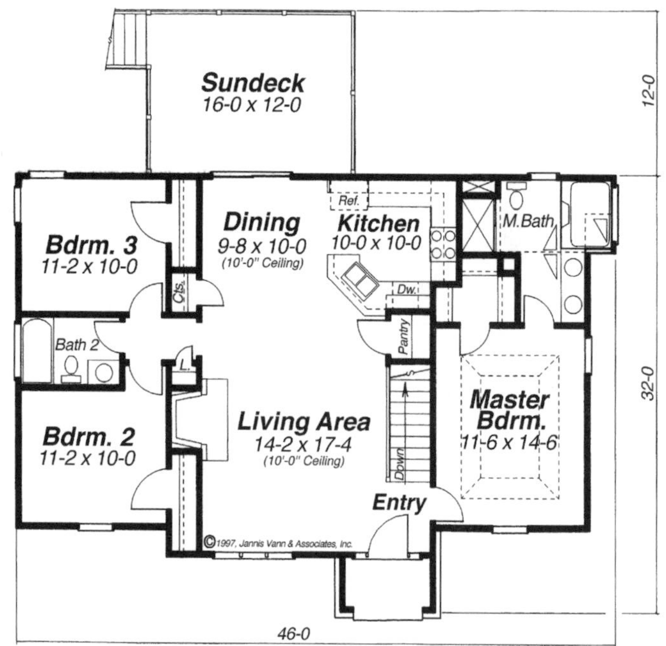

Bright, Spacious And Appealing

Plan #582-022D-0016

Price Code C

Special Features • 1,835 total square feet of living area • The arched entry and vaulted foyer create a welcoming appearance • Divided dining and living rooms continue with vaulted ceilings to provide a distinguished openness • Country kitchen with cozy fireplace and greenhouse windows offer a central gathering area • Open stairway overlooks foyer • All bedrooms are located on the second floor for added privacy • 3 bedrooms, 2 1/2 baths, 2-car garage • Basement foundation

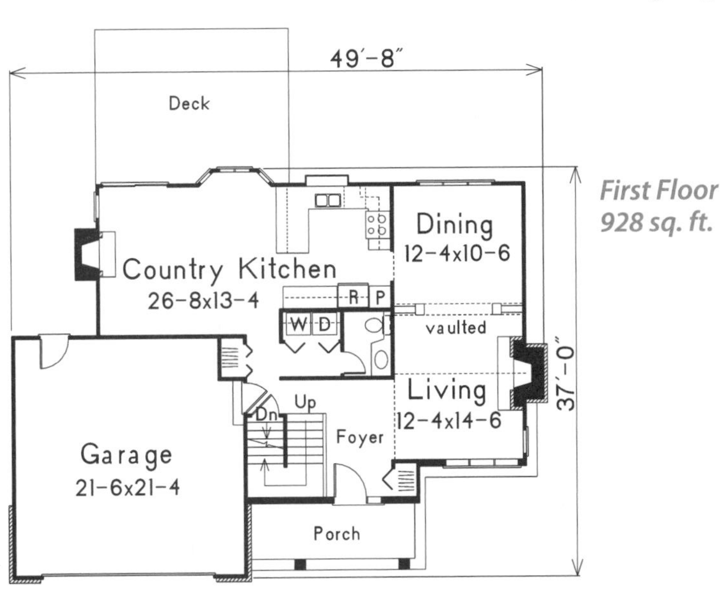

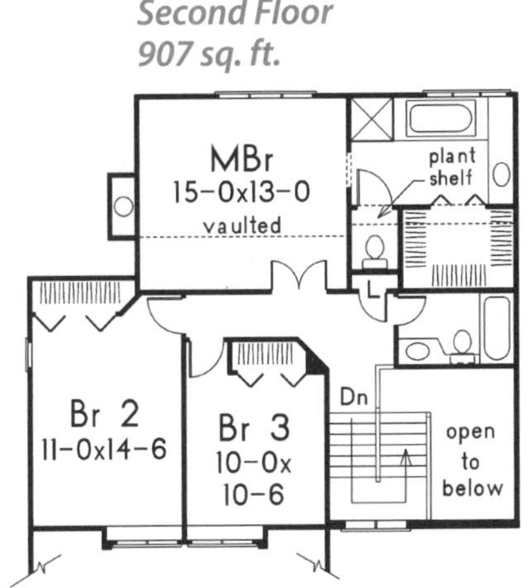

www.houseplansandmore.com

Plan #582-069D-0017

Price Code C

Special Features • 1,926 total square feet of living area • Large covered rear porch is spacious enough for entertaining • L-shaped kitchen is compact yet efficient and includes a snack bar for extra dining space • Oversized utility room has counterspace, extra shelves and space for a second refrigerator • Secluded master suite has a private bath and a large walk-in closet • 3 bedrooms, 2 baths, 2-car side entry garage • Slab or crawl space foundation, please specify when ordering

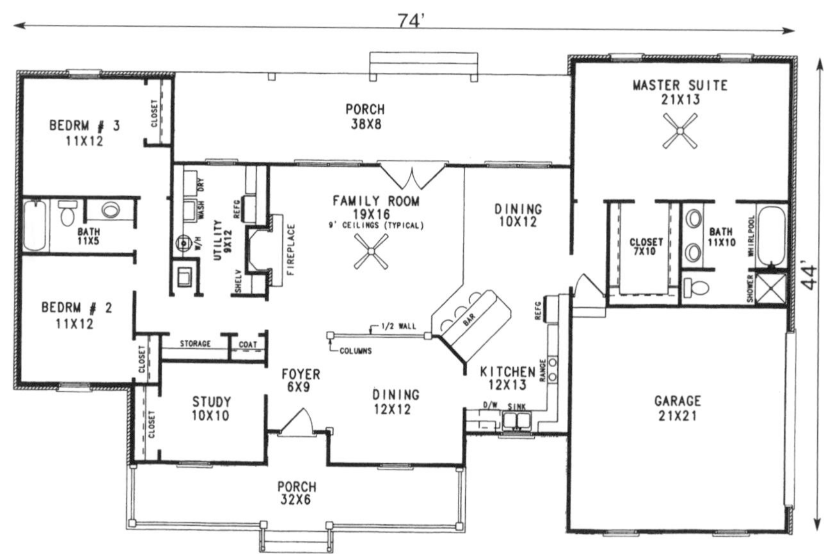

Striking Plant Shelf

Plan #582-011D-0005

Price Code C

Special Features *• 1,467 total square feet of living area • Vaulted ceilings, an open floor plan and a wealth of windows create an inviting atmosphere • Efficiently arranged kitchen has an island with built-in cooktop and a snack counter • Plentiful storage and closet space throughout this home • 3 bedrooms, 2 baths, 2-car garage • Crawl space foundation*

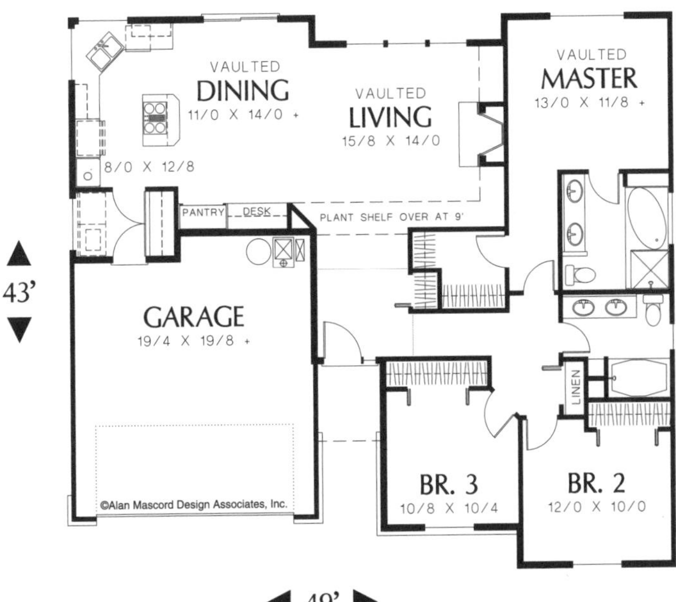

Plan #582-078D-0001

Price Code D

Special Features • 1,695 total square feet of living area • Dramatic sloping rooflines and stone decorate the exterior • Stair location offers privacy to the second floor • The elegant dining room features large French doors that open onto a patio • The living room is warmed by a raised-hearth fireplace • 2 bedrooms, 2 baths, 1-car attached carport with storage • Slab foundation

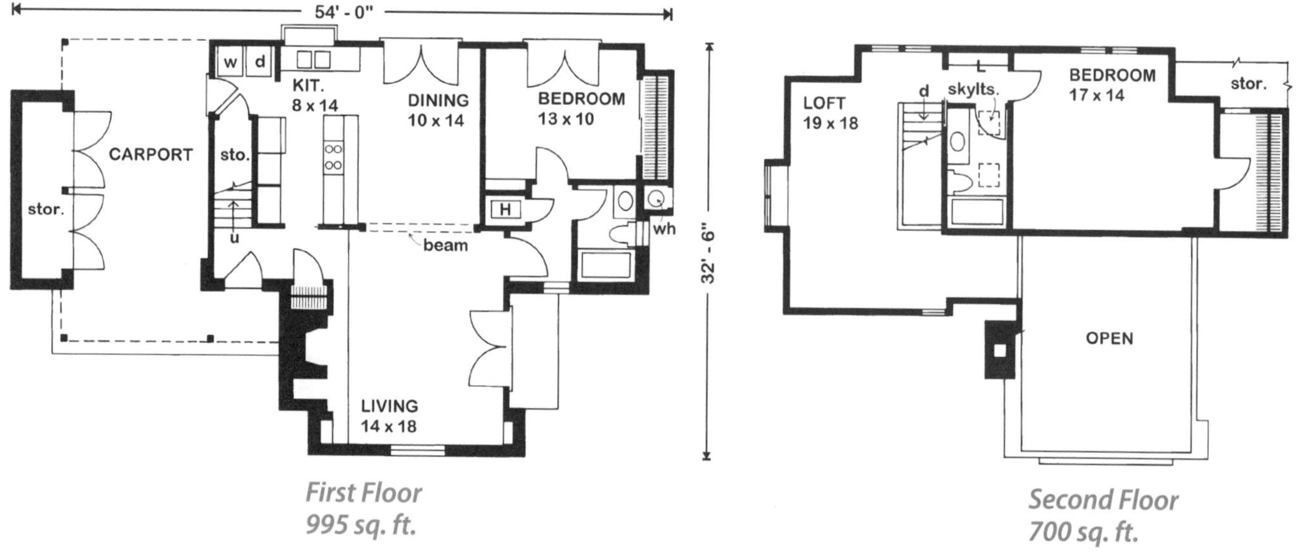

First Floor
995 sq. ft.

Second Floor
700 sq. ft.

Economical Ranch For Easy Living

47'-0"
54'-0"
Patio
Br 2 10-0x9-10
Br 3 10-0x9-10
Kit 10-0x9-10
Dining 11-0x11-0 vaulted
R
P
Dn
L
Living 15-6x15-0 vaulted
MBr 10-0x14-2
D
W
Porch depth 6-0
Garage 20-4x21-8

Plan #582-014D-0005 **Price Code A**

Special Features • *1,314 total square feet of living area* • *Energy efficient home with 2" x 6" exterior walls* • *Covered porch adds immediate appeal and welcoming charm* • *Open floor plan combined with a vaulted ceiling offers spacious living* • *Functional kitchen is complete with a pantry and eating bar* • *Cozy fireplace in the living room* • *Private master bedroom features a large walk-in closet and bath* • *3 bedrooms, 2 baths, 2-car garage* • *Basement foundation*

This Home Has Alpine Appeal

Plan #582-062D-0029

Price Code B

Special Features • 1,670 total square feet of living area • Living and dining areas combine making an ideal space for entertaining • Master bedroom accesses rear verandah through sliding glass doors • Second floor includes cozy family room with patio deck just outside of the secondary bedrooms • 3 bedrooms, 2 baths • Crawl space foundation

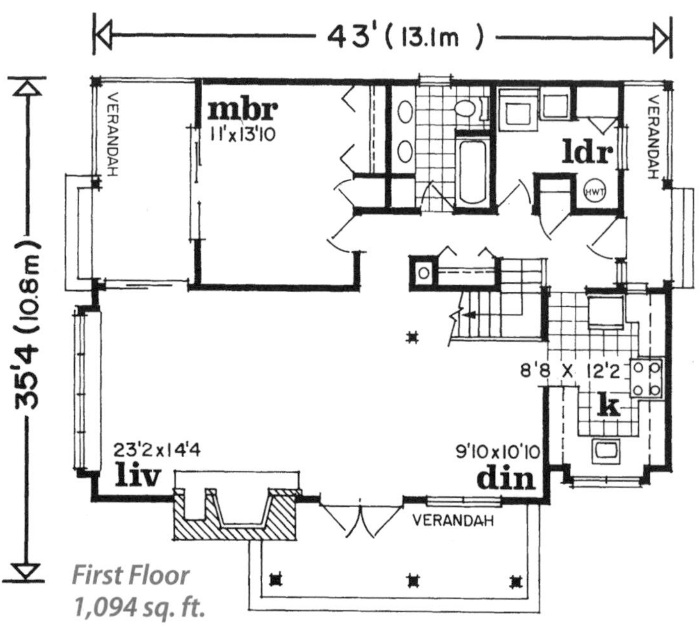

First Floor
1,094 sq. ft.

Second Floor
576 sq. ft.

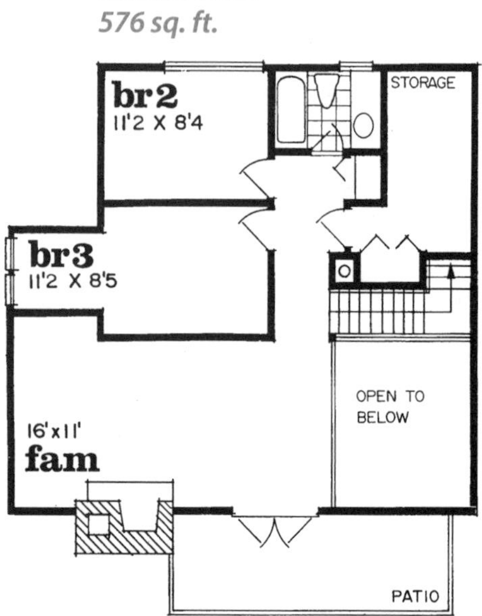

Gables Accent This Home

Plan #582-041D-0005

Price Code A

Special Features • 1,239 total square feet of living area • Master bedroom has a private bath and walk-in closet • Convenient coat closet and pantry are located near the garage entrance • Dining area accesses deck • Stairway with sloped ceiling creates an open atmosphere in the great room • 3 bedrooms, 2 1/2 baths, 2-car garage • Basement foundation

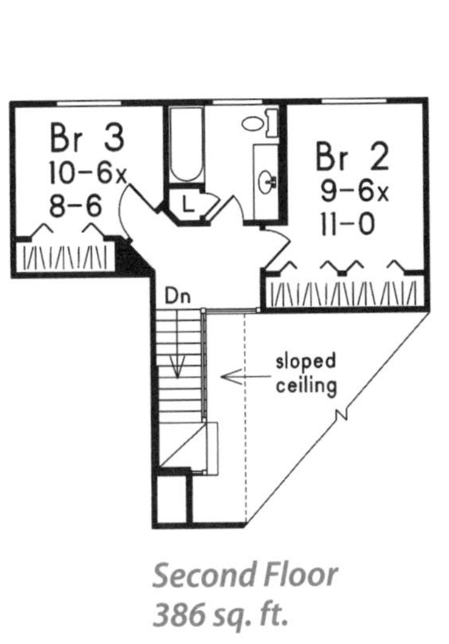

Second Floor
386 sq. ft.

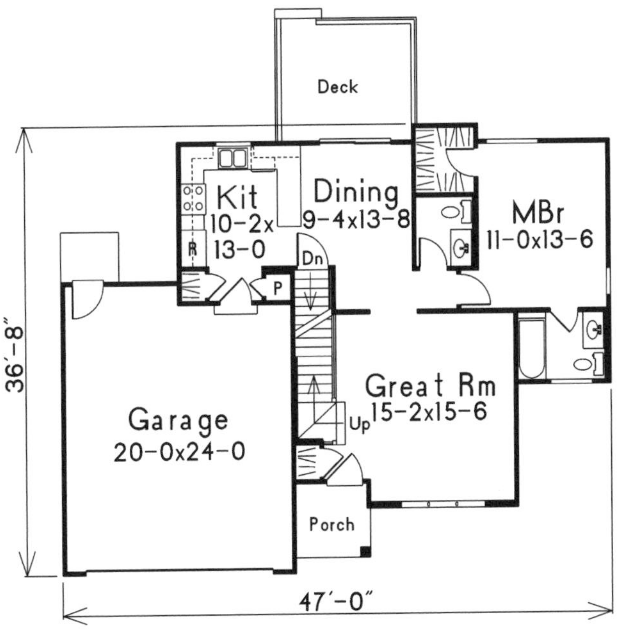

First Floor
853 sq. ft.

Comfortable Vacation Retreat

Plan #582-058D-0013

Price Code AA

Special Features • *1,073 total square feet of living area* • *Home includes a lovely covered front porch and a screened porch off dining area* • *Attractive box window brightens the kitchen* • *Space for efficiency washer and dryer is located conveniently between the bedrooms* • *Family room is spotlighted by a fireplace with flanking bookshelves and spacious vaulted ceiling* • *2 bedrooms, 1 bath* • *Crawl space foundation*

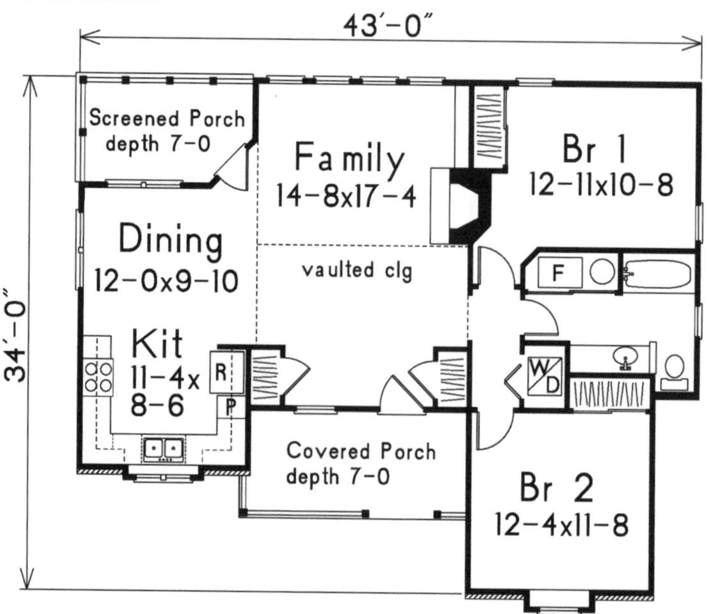

Country-Style With Spacious Rooms

Plan #582-001D-0045

Price Code AA

Special Features *• 1,197 total square feet of living area • U-shaped kitchen includes ample workspace, breakfast bar, laundry area and direct access to the outdoors • Large living room with convenient coat closet • Bedroom #1 features a large walk-in closet • 3 bedrooms, 1 bath • Crawl space foundation, drawings also include basement and slab foundations*

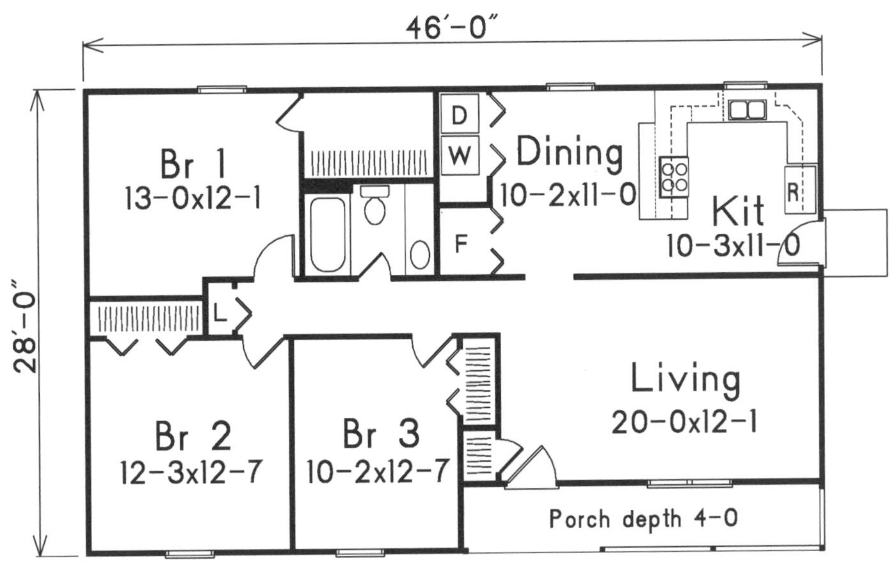

Upscale Ranch With Formal And Informal Areas

Plan #582-068D-0004

Price Code C

Special Features • *1,969 total square feet of living area • Master bedroom boasts luxurious bath with double sinks, two walk-in closets and an oversized tub • Corner fireplace warms a conveniently located family area • Formal living and dining areas in the front of the home lend a touch of privacy when entertaining • Spacious utility room has counterspace and a sink • 3 bedrooms, 2 baths, 2-car garage • Crawl space foundation, drawings also include slab foundation*

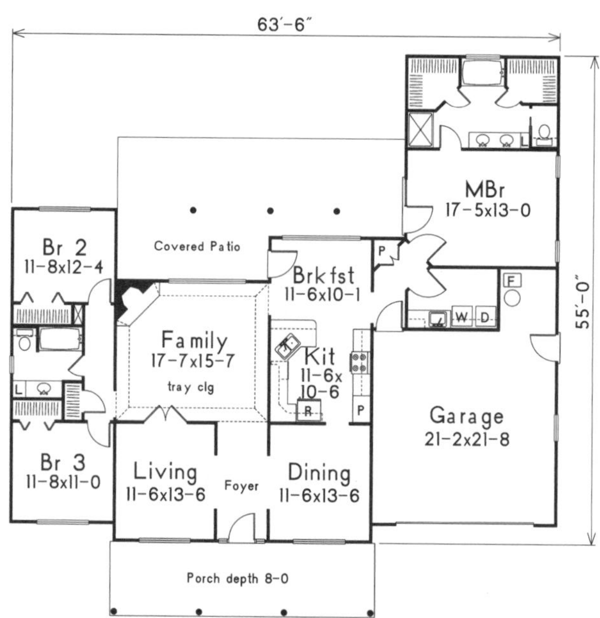

Blends Open And Private Living Areas

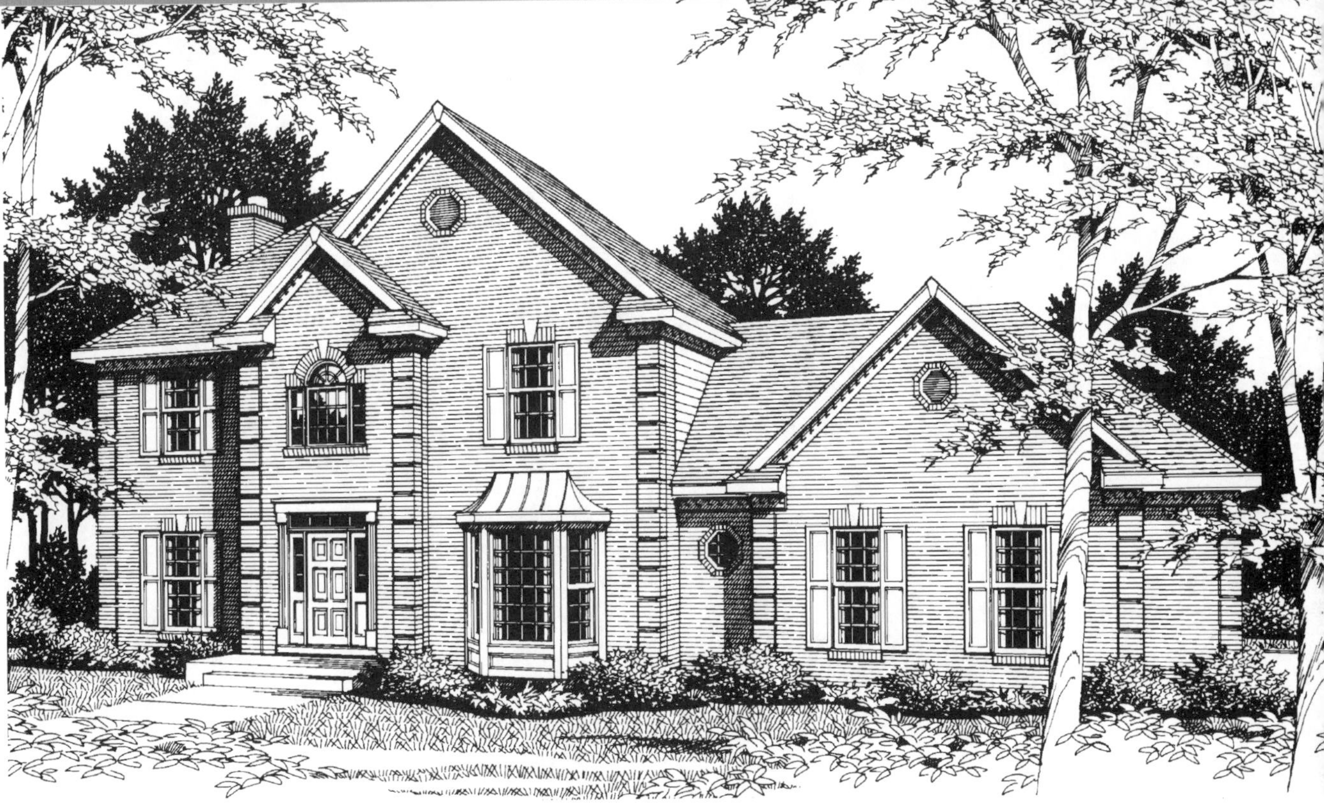

Plan #582-006D-0004

Price Code C

Special Features • *1,996 total square feet of living area • Dining area features an octagon-shaped coffered ceiling and built-in china cabinet • Both the master bath and second floor bath have cheerful skylights • Family room includes a wet bar and fireplace flanked by attractive quarter round windows • 9' ceilings throughout the first floor with plant shelving in foyer and dining area • 3 bedrooms, 2 1/2 baths, 2-car side entry garage • Basement foundation, drawings also include crawl space and slab foundations*

Second Floor
859 sq. ft.

First Floor
1,137 sq. ft.

www.houseplansandmore.com

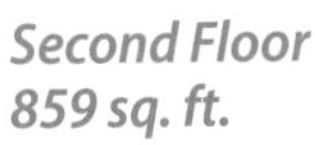

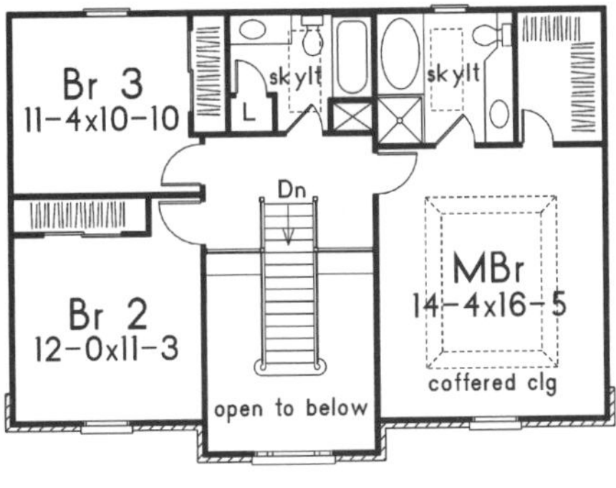

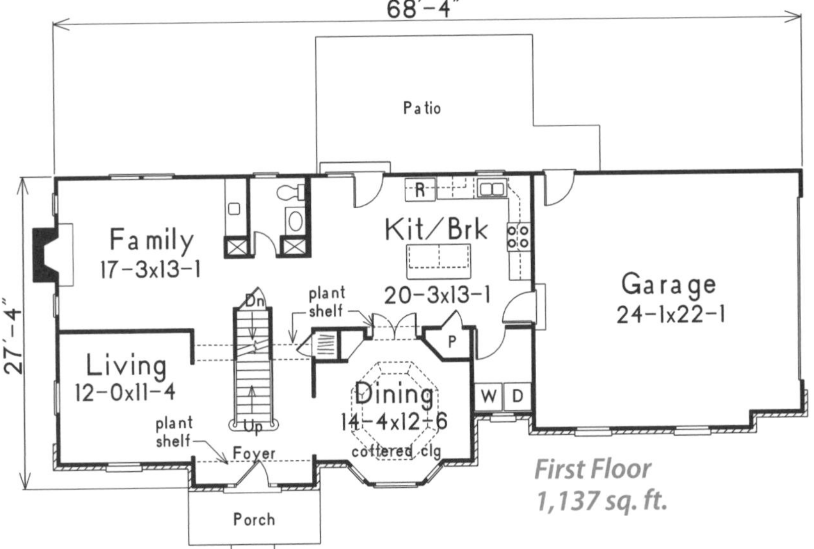

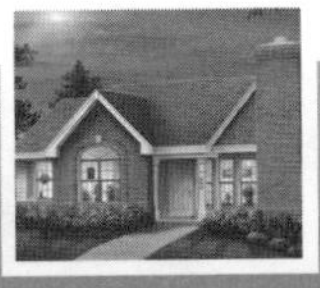

Unique Step Up From Entry To Living Space

Plan #582-053D-0049

Price Code A

Special Features • *1,261 total square feet of living area* • *Great room, brightened by windows and doors, features vaulted ceiling, fireplace and access to deck* • *Vaulted master bedroom enjoys a private bath* • *Split-level foyer leads to living space or basement* • *Centrally located laundry area is near bedrooms* • *3 bedrooms, 2 baths, 2-car drive under garage* • *Basement foundation*

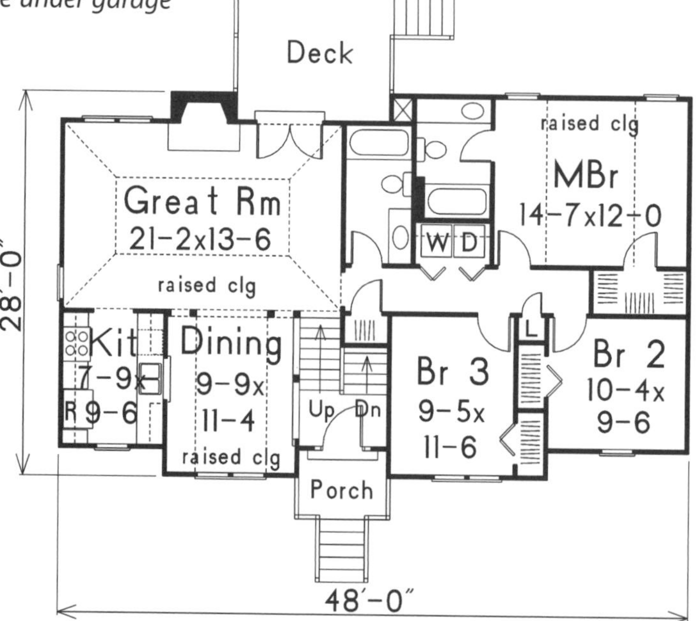

Plan #582-048D-0001

Price Code D

Special Features • 1,865 total square feet of living area • Large foyer opens into an expansive dining area and great room • Home features vaulted ceilings throughout • Master bedroom features an angled entry, vaulted ceiling, plant shelf and bath with double vanity, tub and shower • 4 bedrooms, 2 baths, 2-car garage • Slab foundation, drawings also include crawl space foundation

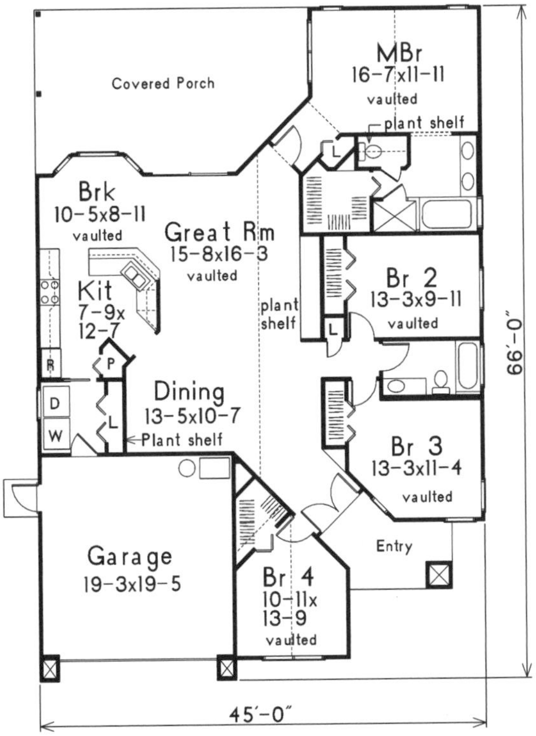

Covered Porch
MBr 16-7x11-11 vaulted
plant shelf
Brk 10-5x8-11 vaulted
Great Rm 15-8x16-3 vaulted
Kit 7-9x 12-7
plant shelf
Br 2 13-3x9-11 vaulted
Dining 13-5x10-7
Plant shelf
Br 3 13-3x11-4 vaulted
Garage 19-3x19-5
Br 4 10-11x 13-9 vaulted
Entry
66'-0"
45'-0"

Secluded Bedroom Makes Great Guest Quarters

Plan #582-001D-0090

Price Code A

Special Features • *1,300 total square feet of living area* • *Combination kitchen/dining area creates an open atmosphere* • *Isolated master bedroom has a private bath* • *Kitchen includes a side entrance, pantry, closet and convenient laundry area* • *4 bedrooms, 2 baths* • *Crawl space foundation, drawings also include basement and slab foundations*

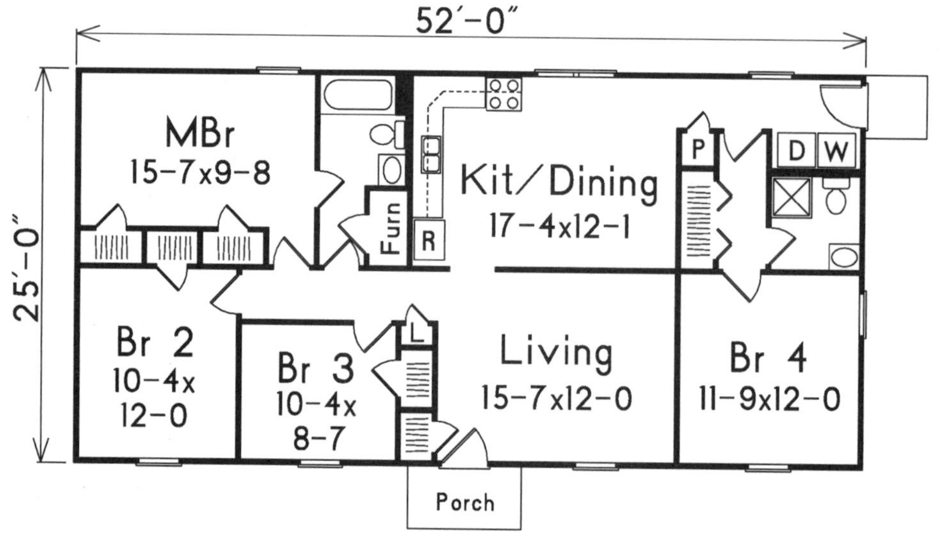

Distinctive Ranch Has A Larger Look

Plan #582-022D-0005

Price Code A

Special Features • *1,360 total square feet of living area* • *Double-gabled front facade frames large windows* • *Entry area is open to a vaulted great room, fireplace and rear deck creating an open feel* • *Vaulted ceiling and large windows add openness to the kitchen/breakfast room* • *Bedroom #3 easily converts to a den* • *Plan easily adapts to crawl space or slab construction, with the utilities replacing the stairs* • *3 bedrooms, 2 baths, 2-car garage* • *Basement foundation*

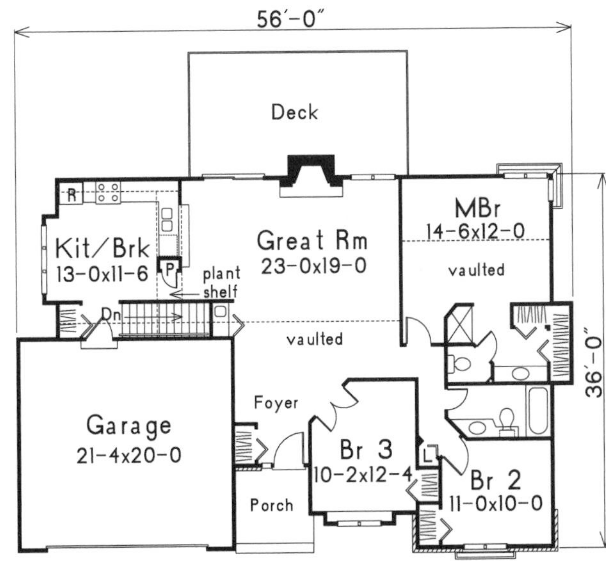

Plan #582-036D-0048

Price Code C

Special Features • *1,830 total square feet of living area* • *Inviting covered verandas in the front and rear of the home* • *Great room has a fireplace and cathedral ceiling* • *Handy service porch allows easy access* • *Master bedroom has a vaulted ceiling and private bath* • *3 bedrooms, 2 baths, 3-car side entry garage* • *Basement, crawl space or slab foundation, please specify when ordering*

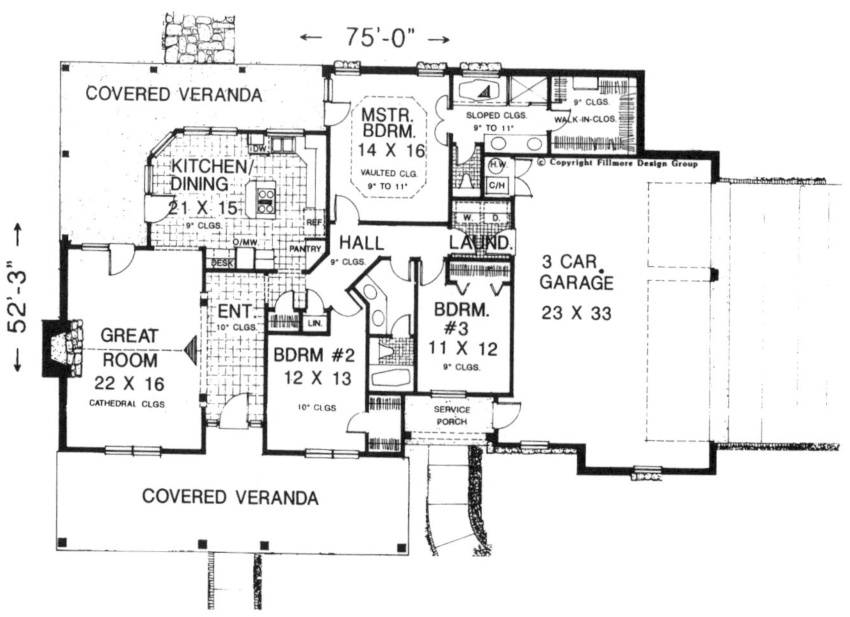

Plan #582-019D-0003

Price Code A

Special Features • 1,310 total square feet of living area • Family room features a corner fireplace adding warmth • Efficiently designed kitchen has a corner sink with windows • Master bedroom includes a large walk-in closet and private bath • 3 bedrooms, 2 baths, 2-car garage • Crawl space foundation, drawings also include slab foundation

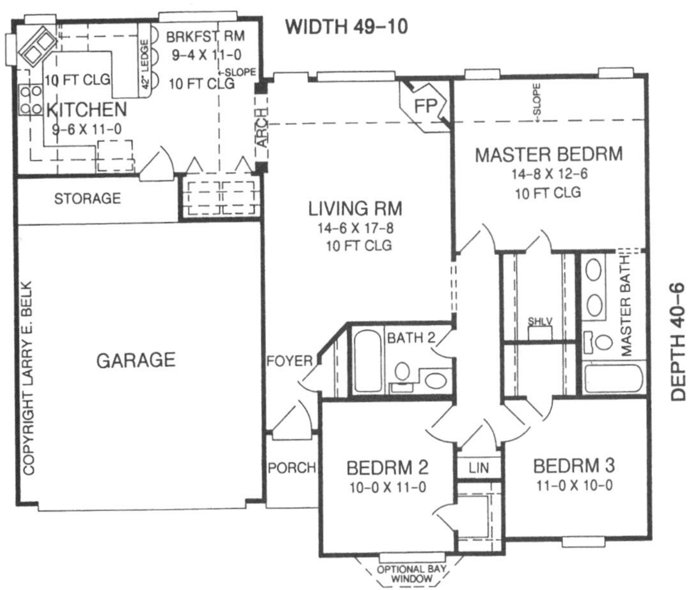

Cheerful Transoms Brighten Great Room

Plan #582-026D-0040 — Price Code A

Special Features • 1,347 total square feet of living area • Efficient snack bar separates kitchen and roomy breakfast room • Elegant master bedroom features a tray ceiling, walk-in closet and a private bath with whirlpool tub • Bedroom #3 can easily be converted to a den • 3 bedrooms, 2 baths, 2-car garage • Basement foundation

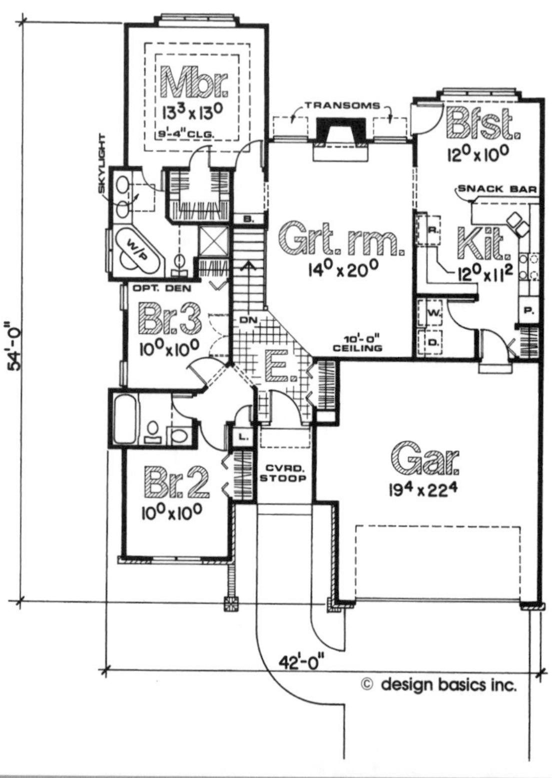

A Charming Home Loaded With Extras

Plan #582-049D-0004

Price Code C

Special Features • 1,997 total square feet of living area • Screened porch leads to a rear terrace with access to the breakfast room • Living and dining rooms combine adding spaciousness to the floor plan • Other welcome amenities include boxed windows in the breakfast and dining rooms, a fireplace in the living room and a pass-through snack bar in the kitchen • 3 bedrooms, 2 1/2 baths • Basement foundation

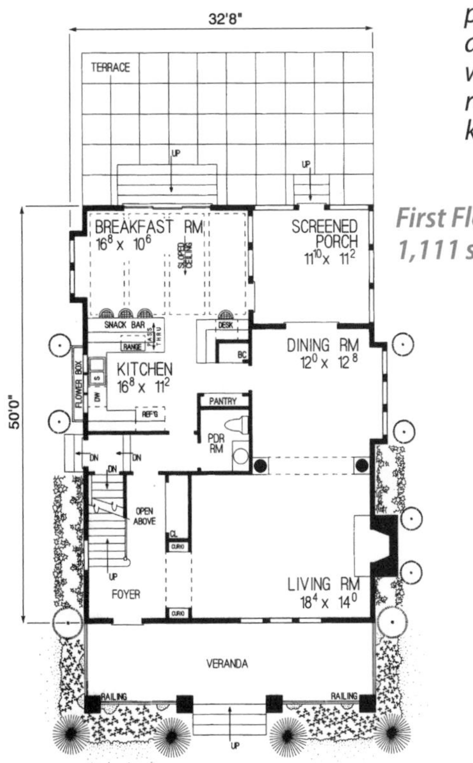

First Floor
1,111 sq. ft.

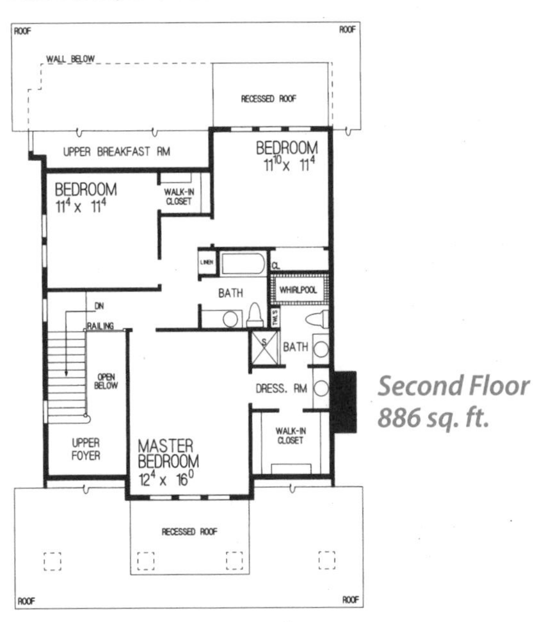

Second Floor
886 sq. ft.

www.houseplansandmore.com

Master Suite With Media Center

Plan #582-030D-0002

Price Code A

Special Features • 1,429 total square feet of living area • Master suite includes a sitting area and private bath with two walk-in closets • Kitchen and dining area overlook the living room • Living room has a fireplace, media center and access to the covered porch • 3 bedrooms, 2 baths, 2-car garage • Slab or crawl space foundation, please specify when ordering

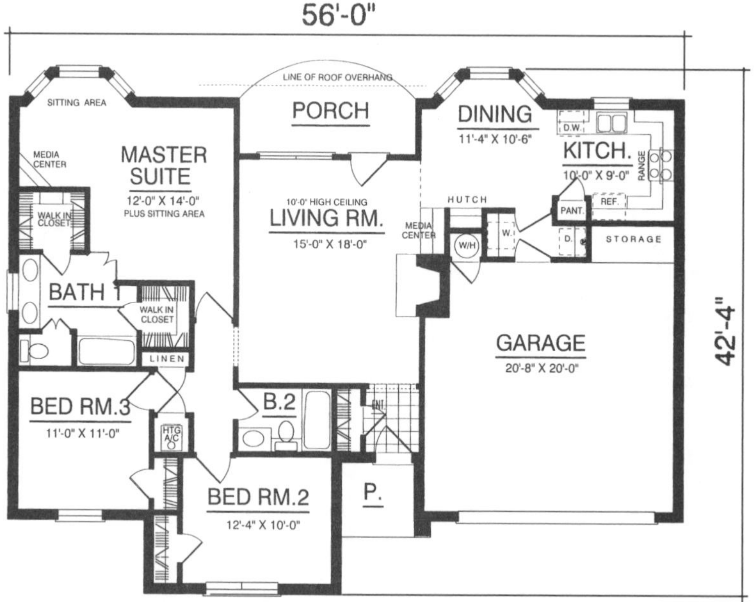

Elaborate Dining Room

Plan #582-035D-0028

Price Code B

Special Features • 1,779 total square feet of living area • Well-designed floor plan has vaulted family room with fireplace and access to the outdoors • Decorative columns separate dining area from foyer • A vaulted ceiling adds spaciousness in master bath with walk-in closet • 3 bedrooms, 2 baths, 2-car garage • Walk-out basement, slab or crawl space foundation, please specify when ordering

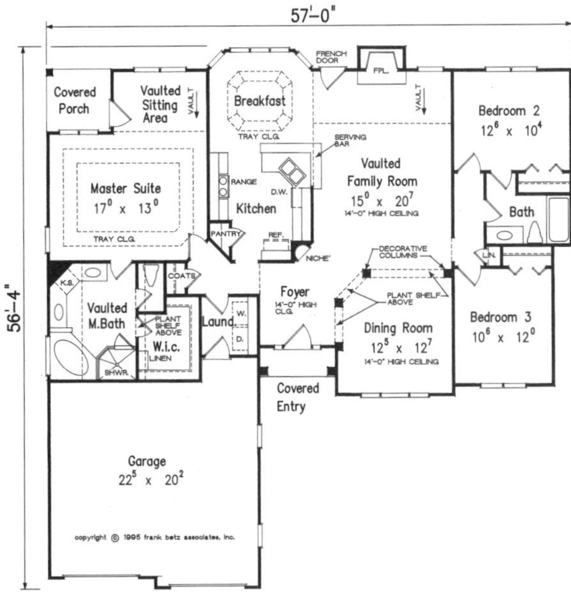

www.houseplansandmore.com

Classic Ranch, Pleasant Covered Front Porch

Plan #582-001D-0021

Price Code A

Special Features • 1,416 total square feet of living area • Excellent floor plan eases traffic • Master bedroom features private bath • Foyer opens to both formal living room and informal great room • Great room has access to the outdoors through sliding doors • 3 bedrooms, 2 baths, 2-car garage • Crawl space foundation, drawings also include basement foundation

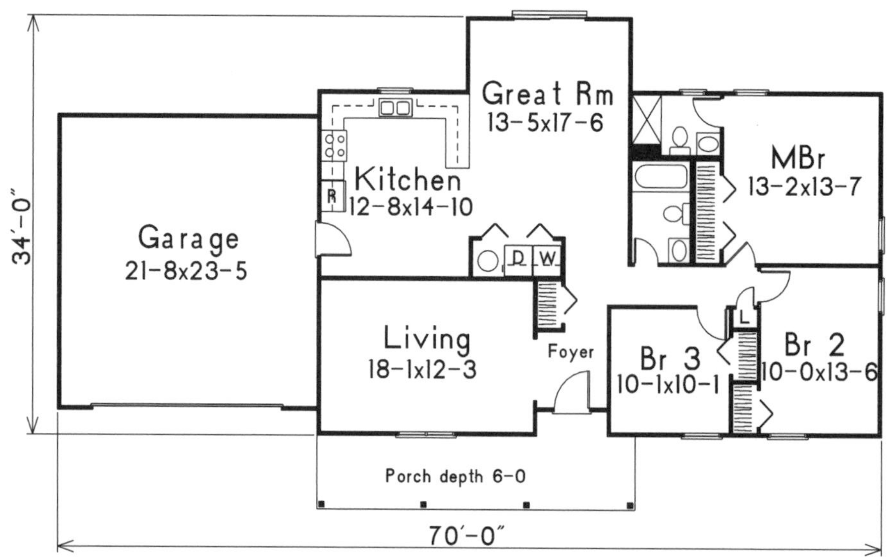

Charming Wrap-Around Porch

Plan #582-058D-0032

Price Code C

Special Features • 1,879 total square feet of living area • Open floor plan on both floors makes home appear larger • Loft area overlooks great room or can become an optional fourth bedroom • Large walk-in pantry in kitchen and large storage in rear of home has access from exterior • 3 bedrooms, 2 baths • Crawl space foundation

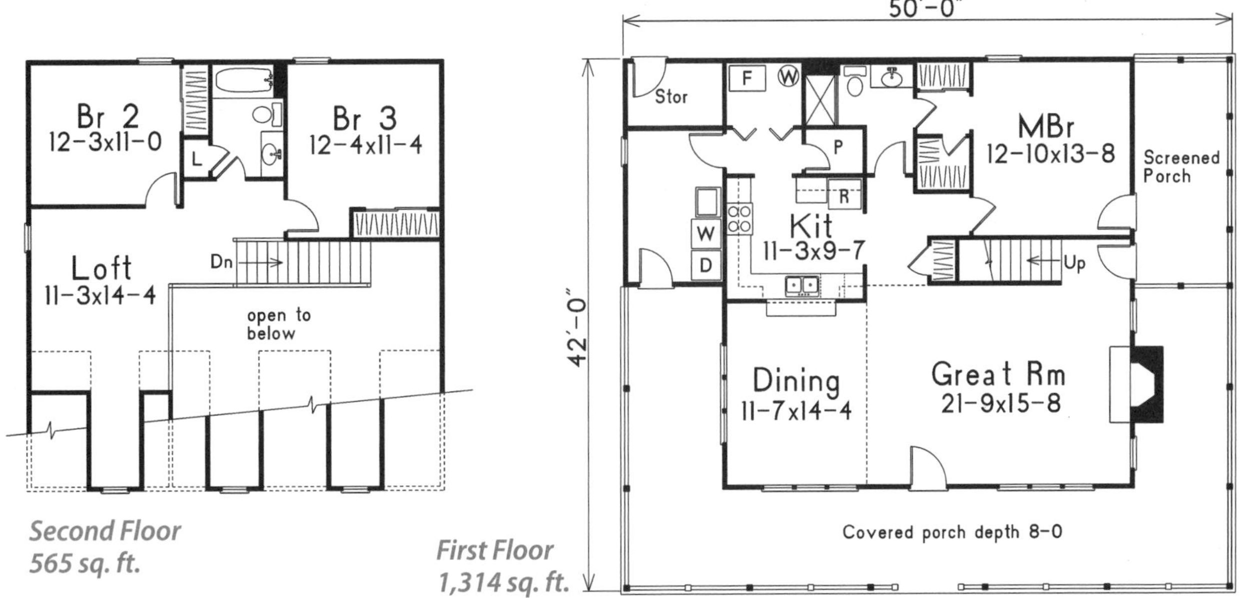

Second Floor
565 sq. ft.

First Floor
1,314 sq. ft.

Columned Breakfast Room Adds Appeal

Plan #582-033D-0005

Price Code D

Special Features • 1,954 total square feet of living area • Living and dining areas include vaulted ceilings and combine for added openness • Convenient access to laundry room from garage • Appealing bay window in family room attracts light • Raised jacuzzi tub featured in master bath • 3 bedrooms, 2 1/2 baths, 2-car garage • Basement foundation

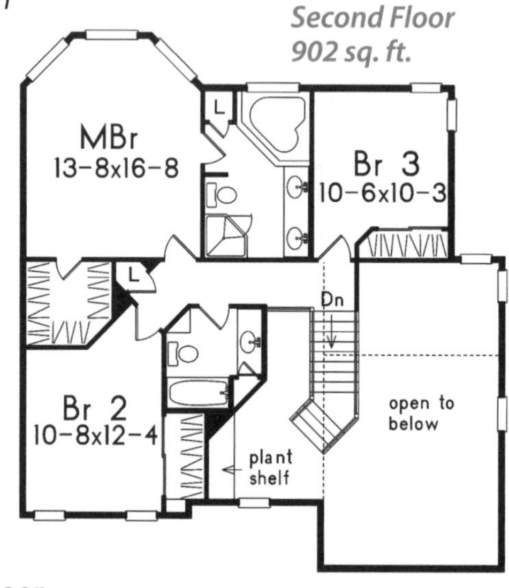

Second Floor
902 sq. ft.

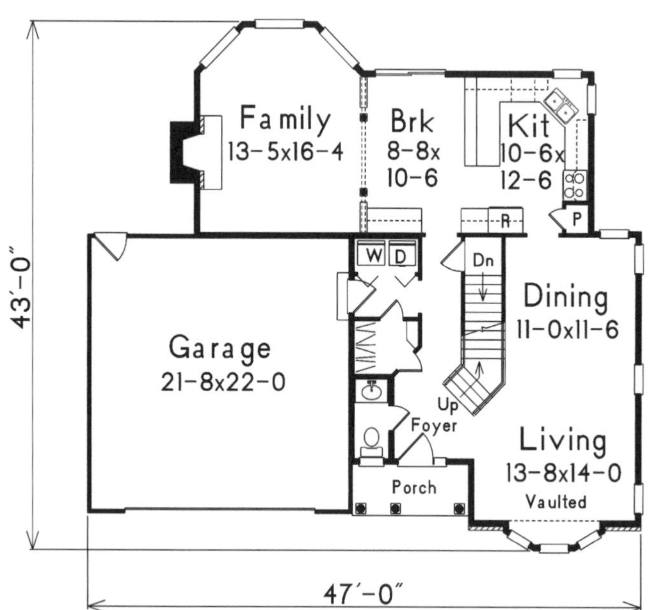

First Floor
1,052 sq. ft.

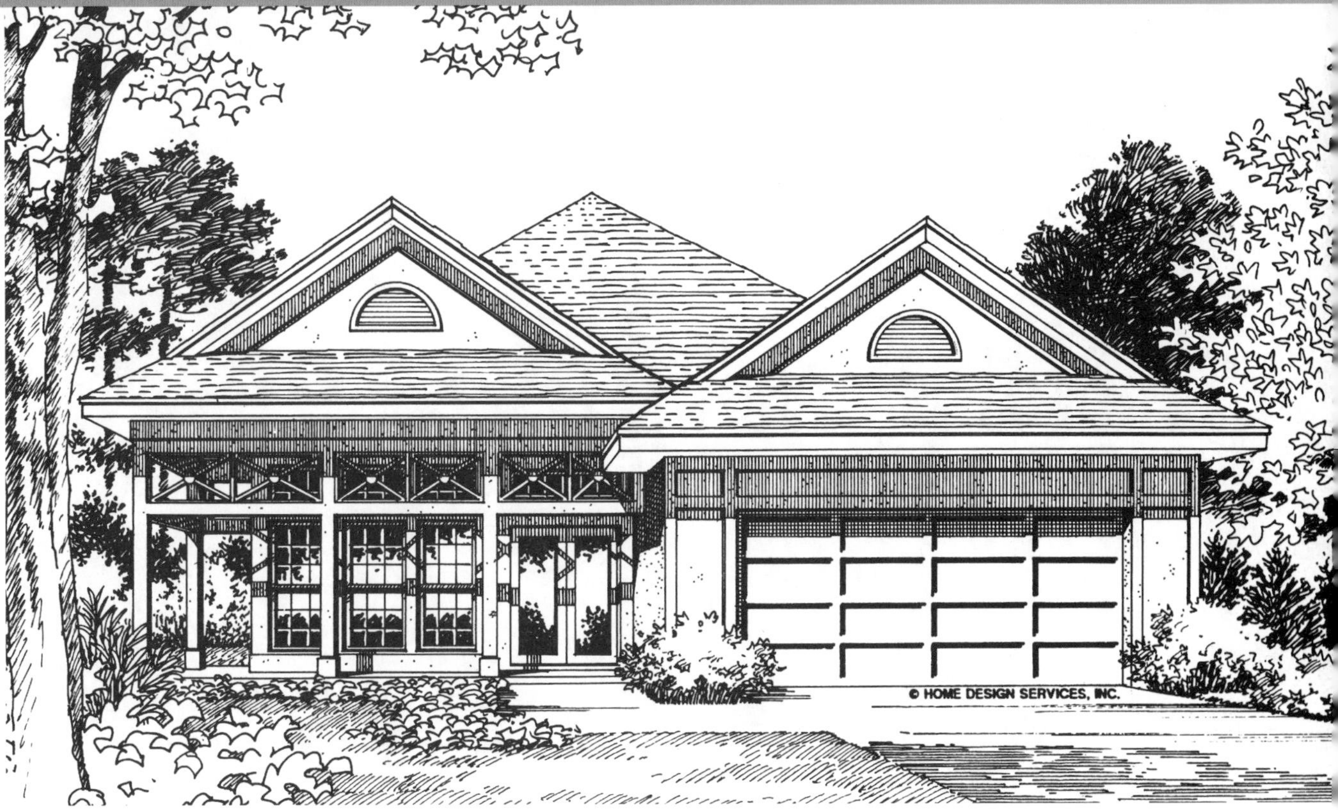

Plan #582-047D-0012 **Price Code B**

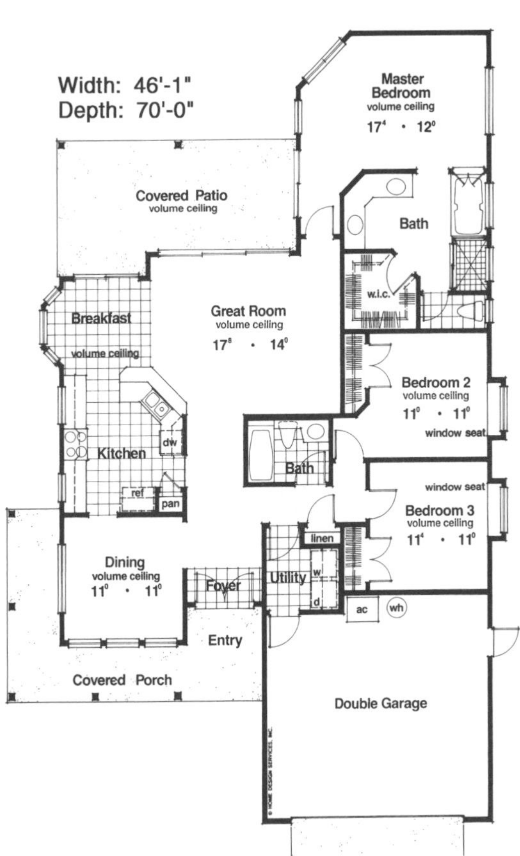

Special Features • 1,627 total square feet of living area • Bay-shaped breakfast room is sunny and bright • Angled window wall and volume ceiling in master bedroom add interest • Box-bay windows are featured in secondary bedrooms • 3 bedrooms, 2 baths, 2-car garage • Slab foundation

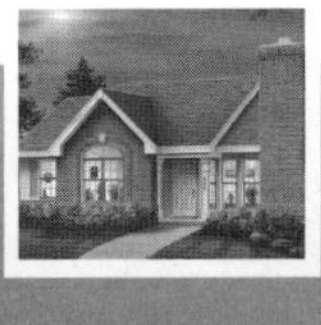

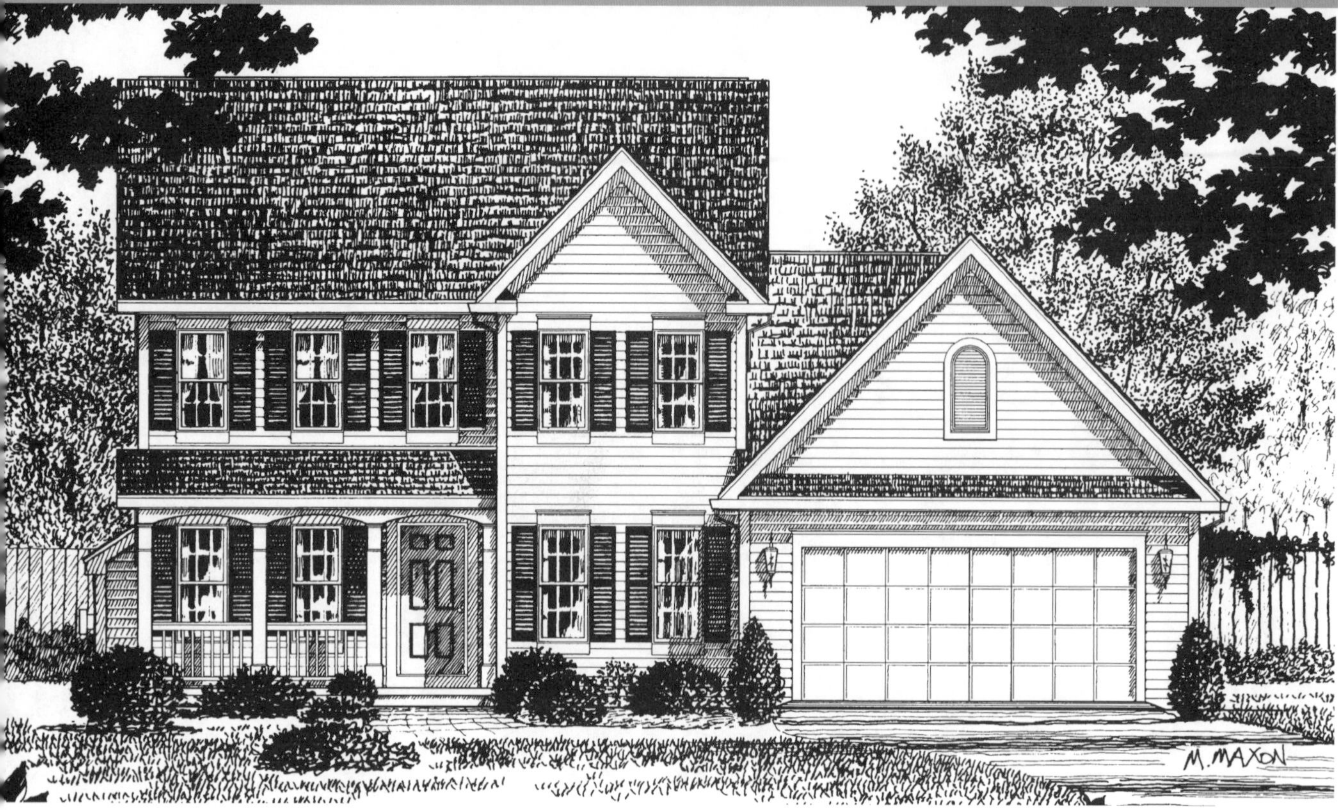

Plan #582-034D-0015

Price Code C

Special Features • 1,868 total square feet of living area • Open floor plan creates an airy feeling • Secluded study makes an ideal home office • Large master bedroom has luxurious private bath with a walk-in closet • Formal dining room has convenient access to kitchen • 3 bedrooms, 2 1/2 baths, 2-car garage • Basement foundation

Width: 52'-8"
Depth: 34'-0"

First Floor
1,020 sq. ft.

Second Floor
848 sq. ft.

1-800-DREAM HOME (373-2646)

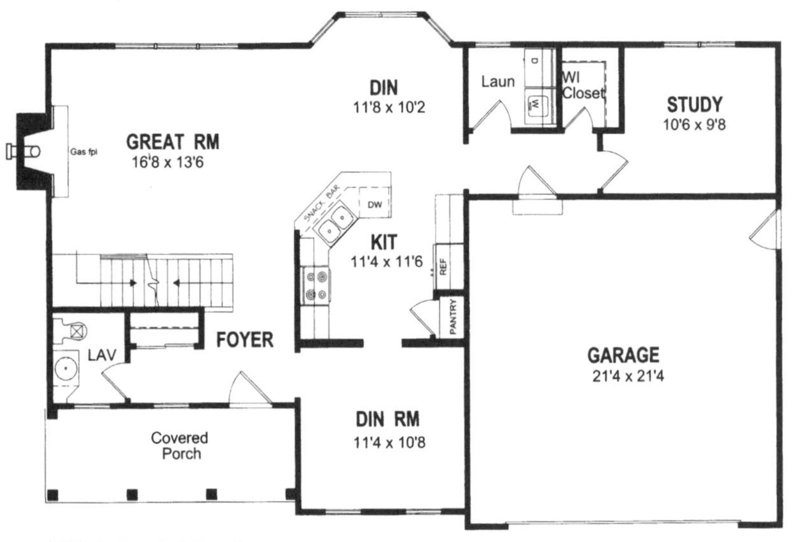

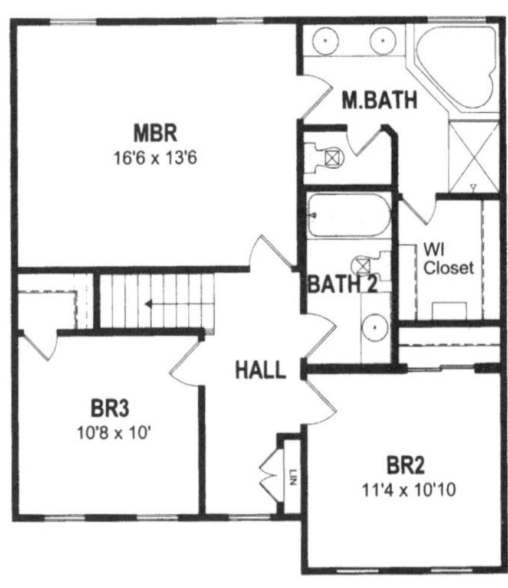

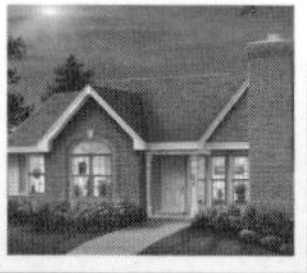

Uncommonly Styled Ranch

Plan #582-013D-0015

Price Code B

Special Features • *1,787 total square feet of living area • Skylights brighten screen porch which connects to the family room and deck outdoors • Master bedroom features a comfortable sitting area, large private bath and direct access to screen porch • Kitchen has a serving bar which extends dining into the family room • 3 bedrooms, 2 baths, 2-car side entry garage • Basement, crawl space or slab foundation, please specify when ordering*

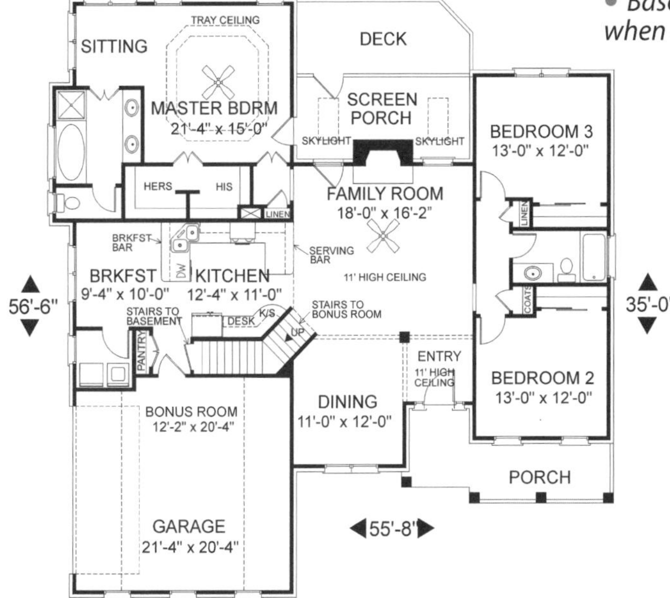

Secluded Master Bedroom

Plan #582-051D-0022 **Price Code A**

Special Features • 1,451 total square feet of living area • The entry opens into the great room with a corner fireplace and vaulted ceiling for an elegant first impression • Convenient coat closets are located near the main and garage entrances • The kitchen wraps around to the dining room which features a cathedral ceiling and access to the outdoors • Two secondary bedrooms are located away from main living areas and share a full bath • 3 bedrooms, 2 baths, 2-car garage • Basement foundation

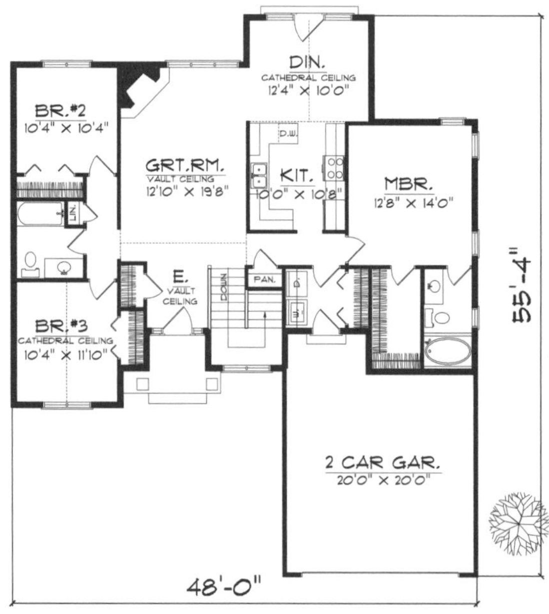

Ranch Style With Many Extras

Plan #582-035D-0050

Price Code A

Special Features • 1,342 total square feet of living area • 9' ceilings throughout the home • Master suite has a tray ceiling and wall of windows that overlook the backyard • Dining room includes a serving bar connecting it to the kitchen and sliding glass doors that lead outdoors • Optional second floor has an additional 350 square feet of living area • 3 bedrooms, 2 baths, 2-car garage • Slab, walk-out basement or crawl space foundation, please specify when ordering

First Floor
1,342 sq. ft.

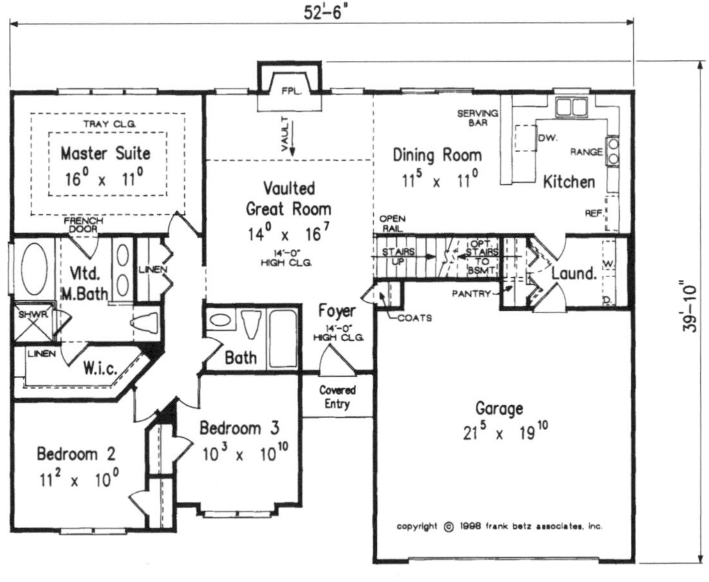

Optional
Second Floor

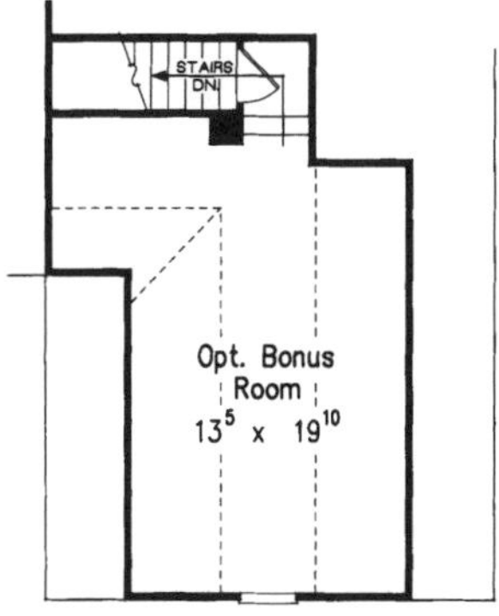

www.houseplansandmore.com

Charming Home Arranged For Open Living

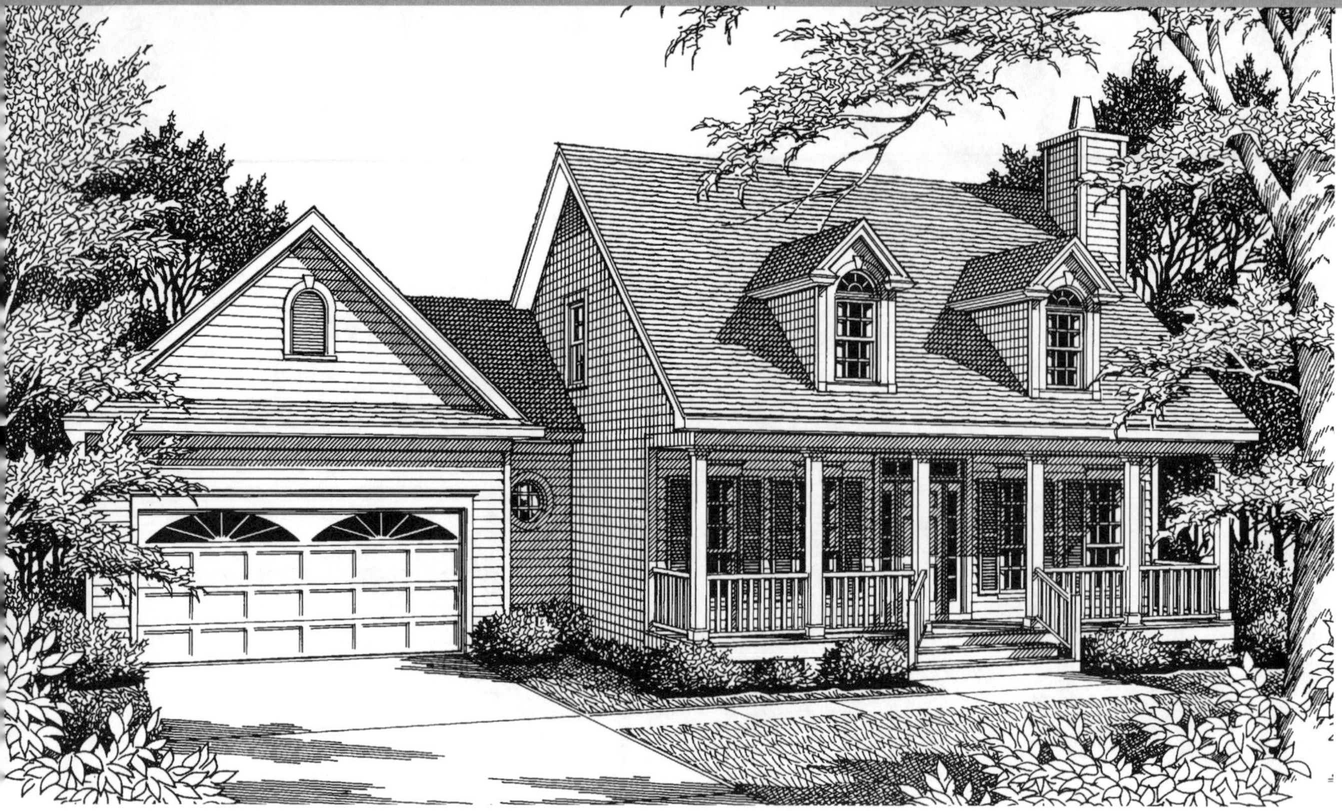

Plan #582-023D-0016

Price Code B

Special Features • 1,609 total square feet of living area • Kitchen captures full use of space with pantry, ample cabinets and workspace • Master bedroom is well-secluded with a walk-in closet and private bath • Large utility room includes a sink and extra storage • Attractive bay window in the dining area provides light • 3 bedrooms, 2 1/2 baths, 2-car garage • Slab foundation

Second Floor
537 sq. ft.

First Floor
1,072 sq. ft.

1-800-DREAM HOME (373-2646)

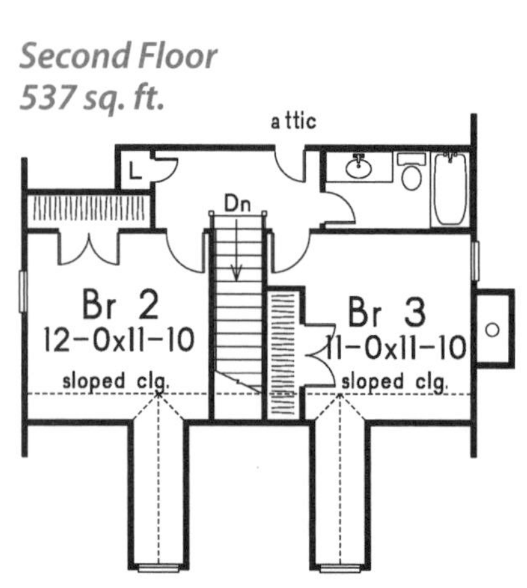

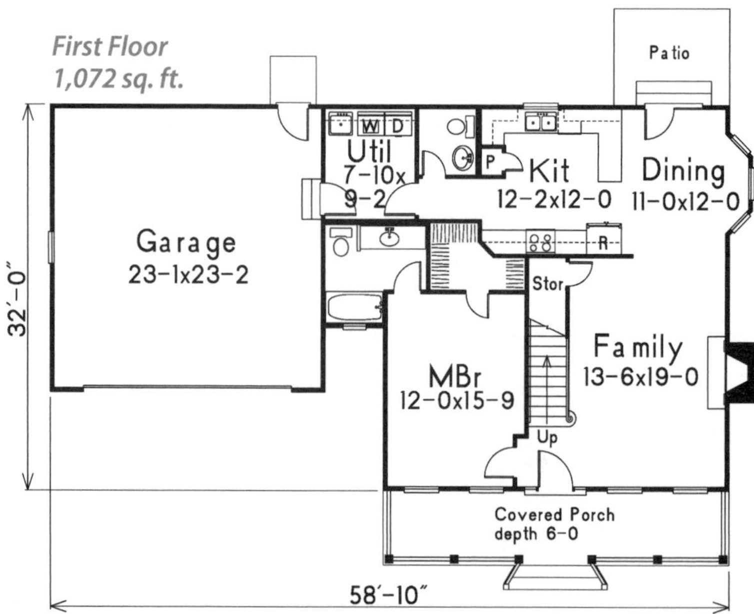

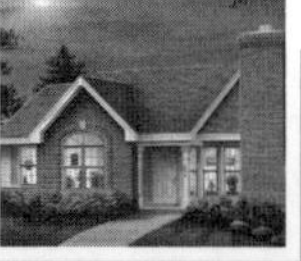

Alpine Style Creates Cozy Cabin Feel

Plan #582-036D-0045

Price Code B

Special Features • 1,577 total square feet of living area • Large living area is a great gathering place with an enormous stone fireplace, cathedral ceiling and kitchen with snack bar nearby • Second floor loft has a half wall creating an open atmosphere • 3 bedrooms, 2 1/2 baths • Crawl space foundation

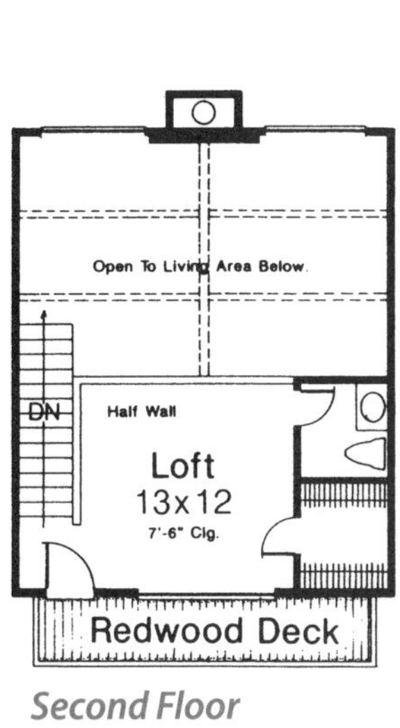

Second Floor
276 sq. ft.

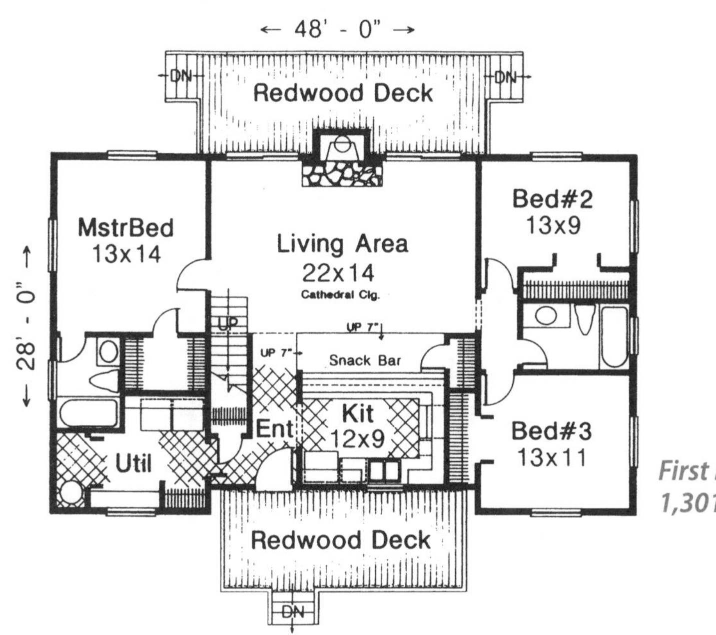

First Floor
1,301 sq. ft.

Plan #582-001D-0058

Price Code B

Special Features • 1,720 total square feet of living area • Lower level includes large family room with laundry area and half bath • L-shaped kitchen has a convenient serving bar and pass-through to dining area • Private half bath in master bedroom • 3 bedrooms, 1 full bath, 2 half baths, 2-car drive under garage • Basement foundation

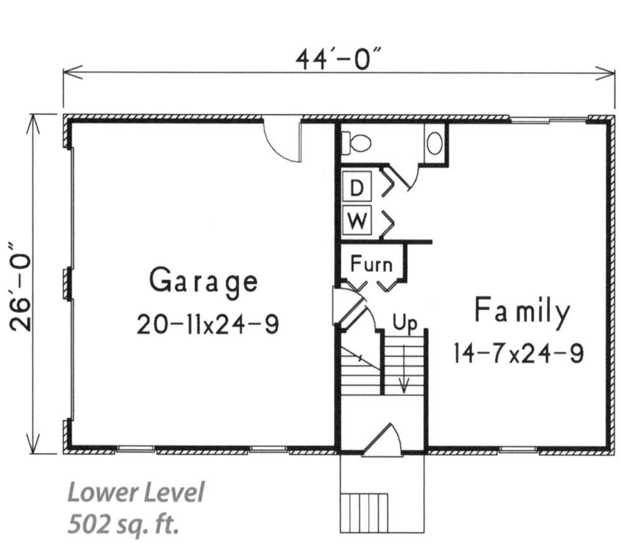

Lower Level
502 sq. ft.

First Floor
1,218 sq. ft.

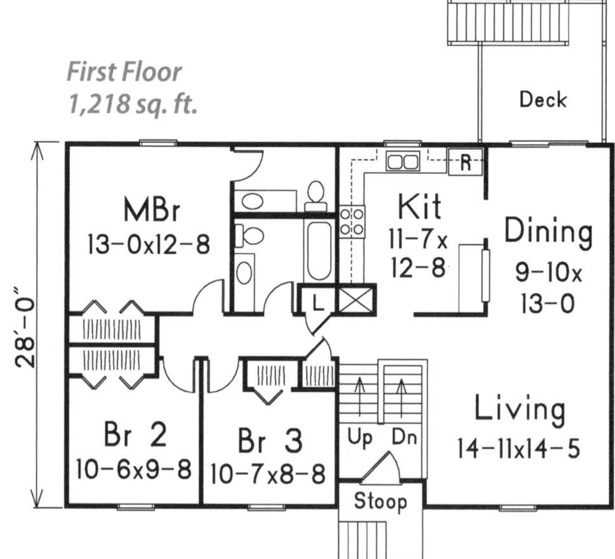

A Great Country Farmhouse

Plan #582-049D-0010

Price Code B

Special Features • 1,669 total square feet of living area • Generous use of windows add exciting visual elements to the exterior as well as plenty of natural light to the interior • Two-story great room has a raised hearth • Second floor loft/study would easily make a terrific home office • 3 bedrooms, 2 baths • Crawl space foundation

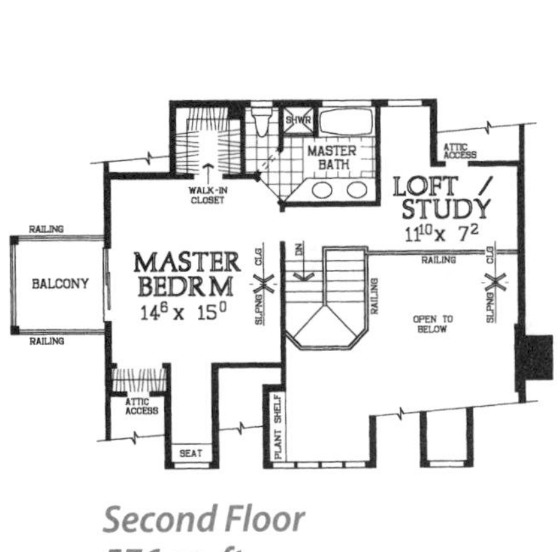

Second Floor 576 sq. ft.

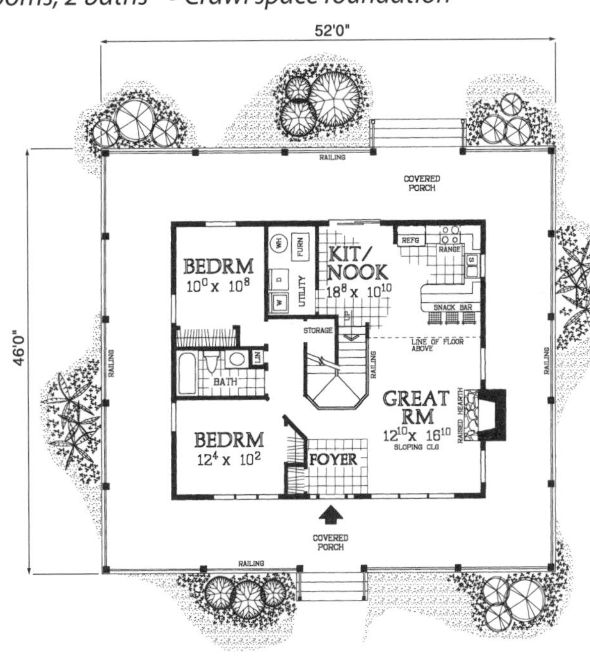

First Floor 1,093 sq. ft.

Secluded Master Bedroom Has Private Patio Area

Plan #582-053D-0047

Price Code A

Special Features • 1,438 total square feet of living area • Vaulted living and dining rooms unite to provide open space for entertaining • Secondary bedrooms share a full bath • Compact kitchen • Vaulted master bedroom includes a private bath, large walk-in closet and access to the patio • 3 bedrooms, 2 baths, 2-car side entry garage • Crawl space foundation, drawings also include slab foundation

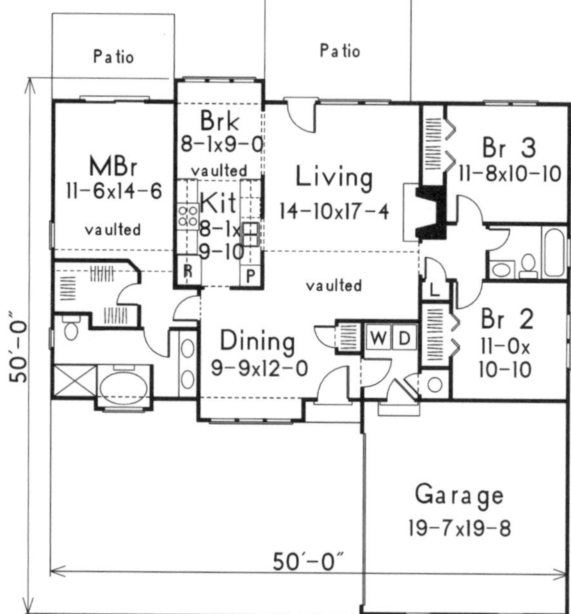

Plan #582-008D-0048

Price Code C

Special Features • *1,948 total square feet of living area* • *Family room offers warmth with an oversized fireplace and rustic beamed ceiling* • *Fully appointed kitchen extends into the family room* • *Practical mud room is adjacent to the kitchen* • *3 bedrooms, 2 1/2 baths* • *Basement foundation, drawings also include crawl space and slab foundations*

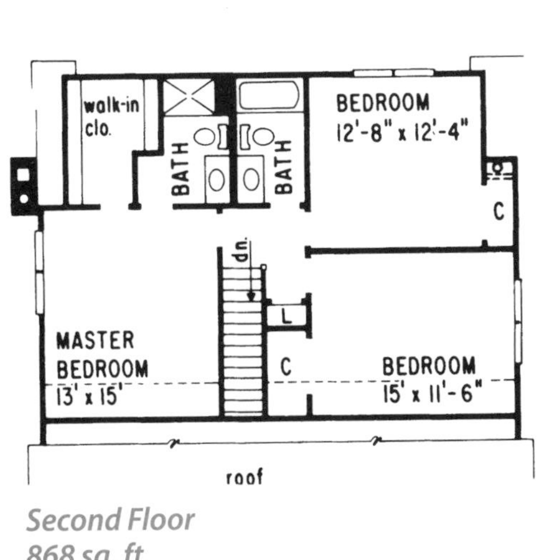

Second Floor 868 sq. ft.

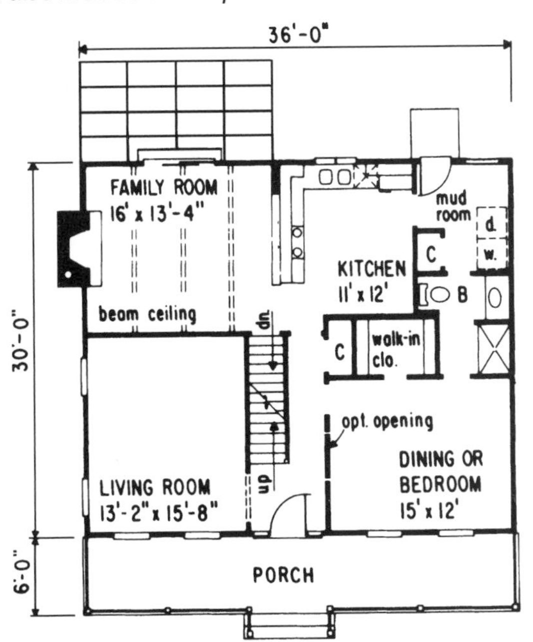

First Floor 1,080 sq. ft.

Covered Rear Porch

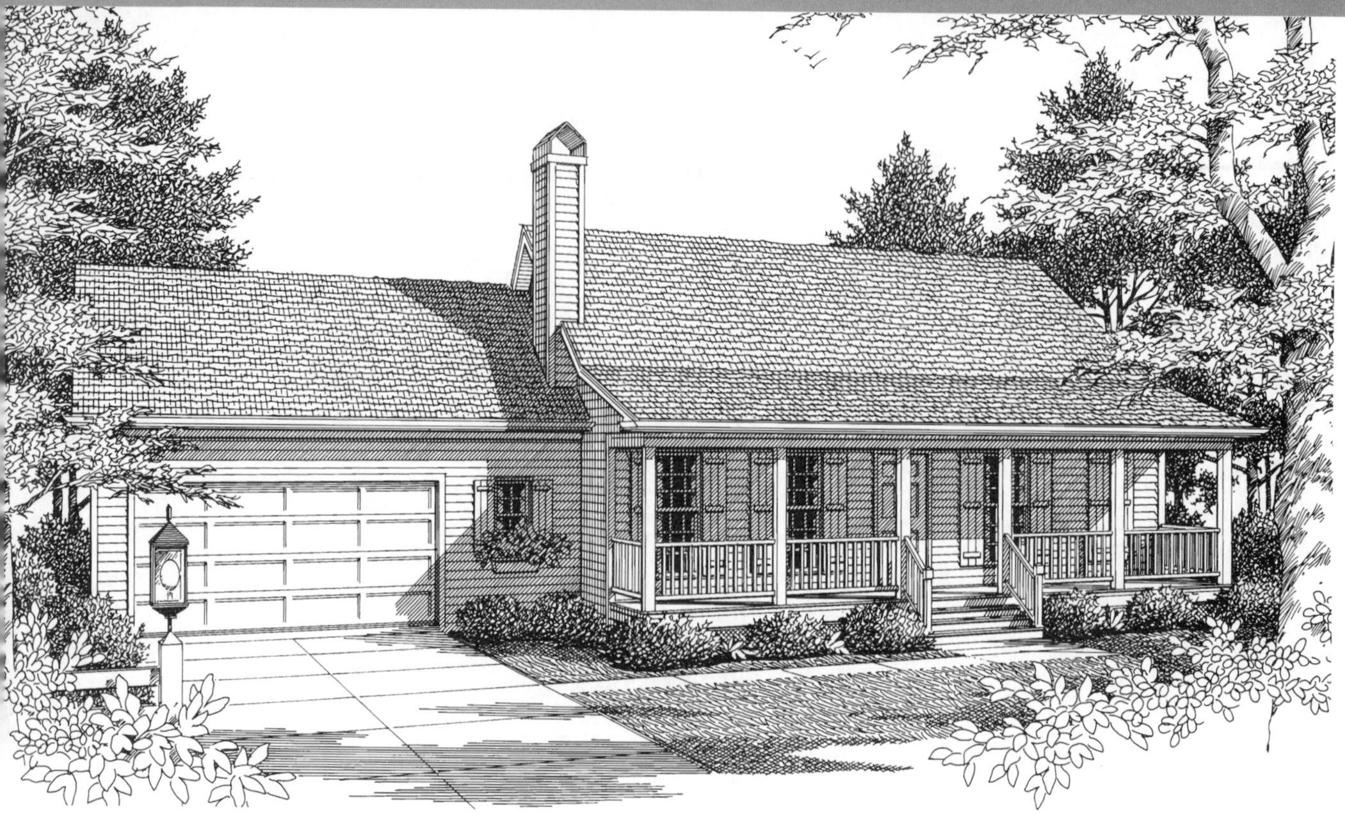

Plan #582-039D-0001

Price Code A

Special Features *• 1,253 total square feet of living area • Sloped ceiling and fireplace in family room add drama • U-shaped kitchen is efficiently designed • Large walk-in closets are found in all the bedrooms • 3 bedrooms, 2 baths, 2-car garage • Crawl space or slab foundation, please specify when ordering*

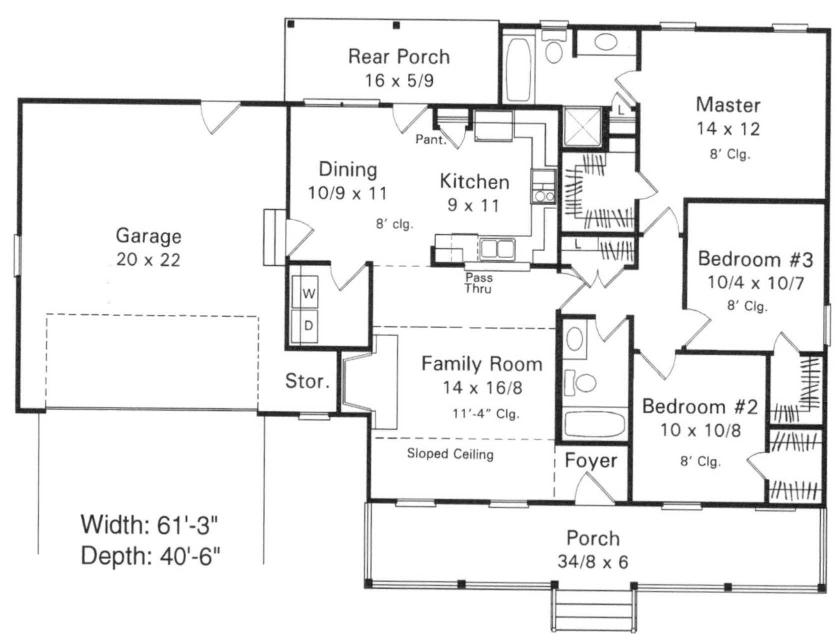

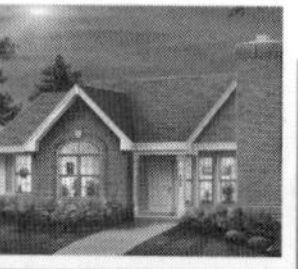

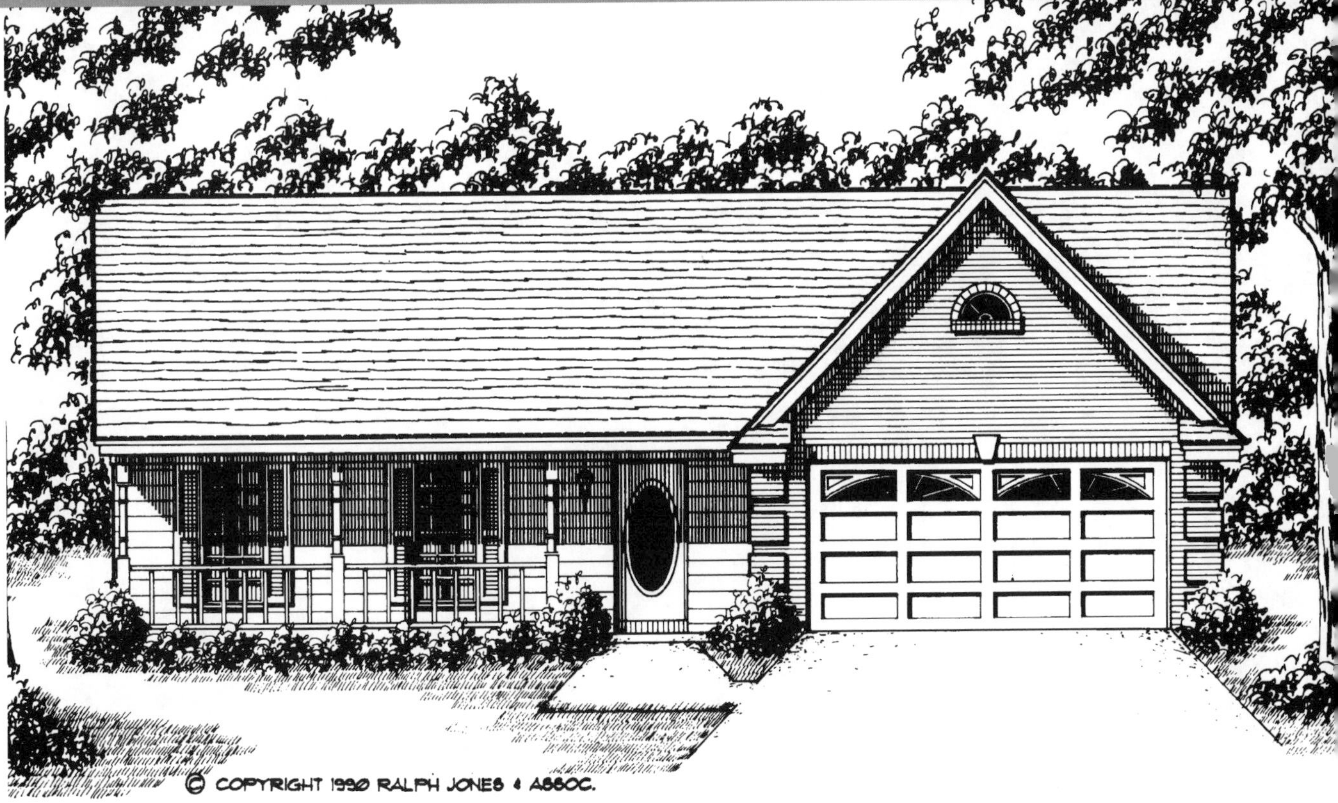

Plan #582-060D-0022

Price Code A

Special Features • 1,436 total square feet of living area • Corner fireplace in great room warms home • Kitchen and breakfast rooms combine for convenience • Centrally located utility room • 3 bedrooms, 2 baths, 2-car garage • Slab foundation

www.houseplansandmore.com

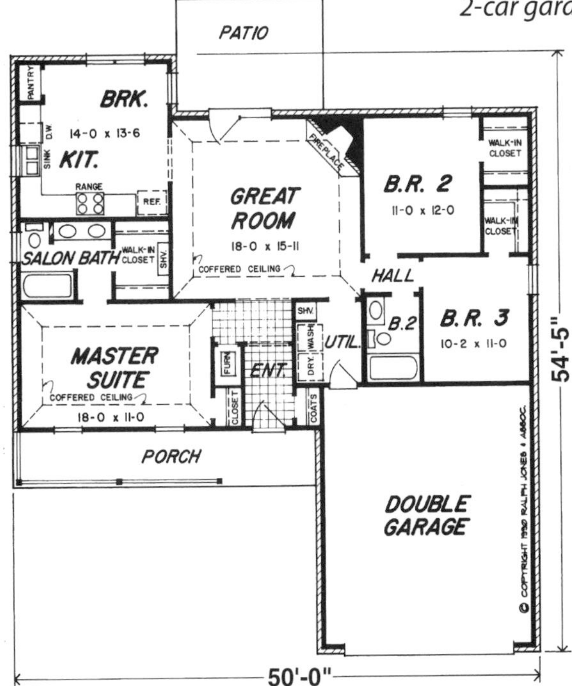

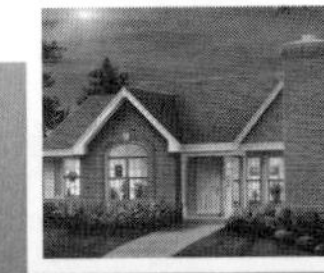

Open Living Area Adds Drama To Home

Plan #582-053D-0044

Price Code A

Special Features • *1,340 total square feet of living area* • *Master bedroom has a private bath and walk-in closet* • *Recessed entry leads to the vaulted family room with see-through fireplace to dining area* • *Garage includes a handy storage area* • *Convenient laundry closet in the kitchen* • *3 bedrooms, 2 baths, 2-car side entry garage* • *Slab foundation, drawings also include crawl space foundation*

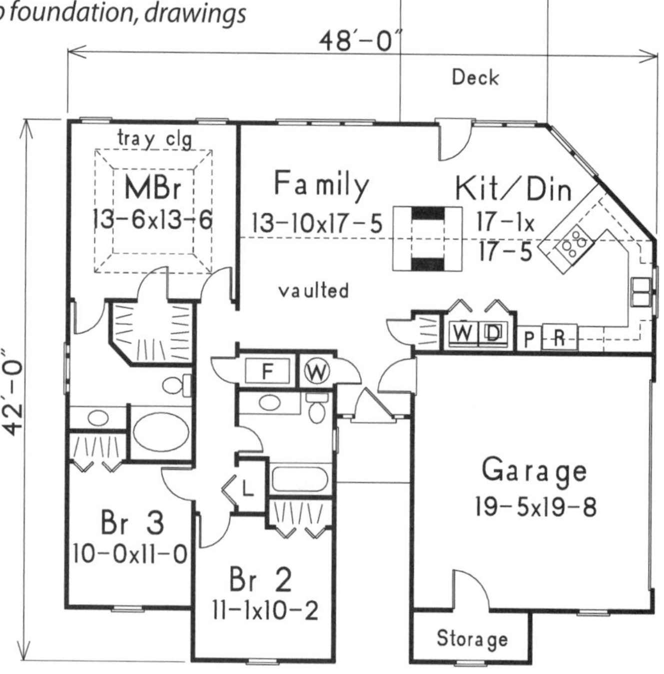

Spacious Dining And Living Areas

Plan #582-001D-0043

Price Code AA

Special Features • *1,104 total square feet of living area* • *Master bedroom includes a private bath* • *Convenient side entrance to dining area/kitchen* • *Laundry area is located near the kitchen* • *Large living area creates a comfortable atmosphere* • *3 bedrooms, 2 baths* • *Crawl space foundation, drawings also include basement and slab foundations*

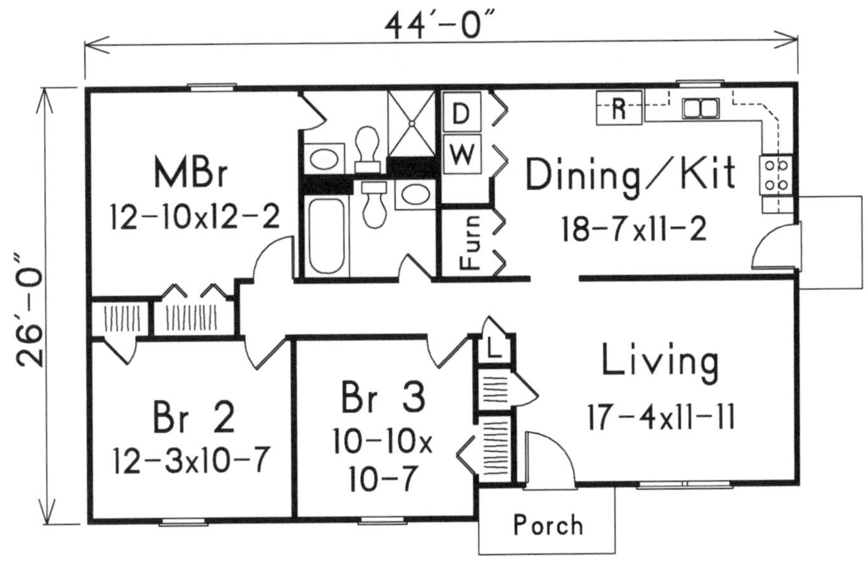

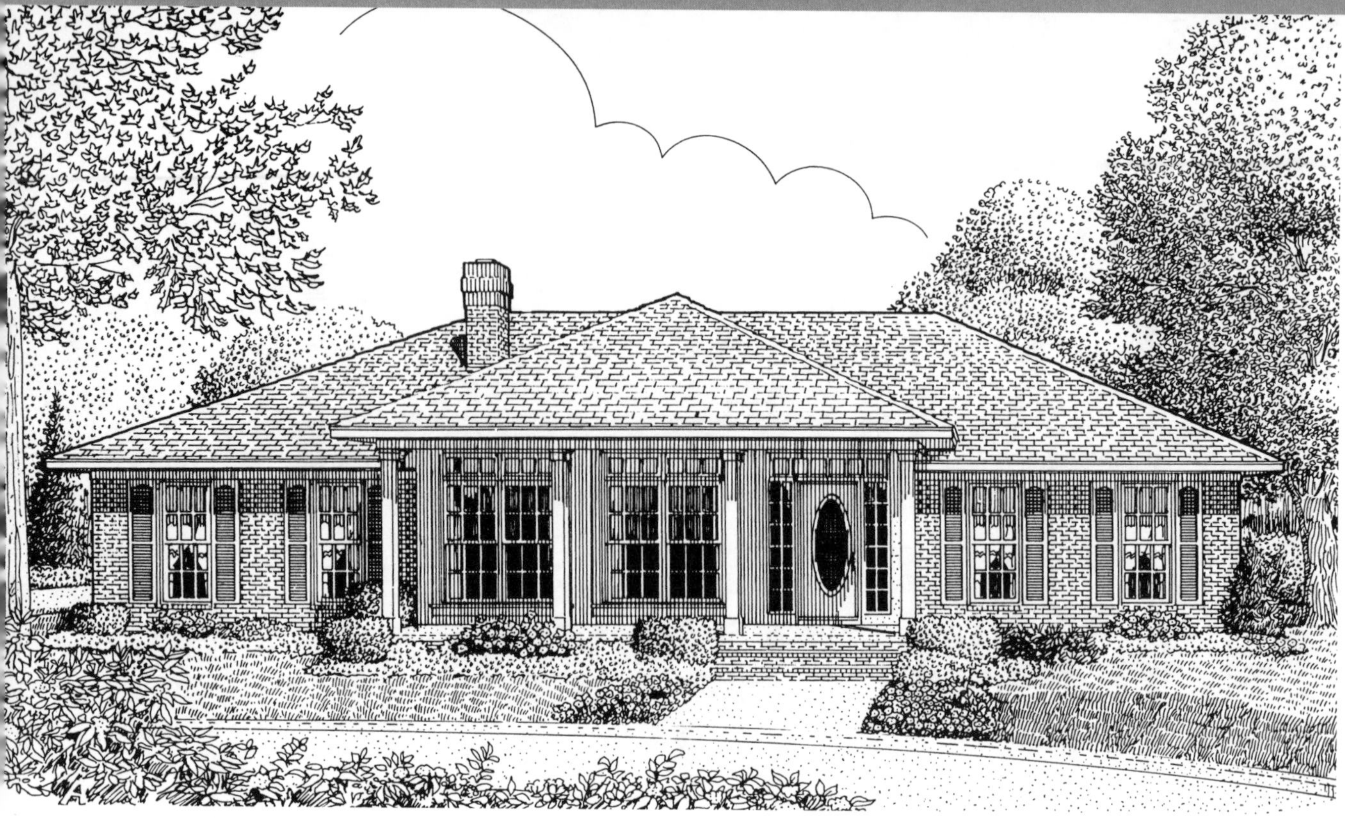

Plan #582-067D-0005

Price Code B

Special Features • *1,698 total square feet of living area* • *Large and open great room adds spaciousness to the living area* • *Cheerful bayed sitting area in the master bedroom* • *Compact, yet efficient kitchen* • *3 bedrooms, 2 1/2 baths, 2-car side entry garage* • *Basement, crawl space or slab foundation, please specify when ordering*

1-800-DREAM HOME (373-2646)

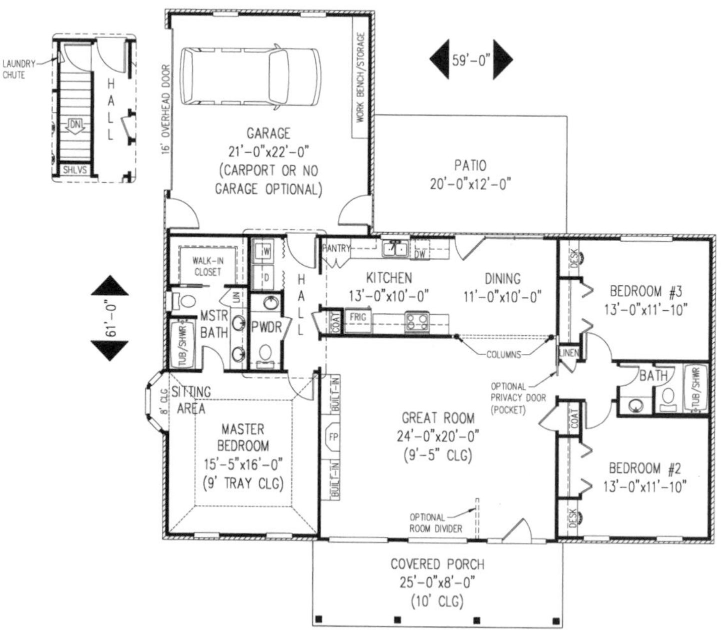

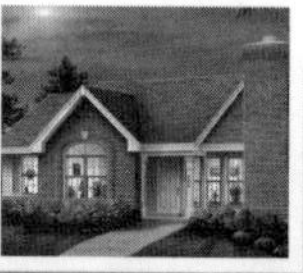

Dormers And Stone Veneer Add Exterior Appeal

Plan #582-053D-0053

Price Code B

Special Features • 1,609 total square feet of living area • Efficient kitchen with corner pantry and adjacent laundry room • Breakfast room boasts plenty of windows and opens onto rear deck • Master bedroom features tray ceiling and private deluxe bath • Entry opens into large living area with fireplace • 4 bedrooms, 2 baths, 2-car garage • Basement foundation

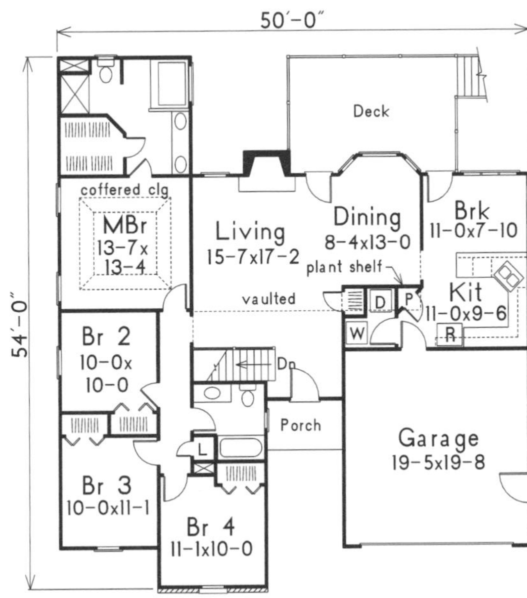

Porch Adds Country Appeal

Plan #582-076D-0004

Price Code B

Special Features • *1,335 total square feet of living area* • *Spacious family room enjoys a grand fireplace* • *The kitchen and dining room combine and feature access onto the rear patio* • *Secondary bedrooms boast generous closet space and share a bath* • *3 bedrooms, 2 baths, 2-car side entry garage* • *Crawl space foundation*

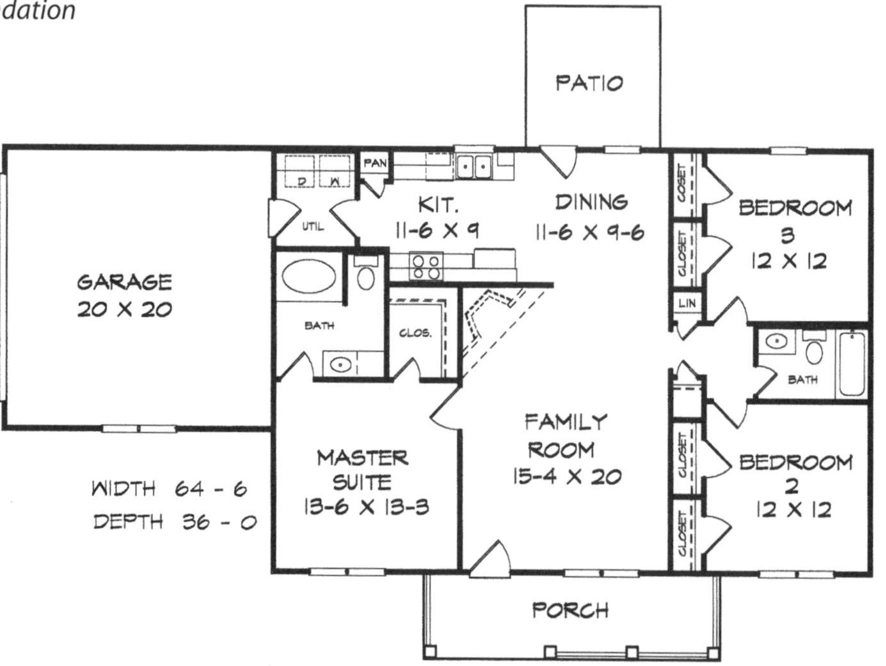

Plan #582-040D-0031

Price Code B

Special Features • 1,687 total square feet of living area • Family room with built-in cabinet and fireplace is the focal point of this home • U-shaped kitchen has a bar that opens to the family room • Back porch opens to the dining room and leads to the garage via a walkway • Convenient laundry room • 4 bedrooms, 2 1/2 baths, 2-car detached garage • Basement foundation

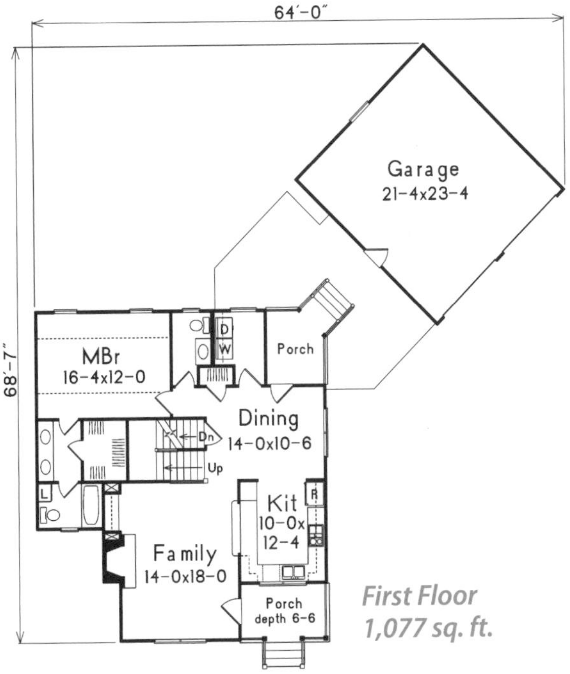

64'-0"
68'-7"
Garage 21-4x23-4
MBr 16-4x12-0
Porch
Dining 14-0x10-6
Dn
Up
Kit 10-0x 12-4
Family 14-0x18-0
Porch depth 6-6

First Floor
1,077 sq. ft.

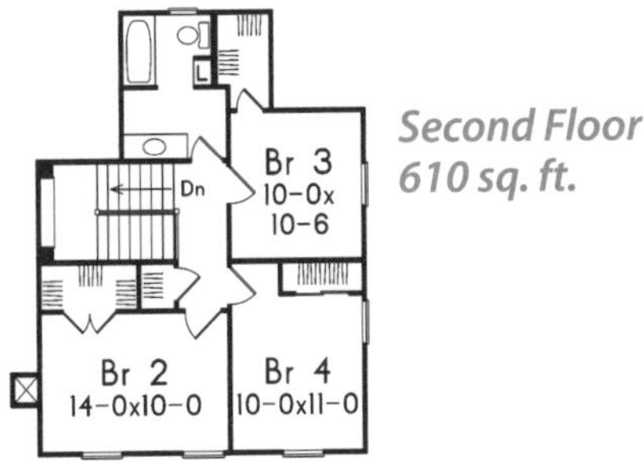

Second Floor
610 sq. ft.

www.houseplansandmore.com

Southern Styling With Covered Porch

Plan #582-035D-0051

Price Code A

Special Features • 1,491 total square feet of living area • Two-story family room has a vaulted ceiling • Well-organized kitchen has serving bar which overlooks family and dining rooms • First floor master suite has a tray ceiling, walk-in closet and master bath • 3 bedrooms, 2 1/2 baths, 2-car drive under garage • Walk-out basement foundation

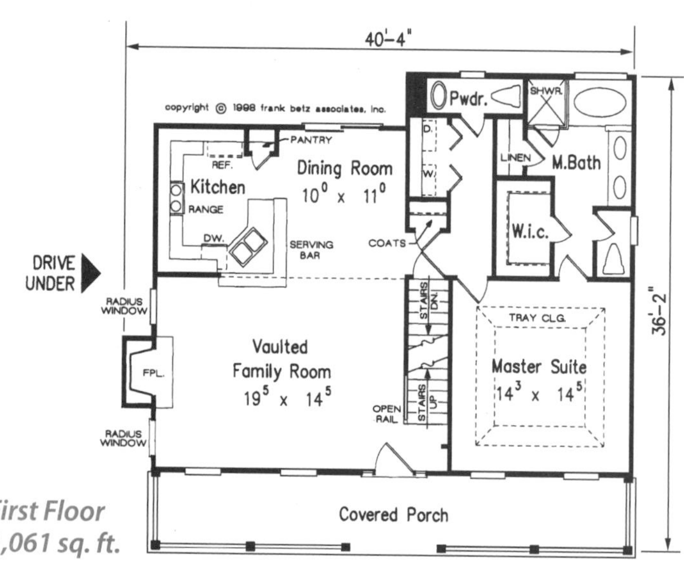

First Floor
1,061 sq. ft.

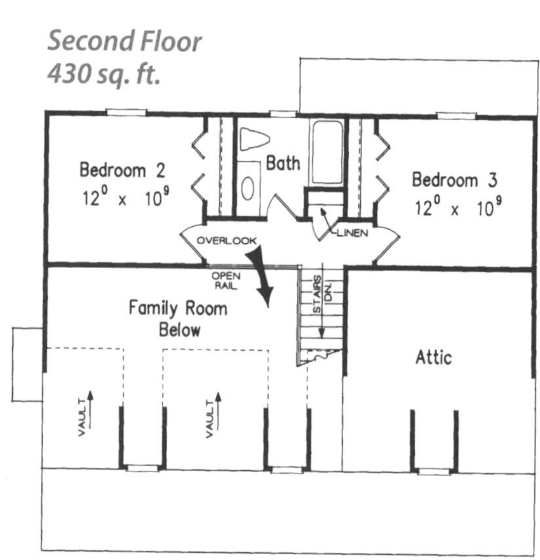

Second Floor
430 sq. ft.

Plan #582-076D-0019

Price Code B

Special Features • 1,083 total square feet of living area • Massive family room with corner fireplace and vaulted ceiling creates a cozy atmosphere • Large utility room includes a convenient coat closet • Charming breakfast area boasts access onto the rear patio • 3 bedrooms, 2 baths, 2-car garage • Slab foundation

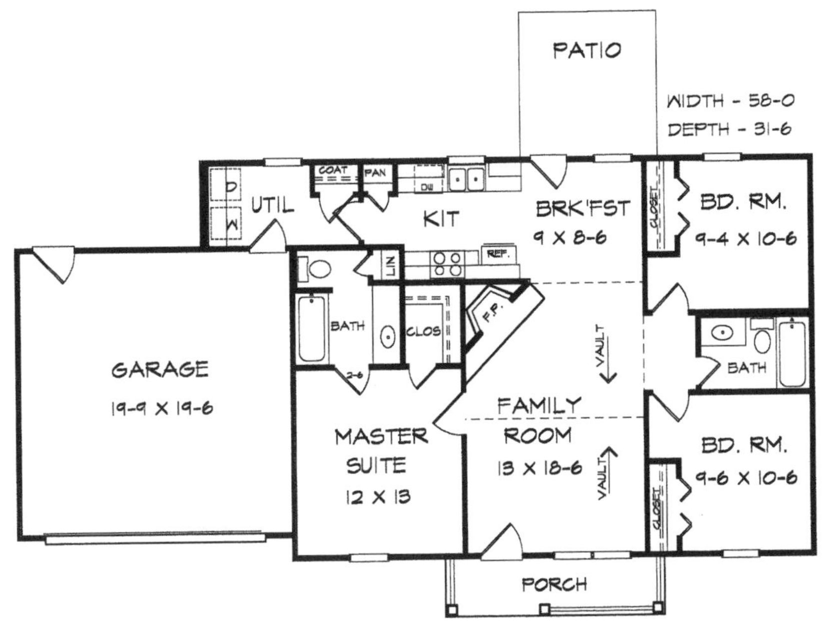

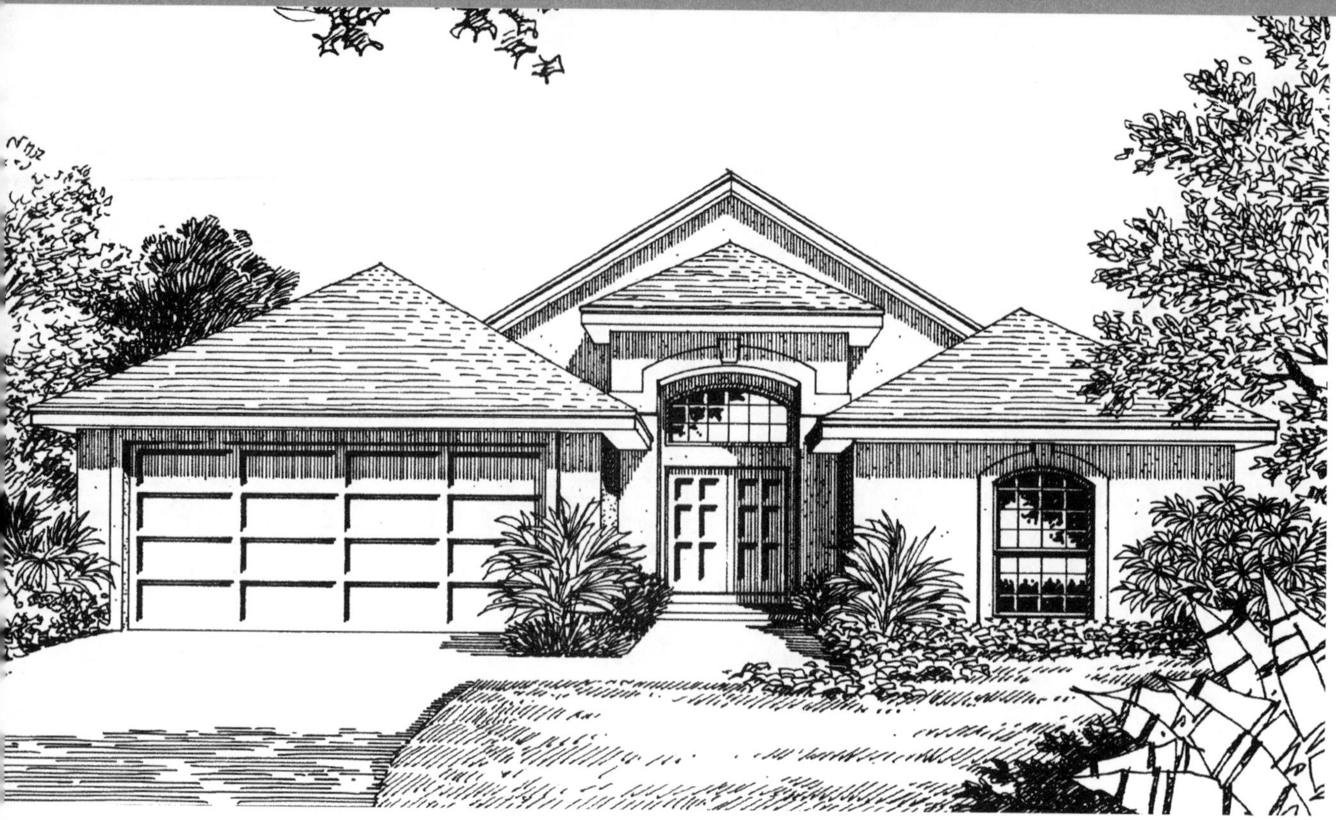

Plan #582-047D-0016 Price Code B

Special Features • *1,703 total square feet of living area* • *Majestic great room has a volume ceiling and sliding glass doors to the covered patio* • *An elegant double-door entry leads to the secluded master bedroom with a private bath and walk-in closet* • *Kitchen is situated between the formal dining area and breakfast room for ultimate convenience* • *3 bedrooms, 2 baths, 2-car garage* • *Slab foundation*

Width: 45'-0"
Depth: 68'-4"

1-800-DREAM HOME (373-2646)

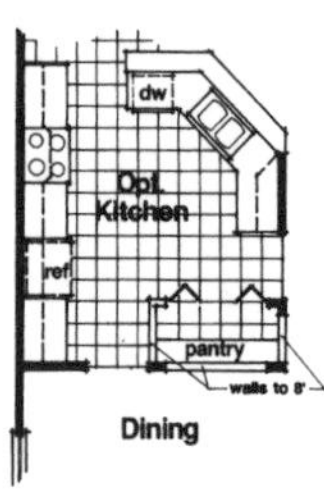

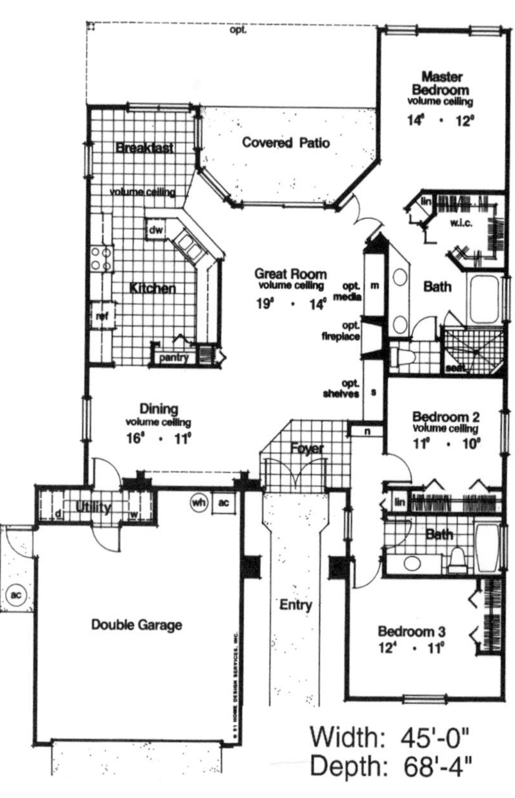

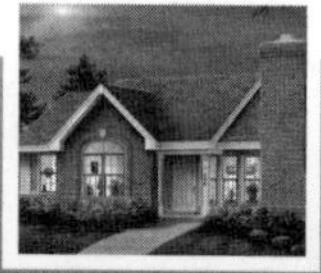

Optional Second Floor Living Quarters

Plan #582-035D-0026

Price Code C

Special Features • 1,845 total square feet of living area • Vaulted living room has a cozy fireplace • Breakfast area and kitchen are lovely gathering places • Dining room overlooks the living room • Optional second floor with bath has an additional 354 square feet of living area • 3 bedrooms, 2 1/2 baths, 2-car side entry garage • Walk-out basement or crawl space foundation, please specify when ordering

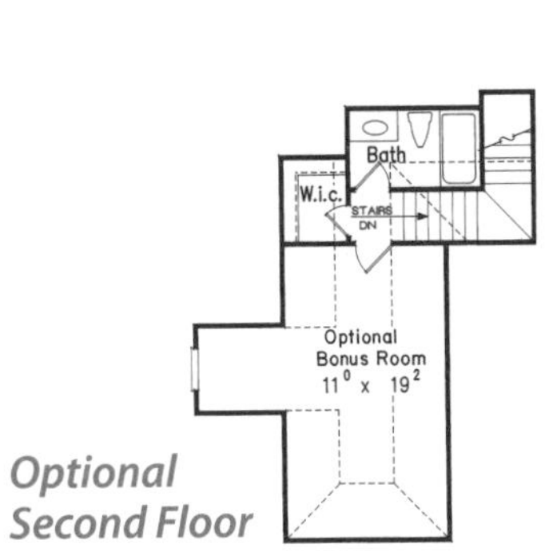

Optional Second Floor

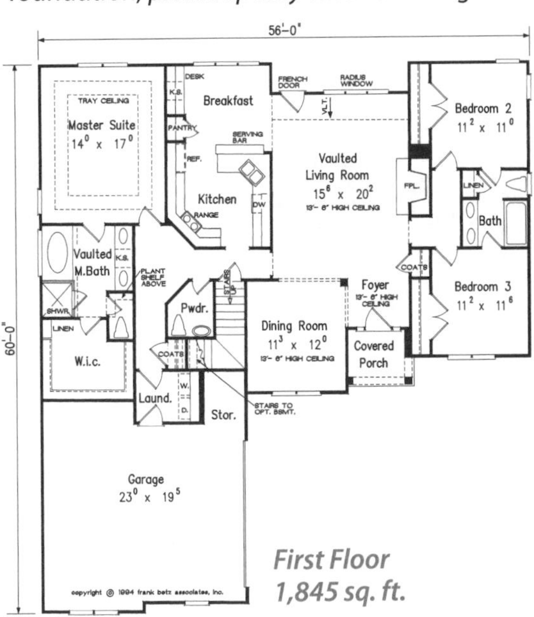

First Floor
1,845 sq. ft.

Roomy Ranch For Easy Living

Plan #582-001D-0023

Price Code A

Special Features • 1,343 total square feet of living area • Separate and convenient family room from living and dining areas • Nice-sized master bedroom suite enjoys a large closet and private bath • Foyer with convenient coat closet opens into combined living and dining rooms • Kitchen has access to the outdoors through sliding glass doors • 3 bedrooms, 2 baths, 2-car garage • Crawl space foundation, drawings also include basement foundation

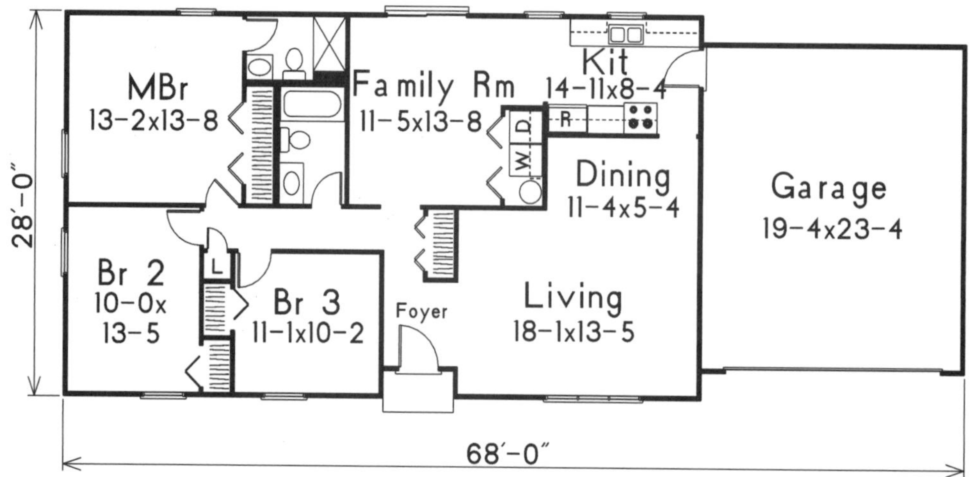

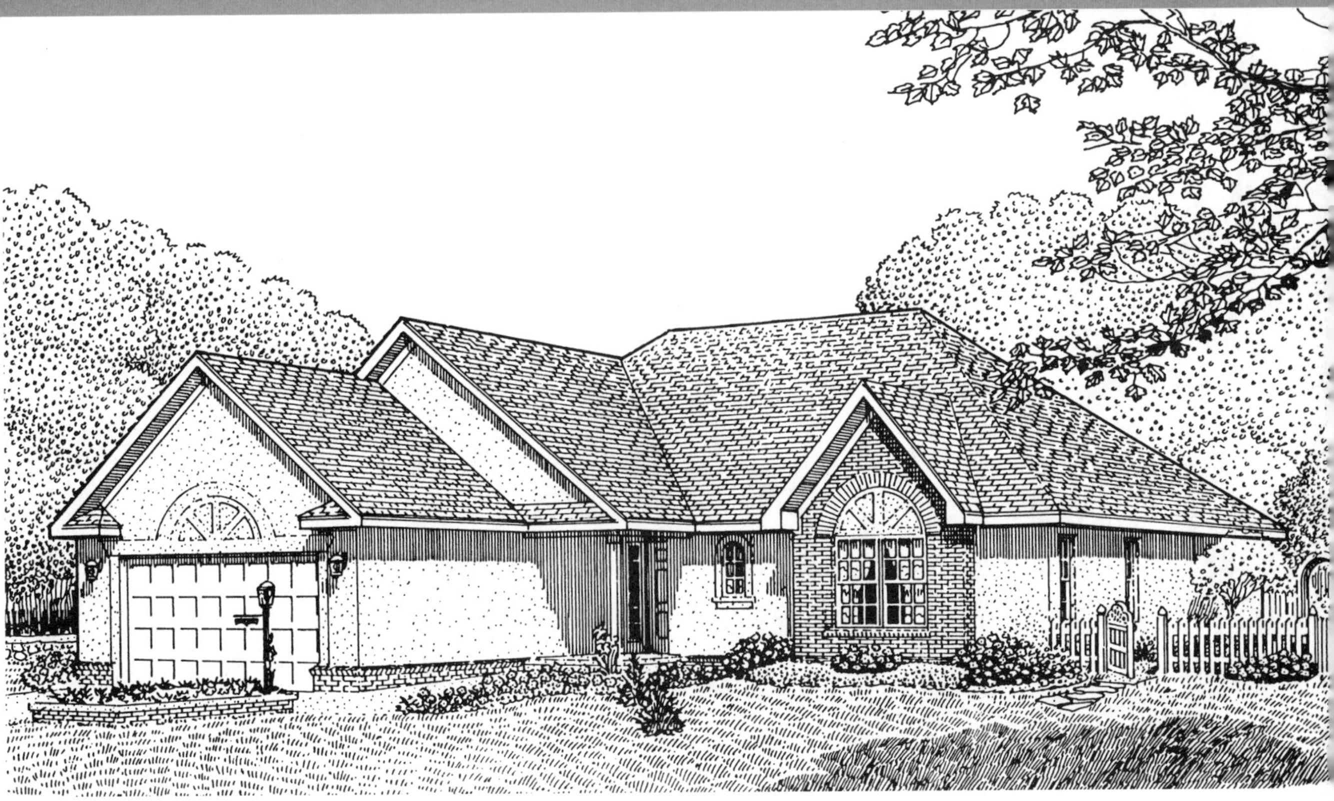

Plan #582-067D-0002

Price Code B

Special Features • 1,627 total square feet of living area • Cathedral ceiling in living room adds drama to this space • Cozy corner dining area just off the kitchen is convenient • Large master bedroom is cheerful with many windows and includes its own bath and walk-in closet • 3 bedrooms, 2 baths, 2-car garage • Crawl space or slab foundation, please specify when ordering

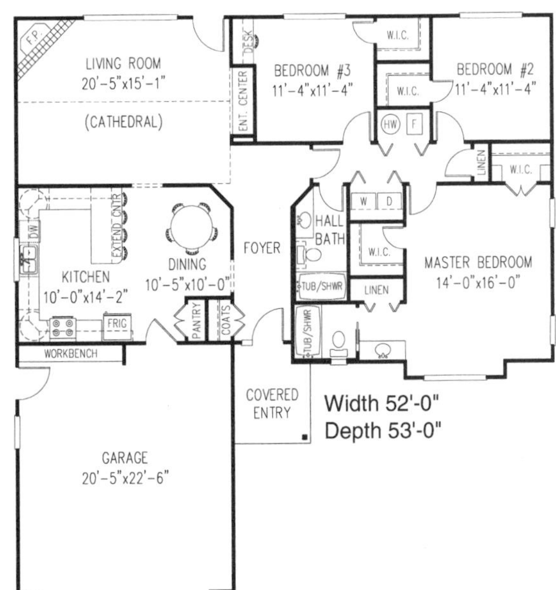

A Ranch Home With A Cottage Feel

Plan #582-060D-0021

Price Code A

Special Features • 1,475 total square feet of living area • Bay window in master suite is appealing and bright • Open kitchen with center island, large pantry with shelves and easy access to breakfast area • Bedroom #2 has an oversized walk-in closet with shelves • 3 bedrooms, 2 baths, optional 2-car garage • Slab or crawl space foundation, please specify when ordering

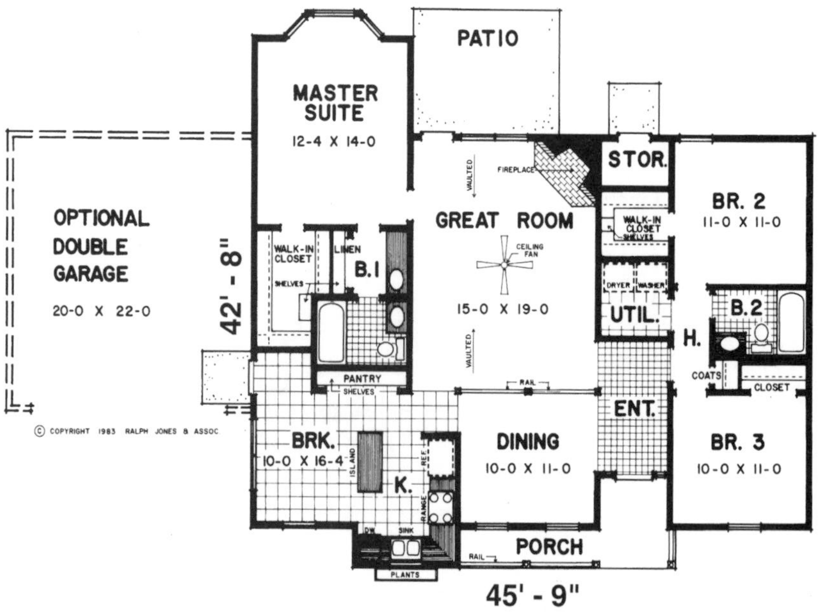

1-800-DREAM HOME (373-2646)

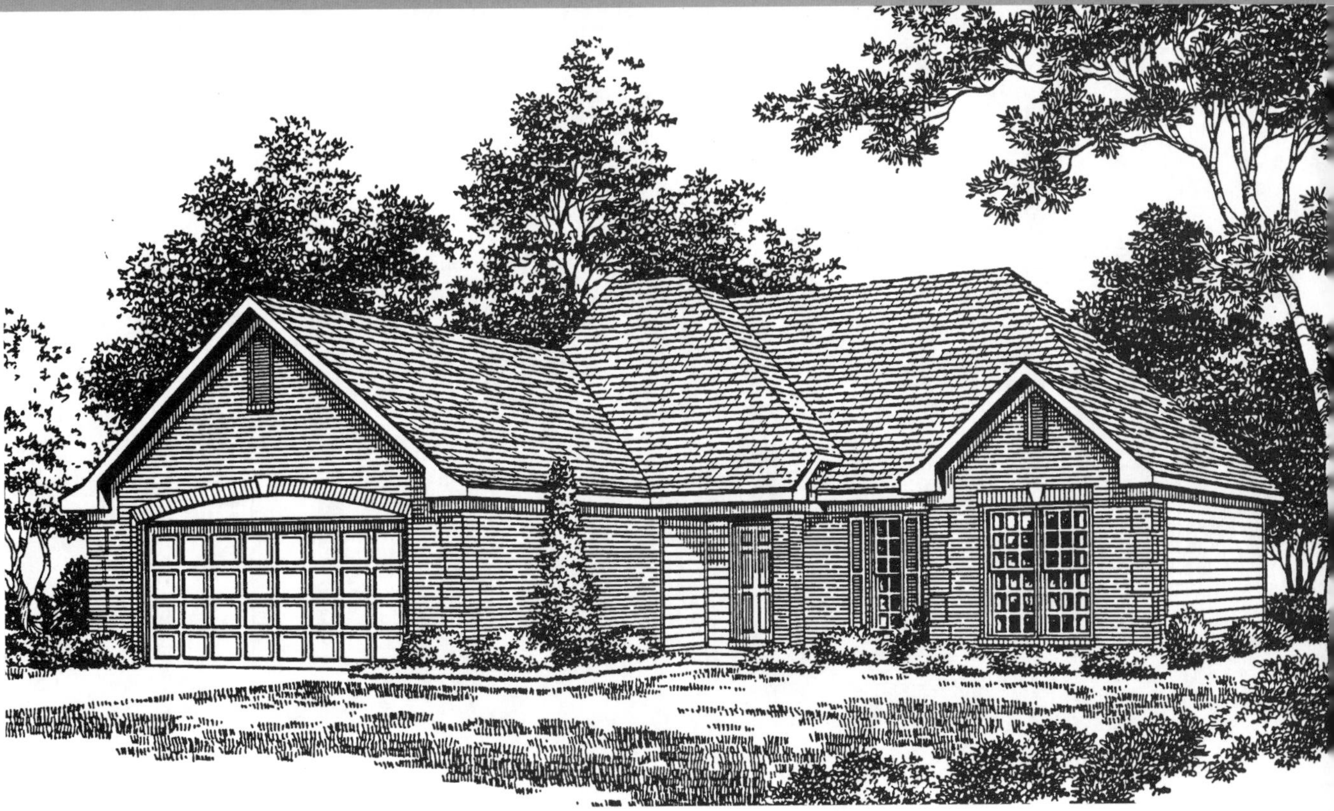

Plan #582-019D-0002

Price Code A

Special Features • 1,282 total square feet of living area • Angled entry creates the illusion of space making the home appear larger • Dining room serves both formal and informal occasions • Master bedroom has a walk-in closet and private bath with whirlpool/shower combination • 3 bedrooms, 2 baths, 2-car garage • Crawl space foundation, drawings also include slab foundation

www.houseplansandmore.com

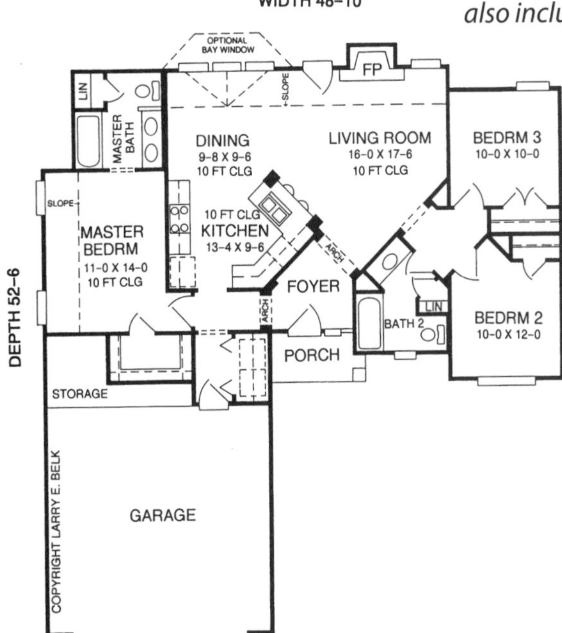

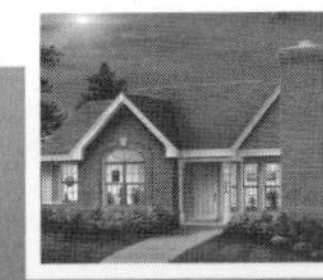

Compact And Convenient Farmhouse

Plan #582-040D-0002

Price Code D

Special Features • 1,958 total square feet of living area • Spacious kitchen and breakfast area are open to the rear deck • Open floor plan with rail that separates the family room from the breakfast area • Dormers add interest and spaciousness in bedroom #2 • Bonus room on the second floor is included in the square footage • 3 bedrooms, 2 1/2 baths, 2-car side entry garage • Basement foundation, drawings also include slab and crawl space foundations

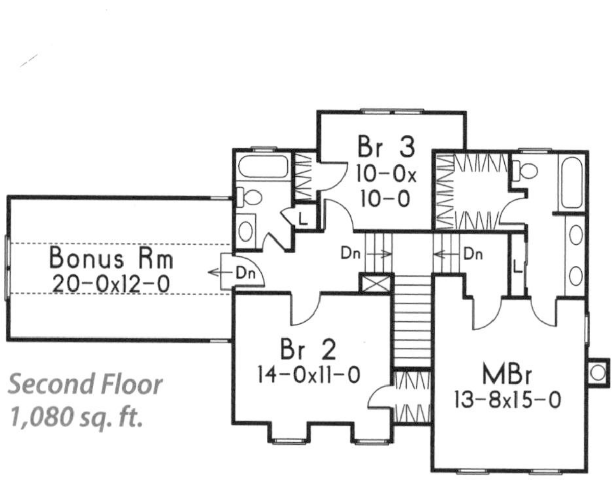

Second Floor
1,080 sq. ft.

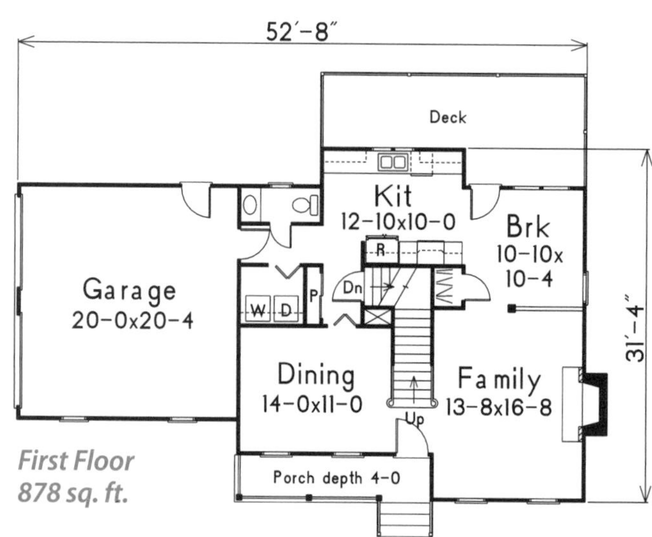

First Floor
878 sq. ft.

Attractive Combination Of Brick And Siding

Plan #582-034D-0014

Price Code B

Special Features • 1,792 total square feet of living area • Traditional styling makes this a popular design • First floor master bedroom maintains privacy • Dining area has sliding glass doors leading to the outdoors • Formal dining and living rooms combine for added gathering space • 3 bedrooms, 2 1/2 baths, 2-car garage • Basement foundation

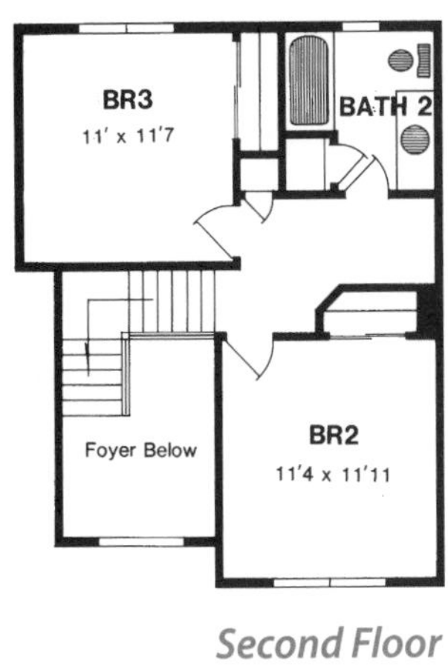

Second Floor
511 sq. ft.

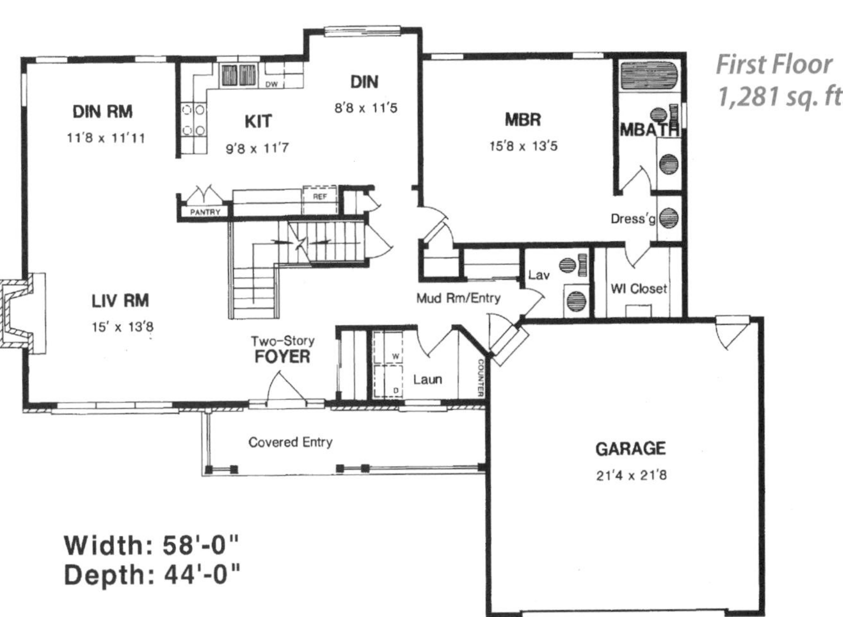

First Floor
1,281 sq. ft.

Width: 58'-0"
Depth: 44'-0"

Charming Two-Story With Dormers And Porch

Plan #582-033D-0009

Price Code C

Special Features • *1,711 total square feet of living area* • *U-shaped kitchen joins breakfast and family rooms for an open living atmosphere* • *Master bedroom has secluded covered porch and private bath* • *Balcony overlooks family room that features a fireplace and accesses deck* • *3 bedrooms, 2 1/2 baths, 2-car garage* • *Basement foundation*

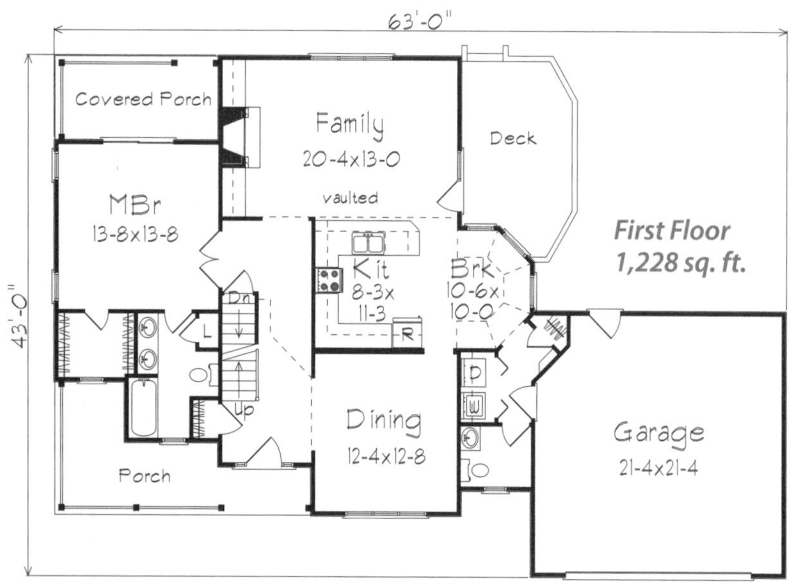

First Floor
1,228 sq. ft.

Second Floor
483 sq. ft.

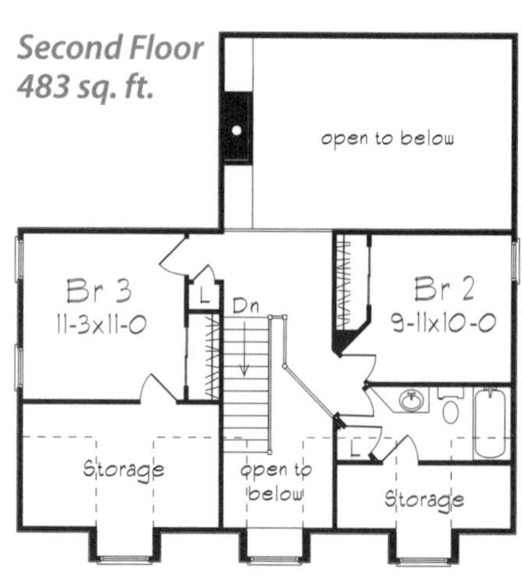

Plan #582-051D-0062

Price Code A

Special Features • 1,342 total square feet of living area • Kitchen/dining area includes a handy desk area • High ceiling in living room adds a spacious feel • First floor master bedroom has a private bath and a large walk-in closet • 3 bedrooms, 2 1/2 baths, 2-car garage • Basement foundation

Second Floor
415 sq. ft.

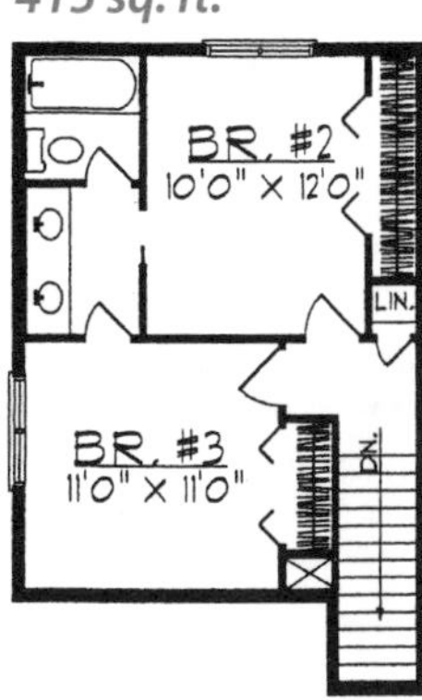

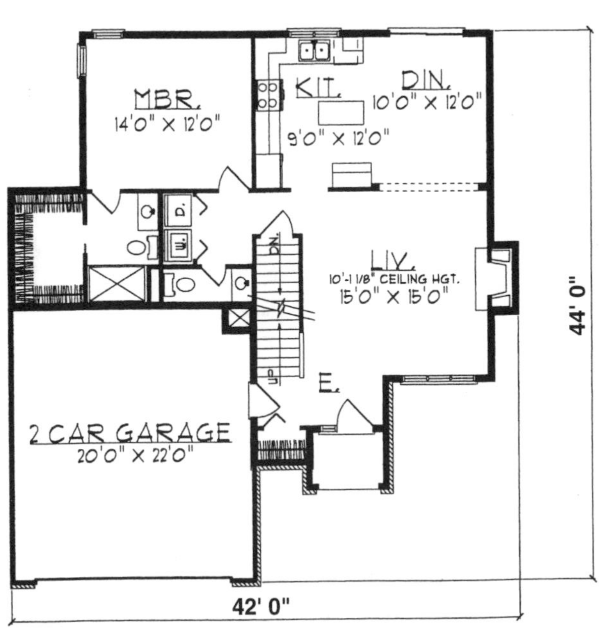

First Floor
927 sq. ft.

Plan #582-030D-0001

Price Code A

Special Features • 1,374 total square feet of living area • Garage has extra storage space • Spacious living room has fireplace • Well-designed kitchen with an adjacent breakfast nook • Separated master suite maintains privacy • 3 bedrooms, 2 baths, 2-car garage • Slab or crawl space foundation, please specify when ordering

Peaceful Shaded Front Porch

Plan #582-001D-0072

Price Code A

Special Features • *1,288 total square feet of living area* • *Kitchen, dining area and great room join to create an open living space* • *Master bedroom includes private bath* • *Secondary bedrooms include ample closet space* • *Hall bath features convenient laundry closet* • *Dining room accesses the outdoors* • *3 bedrooms, 2 baths* • *Crawl space foundation, drawings also include basement and slab foundations*

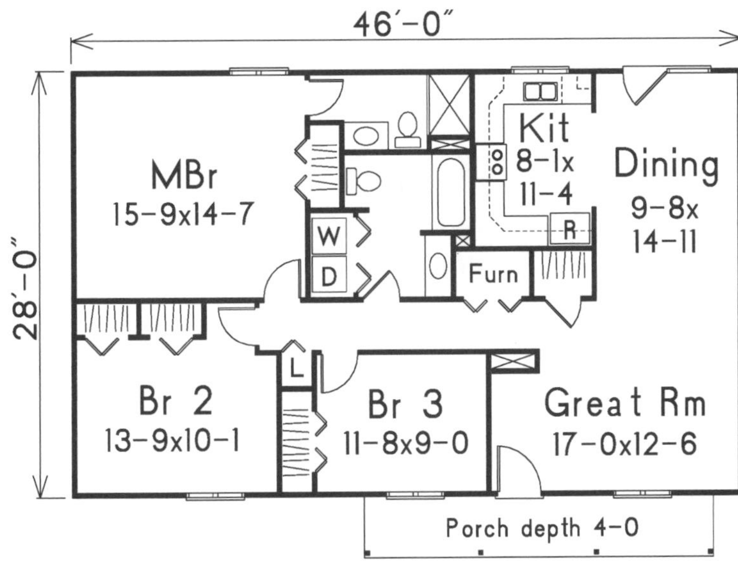

Vaulted Ceilings Throughout Home

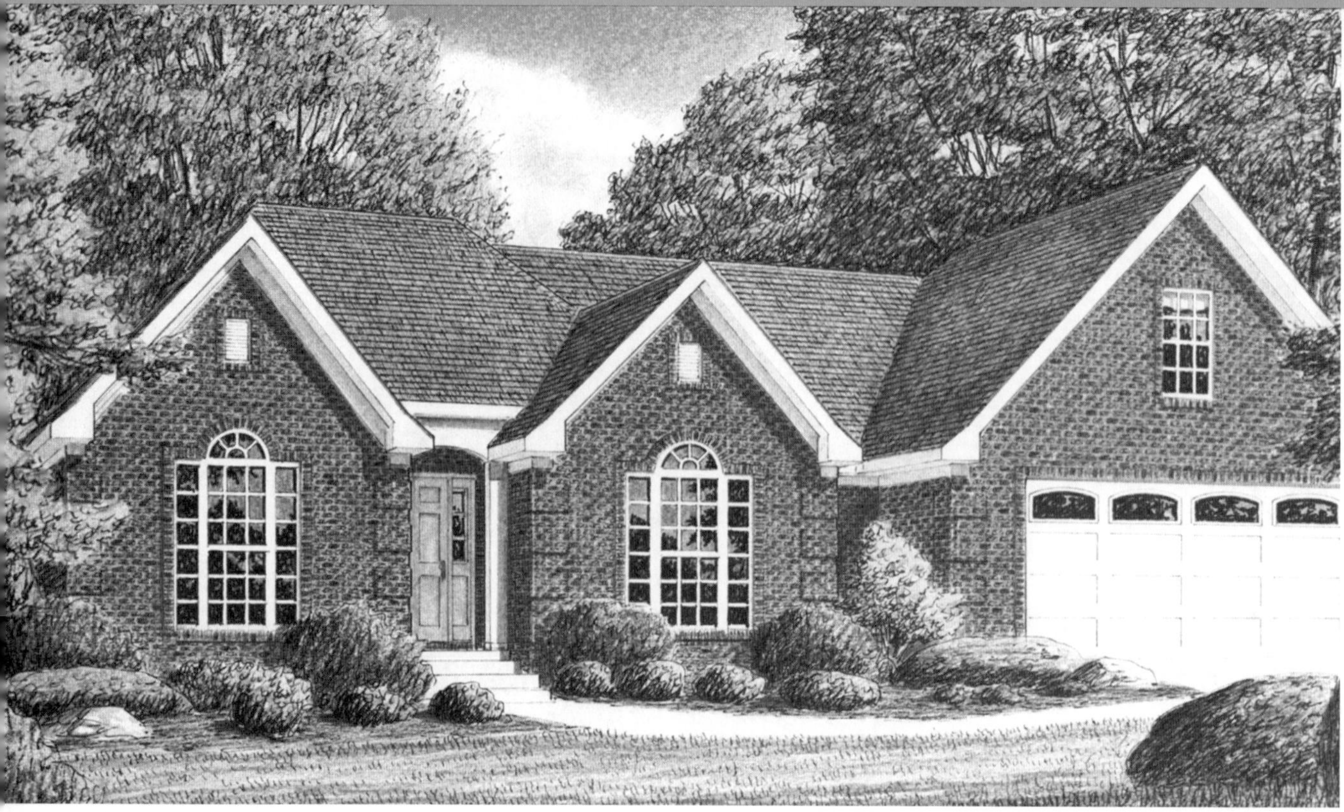

Plan #582-025D-0012

Price Code B

Special Features • 1,634 total square feet of living area • Enter foyer to find a nice-sized dining room to the right and a cozy great room with fireplace straight ahead • Secluded master suite offers privacy from other bedrooms and living areas • Plenty of storage throughout this home • Future playroom on the second floor has an additional 256 square feet of living area • 3 bedrooms, 2 baths, 2-car garage • Slab foundation

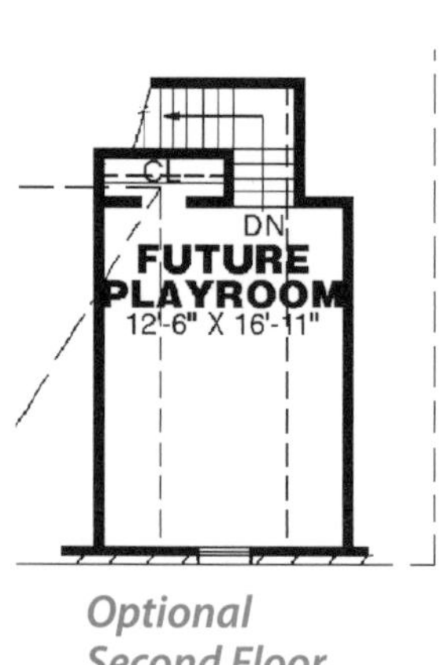

Optional Second Floor

First Floor
1,634 sq. ft.

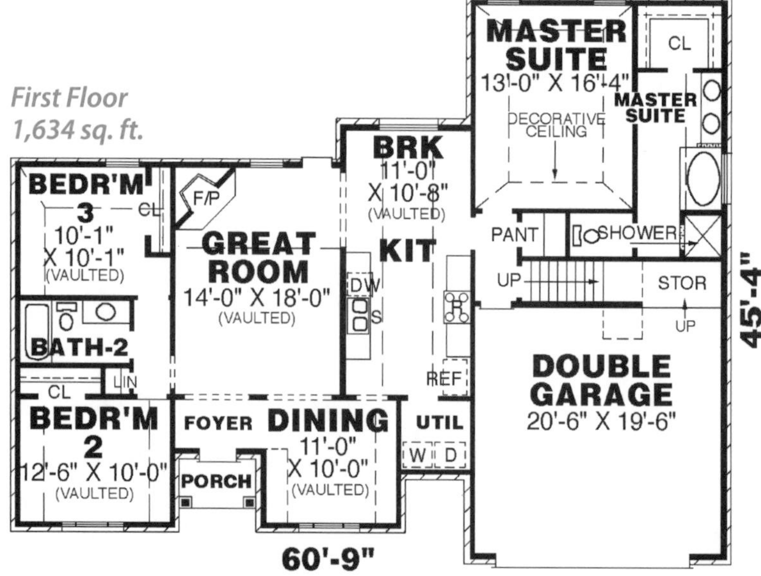

Flexible Design Is Popular

Plan #582-058D-0033

Price Code A

Special Features • 1,440 total square feet of living area • Open floor plan with access to covered porches in front and back • Lots of linen, pantry and closet space throughout • Laundry/mud room between kitchen and garage is a convenient feature • 2 bedrooms, 2 baths, 2-car side entry garage • Basement foundation

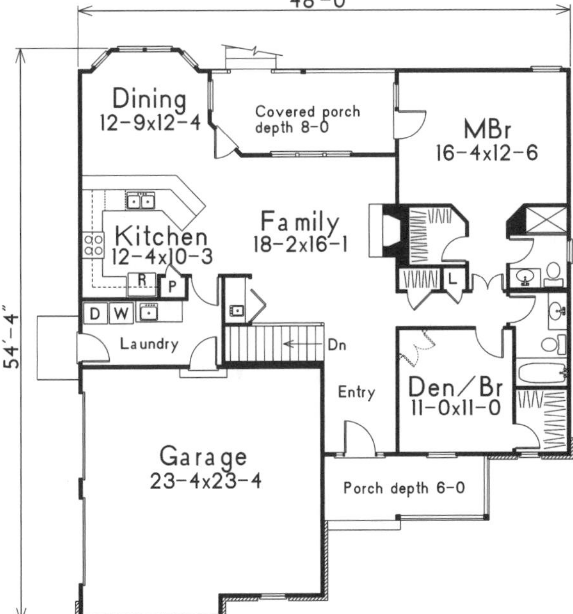

Spacious Master Bedroom Adds Luxury

Plan #582-023D-0017 **Price Code B**

Special Features • 1,596 total square feet of living area • Large corner fireplace enhances living area • Centrally located utility room provides convenient access • Master bath features double walk-in closets, oversized tub and plant shelves • Both the living area and master bedroom are accented with raised ceilings • Bay window in dining area adds interest and light • 3 bedrooms, 2 baths • Slab foundation

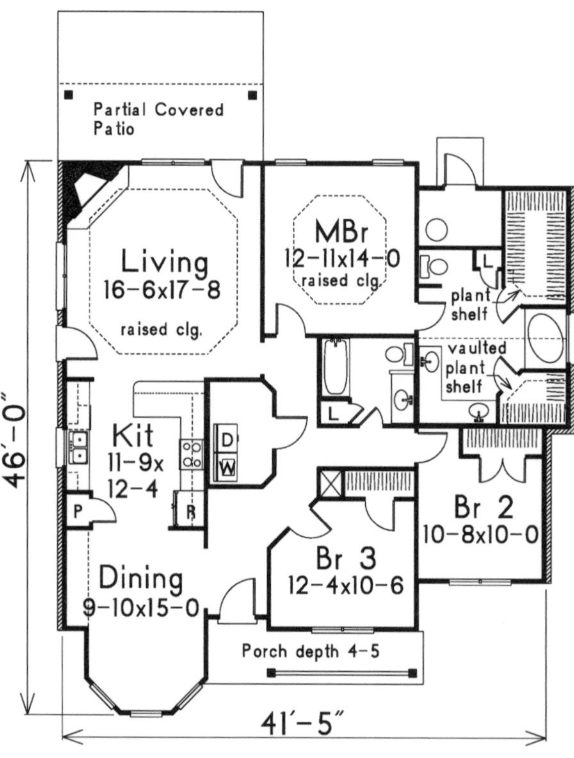

Sheltered Entrance Opens To Stylish Features

Plan #582-037D-0012

Price Code B

Special Features • 1,661 total square feet of living area • Large open foyer with angled wall arrangement and high ceiling adds to spacious living room • The kitchen and dining area have impressive cathedral ceilings and a French door allowing access to the patio • Utility room is conveniently located near the kitchen • Secluded master bedroom has a large walk-in closet, unique brick wall arrangement and 10' ceiling • 3 bedrooms, 2 baths, 2-car garage • Slab foundation

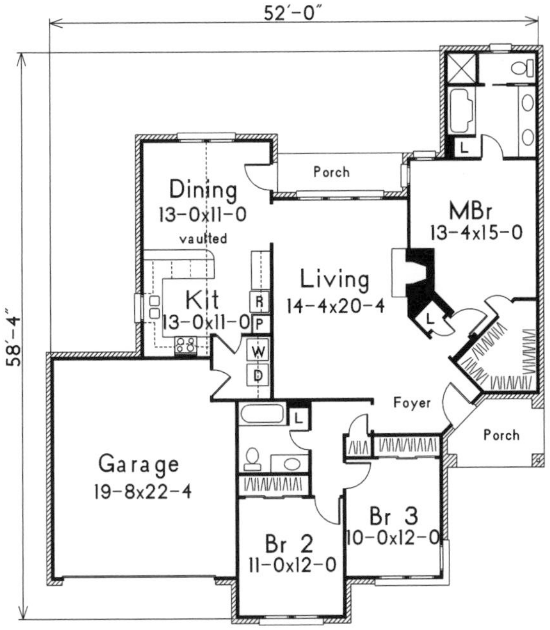

Appealing Charming Porch

Plan #582-013D-0011

Price Code B

Special Features • 1,643 total square feet of living area • First floor master bedroom has a private bath, walk-in closet and easy access to the laundry closet • Comfortable family room features a vaulted ceiling and a cozy fireplace • Two bedrooms on the second floor share a bath • 3 bedrooms, 2 1/2 baths, 2-car drive under garage • Basement or crawl space foundation, please specify when ordering

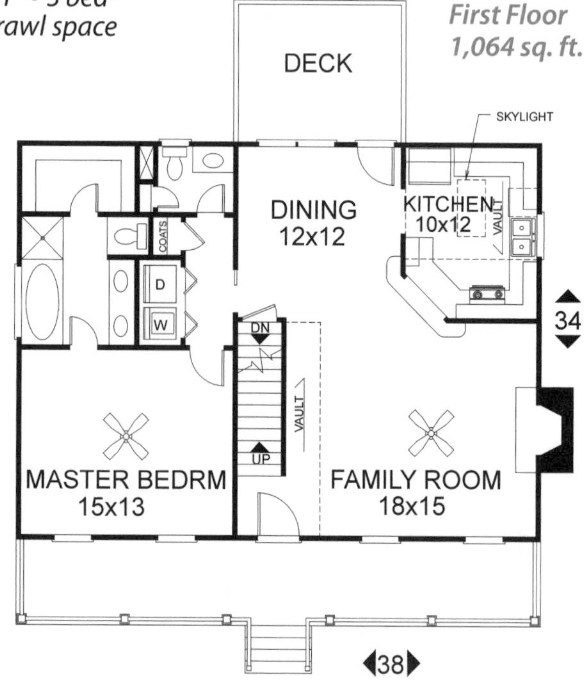

First Floor
1,064 sq. ft.

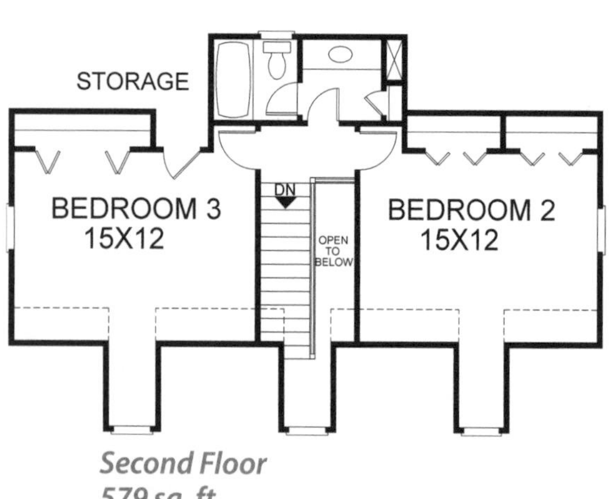

Second Floor
579 sq. ft.

Plan #582-007D-0087

Price Code A

Special Features • 1,332 total square feet of living area • Home offers both basement and first floor entry locations • A dramatic living room features a vaulted ceiling, fireplace, exterior balcony and dining area • An L-shaped kitchen offers spacious cabinetry, breakfast area with bay window and access to the rear patio • 3 bedrooms, 2 baths, 4-car tandem garage • Walk-out basement foundation

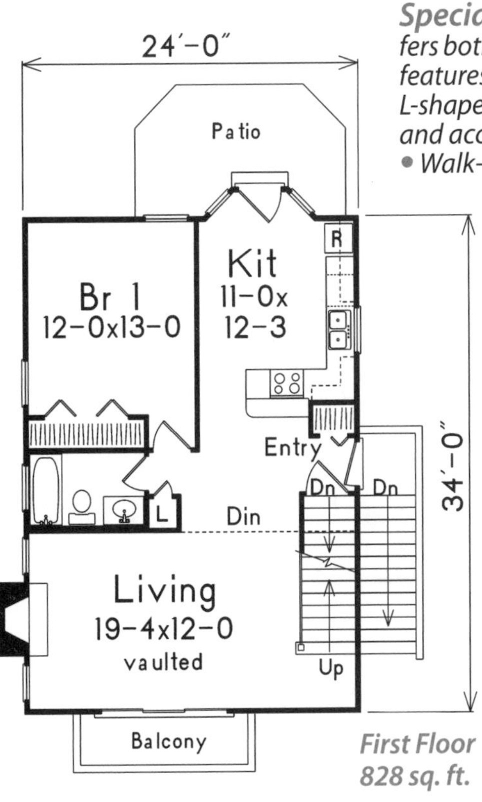

First Floor
828 sq. ft.

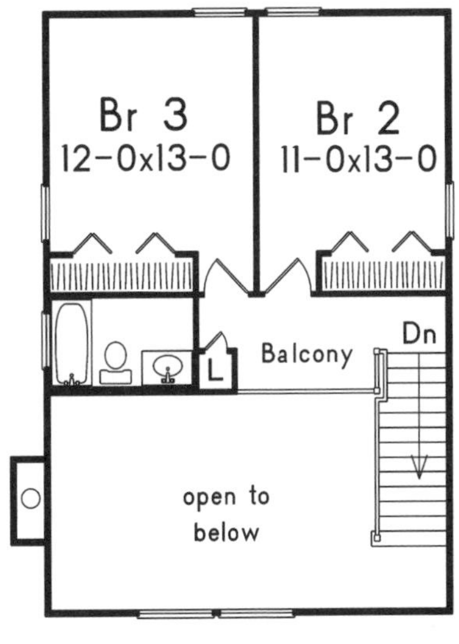

Second Floor
504 sq. ft.

Stonework Entry Adds Character To This Home

Plan #582-010D-0005 Price Code A

Special Features • 1,358 total square feet of living area • Vaulted master bath has walk-in closet, double-bowl vanity, large tub, shower and toilet area • Galley kitchen opens to both the living room and the breakfast area • Vaulted ceiling joins dining and living rooms • Breakfast room has a full wall of windows • 3 bedrooms, 2 baths, 2-car garage • Slab foundation

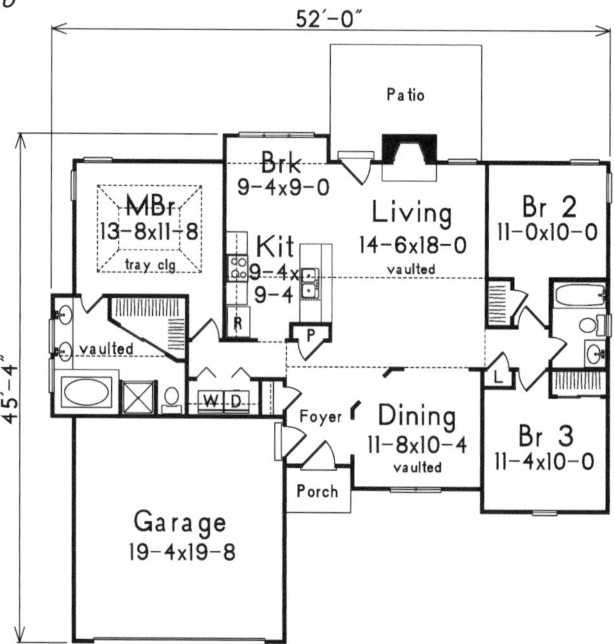

Outdoor Living Area Created By Wrap-Around Covered Porch

Plan #582-068D-0003

Price Code B

Special Features • 1,784 total square feet of living area • Spacious living area with corner fireplace offers a cheerful atmosphere with large windows • Large second floor gathering room is great for kid's play area • Secluded master bedroom has separate porch entrances and a large master bath with walk-in closet • 3 bedrooms, 2 1/2 baths, 1-car garage • Basement foundation, drawings also include crawl space foundation

First Floor
1,112 sq. ft.

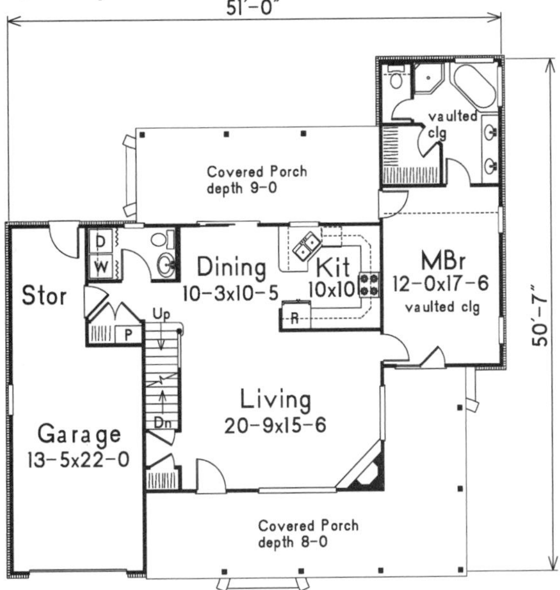

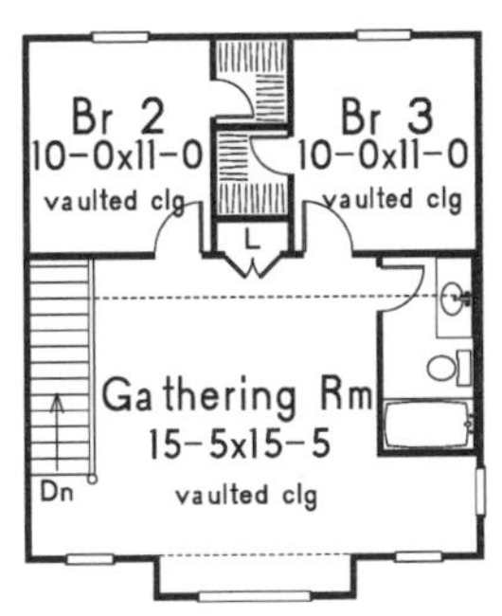

Second Floor
672 sq. ft.

www.houseplansandmore.com

Plan #582-020D-0003

Price Code A

Special Features • 1,420 total square feet of living area • Energy efficient home with 2" x 6" exterior walls • Living room has a 12' ceiling, corner fireplace and atrium doors leading to the covered porch • Secluded master suite has a garden bath and walk-in closet • 3 bedrooms, 2 baths, 2-car garage • Slab foundation, drawings also include crawl space foundation

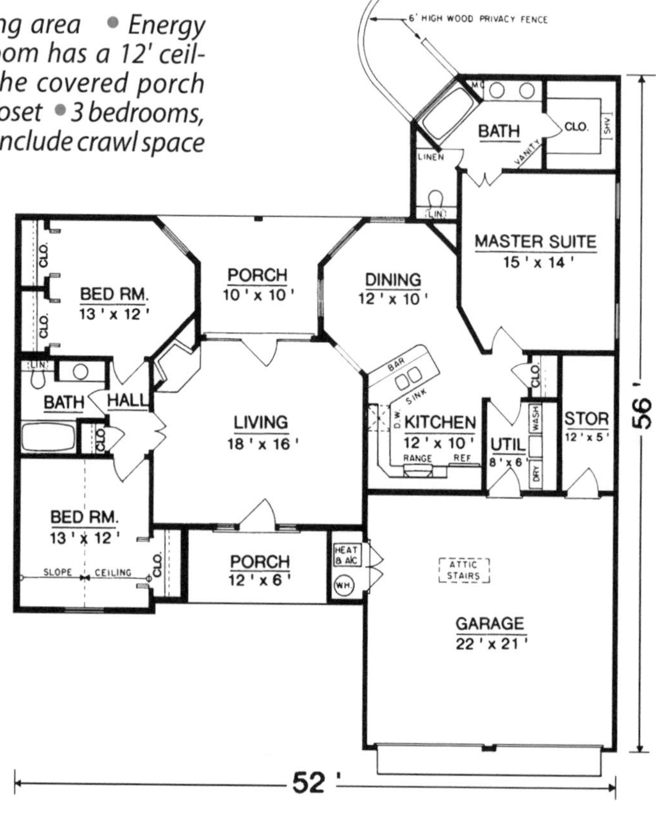

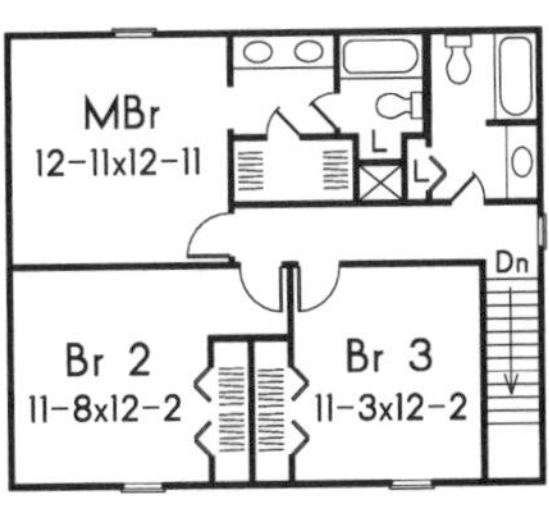

Second Floor
832 sq. ft.

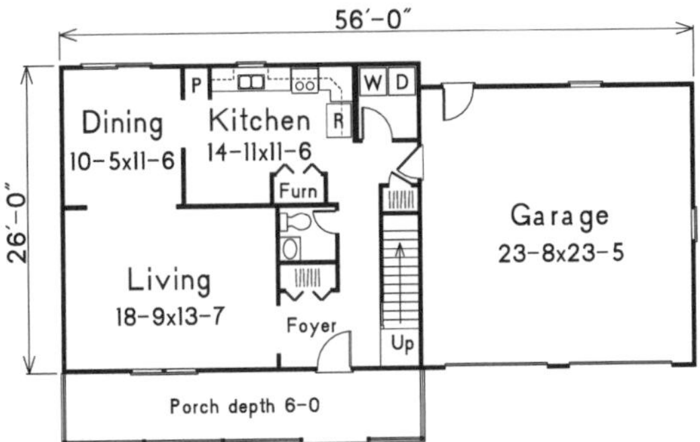

First Floor
832 sq. ft.

Plan #582-001D-0074

Price Code B

Special Features • 1,664 total square feet of living area • L-shaped country kitchen includes pantry and cozy breakfast area • Bedrooms are located on the second floor for privacy • Master bedroom includes a walk-in closet, dressing area and bath • 3 bedrooms, 2 1/2 baths, 2-car garage • Crawl space foundation, drawings also include basement and slab foundations

Study Off Main Entrance

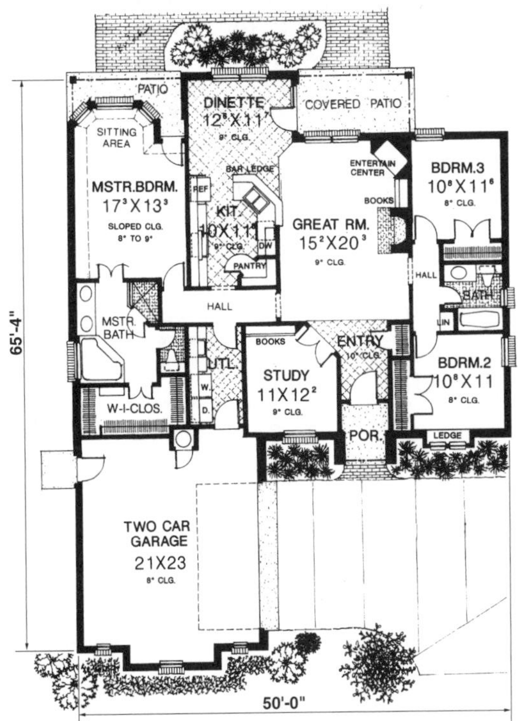

Plan #582-036D-0060

Price Code B

Special Features • 1,760 total square feet of living area • Stone and brick exterior has old-world charm • Master bedroom includes a sitting area and is situated away from other bedrooms for privacy • Kitchen and dinette access the outdoors • Great room includes fireplace, built-in bookshelves and an entertainment center • 3 bedrooms, 2 baths, 2-car side entry garage • Slab foundation

Plan #582-035D-0047

Price Code C

Special Features • 1,818 total square feet of living area • Spacious breakfast area extends into the family room and kitchen • Master suite has a tray ceiling and vaulted bath with walk-in closet • Optional bonus room above the garage has an additional 298 square feet of living area • 3 bedrooms, 2 1/2 baths, 2-car garage • Walk-out basement, slab or crawl space foundation, please specify when ordering

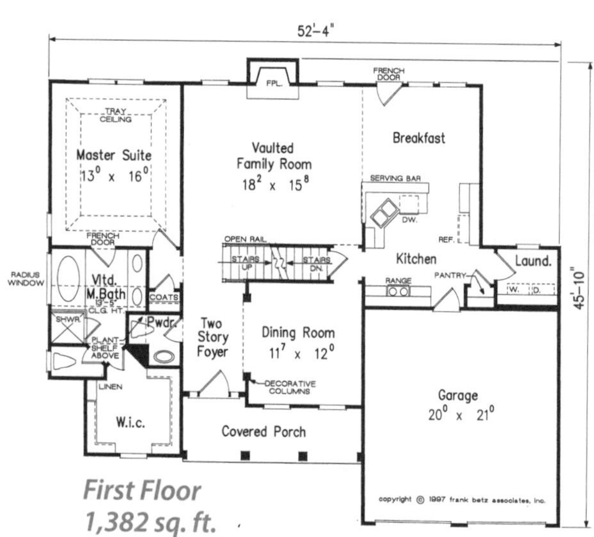

First Floor
1,382 sq. ft.

Second Floor
436 sq. ft.

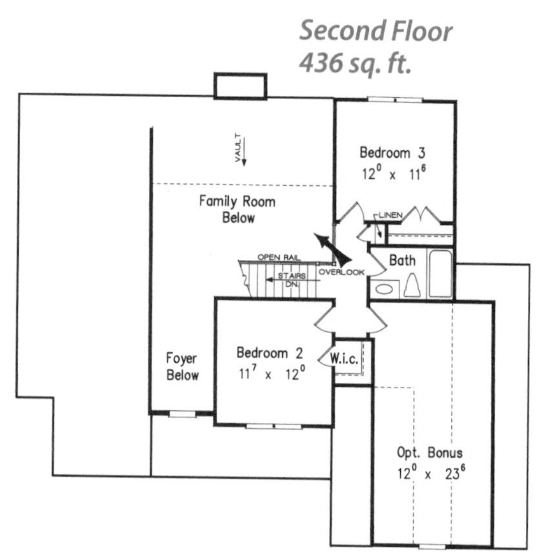

Prestigious Appeal For A Modest Home

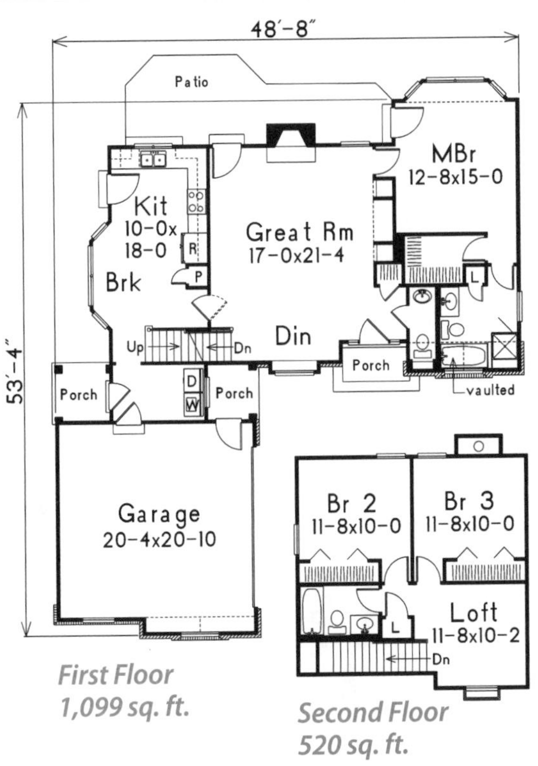

First Floor
1,099 sq. ft.

Second Floor
520 sq. ft.

Plan #582-007D-0035

Price Code B

Special Features • 1,619 total square feet of living area • Home has three quaint porches and a large rear patio • Grand-scale great room has dining area, fireplace with a built-in alcove and shelves creating an entertainment center • Master bedroom has a walk-in closet, bath and access to rear patio • Breakfast room with bay contains staircase leading to second floor • 3 bedrooms, 2 1/2 baths, 2-car side entry garage • Basement foundation

High Ceilings Create A Feeling Of Luxury

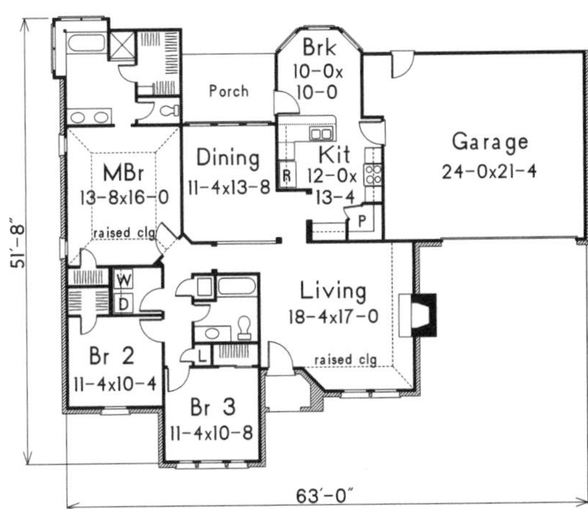

Plan #582-037D-0008

Price Code C

Special Features • 1,707 total square feet of living area • The formal living room off the entry hall has a high sloping ceiling and prominent fireplace • Kitchen and breakfast area allow access to an oversized garage and rear porch • Master bedroom has an impressive vaulted ceiling, luxurious bath, large walk-in closet and separate tub and shower • Utility room is conveniently located near bedrooms • 3 bedrooms, 2 baths, 2-car garage • Slab foundation

Plan #582-043D-0005

Price Code B

Special Features • *1,734 total square feet of living area* • *Large entry with coffered ceiling and display niches* • *Sunken great room has 10' ceiling* • *Kitchen island includes eating counter* • *9' ceiling in master bedroom* • *Master bath features corner tub and double sinks* • *3 bedrooms, 2 baths, 2-car garage* • *Crawl space foundation*

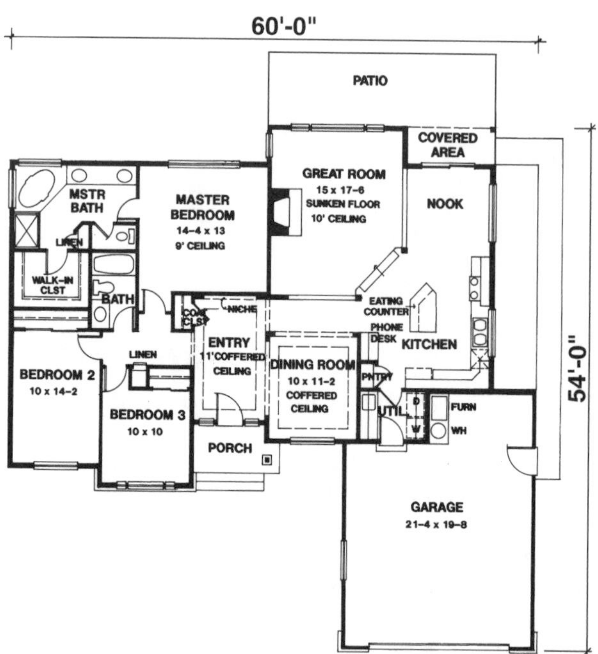

Carport With Storage

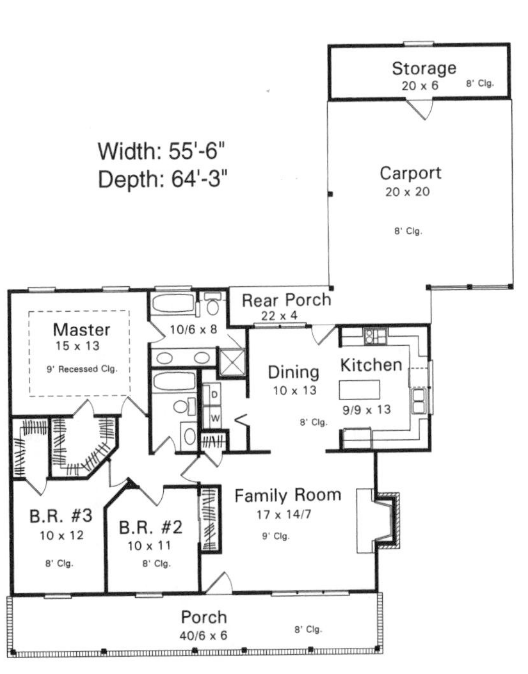

Plan #582-039D-0002

Price Code A

Special Features • 1,333 total square feet of living area • Country charm with a covered front porch • Dining area looks into the family room with fireplace • Master suite has a walk-in closet and private bath • 3 bedrooms, 2 baths, 2-car attached carport • Slab or crawl space foundation, please specify when ordering

Sensational Breakfast Area

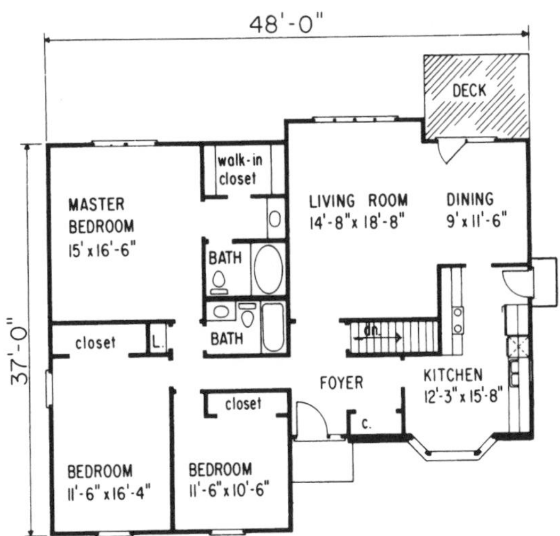

Plan #582-008D-0047

Price Code B

Special Features • 1,610 total square feet of living area • Attractive stone facade wraps around cozy breakfast room bay • Roomy foyer leads to a splendid kitchen with an abundance of storage and counterspace • The spacious living and dining room combination features access to the rear deck • Master bedroom features a walk-in closet and compartmented bath with a luxurious garden tub • 3 bedrooms, 2 baths • Basement foundation, drawings also include crawl space and slab foundations

Plan #582-052D-0011

Price Code A

Special Features • 1,325 total square feet of living area • Sloped ceiling and a fireplace in the living area create a cozy feeling • Formal dining and breakfast areas have an efficiently designed kitchen between them • Master bedroom has a walk-in closet and luxurious private bath • 3 bedrooms, 2 baths, 2-car drive under garage • Basement or crawl space foundation, please specify when ordering

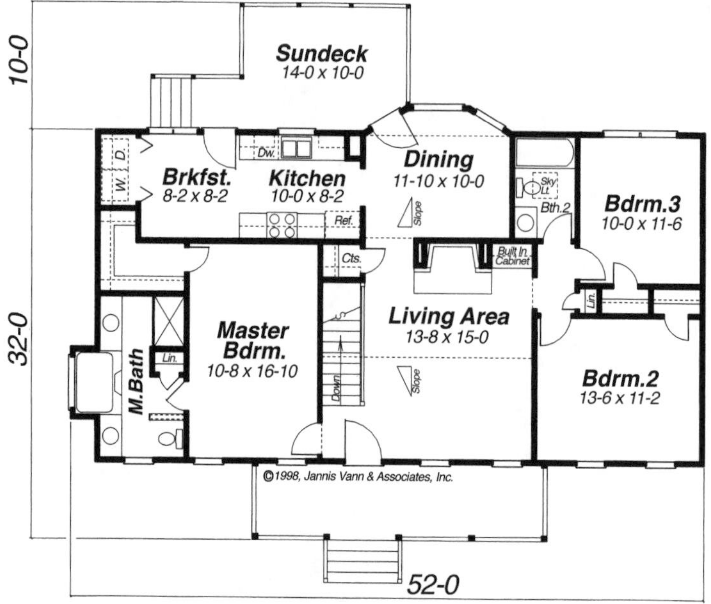

Front Porch Adds Style To This Ranch

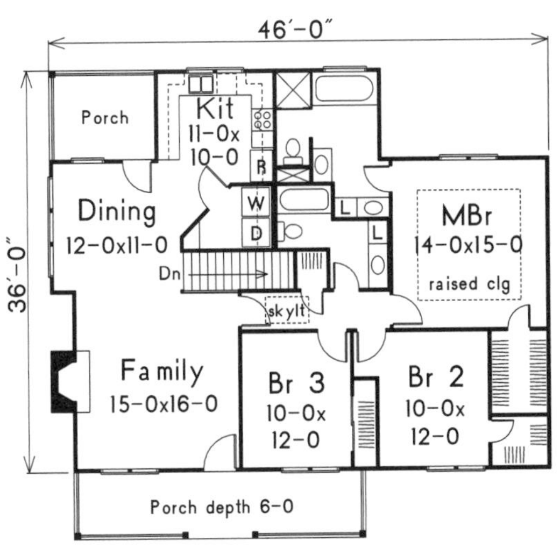

Plan #582-040D-0010

Price Code A

Special Features • *1,496 total square feet of living area • Master bedroom features a tray ceiling, walk-in closet and spacious bath • Vaulted ceiling and fireplace grace family room • Dining room is adjacent to kitchen and features access to rear porch • Convenient access to utility room from kitchen • 3 bedrooms, 2 baths, 2-car drive under garage • Basement foundation*

Triple Dormers Create Terrific Curb Appeal

Plan #582-013D-0022

Price Code C

Special Features • *1,992 total square feet of living area • Interesting angled walls add drama to many of the living areas including family room, master bedroom and breakfast area • Covered porch includes spa and an outdoor kitchen with sink, refrigerator and cooktop • Enter the majestic master bath to find a dramatic corner oversized tub • 4 bedrooms, 3 baths, 2-car side entry garage • Basement, crawl space or slab foundation, please specify when ordering*

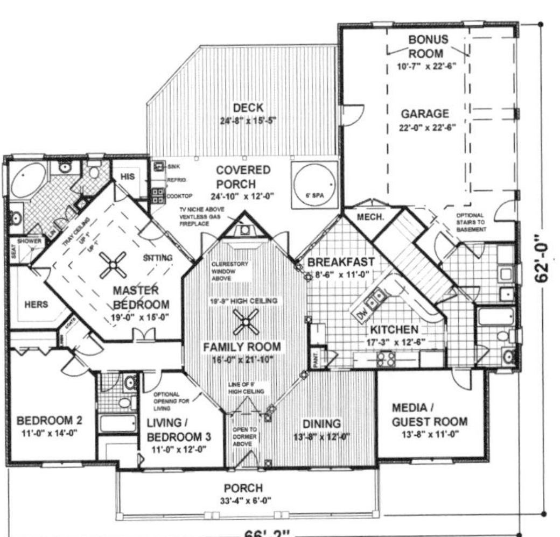

Spacious Living In This Ranch

Plan #582-068D-0005

Price Code A

Special Features • 1,433 total square feet of living area • Vaulted living room includes cozy fireplace and an oversized entertainment center • Bedrooms #2 and #3 share a full bath • Master bedroom has a full bath and large walk-in closet • 3 bedrooms, 2 baths, 2-car garage • Basement foundation, drawings also include crawl space and slab foundations

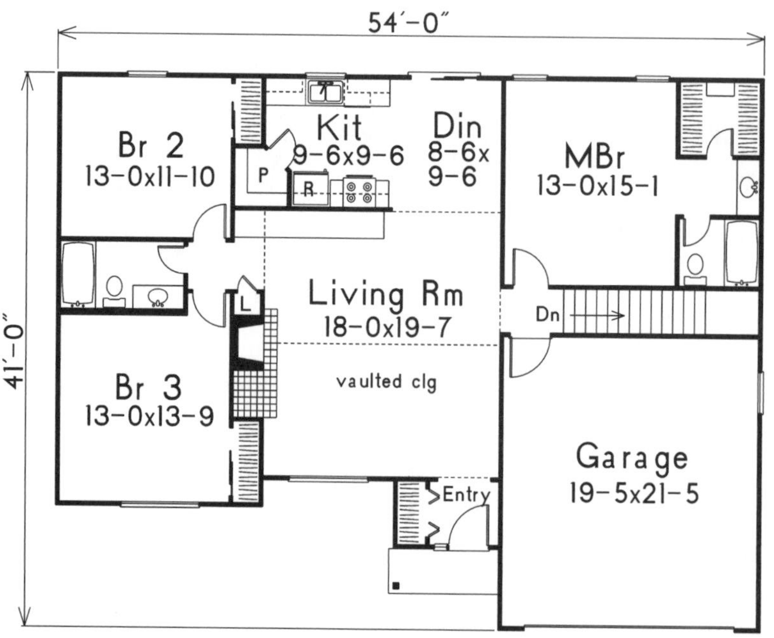

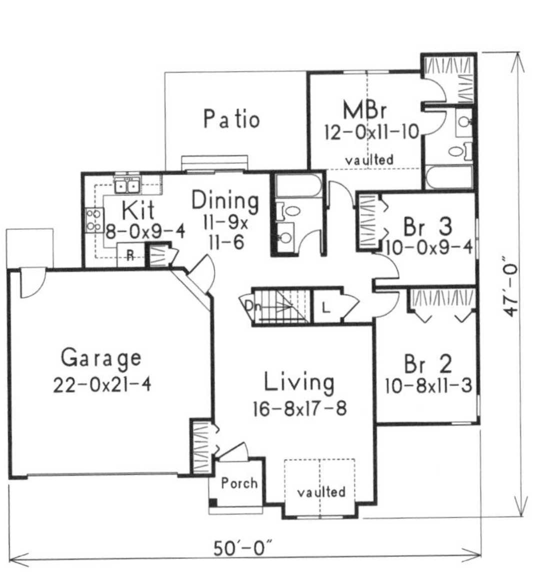

Plan #582-041D-0004

Price Code AA

Special Features • 1,195 total square feet of living area • Dining room opens onto the patio • Master bedroom features a vaulted ceiling, private bath and walk-in closet • Coat closets are located by both the entrances • Convenient secondary entrance is at the back of the garage • 3 bedrooms, 2 baths, 2-car garage • Basement foundation

Wall Of Windows For Terrific Views

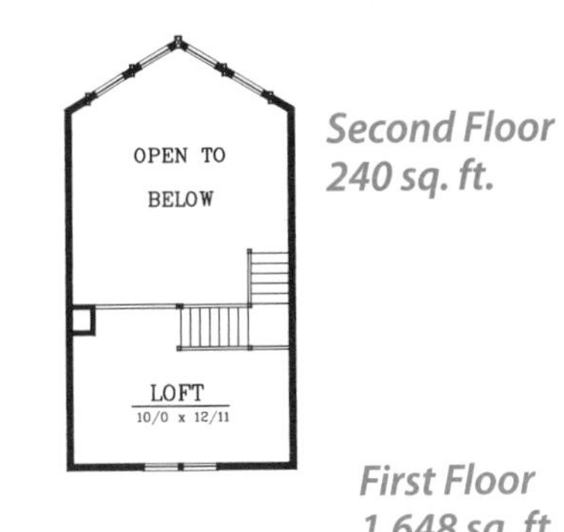

Second Floor
240 sq. ft.

First Floor
1,648 sq. ft.

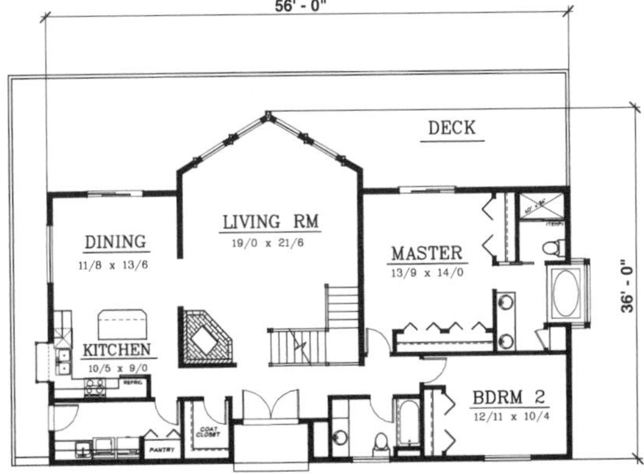

Plan #582-015D-0010

Price Code C

Special Features • 1,888 total square feet of living area • Impressive corner fireplace warms the living room • Second floor loft creates a great entertainment or extra sleeping area • Master bath has a beautiful spa tub flooded with sunlight • 2 bedrooms, 2 baths • Basement foundation

Plan #582-078D-0040 Price Code D

Special Features • 1,905 total square feet of living area • Bright and airy living and dining rooms combine a vaulted ceiling and two pairs of French doors that open onto the front porch • Kitchen features an abundance of counter-space, vaulted ceiling and island counter • Oversized utility room contains a coat closet, pantry and access to the garage • A spiral stairway in the living/dining area leads to a charming loft which has an additional 323 square feet of living area • 3 bedrooms, 2 baths, 3-car rear entry garage • Crawl space foundation

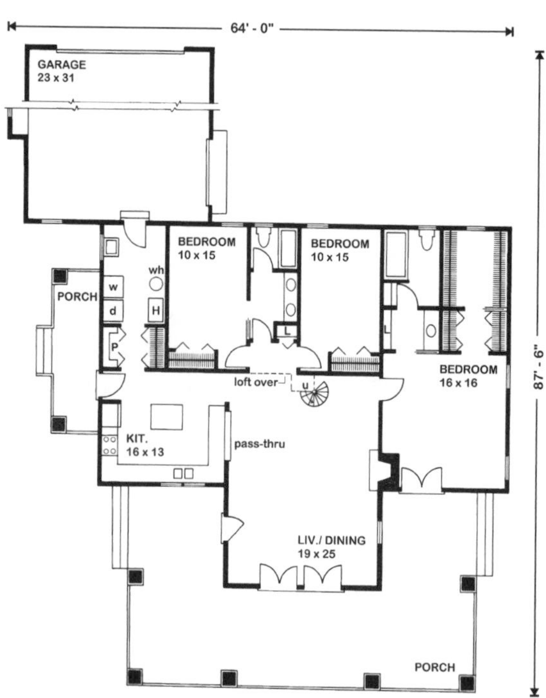

Comfortable One-Story Country Home

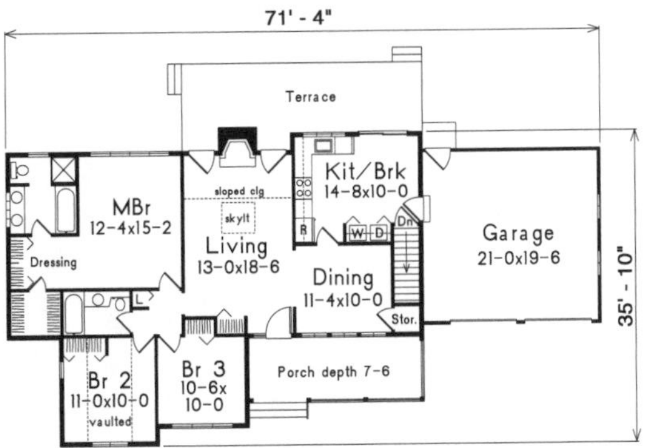

Plan #582-017D-0005

Price Code B

Special Features • 1,367 total square feet of living area • Neat front porch shelters the entrance • Dining room has full wall of windows and convenient storage area • Breakfast area leads to the rear terrace through sliding doors • Large living room with high ceiling, skylight and fireplace • 3 bedrooms, 2 baths, 2-car garage • Basement foundation, drawings also include slab foundation

Formal Living And Dining Rooms

Plan #582-043D-0003

Price Code C

Special Features • 1,890 total square feet of living area • Inviting covered porch • Vaulted ceilings in living, dining and family rooms • Kitchen is open to the family room and nook • Large walk-in pantry in kitchen • Arch accented master bath has spa tub, double sinks and walk-in closet • 3 bedrooms, 2 baths, 2-car garage • Crawl space foundation

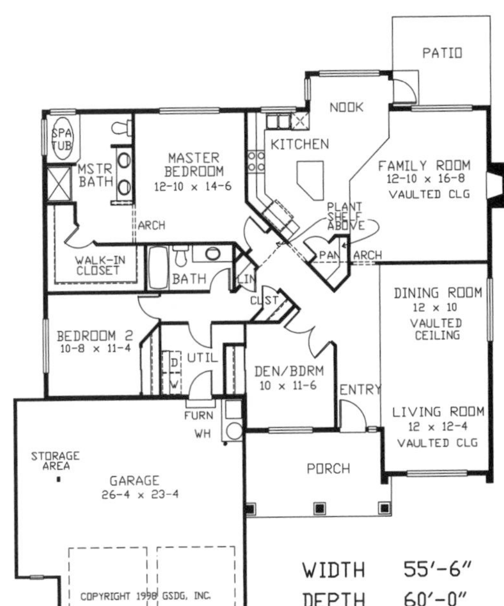

Distinctive Turret Surrounds The Dining Bay

Plan #582-018D-0006

Price Code B

Special Features • *1,742 total square feet of living area* • *Efficient kitchen combines with breakfast area and great room creating a spacious living area* • *Master bedroom includes a private bath with huge walk-in closet, shower and corner tub* • *Great room boasts a fireplace and access outdoors* • *Laundry room is conveniently located near the kitchen and garage* • *3 bedrooms, 2 baths, 2-car garage* • *Slab foundation, drawings also include crawl space foundation*

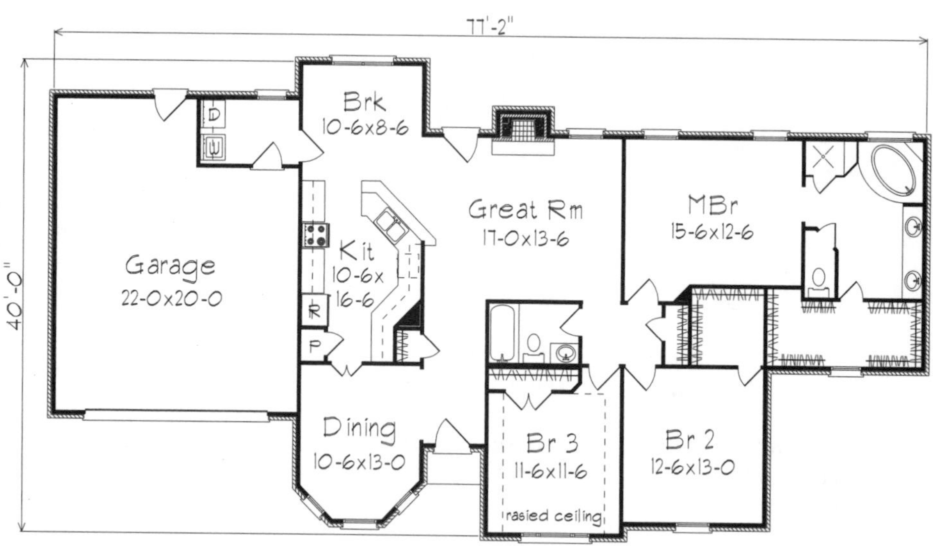

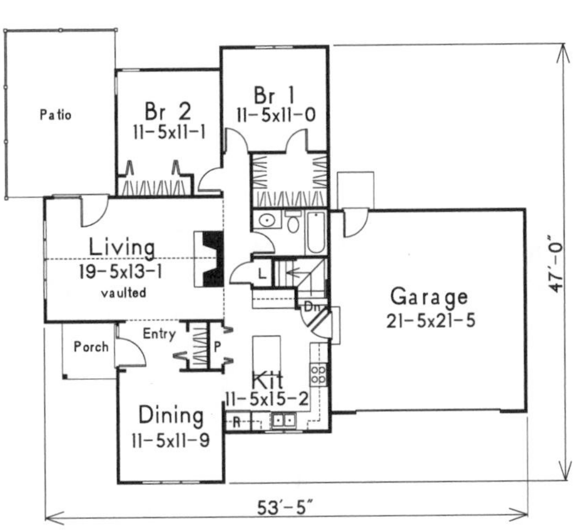

Plan #582-045D-0019

Price Code AA

Special Features • 1,134 total square feet of living area • Kitchen has plenty of counterspace, an island worktop, large pantry and access to the garage • Living room features a vaulted ceiling, fireplace and access to an expansive patio • Bedroom #1 has a large walk-in closet • Convenient linen closet in the hall • 2 bedrooms, 1 bath, 2-car garage • Basement foundation

Circle-Top Details

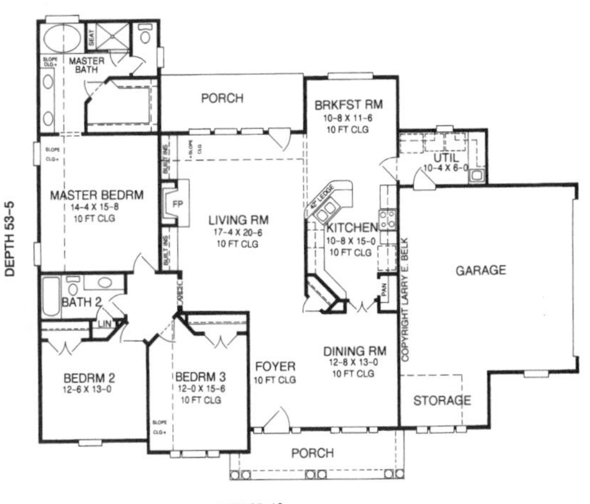

Plan #582-019D-0013

Price Code C

Special Features • 1,932 total square feet of living area • Double arches form entrance to this elegantly styled home • Two palladian windows add distinction to facade • Kitchen has an angled eating bar opening to the breakfast and living rooms • 3 bedrooms, 2 baths, 2-car side entry garage • Crawl space foundation, drawings also include slab foundation

Plan #582-058D-0029

Price Code AA

Special Features • 1,000 total square feet of living area • Large mud room with separate covered porch entrance • Full-length covered front porch • Bedrooms are on opposite sides of the home for privacy • Vaulted ceiling creates an open and spacious feeling • 2 bedrooms, 1 bath • Crawl space foundation

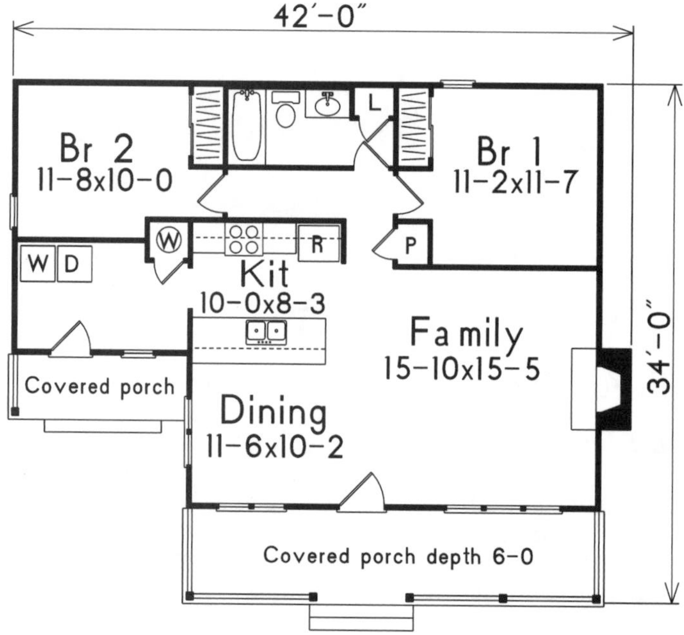

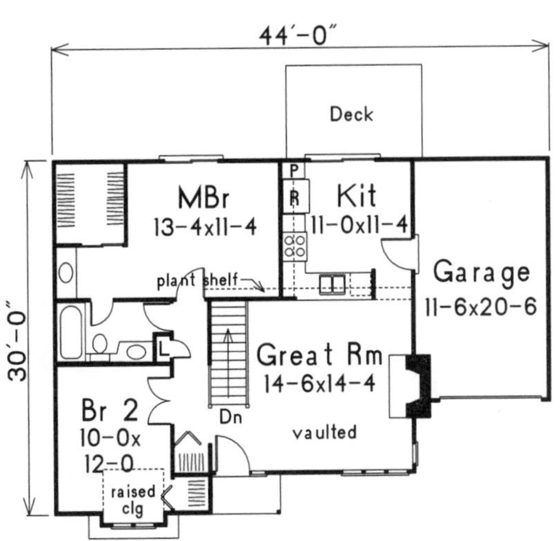

Plan #582-022D-0023

Price Code AA

Special Features • 950 total square feet of living area • Vaulted ceiling, open stairway and fireplace complement the great room • Bedroom #2 with a sloped ceiling and box-bay window can convert to a den • Master bedroom has a walk-in closet, plant shelf, separate dressing area and private access to bath • Kitchen has garage access and opens to great room • 2 bedrooms, 1 bath, 1-car garage • Basement foundation

A Two-Story With Modern Appeal

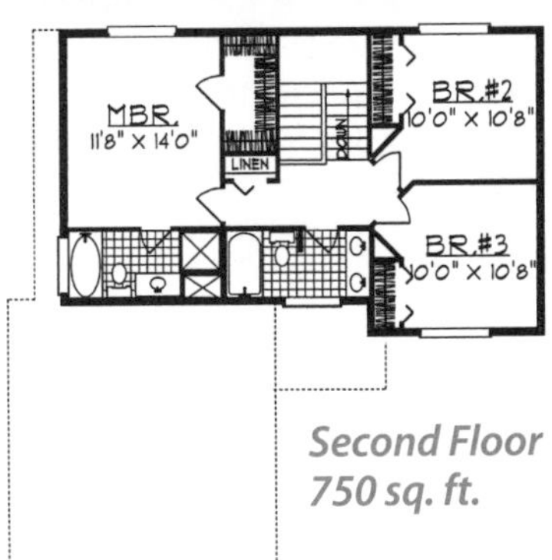

Second Floor
750 sq. ft.

First Floor
786 sq. ft.

Plan #582-051D-0037

Price Code B

Special Features • 1,536 total square feet of living area • 9' ceilings throughout this home • All bedrooms are located on the second floor for privacy from living areas • Spacious great room has a corner fireplace and cheerful wall of windows • 3 bedrooms, 2 1/2 baths, 2-car garage • Basement foundation

Plan #582-001D-0061

Price Code C

Special Features • 1,875 total square feet of living area • Country-style exterior with wrap-around porch and dormers • Large second floor bedrooms share a dressing area and bath • Master bedroom includes a bay window, walk-in closet, dressing area and bath • 3 bedrooms, 2 baths, 2-car side entry garage • Crawl space foundation, drawings also include basement and slab foundations

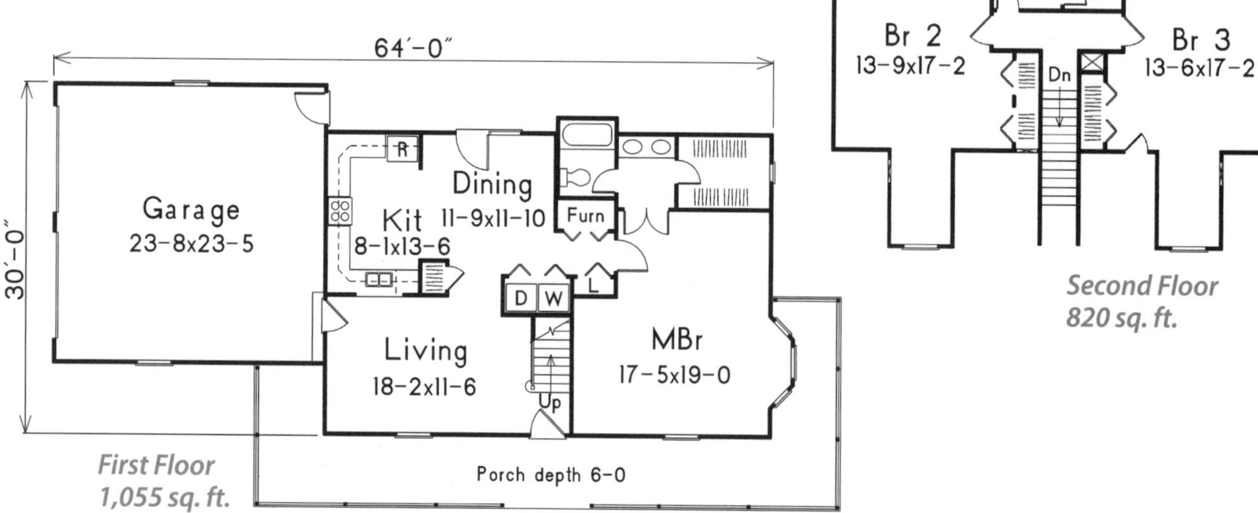

First Floor
1,055 sq. ft.

Second Floor
820 sq. ft.

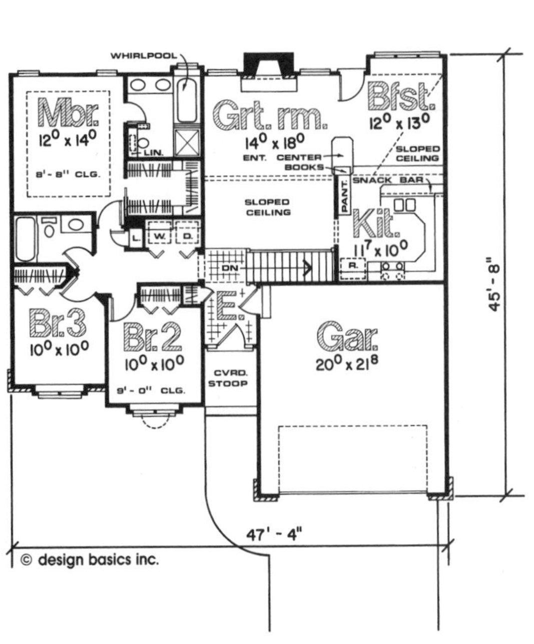

Plan #582-026D-0096

Price Code A

Special Features • 1,341 total square feet of living area • Breakfast area is a cheerful dining retreat • Master bath boasts a whirlpool tub and shower • U-shaped kitchen is designed to have everything within reach • 3 bedrooms, 2 baths, 2-car garage • Basement foundation

Trim Colonial For Practical Living

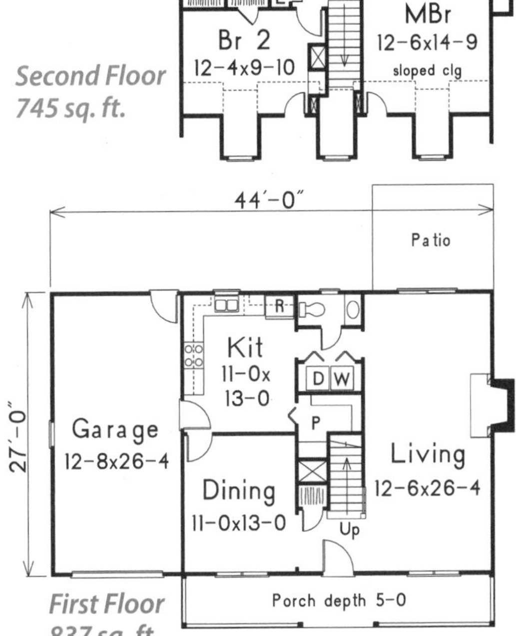

Plan #582-053D-0001

Price Code B

Special Features • 1,582 total square feet of living area • Conservative layout gives privacy to living and dining areas • Large fireplace and windows enhance the living area • Rear door in garage is convenient to the garden and kitchen • Full front porch adds charm • Dormers add light to the foyer and bedrooms • 3 bedrooms, 2 1/2 baths, 1-car garage • Slab foundation, drawings also include crawl space foundation

Upscale Ranch Boasts Both Formal And Casual Areas

Plan #582-061D-0002

Price Code C

Special Features • 1,950 total square feet of living area • Large corner kitchen with island cooktop opens to family room • Master bedroom features double-door entry, raised ceiling, double-bowl vanity and walk-in closet • Plant shelf accents hall • 4 bedrooms, 2 baths, 3-car garage • Crawl space foundation

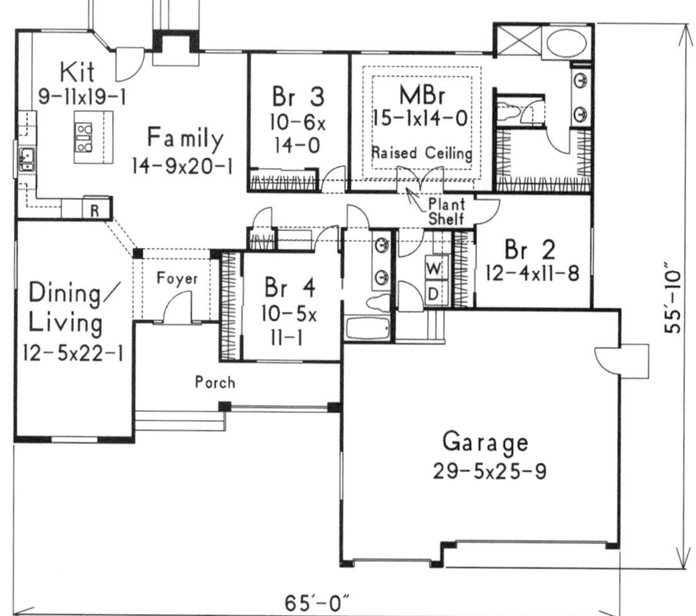

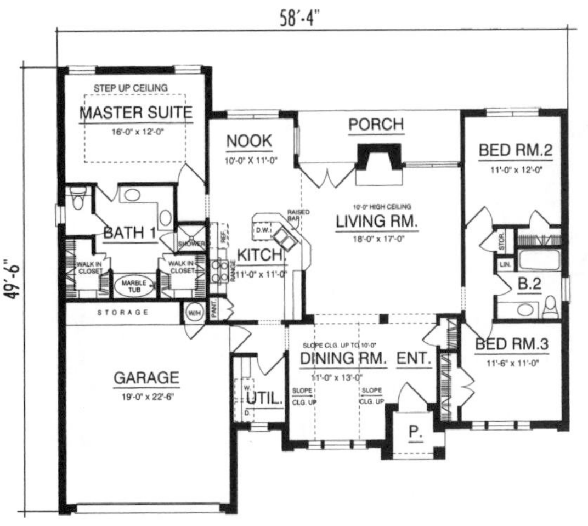

Plan #582-030D-0004

Price Code B

Special Features • 1,791 total square feet of living area • Dining area has a 10' high sloped ceiling • Kitchen opens to large living room with fireplace and has access to a covered porch • Master suite features private bath, double walk-in closets and whirlpool tub • 3 bedrooms, 2 baths, 2-car garage • Slab or crawl space foundation, please specify when ordering

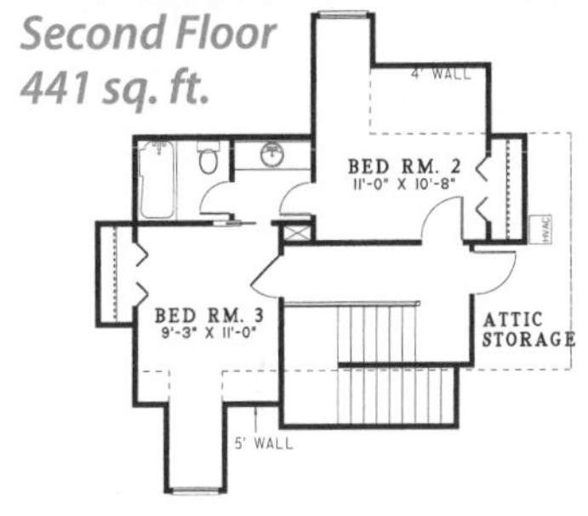

Second Floor
441 sq. ft.

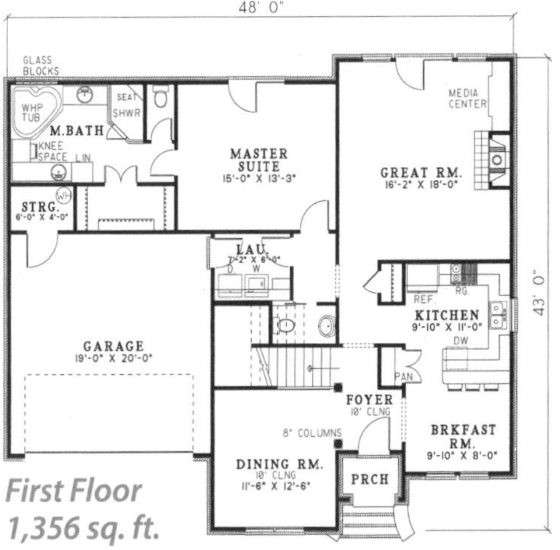

First Floor
1,356 sq. ft.

Plan #582-055D-0044

Price Code B

Special Features • 1,797 total square feet of living area • Great room has outdoor access, media center and a fireplace • Attractive dormers add character to second floor bedrooms • Efficiently designed kitchen • Formal dining area is separated from other areas for entertaining • 3 bedrooms, 2 1/2 baths, 2-car garage • Walk-out basement, basement, crawl space or slab foundation, please specify when ordering

Appealing Ranch Has Attractive Front Dormers

Plan #582-001D-0034

Price Code B

Special Features • 1,642 total square feet of living area • Walk-through kitchen boasts a vaulted ceiling and corner sink overlooking the family room • Vaulted family room features a cozy fireplace and access to the rear patio • Master bedroom includes a sloped ceiling, walk-in closet and private bath • 3 bedrooms, 2 baths, 2-car garage • Basement foundation, drawings also include slab and crawl space foundations

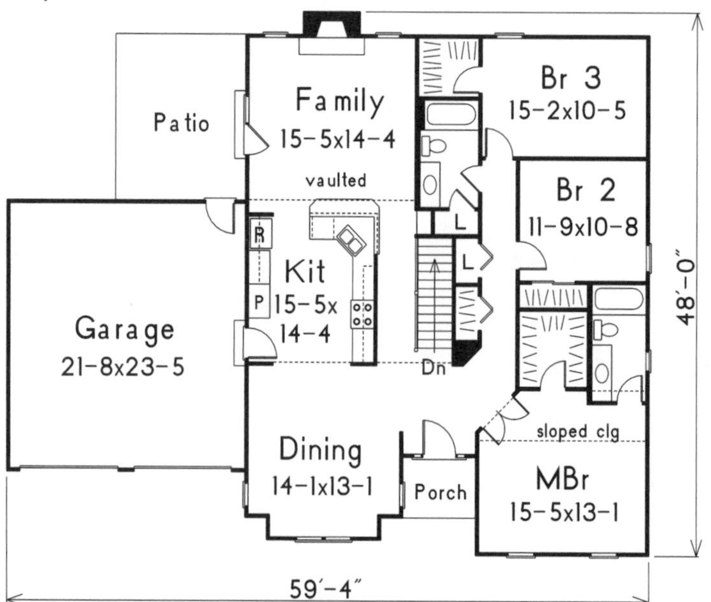

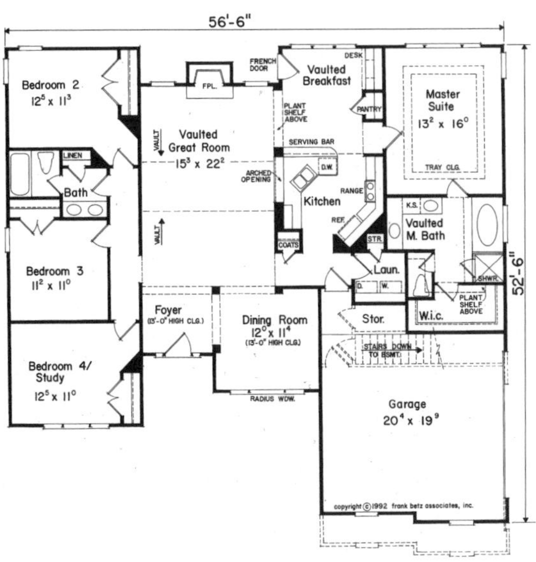

Plan #582-035D-0011

Price Code C

Special Features • 1,945 total square feet of living area • Master suite is separate from other bedrooms for privacy • Vaulted breakfast room is directly off great room • Kitchen includes a built-in desk area • Elegant dining room has an arched window • 4 bedrooms, 2 baths, 2-car side entry garage • Walk-out basement, crawl space or slab foundation, please specify when ordering

Traditional Elegance

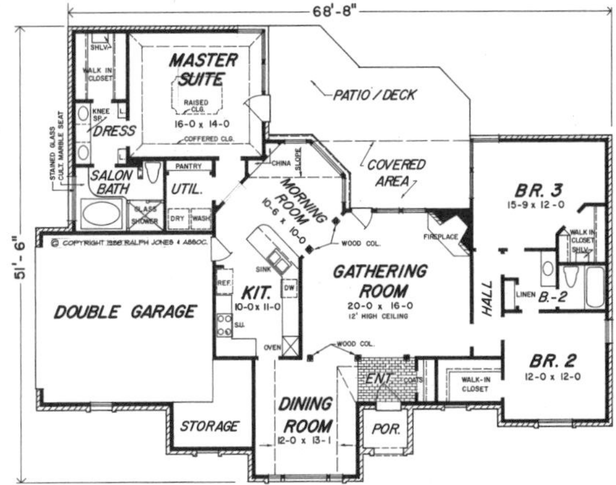

Plan #582-060D-0006

Price Code C

Special Features • 1,945 total square feet of living area • Large gathering room with corner fireplace and 12' high ceiling • Master suite has a coffered ceiling and French door leading to the patio/deck • Master bath has a cultured marble seat, separate shower and tub • All bedrooms have walk-in closets • 3 bedrooms, 2 baths, 2-car side entry garage • Slab or crawl space foundation, please specify when ordering

Plan #582-038D-0036

Price Code A

Special Features • 1,470 total square feet of living area • Vaulted breakfast room is cheerful and sunny • Private second floor master bedroom has a bath and walk-in closet • Large utility room has access to the outdoors • 3 bedrooms, 2 baths • Basement, crawl space or slab foundation, please specify when ordering

Rear View

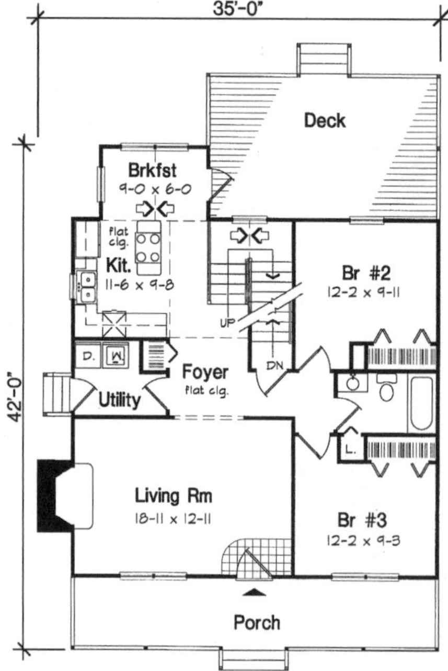

First Floor
1,035 sq. ft.

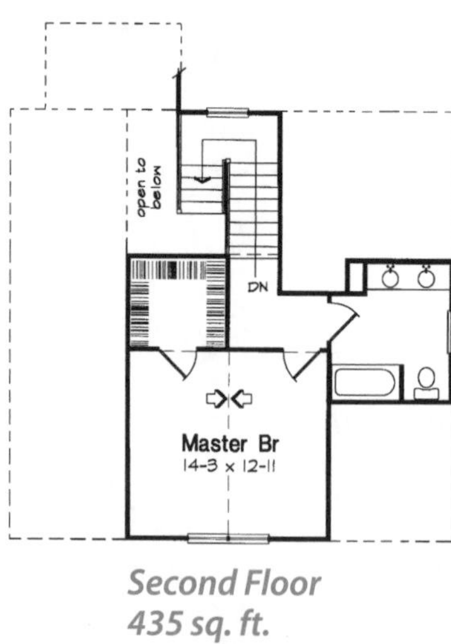

Second Floor
435 sq. ft.

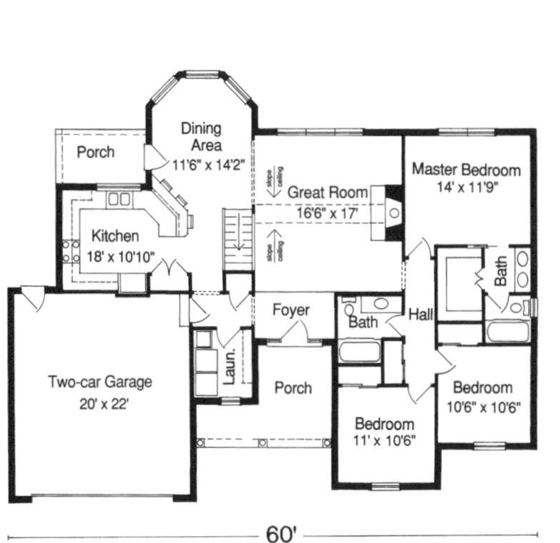

Plan #582-065D-0010

Price Code B

Special Features • 1,508 total square feet of living area • Grand opening between rooms creates a spacious effect • Additional room for quick meals or serving a larger crowd is provided at the breakfast bar • Sunny dining area accesses the outdoors as well • 3 bedrooms, 2 baths, 2-car garage • Basement or crawl space foundation, please specify when ordering

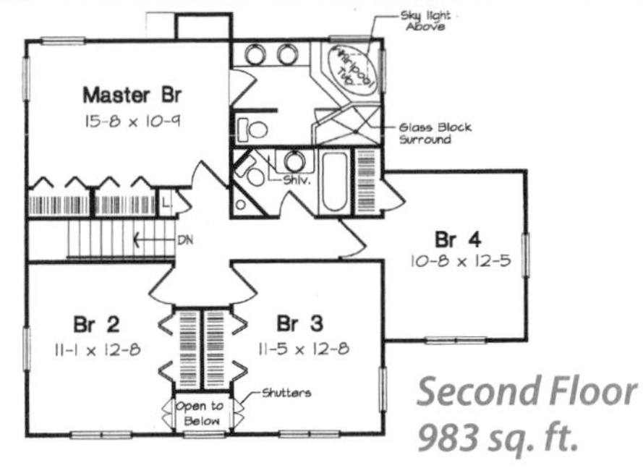

Second Floor
983 sq. ft.

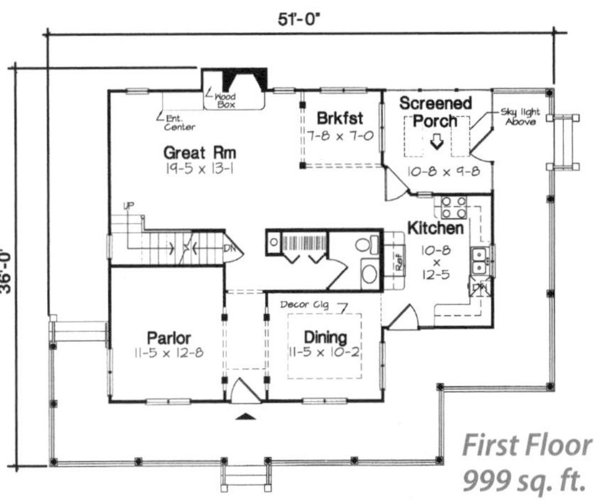

First Floor
999 sq. ft.

Plan #582-038D-0044

Price Code C

Special Features • 1,982 total square feet of living area • Spacious master bedroom has bath with corner whirlpool tub and sunny skylight above • Breakfast area overlooks into great room • Screened porch with skylight above extends the home outdoors and allows for another entertainment area • 4 bedrooms, 2 1/2 baths • Crawl space or slab foundation, please specify when ordering

Plan #582-001D-0019

Price Code A

Special Features • 1,314 total square feet of living area • U-shaped kitchen joins cozy dining area • Family room has direct access into garage • Roomy closets serve the second floor bedrooms • 3 bedrooms, 1 1/2 baths, 2-car garage • Basement foundation, drawings also include crawl space foundation

First Floor
762 sq. ft.

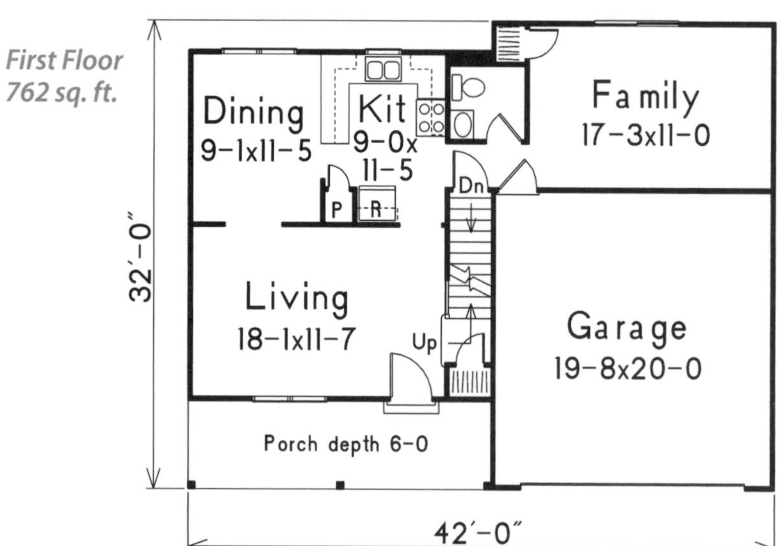

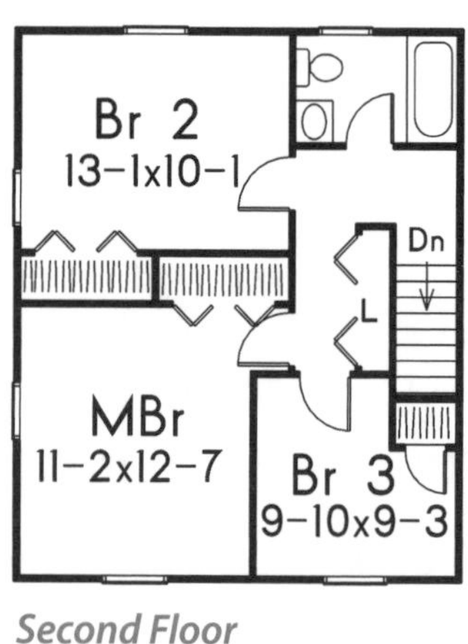

Second Floor
552 sq. ft.

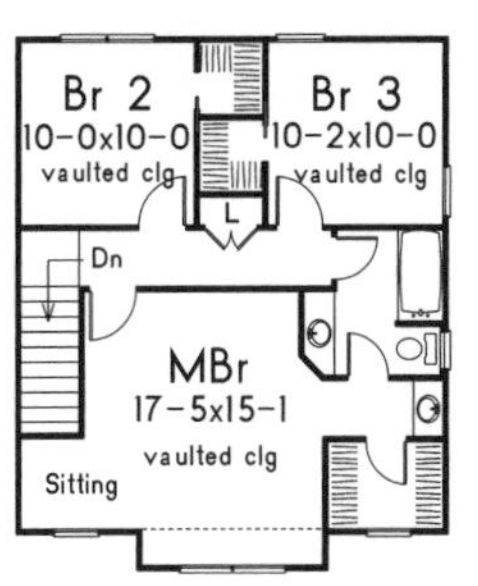

Second Floor
667 sq. ft.

First Floor
732 sq. ft.

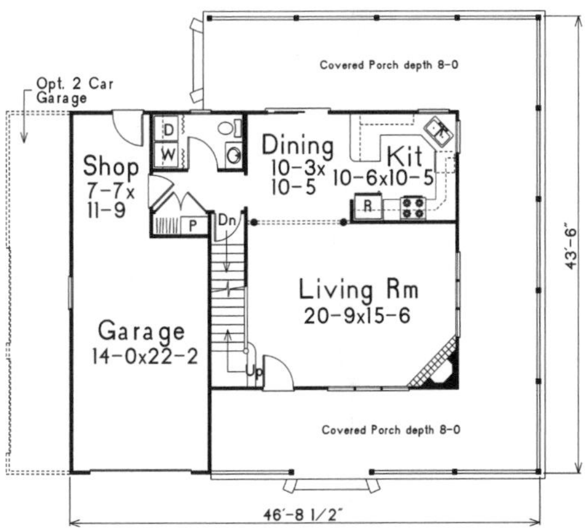

Plan #582-068D-0006

Price Code A

Special Features • 1,399 total square feet of living area • Living room overlooks dining area through arched columns • Laundry room contains handy half bath • Spacious master bedroom includes sitting area, walk-in closet and plenty of sunlight • 3 bedrooms, 1 1/2 baths, 1-car garage • Basement foundation, drawings also include crawl space and slab foundation

Split Entry With Lots Of Room For Future Growth

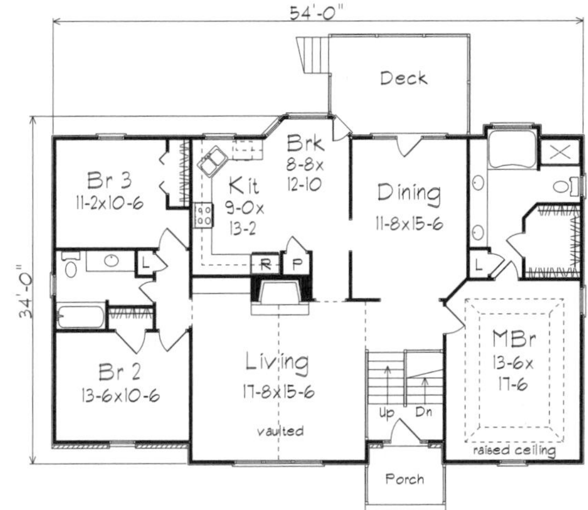

Plan #582-053D-0055

Price Code C

Special Features • 1,803 total square feet of living area • Master bedroom features a raised ceiling and private bath with a walk-in closet, large double-bowl vanity and separate tub and shower • U-shaped kitchen includes a corner sink and convenient pantry • Vaulted living room is complete with a fireplace and built-in cabinet • 3 bedrooms, 2 baths, 3-car drive under garage • Basement foundation

Plan #582-007D-0033

Price Code B

Special Features • *1,618 total square feet of living area* • *Wrap-around porch offers a covered passageway to the garage* • *Dramatic two-story entry, with balcony above and staircase provide an expansive feel with an added decorative oval window* • *Dazzling kitchen features walk-in pantry, convenient laundry and covered rear porch* • *3 bedrooms, 2 1/2 baths, 1-car garage* • *Basement foundation*

Second Floor
754 sq. ft.

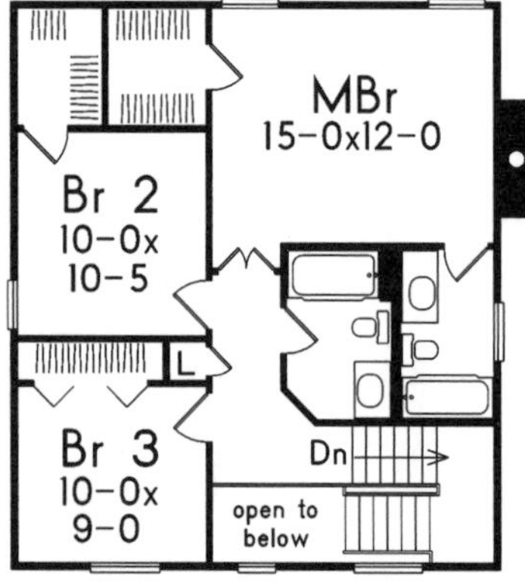

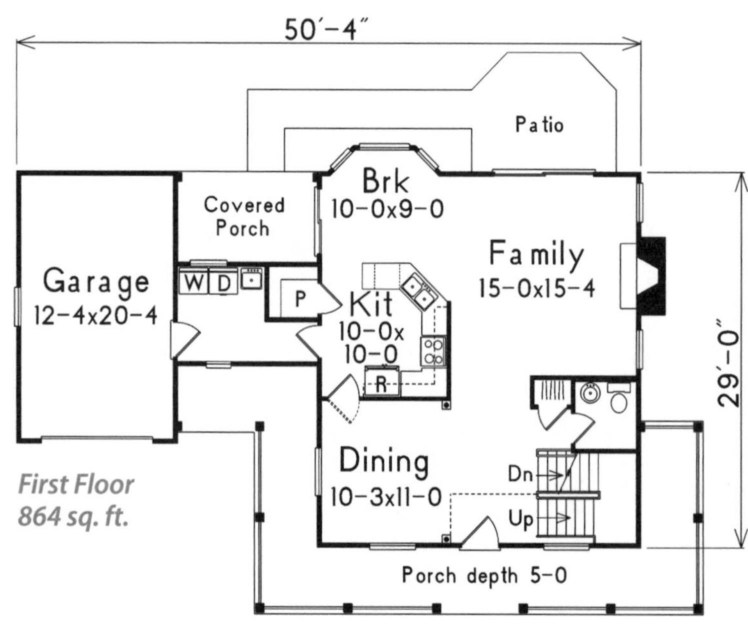

First Floor
864 sq. ft.

Vaulted Ceiling Adds Spaciousness

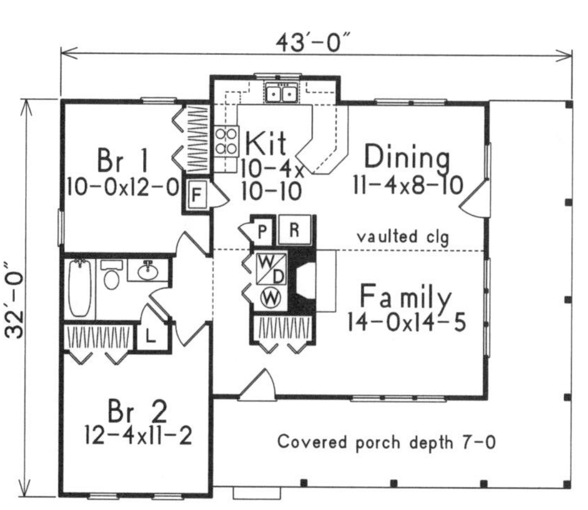

Plan #582-058D-0030

Price Code AA

Special Features • 990 total square feet of living area • Wrap-around porch on two sides of this home • Covered porch surrounding one side of this home maintains privacy • Space for efficiency washer and dryer unit for convenience • 2 bedrooms, 1 bath • Crawl space foundation

Private Master Bedroom

Plan #582-070D-0002

Price Code B

Special Features • 1,700 total square feet of living area • Open and airy dining room • Secondary bedrooms share a central bath • Optional second floor has an additional 268 square feet of living area • 3 bedrooms, 2 baths, 2-car garage • Basement foundation

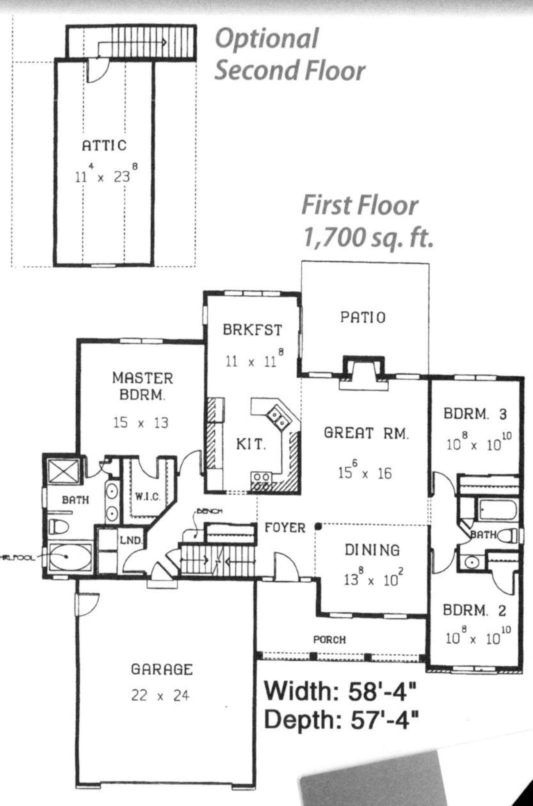

Comfortable Ranch

Plan #582-051D-0040 Price Code A

Special Features • 1,495 total square feet of living area • Dining room has vaulted ceiling creating a large formal gathering area with access to a screen porch • Cathedral ceiling in great room adds spaciousness • Nice-sized entry with coat closet • 3 bedrooms, 2 baths, 2-car garage • Basement foundation

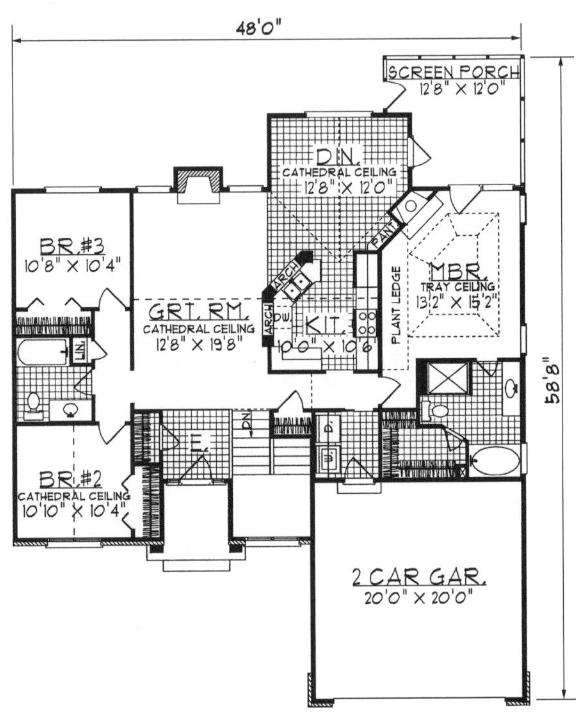

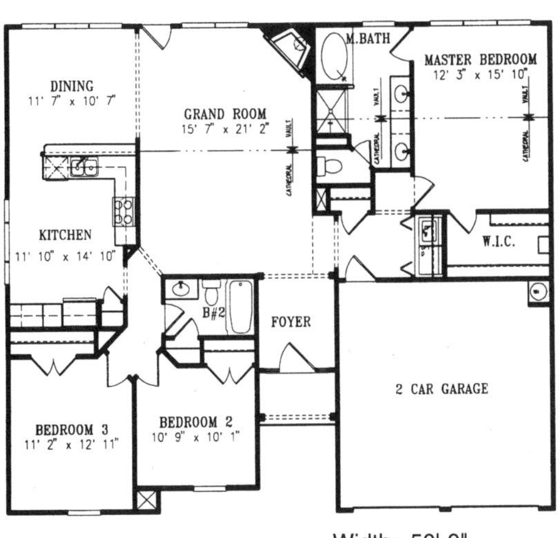

Width: 50'-0"
Depth: 42'-0"

Plan #582-056D-0009

Price Code B

Special Features • 1,606 total square feet of living area • Kitchen has a snack bar which overlooks the dining area for convenience • Master bedroom has lots of windows with a private bath and large walk-in closet • Cathedral vault in great room adds spaciousness • 3 bedrooms, 2 baths, 2-car garage • Slab foundation

Plan #582-076D-0001

Price Code B

Special Features • 1,352 total square feet of living area • The spacious kitchen and breakfast area open into the formal bayed dining room • The grand family room features a fireplace and access onto the rear patio • A whirlpool tub and walk-in closet grace the vaulted master suite • 3 bedrooms, 2 baths, 2-car side entry garage • Slab foundation

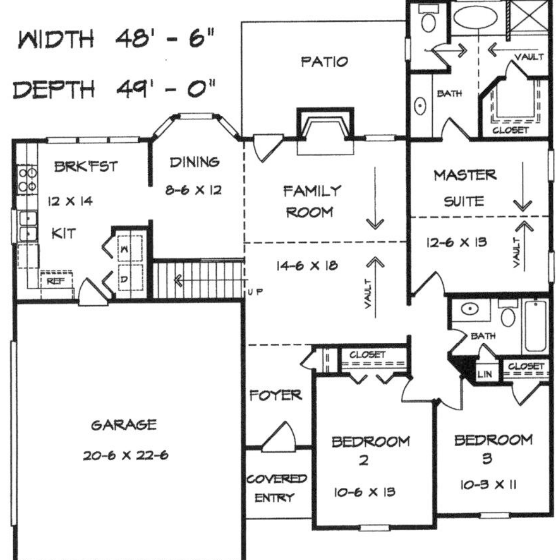

Central Fireplace Warms This Cozy Contemporary

Plan #582-021D-0002

Price Code A

Special Features • 1,442 total square feet of living area • Centrally located living room with recessed fireplace and 10' ceiling • Large U-shaped kitchen offers an eating bar and pantry • Expanded garage provides extra storage and work area • Spacious master bedroom with sitting area and large walk-in closet • 3 bedrooms, 2 baths, 2-car garage • Slab foundation, drawings also include crawl space foundation

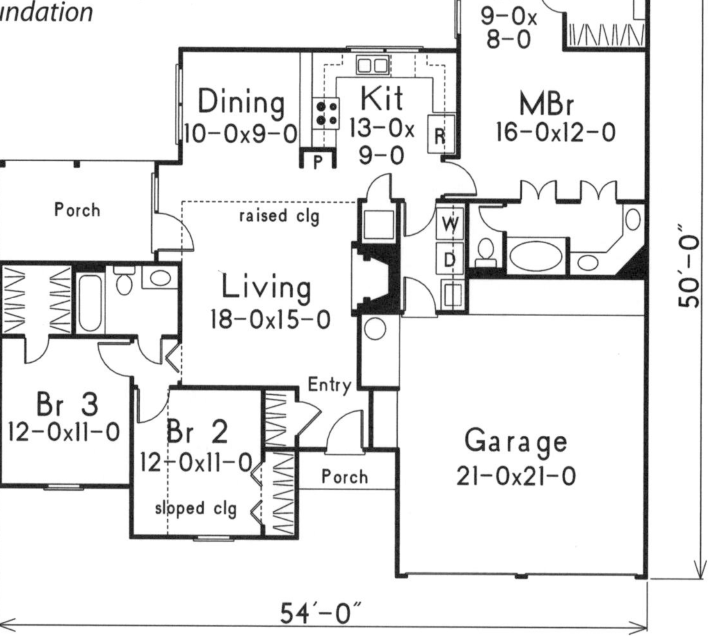

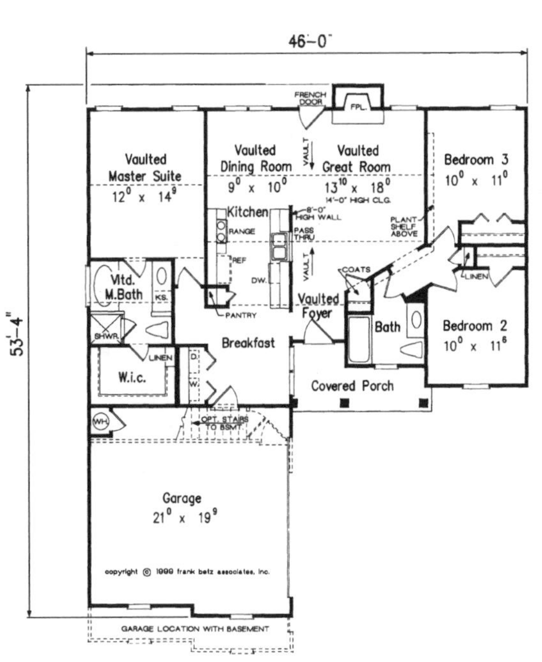

Plan #582-035D-0060

Price Code A

Special Features • 1,290 total square feet of living area • The kitchen is located conveniently between the dining room and breakfast area • Master suite has a luxurious bath with a walk-in closet • Decorative plant shelves throughout this plan add style • 3 bedrooms, 2 baths, 2-car side entry garage • Slab, crawl space or walk-out basement foundation, please specify when ordering

Timeless Classicism

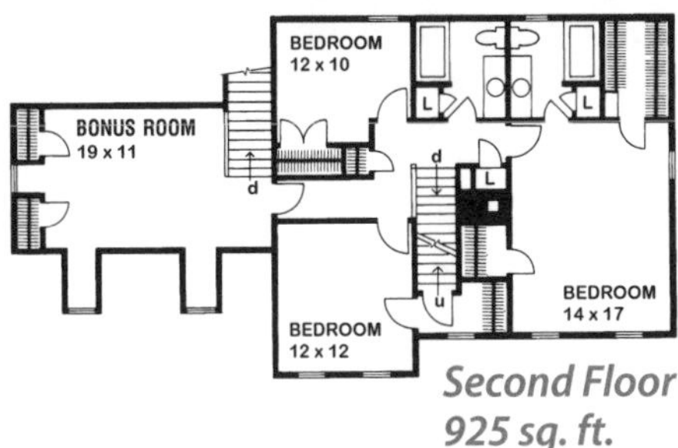

Second Floor
925 sq. ft.

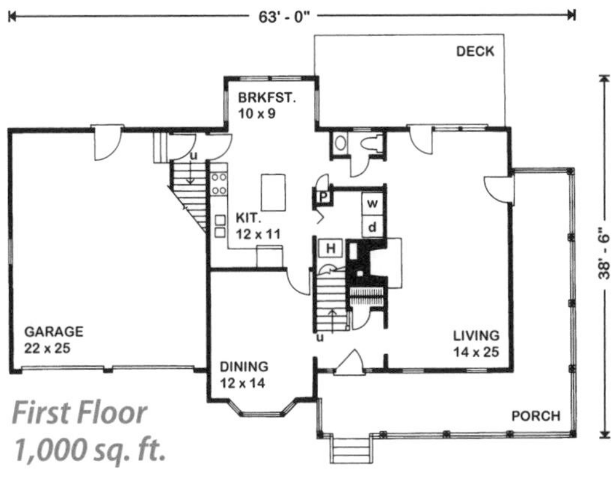

First Floor
1,000 sq. ft.

Plan #582-078D-0002

Price Code D

Special Features • 1,925 total square feet of living area • Spacious foyer is flanked by the formal dining and living rooms • The centrally located kitchen serves the dining room and breakfast nook with ease • Expansive master bedroom enjoys a large walk-in closet and full private bath • The bonus room above the garage has an additional 209 square feet of living area • 3 bedrooms, 2 1/2 baths, 2-car garage • Crawl space foundation

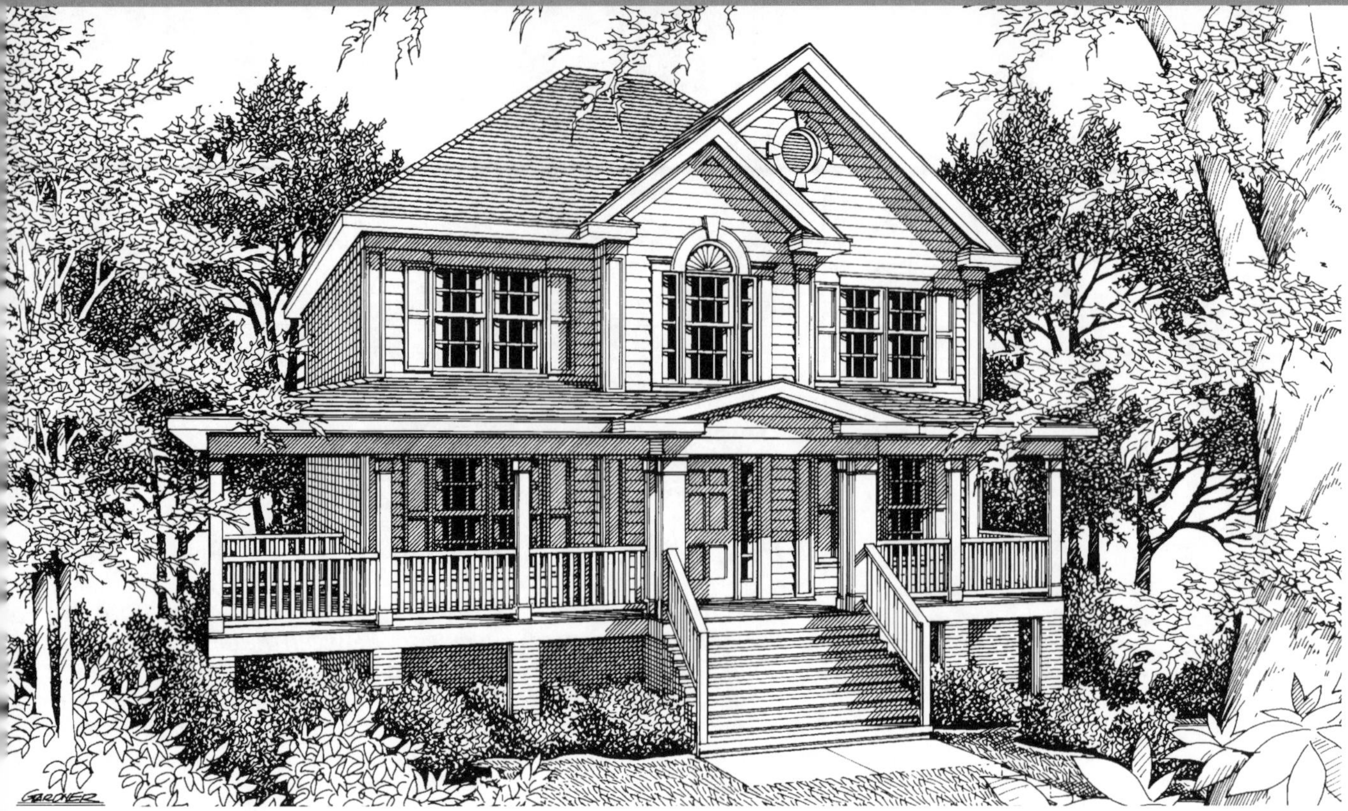

Plan #582-053D-0056

Price Code C

Special Features • *1,880 total square feet of living area* • *Master bedroom is enhanced with a coffered ceiling* • *Generous family and breakfast areas are modern and functional* • *The front porch complements the front facade* • *3 bedrooms, 2 1/2 baths, 2-car drive under garage* • *Basement foundation*

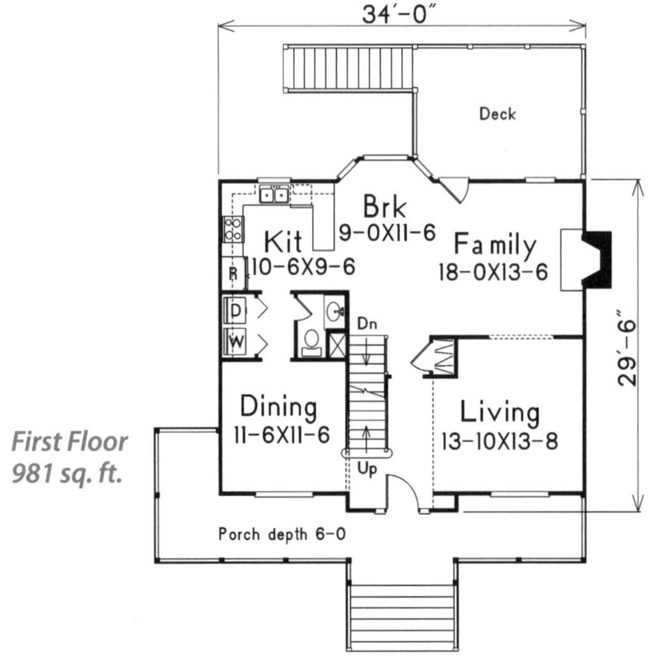

First Floor
981 sq. ft.

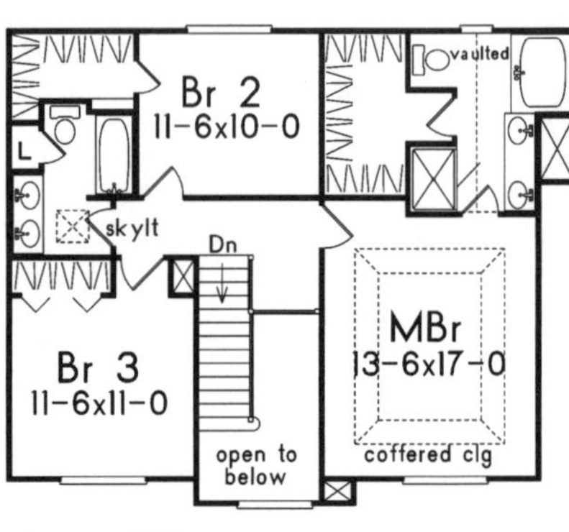

Second Floor
899 sq. ft.

Stone Adds Charm To Exterior

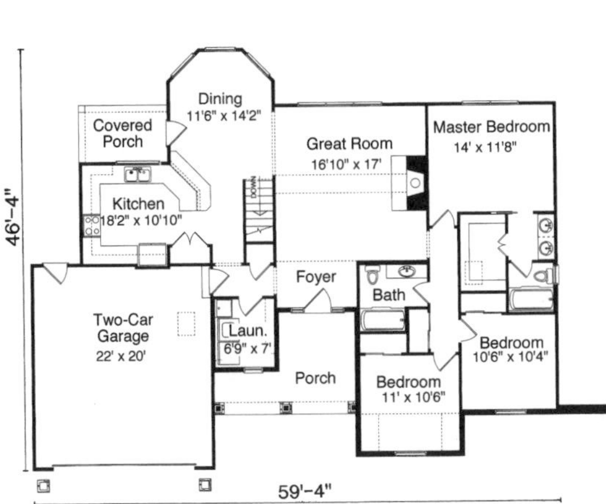

Plan #582-065D-0034 — Price Code B

Special Features • 1,509 total square feet of living area • A grand opening between the great room and dining area visually expands the living space • The kitchen is a delightful place to prepare meals with a snack bar and large pantry • Master bedroom enjoys a private bath with double-bowl vanity and large walk-in closet • 3 bedrooms, 2 baths, 2-car garage • Basement foundation

Beautiful Brickwork Adds Elegance

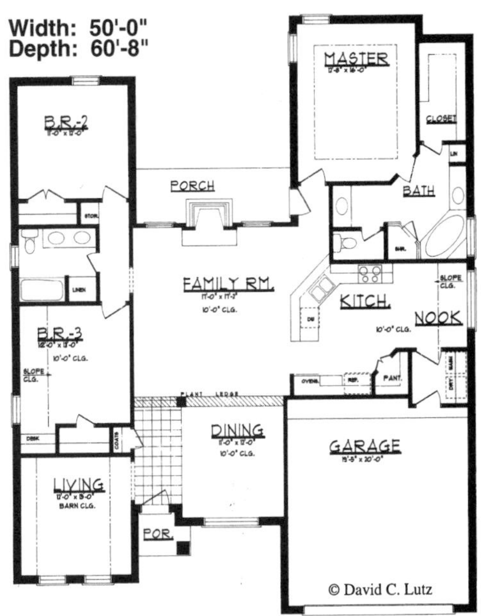

Plan #582-031D-0009 — Price Code C

Special Features • 1,960 total square feet of living area • Open floor plan is suitable for an active family • Desk space in bedroom #3 is ideal for a young student • Effective design creates an enclosed courtyard in the rear of the home • 3 bedrooms, 2 baths, 2-car garage • Slab foundation

Lovely Arched Touches On The Covered Porch

Plan #582-069D-0012

Price Code B

Special Features • 1,594 total square feet of living area • Corner fireplace in the great room creates a cozy feel • Spacious kitchen combines with the dining room creating a terrific gathering place • A handy family and guest entrance is a casual and convenient way to enter the home • 3 bedrooms, 2 baths, 2-car garage • Slab or crawl space foundation, please specify when ordering

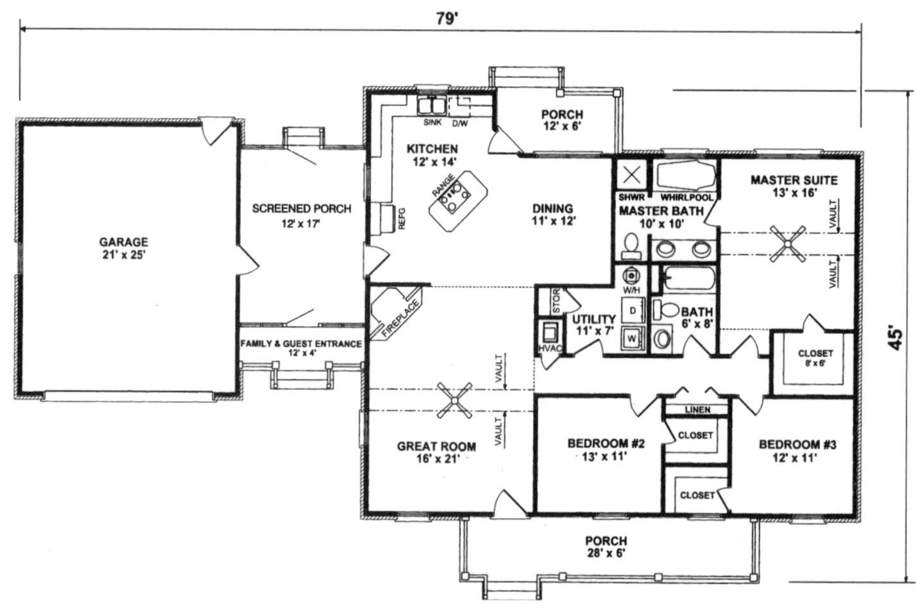

Well-Designed Plan Is Perfect For Entertaining

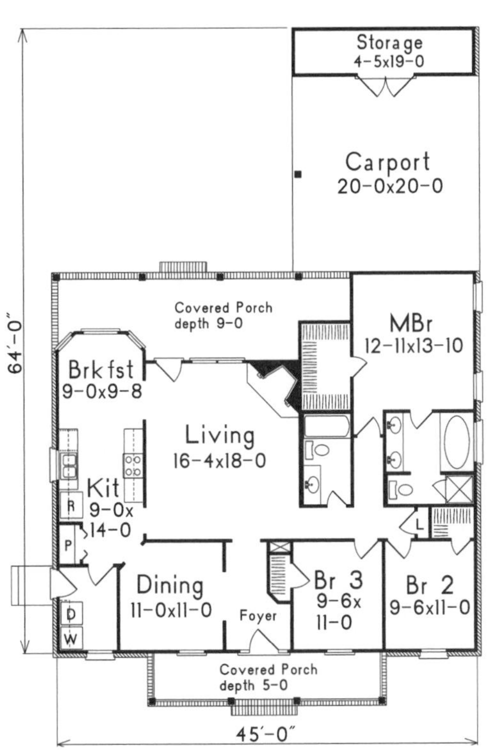

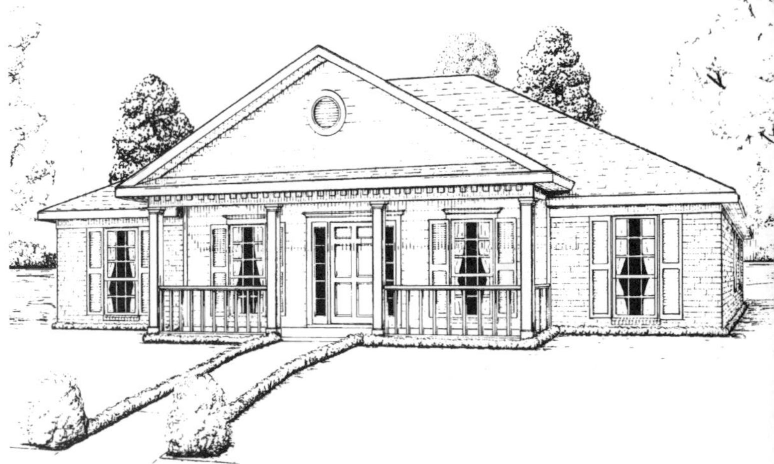

Plan #582-023D-0018

Price Code B

Special Features • 1,556 total square feet of living area • Corner fireplace in the living area warms surroundings • Spacious master bedroom includes a walk-in closet and private bath with double-bowl vanity • Compact kitchen is designed for efficiency • Covered porches in both front and back of home add coziness • 3 bedrooms, 2 baths, 2-car attached carport • Slab foundation

Stunning Triple Dormers And Arches

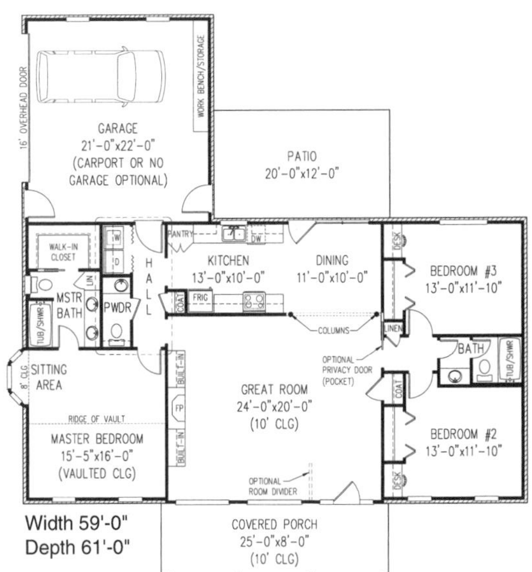

Width 59'-0"
Depth 61'-0"

Plan #582-067D-0004

Price Code B

Special Features • 1,698 total square feet of living area • Vaulted master bedroom has a private bath and a walk-in closet • Decorative columns flank the entrance to the dining room • Open great room is perfect for gathering family together • 3 bedrooms, 2 1/2 baths, 2-car side entry garage with storage • Basement, crawl space or slab foundation, please specify when ordering

Plan #582-049D-0011

Price Code C

Special Features • 1,974 total square feet of living area • Sunny bayed nook invites casual dining and shares its natural light with a snack counter and kitchen • Spacious master bedroom occupies a bay window and offers a sumptuous bath • Both second floor bedrooms have private balconies • 3 bedrooms, 2 1/2 baths • Basement or crawl space foundation, please specify when ordering

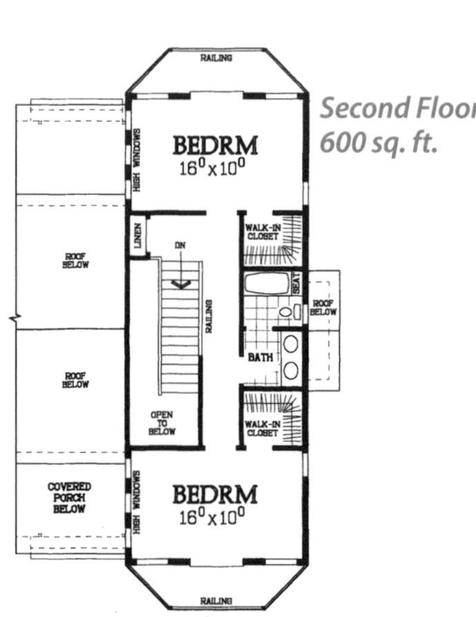

Second Floor
600 sq. ft.

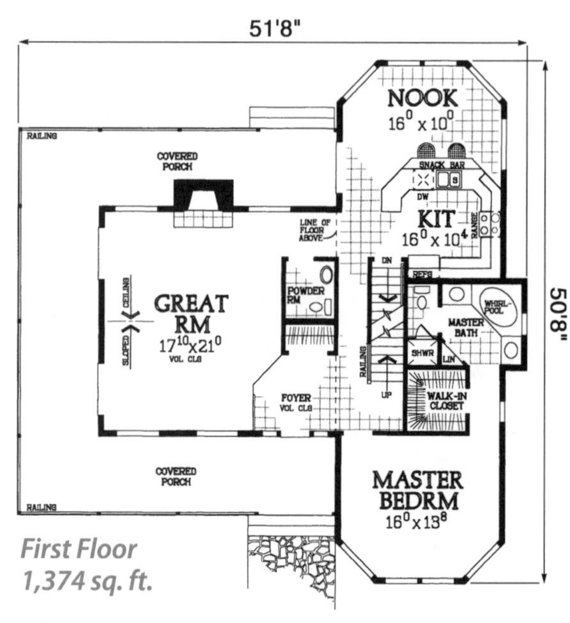

First Floor
1,374 sq. ft.

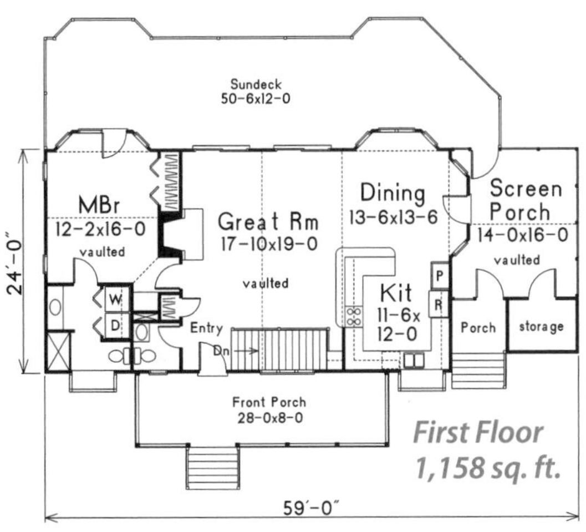

First Floor
1,158 sq. ft.

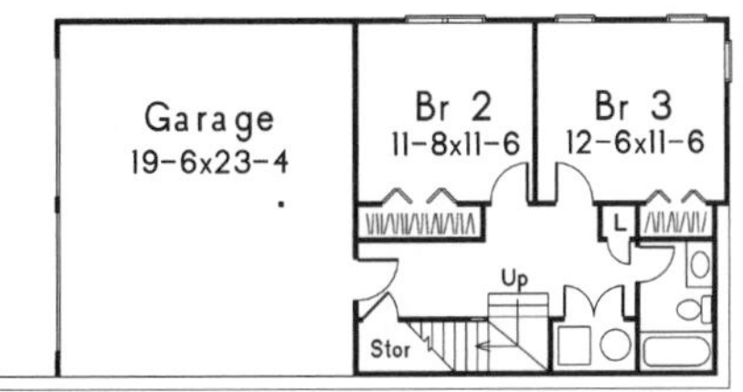

Lower Level 574 sq. ft.

Plan #582-053D-0043

Price Code B

Special Features • 1,732 total square feet of living area • Spacious great room with vaulted ceiling and fireplace overlooks large sundeck • Dramatic dining room boasts extensive windows and angled walls • Vaulted master bedroom includes private bath with laundry area and accesses sundeck • Convenient second entrance leads to screened porch and dining area • 3 bedrooms, 2 1/2 baths, 2-car drive under garage • Basement foundation

A Unique Place To Call Home

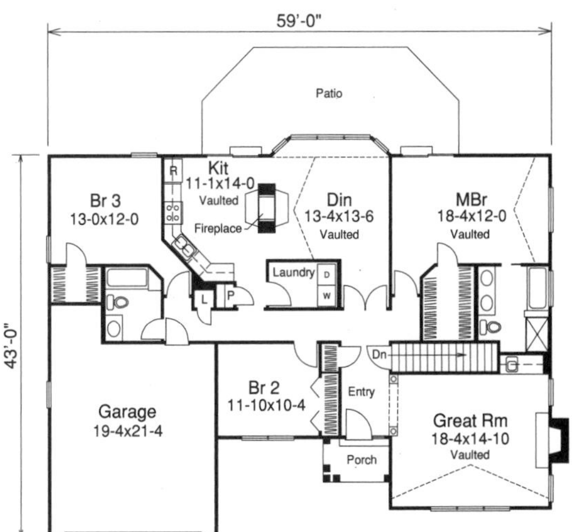

Plan #582-007D-0090

Price Code C

Special Features • 1,826 total square feet of living area • An arched opening with columns invites you into a beautiful great room with fireplace, wet bar and vaulted ceiling • A double-door entry leads into a large vaulted dining room with a fireplace, plant shelves and great view of the rear patio through a sweeping bay window • Every bedroom enjoys private zoning with lots of closet space • 3 bedrooms, 2 baths, 2-car garage • Basement foundation

High-Style Vaulted Ranch

Plan #582-014D-0007

Price Code A

Special Features • 1,453 total square feet of living area • Decorative vents, window trim, shutters and brick blend to create dramatic curb appeal • Energy efficient home with 2" x 6" exterior walls • Kitchen opens to living area and includes salad sink in the island, pantry and handy laundry room • Exquisite master bedroom is highlighted by a vaulted ceiling, dressing area with walk-in closet, private bath and spa tub/shower • 3 bedrooms, 2 baths, 2-car garage • Basement foundation, drawings also include crawl space foundation

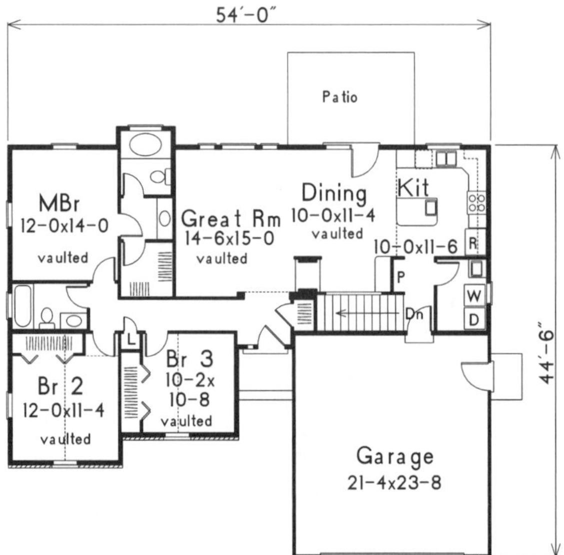

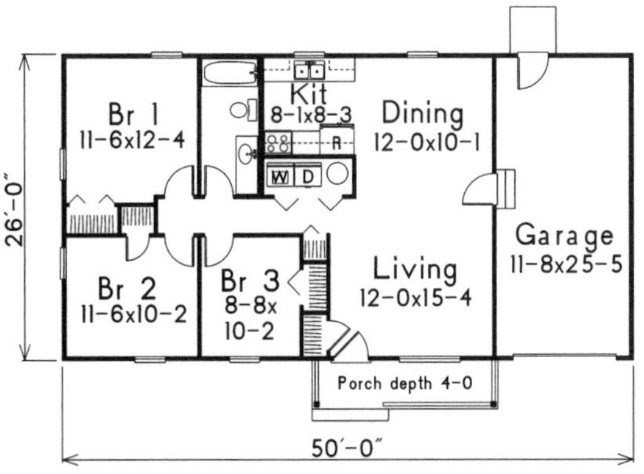

Plan #582-001D-0018

Price Code AA

Special Features • 988 total square feet of living area • Pleasant covered porch entry • The kitchen, living and dining areas are combined to maximize space • Entry has convenient coat closet • Laundry closet is located adjacent to bedrooms • 3 bedrooms, 1 bath, 1-car garage • Basement foundation, drawings also include crawl space foundation

Stately And Functional Family Room

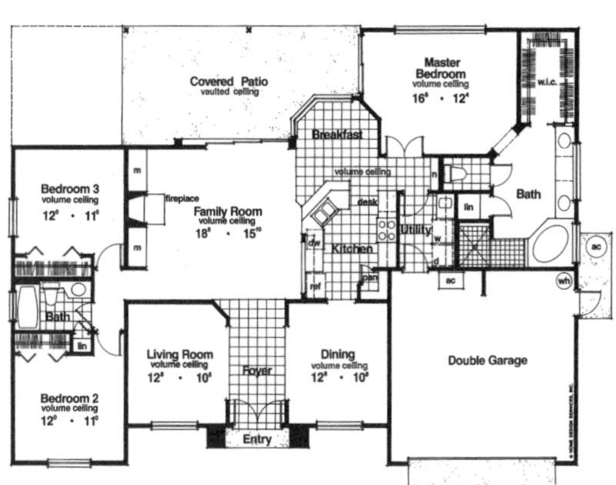

Width: 60'-0"
Depth: 45'-0"

Plan #582-047D-0020

Price Code B

Special Features • 1,783 total square feet of living area • Formal living and dining rooms in the front of the home • Kitchen overlooks breakfast area • Conveniently located laundry area near kitchen and master bedroom • 3 bedrooms, 2 baths, 2-car garage • Slab foundation

Two-Story Country Home Features Large Living Areas

Plan #582-001D-0025

Price Code D

Special Features • *1,998 total square feet of living area • Large family room features a fireplace and access to the kitchen and dining area • Skylights add daylight to second floor baths • Utility room is conveniently located near the garage and kitchen • Kitchen/breakfast area includes pantry, island workspace and easy access to the patio • 3 bedrooms, 2 1/2 baths, 2-car side entry garage • Basement foundation, drawings also include crawl space and slab foundations*

Second Floor
938 sq. ft.

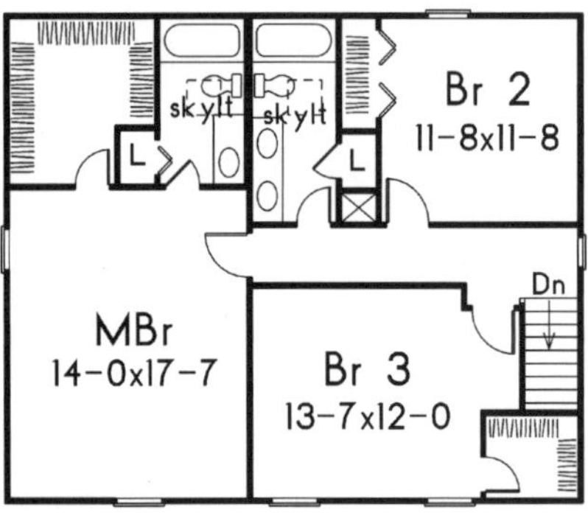

First Floor
1,060 sq. ft.

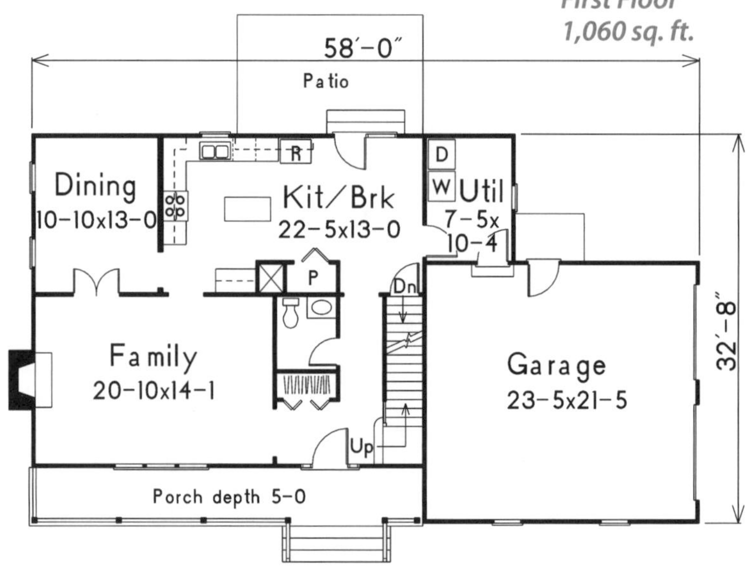

Plan #582-037D-0002

Price Code C

Special Features • 1,816 total square feet of living area • Two-way living room fireplace with large nearby window seat • Wrap-around dining room windows create sunroom appearance • Master bedroom has abundant closet and storage space • Rear dormers, closets and desk areas create an interesting and functional second floor • 3 bedrooms, 2 1/2 baths, 2-car detached garage • Slab foundation, drawings also include crawl space foundation

First Floor
1,330 sq. ft.

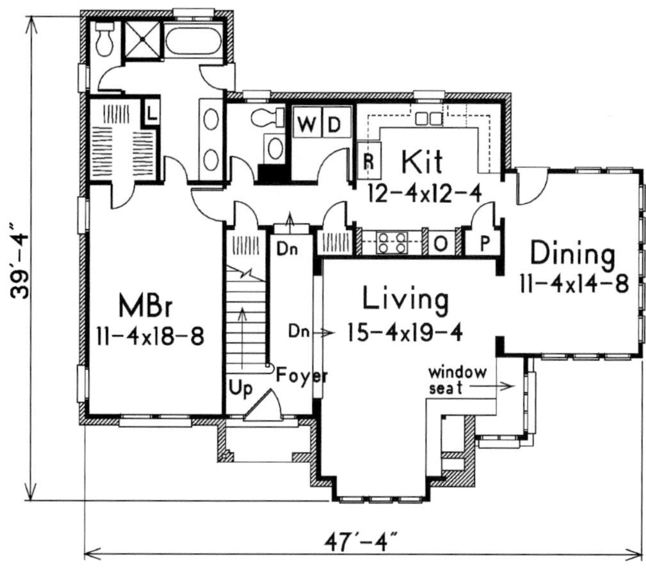

Second Floor
486 sq. ft.

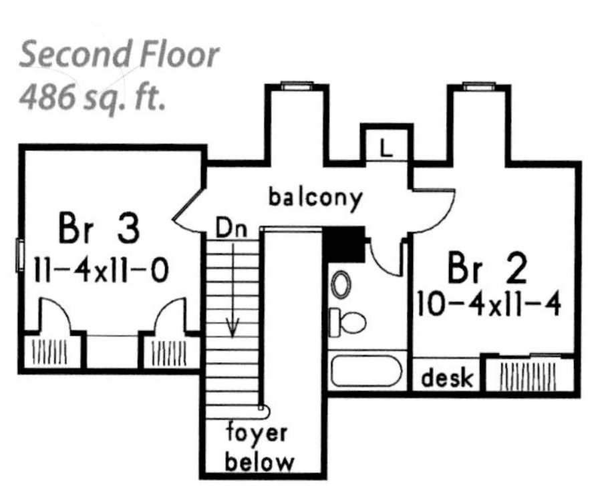

www.houseplansandmore.com

Traditional Exterior, Handsome Accents

Plan #582-001D-0013

Price Code D

Special Features • 1,882 total square feet of living area • Wide, handsome entrance opens to the vaulted great room with fireplace • Living and dining areas are conveniently joined but still allow privacy • Private covered porch extends breakfast area • Practical passageway runs through the laundry and mud room from the garage to the kitchen • Vaulted ceiling in master bedroom • 3 bedrooms, 2 baths, 2-car garage • Basement foundation

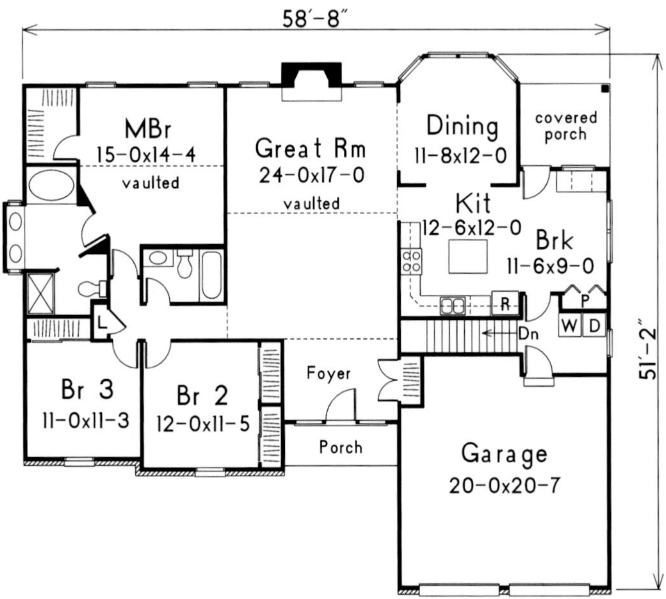

Two-Sided Fireplace Warms This Home

Plan #582-038D-0034

Price Code B

Special Features • 1,625 total square feet of living area • An interesting double-door entry leads to the den/guest room • Spacious master bath has both a whirlpool tub and a shower • Welcoming planter boxes in front add curb appeal • 3 bedrooms, 2 baths, 2-car garage • Basement or crawl space foundation, please specify when ordering

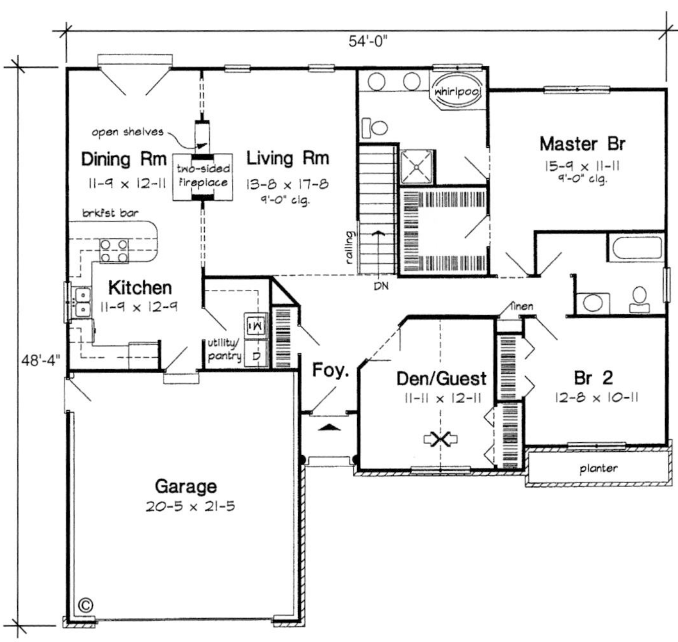

Enchanting Country Cottage

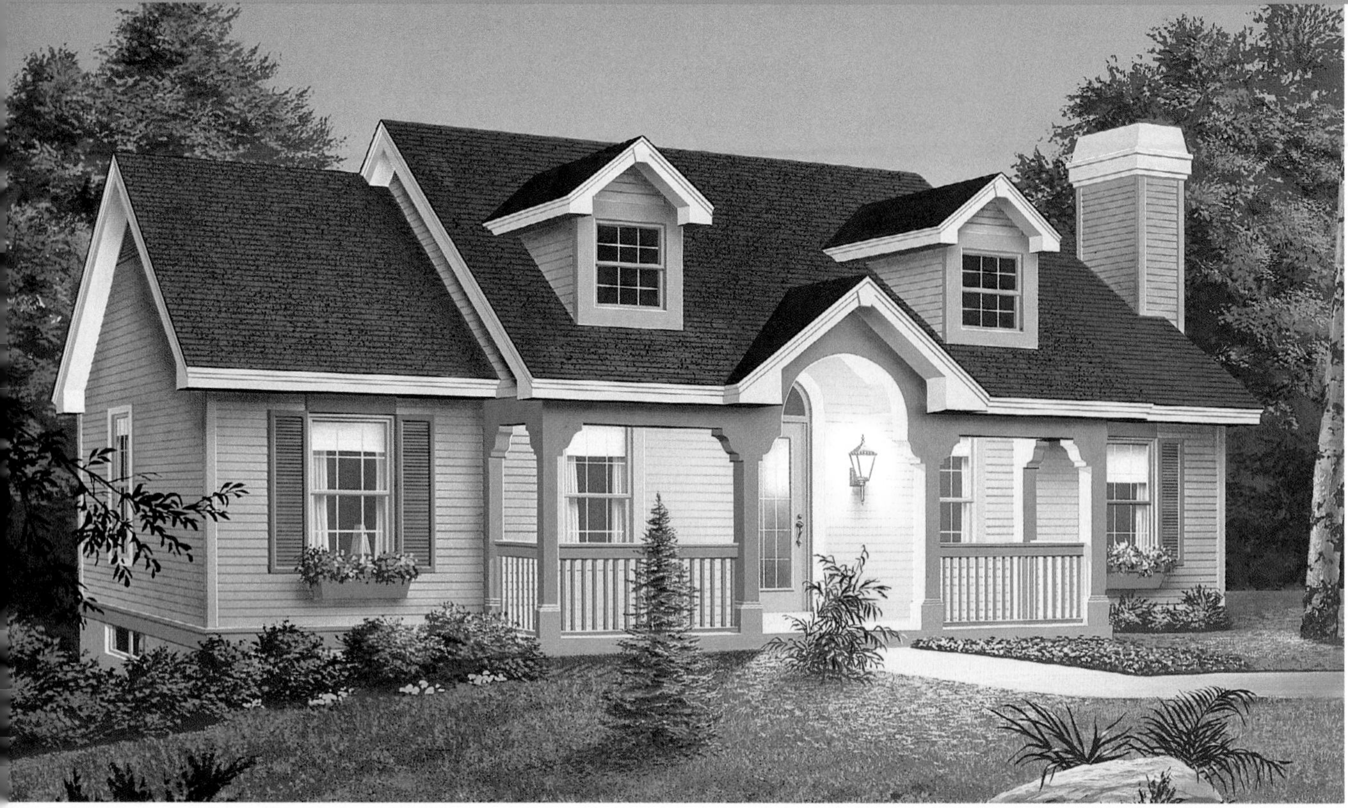

Plan #582-007D-0030

Price Code AA

Special Features • *1,140 total square feet of living area* • *Open and spacious living and dining areas for family gatherings* • *Well-organized kitchen with an abundance of cabinetry and a built-in pantry* • *Roomy master bath features double-bowl vanity* • *3 bedrooms, 2 baths, 2-car drive under garage* • *Basement foundation*

1-800-DREAM HOME (373-2646)

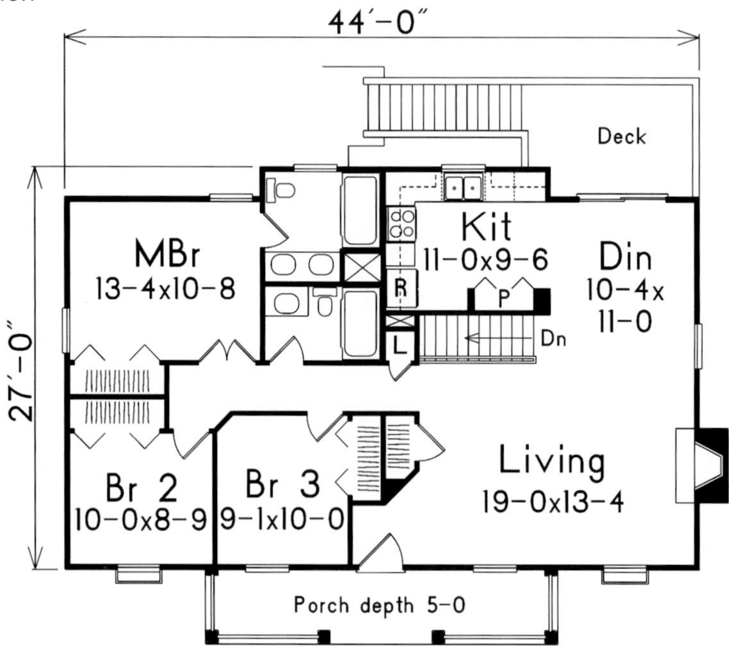

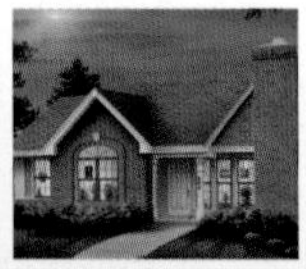

Compact Ranch Loaded With Extras

Plan #582-052D-0003

Price Code A

Special Features • 1,208 total square feet of living area • Master bath is graced with an oversized tub and a double vanity • A U-shaped kitchen promotes organization while easily accessing the dining area • Hall bath includes a laundry closet for your convenience • 3 bedrooms, 2 baths, 2-car drive under garage • Basement foundation

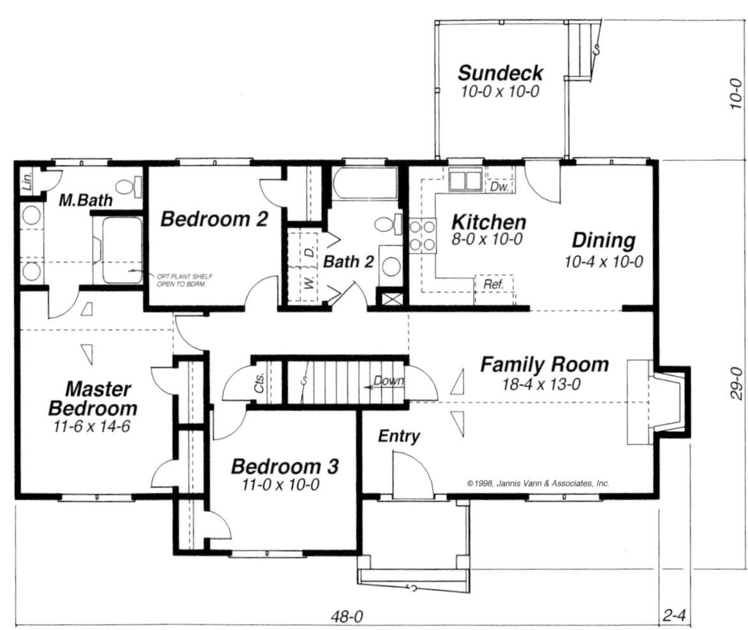

Two-Story Foyer Adds Spacious Feeling

Plan #582-040D-0001

Price Code D

Special Features • 1,814 total square feet of living area • Large master bedroom includes a spacious bath with garden tub, separate shower and large walk-in closet • The spacious kitchen and dining area are brightened by large windows and patio access • Detached two-car garage with walkway leading to house adds charm to this country home • Large front porch • 3 bedrooms, 2 1/2 baths, 2-car detached side entry garage • Crawl space foundation, drawings also include slab foundation

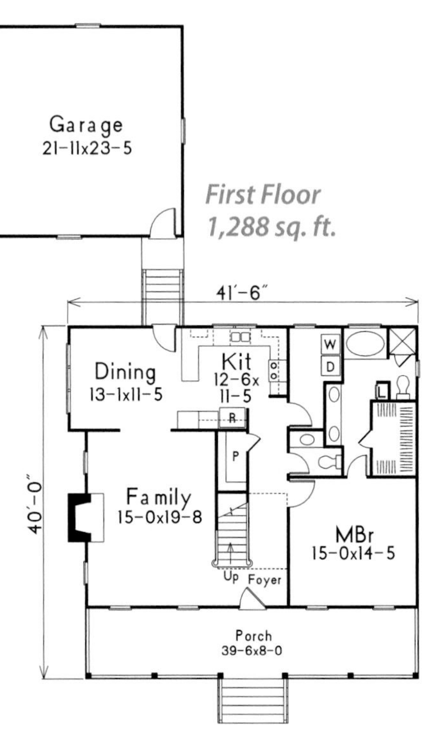

First Floor
1,288 sq. ft.

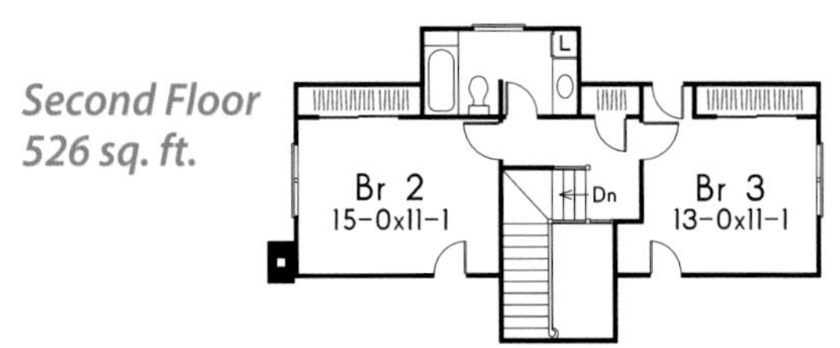

Second Floor
526 sq. ft.

Wrap-Around Porch Adds To Farmhouse Style

Plan #582-016D-0049

Price Code B

Special Features • 1,793 total square feet of living area • Beautiful foyer leads into the great room that has a fireplace flanked by two sets of beautifully transomed doors both leading to a large covered porch • Dramatic eat-in kitchen includes an abundance of cabinets and work-space in an exciting angled shape • Delightful master bedroom has many amenities • Optional bonus room above the garage has an additional 779 square feet of living area • 3 bedrooms, 2 baths, 2-car side entry garage • Basement, crawl space or slab foundation, please specify when ordering

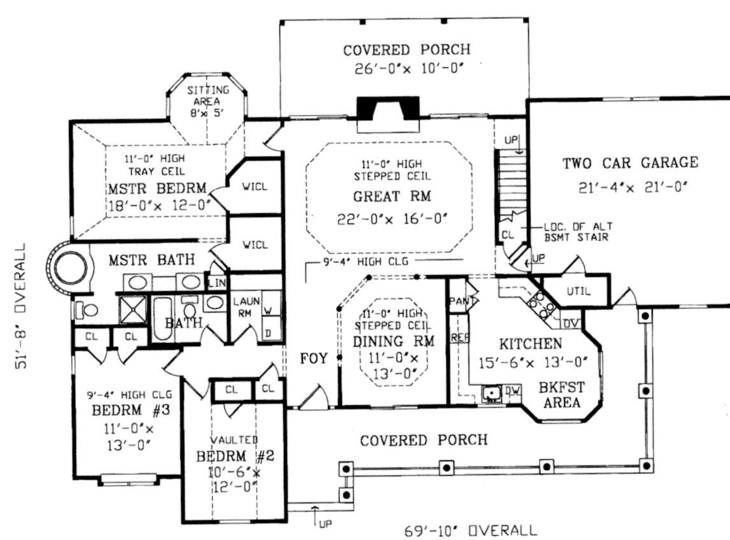

Cheerful And Sunny Kitchen

Plan #582-008D-0045

Price Code B

Special Features • 1,540 total square feet of living area • Porch entrance into foyer leads to an impressive dining area with full window and a half-circle window above • Kitchen/breakfast room features a center island and cathedral ceiling • Great room with cathedral ceiling and exposed beams is accessible from foyer • Master bedroom includes a full bath and walk-in closet • Two additional bedrooms share a full bath • 3 bedrooms, 2 baths, 2-car garage • Basement foundation, drawings also include crawl space and slab foundations

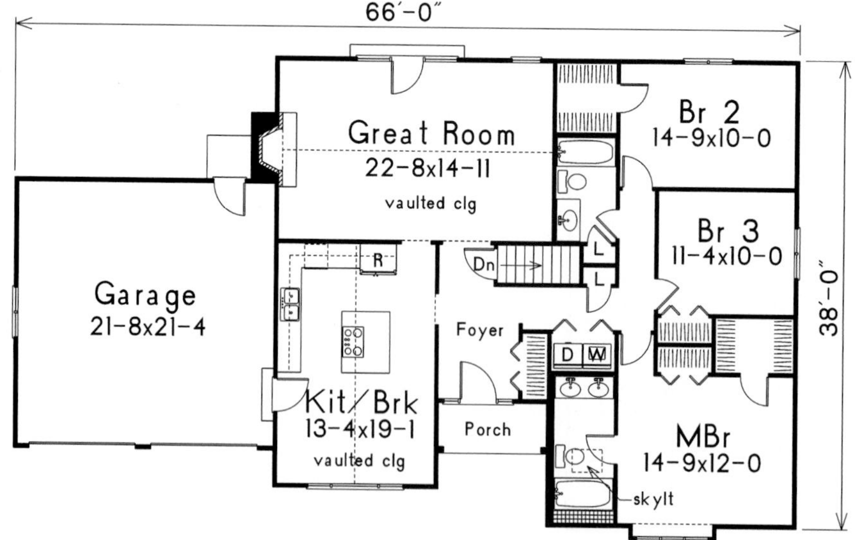

Casual Living With This Family Design

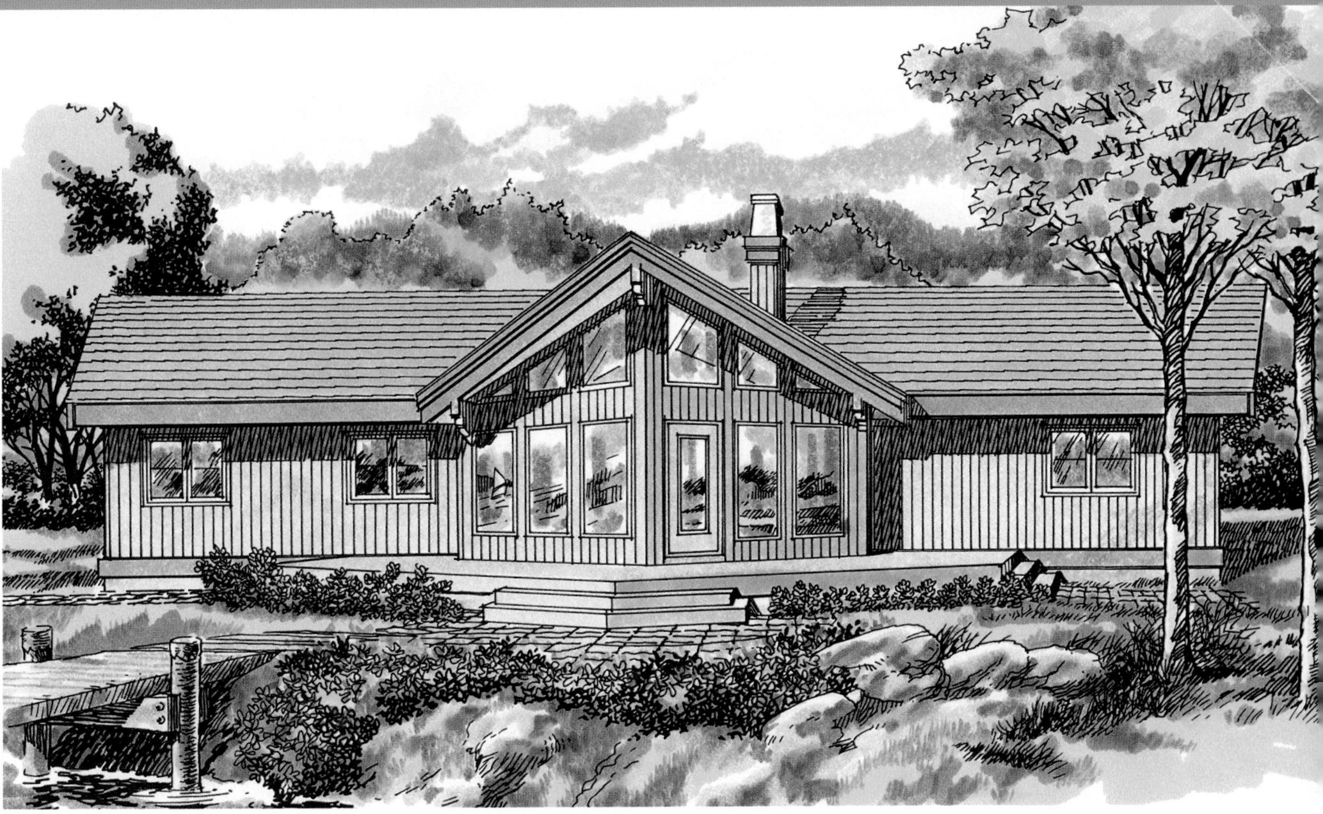

Plan #582-062D-0053

Price Code A

Special Features • *1,405 total square feet of living area* • *An expansive wall of glass gives a spectacular view to the great room and accentuates the high vaulted ceilings throughout the design* • *Great room is warmed by a woodstove and is open to the dining room and L-shaped kitchen* • *Triangular snack bar graces kitchen* • *3 bedrooms, 2 baths* • *Basement or crawl space foundation, please specify when ordering*

Width: 62'-0"
Depth: 29'-0"

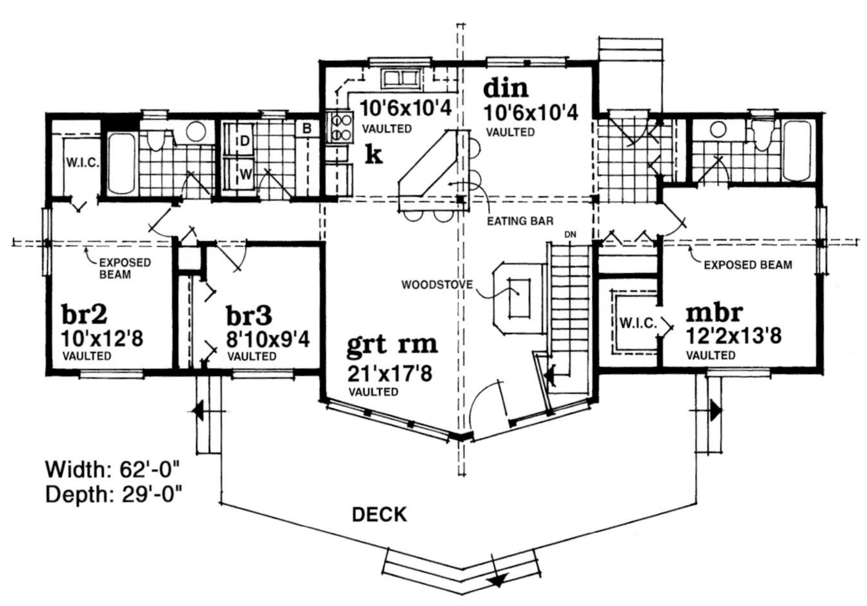

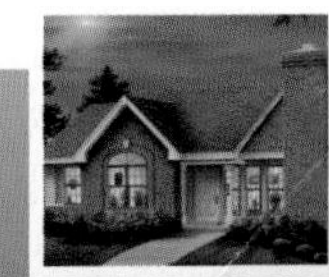

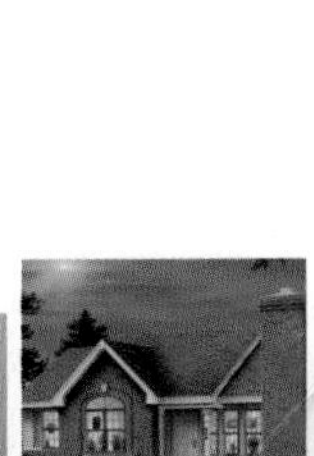

Inviting Covered Entry

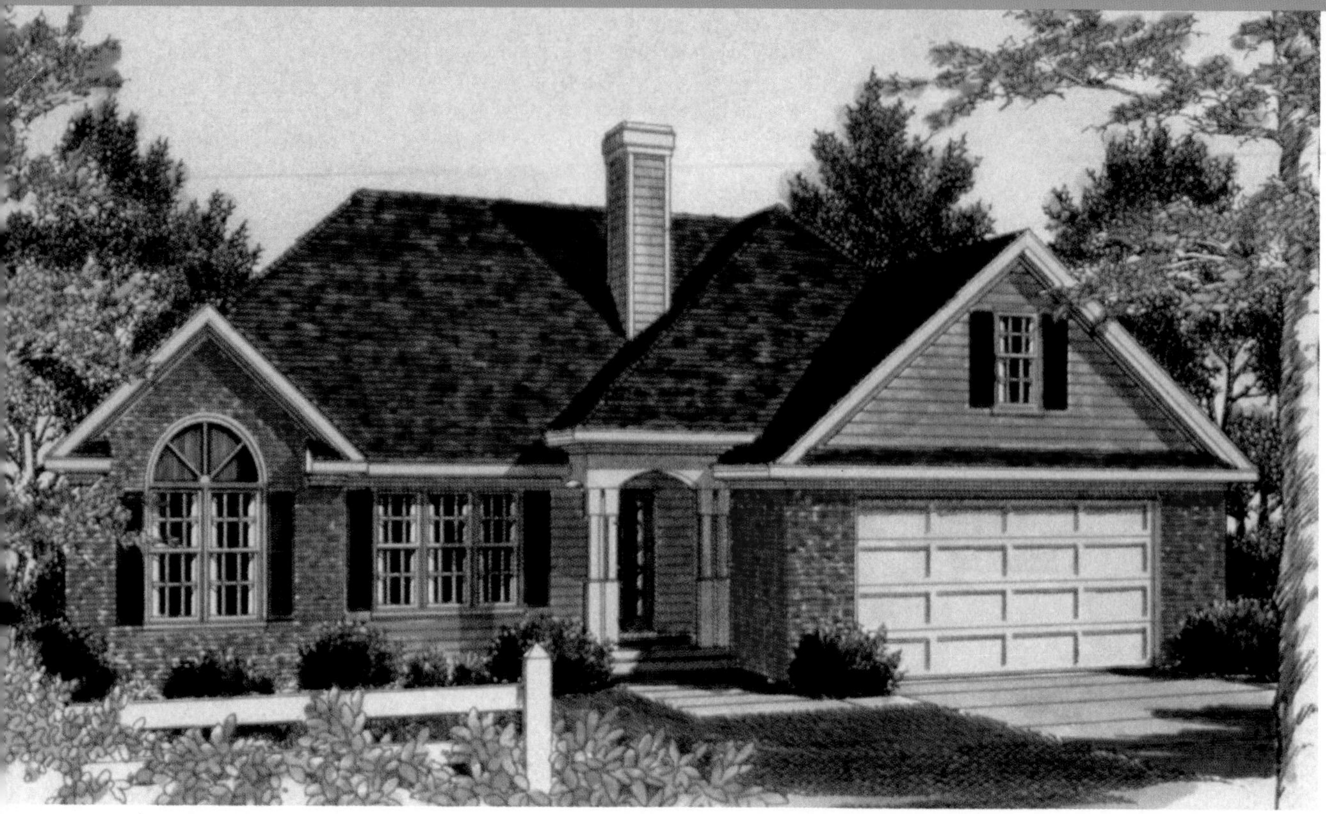

Plan #582-076D-0005

Price Code B

Special Features • *1,322 total square feet of living area* • *Wrap-around counter connects kitchen to dining and family rooms creating an open atmosphere* • *The private master bedroom boasts a deluxe bath with a double vanity, whirlpool tub and large walk-in closet* • *Bonus room above the garage has an additional 294 square feet of living area* • *3 bedrooms, 2 baths, 2-car garage* • *Slab foundation*

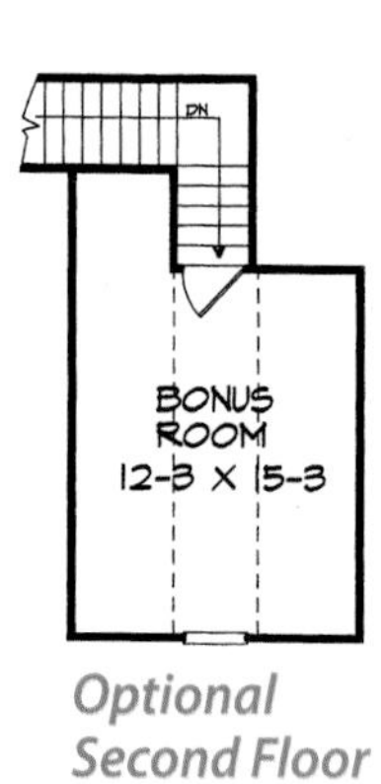

Optional
Second Floor

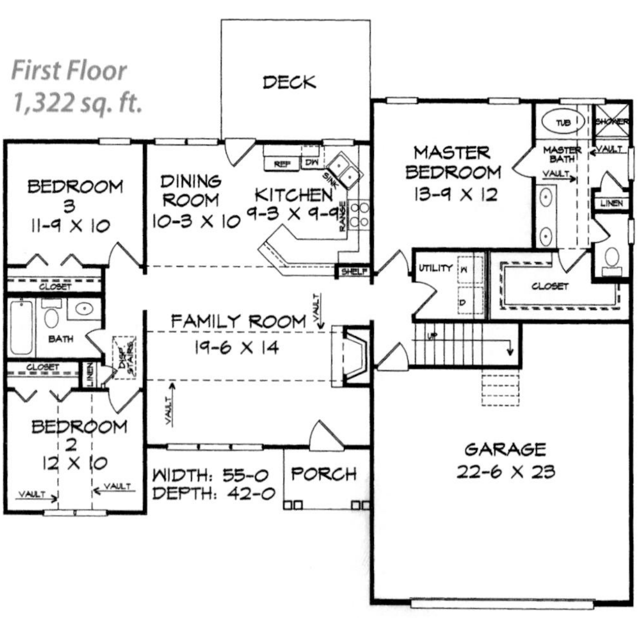

First Floor
1,322 sq. ft.

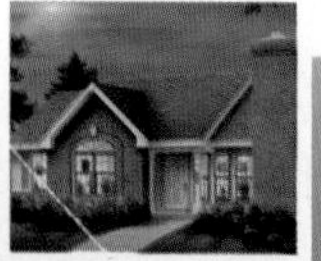

Comfortable Family Living In This Ranch

Plan #582-037D-0020

Price Code D

Special Features • 1,994 total square feet of living area • Convenient entrance from the garage into the main living area through the utility room • Bedroom #2 features a 12' vaulted ceiling and the dining room boasts a 10' ceiling • Master bedroom offers a full bath with an oversized tub, separate shower and walk-in closet • Entry leads to the formal dining room and attractive living room with double French doors and fireplace • 3 bedrooms, 2 baths, 2-car garage • Slab foundation

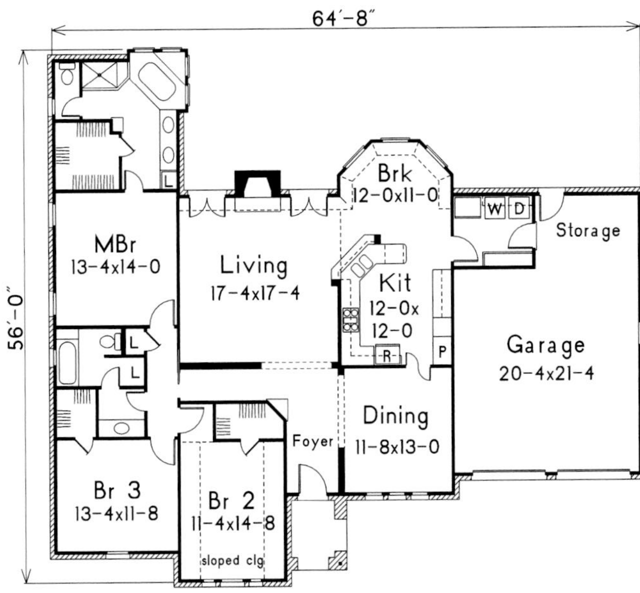

Great Room And Kitchen Symmetry Dominates Design

Plan #582-007D-0046

Price Code B

Special Features • *1,712 total square feet of living area* • *Stylish stucco exterior enhances curb appeal* • *Sunken great room offers corner fireplace flanked by 9' wide patio doors* • *Well-designed kitchen features ideal view of the great room and fireplace through breakfast bar opening* • *3 bedrooms, 2 1/2 baths, 2-car garage* • *Crawl space foundation*

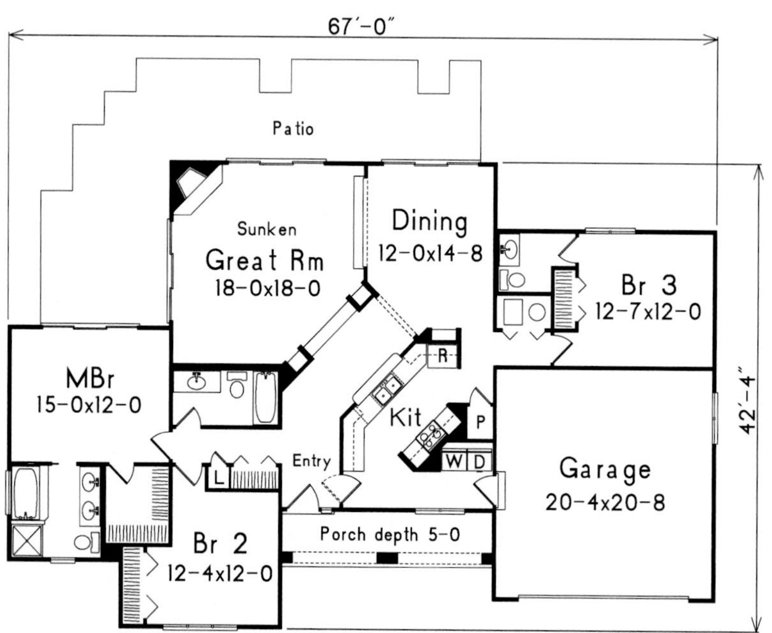

Plan #582-078D-0012

Price Code D

Special Features • 1,575 total square feet of living area • The sunken living room features an exposed beam vaulted ceiling, bay windows and an expansive brick fireplace flanked by built-in cabinets • The open kitchen adjoins the formal dining area • The luxurious master bedroom boasts French doors leading to the porch, a full bath and two closets • 3 bedrooms, 2 baths, 2-car rear entry garage • Basement or crawl space foundation, please specify when ordering

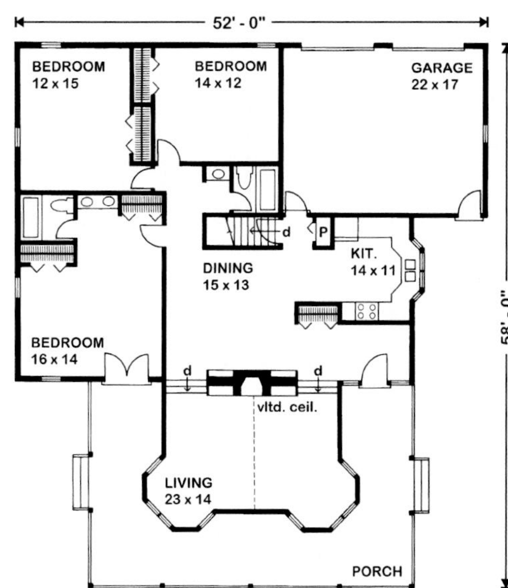

Plan #582-038D-0009

Price Code B

Special Features • *1,893 total square feet of living area* • *A plant ledge graces the dining area* • *Double walk-in closets in the master bath flank a step-up tub* • *Sloped ceilings add interest to the living and dining rooms* • *3 bedrooms, 2 1/2 baths, 2-car garage* • *Basement, crawl space or slab foundation, please specify when ordering*

First Floor
1,277 sq. ft.

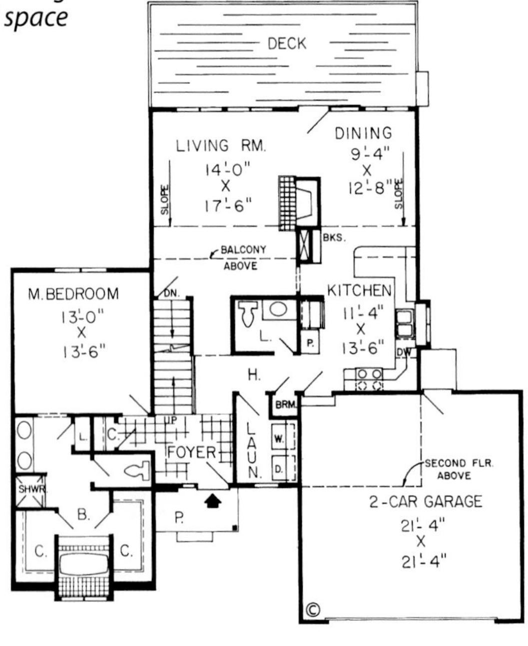

49'-0"

50'-0"

Second Floor
616 sq. ft.

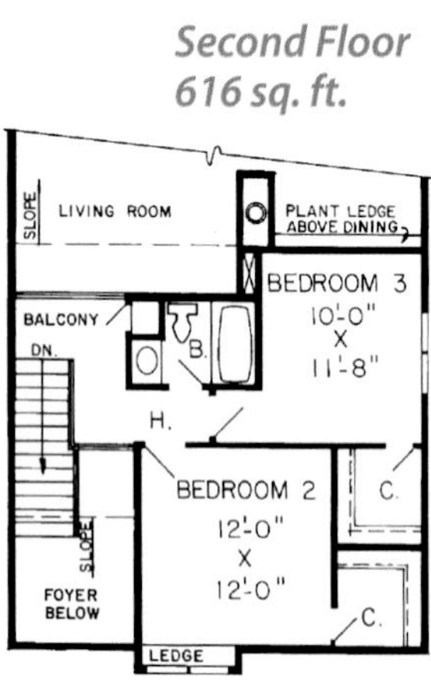

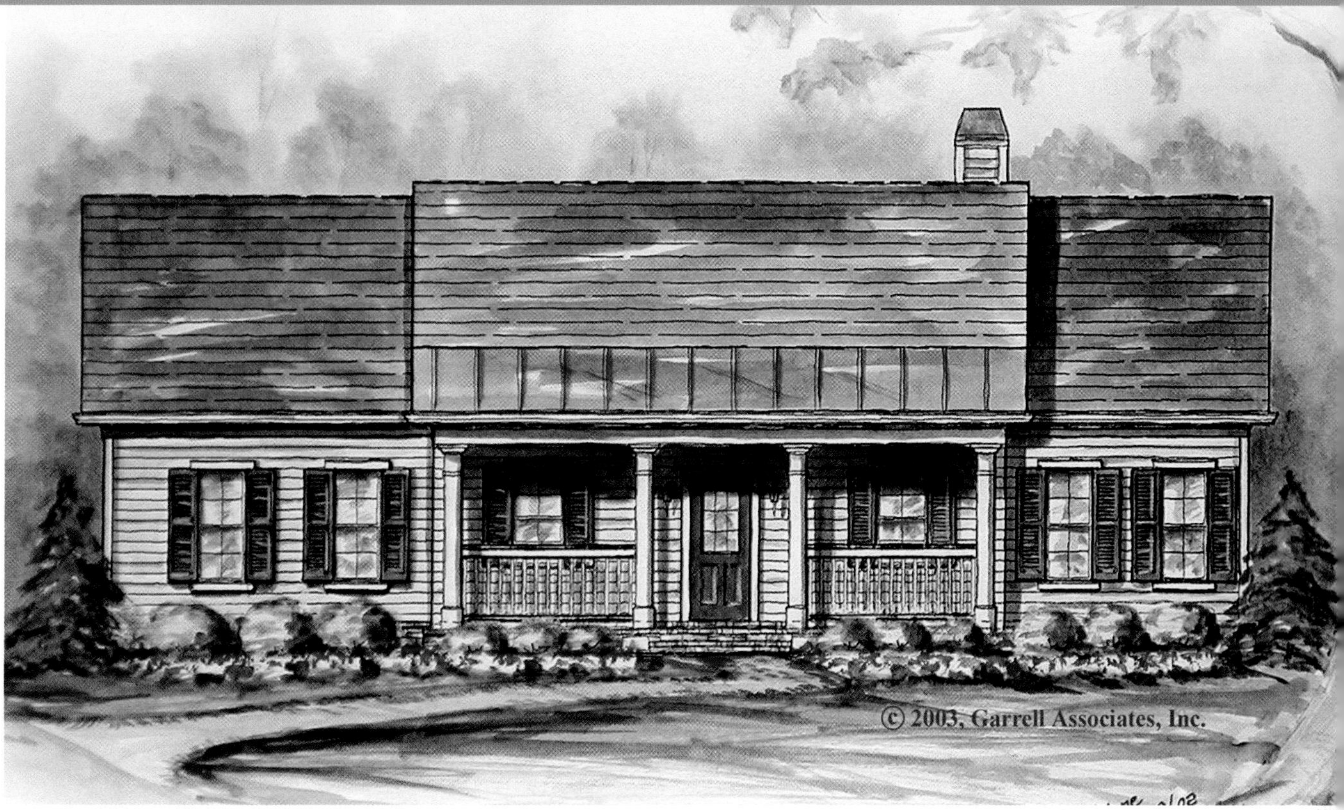

Plan #582-056D-0001

Price Code E

Special Features • *1,624 total square feet of living area* • *Large covered deck leads to two uncovered decks accessible by the master bedroom and bedroom #3* • *Well-organized kitchen overlooks into the breakfast area and family room* • *Laundry closet is located near the secondary bedrooms* • *3 bedrooms, 2 baths* • *Crawl space or slab foundation, please specify when ordering*

Width 56'-0"
Depth 30'-0"

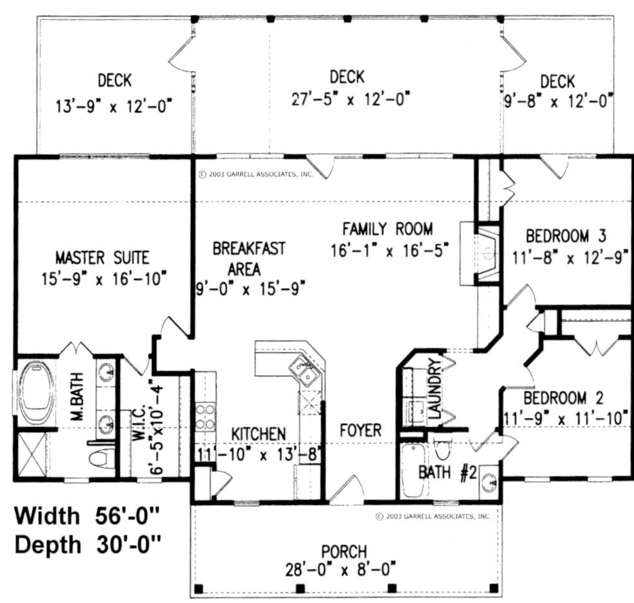

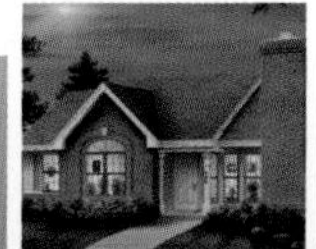

Rambling Country Bungalow

Plan #582-040D-0003 Price Code B

Special Features • 1,475 total square feet of living area • Family room features a high ceiling and prominent corner fireplace • Kitchen with island counter and garden window makes a convenient connection between the family and dining rooms • Hallway leads to three bedrooms all with large walk-in closets • Covered breezeway joins main house and garage • Full-width covered porch entry lends a country touch • 3 bedrooms, 2 baths, 2-car side entry garage • Slab foundation, drawings also include crawl space foundation

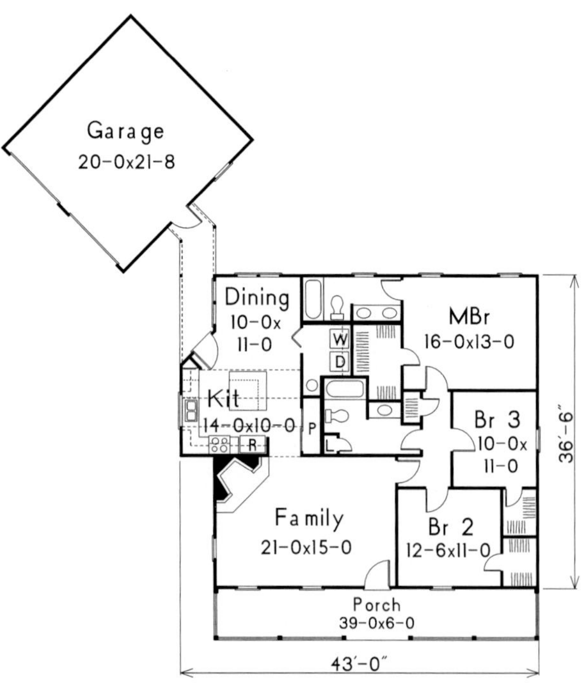

Cozy And Convenient Cottage

Plan #582-065D-0035 Price Code B

Special Features • 1,798 total square feet of living area • The expansive great room enjoys a fireplace and has access onto the rear patio • The centrally located kitchen is easily accessible to the dining room and breakfast area • The master bedroom boasts a sloped ceiling and deluxe bath with a corner whirlpool tub and large walk-in closet • A screened porch offers relaxing outdoor living • 3 bedrooms, 2 baths, 2-car garage • Basement foundation

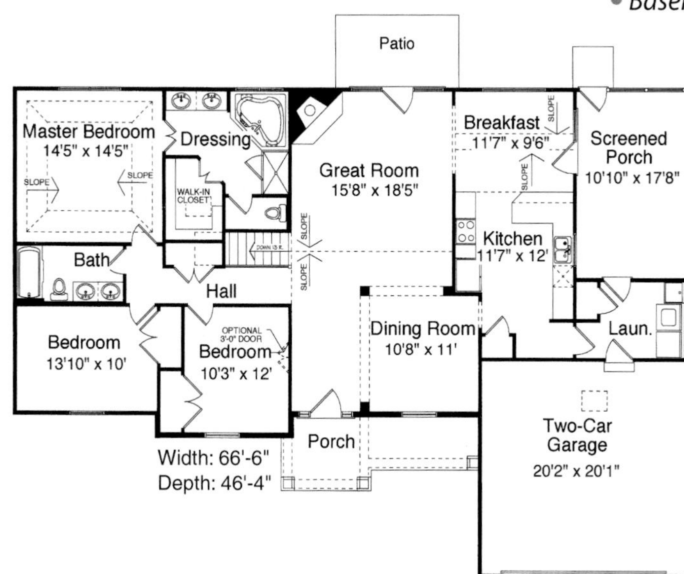

Covered Front Porch Is A Terrific Focal Point

Plan #582-055D-0046 **Price Code C**

Special Features • 1,934 total square feet of living area • Private master suite has access onto covered porch, a private bath and double walk-in closets • Extra storage in the garage • Centralized laundry area • 3 bedrooms, 2 baths, 2-car rear entry garage • Crawl space or slab foundation, please specify when ordering

Gables Add Warmth To Exterior

Plan #582-077D-0001

Price Code C

Special Features • 1,638 total square feet of living area • Great room features a fireplace with flanking doors that access the covered porch • The centrally located kitchen serves the breakfast and dining areas with ease • Plenty of storage area is located in the garage • 3 bedrooms, 2 baths, 2-car side entry garage • Basement, crawl space or slab foundation, please specify when ordering

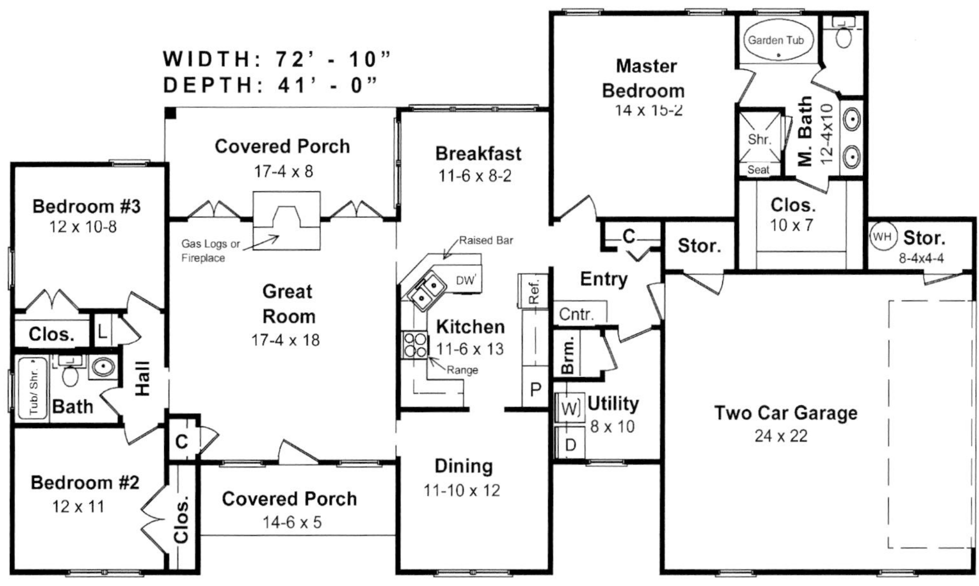

Small Ranch For A Perfect Country Haven

Plan #582-007D-0067

Price Code B

Special Features • 1,761 total square feet of living area • Exterior window dressing, roof dormers and planter boxes provide visual warmth and charm • Great room boasts a vaulted ceiling, fireplace and opens to a pass-through kitchen • Master bedroom is vaulted with luxury bath and walk-in closet • Home features eight separate closets with an abundance of storage • 4 bedrooms, 2 baths, 2-car side entry garage • Basement foundation

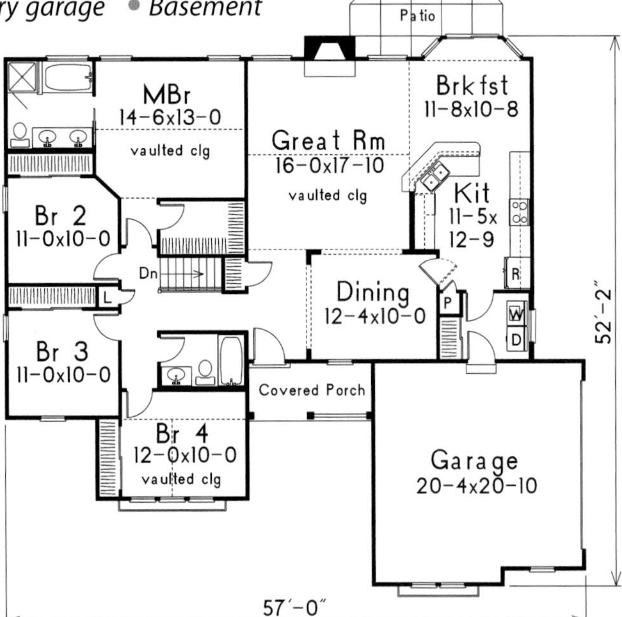

Plan #582-048D-0011

Price Code B

Special Features • 1,550 total square feet of living area • Cozy corner fireplace provides a focal point in the family room • Master bedroom features a large walk-in closet, skylight and separate tub and shower • Convenient laundry closet • Kitchen with pantry and breakfast bar connects to the family room • Family room and master bedroom access the covered patio • 3 bedrooms, 2 baths, 2-car garage • Slab foundation

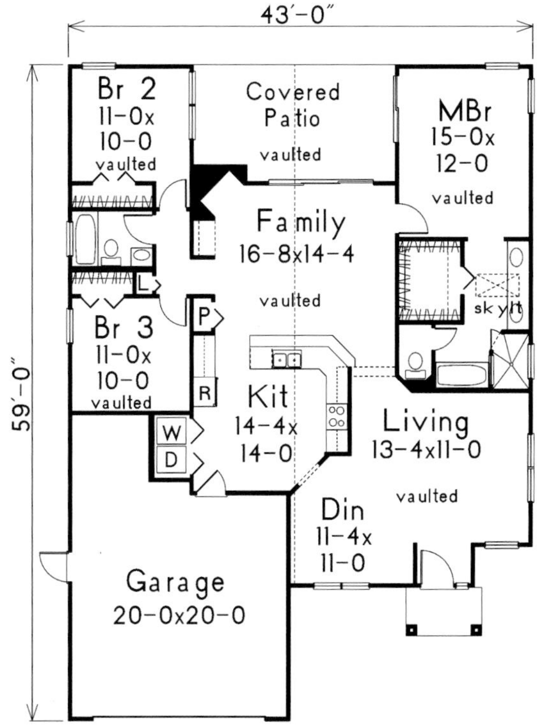

Country-Style With Wrap-Around Porch

Plan #582-040D-0027

Price Code C

Special Features • 1,597 total square feet of living area • Spacious family room includes fireplace and coat closet • Open kitchen and dining room provide breakfast bar and access to the outdoors • Convenient laundry area is located near kitchen • Secluded master bedroom with walk-in closet and private bath • 4 bedrooms, 2 1/2 baths, 2-car detached garage • Basement foundation

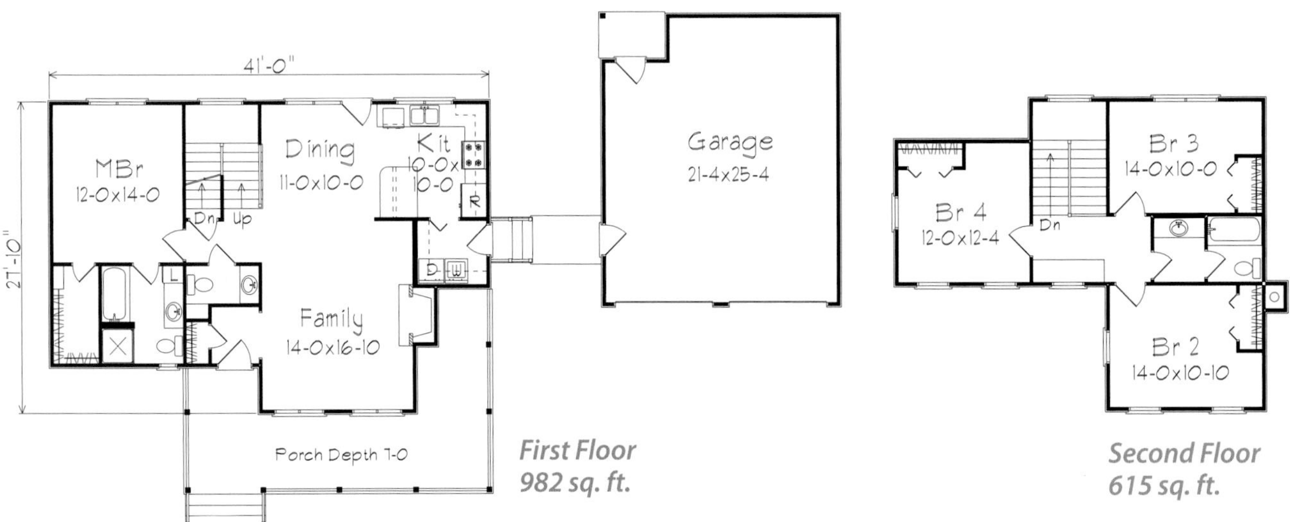

First Floor
982 sq. ft.

Second Floor
615 sq. ft.

Plan #582-016D-0001

Price Code D

Special Features • 1,783 total square feet of living area • The front to rear flow of the great room, with built-ins on one side is a furnishing delight • Bedrooms are all quietly zoned on one side • The master bedroom is separated for privacy • Every bedroom features a walk-in closet • 3 bedrooms, 2 baths, 2-car side entry garage • Basement, crawl space or slab foundation, please specify when ordering

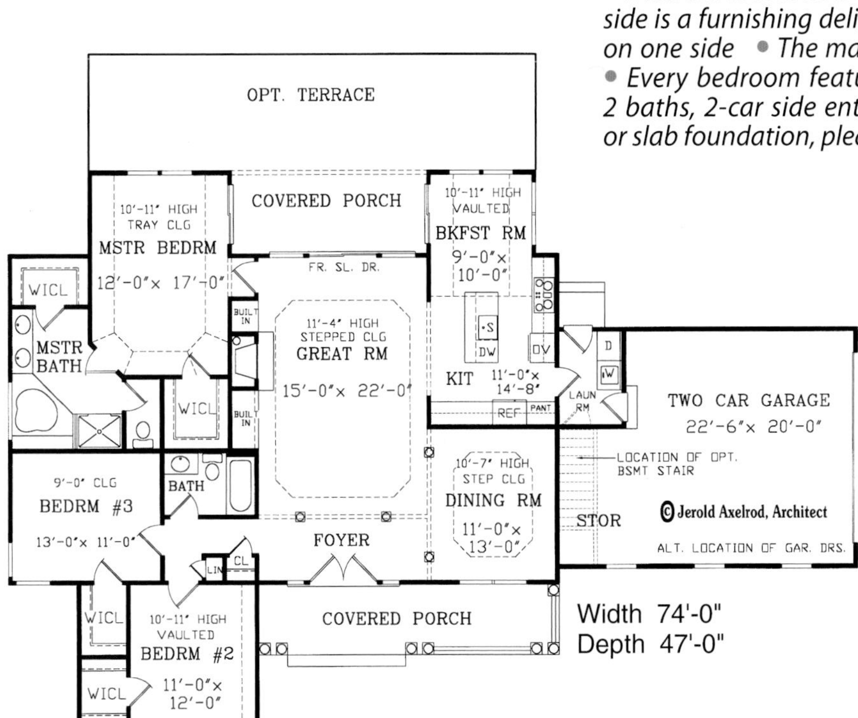

Width 74'-0"
Depth 47'-0"

Ranch Offers Country Elegance

Plan #582-007D-0085

Price Code B

Special Features • 1,787 total square feet of living area • Large great room with fireplace and vaulted ceiling features three large skylights and windows galore • Cooking is sure to be a pleasure in this L-shaped well-appointed kitchen which includes bayed breakfast area with access to rear deck • Every bedroom offers a spacious walk-in closet with a convenient laundry room just steps away • 415 square feet of optional living area available on the lower level • 3 bedrooms, 2 baths, 2-car drive under garage • Walk-out basement foundation

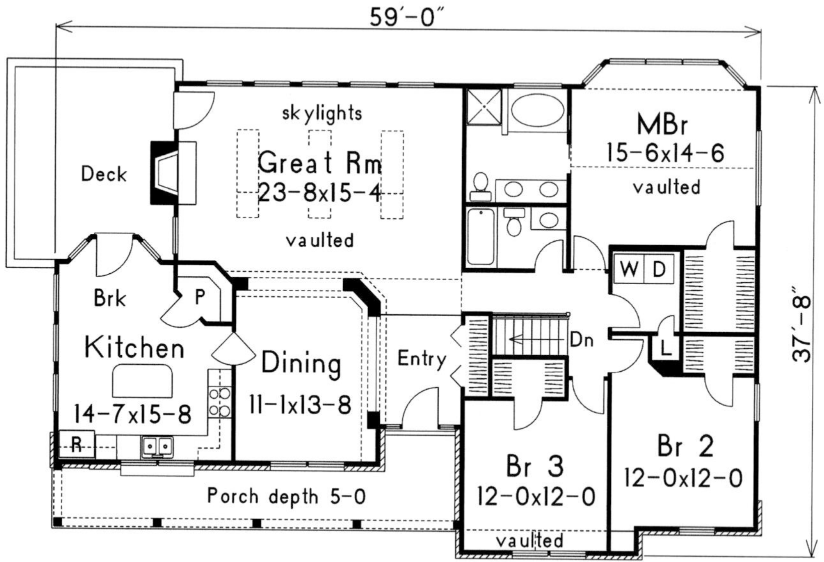

Plan #582-056D-0013

Price Code E

Special Features • *1,404 total square feet of living area* • *Dining area and kitchen connect allowing for convenience and ease* • *Well-located laundry area is within steps of bedrooms and baths* • *Vaulted grand room creates a feeling of spaciousness for this gathering area* • *3 bedrooms, 2 1/2 baths, 2-car garage* • *Slab foundation*

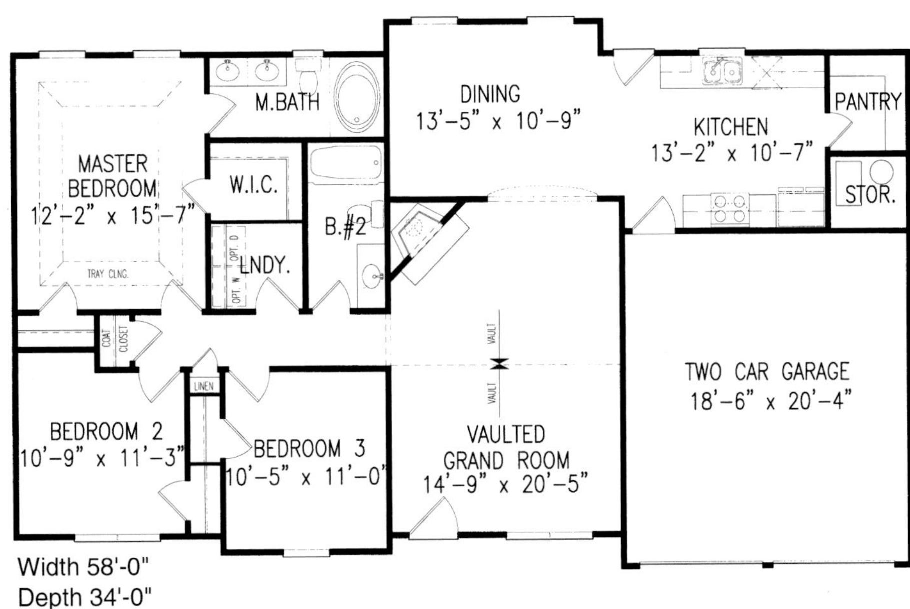

Width 58'-0"
Depth 34'-0"

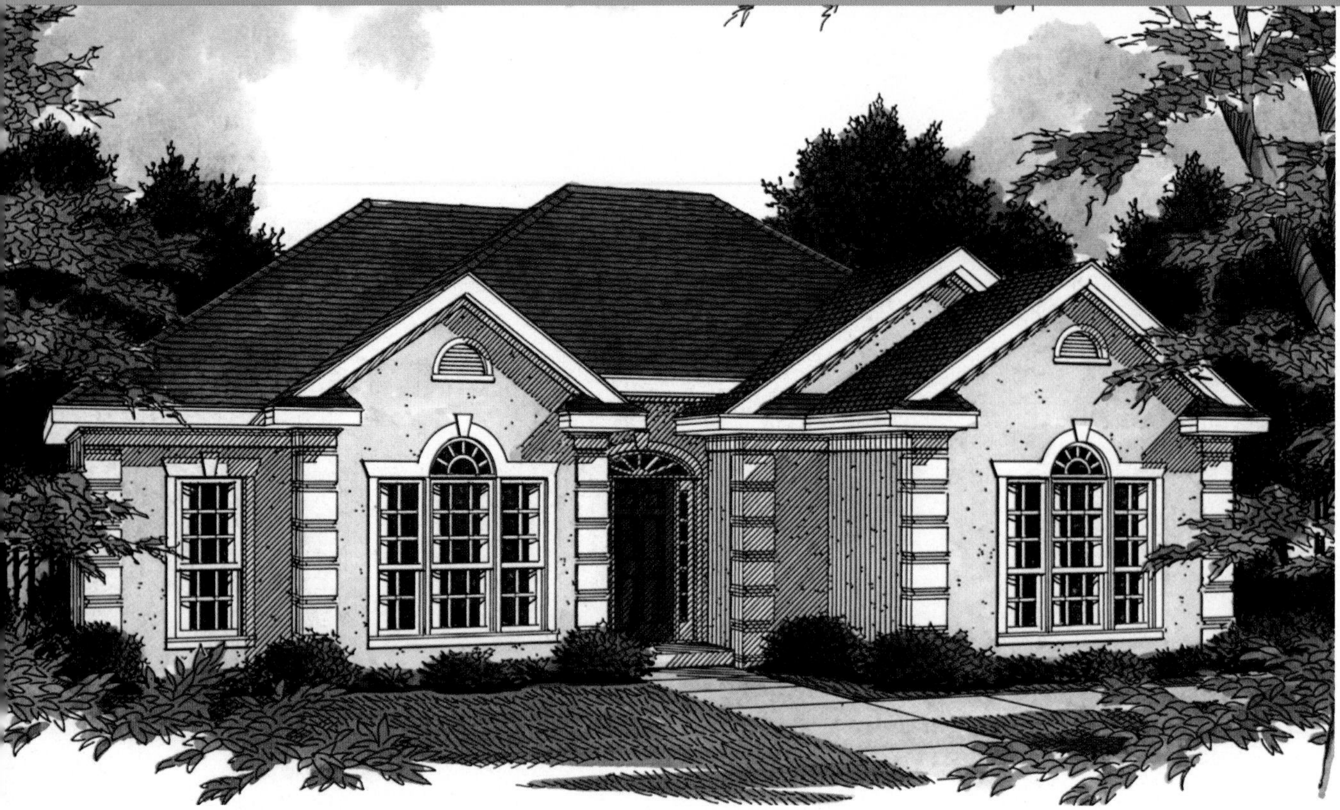

Plan #582-024D-0009

Price Code B

Special Features • *1,704 total square feet of living area* • *Open floor plan combines foyer, dining and living rooms together for an open airy feeling* • *Kitchen has island that adds workspace and storage* • *Bedrooms are situated together and secluded from the rest of the home* • *3 bedrooms, 2 baths* • *Slab foundation*

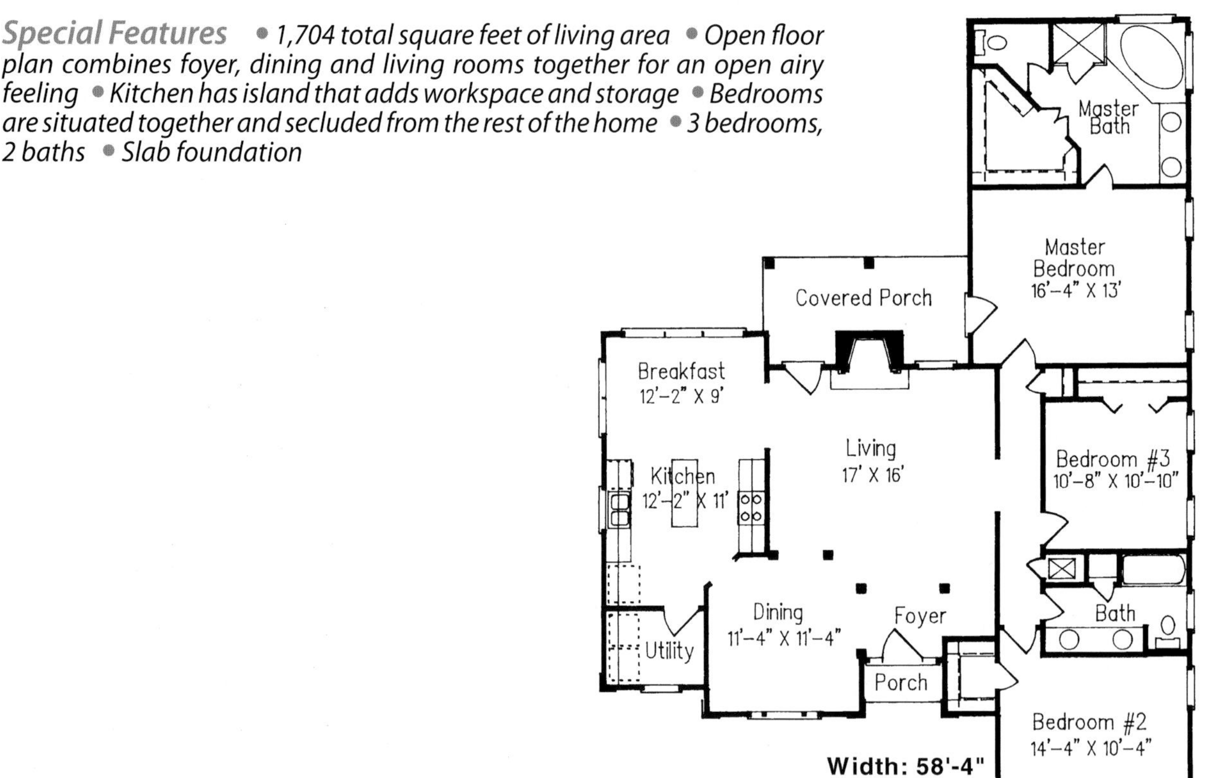

Bay Window Graces Luxury Master Bedroom

Plan #582-053D-0002

Price Code C

Special Features • 1,668 total square feet of living area • Large bay windows in breakfast area, master bedroom and dining room • Extensive walk-in closets and storage spaces throughout the home • Handy covered entry porch • Large living room has a fireplace, built-in bookshelves and sloped ceiling • 3 bedrooms, 2 baths, 2-car drive under garage • Basement foundation

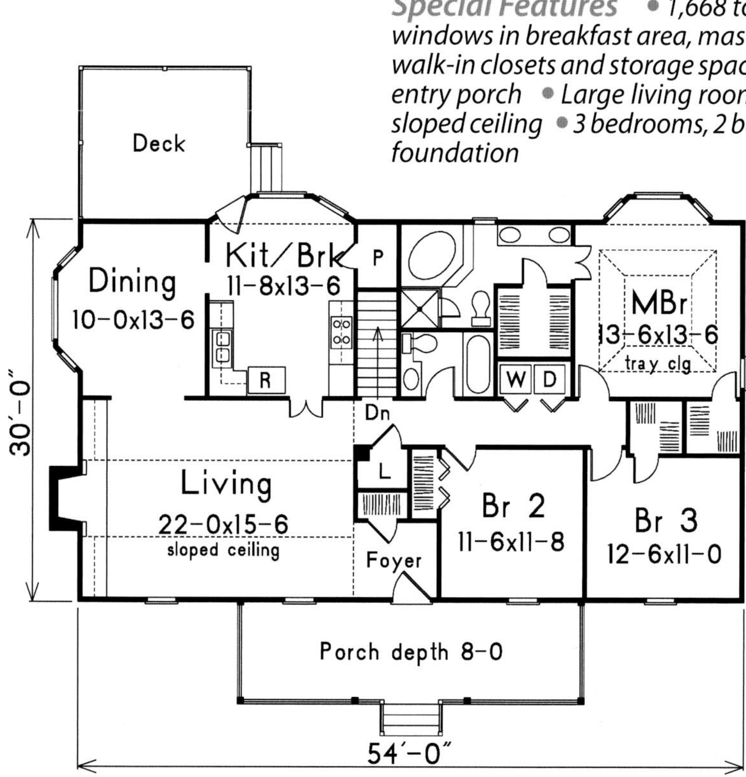

Plan #582-033D-0002

Price Code D

Special Features • 1,859 total square feet of living area • Fireplace highlights vaulted great room • Master bedroom includes large closet and private bath • Kitchen adjoins breakfast room providing easy access to the outdoors • 3 bedrooms, 2 1/2 baths, 2-car garage • Basement foundation

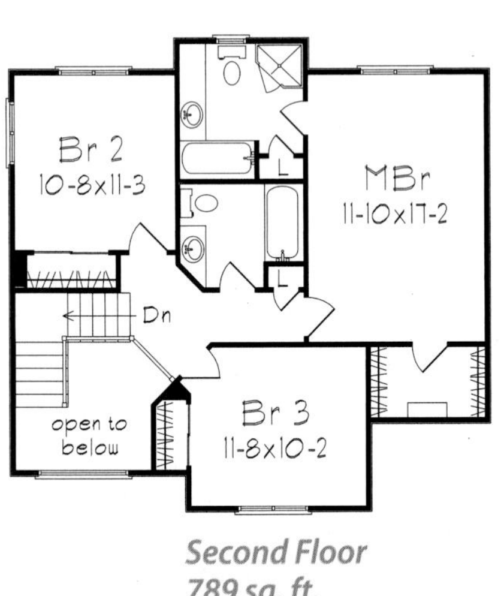

Second Floor
789 sq. ft.

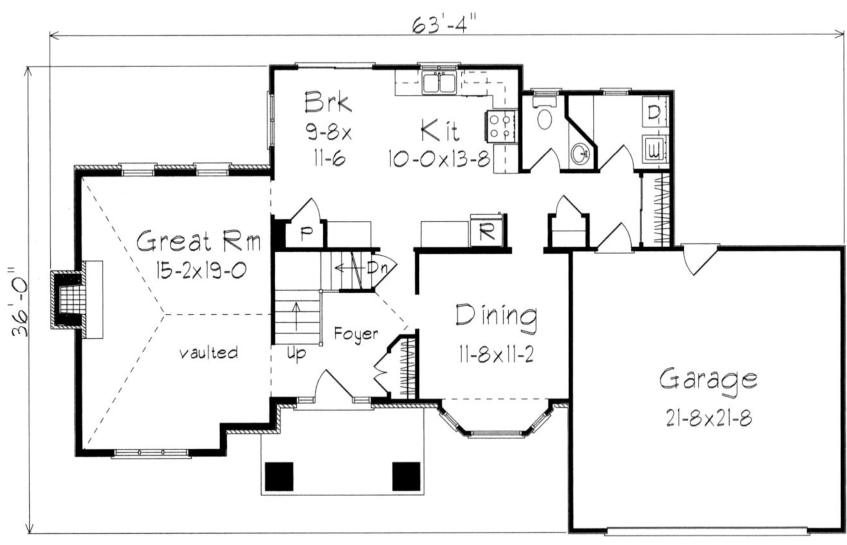

First Floor
1,070 sq. ft.

Quaint Porch Adds Charm

Plan #582-052D-0031

Price Code B

Special Features • 1,735 total square feet of living area • Angled kitchen wall expands space into the dining room • Second floor has cozy sitting area with cheerful window • Two spacious bedrooms on second floor share a bath • 3 bedrooms, 2 1/2 baths, 2-car drive under garage • Basement foundation

Second Floor
690 sq. ft.

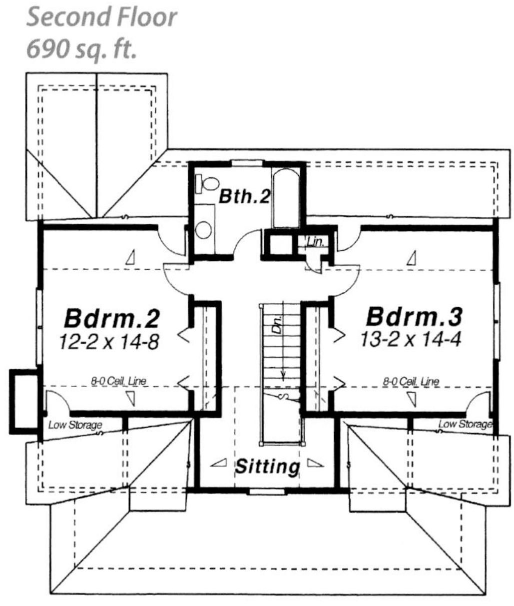

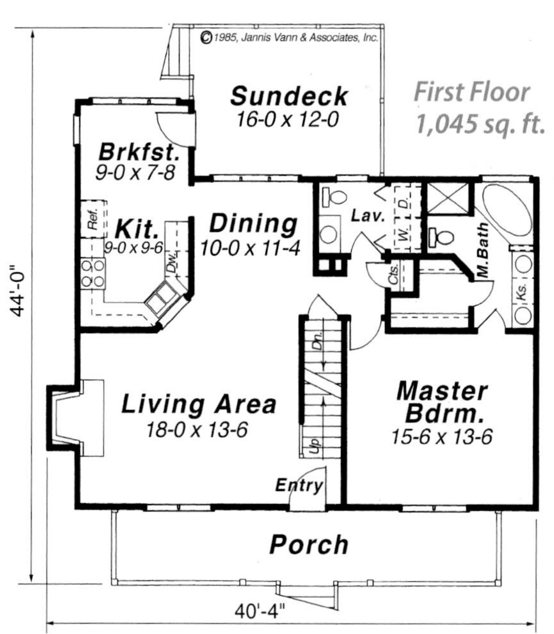

First Floor
1,045 sq. ft.

Relaxing Bayed Dining Area

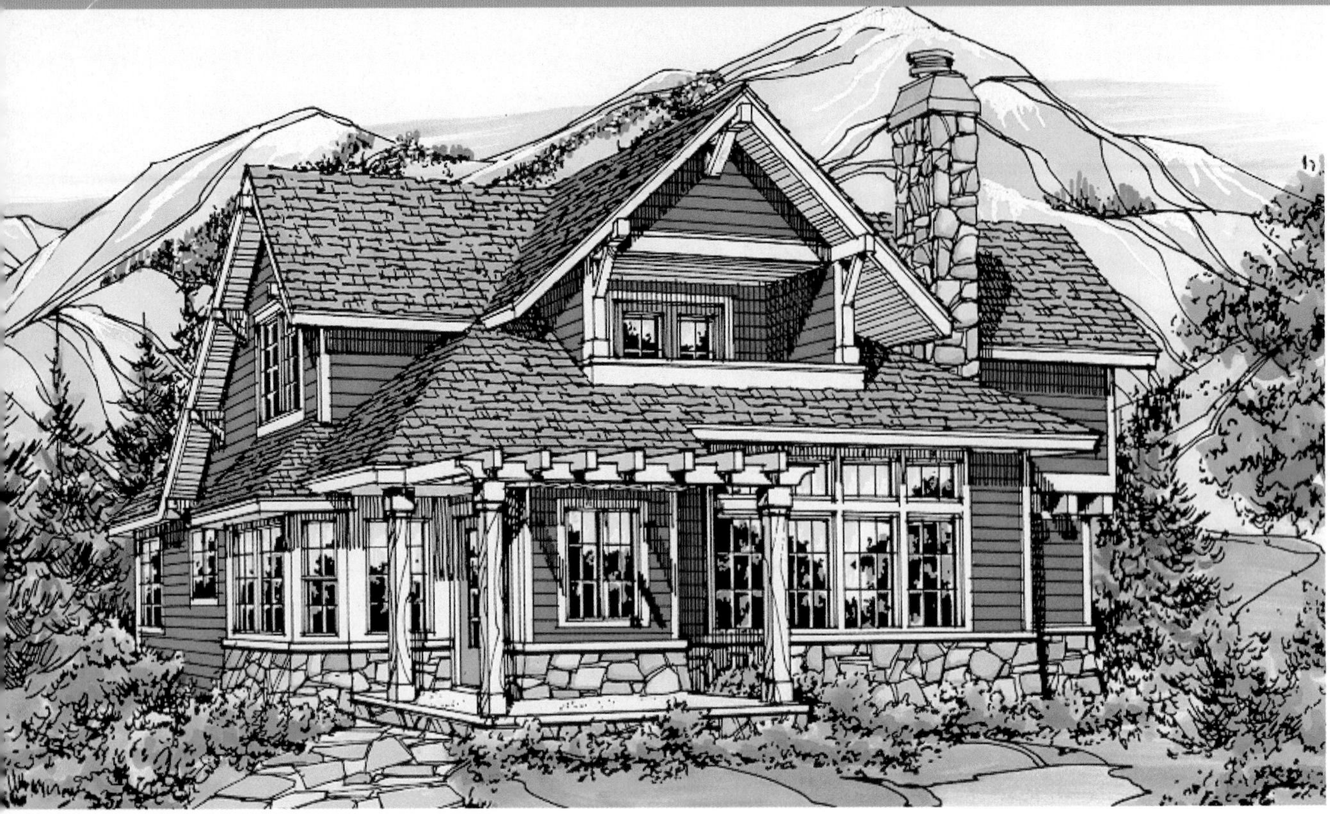

Plan #582-078D-0035

Price Code D

Special Features • 1,635 total square feet of living area • Entry features a cozy window seat and convenient coat closet • Airy living room boasts a grand fireplace • Kitchen opens to the bayed breakfast area and includes a laundry closet • Two second floor bedrooms flank a sitting area where French doors open to a covered porch • 3 bedrooms, 2 baths • Crawl space foundation

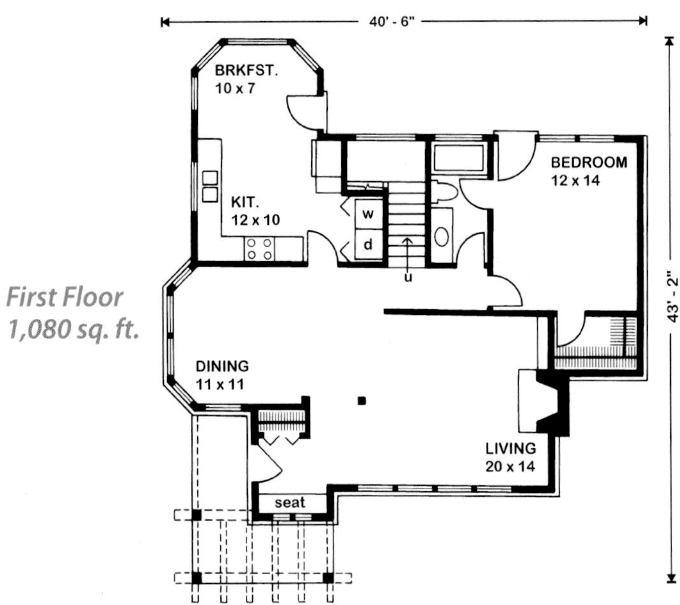

First Floor
1,080 sq. ft.

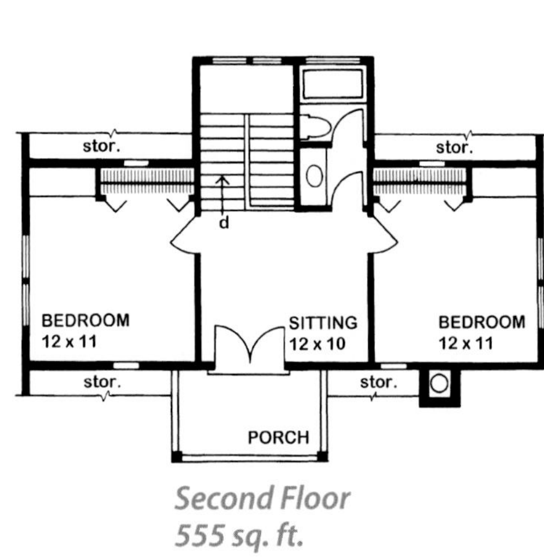

Second Floor
555 sq. ft.

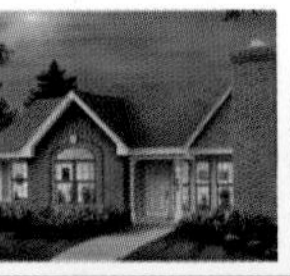

Plan #582-003D-0005

Price Code B

Special Features • 1,708 total square feet of living area • Massive family room is enhanced with several windows, a fireplace and access to the porch • Deluxe master bath is accented by a step-up corner tub flanked by double vanities • Closets throughout maintain organized living • Bedrooms are isolated from living areas • 3 bedrooms, 2 baths, 2-car garage • Basement foundation, drawings also include crawl space foundation

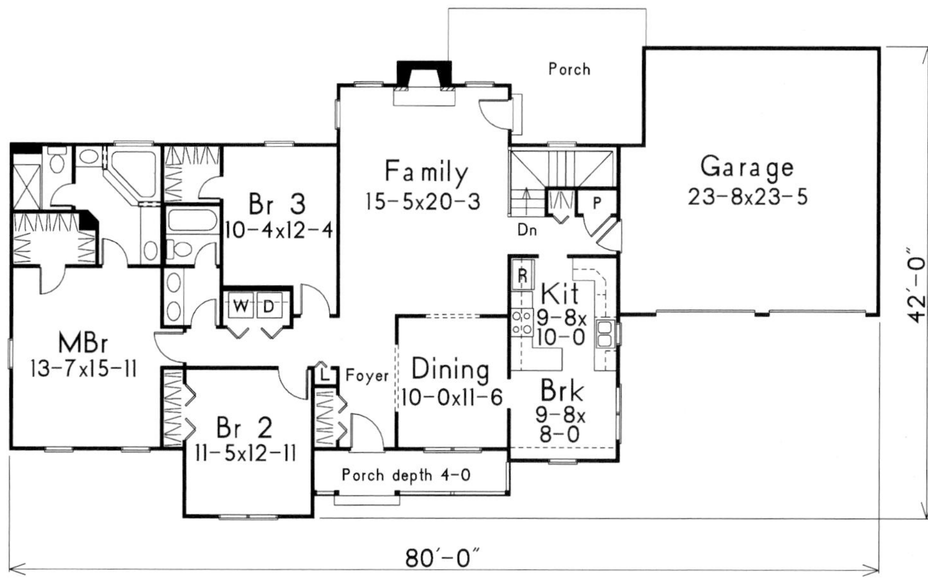

Plan #582-028D-0004

Price Code B

Special Features • 1,785 total square feet of living area • 9' ceilings throughout home • Luxurious master bath includes whirlpool tub and separate shower • Cozy breakfast area is convenient to kitchen • 3 bedrooms, 3 baths, 2-car detached garage • Basement, crawl space or slab foundation, please specify when ordering

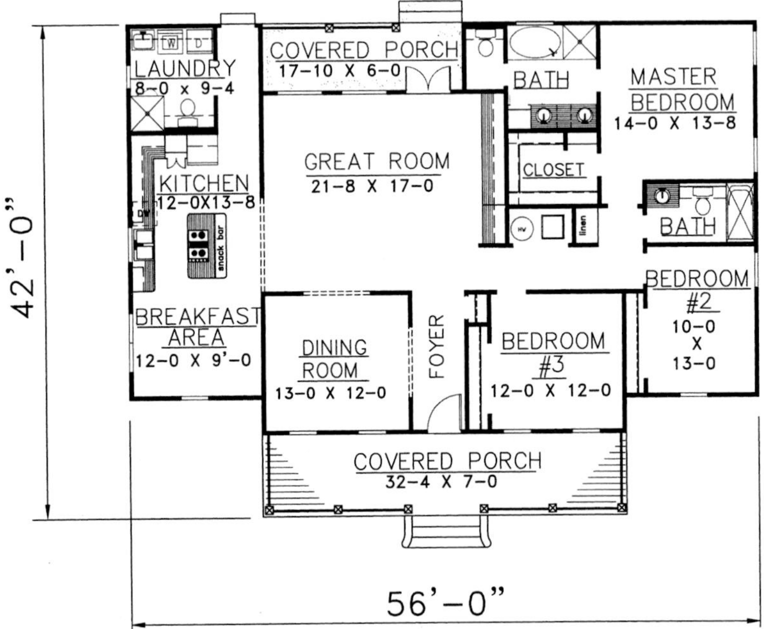

Lovely Ranch Living

Plan #582-056D-0023

Price Code E

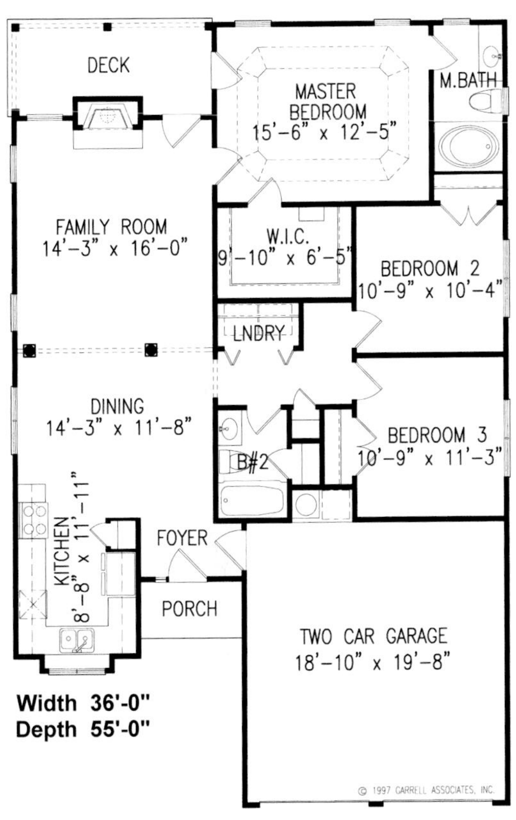

Special Features • 1,277 total square feet of living area • Both the family room and master bedroom have direct access to an outdoor deck • The kitchen is compact, yet efficient • Columns add distinction between dining and family rooms • 3 bedrooms, 2 baths, 2-car garage • Slab foundation

Tranquility Of An Atrium Cottage

Plan #582-007D-0068

Price Code B

Rear View

Special Features • 1,384 total square feet of living area • Wrap-around country porch for peaceful evenings • Vaulted great room enjoys a large bay window, stone fireplace, pass-through kitchen and awesome rear views through atrium window wall • Master bedroom features a double-door entry, walk-in closet and a fabulous bath • Atrium opens to 611 square feet of optional living area below • 2 bedrooms, 2 baths, 1-car side entry garage • Walk-out basement foundation

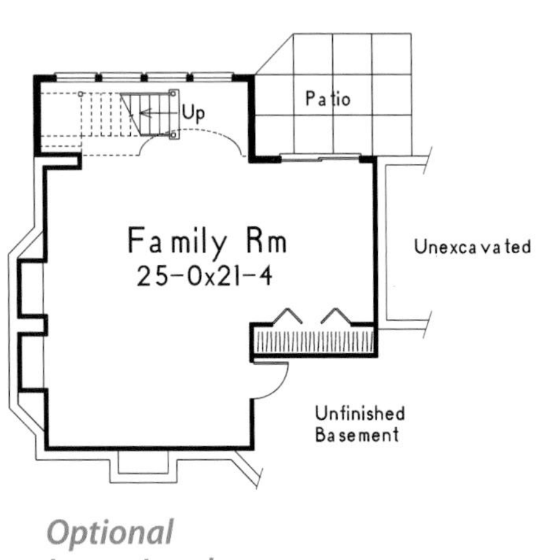

Optional Lower Level

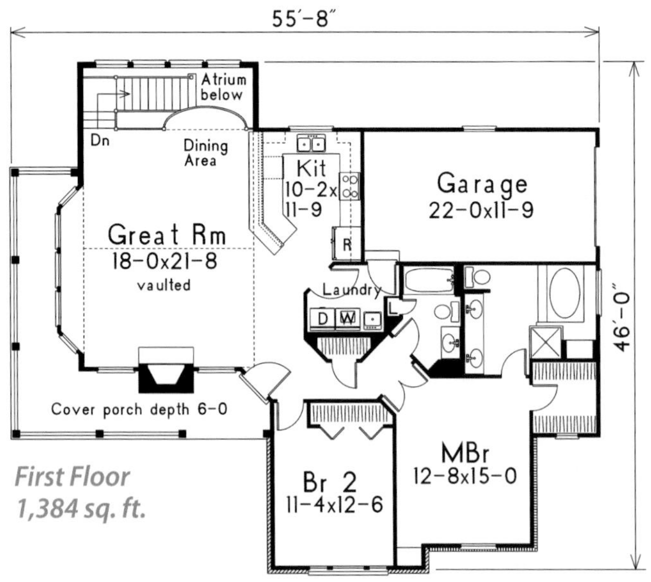

First Floor 1,384 sq. ft.

Warm And Inviting Ranch

Plan #582-065D-0040

Price Code C

Special Features • *1,874 total square feet of living area • The bayed dining area, kitchen and great room with a fireplace combine for an open living area • The master bedroom pampers with a corner whirlpool tub, double vanity and walk-in closet • 9' ceilings throughout home add to the spaciousness • Optional lower level has an additional 1,175 square feet of living area • 3 bedrooms, 2 baths, 3-car side entry garage • Basement or walk-out basement foundation, please specify when ordering*

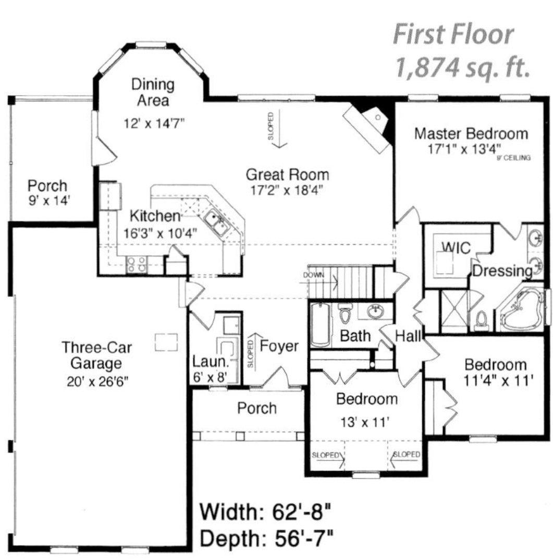

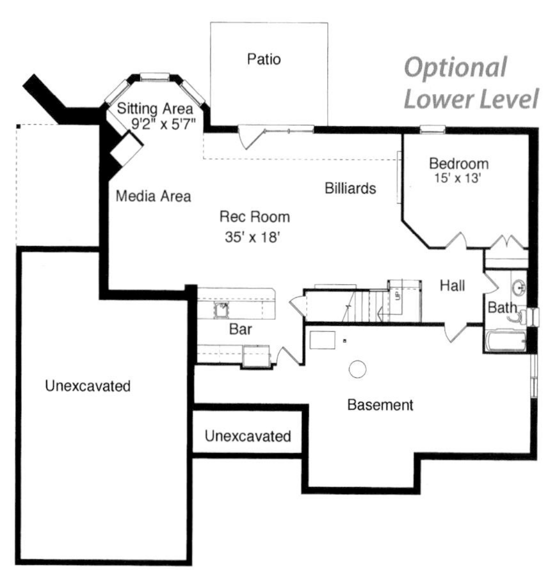

www.houseplansandmore.com

A Great Plan With Cozy Charm

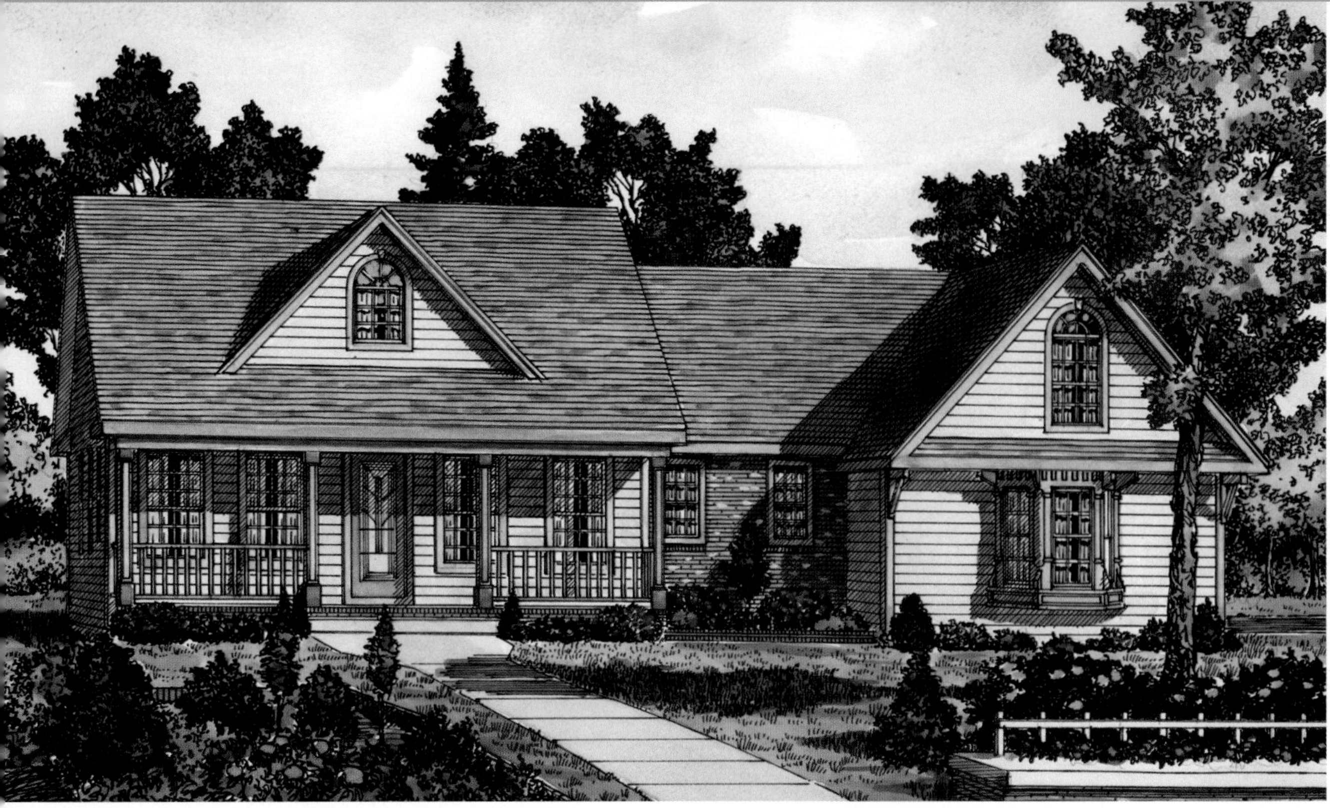

Plan #582-016D-0021

Price Code D

Special Features • 1,892 total square feet of living area • Victorian home includes folk charm • This split bedroom plan places a lovely master bedroom on the opposite end of the other two bedrooms for privacy • Central living and dining areas combine creating a great place for entertaining • Bonus room on the second floor has an additional 285 square feet of living area • 3 bedrooms, 2 1/2 baths, 2-car side entry garage • Basement, crawl space or slab foundation, please specify when ordering

Width 65'-0"
Depth 45'-0"

First Floor
1,892 sq. ft.

Optional Second Floor

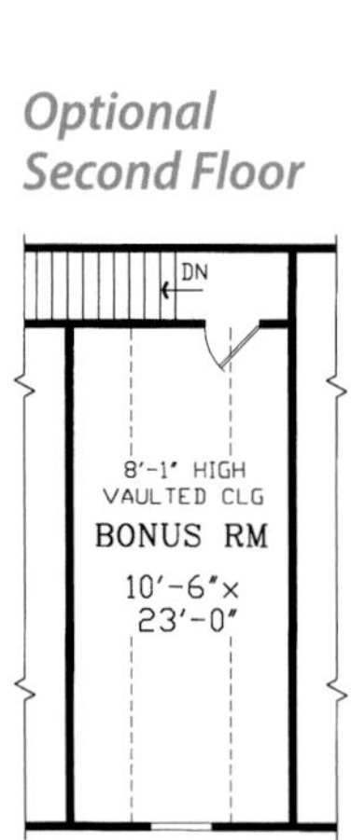

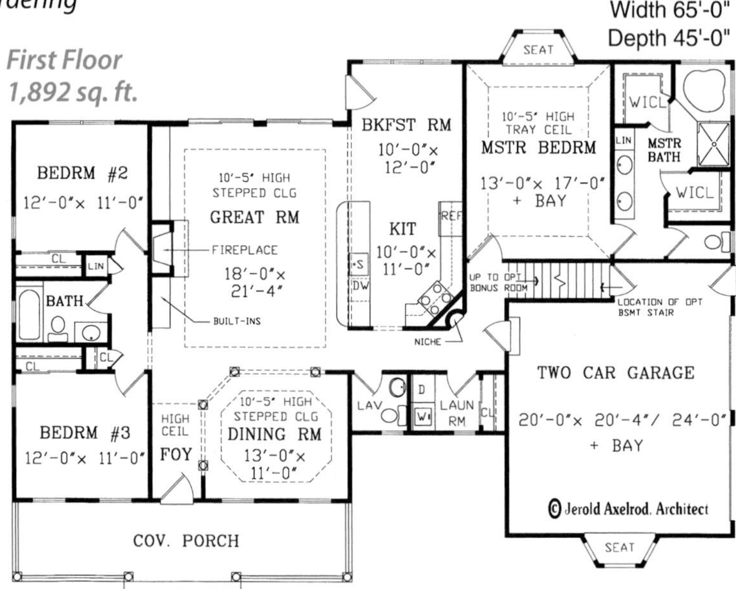

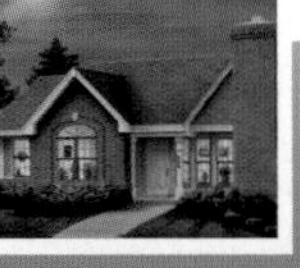

Plan #582-065D-0038

Price Code B

Special Features • 1,663 total square feet of living area • The open great room, dining area and kitchen combine to form the main living area • An 11' ceiling tops the great room and foyer for added openness • The rear covered porch provides a cozy and relaxing atmosphere • The master bedroom enjoys a sloped ceiling and a private entrance to the covered porch • 3 bedrooms, 2 baths, 2-car side entry garage • Basement foundation

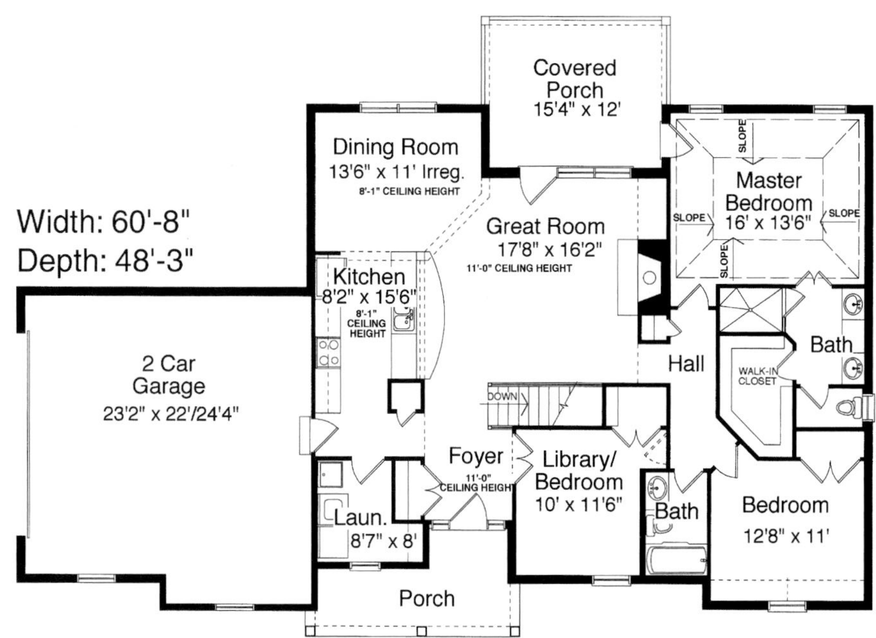

Entertainment Center In Great Room

Plan #582-070D-0004

Price Code B

Special Features • 1,791 total square feet of living area • A whirlpool tub adds luxury to the master bath • Breakfast nook leads to a covered porch • Double closets create plenty of storage in the foyer • 3 bedrooms, 2 baths, 2-car side entry garage • Basement foundation

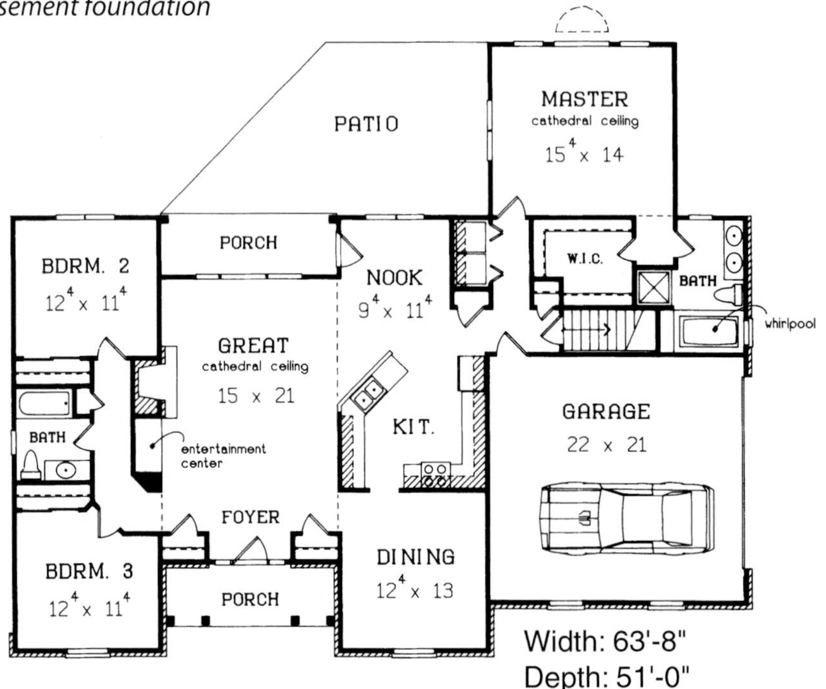

Plan #582-077D-0002

Price Code D

Special Features • 1,855 total square feet of living area • The great room boasts a 12' ceiling and corner fireplace • Bayed breakfast area adjoins kitchen that features a walk-in pantry • The relaxing master bedroom includes a private bath with walk-in closet and garden tub • Optional second floor has an additional 352 square feet of living area • 3 bedrooms, 2 1/2 baths, 2-car side entry garage • Basement, crawl space or slab foundation, please specify when ordering

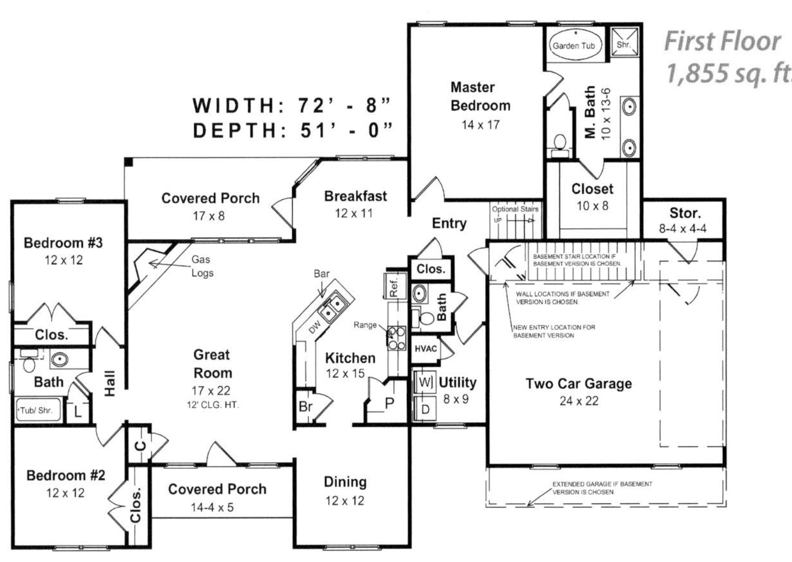

First Floor
1,855 sq. ft.

Optional
Second Floor

An Enhancement To Any Neighborhood

Plan #582-008D-0010 **Price Code A**

Special Features • 1,440 total square feet of living area • Foyer adjoins massive-sized great room with sloping ceiling and tall masonry fireplace • Kitchen connects to the spacious dining room and features a pass-through breakfast bar • Master bedroom enjoys a private bath and two closets • An oversized two-car side entry garage offers plenty of storage for bicycles, lawn equipment, etc. • 3 bedrooms, 2 baths, 2-car side entry garage • Basement foundation, drawings also include crawl space and slab foundations

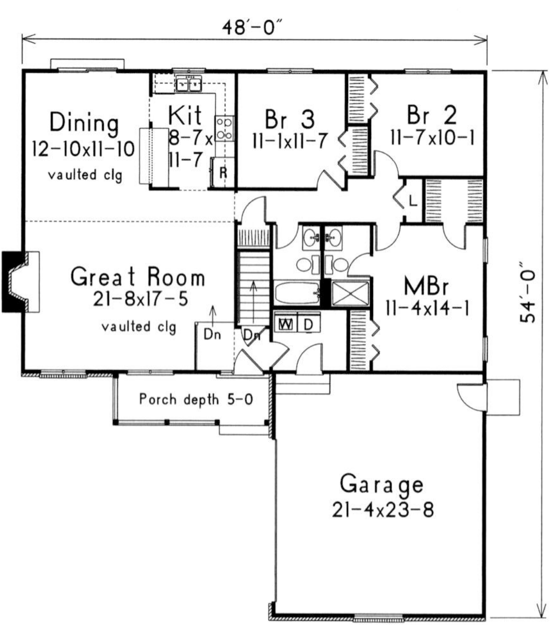

Summer Home Or Year-Round

Plan #582-007D-0037

Price Code A

Special Features • *1,403 total square feet of living area* • *Impressive living areas for a modest-sized home* • *Special master/hall bath has linen storage, step-up tub and lots of window light* • *Spacious closets everywhere you look* • *3 bedrooms, 2 baths, 2-car drive under garage* • *Basement foundation*

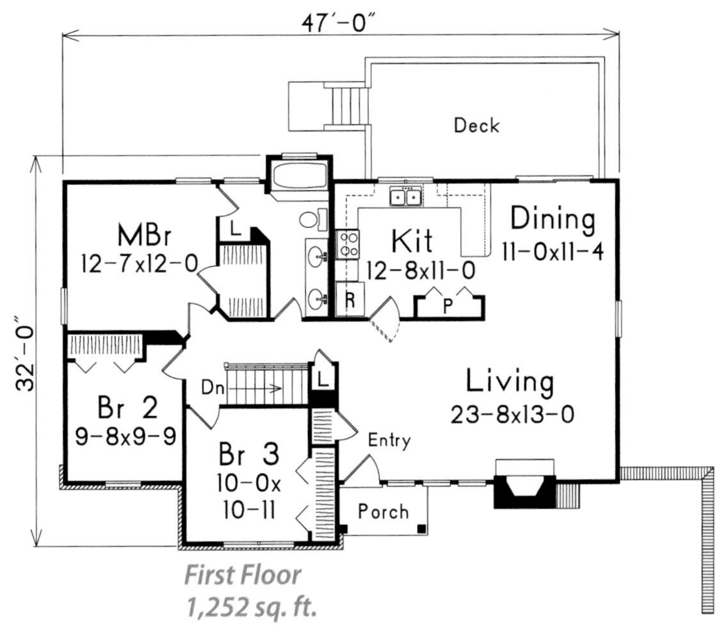

First Floor
1,252 sq. ft.

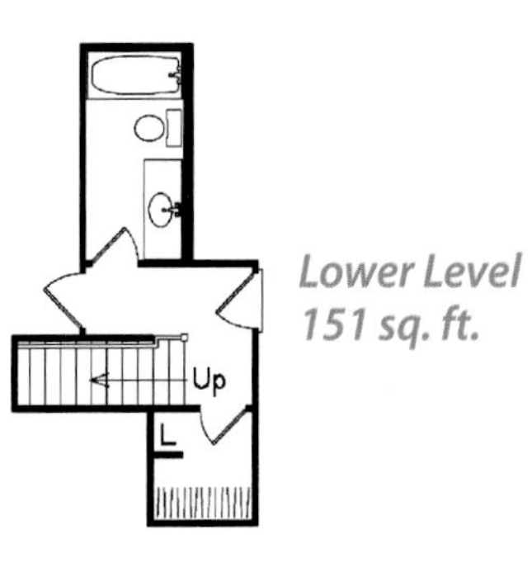

Lower Level
151 sq. ft.

www.houseplansandmore.com

Plan #582-028D-0003

Price Code B

Special Features • *1,716 total square feet of living area* • *Great room boasts a fireplace and access to the kitchen/breakfast area through a large arched opening* • *Master bedroom includes a huge walk-in closet and French doors that lead onto an L-shaped porch* • *Bedrooms #2 and #3 share a bath and linen closet* • *3 bedrooms, 2 baths, 2-car detached garage* • *Crawl space or slab foundation, please specify when ordering*

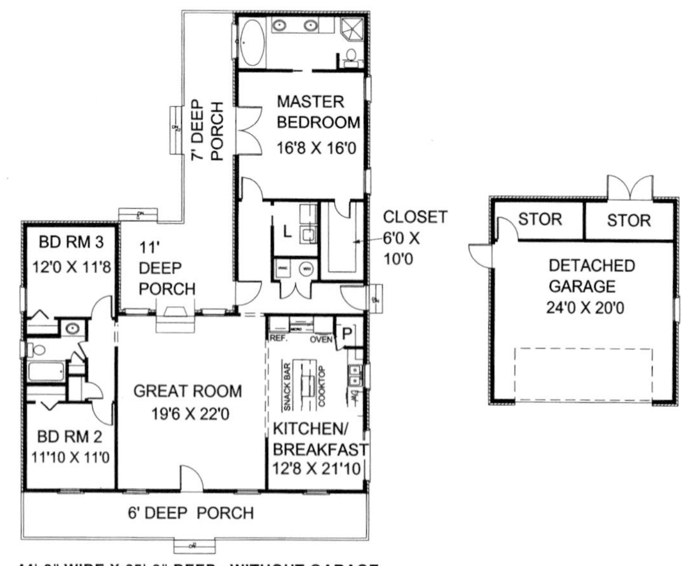

44'-0" WIDE X 65'-0" DEEP - WITHOUT GARAGE

Bayed Dining Room

Plan #582-055D-0026

Price Code B

Special Features • 1,538 total square feet of living area • Dining and great rooms highlighted in this design • Master suite has many amenities • Kitchen and laundry room are accessible from any room in the house • 3 bedrooms, 2 baths, 2-car garage • Walk-out basement, basement, crawl space or slab foundation, please specify when ordering

Distinctive Stone And Stucco Facade

Plan #582-025D-0010

Price Code B

Special Features • 1,677 total square feet of living area • Master suite has a secluded feel with a private and remote location from other bedrooms • Great room is complete with fireplace and beautiful windows • Optional second floor has an additional 350 square feet of living area • 3 bedrooms, 2 baths, 2-car side entry garage • Slab foundation

First Floor
1,677 sq. ft.

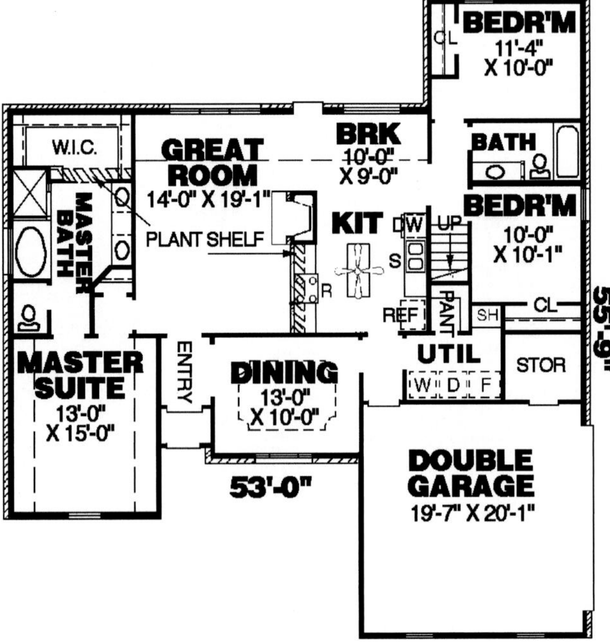

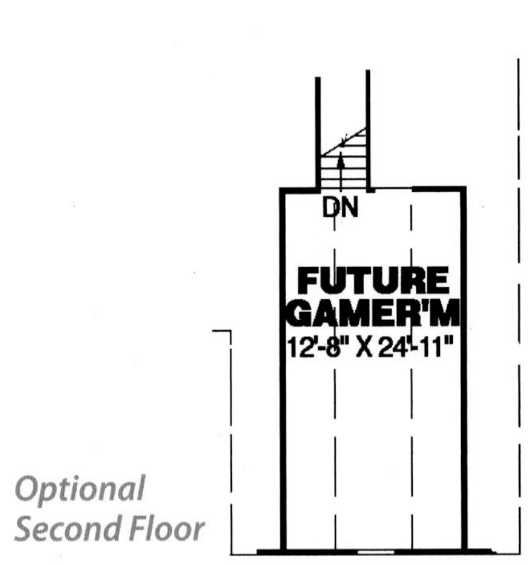

Optional
Second Floor

Vaulted Living And Dining Areas

Plan #582-078D-0005

Price Code D

Special Features • *1,525 total square feet of living area • Back-to-back fireplaces warm both the living room and kitchen/breakfast area • Kitchen features a corner sink, center island and a side deck which offers outdoor dining opportunities • One secluded bedroom offers a quiet retreat with a walk-in closet and private bath making it a perfect master bedroom • 3 bedrooms, 2 baths • Basement or crawl space foundation, please specify when ordering*

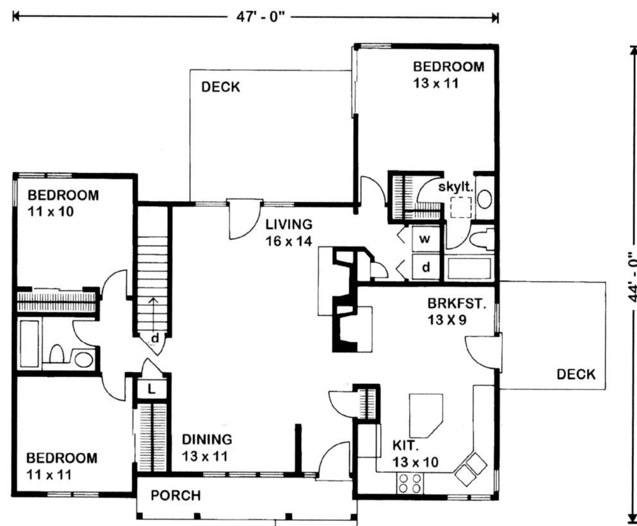

Sculptured Roof Line And Facade Add Charm

Plan #582-006D-0003

Price Code B

Special Features • 1,674 total square feet of living area • Vaulted great room, dining area and kitchen all enjoy a central fireplace and log bin • Convenient laundry/mud room is located between the garage and family area with handy stairs to the basement • Easily expandable screened porch and adjacent patio are accessed from the dining area • Master bedroom features a full bath with tub, separate shower and walk-in closet • 3 bedrooms, 2 baths, 2-car garage • Basement foundation, drawings also include crawl space and slab foundations

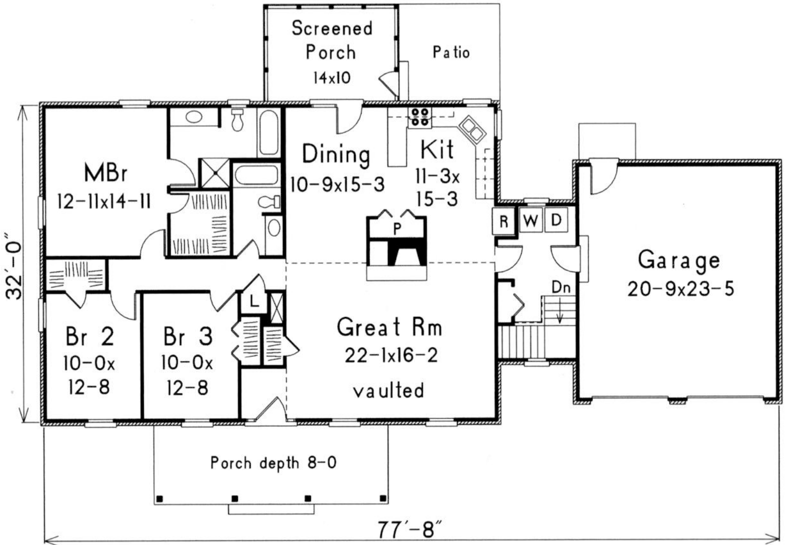

Stone And Stucco Accent This Old-World Cottage

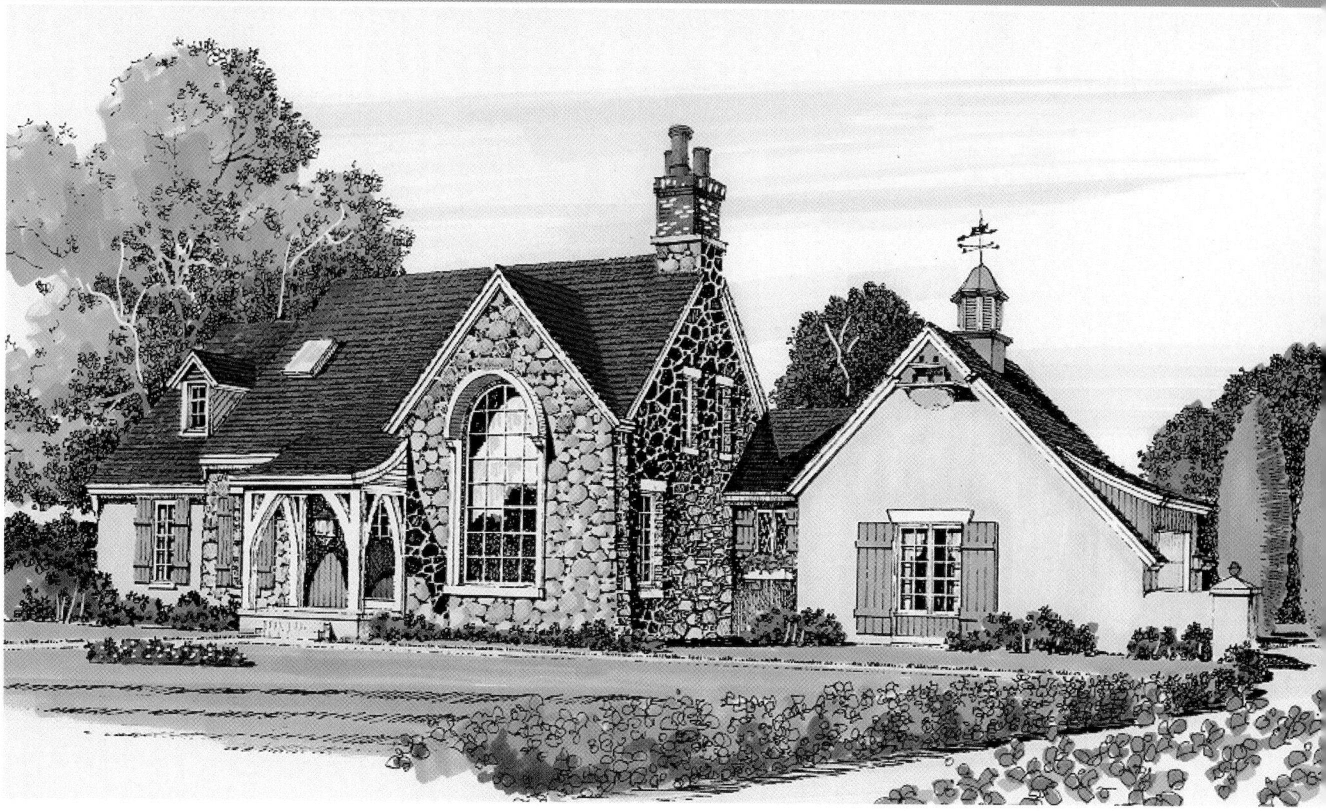

Plan #582-078D-0016

Price Code D

Special Features • 1,655 total square feet of living area • The kitchen, living and dining rooms combine to form an expansive open area • Bedrooms are situated away from the main living area for privacy • The second floor has a spacious loft with its own bath and balcony overlooking the living room • 3 bedrooms, 2 baths, 2-car side entry garage • Basement or crawl space foundation, please specify when ordering

First Floor
1,275 sq. ft.

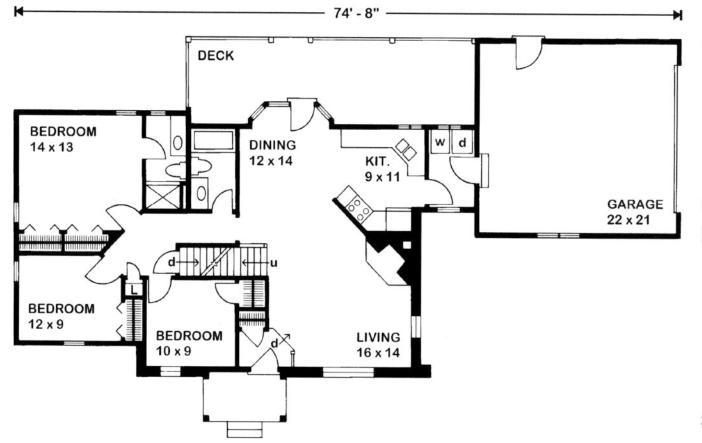

Second Floor
380 sq. ft.

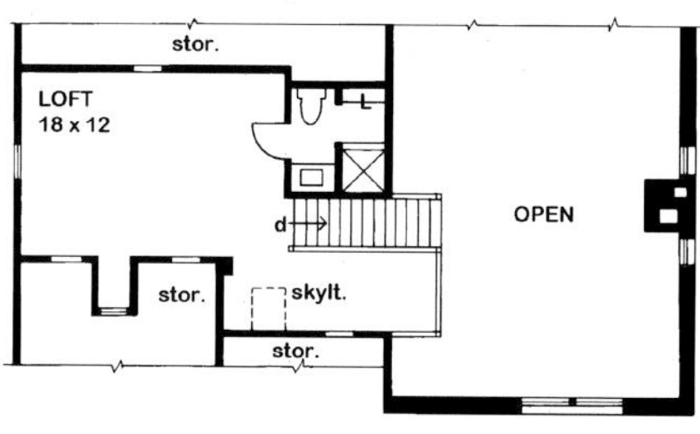

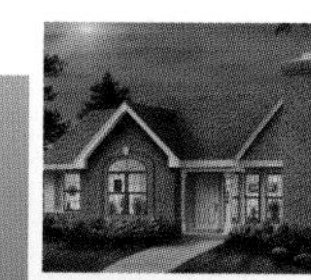

Charming Country Facade

Plan #582-008D-0004

Price Code B

Special Features • 1,643 total square feet of living area • An attractive front entry porch gives this ranch a country accent • Spacious family/dining room is the focal point of this design • Kitchen and utility room are conveniently located near gathering areas • Formal living room in the front of the home provides area for quiet and privacy • Master bedroom has view to the rear of the home and a generous walk-in closet • 3 bedrooms, 2 baths, 2-car garage • Basement foundation, drawings also include crawl space and slab foundations

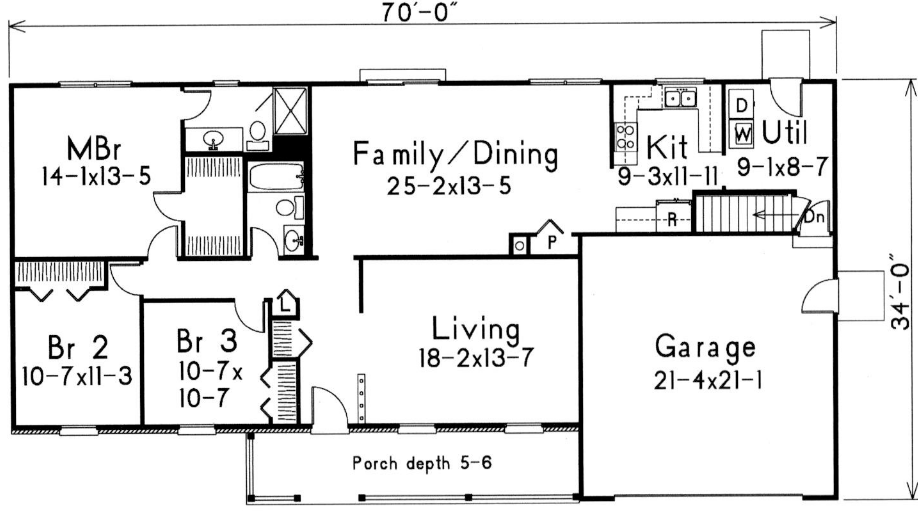

Double Bay Enhances Front Entry

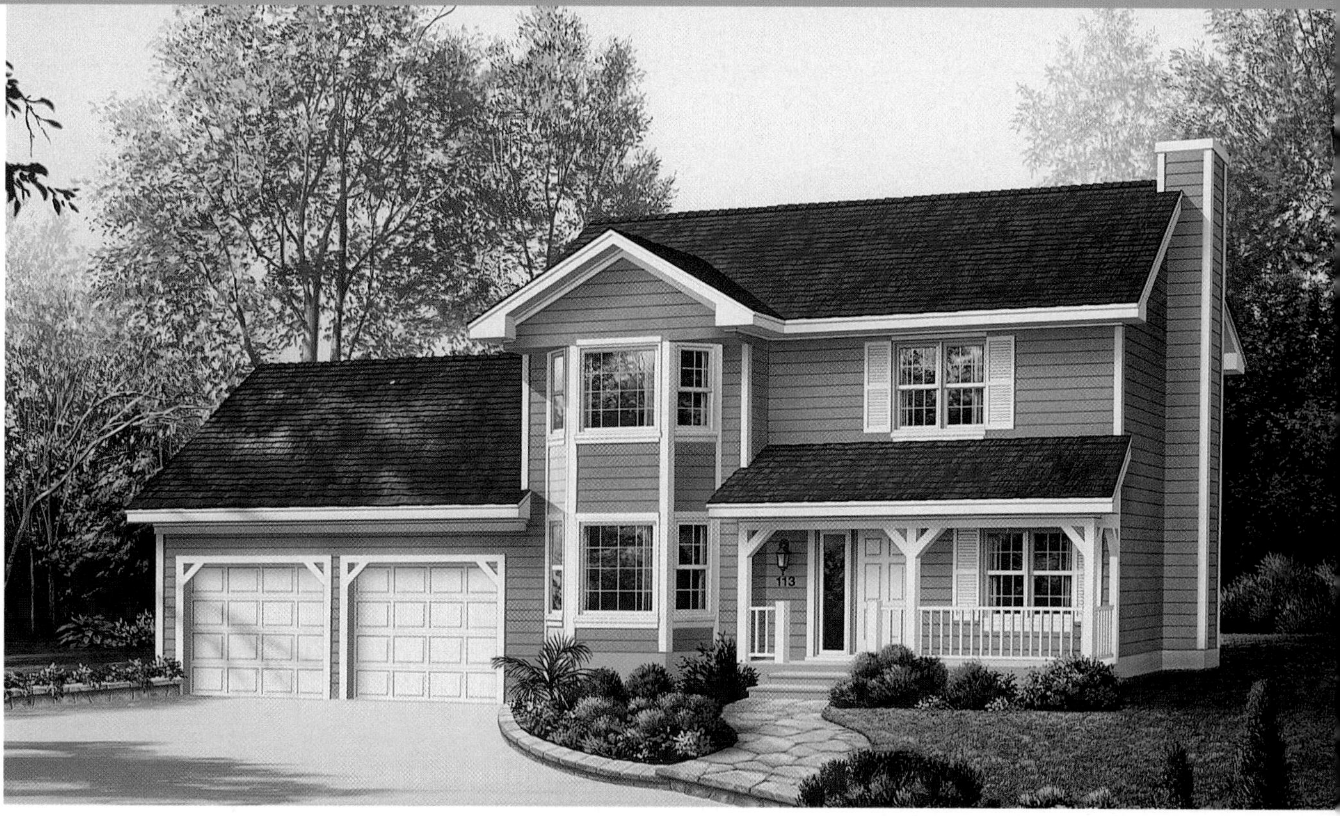

Plan #582-053D-0003

Price Code C

Special Features • *1,992 total square feet of living area* • *Distinct living, dining and breakfast areas* • *Master bedroom boasts a full-end bay window and a cathedral ceiling* • *Storage and laundry area are located adjacent to the garage* • *Bonus room over the garage for future office or playroom is included in the square footage* • *3 bedrooms, 2 1/2 baths, 2-car garage* • *Crawl space foundation, drawings also include basement foundation*

First Floor
868 sq. ft.

Second Floor
1,124 sq. ft.

www.houseplansandmore.com

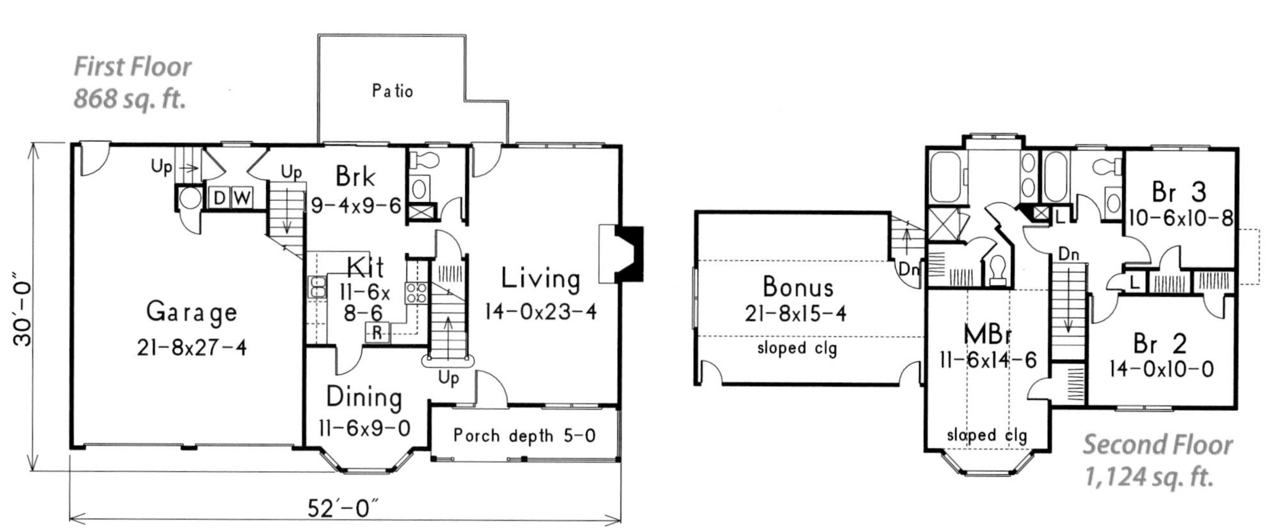

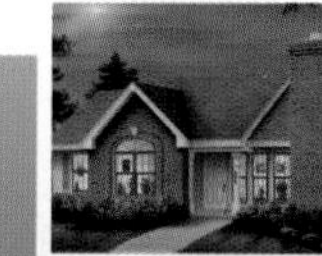

Plan #582-032D-0019

Price Code C

Special Features • *1,995 total square feet of living area* • *First floor solarium creates a sunny atmosphere* • *Second floor office is tucked away from traffic areas for privacy* • *Energy efficient home with 2" x 6" exterior walls* • *Bonus room above the garage provides an additional 285 square feet of living area* • *3 bedrooms, 2 1/2 baths, 2-car side entry garage* • *Basement foundation*

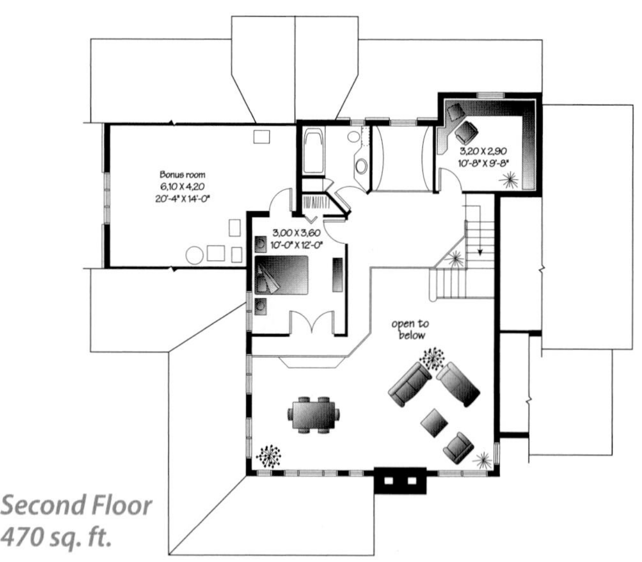

Second Floor
470 sq. ft.

First Floor
1,525 sq. ft.

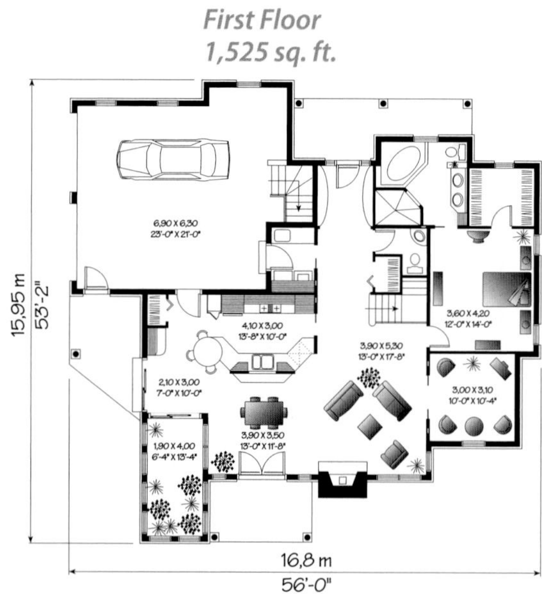

Double Gables Add Warmth To Exterior

Plan #582-070D-0001

Price Code A

Special Features • 1,300 total square feet of living area • Bayed dining room has sliding glass doors that open onto an outdoor patio • Large bedroom #2 has a built-in desk • Charming wrap-around front porch • 3 bedrooms, 2 baths, 2-car garage • Basement foundation

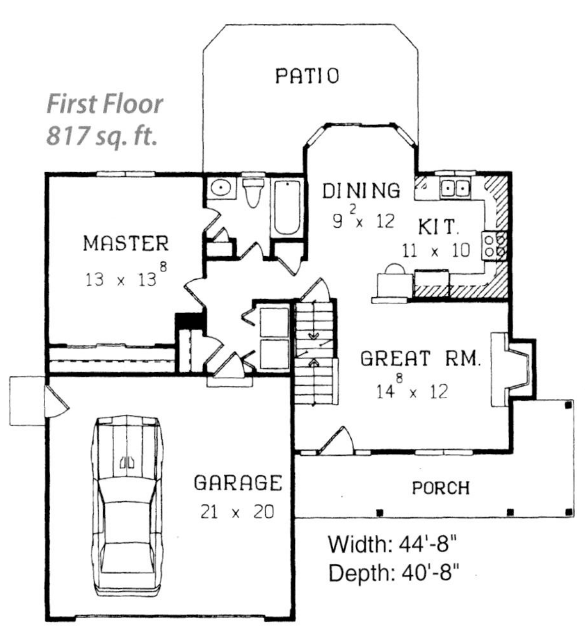

First Floor
817 sq. ft.

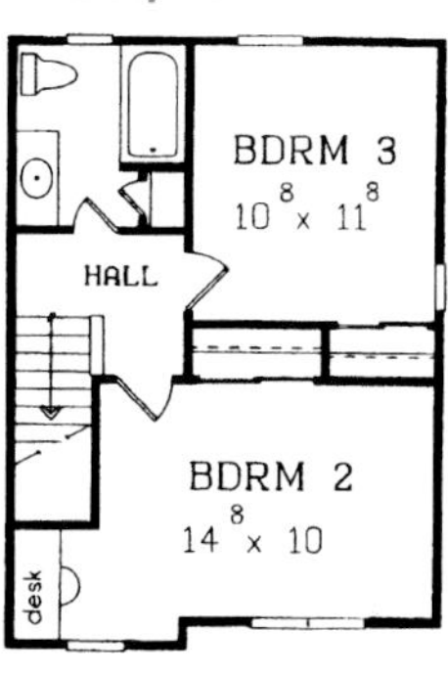

Second Floor
483 sq. ft.

Central Fireplace Dominates Living Area

Plan #582-021D-0010

Price Code A

Special Features • *1,444 total square feet of living area* • *11' ceilings in the living and dining rooms combine with a central fireplace to create a large open living area* • *Both secondary bedrooms have large walk-in closets* • *Large storage area in the garage is suitable for a workshop or play area* • *Front and rear covered porches add a cozy touch* • *U-shaped kitchen includes a laundry closet and serving bar* • *3 bedrooms, 2 baths, 2-car side entry garage* • *Slab foundation, drawings also include crawl space foundation*

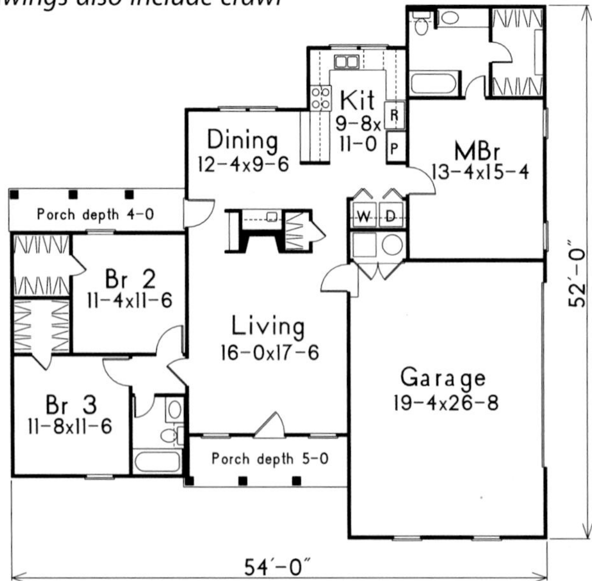

Large Corner Deck Lends Way To Outdoor Living Area

Plan #582-022D-0019

Price Code A

Special Features • 1,283 total square feet of living area • Vaulted breakfast room has sliding doors that open onto deck • Kitchen features convenient corner sink and pass-through to dining room • Open living atmosphere in dining area and great room • Vaulted great room features a fireplace • 3 bedrooms, 2 baths, 2-car garage • Basement foundation

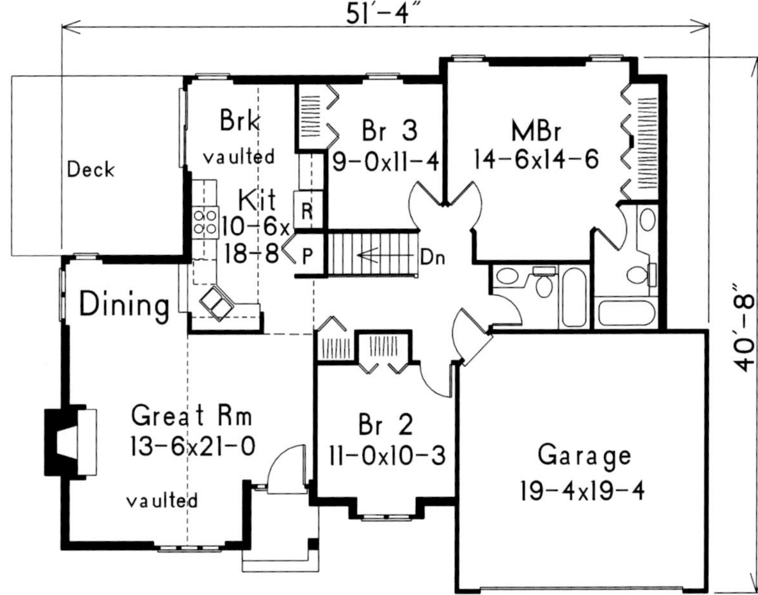

Exquisite Arched Windows

Plan #582-038D-0032

Price Code B

Special Features • *1,554 total square feet of living area* • *Bay-shaped kitchen has enough space for dining as well as a convenient closet for the washer and dryer* • *A half wall divides the dining and living rooms creating privacy while maintaining a feeling of openness* • *A cheerful sun room graces the front entry* • *3 bedrooms, 2 1/2 baths, 2-car garage* • *Basement, crawl space or slab foundation, please specify when ordering*

Second Floor
748 sq. ft.

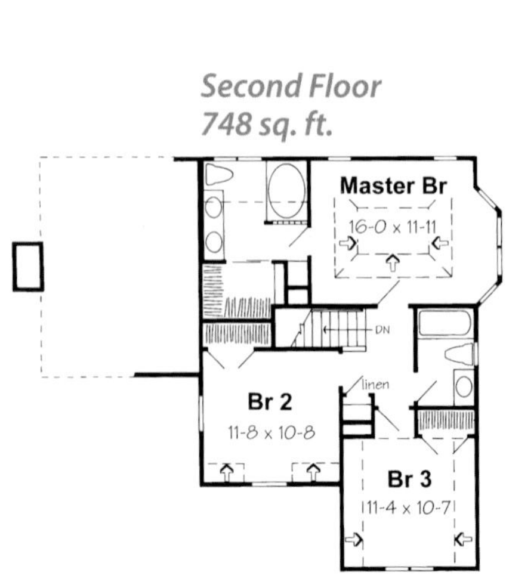

First Floor
806 sq. ft.

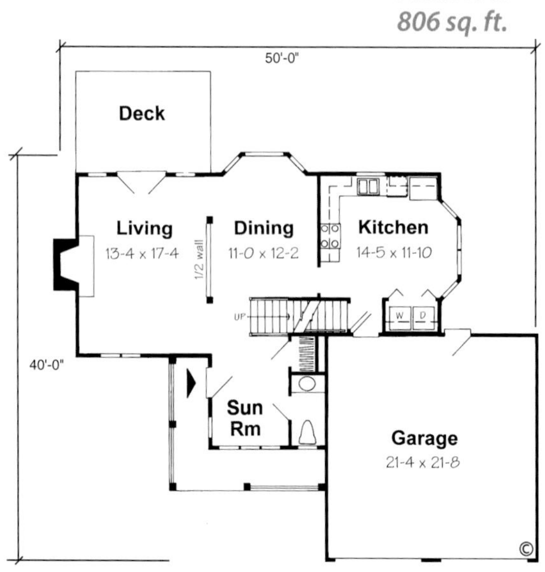

Enchanting French-Country Chateau

Plan #582-078D-0019

Price Code D

Special Features • *1,895 total square feet of living area* • *The spacious living room boasts a grand fireplace flanked by built-in shelves* • *Luxurious first floor master bedroom enjoys a private patio, two walk-in closets and a bath* • *Bayed dining room provides a formal area for entertaining* • *4 bedrooms, 2 1/2 baths, 2-car side entry garage* • *Basement or crawl space foundation, please specify when ordering*

First Floor
1,180 sq. ft.

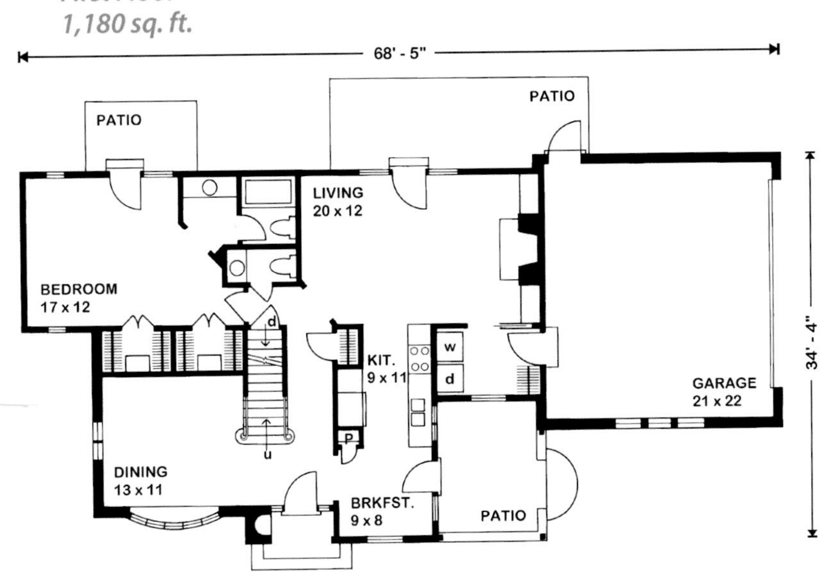

Second Floor
715 sq. ft.

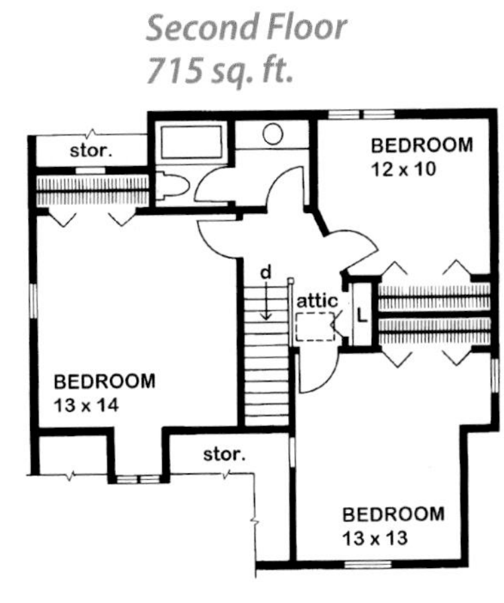

Plan #582-016D-0051

Price Code D

Special Features • 1,945 total square feet of living area • Great room has a stepped ceiling and a fireplace • Bayed dining area with stepped ceiling and French door leads to a covered porch • Master bedroom has a tray ceiling, bay window and large walk-in closet • 3 bedrooms, 2 1/2 baths, 2-car side entry garage • Basement, crawl space or slab foundation, please specify when ordering

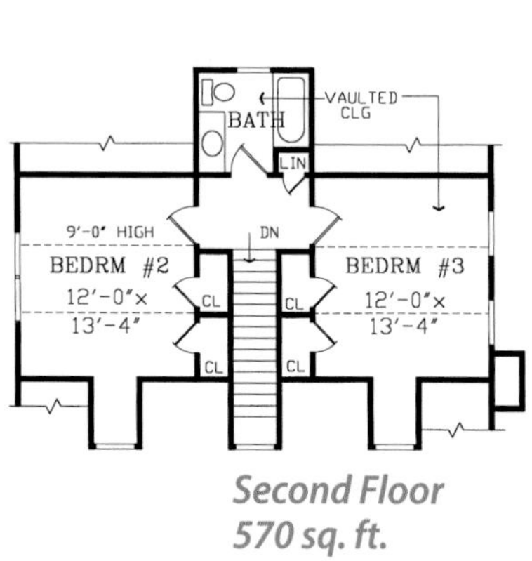

Second Floor
570 sq. ft.

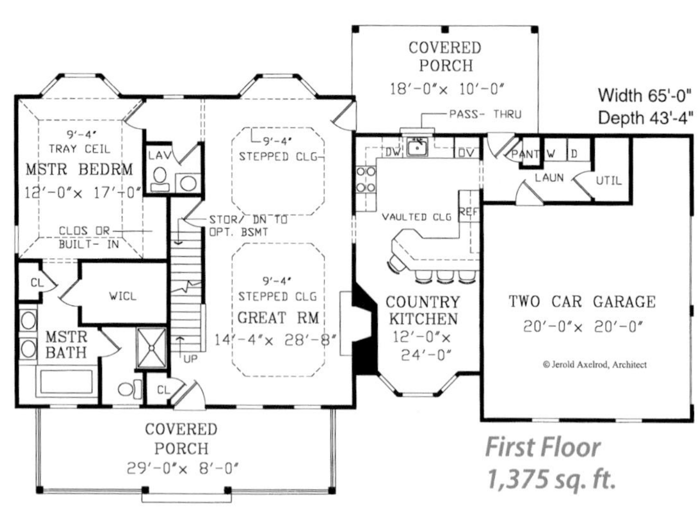

First Floor
1,375 sq. ft.

Christine Canova 9/02

Plan #582-056D-0008

Price Code E

Special Features • *1,821 total square feet of living area* • *9' ceilings throughout first floor* • *Master suite is secluded for privacy and has a spacious bath* • *Sunny breakfast room features bay window* • *Bonus room on the second floor has an additional 191 square feet of living area* • *3 bedrooms, 2 baths, 2-car side entry garage* • *Basement or slab foundation, please specify when ordering*

First Floor
1,821 sq. ft.

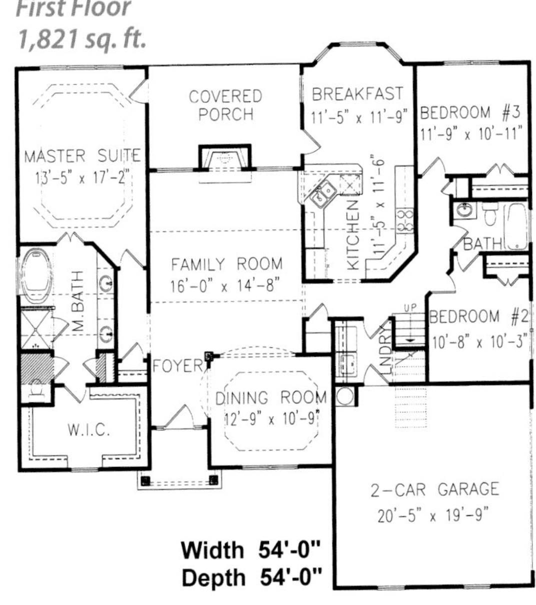

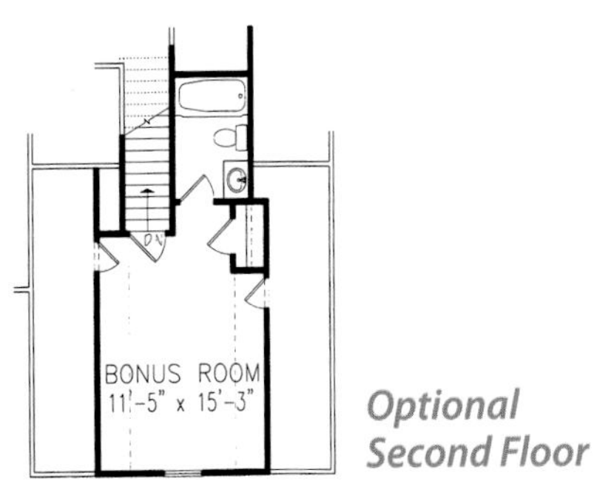

Optional Second Floor

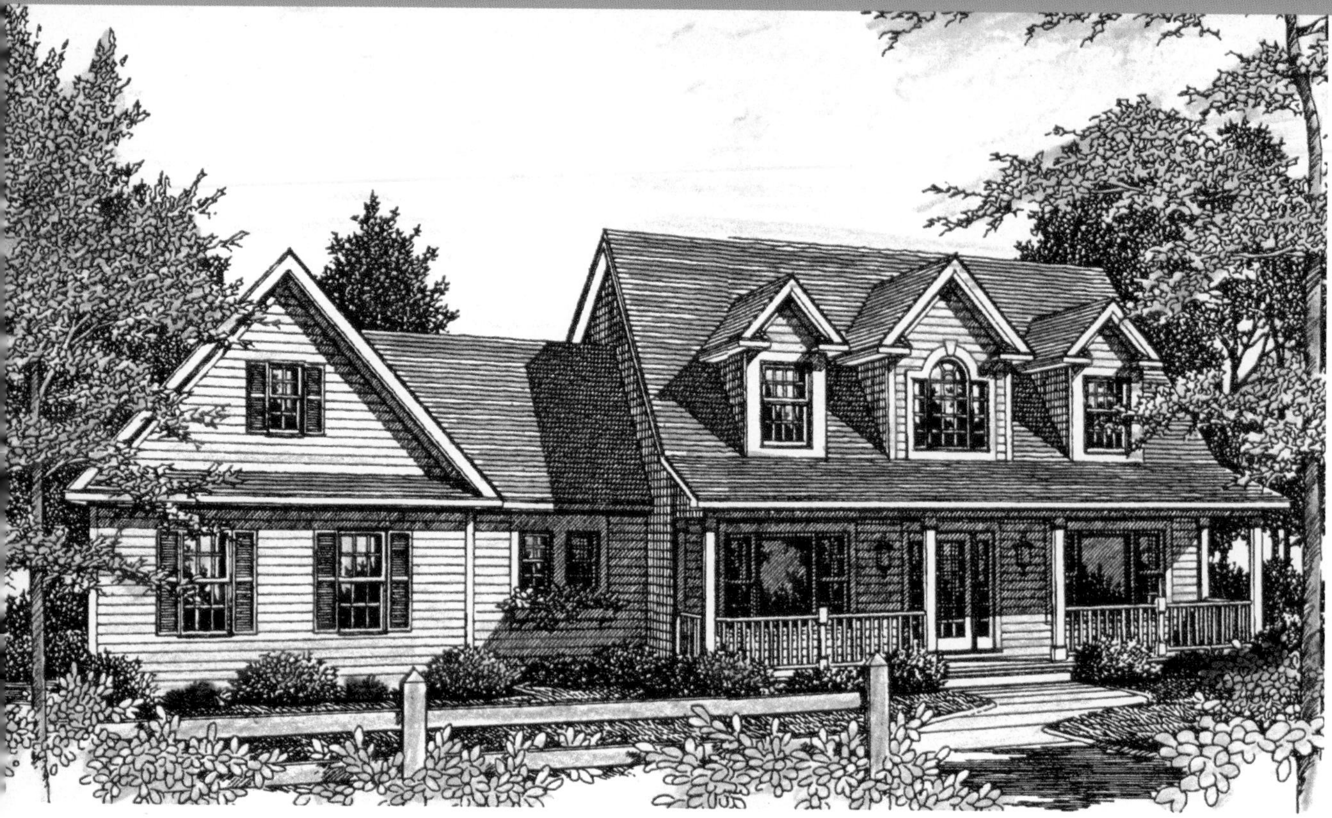

Plan #582-070D-0006

Price Code C

Special Features • 1,841 total square feet of living area • Sunny bayed breakfast room is cheerful for meals • The master suite remains separate from the other bedrooms for privacy • Bonus rooms on the second floor have a total of 295 additional square feet of living area • 3 bedrooms, 2 1/2 baths, 2-car side entry garage • Basement foundation

Second Floor
509 sq. ft.

First Floor
1,332 sq. ft.

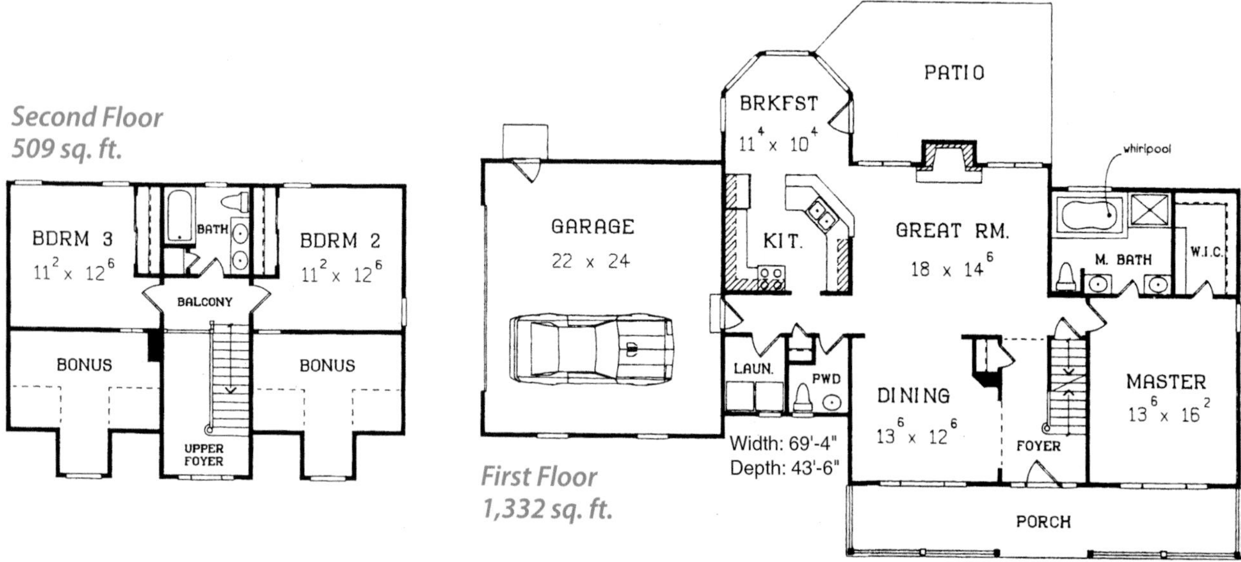

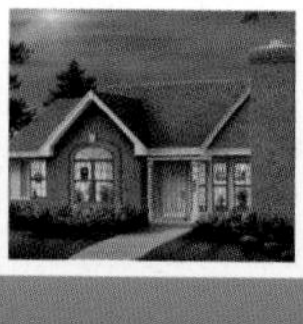

Screened Porch For Outdoor Enjoyment

Plan #582-055D-0100

Price Code A

Special Features • 1,294 total square feet of living area • Second floor bedroom #2/loft has its own bath and a vaulted ceiling overlooking to the great room below • Great room has a cozy fireplace and accesses both the front and the rear of the home • Laundry area on the first floor is convenient to the kitchen • 2 bedrooms, 2 baths, 2-car garage • Crawl space or slab foundation, please specify when ordering

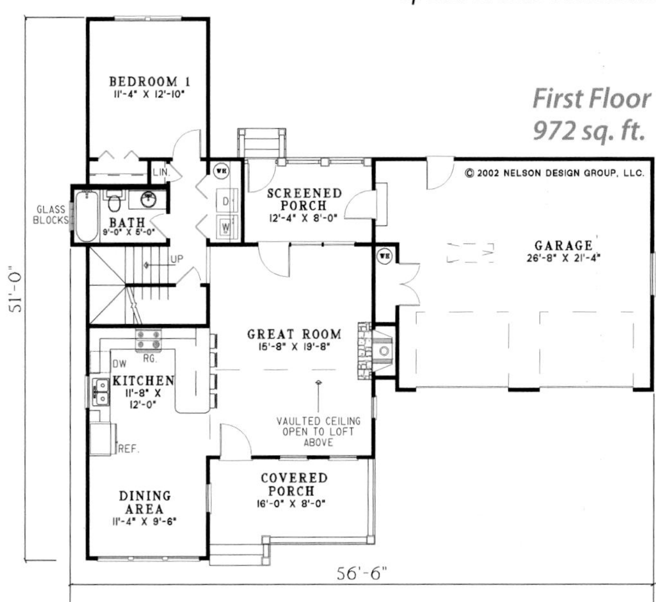

First Floor
972 sq. ft.

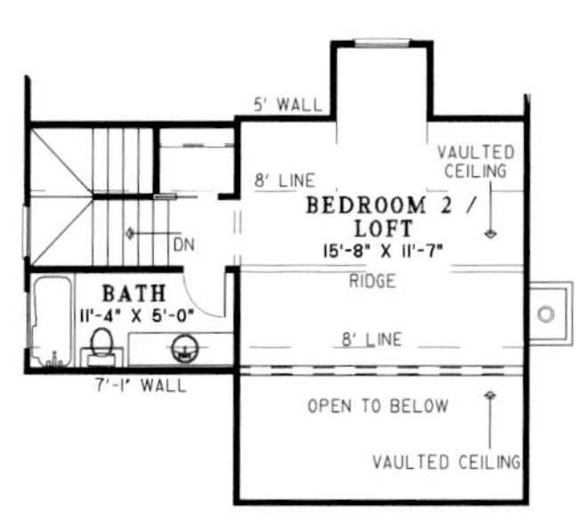

Second Floor
322 sq. ft.

A Beautifully Balanced Facade

Plan #582-016D-0011

Price Code D

Special Features • 1,815 total square feet of living area • The great room features a 10' ceiling, built-in fireplace and a bright airy feeling from several windows • The kitchen and breakfast area are visually connected and the formal dining room is nearby for convenience • Optional bonus room has an additional 323 square feet of living area • 3 bedrooms, 2 baths, 2-car side entry garage • Basement, crawl space or slab foundation, please specify when ordering

First Floor
1,815 sq. ft.

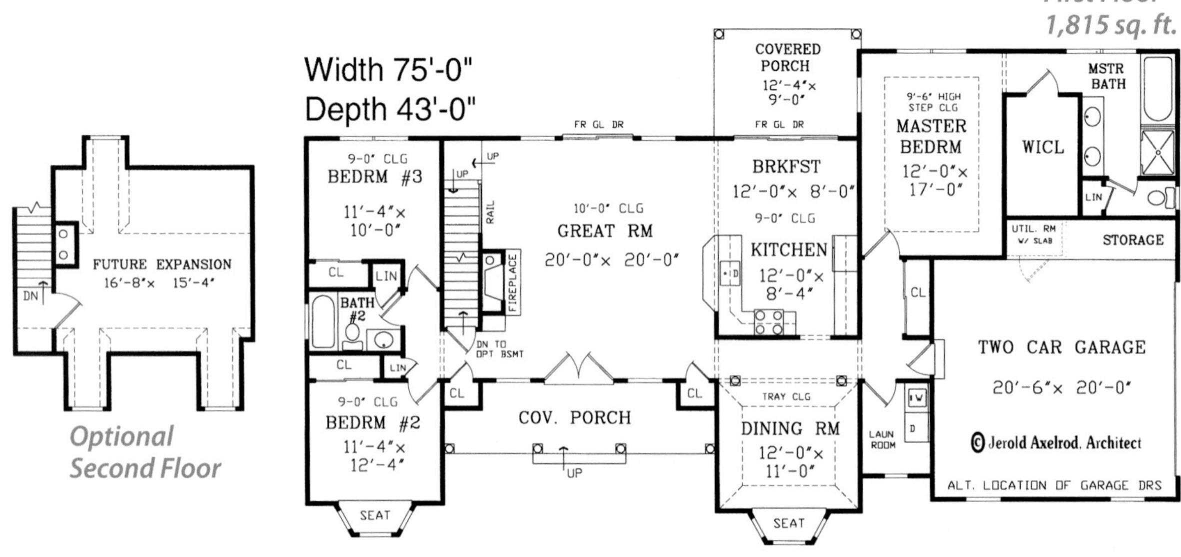

Optional
Second Floor

Stylish Features Enhance Open Living

Plan #582-037D-0011 — Price Code C

Special Features • 1,846 total square feet of living area • Enormous living area combines with the dining and breakfast rooms that are both complemented by windows and high ceilings • Master bedroom has a walk-in closet, display niche and deluxe bath • Secondary bedrooms share a bath and feature large closet space • Oversized two-car garage has plenty of storage and workspace with handy access to the kitchen through the utility area • 3 bedrooms, 2 baths, 2-car garage • Slab foundation

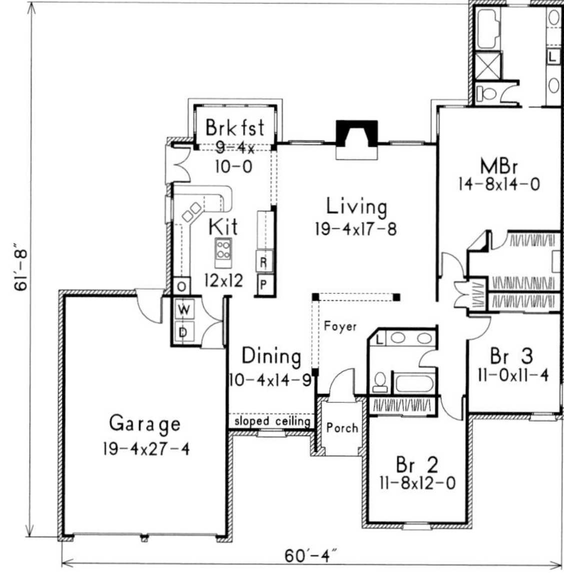

Plan #582-021D-0006

Price Code C

Special Features • *1,600 total square feet of living area* • *Energy efficient home with 2" x 6" exterior walls* • *Impressive sunken living room features a massive stone fireplace and 16' vaulted ceiling* • *Dining room is conveniently located next to kitchen and divided for privacy* • *Special amenities include sewing room, glass shelves in kitchen and master bath and a large utility area* • *Sunken master bedroom features a distinctive sitting room* • *3 bedrooms, 2 baths, 2-car side entry garage* • *Slab foundation, drawings also include crawl space and basement foundations*

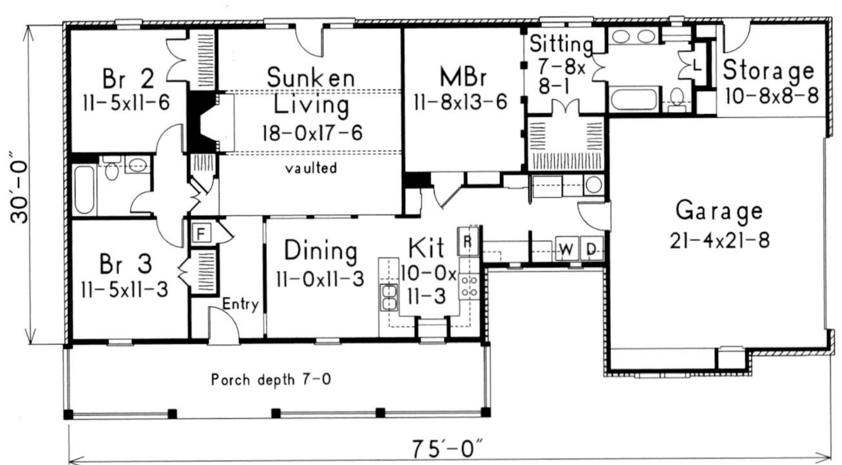

Well-Planned Ranch Home

Plan #582-052D-0038

Price Code B

Special Features • 1,787 total square feet of living area • Private master bedroom features an enormous tub, walk-in closet and close proximity to the laundry room • A Jack and Jill style bath is shared by bedrooms #2 and #3 • 12' ceiling in foyer makes a dramatic entrance • 3 bedrooms, 2 1/2 baths, 2-car garage • Basement foundation

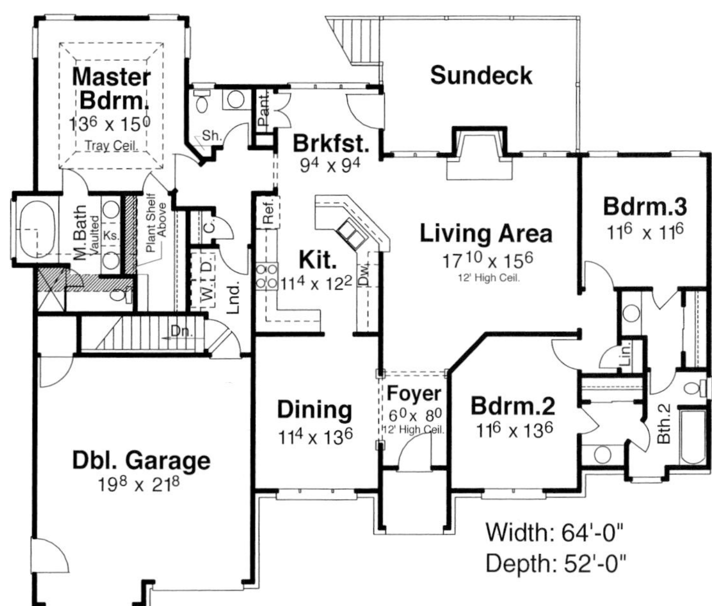

Width: 64'-0"
Depth: 52'-0"

Functional Layout For Comfortable Living

Plan #582-001D-0024

Price Code A

Special Features • *1,360 total square feet of living area • Kitchen/dining room features island workspace and plenty of dining area • Master bedroom has a large walk-in closet and private bath • Laundry room is adjacent to the kitchen for easy access • Convenient workshop in garage • Large closets in secondary bedrooms • 3 bedrooms, 2 baths, 2-car side entry garage • Basement foundation, drawings also include crawl space and slab foundations*

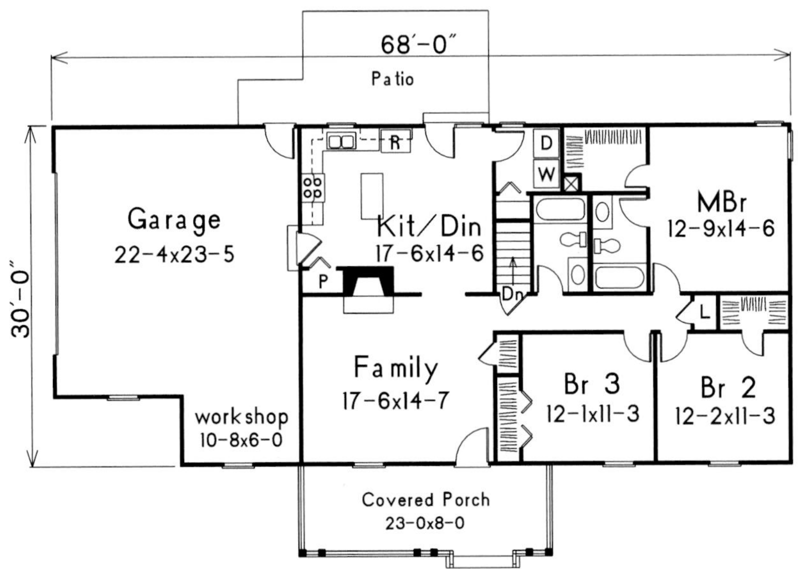

Dramatic Expanse Of Windows

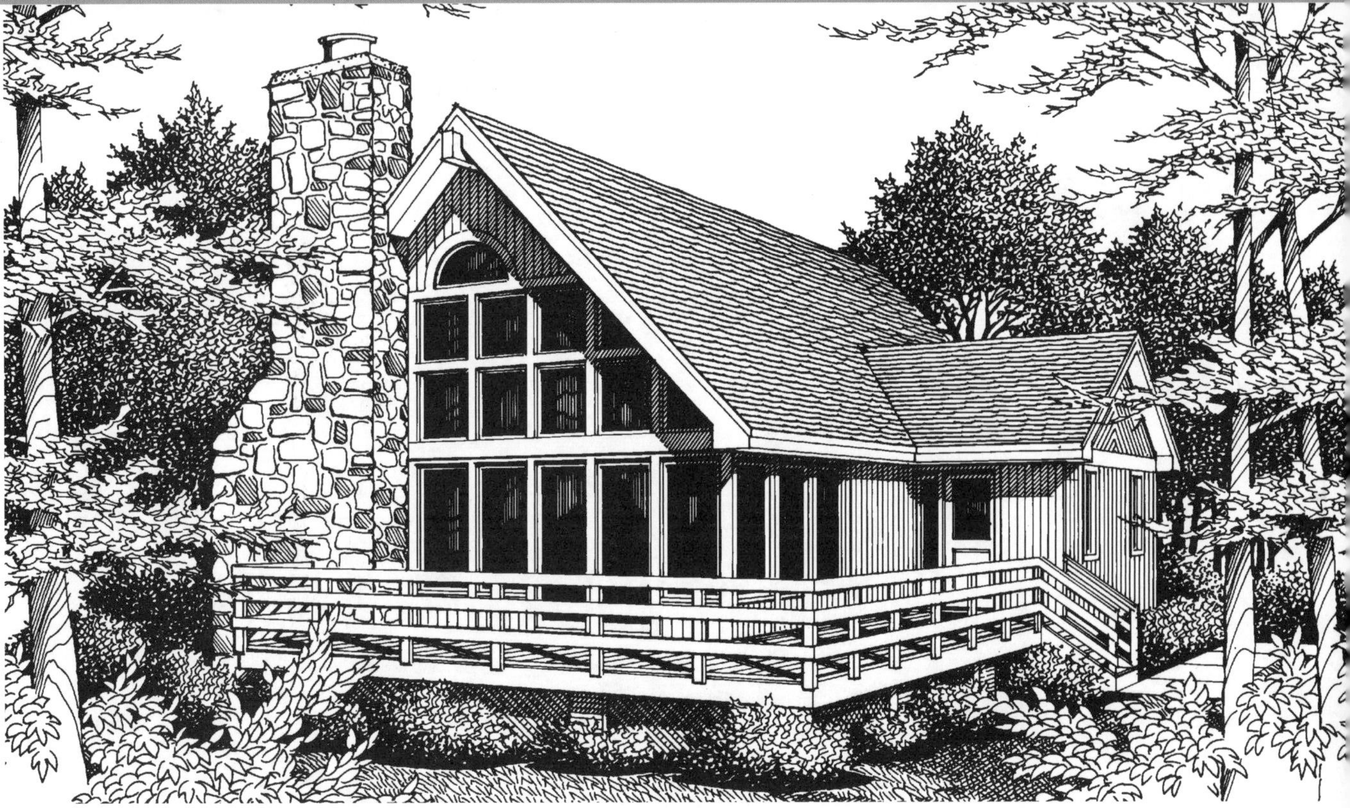

Plan #582-017D-0010

Price Code C

Special Features • 1,660 total square feet of living area • Convenient gear and equipment room • Spacious living and dining rooms look even larger with the openness of the foyer and kitchen • Large wrap-around deck is a great plus for outdoor living • Broad balcony overlooks living and dining rooms • 3 bedrooms, 3 baths • Partial basement/crawl space foundation, drawings also include slab foundation

First Floor
1,292 sq. ft.

Second Floor
368 sq. ft.

www.houseplansandmore.com

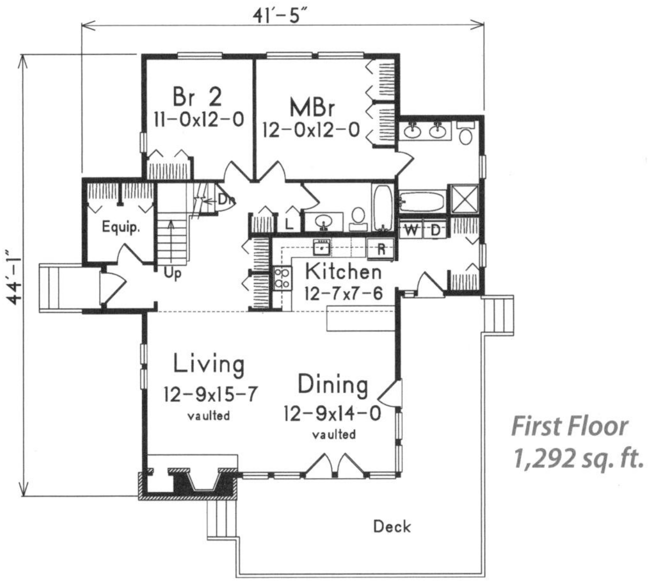

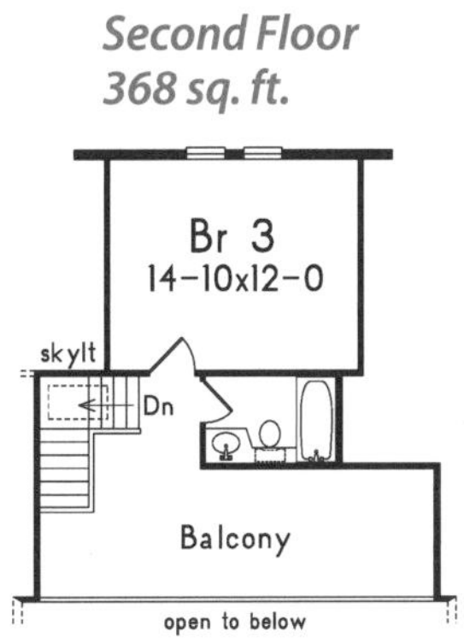

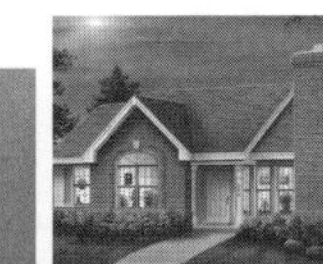

Plan #582-001D-0080

Price Code C

Special Features • 1,832 total square feet of living area • Distinctive master bedroom is enhanced by skylights, garden tub, separate shower and walk-in closet • U-shaped kitchen features a convenient pantry, laundry area and full view to breakfast room • Foyer opens into spacious living room • Large front porch creates enjoyable outdoor living • 3 bedrooms, 2 baths, 2-car detached garage • Crawl space foundation, drawings also include basement and slab foundations

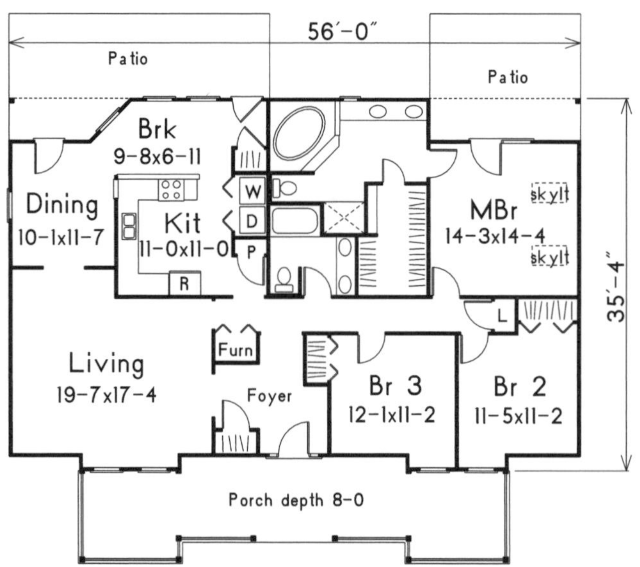

Plan #582-026D-0155 **Price Code B**

Special Features • *1,691 total square feet of living area* • *Bay windowed breakfast room allows for plenty of sunlight* • *Large inviting covered porch in the front of the home* • *Great room fireplace is surrounded by windows* • *3 bedrooms, 2 baths, 2-car garage* • *Basement foundation*

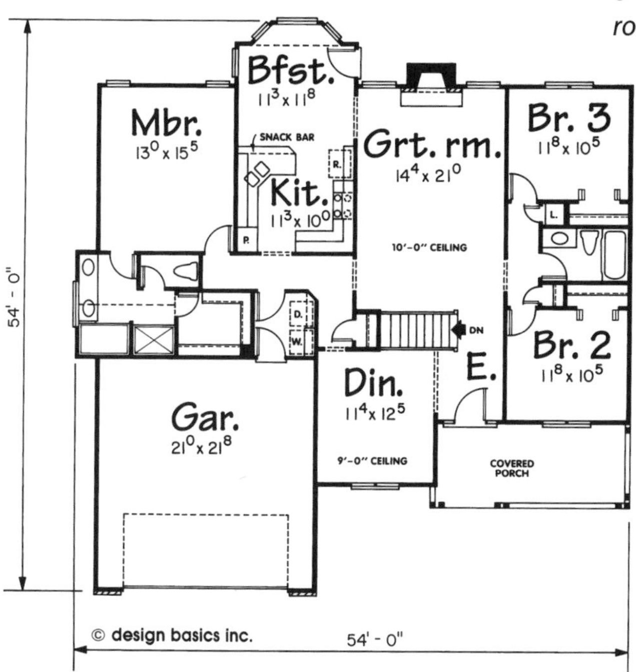

Plan #582-051D-0060

Price Code B

Special Features • 1,591 total square feet of living area • Fireplace in great room is accented by windows on both sides • Practical kitchen is splendidly designed for organization • Large screen porch for three-season entertaining • 3 bedrooms, 2 baths, 3-car garage • Basement foundation

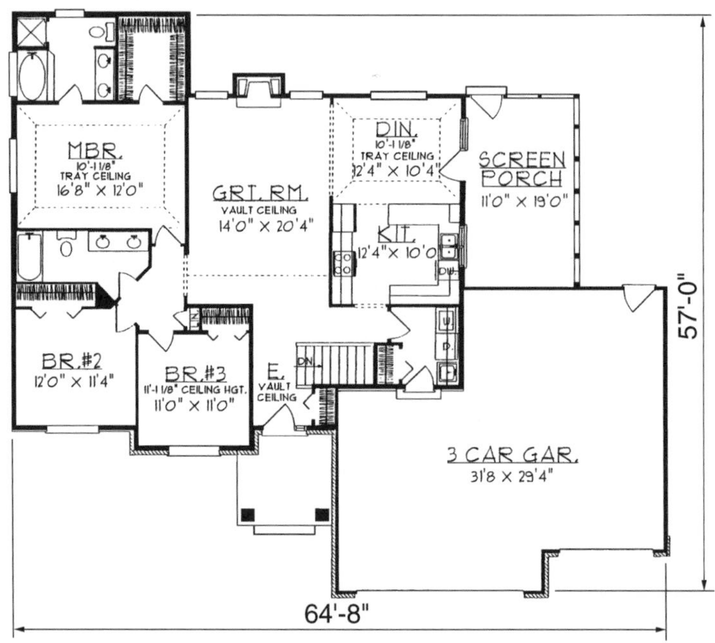

Cozy Home For Family Living

Plan #582-025D-0006

Price Code B

Special Features • 1,612 total square feet of living area • Covered porch in rear of home creates an outdoor living area • Master suite is separated from other bedrooms for privacy • Eating bar in kitchen extends into breakfast area for additional seating • 3 bedrooms, 2 baths, 2-car side entry garage • Slab foundation

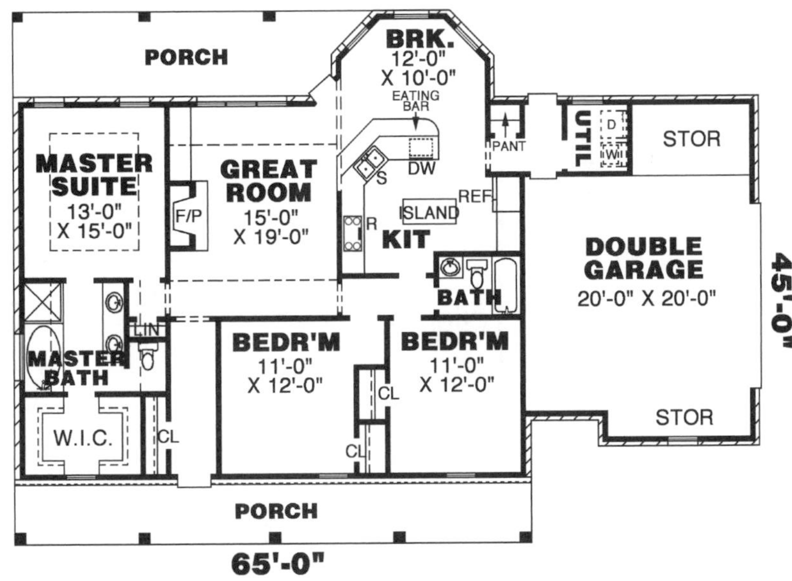

Plan #582-056D-0022

Price Code C

Special Features • 1,817 total square feet of living area • Two-story foyer is accented with a plant shelf • Living and dining rooms are separated by distinctive columns • Laundry area is located on the second floor near the bedrooms • Two-story grand room has a fireplace and second floor balcony • 3 bedrooms, 2 1/2 baths, 2-car garage • Basement or slab foundation, please specify when ordering

First Floor
974 sq. ft.

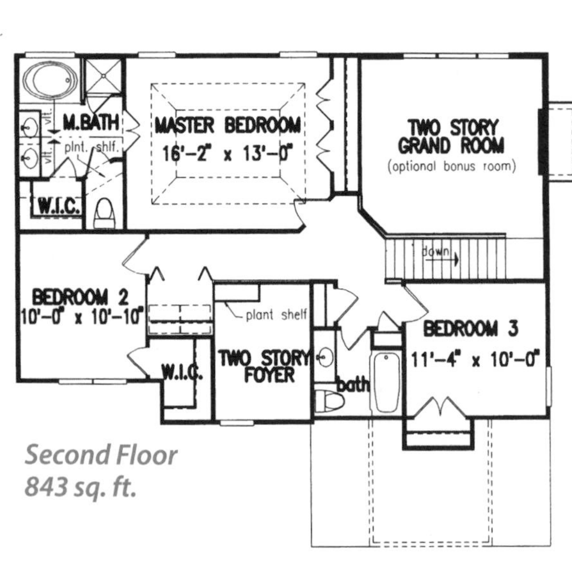

Second Floor
843 sq. ft.

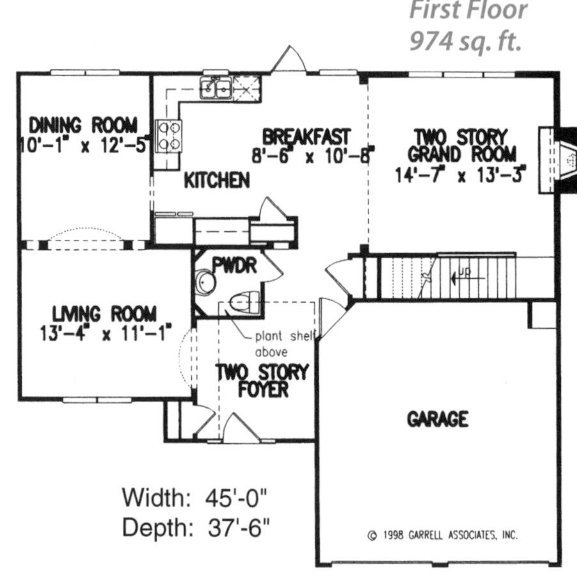

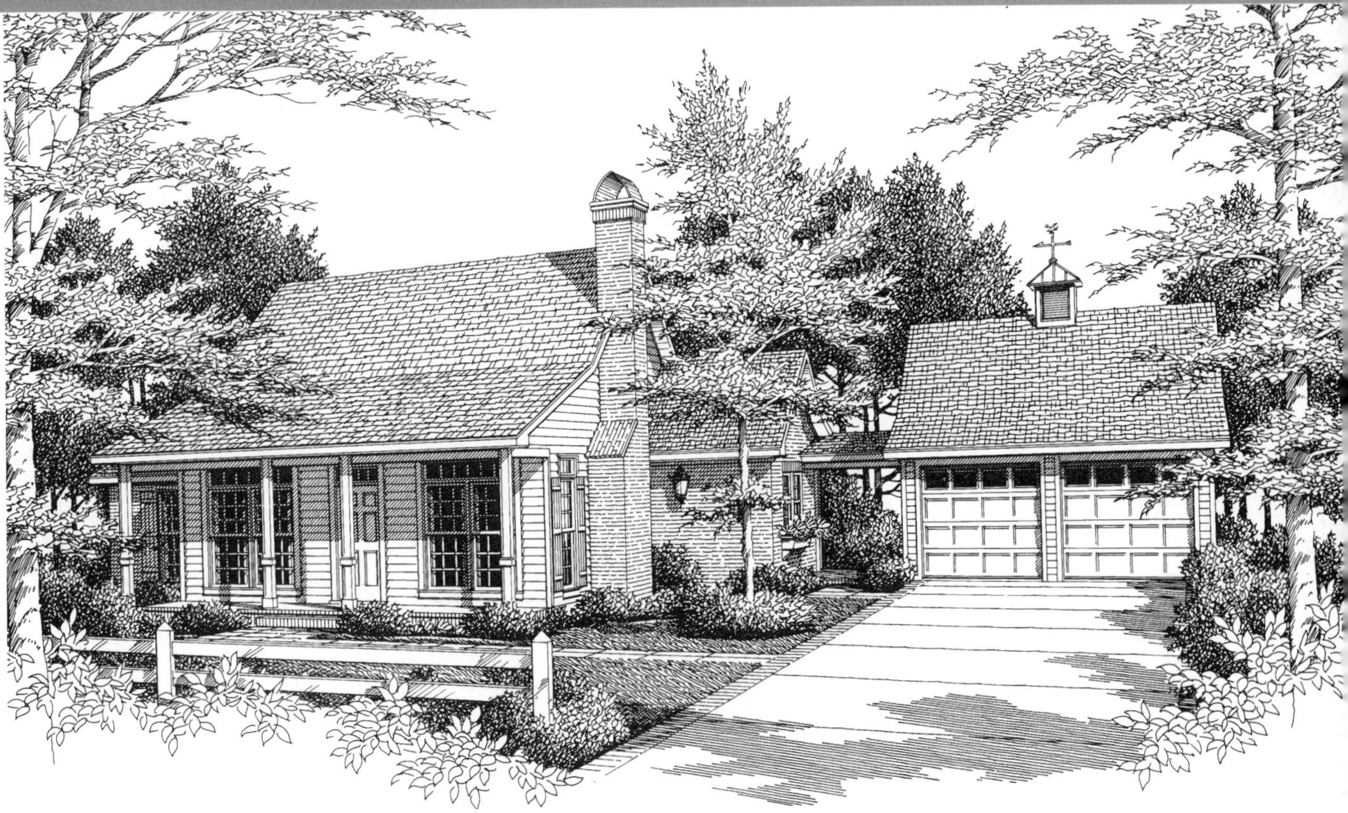

Plan #582-039D-0004

Price Code A

Special Features • 1,406 total square feet of living area • Master bedroom has a sloped ceiling • Kitchen and dining area merge becoming a gathering place • Enter the family room from the charming covered front porch to find a fireplace and lots of windows • 3 bedrooms, 2 baths, 2-car detached garage • Slab or crawl space foundation, please specify when ordering

With Garage
Width: 76'-6"
Depth: 57'-1"

Without Garage
Width: 47'-0"
Depth: 46'-0"

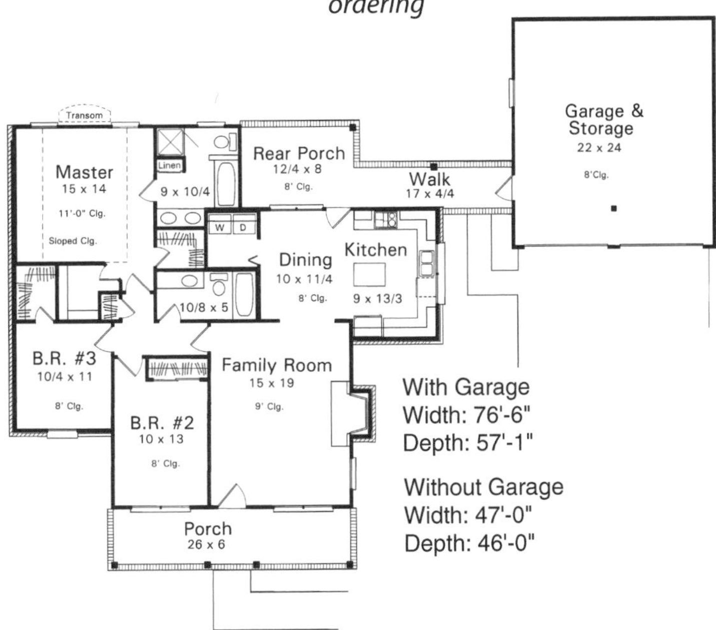

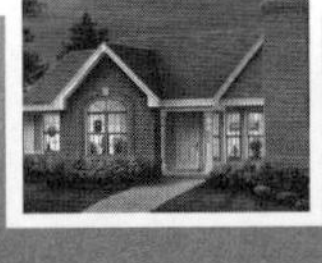

Stylish Ranch With Rustic Charm

Plan #582-001D-0053

Price Code A

Special Features • *1,344 total square feet of living area • Family/dining room has sliding glass doors to the outdoors • Master bedroom has a private bath with shower • Hall bath includes double vanity for added convenience • U-shaped kitchen features a large pantry and laundry area • 3 bedrooms, 2 baths, 2-car garage • Crawl space foundation, drawings also include basement and slab foundations*

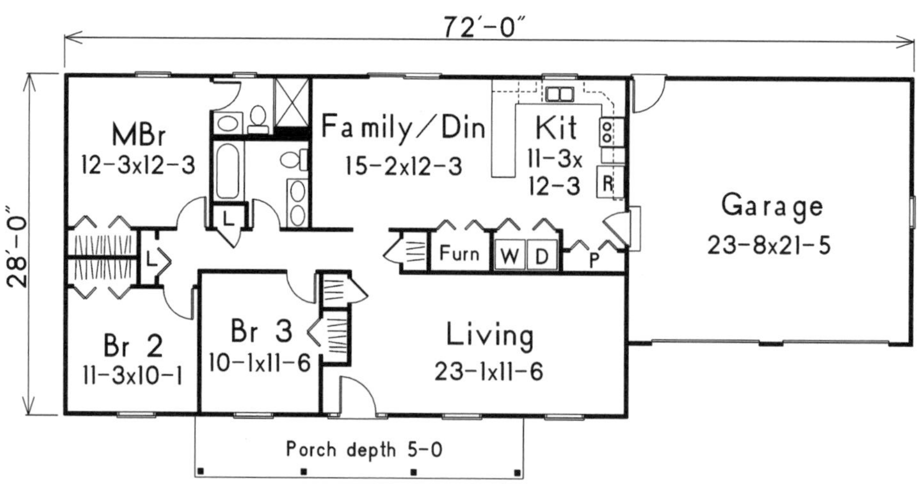

Plan #582-049D-0008

Price Code C

Special Features • 1,937 total square feet of living area • Upscale great room offers a sloped ceiling, fireplace with extended hearth and built-in shelves for an entertainment center • Gourmet kitchen includes a cooktop island counter and a quaint morning room • Master suite features a sloped ceiling, cozy sitting room, walk-in closet and a private bath with whirlpool tub • 3 bedrooms, 2 baths, 2-car side entry garage • Crawl space foundation

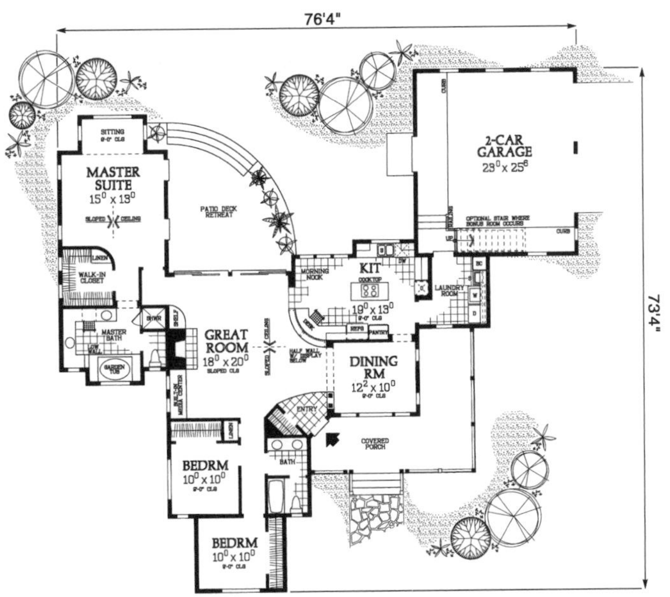

www.houseplansandmore.com

Plan #582-069D-0010

Price Code A

Special Features • 1,458 total square feet of living area • Divider wall allows for some privacy in the formal dining area while maintaining openness • Two secondary bedrooms share a full bath • Covered front and rear porches create enjoyable outdoor living spaces • 3 bedrooms, 2 baths, 2-car garage • Slab or crawl space foundation, please specify when ordering

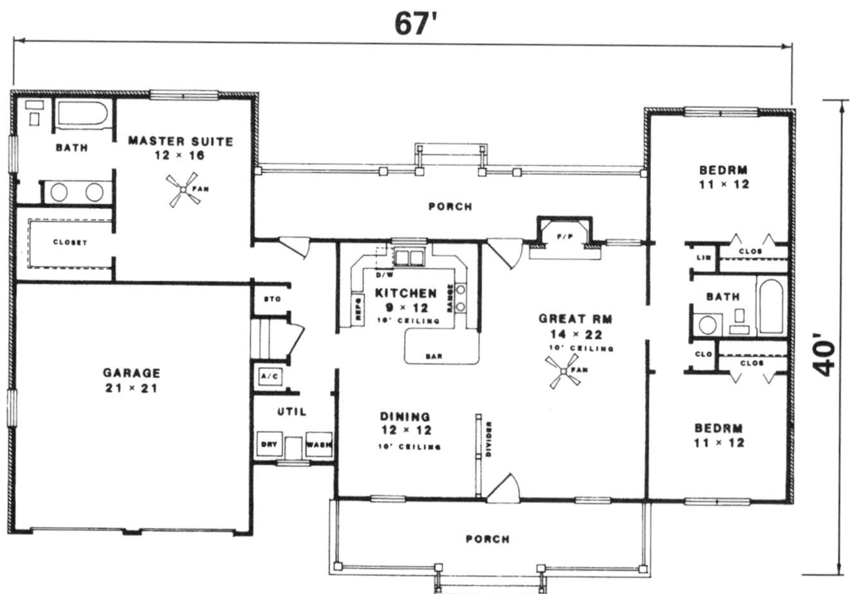

Contemporary Elegance With Efficiency

Plan #582-007D-0045

Price Code A

Special Features • 1,321 total square feet of living area • Rear entry garage and elongated brick wall add to appealing facade • Dramatic vaulted living room includes corner fireplace and towering feature windows • Breakfast room is immersed in light from two large windows and glass sliding doors • 3 bedrooms, 2 baths, 1-car rear entry garage • Basement foundation

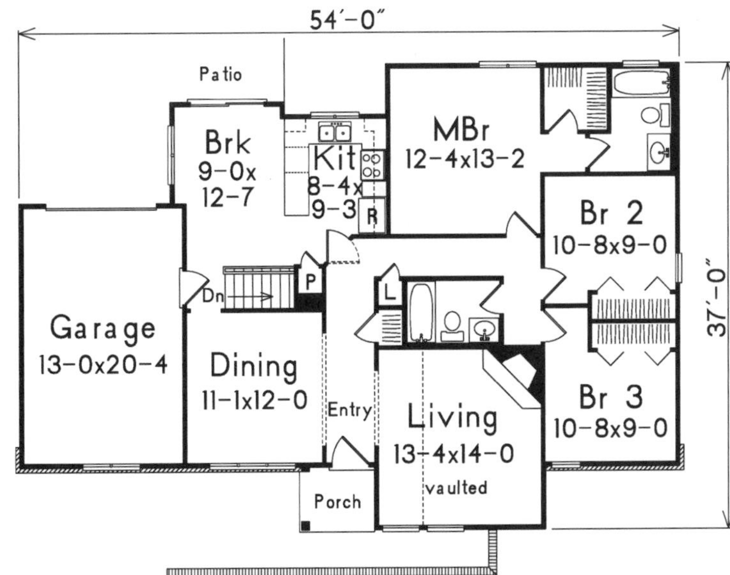

Plan #582-019D-0005

Price Code B

Special Features • *1,575 total square feet of living area* • *Decorative columns separate dining room from living room and foyer* • *Kitchen has plenty of workspace* • *Spacious walk-in closet in master bedroom* • *3 bedrooms, 2 baths, 2-car garage* • *Crawl space foundation, drawings also include slab foundation*

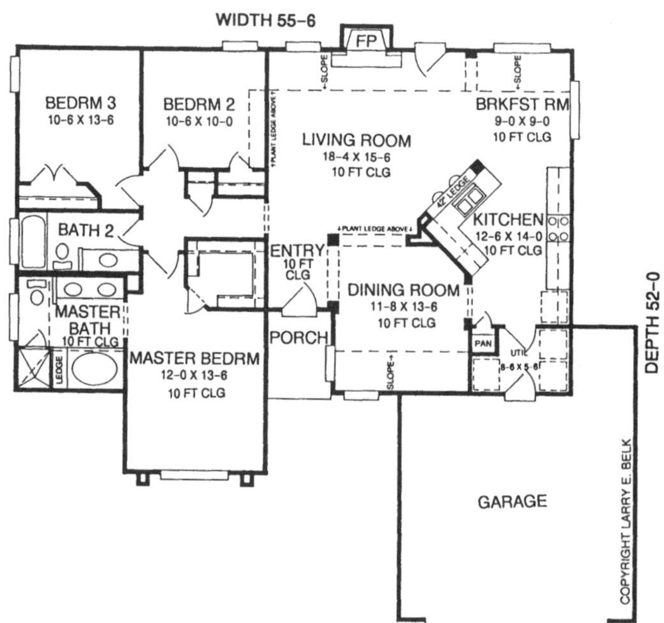

Circle-Top Windows Grace The Facade Of This Home

Plan #582-021D-0012

Price Code C

Special Features •1,672 total square feet of living area • Vaulted master bedroom features a walk-in closet and adjoining bath with separate tub and shower • Energy efficient home with 2" x 6" exterior walls • Covered front and rear porches • 12' ceilings in living room, kitchen and bedroom #2 • Kitchen is complete with pantry, angled bar and adjacent eating area • 3 bedrooms, 2 baths, 2-car side entry garage • Crawl space foundation, drawings also include basement and slab foundations

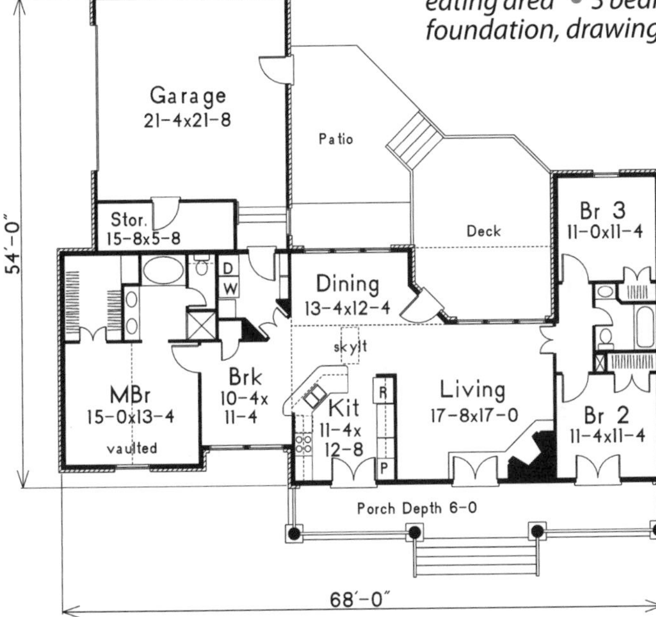

Exciting Split-Foyer Entrance

Plan #582-053D-0040

Price Code A

Special Features • *1,407 total square feet of living area* • *Large living room has a fireplace and access to the rear deck* • *Kitchen and dining area combine to create an open gathering area* • *Convenient laundry room and broom closet* • *Master bedroom includes a private bath with large vanity and separate tub and shower* • *3 bedrooms, 2 baths, 2-car drive under garage* • *Basement foundation*

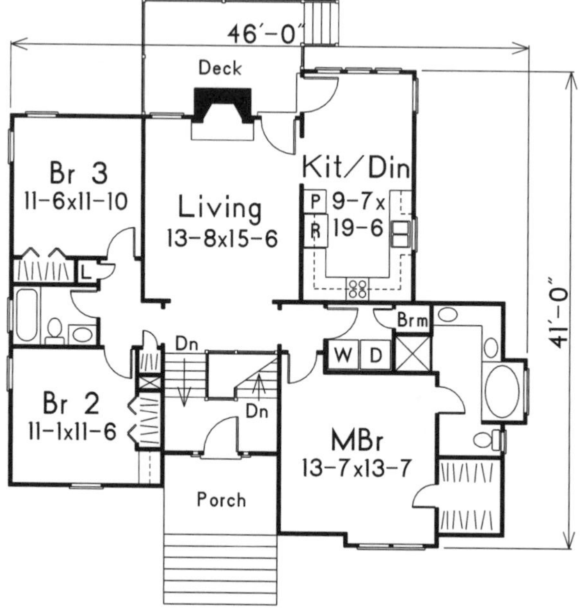

Bedrooms Are Separate From Rest Of Home

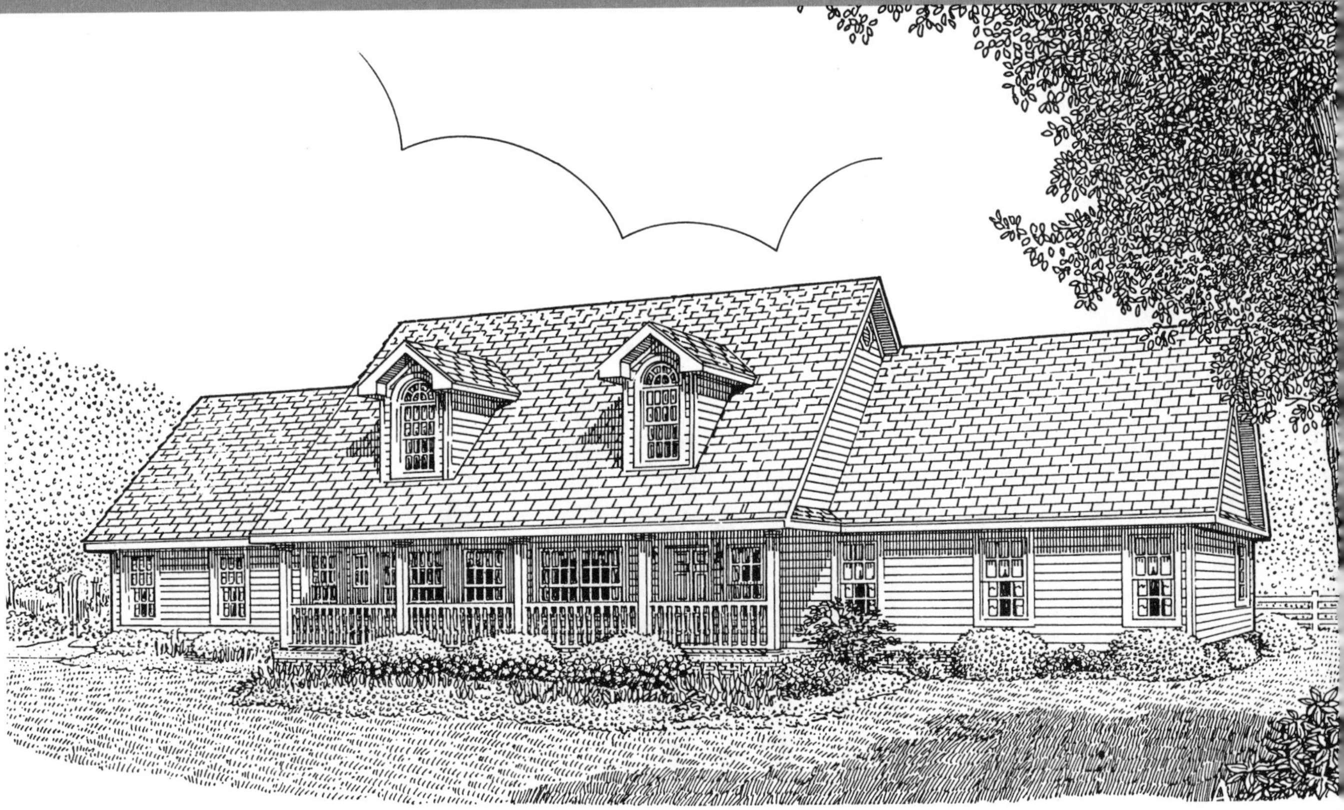

Plan #582-068D-0010

Price Code C

Special Features • 1,849 total square feet of living area • Enormous laundry/mud room has many extras including storage area and half bath • Lavish master bath has corner jacuzzi tub, double sinks and a walk-in closet • Secondary bedrooms include walk-in closets • Kitchen has wrap-around eating counter and is positioned between formal dining area and breakfast room for convenience • 3 bedrooms, 2 1/2 baths, 2-car side entry garage • Slab foundation, drawings also include crawl space foundation

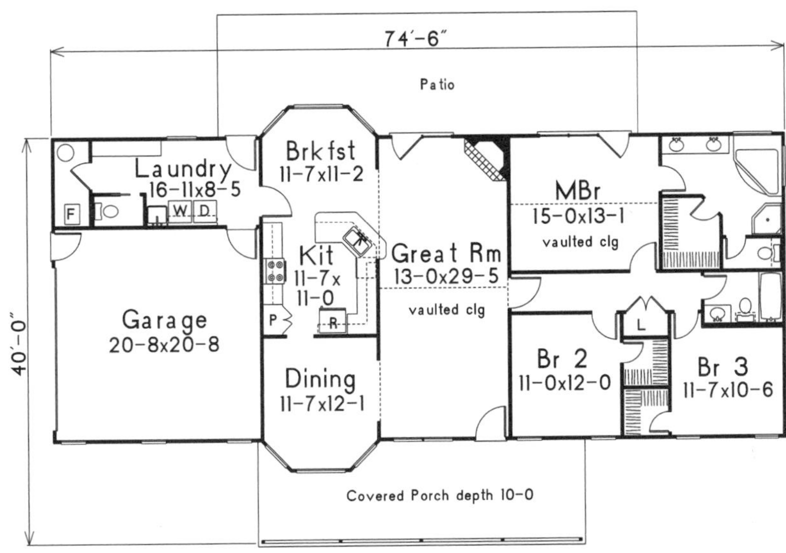

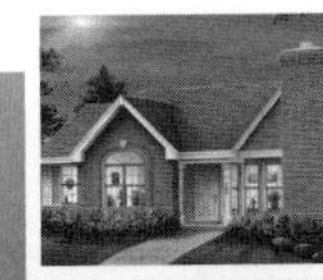

Cottage Style Adds Charm

Plan #582-043D-0008

Price Code A

Special Features • 1,496 total square feet of living area • Large utility room with sink and extra counterspace • Covered patio off breakfast nook extends dining to the outdoors • Eating counter in kitchen overlooks vaulted family room • 3 bedrooms, 2 baths, 2-car side entry garage • Crawl space foundation

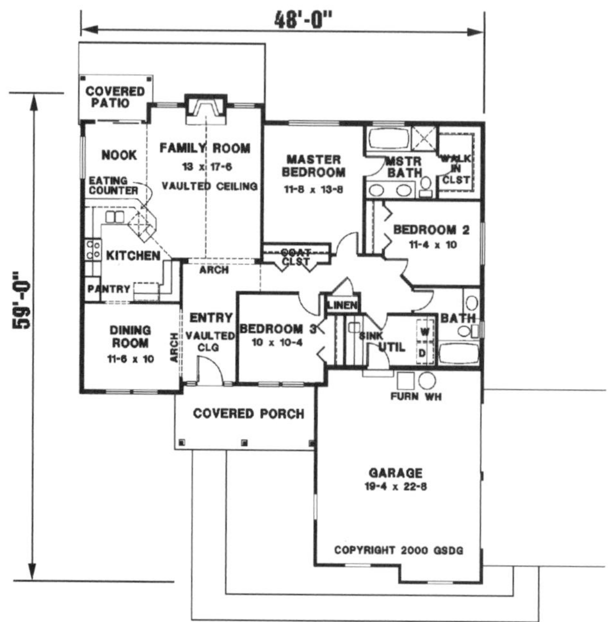

Exterior Accents Add Charm To This Compact Cottage

Plan #582-022D-0004

Price Code A

Special Features • 1,359 total square feet of living area • Covered porch, stone chimney and abundant windows lend an outdoor appeal • Spacious and bright kitchen has pass-through to formal dining room • Large walk-in closets in all bedrooms • Extensive deck expands dining and entertaining areas • 3 bedrooms, 2 1/2 baths, 2-car garage • Basement foundation

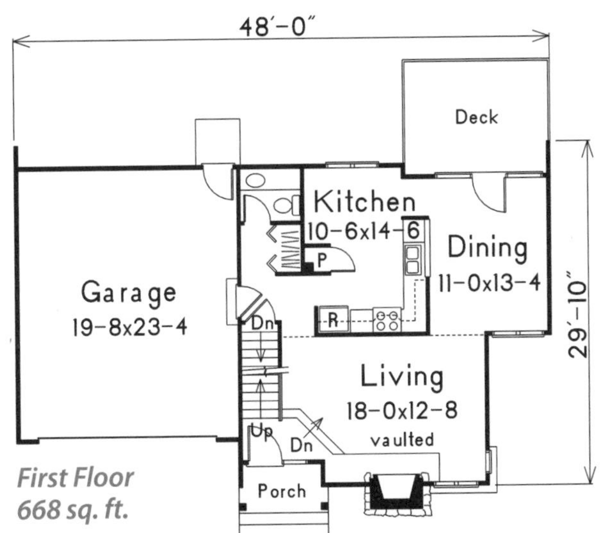

First Floor
668 sq. ft.

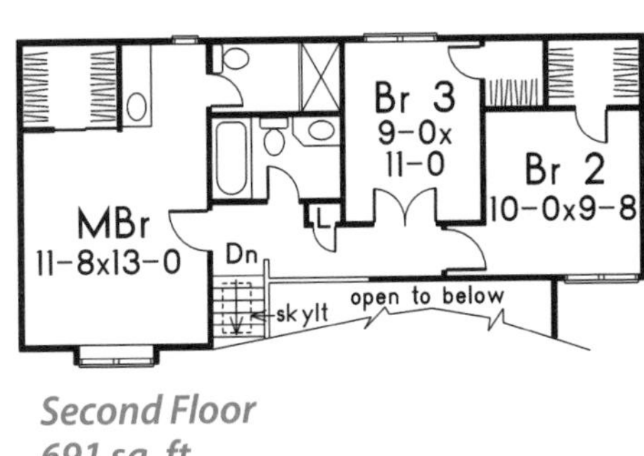

Second Floor
691 sq. ft.

Country Flair In A Flexible Ranch

Plan #582-051D-0053

Price Code A

Special Features • 1,461 total square feet of living area • Casual dining room • Cathedral ceilings in the great room and dining area give the home a spacious feel • Relaxing master bedroom boasts an expansive bath and large walk-in closet • 3 bedrooms, 2 baths, 2-car garage • Basement foundation

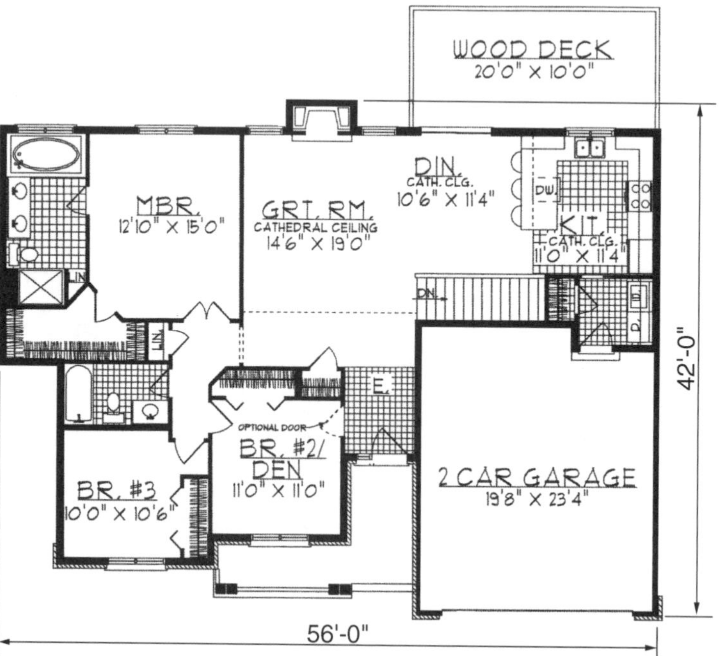

L-Shaped Ranch With Many Amenities

Plan #582-001D-0071 **Price Code A**

Special Features • *1,440 total square feet of living area* • *Spaciousness is created with open living and dining areas* • *Entry foyer features a coat closet and half wall leading into the living area* • *Walk-in pantry adds convenience to the U-shaped kitchen* • *Spacious utility room is adjacent to the garage* • *3 bedrooms, 2 baths, 2-car side entry garage* • *Crawl space foundation, drawings also include basement and slab foundations*

48'-0"
56'-0"
Dining 11-9x15-10
Kit 11-1x 12-2
Br 3 10-5x9-9
Br 2 13-3x9-9
P
Furn
L
L
Living 16-9x13-6
MBr 13-3x14-7
Foyer
W
D
R
Garage 23-5x25-8

Plan #582-035D-0005

Price Code A

Special Features • 1,281 total square feet of living area • Spacious master suite has a tray ceiling, double closets and a private bath • Vaulted family room has lots of sunlight from multiple windows and a fireplace • Plant shelf above kitchen and dining room is a nice decorative touch • 3 bedrooms, 2 baths, 2-car drive under garage • Walk-out basement foundation

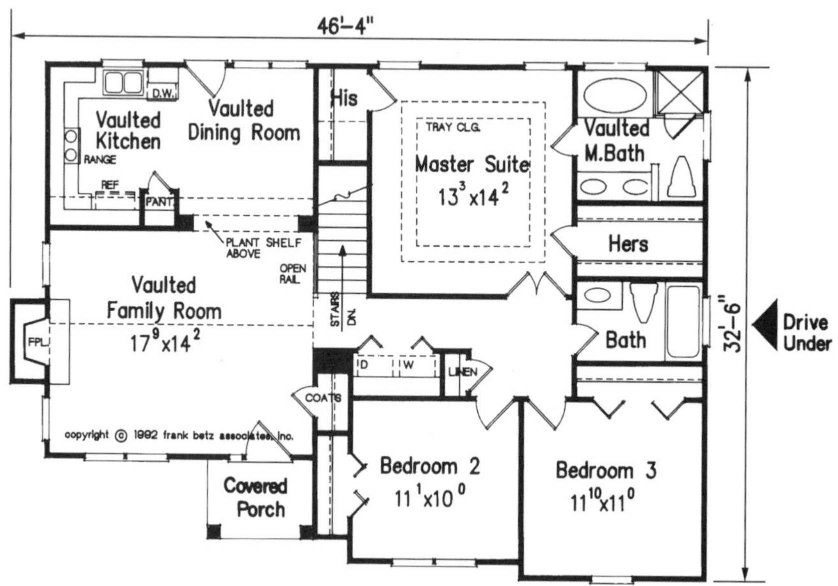

Plan #582-058D-0038

Price Code B

Special Features • 1,680 total square feet of living area • Compact and efficient layout in an affordable package • Second floor has three bedrooms all with oversized closets • All bedrooms on second floor for privacy • 3 bedrooms, 2 1/2 baths, 2-car garage • Basement foundation

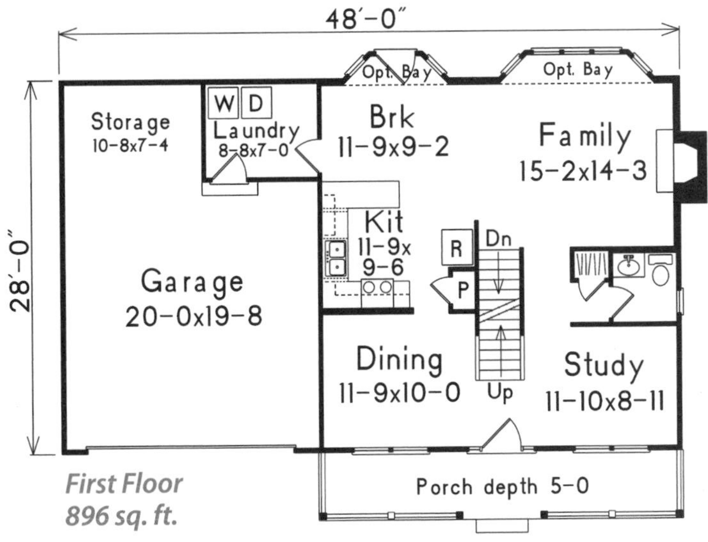

First Floor
896 sq. ft.

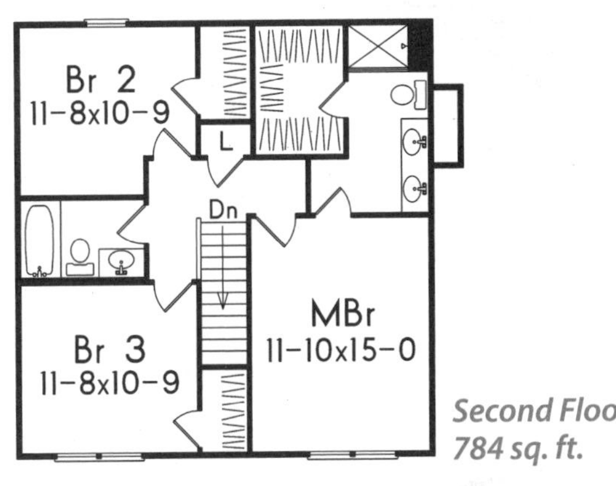

Second Floor
784 sq. ft.

Old-Fashioned Comfort And Privacy

Plan #582-037D-0006

Price Code C

Special Features • 1,772 total square feet of living area • Extended porches in front and rear provide a charming touch • Large bay windows lend distinction to dining room and bedroom #3 • Efficient U-shaped kitchen • Master bedroom includes two walk-in closets • Full corner fireplace in family room • 3 bedrooms, 2 baths, 2-car detached garage • Slab foundation, drawings also include crawl space foundation

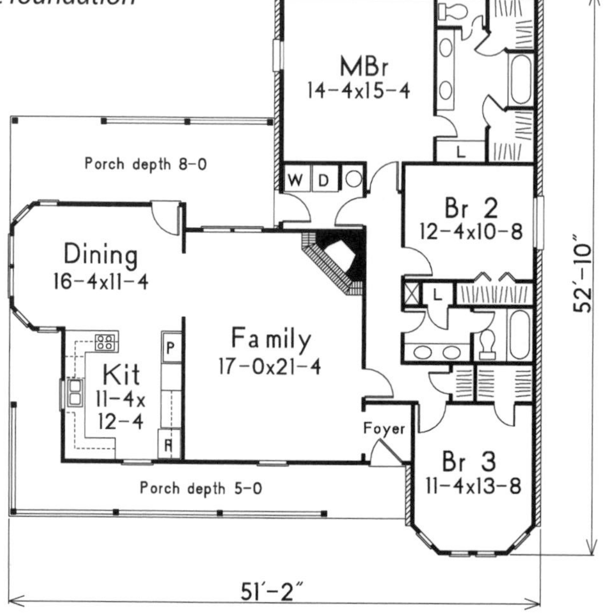

Handsome Columns And Trim Details

Plan #582-026D-0162

Price Code B

Special Features • 1,575 total square feet of living area • A half bath is tucked away in the laundry area for convenience • Second floor hall has a handy desk • Bonus area on the second floor has an additional 353 square feet of living area • 3 bedrooms, 2 1/2 baths, 2-car garage • Basement foundation

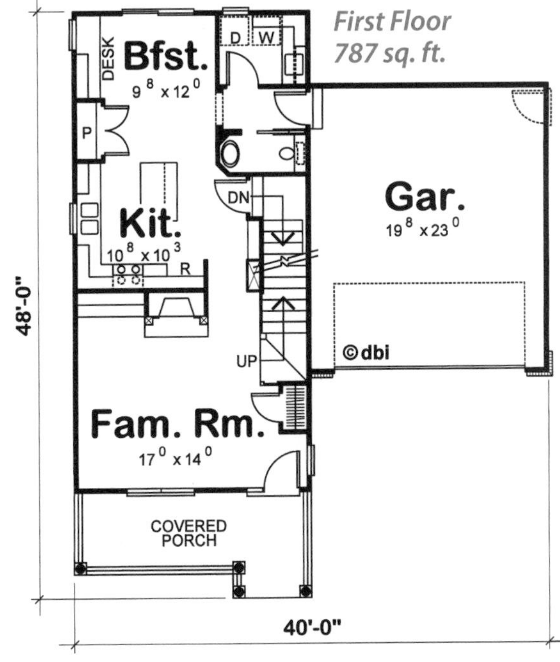

First Floor
787 sq. ft.

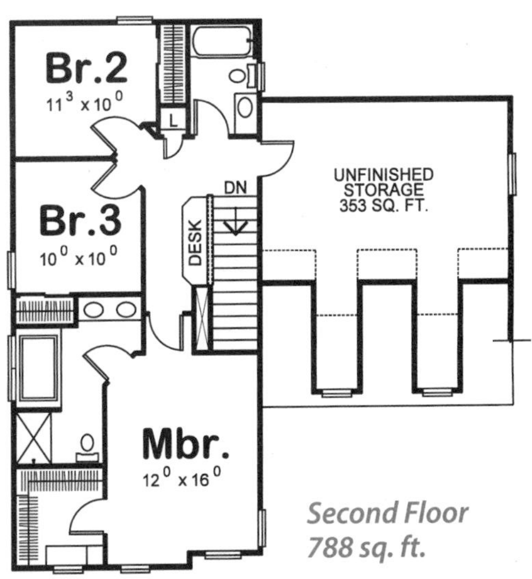

Second Floor
788 sq. ft.

Affordable, Upscale And Amenity Full

Plan #582-006D-0001

Price Code B

Special Features • 1,643 total square feet of living area • Family room has a vaulted ceiling, open staircase and arched windows allowing for plenty of light • Kitchen captures full use of space, with a pantry, storage, ample counterspace and work island • Large closets and storage areas throughout • Roomy master bath has a skylight for natural lighting plus a separate tub and shower • Rear of house provides ideal location for future screened-in porch • 3 bedrooms, 2 baths, 2-car side entry garage • Basement foundation, drawings also include slab and crawl space foundations

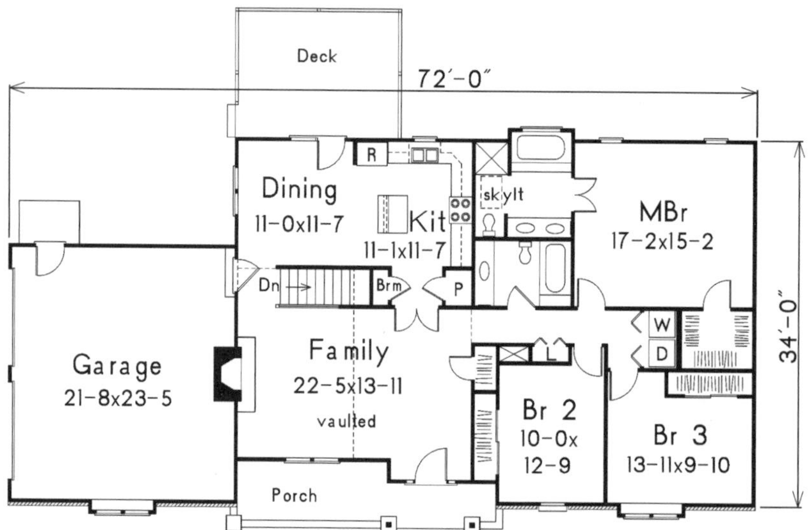

Plan #582-031D-0005

Price Code B

Special Features • 1,735 total square feet of living area • Luxurious master bath has a spa tub, shower, double vanity and large walk-in closet • Peninsula in the kitchen has a sink and dishwasher • Massive master bedroom has a step-up ceiling and private location • 3 bedrooms, 2 baths, 2-car garage • Slab foundation

Family Living Focuses Around Central Fireplace

Plan #582-053D-0037

Price Code A

Special Features • 1,408 total square feet of living area • Handsome see-through fireplace offers a gathering point for the kitchen, family and breakfast rooms • Vaulted ceiling and large bay window in the master bedroom add charm to this room • A dramatic angular wall and large windows add brightness to the kitchen and breakfast room • Kitchen, breakfast and family rooms have vaulted ceilings, adding to this central living area • 3 bedrooms, 2 baths, 2-car garage • Crawl space foundation, drawings also include slab foundation

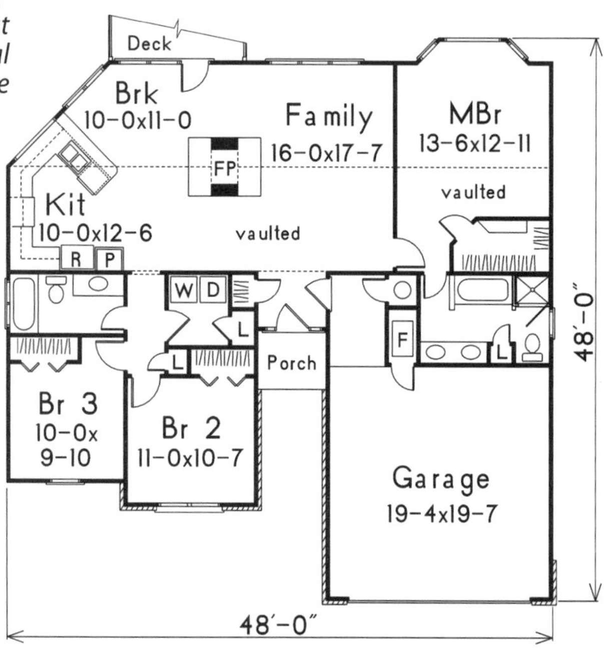

Plan #582-008D-0126

Price Code B

Special Features • *1,605 total square feet of living area* • *Detailed entry is highlighted with a stone floor and double guest closets* • *Kitchen is well-designed and includes an open view to the family room* • *The third bedroom can be easily utilized as a den with optional bi-fold doors off the entry* • *3 bedrooms, 2 baths, 2-car garage* • *Basement foundation, drawings also include crawl space and slab foundations*

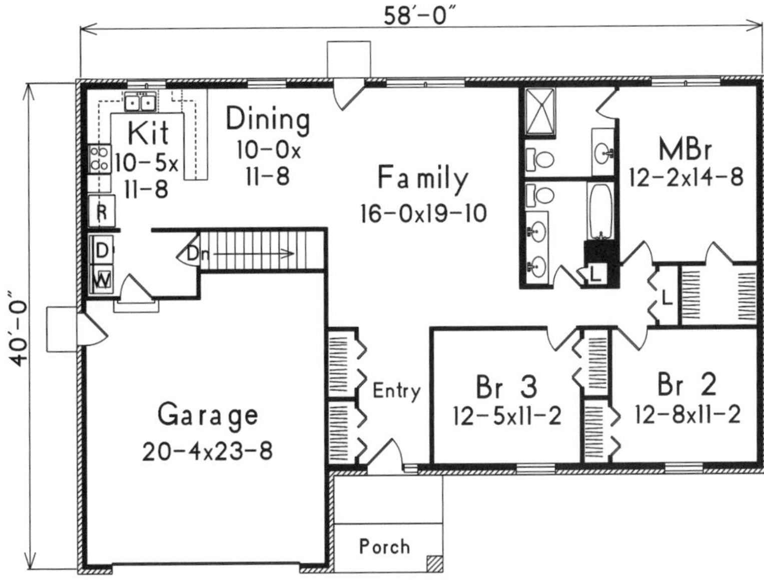

Well-Sculptured Design, Inside And Out

Plan #582-040D-0006

Price Code B

Special Features • 1,759 total square feet of living area • The striking entry is created by a unique stair layout, an open high ceiling and a fireplace • Bonus area over garage, which is included in the square footage, could easily convert to a fourth bedroom or activity center • Second floor bedrooms share a private dressing area and bath • 3 bedrooms, 2 1/2 baths, 2-car garage • Basement foundation

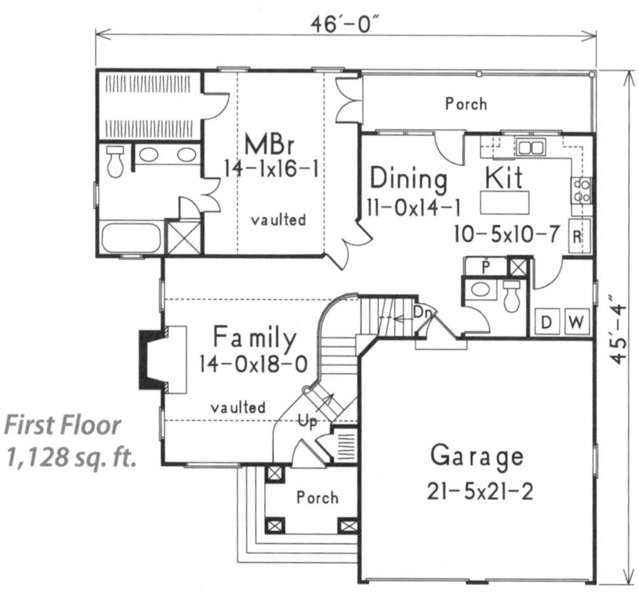

First Floor
1,128 sq. ft.

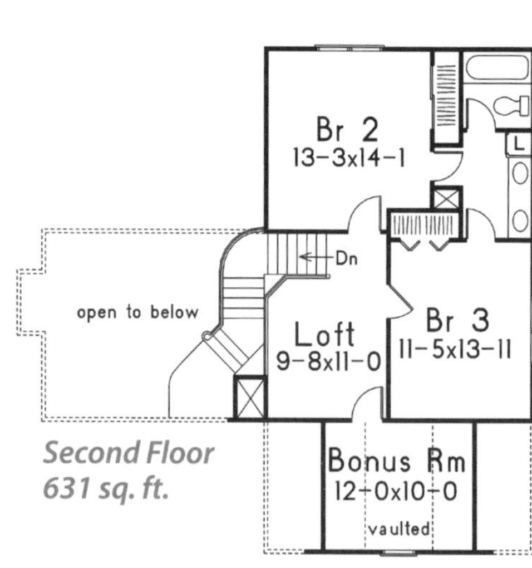

Second Floor
631 sq. ft.

Modest Ranch Style

Plan #582-060D-0015

Price Code AA

Special Features • 1,192 total square feet of living area • Kitchen eating bar overlooks well-designed great room • Private bath in master suite • Extra storage space in garage • 3 bedrooms, 2 baths, 2-car garage • Slab or crawl space foundation, please specify when ordering

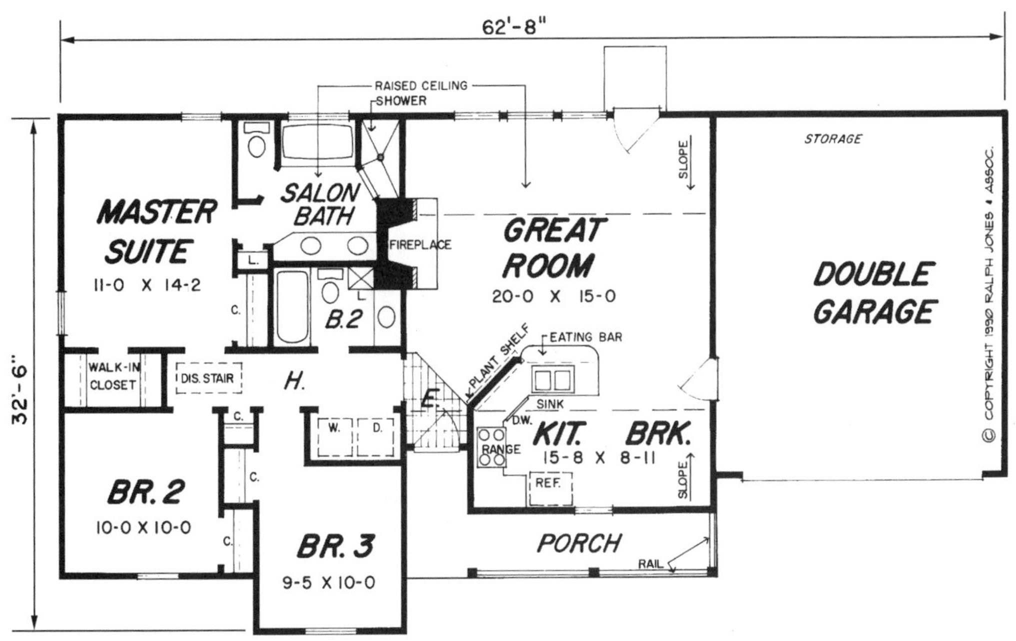

Plan #582-020D-0001

Price Code A

Special Features • 1,375 total square feet of living area • Master bedroom has a private bath and walk-in closet • Kitchen and dining room are located conveniently near the utility and living rooms • Cathedral ceiling in living room adds spaciousness • 3 bedrooms, 2 baths, 2-car carport • Slab foundation

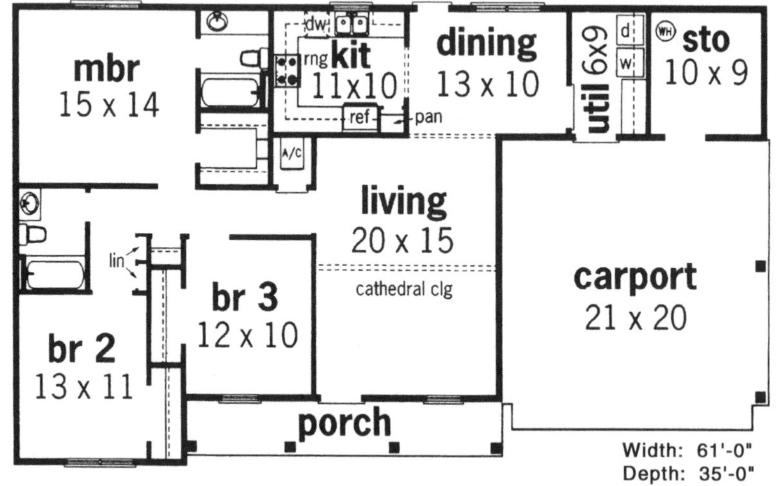

Luxurious Master Bath

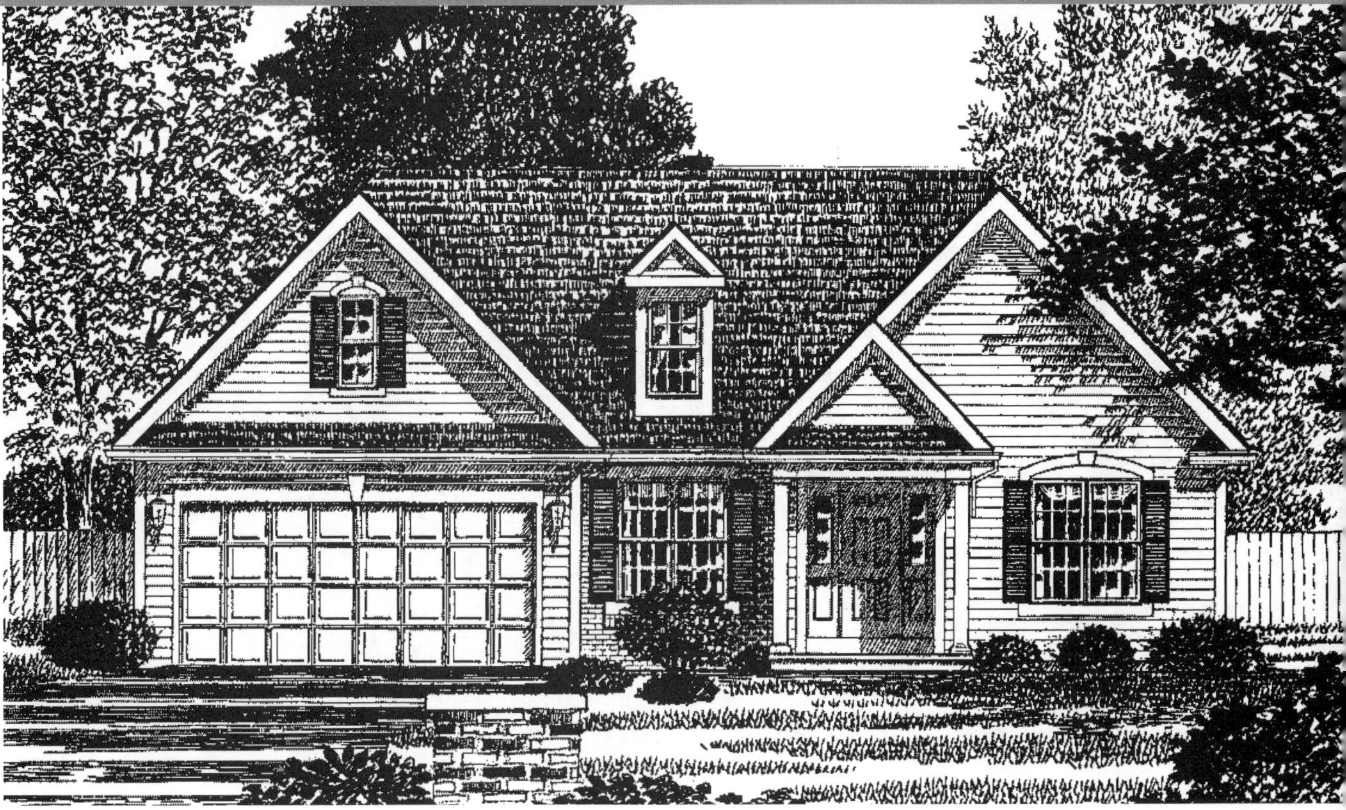

Plan #582-034D-0002

Price Code A

Special Features • 1,456 total square feet of living area • Open floor plan adds spaciousness to this design • Bayed dining area creates a cheerful setting • Corner fireplace in great room is a terrific focal point • 3 bedrooms, 2 baths, 2-car garage • Basement foundation

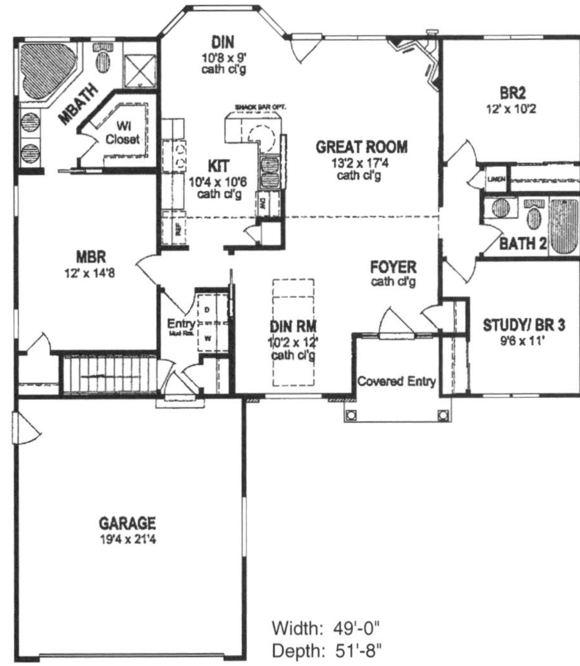

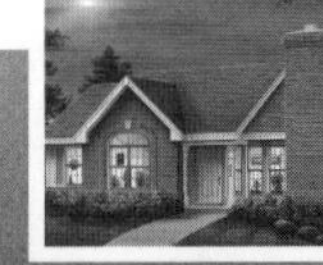

Central Fireplace Warms Living Area

Plan #582-001D-0029

Price Code A

Special Features • 1,260 total square feet of living area • Spacious kitchen and dining area feature a large pantry, storage area, easy access to garage and laundry room • Pleasant covered front porch adds a practical touch • Master bedroom with a private bath adjoins two other bedrooms, all with plenty of closet space • 3 bedrooms, 2 baths, 2-car garage • Basement foundation, drawings also include crawl space and slab foundations

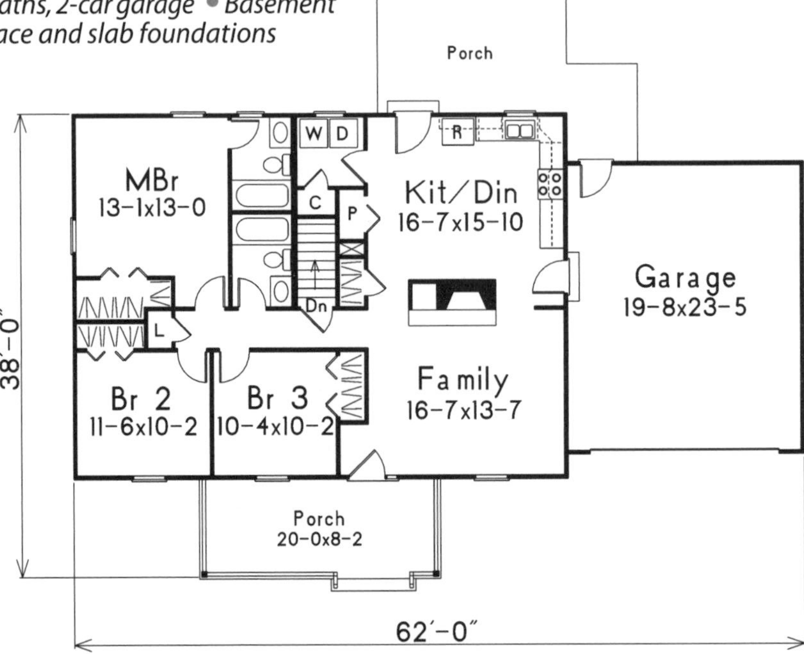

Country Home With Plenty Of Style

Plan #582-040D-0033

Price Code C

Special Features *• 1,829 total square feet of living area • Entry foyer with coat closet opens to a large family room with fireplace • Two second floor bedrooms share a full bath • Optional bedroom #4 on the second floor has an additional 145 square feet of living area • Cozy porch provides convenient side entrance into home • 3 bedrooms, 2 1/2 baths, 2-car side entry garage • Partial basement/crawl space foundation*

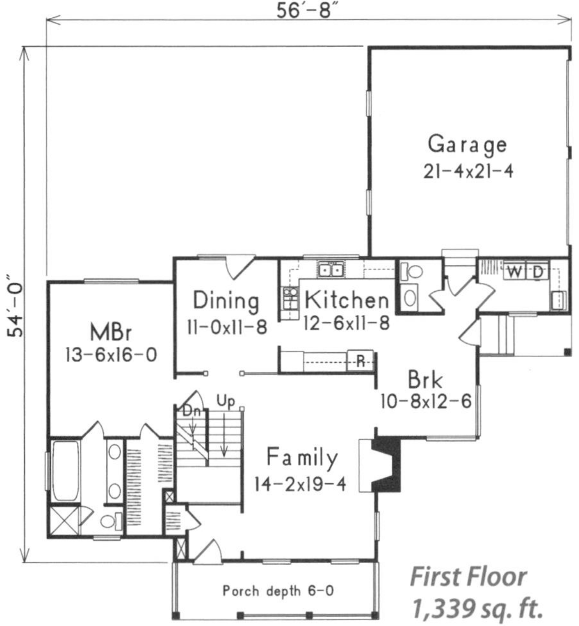

First Floor 1,339 sq. ft.

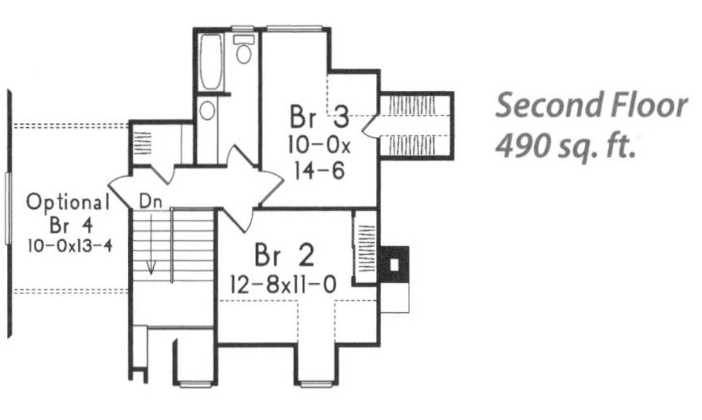

Second Floor 490 sq. ft.

Graciously Designed Ranch

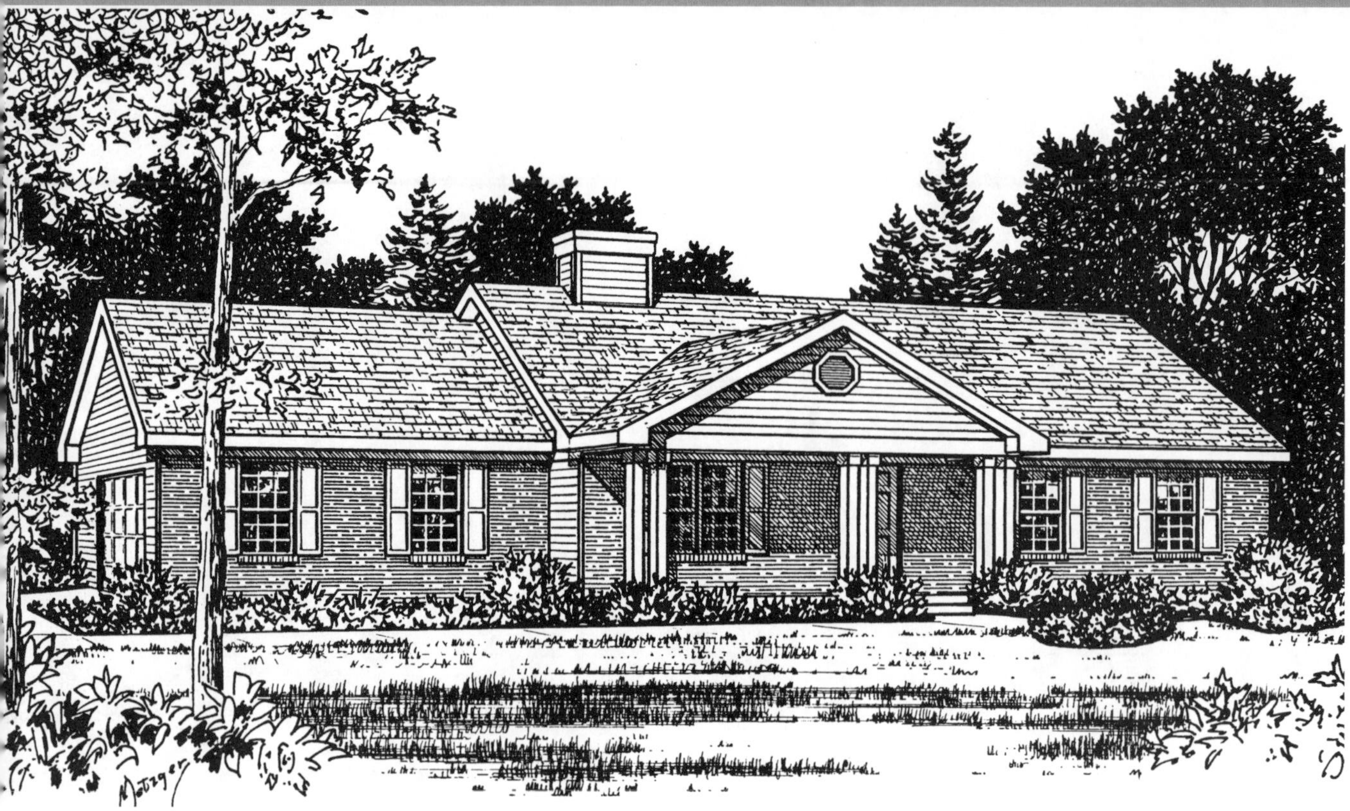

Plan #582-058D-0021

Price Code A

Special Features • *1,477 total square feet of living area* • *Oversized porch provides protection from the elements* • *Innovative kitchen employs step-saving design* • *Kitchen has snack bar which opens to the breakfast room with bay window* • *3 bedrooms, 2 baths, 2-car side entry garage with storage area* • *Basement foundation*

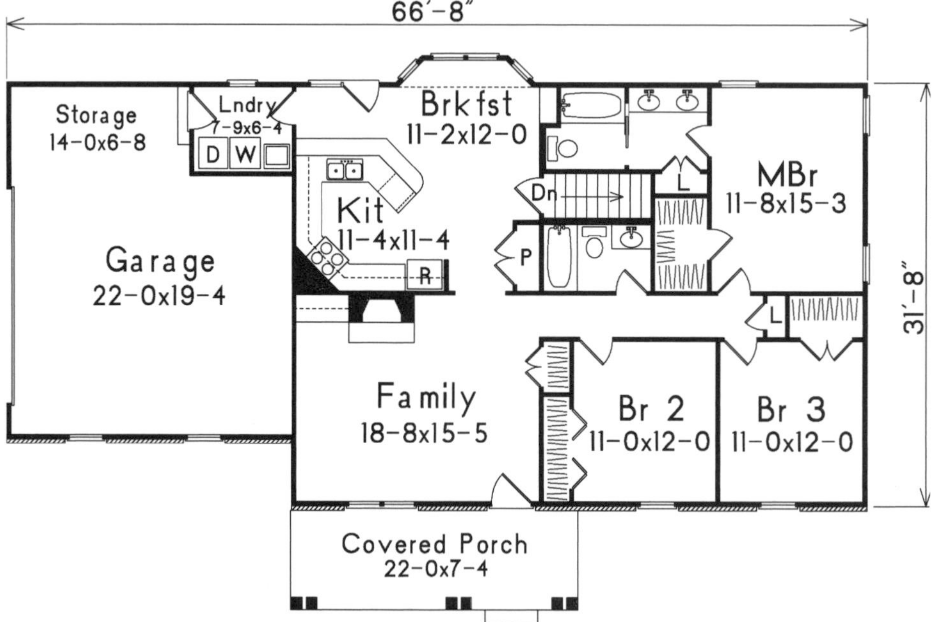

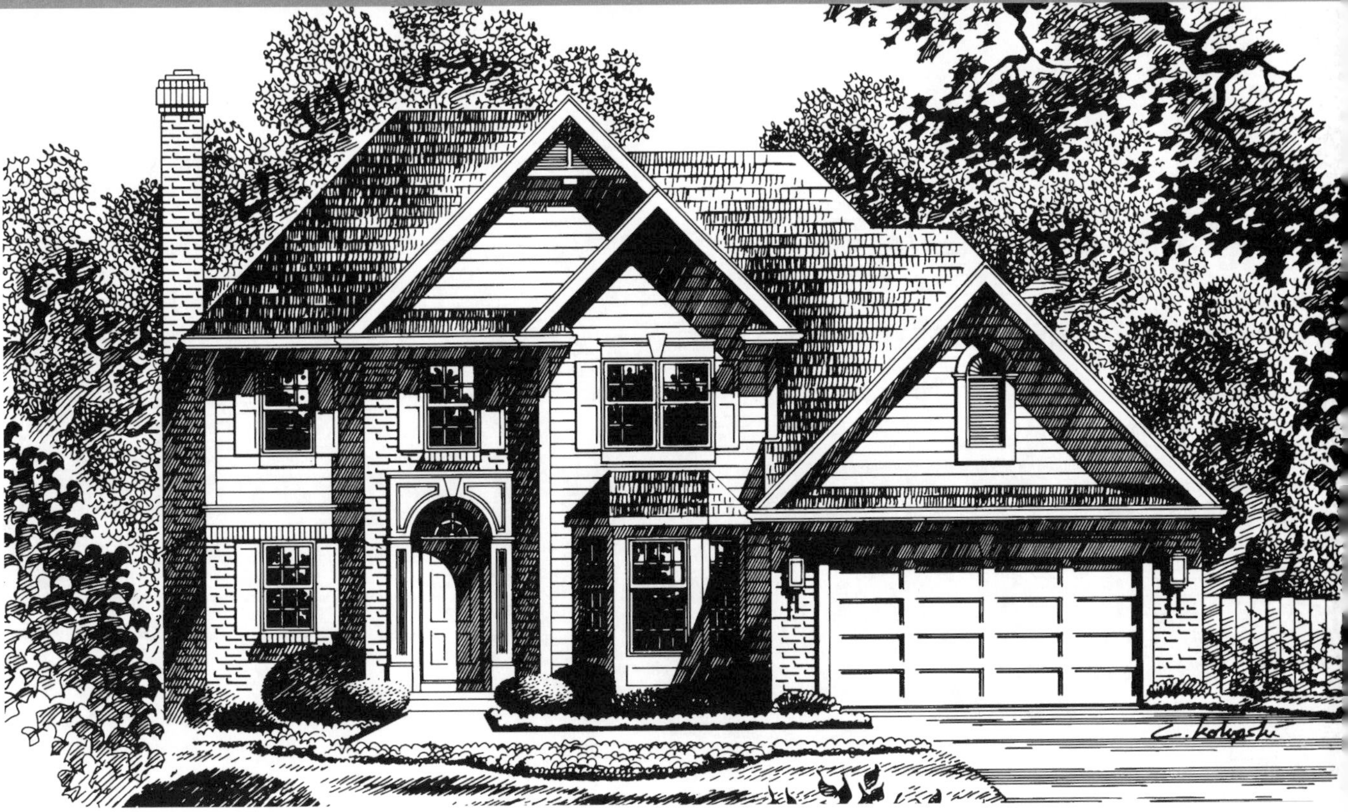

Plan #582-034D-0016

Price Code C

Special Features • 1,873 total square feet of living area • Formal dining area in the front of the house is conveniently located near kitchen • Large great room has fireplace and lots of windows • Master bedroom has double-door entry with a private bath • 3 bedrooms, 2 1/2 baths, 2-car garage • Basement foundation

Second Floor
942 sq. ft.

First Floor
931 sq. ft.

Width: 50-4"
Depth: 38'-0"

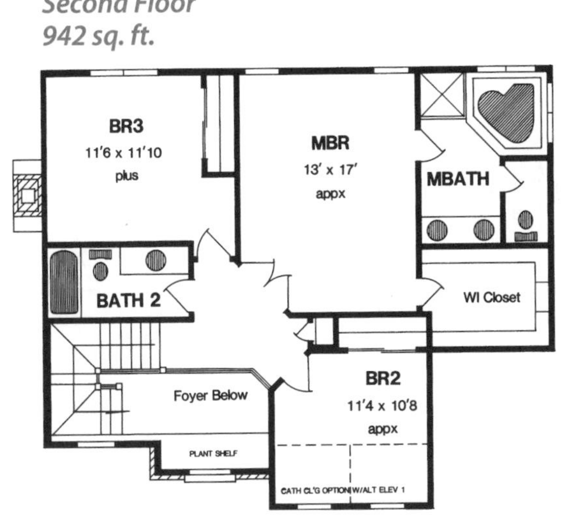

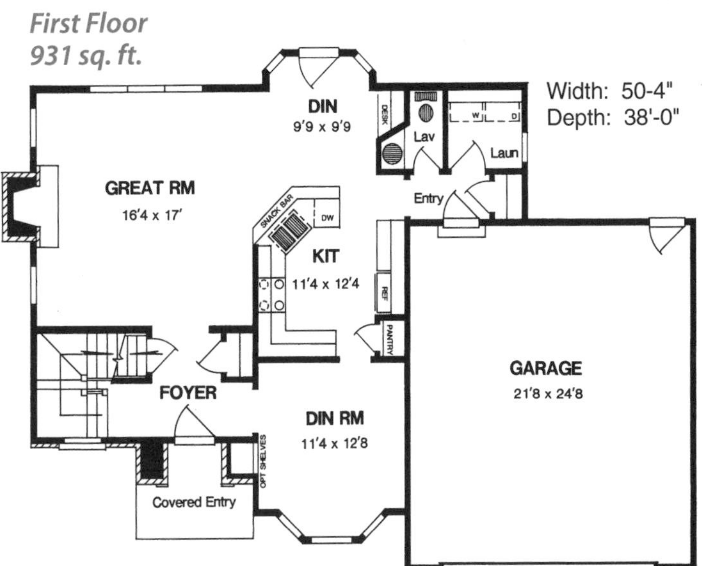

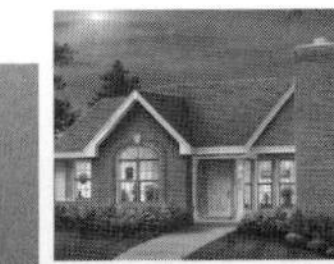

Plan #582-008D-0042 Price Code B

Special Features • 1,668 total square feet of living area • Simple, but attractively styled ranch home is perfect for a narrow lot • Front entry porch flows into foyer which connects to living room • Garage entrance to home leads to kitchen through mud room/laundry area • U-shaped kitchen opens to dining area and family room • Three bedrooms are situated at the rear of the home with two full baths • Master bedroom has walk-in closet • 3 bedrooms, 2 baths, 2-car garage • Partial basement/crawl space foundation, drawings also include crawl space and slab foundations

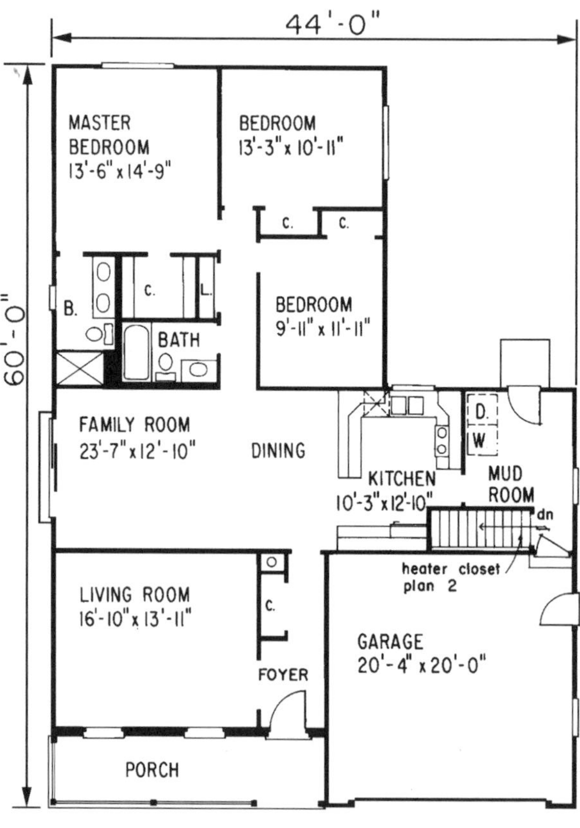

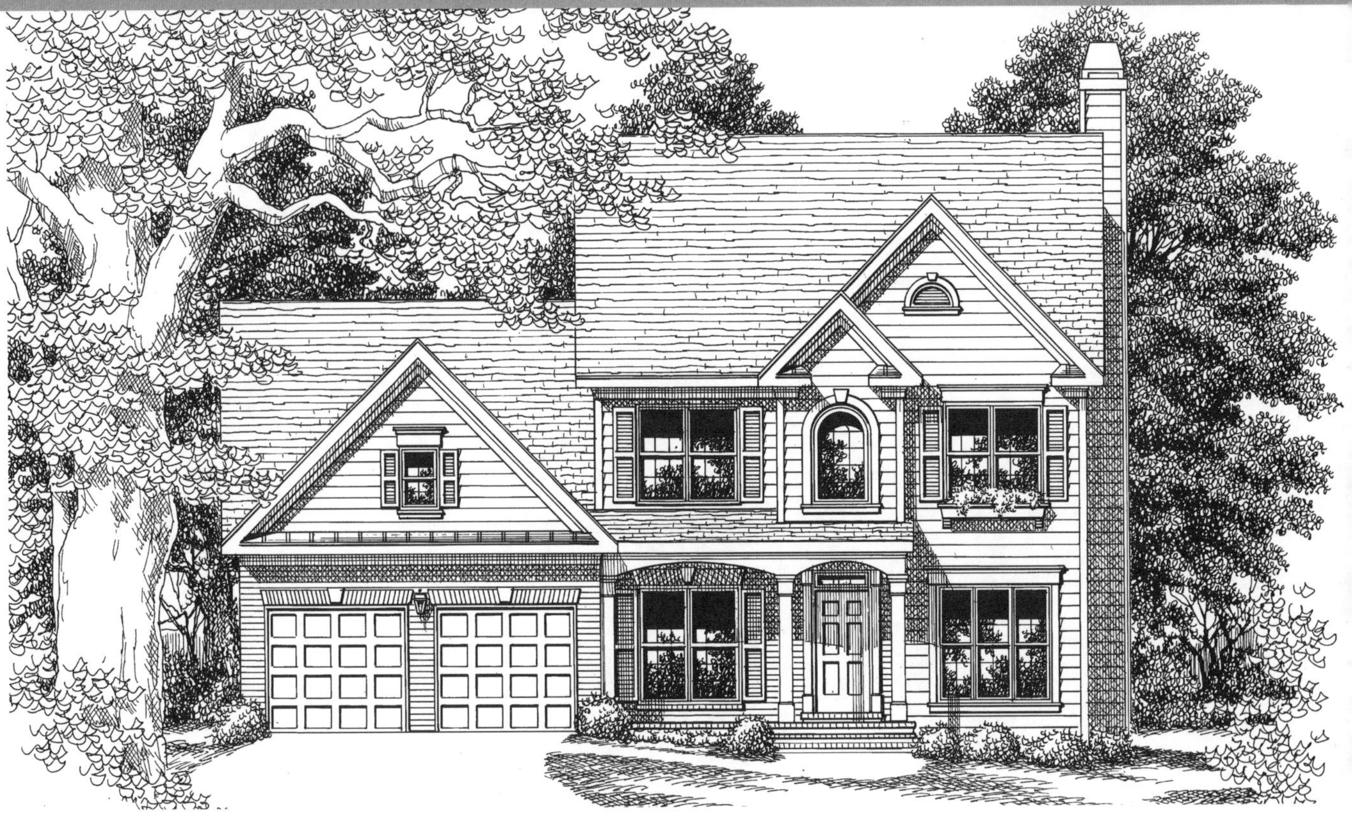

Plan #582-035D-0038

Price Code C

Special Features • 1,862 total square feet of living area • Dining and living rooms flank grand two-story foyer • Open floor plan combines kitchen, breakfast and family rooms • Study is tucked away on first floor for privacy • Second floor bedrooms have walk-in closets • 4 bedrooms, 3 baths, 2-car garage • Walk-out basement or crawl space foundation, please specify when ordering

Second Floor
759 sq. ft.

First Floor
1,103 sq. ft.

www.houseplansandmore.com

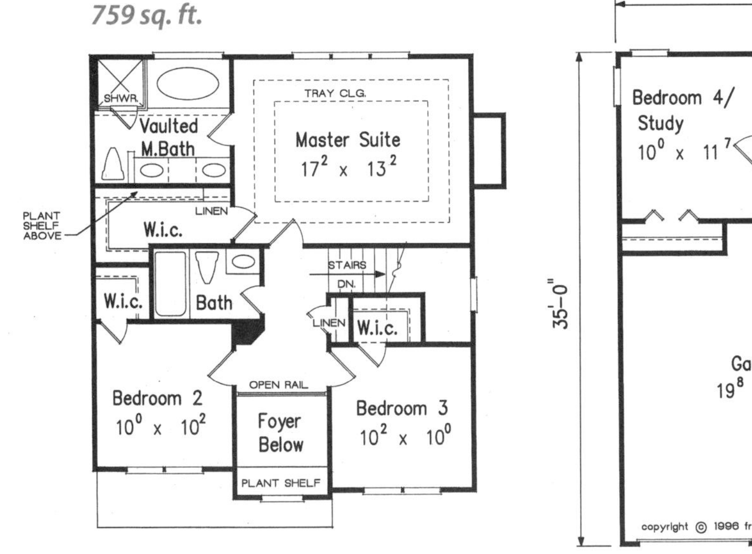

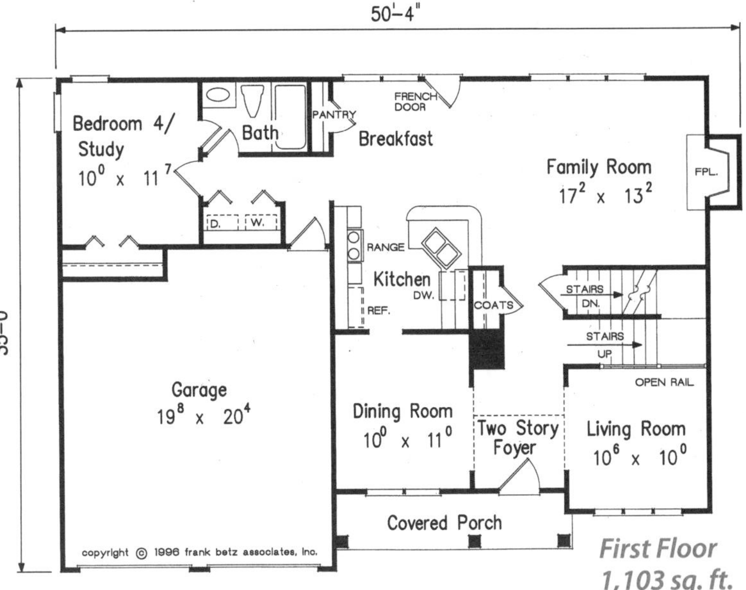

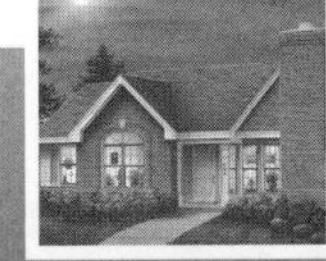

Plan #582-076D-0009

Price Code B

Special Features • 1,251 total square feet of living area • The kitchen provides an abundance of counterspace and opens into the large breakfast area • A grand corner fireplace graces the vaulted family room • Secondary bedrooms are generously sized and are secluded from the main living area • The bonus room on the second floor has 261 square feet of additional living area • 3 bedrooms, 2 baths, 2-car garage • Crawl space or slab foundation, please specify when ordering

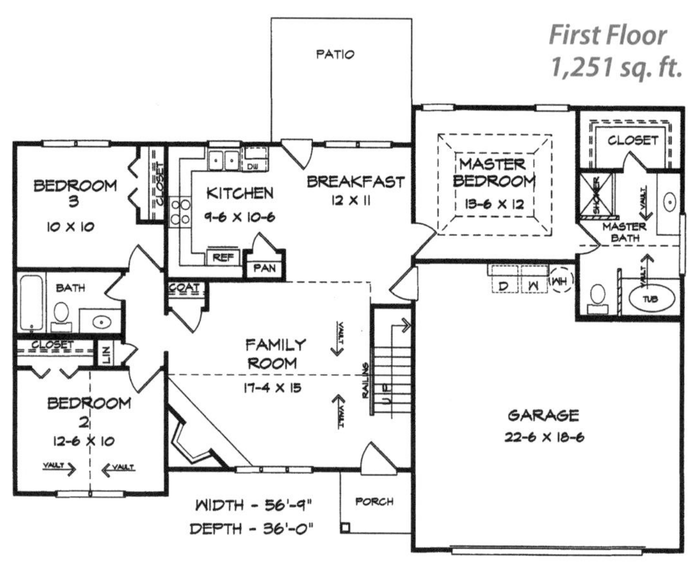

First Floor
1,251 sq. ft.

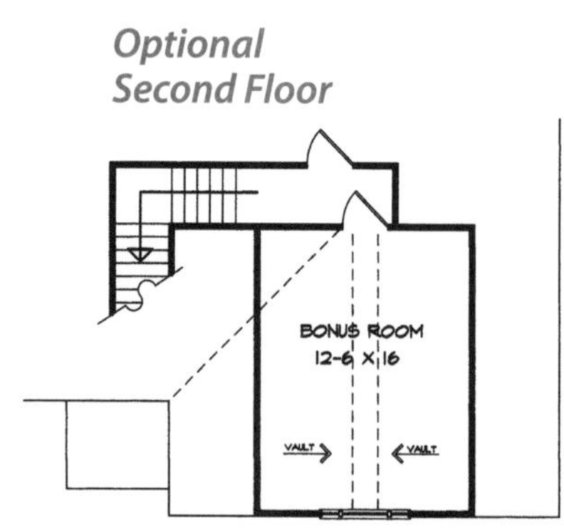

Optional
Second Floor

Dormers Accent Country Home

Plan #582-053D-0058 — Price Code C

Special Features • 1,818 total square feet of living area • Breakfast room is tucked behind the kitchen and has a laundry closet and deck access • Living and dining areas share a vaulted ceiling and fireplace • Master bedroom has two closets, a large double-bowl vanity, separate tub and shower • Large front porch wraps around home • 4 bedrooms, 2 1/2 baths, 2-car drive under garage • Basement foundation

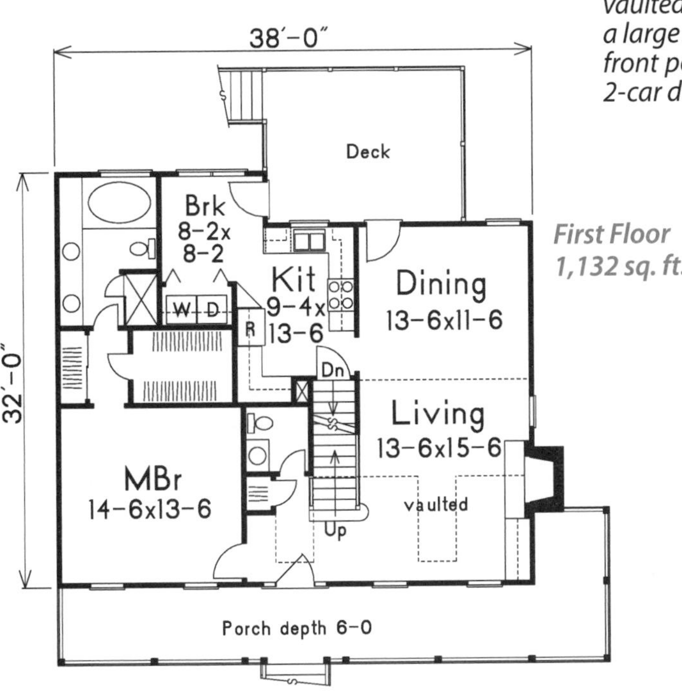

First Floor
1,132 sq. ft.

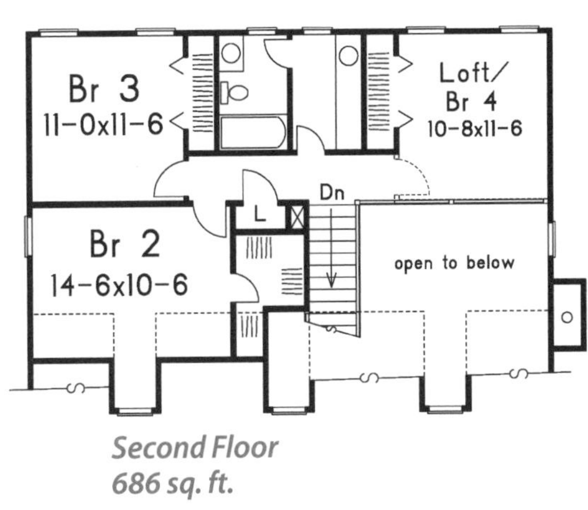

Second Floor
686 sq. ft.

www.houseplansandmore.com

Plan #582-001D-0091

Price Code A

Special Features • 1,344 total square feet of living area • Kitchen has side entry, laundry area, pantry and joins family/dining area • Master bedroom includes a private bath • Linen and storage closets in hall • Covered porch opens to the spacious living room with a handy coat closet • 3 bedrooms, 2 baths • Crawl space foundation, drawings also include basement and slab foundations

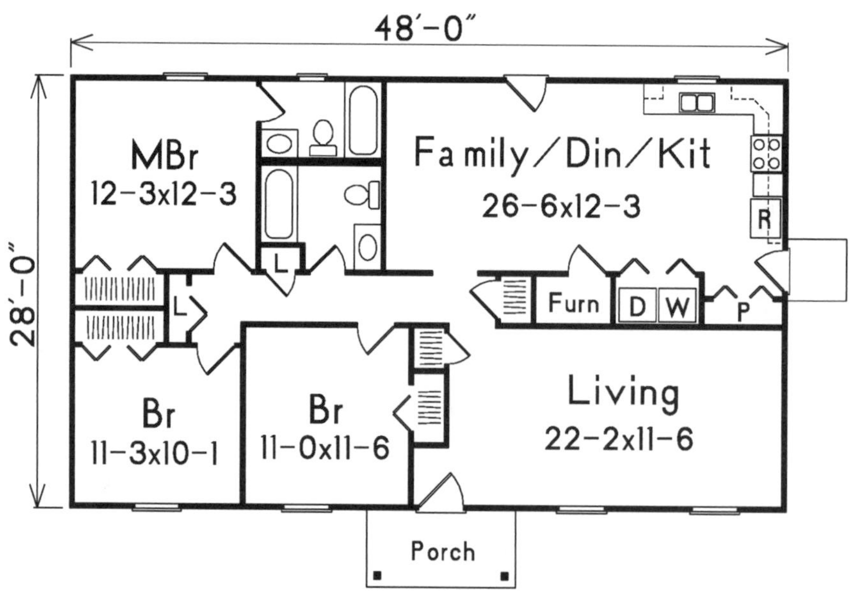

Exterior Accents Make This A Standout

Plan #582-035D-0053

Price Code A

Special Features • 1,467 total square feet of living area • 9' ceilings throughout this home • Two-story family and dining rooms are open and airy • Bonus room above the garage has an additional 292 square feet of living area • 3 bedrooms, 2 1/2 baths, 2-car garage • Walk-out basement or crawl space foundation, please specify when ordering

Second Floor
466 sq. ft.

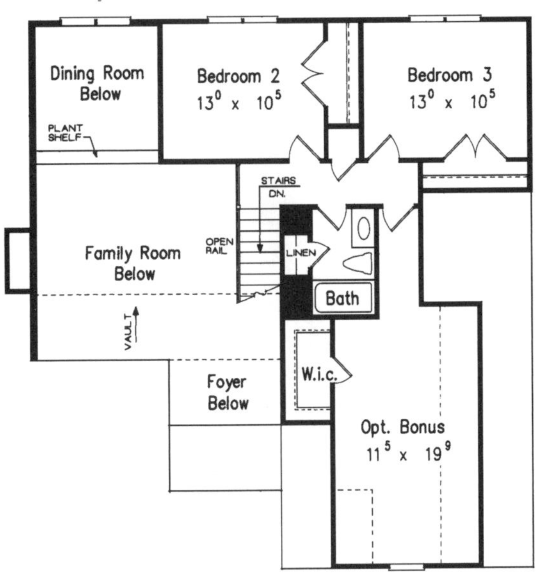

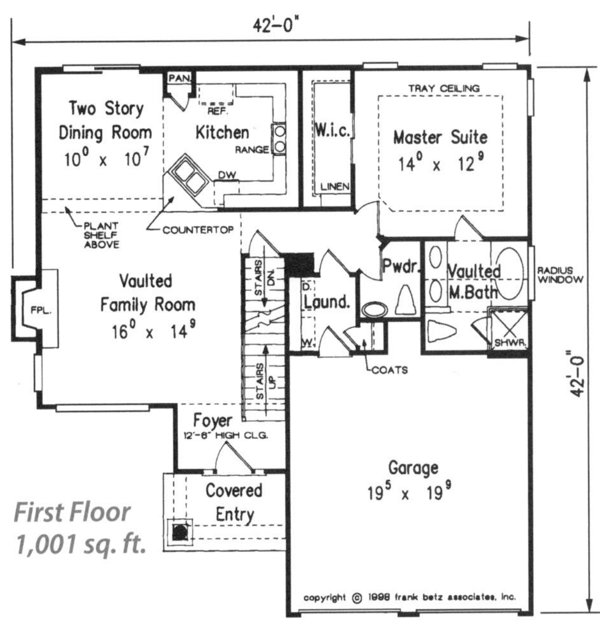

First Floor
1,001 sq. ft.

www.houseplansandmore.com

Plan #582-045D-0009 Price Code B

Special Features • 1,684 total square feet of living area • The bayed dining room boasts convenient double-door access to the large deck • The family room features several large windows for brightness • Bedrooms are separate from living areas for privacy • Master bedroom offers a bath with walk-in closet, double-bowl vanity and both a shower and a whirlpool tub • 3 bedrooms, 2 1/2 baths, 2-car garage • Basement foundation

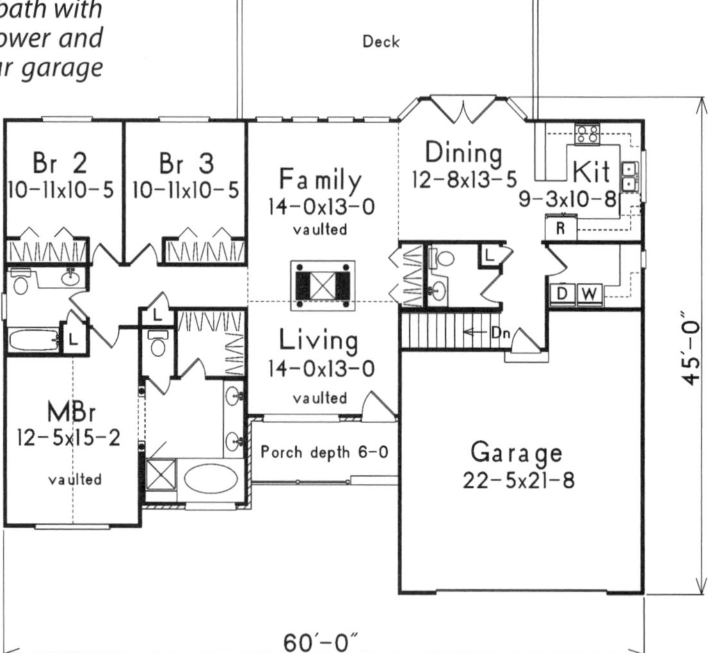

Ornate Corner Porch Catches The Eye

Plan #582-022D-0012

Price Code B

Special Features • 1,550 total square feet of living area • Impressive front entrance with a wrap-around covered porch and raised foyer • Corner fireplace provides a focal point in the vaulted great room • Loft is easily converted to a third bedroom or activity center • Large kitchen/family room includes greenhouse windows and access to the deck and utility area • The secondary bedroom has a large dormer and window seat • 2 bedrooms, 2 1/2 baths, 2-car garage • Basement foundation

First Floor
818 sq. ft.

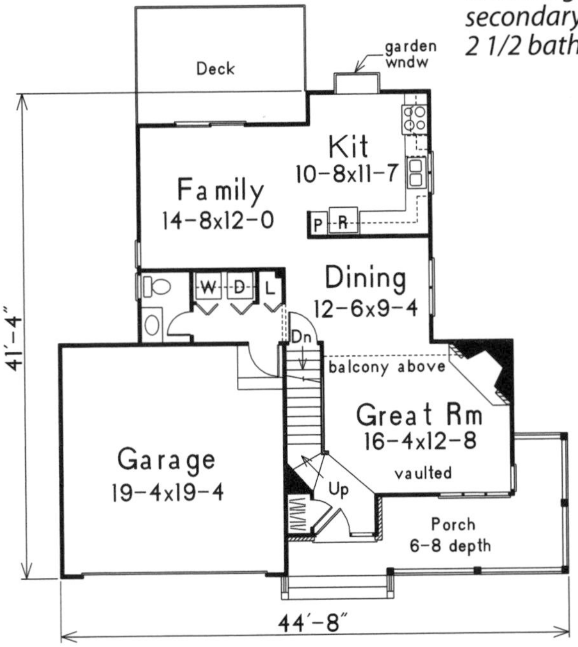

Deck
garden wndw
Kit 10-8x11-7
Family 14-8x12-0
P R
Dining 12-6x9-4
W D L
Dn
balcony above
Great Rm 16-4x12-8 vaulted
Garage 19-4x19-4
Up
Porch 6-8 depth
41'-4"
44'-8"

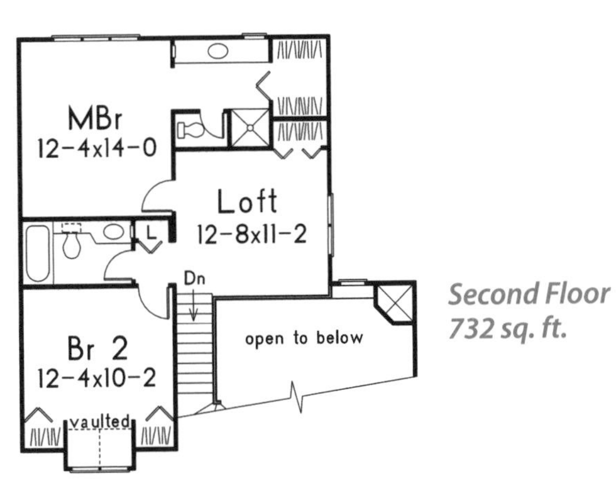

Second Floor
732 sq. ft.

www.houseplansandmore.com

Plan #582-058D-0024

Price Code B

Special Features • 1,598 total square feet of living area • Additional storage area in garage • Double-door entry into master bedroom with luxurious master bath • Entry opens into large family room with vaulted ceiling and open stairway to basement • 3 bedrooms, 2 baths, 2-car garage • Basement foundation

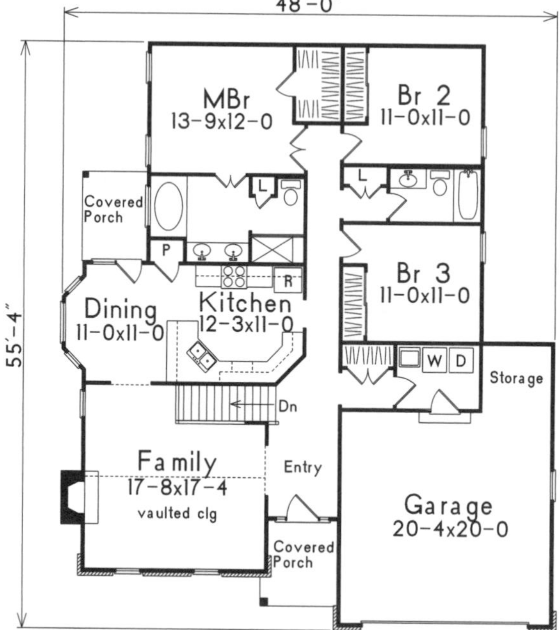

Plan #582-026D-0141

Price Code C

Special Features • 1,814 total square feet of living area • Handy bench located outside laundry area for changing • Charming garden room located off great room brings in the outdoors • Kitchen features lots of cabinetry and counterspace • 4 bedrooms, 2 1/2 baths, 3-car garage • Basement foundation

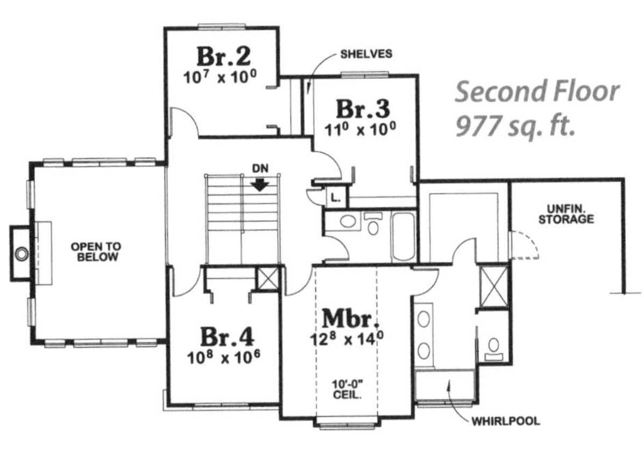

Second Floor
977 sq. ft.

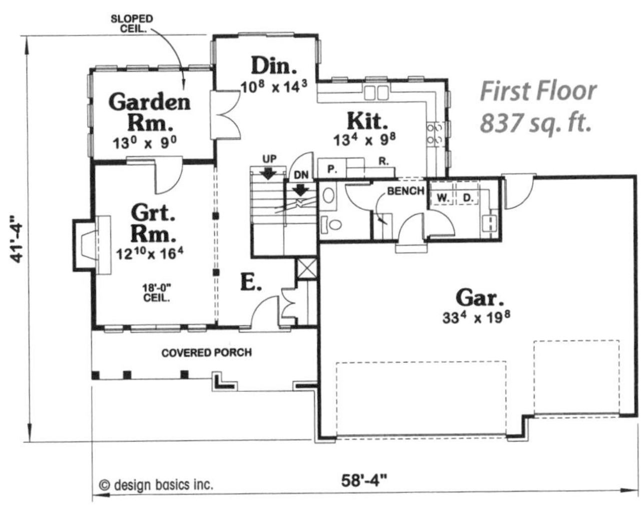

First Floor
837 sq. ft.

Plan #582-039D-0015

Price Code C

Special Features • 1,855 total square feet of living area • Angled stairs add character to the two-story foyer • Secluded dining area is formal and elegant • Sunny master bedroom has all the luxuries • A half bath is conveniently located off the kitchen and breakfast area • 3 bedrooms, 2 1/2 baths, 2-car garage • Basement foundation

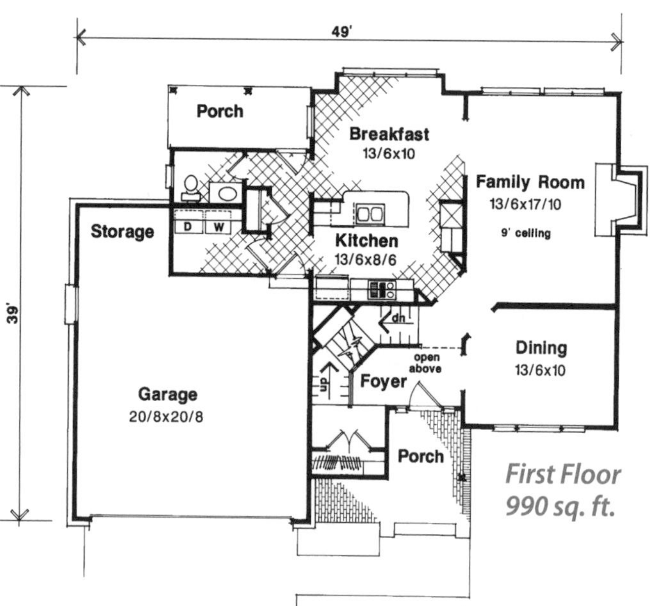

First Floor
990 sq. ft.

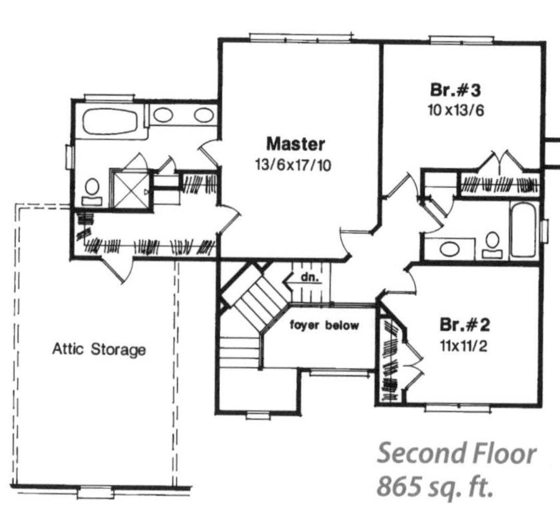

Second Floor
865 sq. ft.

Spacious Interior For Open Living

Plan #582-001D-0048

Price Code A

Special Features • 1,400 total square feet of living area • Front porch offers warmth and welcome • Large great room opens into dining room creating an open living atmosphere • Kitchen features convenient laundry area, pantry and breakfast bar • 3 bedrooms, 2 baths, 2-car garage • Crawl space foundation, drawings also include basement and slab foundations

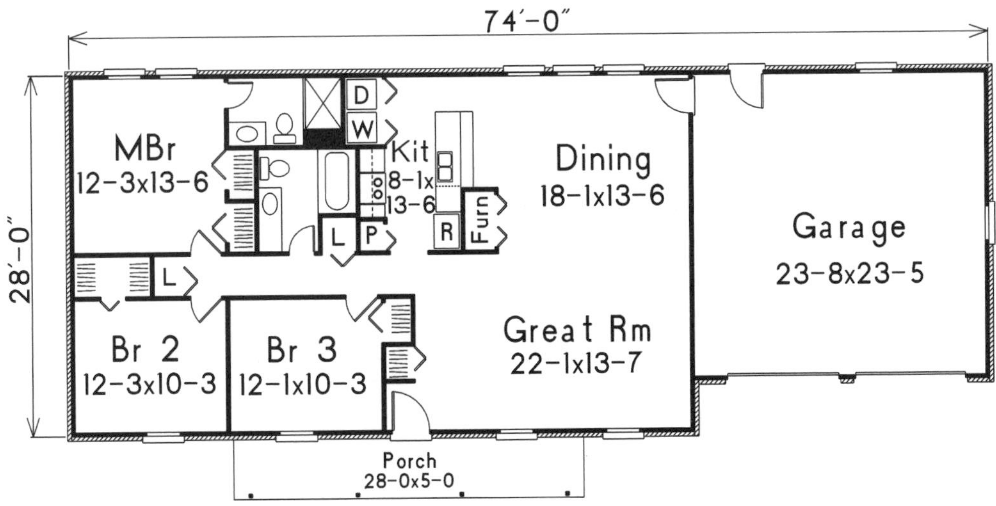

www.houseplansandmore.com

Plan #582-028D-0006

Price Code B

Special Features • 1,700 total square feet of living area • Oversized laundry room has large pantry and storage area as well as access to the outdoors • Master bedroom is separated from other bedrooms for privacy • Raised snack bar in kitchen allows extra seating for dining • 3 bedrooms, 2 baths • Crawl space foundation

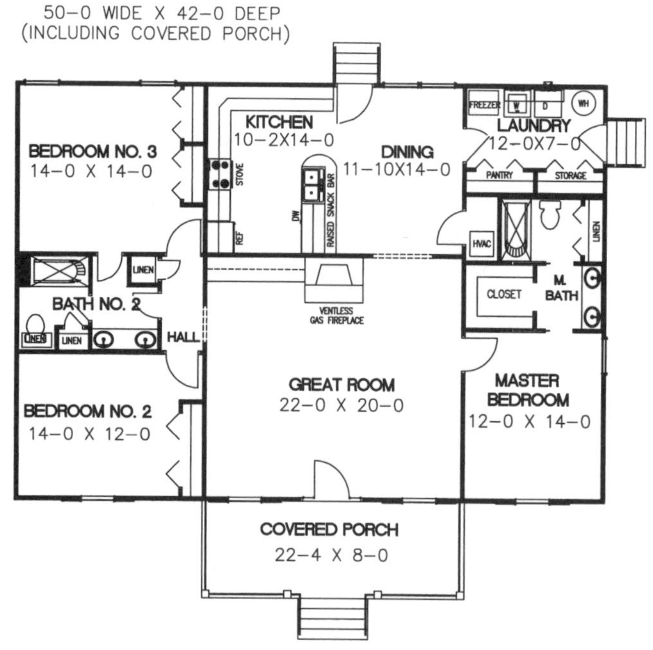

1-800-DREAM HOME (373-2646)

Bayed Breakfast Room

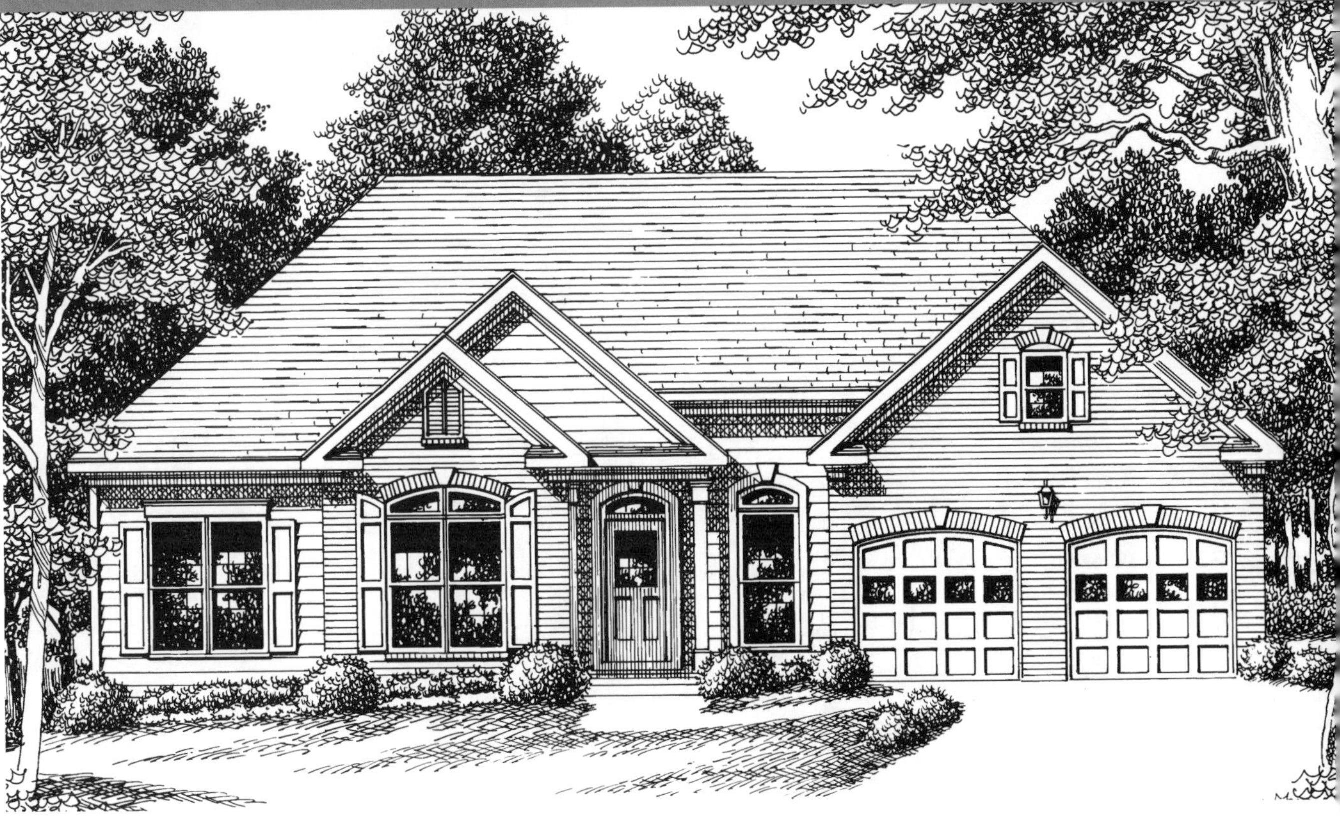

Plan #582-035D-0048 Price Code C

Special Features • *1,915 total square feet of living area* • *Large breakfast area overlooks vaulted great room* • *Master suite has cheerful sitting room and a private bath* • *Plan features unique in-law suite with private bath and walk-in closet* • *4 bedrooms, 3 baths, 2-car garage* • *Walk-out basement, slab or crawl space foundation, please specify when ordering*

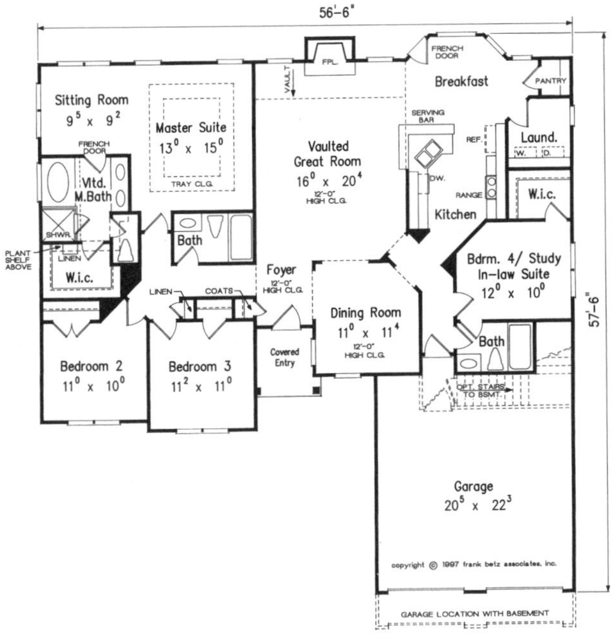

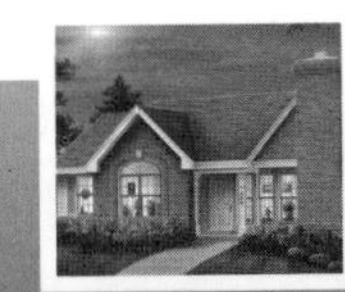

Plan #582-017D-0008

Price Code B

Special Features • 1,466 total square feet of living area • Energy efficient home with 2" x 6" exterior walls • Foyer separates the living room from the dining room and contains a generous coat closet • Large living room features a corner fireplace, bay window and pass-through to the kitchen • Informal breakfast area opens to a large terrace through sliding glass doors which brighten area • Master bedroom has a large walk-in closet and private bath • 3 bedrooms, 2 baths, 2-car garage • Basement foundation, drawings also include slab foundation

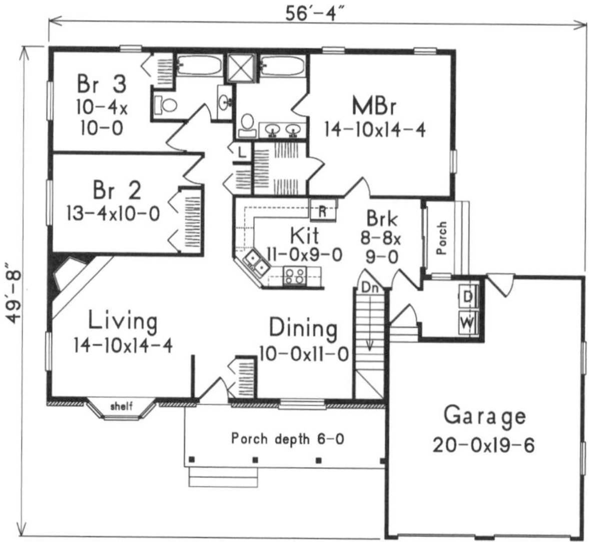

Covered Porch Is Focal Point Of Entry

Plan #582-040D-0014

Price Code B

Special Features • 1,595 total square feet of living area • Dining room has convenient built-in desk and provides access to the outdoors • L-shaped kitchen area features island cooktop • Family room has high ceiling and a fireplace • Private master bedroom includes large walk-in closet and bath with separate tub and shower units • 3 bedrooms, 2 baths, 2-car side entry garage • Slab foundation, drawings also include crawl space foundation

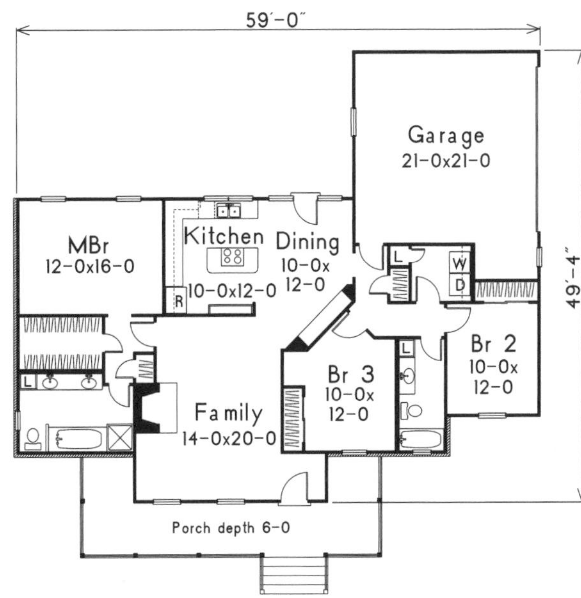

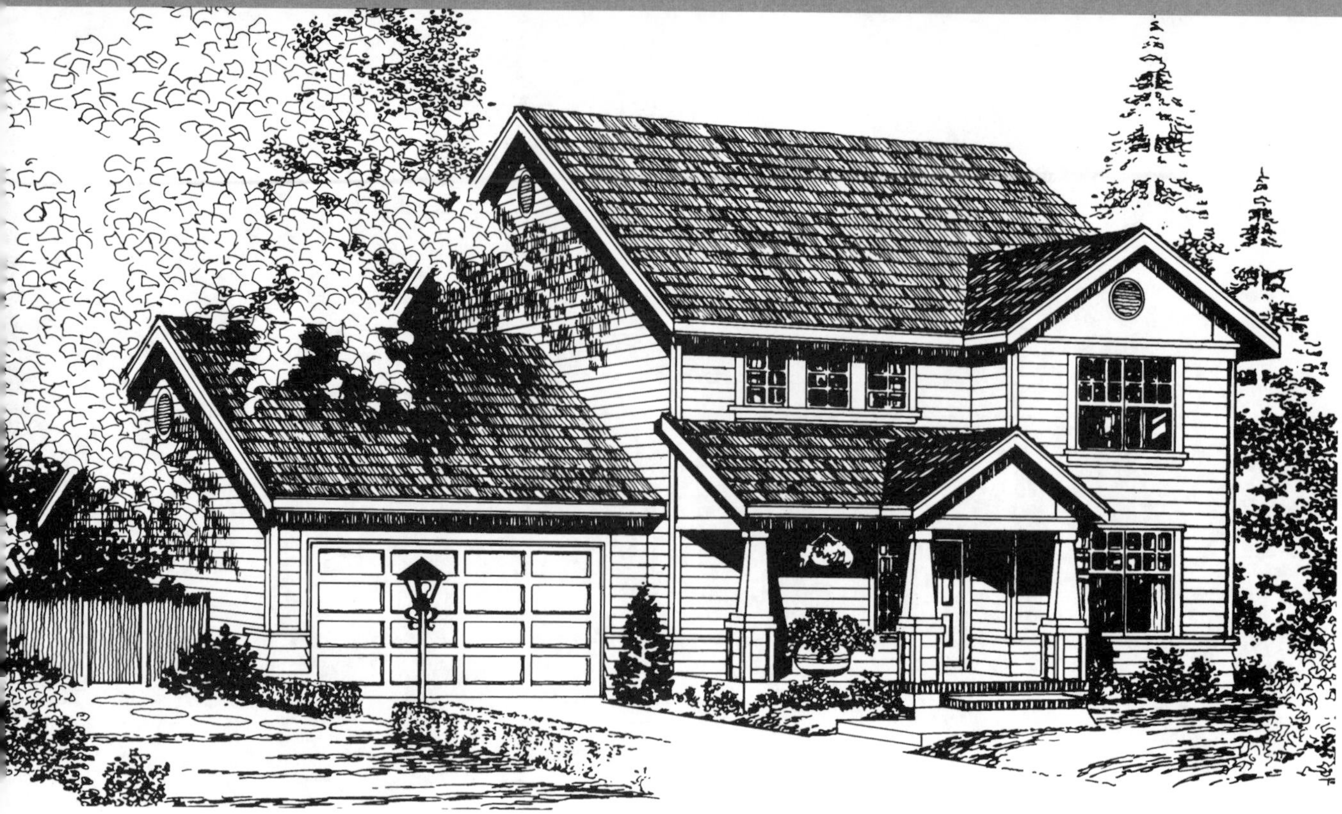

Plan #582-043D-0009

Price Code B

Special Features • *1,751 total square feet of living area* • *Charming covered front porch* • *Elegant two-story entry* • *Beautifully designed great room with fireplace opens to kitchen* • *Large eating counter and walk-in pantry* • *Second floor study area is perfect for a growing family* • *3 bedrooms, 2 1/2 baths, 2-car garage* • *Crawl space foundation*

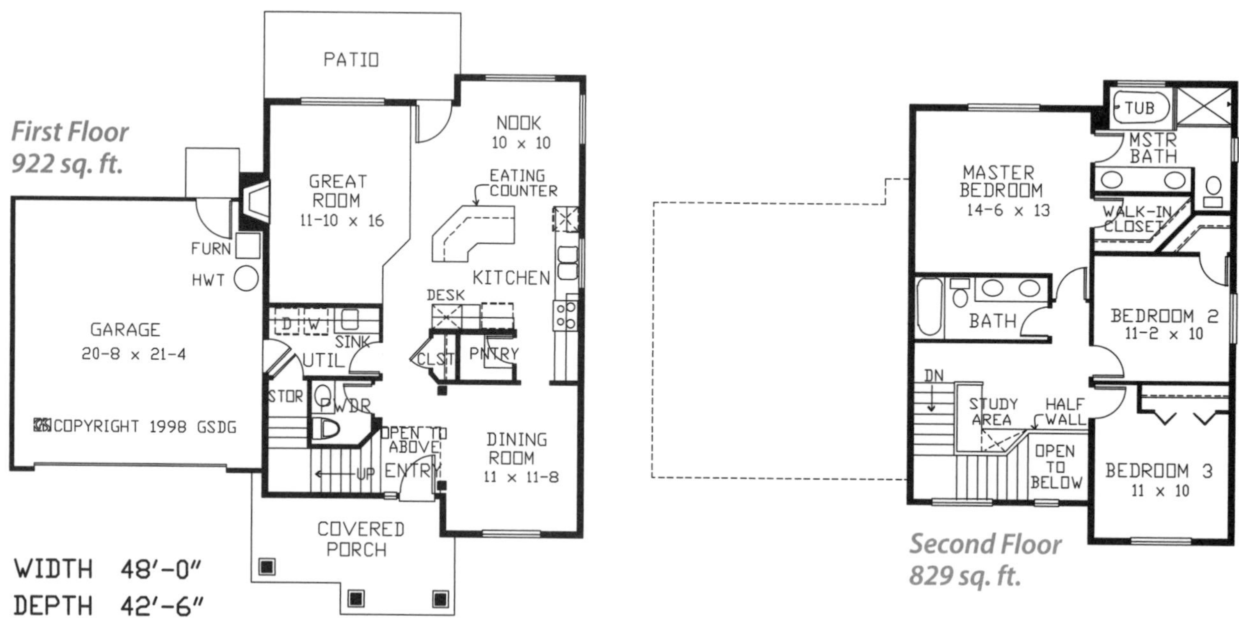

Plan #582-060D-0026

Price Code A

Special Features • 1,497 total square feet of living area • Open living area has a kitchen counter overlooking a cozy great room with fireplace • Sloped ceiling accents dining room • Master suite has privacy from other bedrooms • 3 bedrooms, 2 baths, 2-car garage • Slab foundation

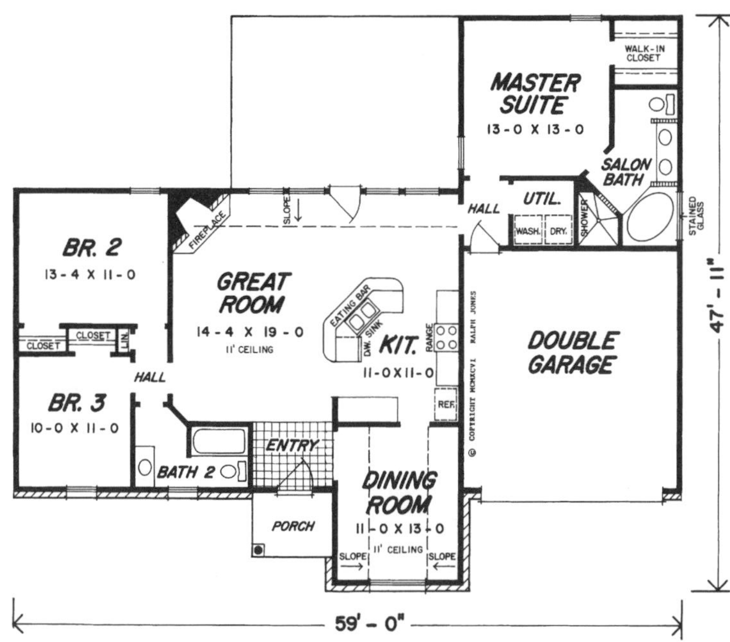

Compact Home Is Charming And Functional

Plan #582-053D-0032

Price Code A

Special Features • 1,404 total square feet of living area • Split-foyer entrance • Bayed living area features a unique vaulted ceiling and fireplace • Wrap-around kitchen has corner windows for added sunlight and a bar that overlooks dining area • Master bath features a garden tub with separate shower • Rear deck provides handy access to dining room and kitchen • 3 bedrooms, 2 baths, 2-car drive under garage • Basement foundation, drawings also include partial crawl space foundation

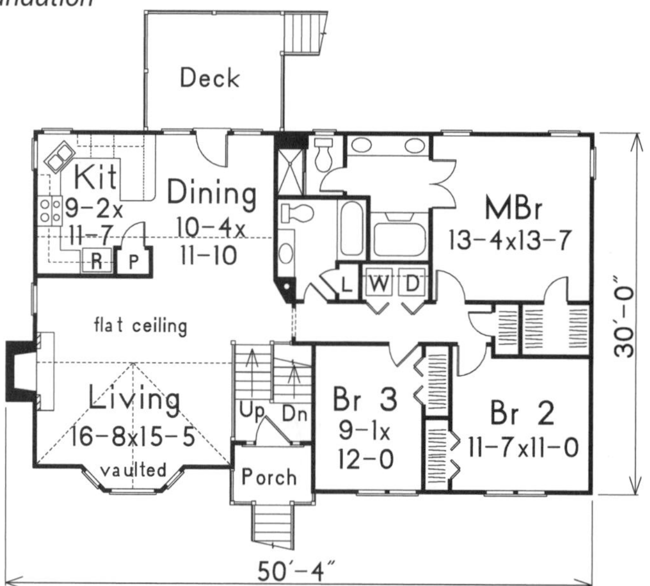

Gables Decorate Facade

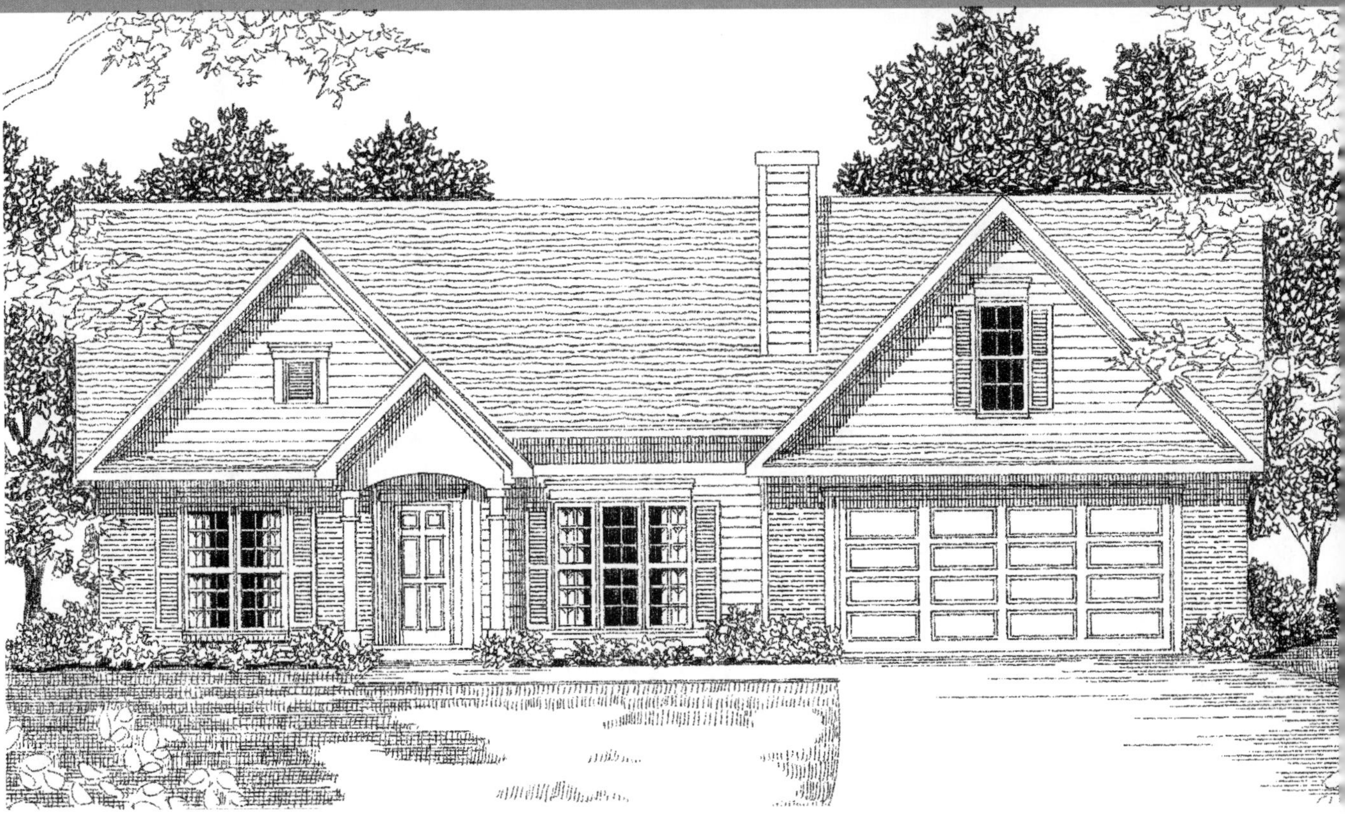

Plan #582-076D-0010

Price Code B

Special Features • 1,236 total square feet of living area • U-shaped kitchen opens into dining area with patio access • Private master suite features a vaulted bath and walk-in closet • Two secondary bedrooms are located away from the main living areas and share a bath • Optional bonus room above the garage has an additional 298 square feet of living area • 3 bedrooms, 2 baths, 2-car garage • Slab foundation

First Floor
1,236 sq. ft.

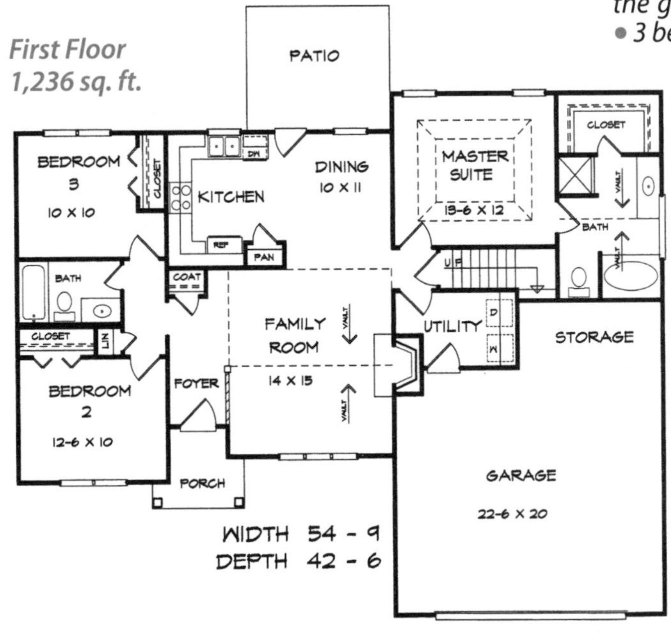

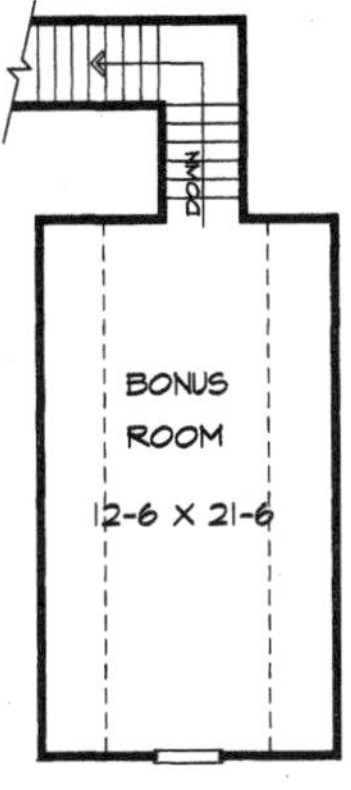

Optional
Second Floor

www.houseplansandmore.com

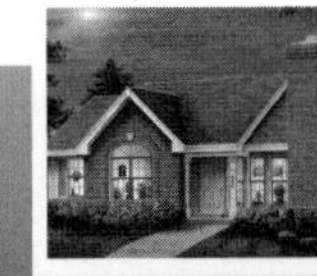

Plan #582-036D-0047

Price Code B

Special Features • *1,702 total square feet of living area* • *Second floor loft has a wall of windows making this space functional and bright* • *Sloped ceilings in both bedrooms* • *Kitchen and dining area combine to create a terrific gathering space* • *2 bedrooms, 2 baths, 2-car garage* • *Slab foundation*

Second Floor
314 sq. ft.

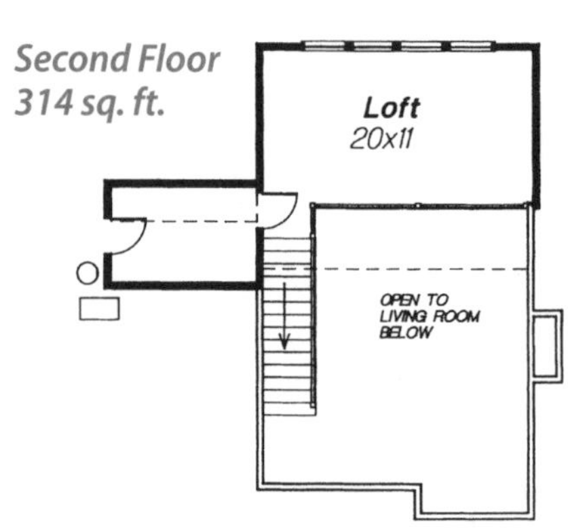

First Floor
1,388 sq. ft.

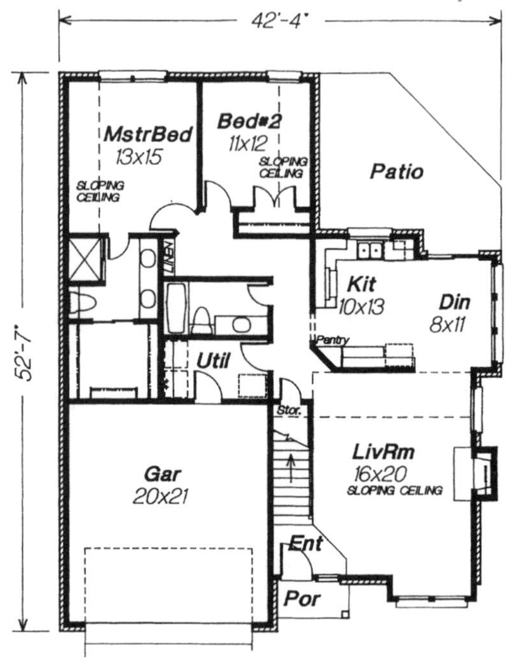

Plan #582-047D-0018

Price Code B

Special Features • 1,750 total square feet of living area • The dining and living rooms in the front of the home combine creating a wonderful area for entertaining away from the more casual living spaces • Master bedroom maintains lots of privacy from other bedrooms • Large kitchen includes a breakfast nook for convenient dining • 3 bedrooms, 2 baths, 2-car garage • Slab foundation

Width: 42'-6"
Depth: 55'-0"

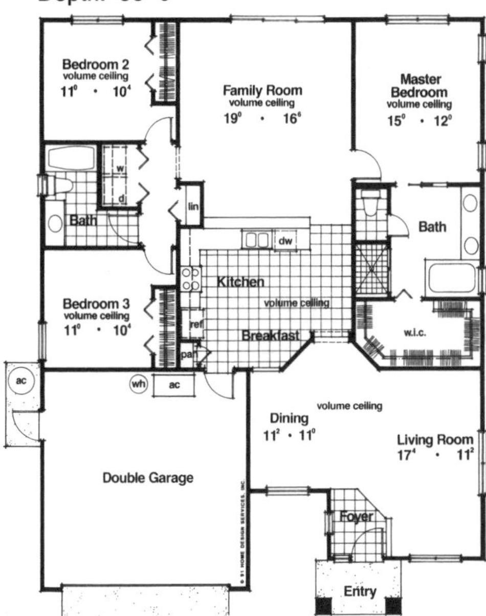

Vaulted Ceilings Create Spacious Feeling

Plan #582-001D-0001

Price Code B

Special Features • 1,605 total square feet of living area • Vaulted ceilings in great room, kitchen and breakfast area • Spacious great room features a large bay window, fireplace, built-in bookshelves and a convenient wet bar • The formal dining room and breakfast area are perfect for entertaining or everyday living • Master bedroom has a spacious bath with oval tub and separate shower • 3 bedrooms, 2 baths, 2-car garage • Basement foundation, drawings also include slab and crawl space foundations

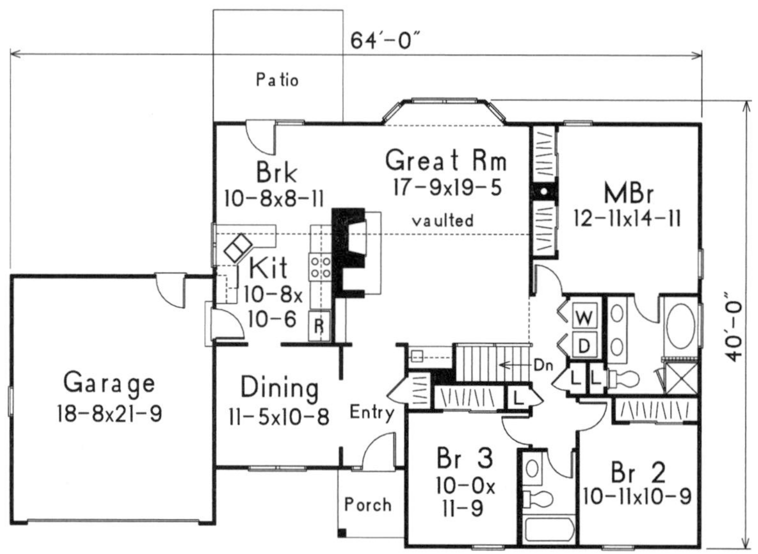

Luxurious Master Suite

Plan #582-035D-0046

Price Code AA

Special Features • 1,080 total square feet of living area • Secondary bedrooms are separate from master suite allowing privacy • Compact kitchen is well-organized • The laundry closet is conveniently located next to the secondary bedrooms • 3 bedrooms, 2 baths, 2-car garage • Walk-out basement or crawl space foundation, please specify when ordering

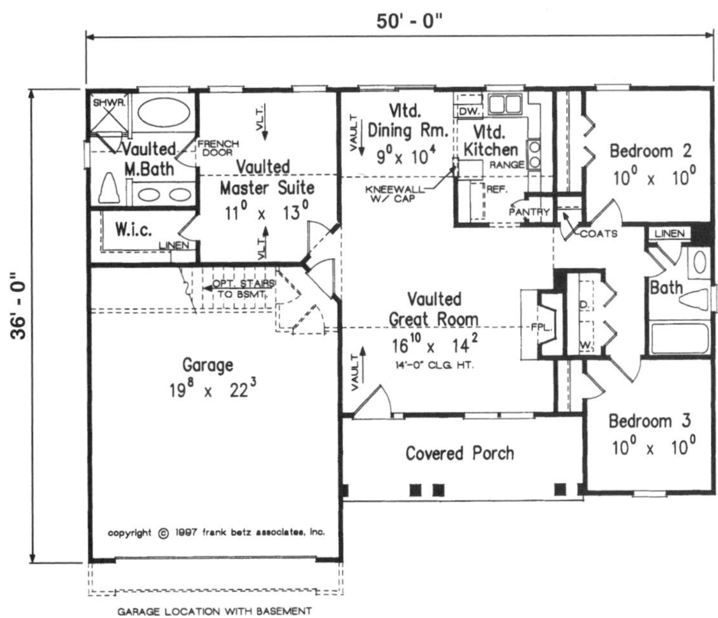

Impressive Corner Fireplace Highlights The Living Area

Plan #582-053D-0042

Price Code A

Special Features • *1,458 total square feet of living area • Convenient snack bar joins kitchen with breakfast room • Large living room has a fireplace, plenty of windows, vaulted ceiling and nearby plant shelf • Master bedroom offers a private bath, walk-in closet, plant shelf and coffered ceiling • Corner windows provide abundant light in breakfast room • 3 bedrooms, 2 baths, 2-car garage • Crawl space foundation, drawings also include slab foundation*

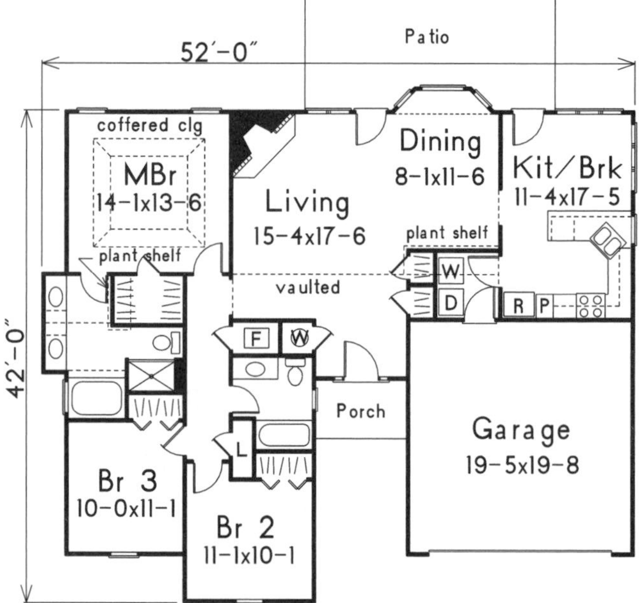

Plan #582-030D-0005

Price Code C

Special Features • 1,815 total square feet of living area • Well-designed kitchen opens to dining room and features raised breakfast bar • First floor master suite has walk-in closet • Front and back porches unite this home with the outdoors • 3 bedrooms, 2 baths, 2-car side entry garage • Basement, crawl space or slab foundation, please specify when ordering

First Floor
1,245 sq. ft.

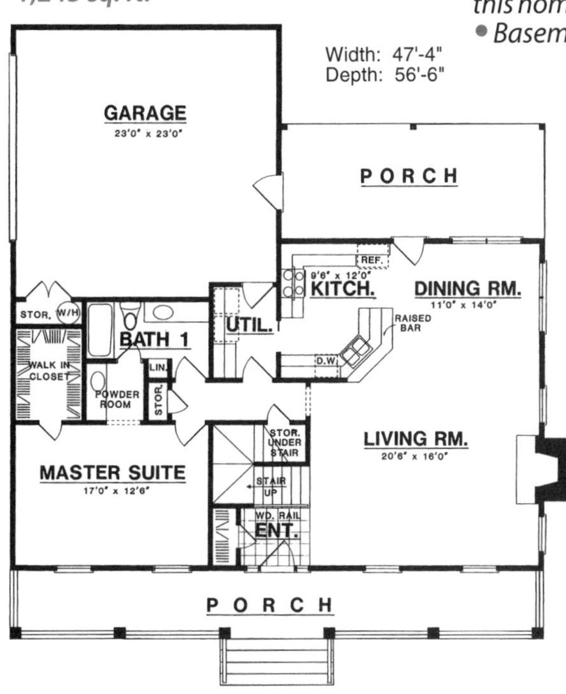

Second Floor
570 sq. ft.

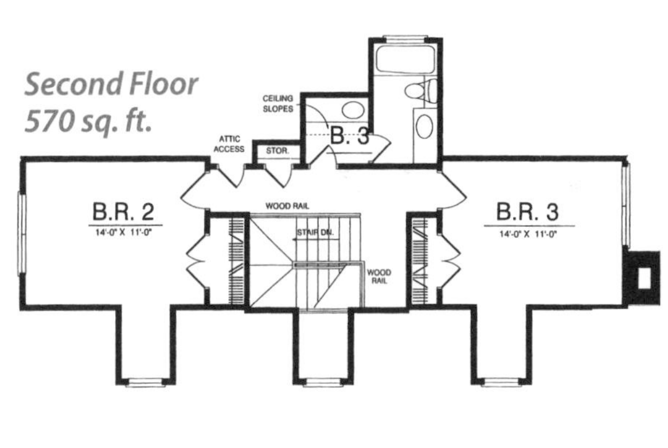

www.houseplansandmore.com

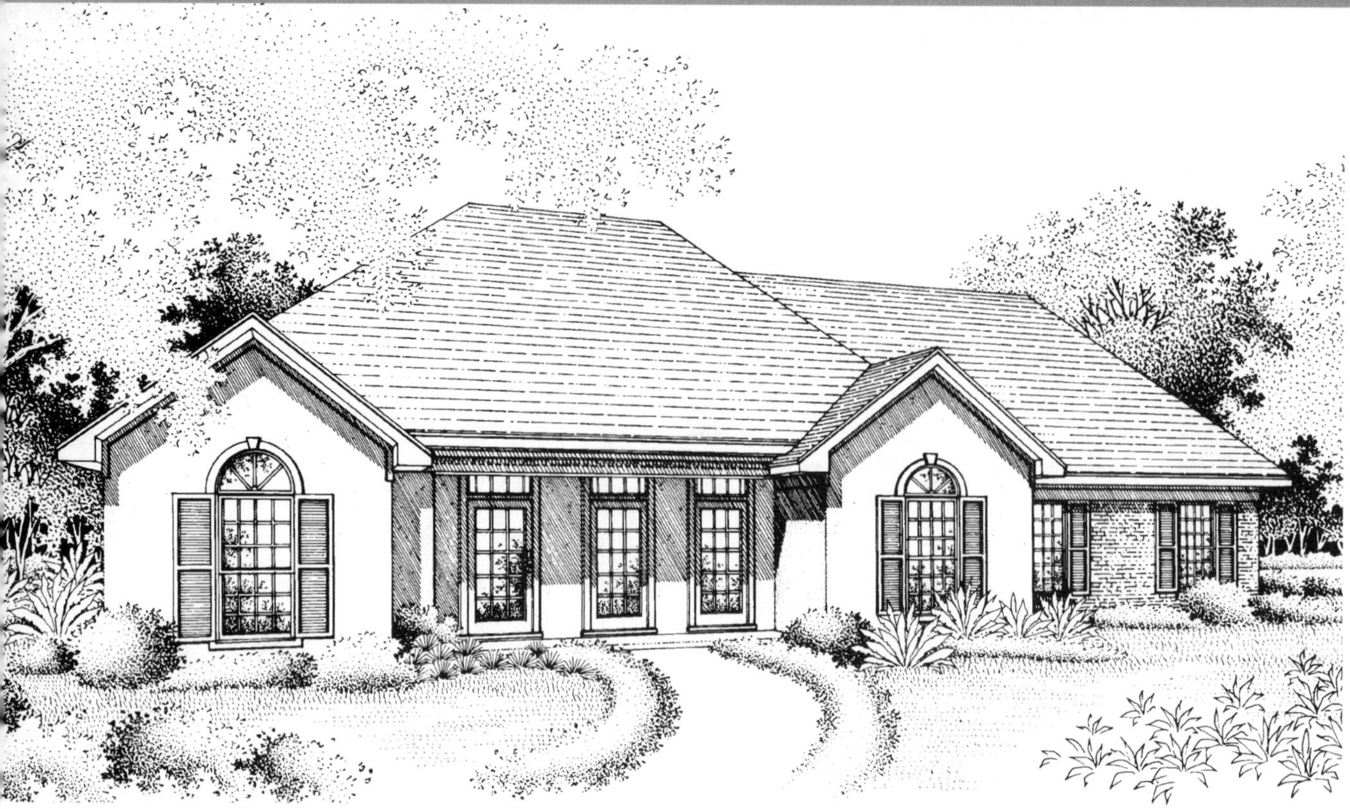

Plan #582-021D-0007

Price Code D

Special Features • 1,868 total square feet of living area • Luxurious master bath is impressive with an angled quarter-circle tub, separate vanities and large walk-in closet • Energy efficient home with 2" x 6" exterior walls • Dining room is surrounded by a series of arched openings which complement the open feeling of this design • Living room has a 12' ceiling accented by skylights and a large fireplace flanked by sliding doors • Large storage areas • 3 bedrooms, 2 baths, 2-car side entry garage • Slab foundation, drawings also include crawl space foundation

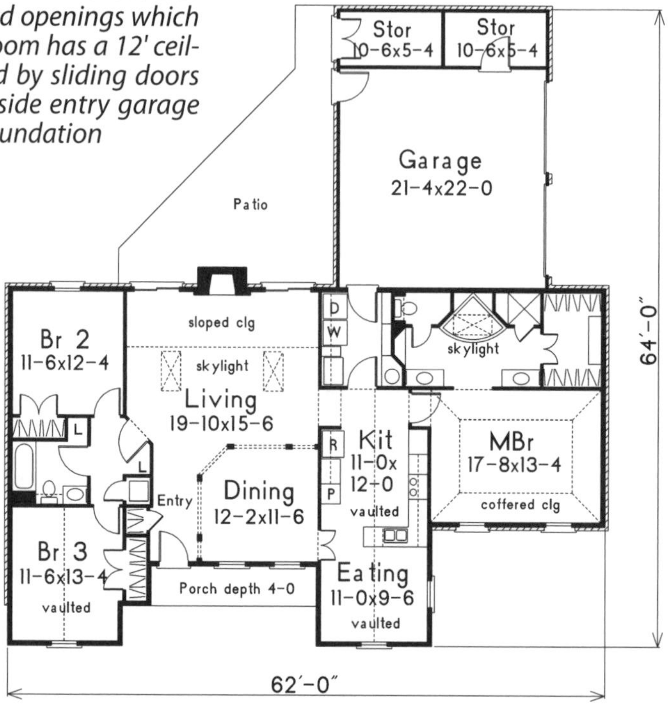
Stor 10-6x5-4
Stor 10-6x5-4
Garage 21-4x22-0
Patio
sloped clg
skylight
Living 19-10x15-6
Br 2 11-6x12-4
Br 3 11-6x13-4 vaulted
Entry
Dining 12-2x11-6
Porch depth 4-0
Kit 11-0x 12-0 vaulted
Eating 11-0x9-6 vaulted
skylight
MBr 17-8x13-4
coffered clg
64'-0"
62'-0"

1-800-DREAM HOME (373-2646)

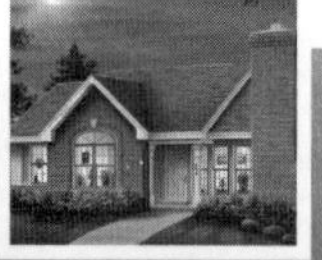

Plan #582-019D-0010

Price Code C

Special Features • *1,890 total square feet of living area* • *10' ceilings give this home a spacious feel* • *Efficient kitchen has breakfast bar which overlooks living room* • *Master bedroom has a private bath with walk-in closet* • *3 bedrooms, 2 baths, 2-car side entry garage* • *Crawl space foundation, drawings also include slab foundation*

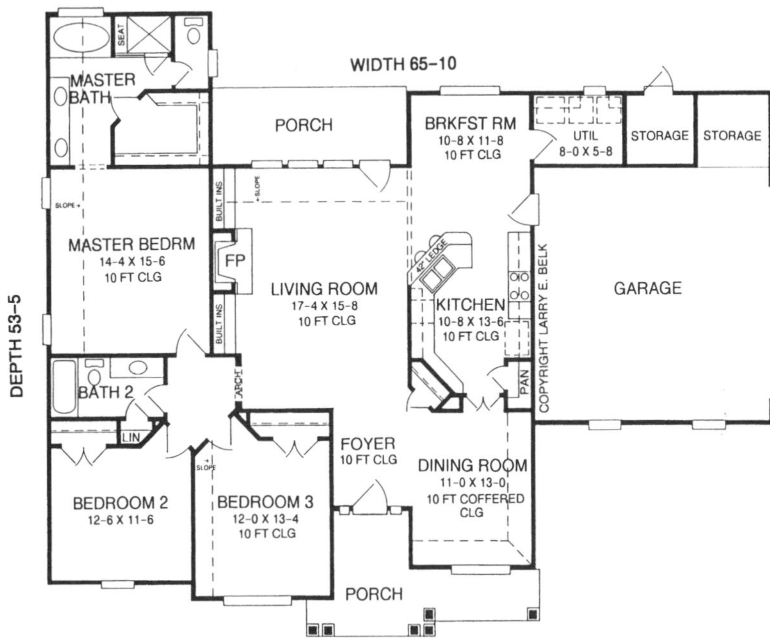

Well-Designed Ranch Style With Wrap-Around Porch

Plan #582-004D-0002

Price Code C

Special Features • 1,823 total square feet of living area • Vaulted living room is spacious and easily accesses the dining area • The master bedroom boasts a tray ceiling, large walk-in closet and a private bath with a corner whirlpool tub • Cheerful dining area is convenient to the U-shaped kitchen and also enjoys patio access • Centrally located laundry room connects the garage to the living areas • 3 bedrooms, 2 baths, 2-car garage • Basement foundation

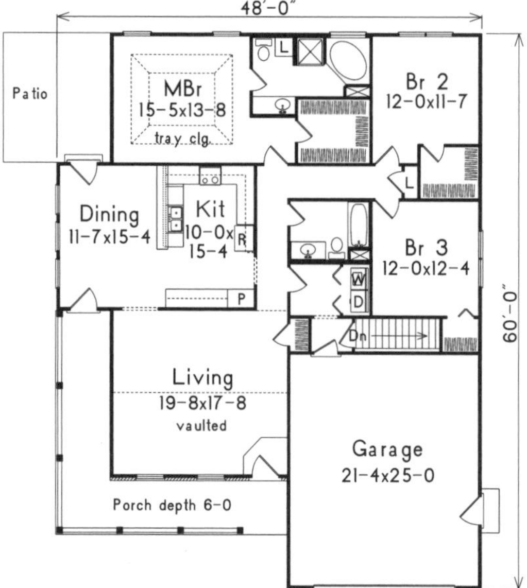

Beautiful Window Adds Curb Appeal

Plan #582-076D-0014

Price Code B

Special Features • 1,163 total square feet of living area • Side entrance makes home ideal for a narrow lot • Bayed breakfast area adjoins kitchen creating a cheerful dining space • Dining and family rooms combine to form an expansive living area warmed by a grand fireplace • 3 bedrooms, 2 baths, 1-car garage • Crawl space or slab foundation, please specify when ordering

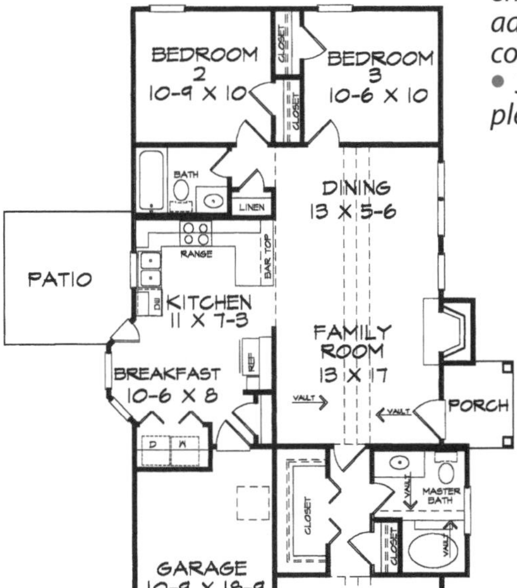

Roomy Two-Story Has Screened-In Rear Porch

Plan #582-021D-0016

Price Code B

Special Features • 1,600 total square feet of living area • Energy efficient home with 2" x 6" exterior walls • First floor master bedroom is accessible from two points of entry • Master bath dressing area includes separate vanities and a mirrored makeup counter • Second floor bedrooms have generous storage space and share a full bath • 3 bedrooms, 2 baths, 2-car side entry garage • Crawl space foundation, drawings also include slab foundation

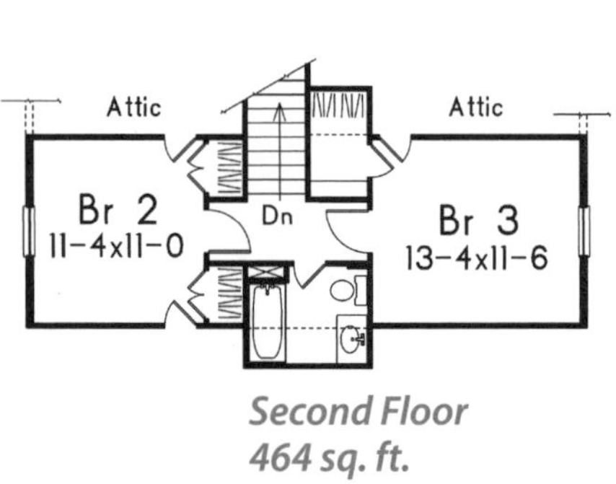

Second Floor
464 sq. ft.

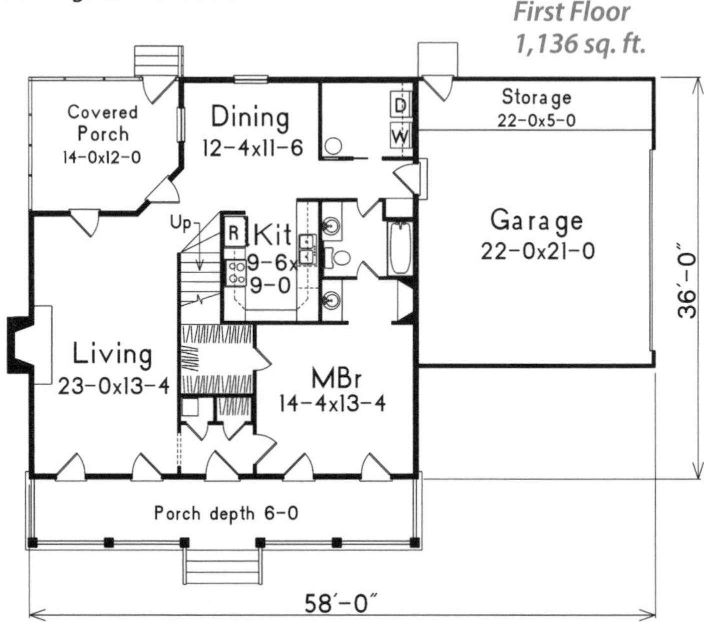

First Floor
1,136 sq. ft.

Plan #582-076D-0023 **Price Code B**

Special Features • *1,318 total square feet of living area • Enter the elegant vaulted family room with fireplace through grand columns • The kitchen opens to the expansive vaulted breakfast area • All the bedrooms are located away from the main living areas and are near the convenient laundry area • 3 bedrooms, 2 baths, 2-car garage • Crawl space or slab foundation, please specify when ordering*

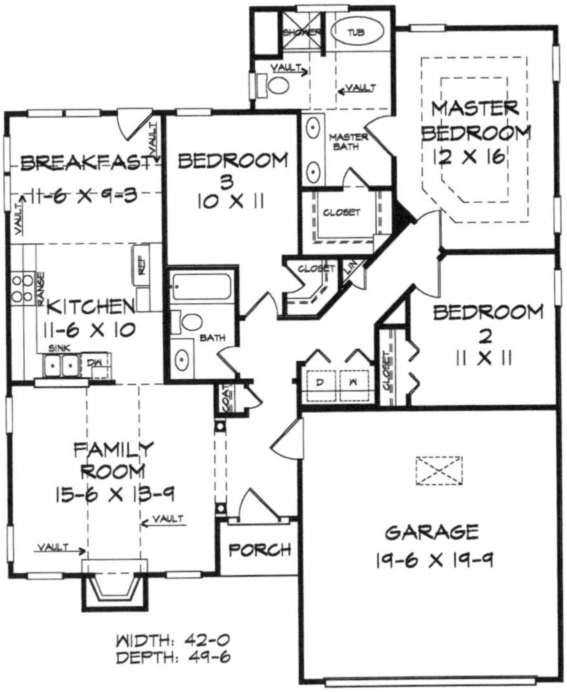

WIDTH: 42-0
DEPTH: 49-6

Elegant Window Graces Exterior

Plan #582-076D-0020

Price Code B

Special Features • 1,072 total square feet of living area • The vaulted family room features a 12' ceiling and a grand fireplace • The breakfast area boasts a vaulted ceiling, access onto the rear patio and a laundry area • Bedrooms are located away from main living areas for privacy • 3 bedrooms, 2 baths, 2-car side entry garage • Slab foundation

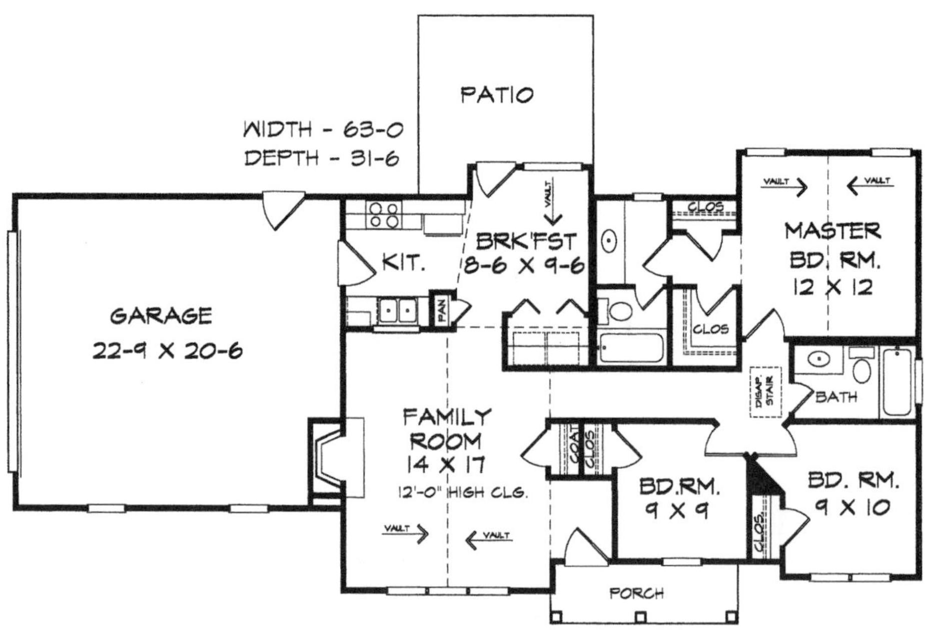

Fireplace Is Focal Point In Living Room

Plan #582-037D-0022

Price Code B

Special Features • *1,539 total square feet of living area* • *Standard 9' ceilings* • *Master bedroom features 10' tray ceiling, access to porch, ample closet space and full bath* • *Serving counter separates kitchen and dining room* • *Foyer with handy coat closet opens to living area with fireplace* • *Handy utility room near kitchen* • *3 bedrooms, 2 baths, 2-car garage* • *Slab foundation*

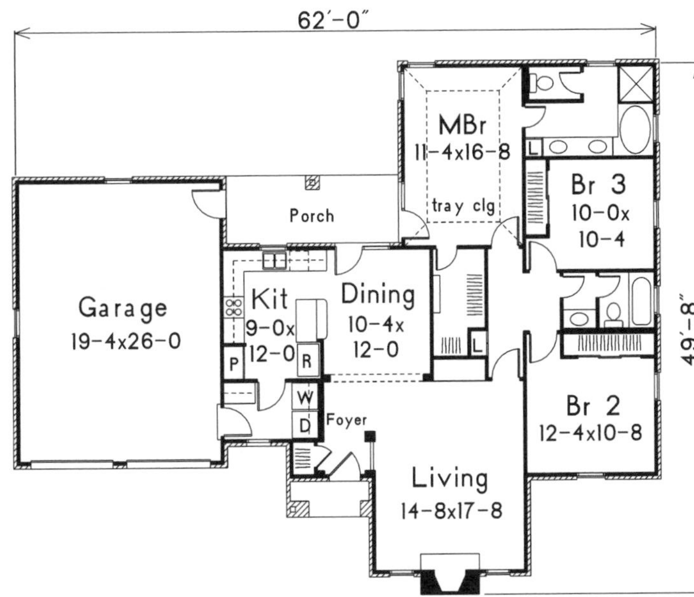

Plan #582-008D-0054

Price Code B

Special Features • 1,574 total square feet of living area • Foyer enters into open great room with corner fireplace and rear dining room with adjoining kitchen • Two secondary bedrooms share a full bath • Master bedroom has a spacious private bath • Garage accesses home through mud room/laundry • 3 bedrooms, 2 baths, 2-car garage • Basement foundation, drawings also include crawl space foundation

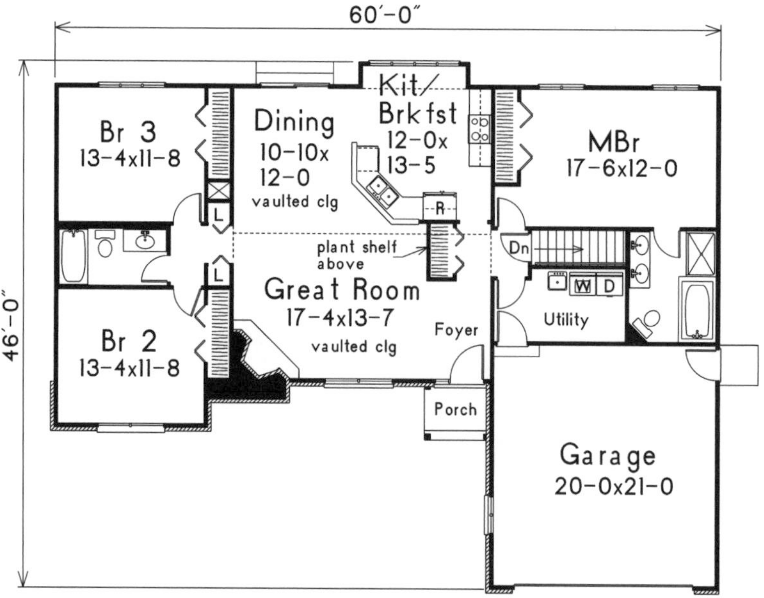

Vaulted Ceilings Add Spaciousness

Plan #582-076D-0021

Price Code B

Special Features • 1,053 total square feet of living area • The spacious master bedroom enjoys two closets and a private bath • The kitchen combines with the vaulted breakfast area for a cozy dining space • A convenient coat closet is located off the entry • 3 bedrooms, 2 baths, 2-car side entry garage • Slab foundation

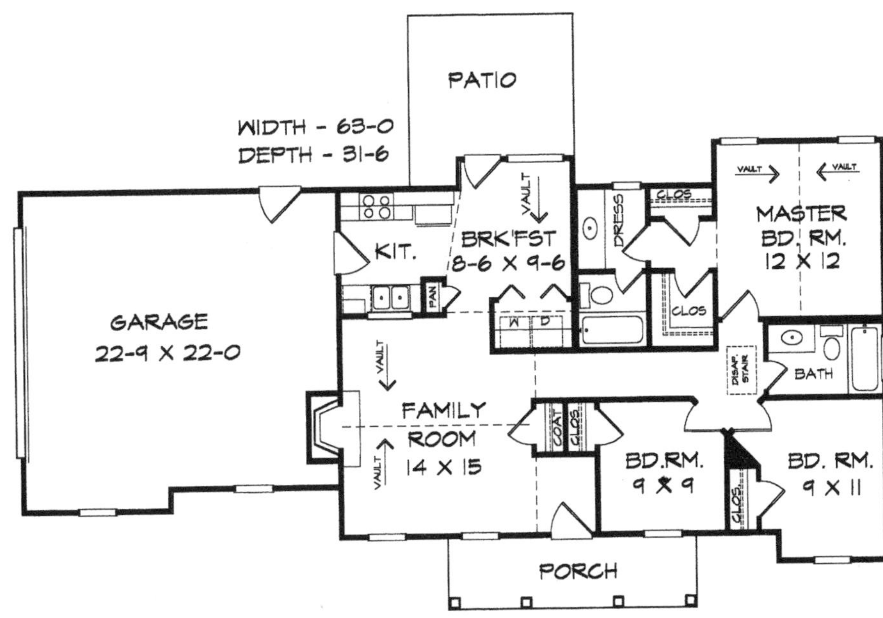

Quaint And Cozy

Plan #582-020D-0015

Price Code AA

Special Features • 1,191 total square feet of living area • Energy efficient home with 2" x 6" exterior walls • Master bedroom is located near living areas for maximum convenience • Living room has a cathedral ceiling and stone fireplace • 3 bedrooms, 2 baths, 2-car side entry garage • Slab foundation, drawings also include crawl space foundation

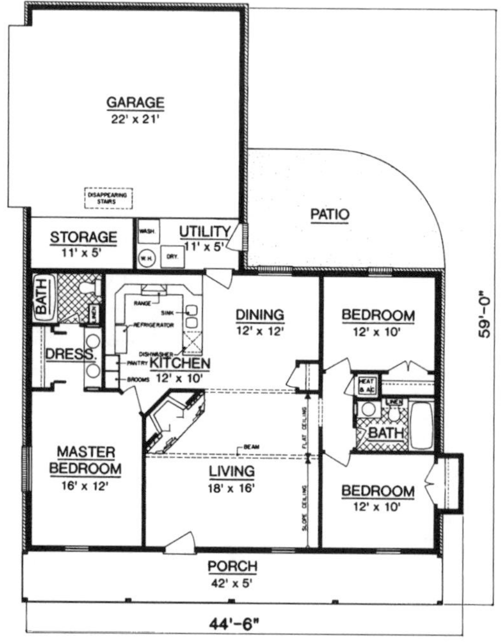

Plan #582-076D-0022

Price Code B

Special Features • 1,342 total square feet of living area • Bayed dining area provides a cheerful setting and opens to the vaulted family room • Vaulted master suite is a glorious retreat with a private bath and walk-in closet • Laundry area is conveniently located off of the kitchen • Second-floor bonus room provides an additional 266 square feet of living area • 3 bedrooms, 2 baths, 2-car side entry garage • Slab foundation

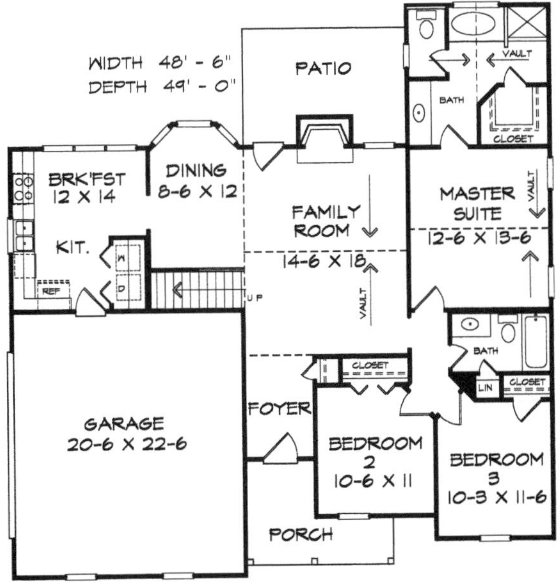

First Floor
1,342 sq. ft.

Optional
Second Floor

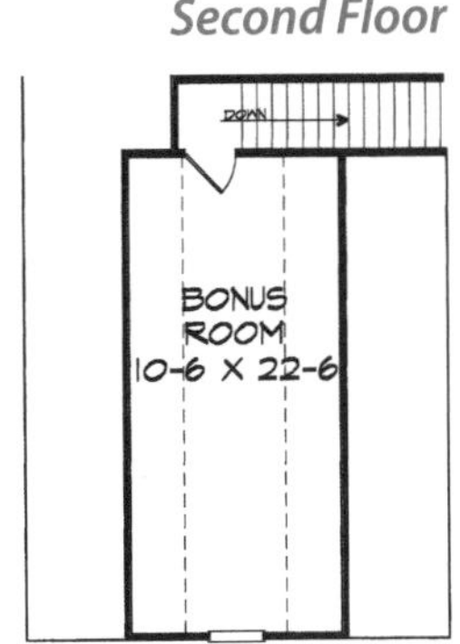

Plan #582-035D-0032

Price Code C

Special Features • 1,856 total square feet of living area • Beautiful covered porch creates a Southern accent • Kitchen has an organized feel with lots of cabinetry • Large foyer has a grand entrance and leads into family room through columns and an arched opening • 3 bedrooms, 2 baths, 2-car side entry garage • Walk-out basement, crawl space or slab foundation, please specify when ordering

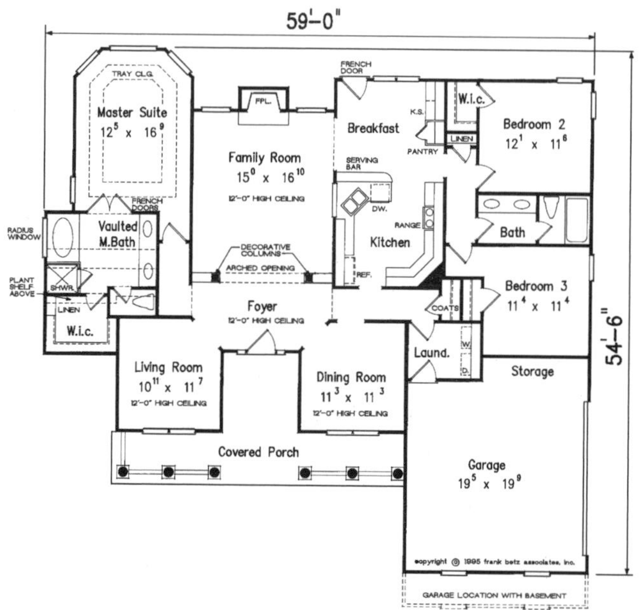

Charming Ranch Home

Plan #582-060D-0016

Price Code A

Special Features • 1,214 total square feet of living area • Sloped ceiling in great room adds drama • Utility closet is well-located near bedrooms • Open kitchen and breakfast area has cheerful window with seat • 3 bedrooms, 2 baths, optional 2-car garage • Slab or crawl space foundation, please specify when ordering

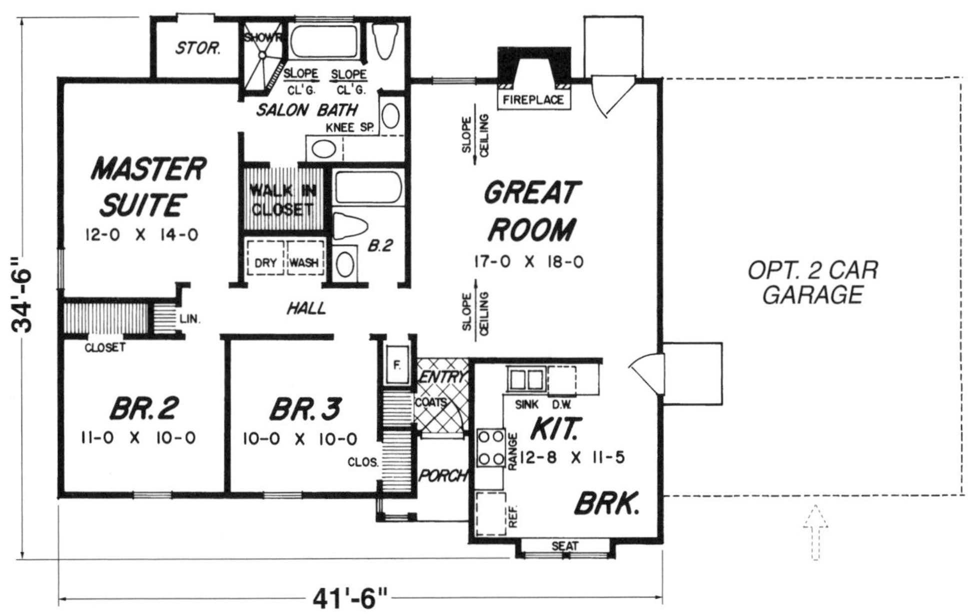

Plan #582-058D-0022

Price Code B

Special Features • 1,578 total square feet of living area • Plenty of closet, linen and storage space • Covered porches in the front and rear of home add charm to this design • Open floor plan has unique angled layout • 3 bedrooms, 2 baths, 2-car garage • Basement foundation

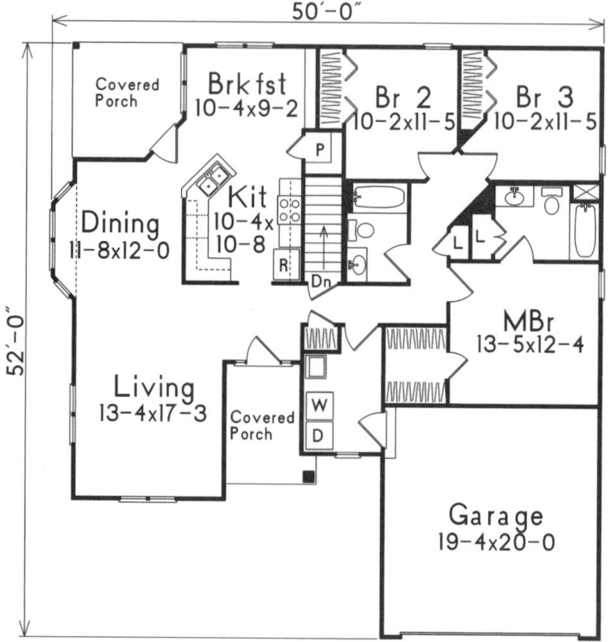

Secluded Living Room

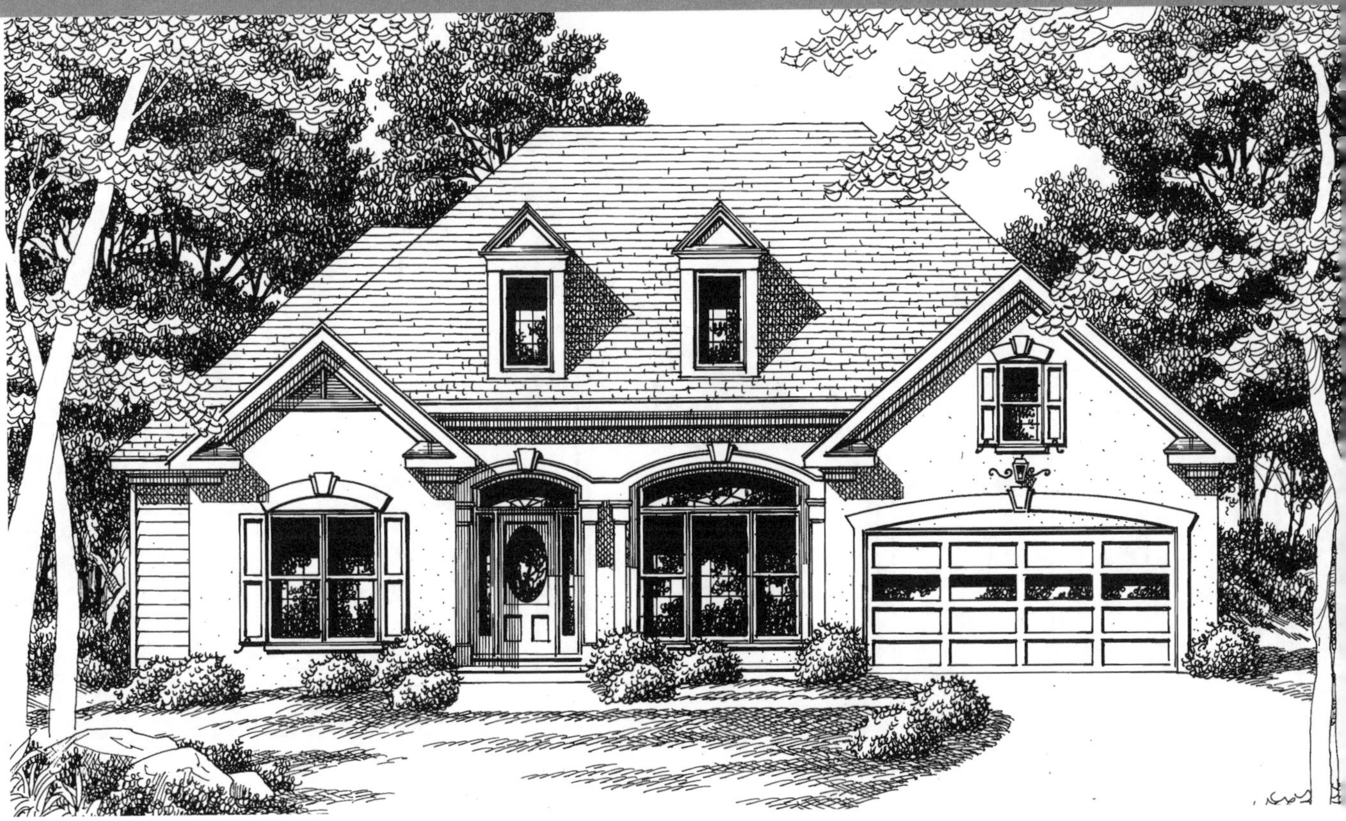

Plan #582-035D-0021

Price Code C

Special Features • 1,978 total square feet of living area • Elegant arched openings throughout interior • Vaulted living room off foyer • Master suite features a cheerful sitting room and a private bath • 3 bedrooms, 2 1/2 baths, 2-car garage • Walk-out basement, slab or crawl space foundation, please specify when ordering

www.houseplansandmore.com

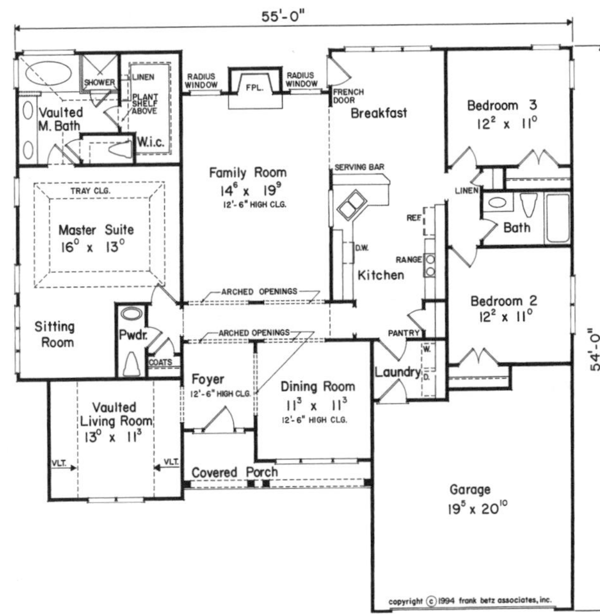

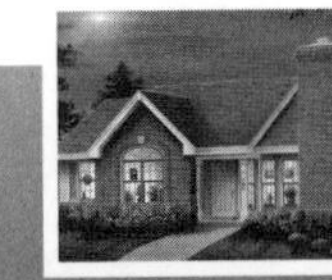

Plan #582-017D-0009

Price Code B

Special Features • 1,432 total square feet of living area • Enter the two-story foyer from the covered porch or garage • Living room has a square bay window with seat, glazed end wall with floor-to-ceiling windows and access to the deck • Kitchen/dining room also opens to the deck for added convenience • 3 bedrooms, 2 baths, 1-car garage • Basement foundation, drawings also include slab foundation

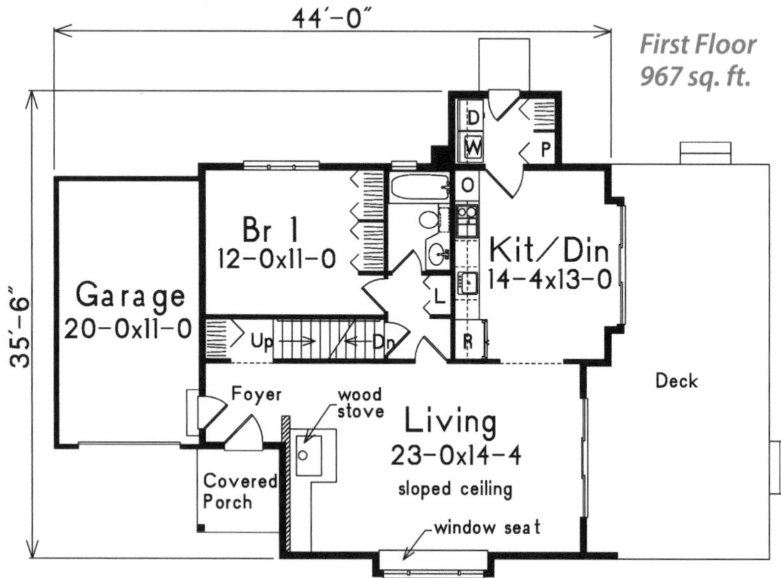

First Floor
967 sq. ft.

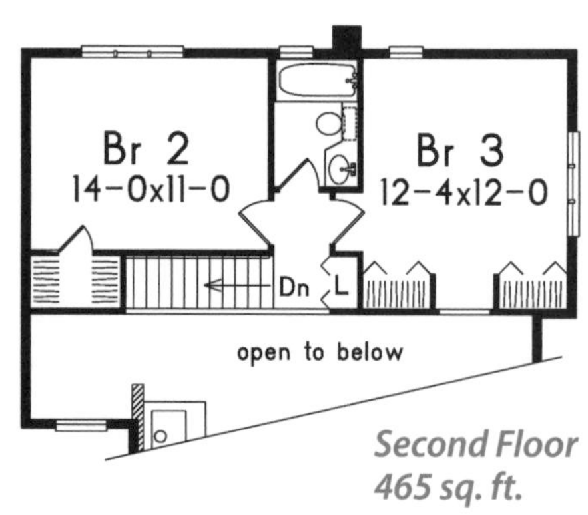

Second Floor
465 sq. ft.

Plan #582-060D-0027

Price Code B

Special Features • 1,628 total square feet of living area • Large circle transom over the front door gives this house a classic look • 9' ceilings on the first floor • Salon bath has a tub, separate shower, a double vanity and a large walk-in closet • Well-lit breakfast area has view to the backyard with large patio area • Future play room on the second floor has an additional 354 square feet of living area • 3 bedrooms, 2 1/2 baths, 2-car garage • Slab foundation

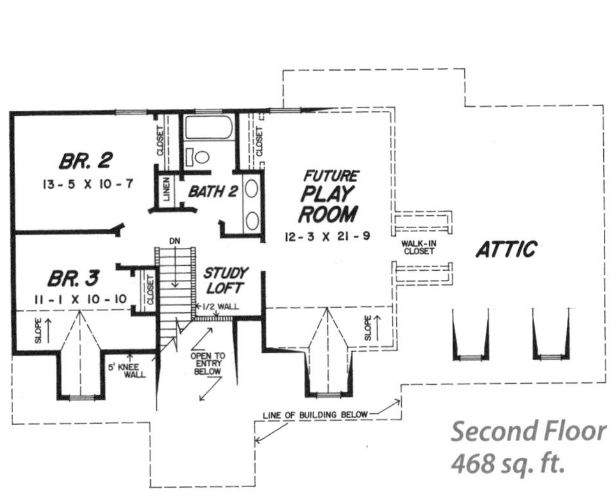

Second Floor
468 sq. ft.

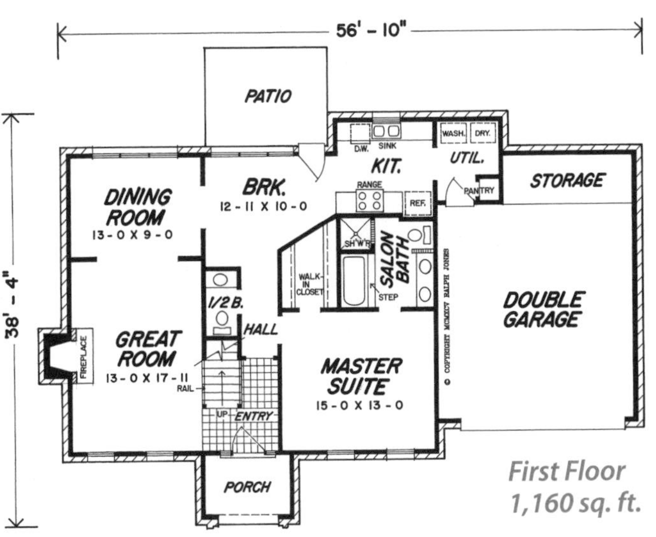

First Floor
1,160 sq. ft.

www.houseplansandmore.com

Trio Of Dormers Adds Light

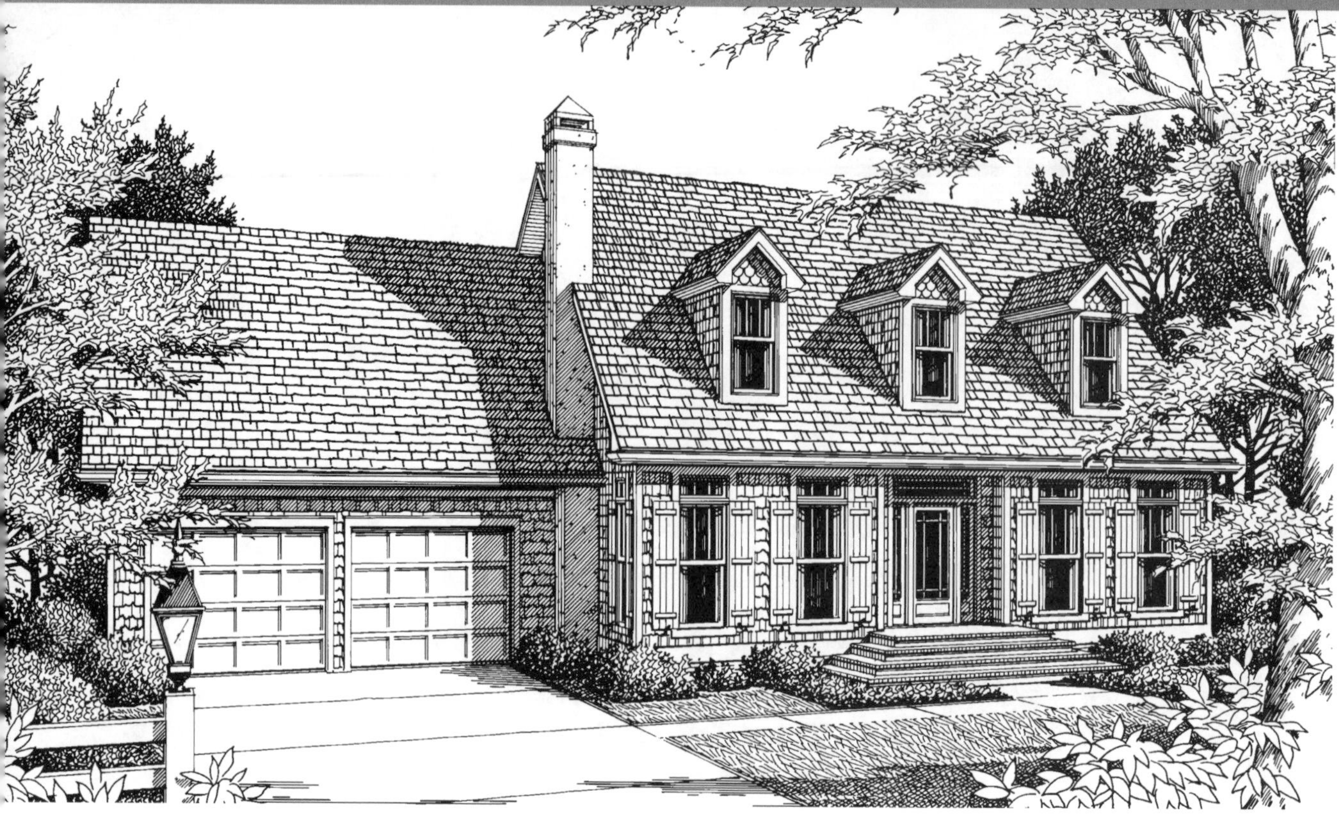

Plan #582-039D-0011

Price Code B

Special Features • 1,780 total square feet of living area • Traditional styling with all the comforts of home • First floor master bedroom has walk-in closet and bath • Large kitchen and dining area open to deck • 3 bedrooms, 2 1/2 baths, 2-car garage • Basement, crawl space or slab foundation, please specify when ordering

First Floor
1,229 sq. ft.

Second Floor
551 sq. ft.

1-800-DREAM HOME (373-2646)

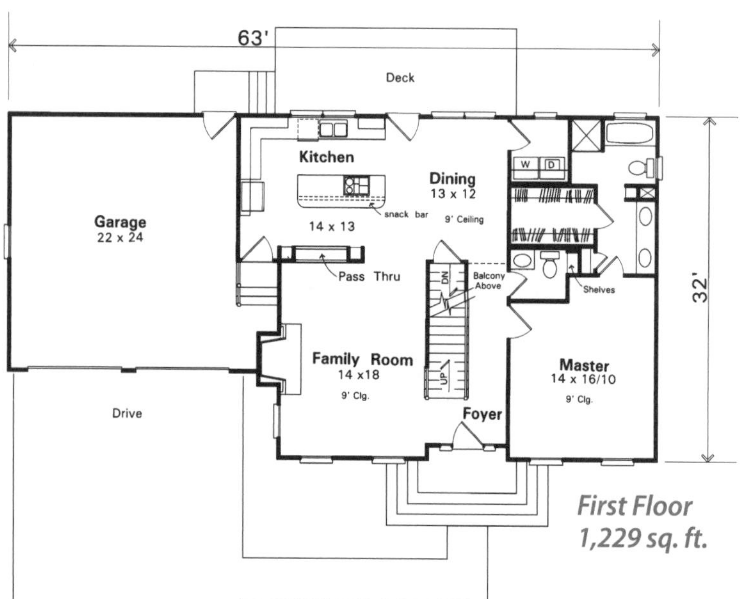

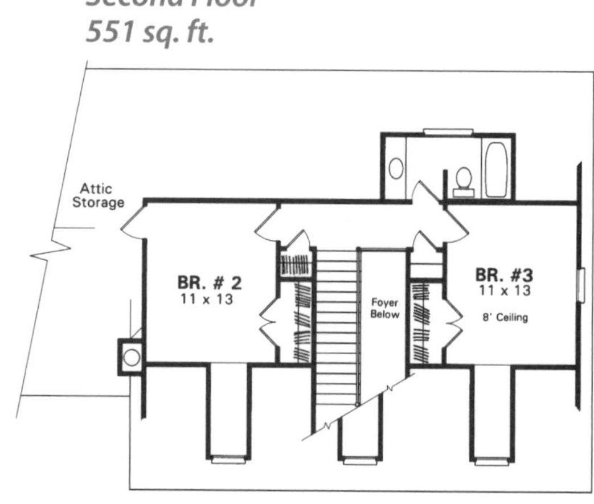

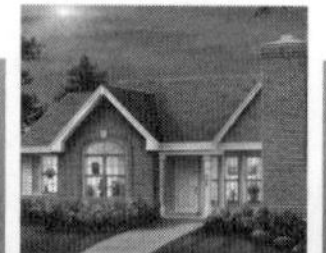

Large Living And Dining Areas

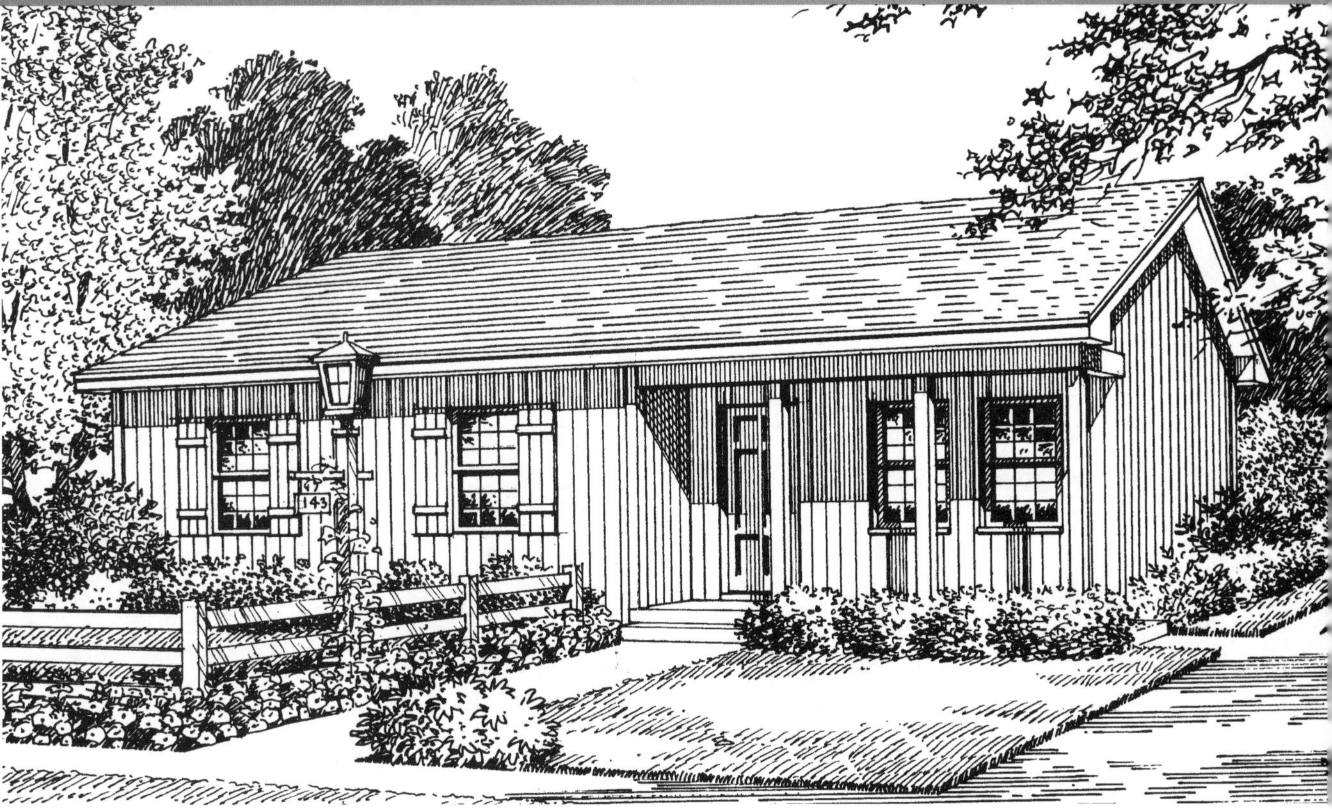

Plan #582-001D-0081

Price Code AA

Special Features • 1,160 total square feet of living area • U-shaped kitchen includes breakfast bar and convenient laundry area • Master bedroom features private half bath and large closet • Dining room has outdoor access • Dining and great rooms combine to create an open living atmosphere • 3 bedrooms, 1 1/2 baths • Crawl space foundation, drawings also include basement and slab foundations

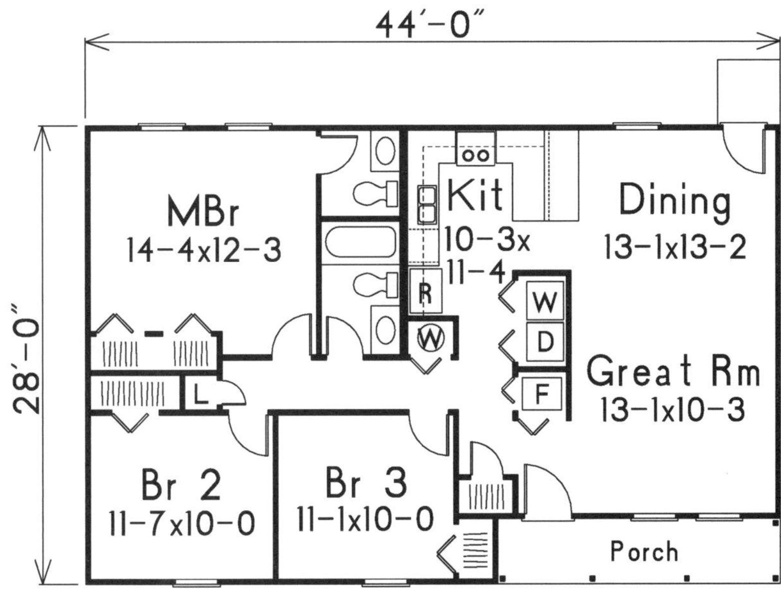

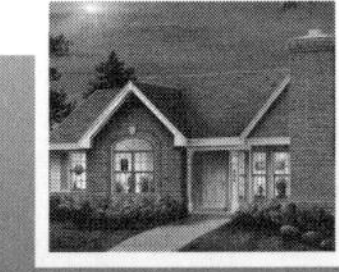

Stylish Master Bedroom Off By Itself

Plan #582-022D-0008

Price Code B

Special Features • 1,565 total square feet of living area • Highly-detailed exterior adds value • Large vaulted great room with a full wall of glass opens onto the corner deck • Loft balcony opens to rooms below and adds to the spacious feeling • Bay-windowed kitchen with a cozy morning room • Master bath with platform tub, separate shower and a large walk-in closet • 3 bedrooms, 2 1/2 baths, 2-car garage • Basement foundation

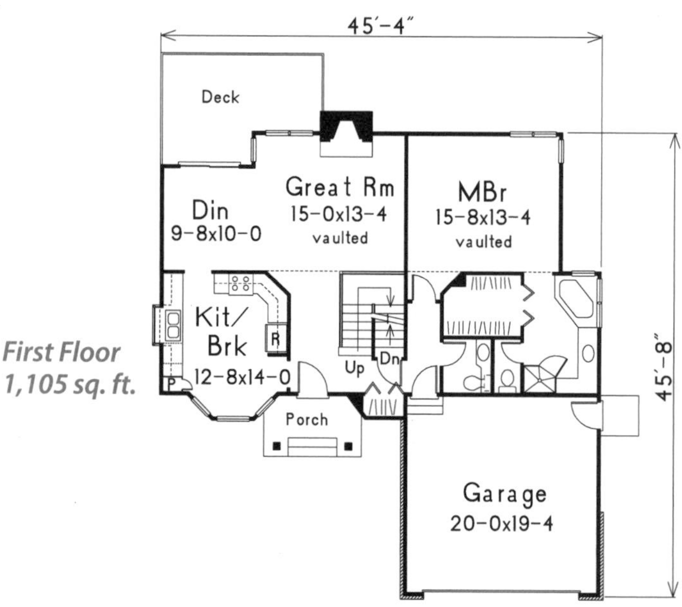

First Floor
1,105 sq. ft.

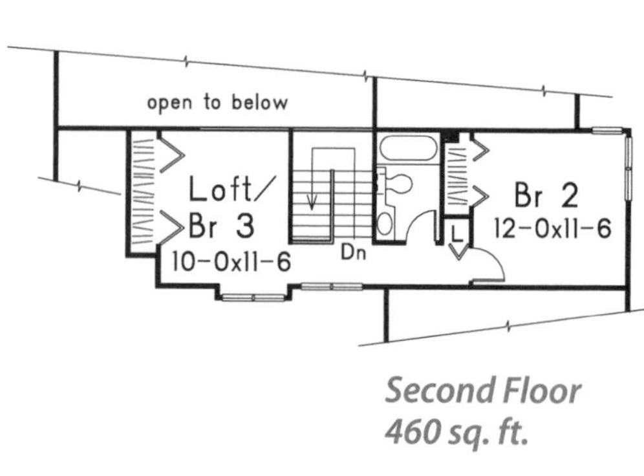

Second Floor
460 sq. ft.

Plan #582-049D-0006

Price Code B

Special Features • 1,771 total square feet of living area • Efficient country kitchen shares space with a bayed eating area • Two-story family/great room is warmed by a fireplace in winter and open to outdoor country comfort in the summer with double French doors • First floor master suite offers a bay window and access to the porch through French doors • 3 bedrooms, 2 1/2 baths, optional 2-car detached garage • Basement foundation

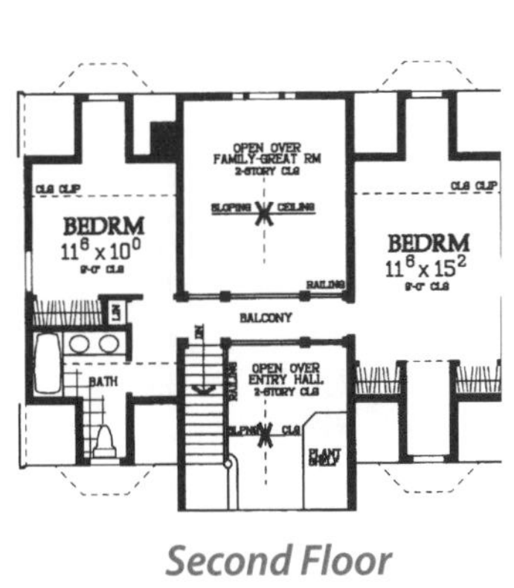

Second Floor
600 sq. ft.

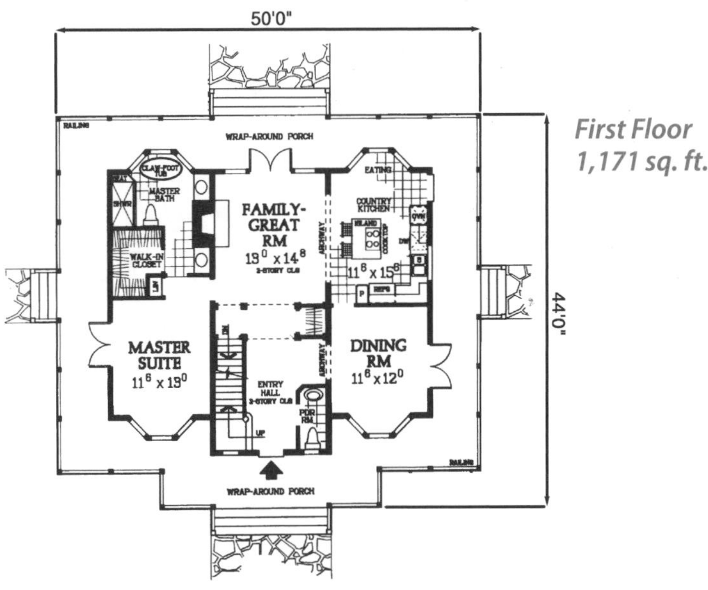

First Floor
1,171 sq. ft.

www.houseplansandmore.com

Comfortable Living In This Ranch

Plan #582-025D-0003

Price Code A

Special Features • 1,379 total square feet of living area • Vaulted great room makes a lasting impression with corner fireplace and windows • Formal dining room easily connects to kitchen making entertaining easy • Master bath includes all the luxuries such as a spacious walk-in closet, oversized tub and separate shower • 3 bedrooms, 2 baths, 2-car garage • Slab foundation

Cozy Covered Front Porch

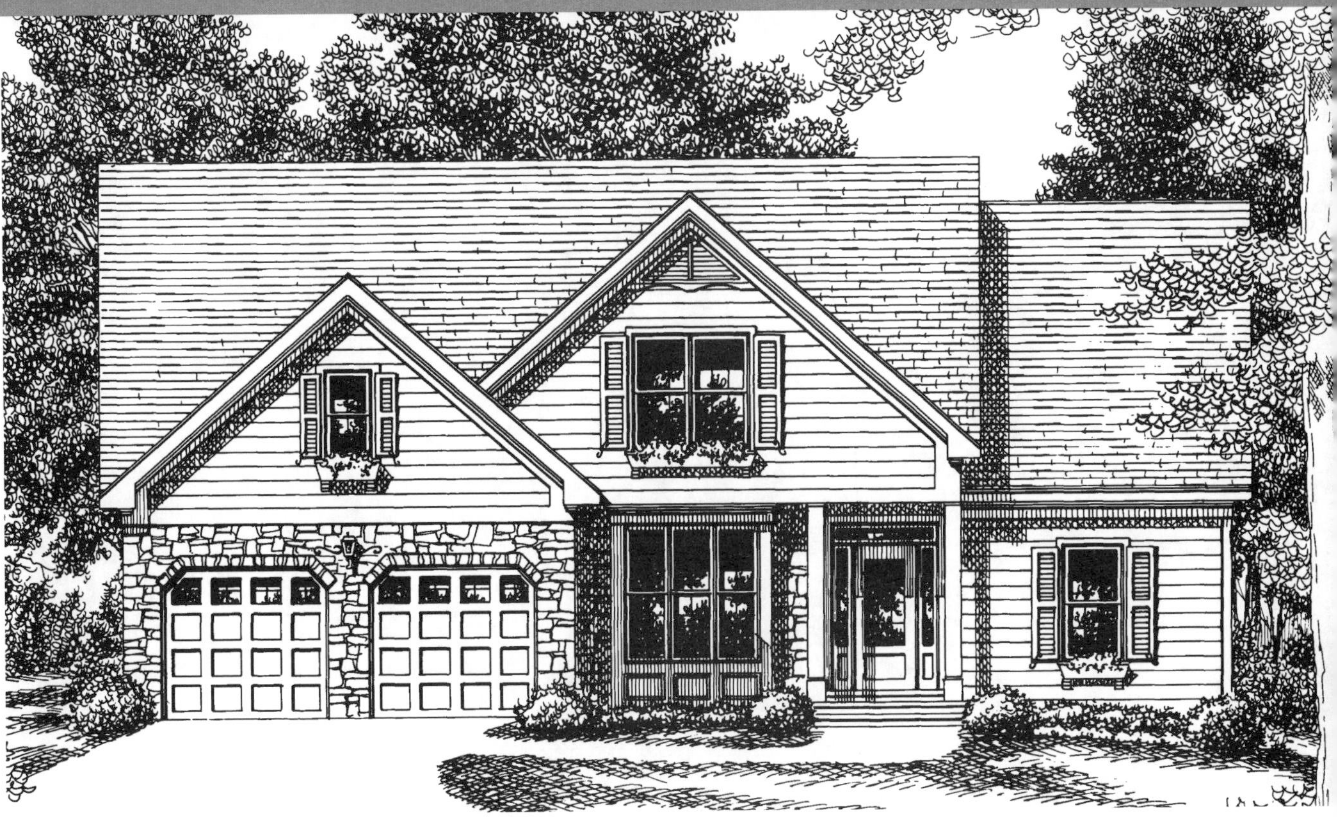

Plan #582-035D-0055

Price Code B

Special Features • 1,583 total square feet of living area • 9' ceilings throughout this home • Additional bedrooms are located away from the master suite for privacy • Optional second floor has an additional 532 square feet of living area • 3 bedrooms, 2 baths, 2-car garage • Walk-out basement or crawl space foundation, please specify when ordering

Optional Second Floor

First Floor
1,583 sq. ft.

www.houseplansandmore.com

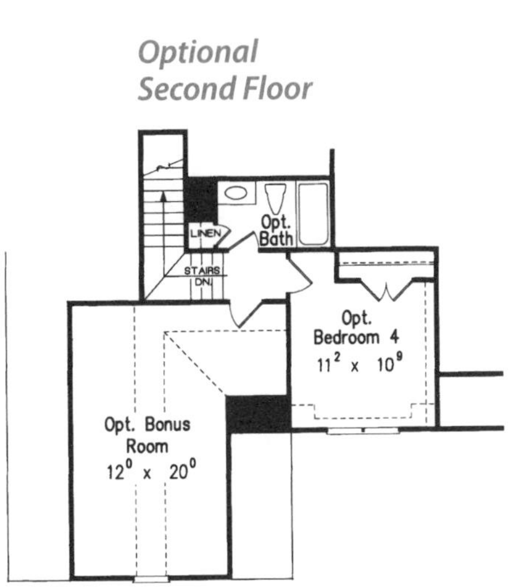

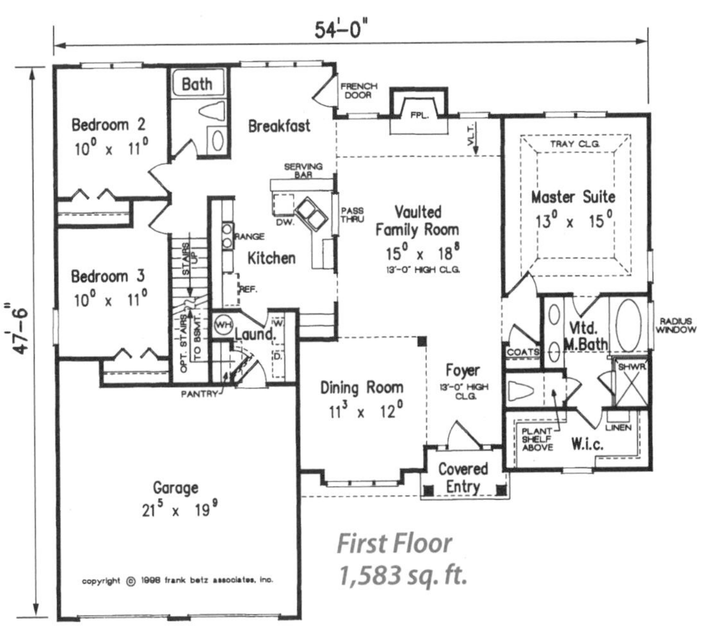

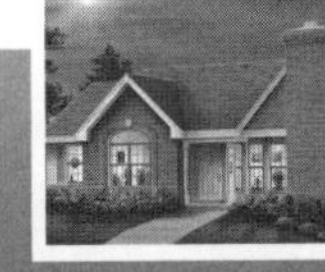

Plan #582-040D-0024

Price Code C

Special Features • 1,874 total square feet of living area • 9' ceilings throughout first floor • Two-story foyer opens into large family room with fireplace • First floor master bedroom includes private bath with tub and shower • 4 bedrooms, 2 1/2 baths, 2-car garage • Basement foundation, drawings also include slab foundation

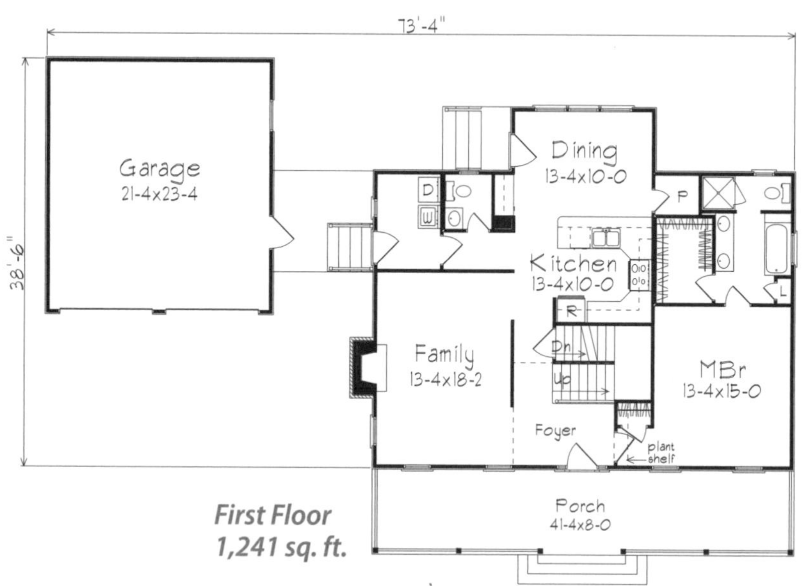

First Floor
1,241 sq. ft.

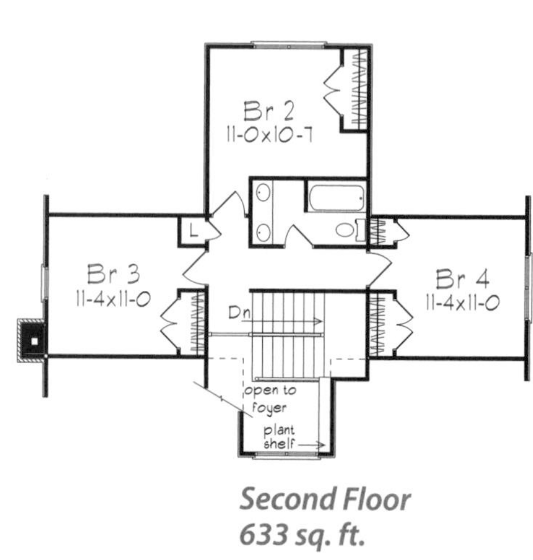

Second Floor
633 sq. ft.

Porch Adds Country Charm To Home

Plan #582-076D-0006

Price Code B

Special Features • 1,277 total square feet of living area • Spacious family room enjoys grand corner fireplace • Bayed dining area connects with the kitchen and family room for added openness • Optional lower level has an additional 633 square feet of living area with a recreation area and bonus room • 3 bedrooms, 3 baths, 2-car drive under garage • Basement foundation

First Floor
1,277 sq. ft.

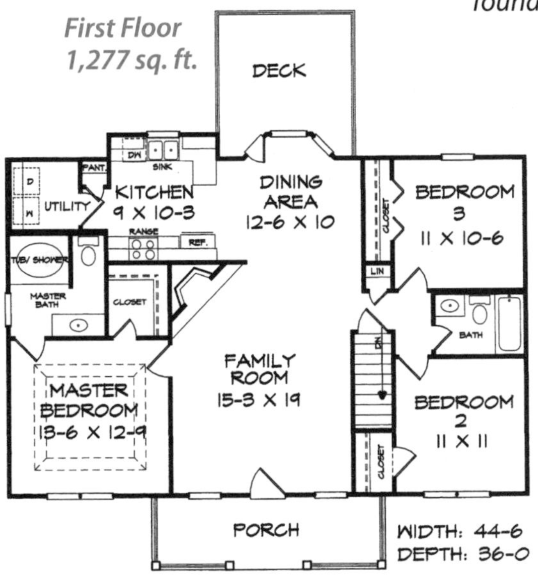

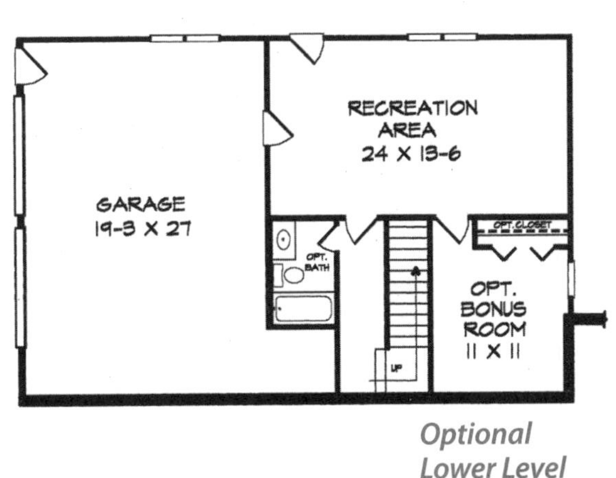

Optional
Lower Level

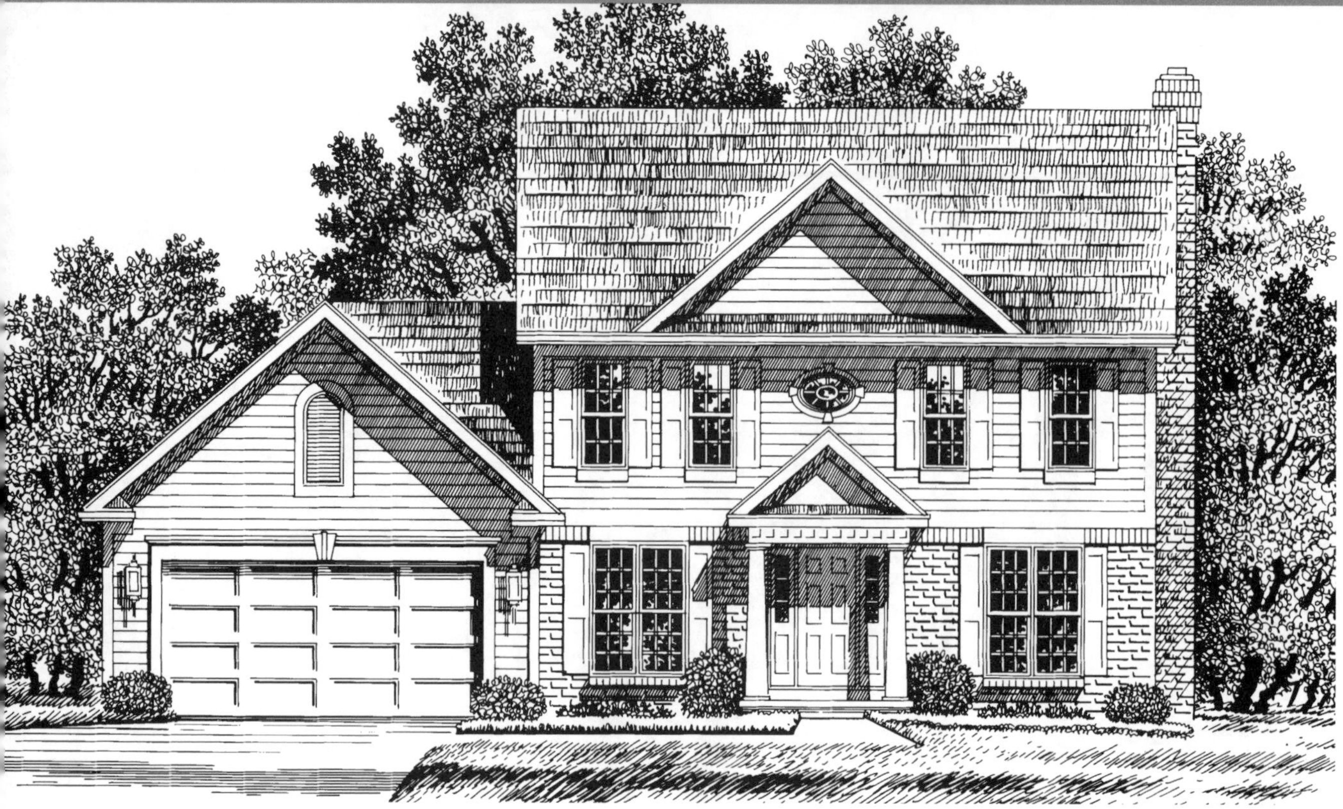

Plan #582-034D-0019

Price Code C

Special Features • 1,992 total square feet of living area • Sunny family room has lots of windows and a large fireplace • Octagon-shaped dining area is adjacent to kitchen for easy access • The family room features a double-door entry into the formal living room • Master bedroom has a private bath with dressing area and walk-in closet • 4 bedrooms, 2 1/2 baths, 2-car garage • Basement foundation

Width: 52'-8"
Depth: 41'-8"

First Floor
1,100 sq. ft.

Second Floor
892 sq. ft.

1-800-DREAM HOME (373-2646)

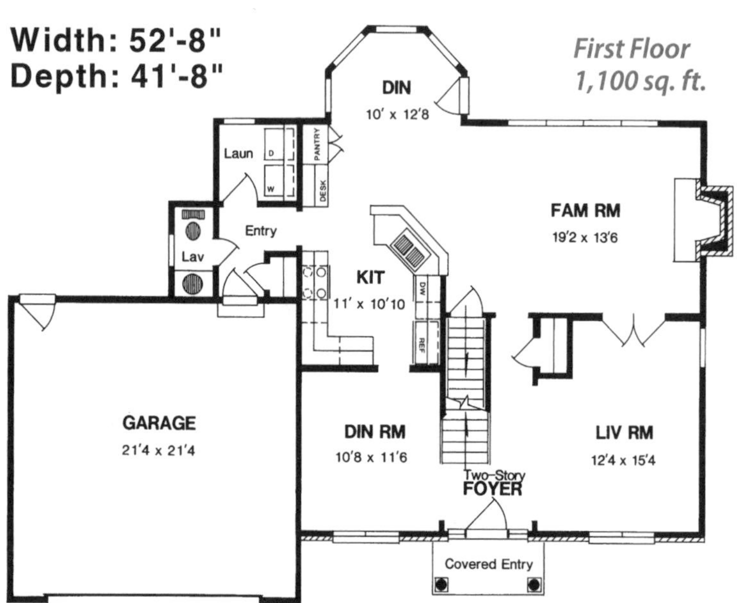

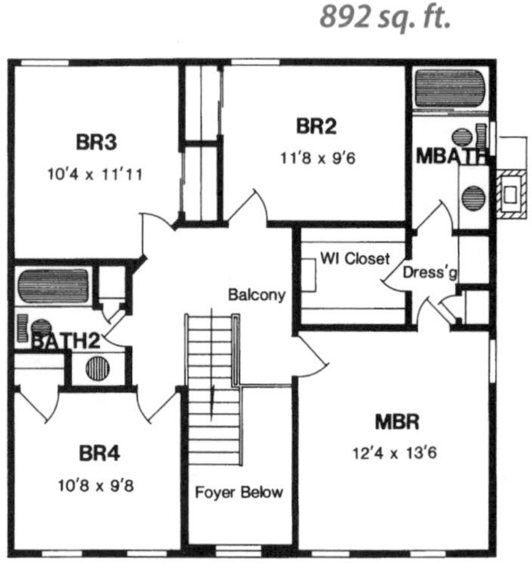

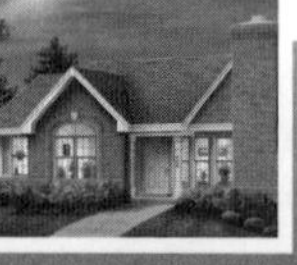

Plan #582-008D-0012

Price Code A

Special Features • 1,232 total square feet of living area • Ideal porch for quiet quality evenings • Great room opens to dining room for those large dinner gatherings • Functional L-shaped kitchen includes broom cabinet • Master bedroom contains large walk-in closet and compartmented bath • 3 bedrooms, 1 bath, optional 2-car garage • Basement foundation, drawings also include crawl space and slab foundations

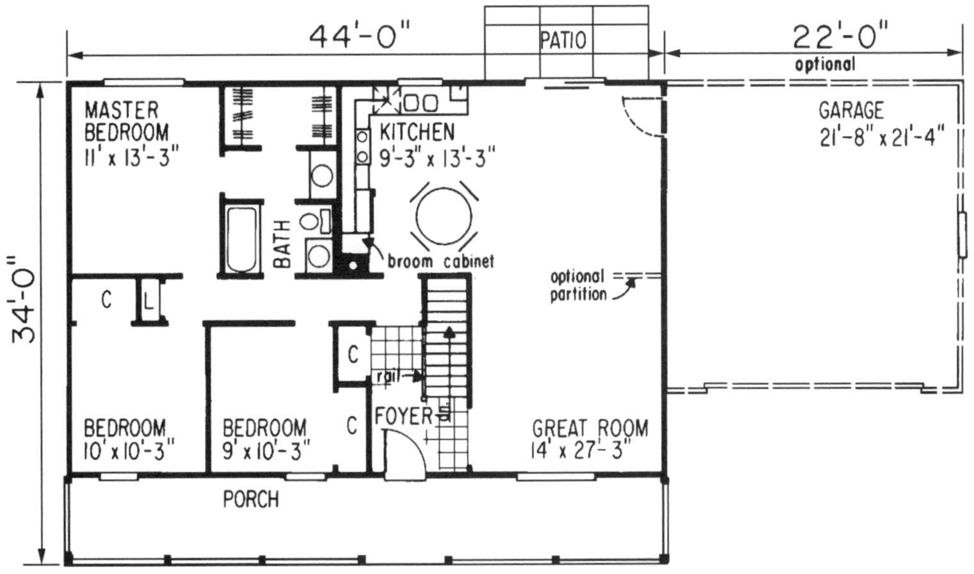

Plan #582-047D-0026 Price Code C

Special Features • 1,817 total square feet of living area • Master bedroom has its own sitting area flooded with sunlight from windows all around • Family room has a fireplace flanked by bookshelves • An open and airy dining room flows into the family room • 3 bedrooms, 2 baths, 2-car garage • Slab foundation

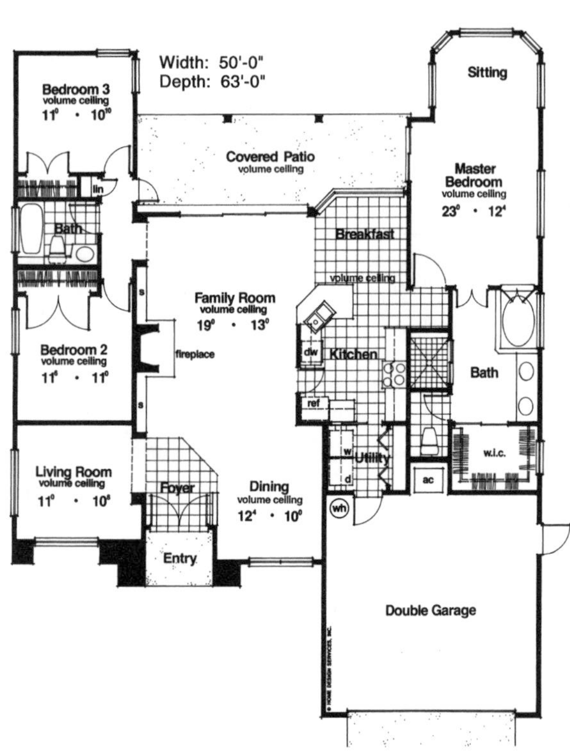

Large Built-In Desk On Second Floor

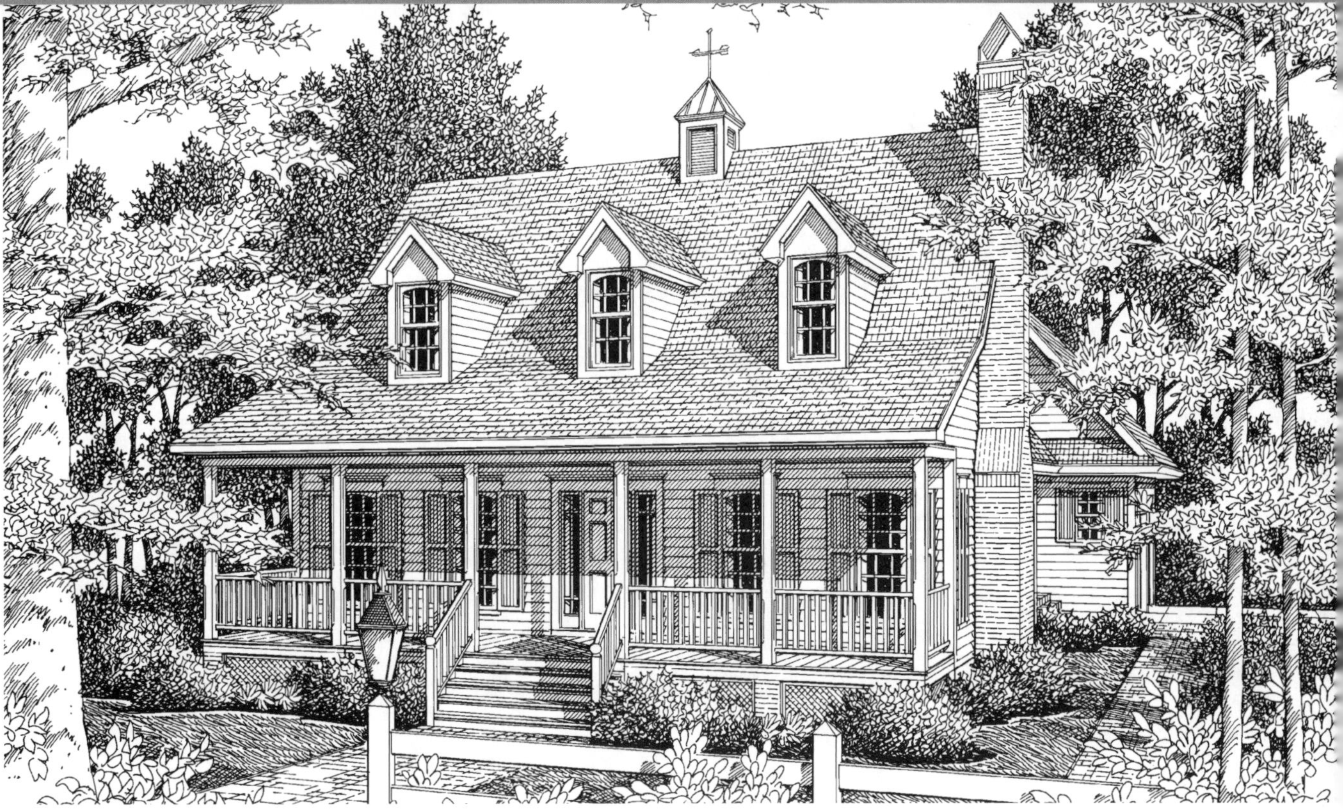

Plan #582-039D-0012 — Price Code C

Special Features • 1,815 total square feet of living area • Second floor has built-in desk in hall that is ideal as a computer work station or mini office area • Two doors into laundry area make it handy from the master bedroom and the rest of the home • Inviting covered porch • Lots of counterspace and cabinetry in kitchen • 3 bedrooms, 2 1/2 baths, 2-car side entry garage • Basement foundation

Width: 43'-0"
Depth: 74'-0"

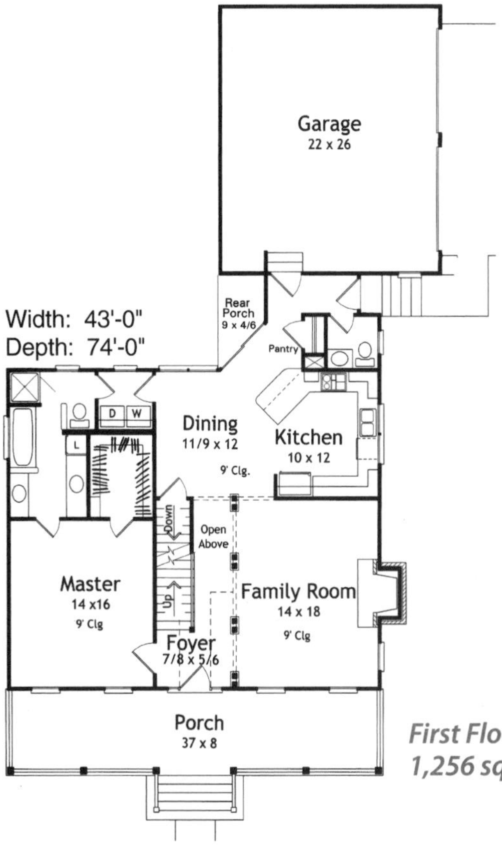

First Floor
1,256 sq. ft.

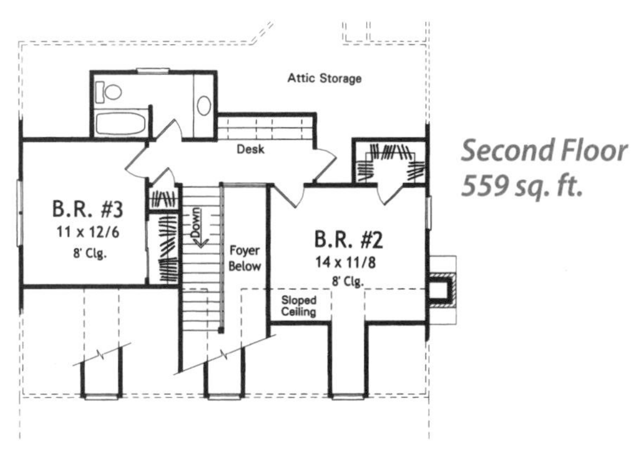

Second Floor
559 sq. ft.

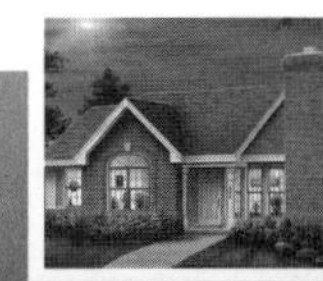

Great Plan For Formal And Informal Entertaining

Plan #582-033D-0013

Price Code D

Special Features • 1,813 total square feet of living area • Bedrooms are located on the second floor for privacy • Living room with large bay window joins dining room for expansive formal entertaining • The family room, dinette and kitchen combine for an impressive living area • Two-story foyer and L-shaped stairs create a dramatic entry • Inviting covered porch • 3 bedrooms, 2 1/2 baths, 2-car garage • Basement foundation

Second Floor
719 sq. ft.

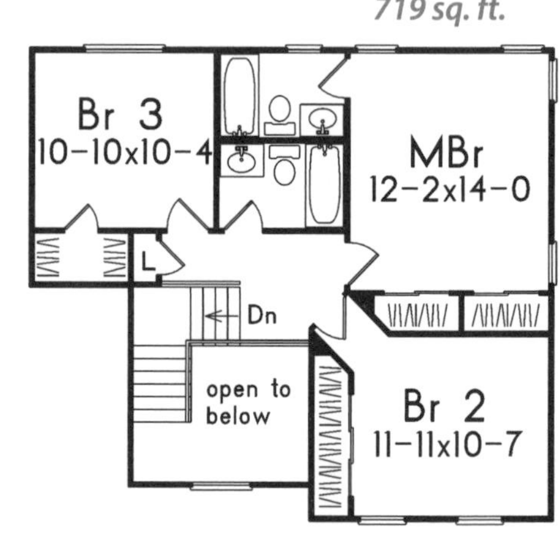

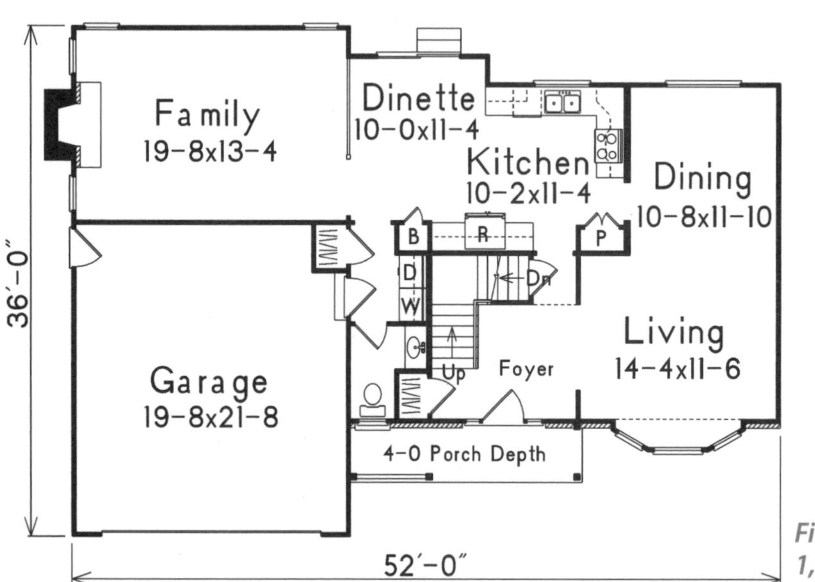

First Floor
1,094 sq. ft.

Plan #582-049D-0009

Price Code B

Special Features • 1,673 total square feet of living area • Great room flows into the breakfast nook with outdoor access and beyond to an efficient kitchen • Master bedroom on second floor has access to loft/study, private balcony and bath • Covered porch surrounds the entire home for outdoor living area • 3 bedrooms, 2 baths • Crawl space foundation

Second Floor
580 sq. ft.

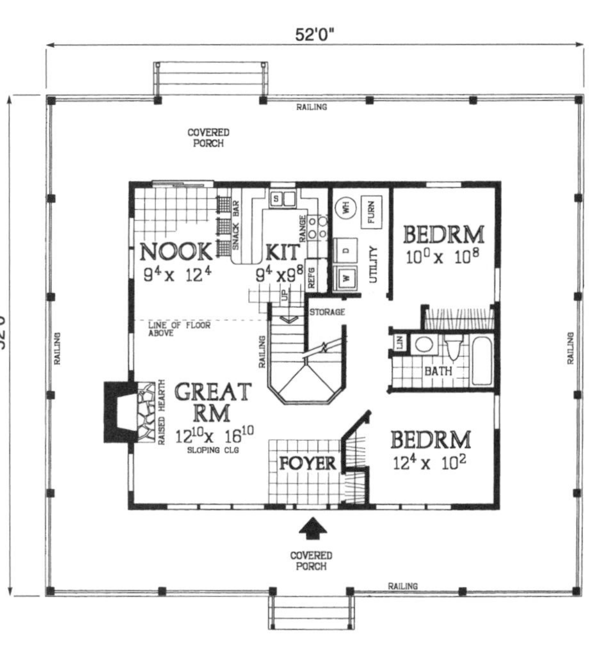

First Floor
1,093 sq. ft.

Plan #582-030D-0006

Price Code C

Special Features • 1,896 total square feet of living area • Living room has lots of windows, a media center and a fireplace • Centrally located kitchen with breakfast nook • Extra storage in garage • Covered porch in front and rear of home • Optional balcony on second floor • 4 bedrooms, 2 1/2 baths, 2-car garage • Basement, crawl space or slab foundation, please specify when ordering

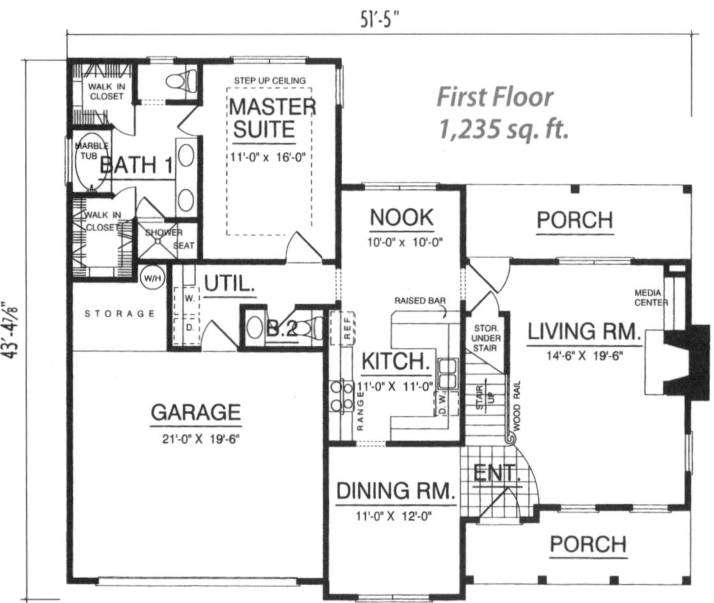

First Floor
1,235 sq. ft.

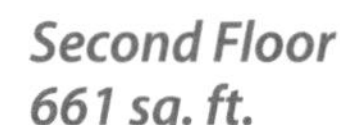

Second Floor
661 sq. ft.

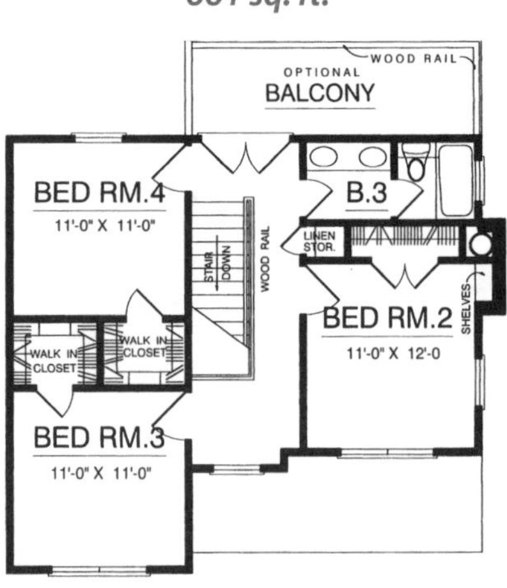

Open Floor Plan Makes Home Feel Larger

Plan #582-058D-0043

Price Code A

Special Features • 1,277 total square feet of living area • Vaulted ceilings in master bedroom, great room, kitchen and dining room • Laundry closet is located near bedrooms for convenience • Compact, yet efficient kitchen • 3 bedrooms, 2 baths, 2-car garage • Basement foundation

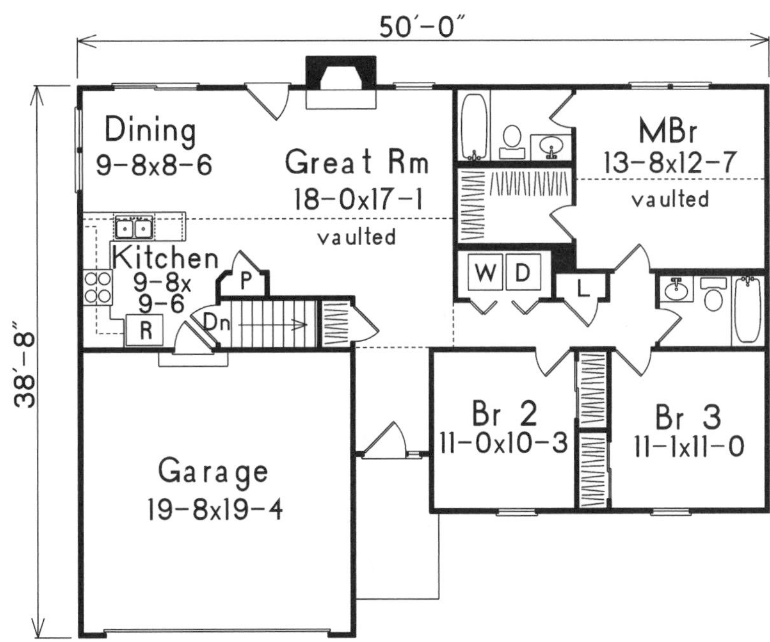

Vaulted Ceilings Show Off This Ranch

Plan #582-014D-0008

Price Code AA

Special Features • 1,135 total square feet of living area • Living and dining rooms feature vaulted ceilings and a corner fireplace • Energy efficient home with 2" x 6" exterior walls • Master bedroom offers a vaulted ceiling, private bath and generous closet space • Compact but functional kitchen complete with pantry and adjacent utility room • 3 bedrooms, 2 baths, 2-car garage • Basement foundation, drawings also include crawl space foundation

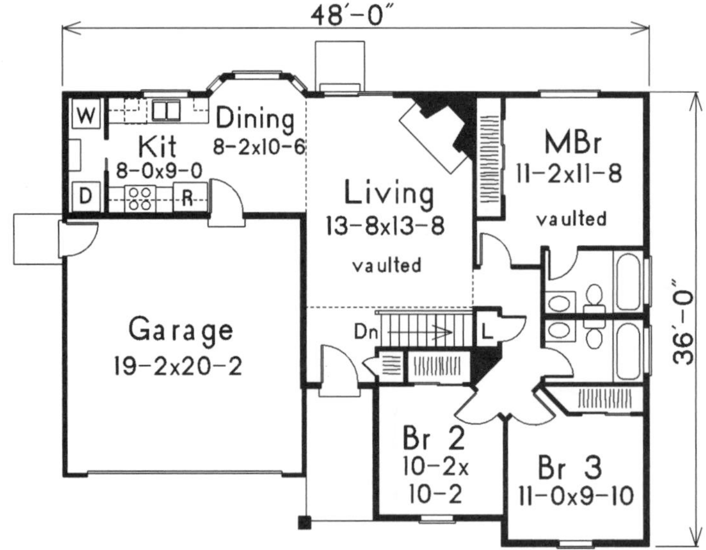

Plan #582-026D-0137

Price Code B

Special Features • 1,758 total square feet of living area • Secluded covered porch off breakfast area is a charming touch • Great room and dining area combine for terrific entertaining possibilities • Master bedroom has all the amenities • Spacious foyer opens into a large great room with 11' ceiling • 3 bedrooms, 2 baths, 2-car garage • Basement foundation

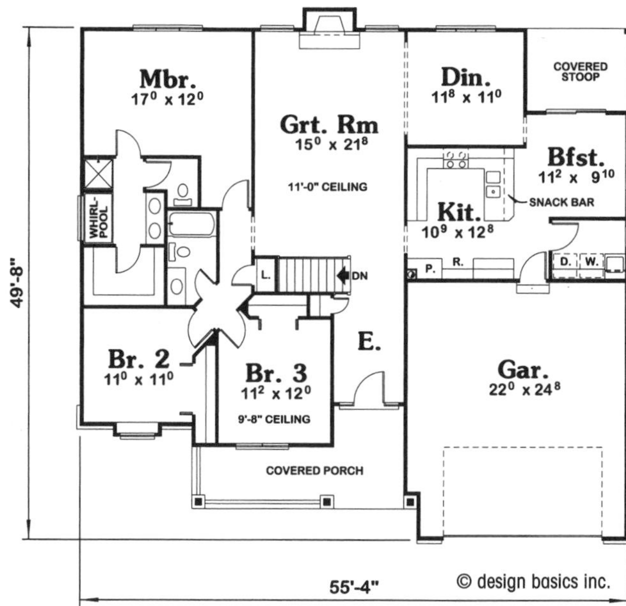

Plan #582-060D-0018

Price Code A

Special Features • 1,398 total square feet of living area • Country kitchen has a vaulted ceiling, spacious eating bar and lots of extra space for dining • Enormous vaulted great room has cozy fireplace flanked by windows and ceiling beams for an added rustic appeal • Master suite bath has a shower and step-up tub with stained glass ledge and plant niche accents • 3 bedrooms, 2 baths, 2-car garage • Slab or crawl space foundation, please specify when ordering

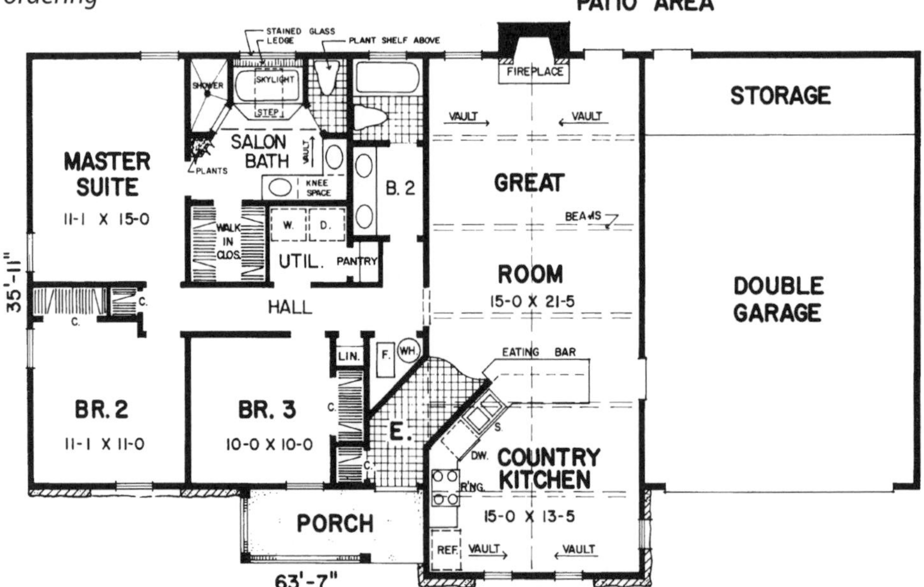

1-800-DREAM HOME (373-2646)

Tall Windows, Sweeping Roof Lines Make An Impression

Plan #582-022D-0003

Price Code A

Special Features • 1,351 total square feet of living area • Roof lines and vaulted ceilings make this home appear larger • Central fireplace provides a focal point for dining and living areas • Master bedroom features a roomy window seat and a walk-in closet • Loft can easily be converted to a third bedroom • 2 bedrooms, 2 1/2 baths, 2-car garage • Basement foundation

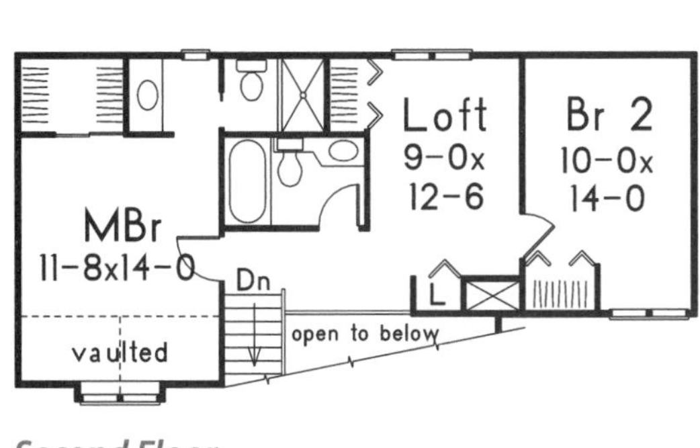

Second Floor
677 sq. ft.

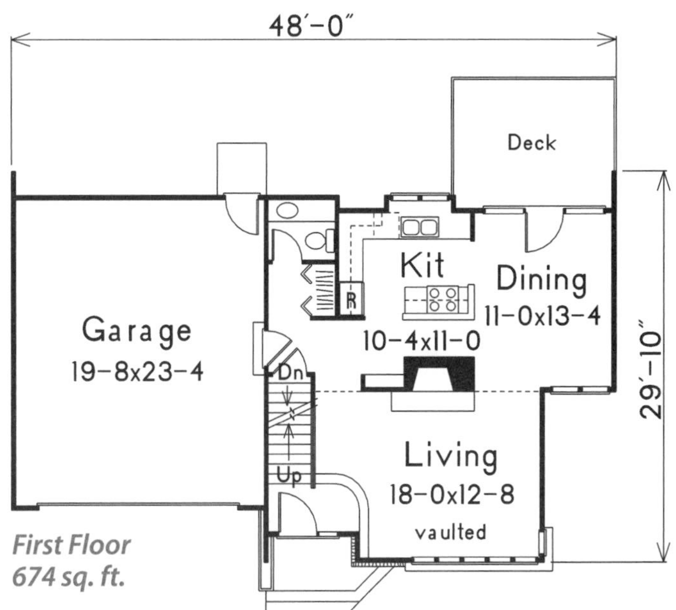

First Floor
674 sq. ft.

Well-Arranged For Cozy Open Living

Plan #582-053D-0035

Price Code B

Special Features • 1,527 total square feet of living area • Convenient laundry room is located off the garage • Vaulted ceiling in living room slopes to foyer and dining area creating a spacious entrance • Galley kitchen provides easy passage to both breakfast and dining areas • Master bedroom is complete with a large master bath, platform tub and shower, plus roomy walk-in closets • 3 bedrooms, 2 baths, 2-car side entry garage • Basement foundation, drawings also include slab and crawl space foundations

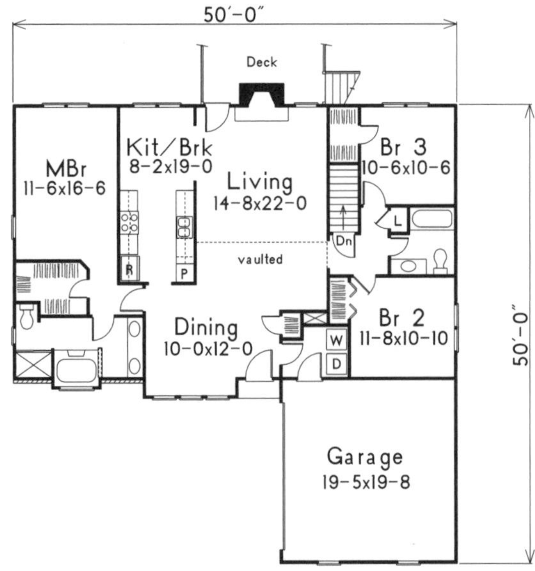

Plan #582-040D-0032

Price Code C

Special Features • *1,808 total square feet of living area* • *Master bedroom has a walk-in closet, double vanities and a separate tub and shower* • *Two second floor bedrooms share a study area and full bath* • *Partially covered patio is complete with a skylight* • *Side entrance opens to utility room with convenient counterspace and laundry sink* • *3 bedrooms, 2 1/2 baths, 2-car side entry garage* • *Basement foundation*

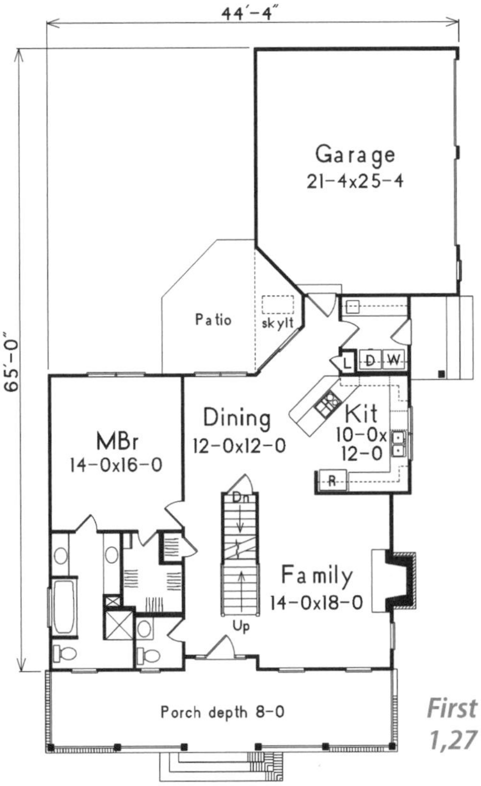

First Floor
1,271 sq. ft.

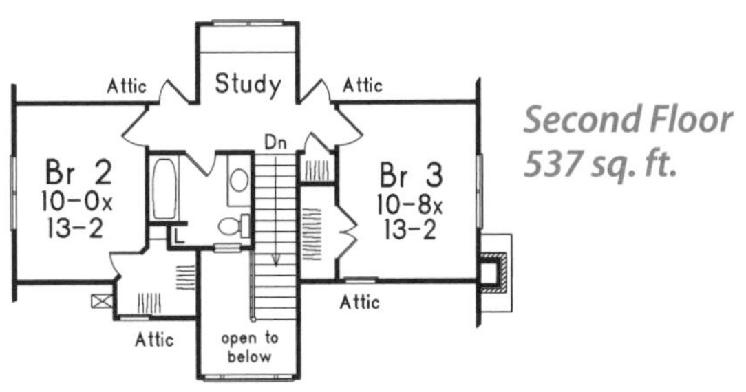

Second Floor
537 sq. ft.

Gabled Front Porch Gives A Country Flair

Plan #582-052D-0013

Price Code A

Special Features • 1,379 total square feet of living area • Living area has a spacious feel with 11'-6" ceiling • Kitchen has eat-in breakfast bar open to dining area • Laundry area is located near the bedrooms • Large cased opening with columns opens to the living and dining areas • 3 bedrooms, 2 baths, 2-car drive under garage • Basement foundation

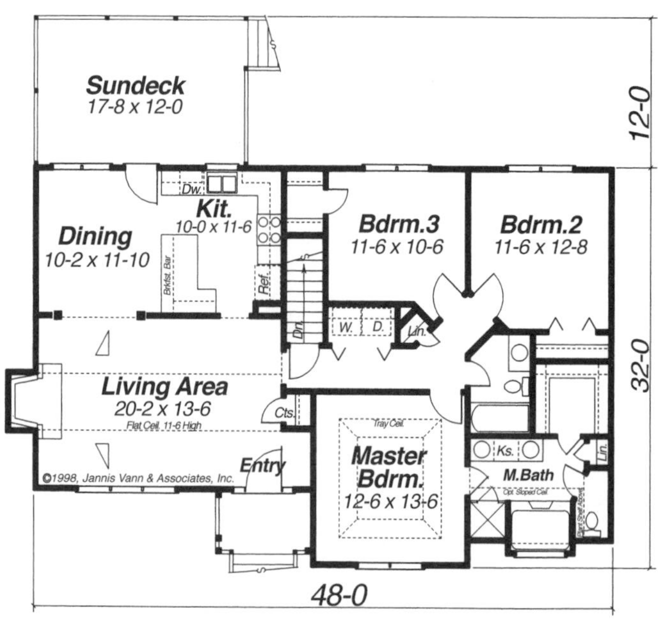

Openness Reflects Relaxed Lifestyle

Plan #582-007D-0036

Price Code A

Special Features • *1,330 total square feet of living area* • *Vaulted living room is open to bayed dining room and kitchen creating an ideal space for entertaining* • *Two bedrooms, a bath and linen closet complete the first floor and are easily accessible* • *The second floor offers two bedrooms with walk-in closets, a very large storage room and an opening with louvered doors which overlooks the living room* • *4 bedrooms, 2 baths, 1-car garage* • *Basement foundation*

First Floor
884 sq. ft.

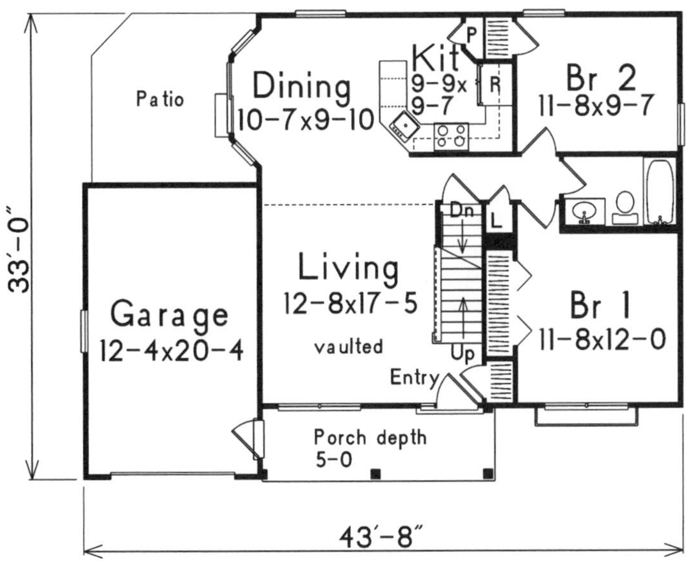

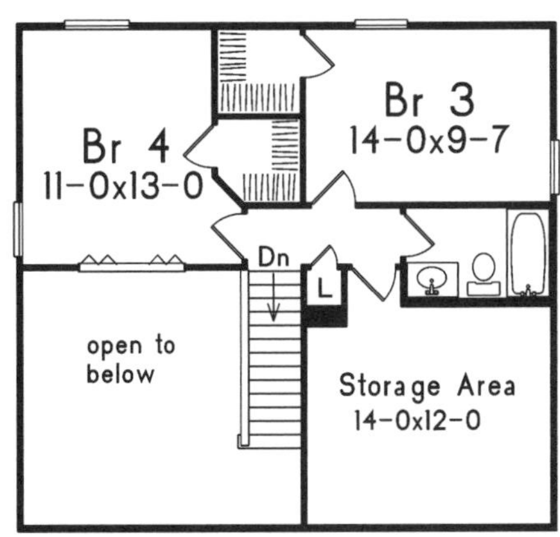

Second Floor
446 sq. ft.

www.houseplansandmore.com

Farmhouse Style Offers Great Privacy

Plan #582-017D-0002

Price Code D

Special Features • 1,805 total square feet of living area • Energy efficient home with 2" x 6" exterior walls • Master bedroom forms its own wing • Second floor bedrooms share a hall bath • Large great room with fireplace blends into the formal dining room • 3 bedrooms, 2 1/2 baths, 2-car side entry garage • Basement foundation, drawings also include slab foundation

First Floor
1,245 sq. ft.

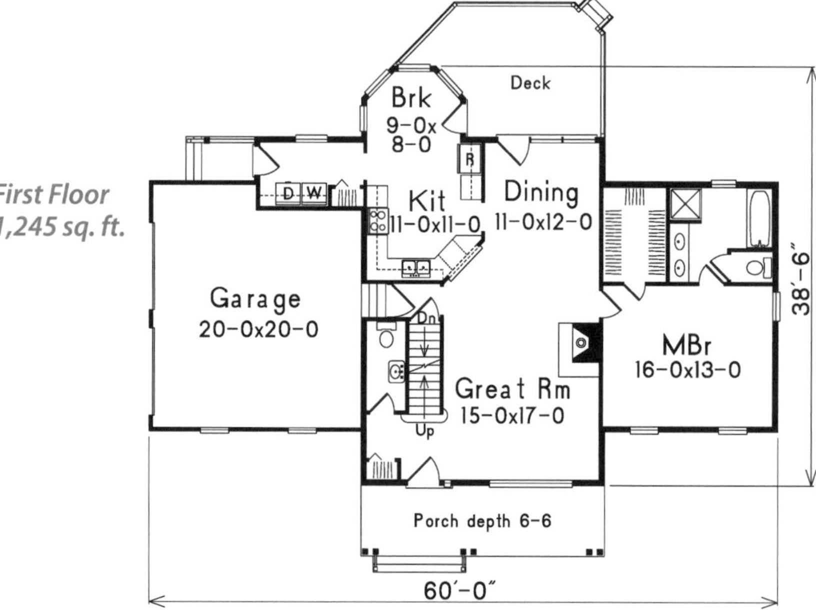

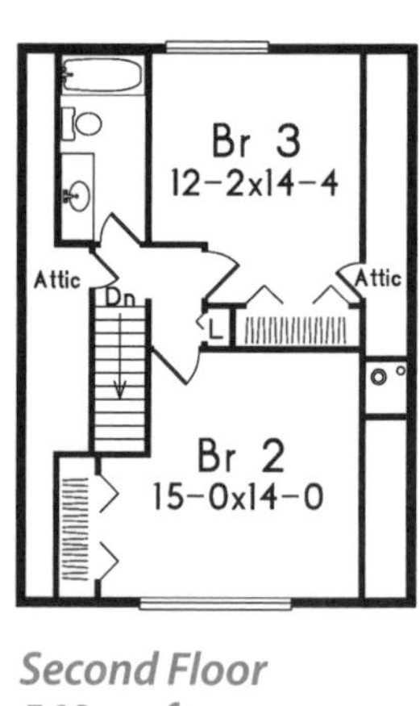

Second Floor
560 sq. ft.

Spacious And Centrally Located Family Area

Plan #582-023D-0019

Price Code B

Special Features • 1,539 total square feet of living area • Large master bedroom has a private bath with access to patio • Convenient laundry room is located between carport and kitchen • Bedrooms are secluded from living areas for added privacy • Private dining area features a bay window for elegant entertaining • Attached carport offers an additional roomy storage area • 3 bedrooms, 2 baths, 2-car attached carport • Slab foundation

Storage
Carport
Patio
MBr
15-4x14-6
Family
14-10x19-6
Kit
8-6x
9-6
Dining
11-4x10-6
Br 2
11-10x11-0
Foyer
Porch
Br 3
12-10x11-8
65'-4"
50'-10"

Simple, But Elegant Ranch

Plan #582-051D-0058

Price Code A

Special Features • *1,462 total square feet of living area • Spacious great room has a marvelous cathedral ceiling • Kitchen with breakfast bar opens to the great room and dining area • Cheerful master bedroom features a wall of windows • 3 bedrooms, 2 baths, 2-car garage • Basement foundation*

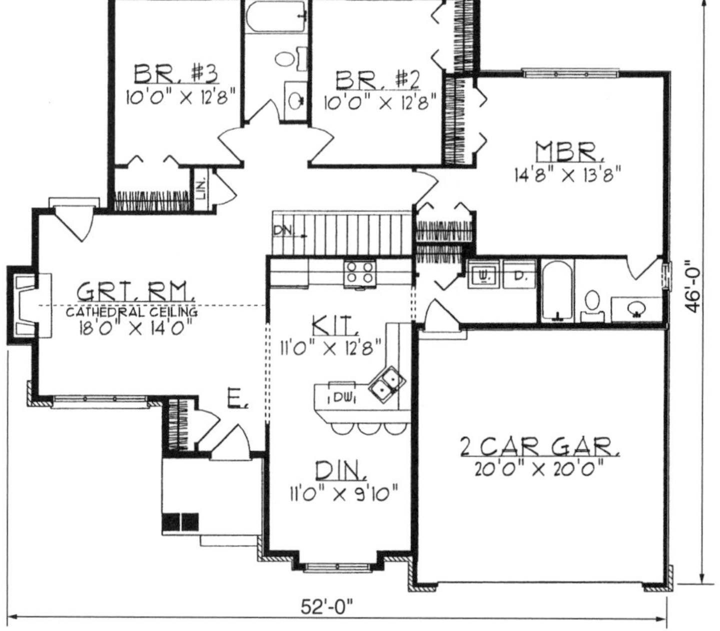

Spacious And Open Family Living Area

Plan #582-001D-0030

Price Code A

Special Features • 1,416 total square feet of living area • Family room includes fireplace, elevated plant shelf and vaulted ceiling • Patio is accessible from dining area and garage • Centrally located laundry area • Oversized walk-in pantry • 3 bedrooms, 2 baths, 2-car garage • Basement foundation, drawings also include crawl space and slab foundations

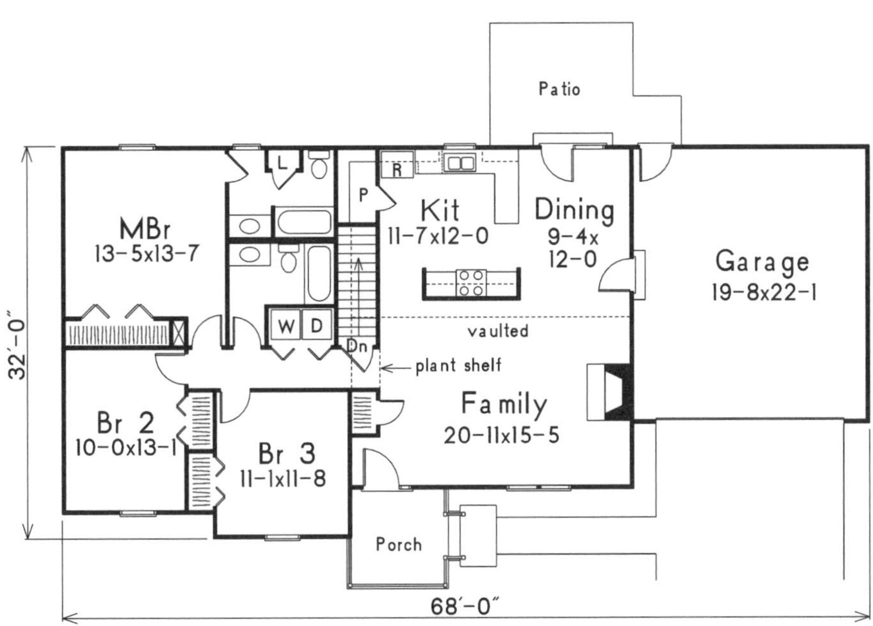

A Trim Arrangement Of Living Areas

Plan #582-037D-0010 Price Code B

Special Features • 1,770 total square feet of living area • Distinctive covered entrance leads into spacious foyer • Master bedroom, living and dining rooms feature large windows for plenty of light • Oversized living room has a high ceiling and large windows that flank the fireplace • Kitchen includes a pantry and large planning center • Master bedroom has a high vaulted ceiling, deluxe bath, and private access outdoors • 3 bedrooms, 2 baths, 2-car garage • Slab foundation

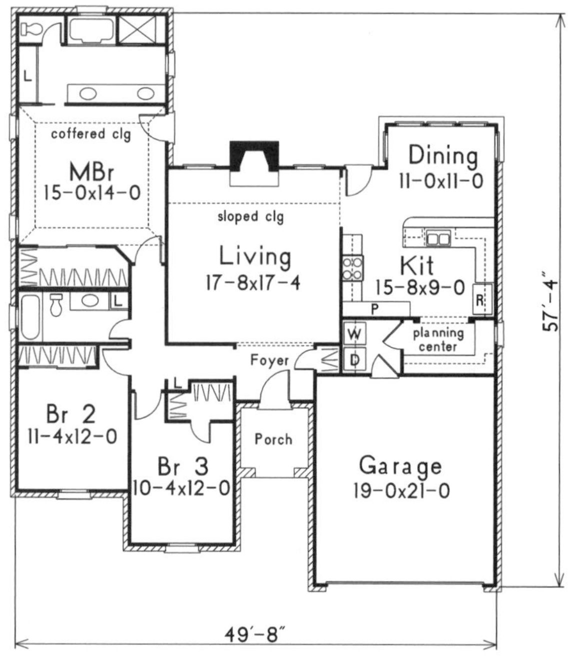

Stylish Ranch

Plan #582-069D-0005

Price Code A

Special Features • 1,267 total square feet of living area • 10' vaulted ceiling in great room • Open floor plan creates a spacious feeling • Master suite is separated from other bedrooms for privacy • 3 bedrooms, 2 baths, 2-car garage • Slab or crawl space foundation, please specify when ordering

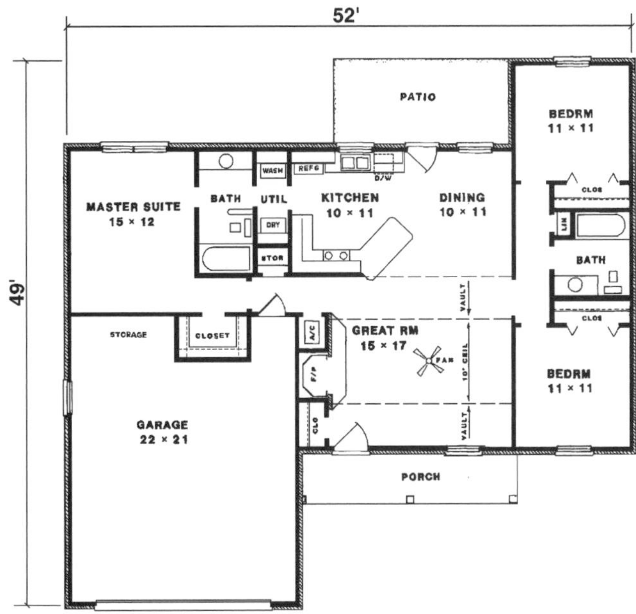

Plan #582-019D-0009

Price Code C

Special Features • 1,862 total square feet of living area • Comfortable traditional has all the amenities of a larger plan in a compact layout • Angled eating bar separates kitchen and great room while leaving these areas open to one another for entertaining • 3 bedrooms, 2 baths, 2-car garage • Crawl space foundation, drawings also include slab foundation

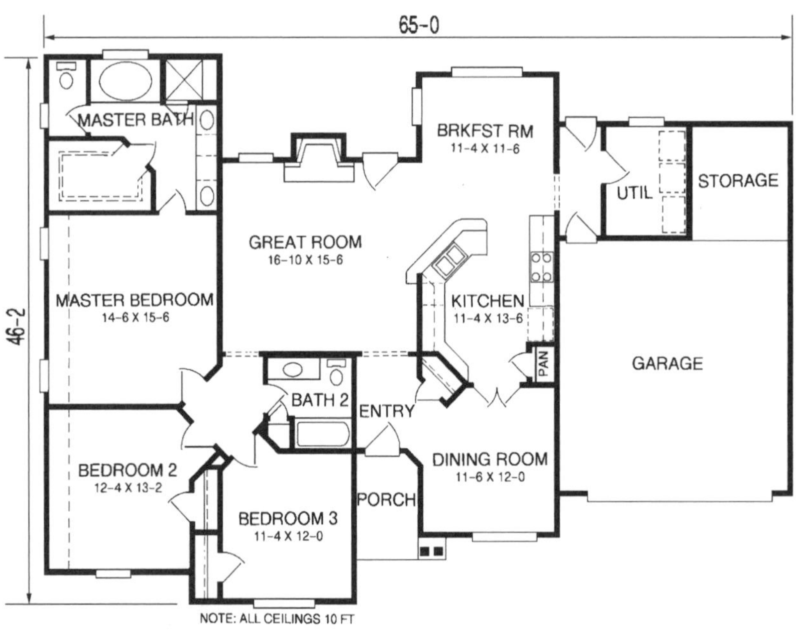

Multiple Gabled Roofs Add Drama

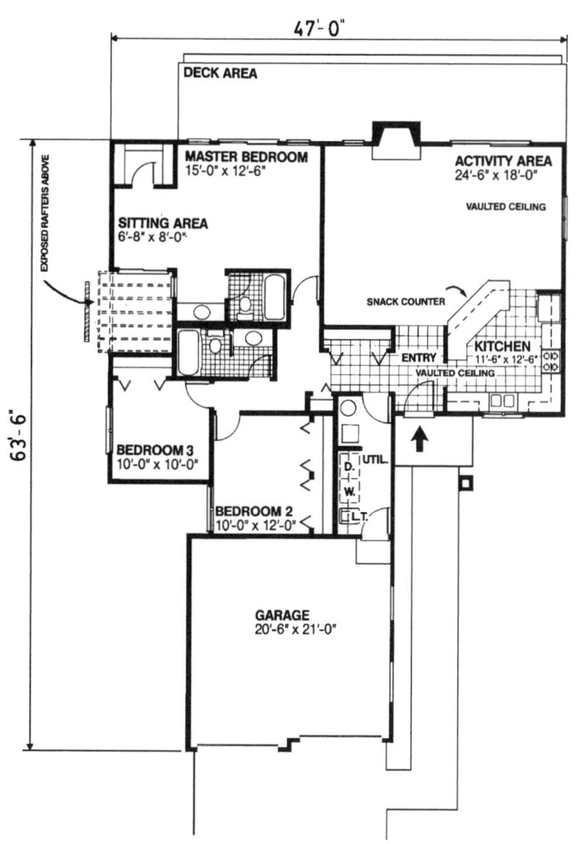

Plan #582-008D-0069 — Price Code B

Special Features • 1,533 total square feet of living area • Master bedroom accesses the outdoors through sliding glass doors onto a deck • Sloped ceiling adds volume to the large activity area • Activity area has a fireplace, snack bar and access to the outdoors • Convenient utility room is located near the garage • 3 bedrooms, 2 baths, 2-car garage • Partial basement foundation, drawings also include crawl space foundation

Large Windows Grace This Split-Level Home

Plan #582-010D-0007

Price Code A

Special Features • 1,427 total square feet of living area • Practical storage space is situated in the garage • Convenient laundry closet is located on the lower level • Kitchen and dining area both have sliding doors that access the deck • Large expansive space created by vaulted living and dining rooms • 3 bedrooms, 2 baths, 2-car drive under garage • Basement foundation

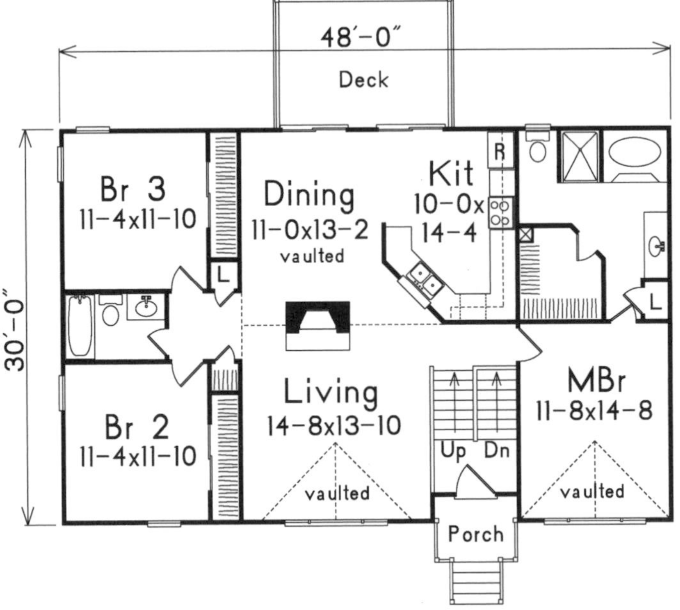

Small Home Is Remarkably Spacious

Plan #582-007D-0042

Price Code AA

Special Features • 914 total square feet of living area • Large porch for leisure evenings • Dining area with bay window, open stair and pass-through kitchen create openness • Basement includes generous garage space, storage area, finished laundry and mechanical room • 2 bedrooms, 1 bath, 2-car drive under garage • Basement foundation

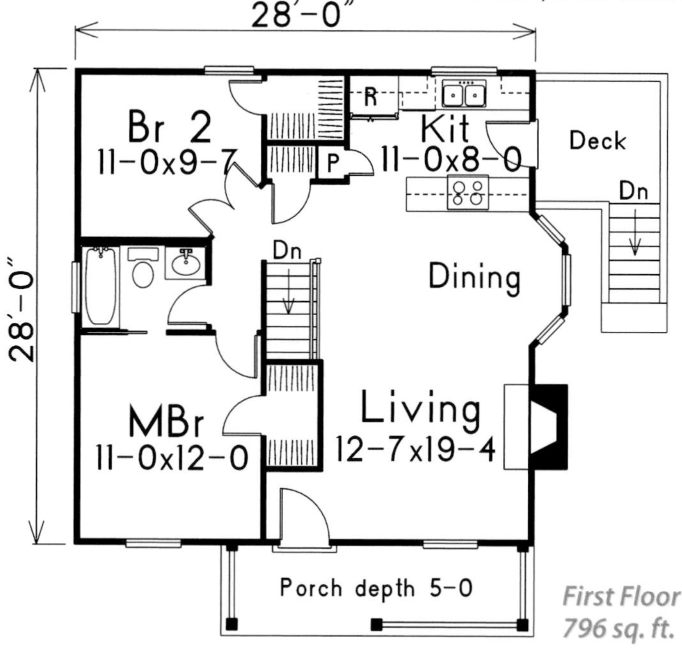

First Floor
796 sq. ft.

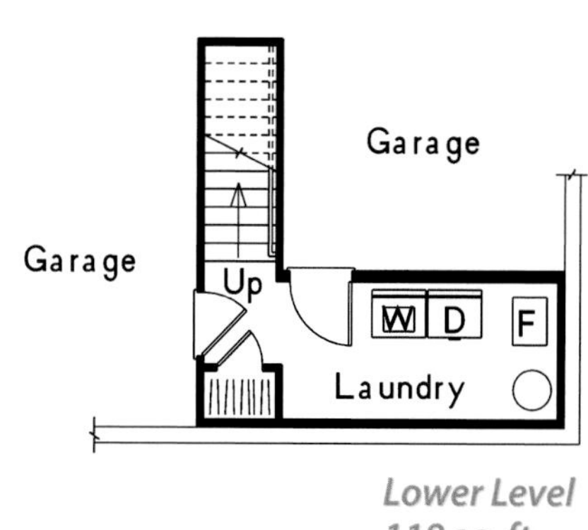

Lower Level
118 sq. ft.

Family Home Ideal For Narrow Lots

Plan #582-076D-0018

Price Code B

Special Features • 1,116 total square feet of living area • Centrally located kitchen serves breakfast and dining areas with ease • Fireplace warms the vaulted family room which is open and spacious • Vaulted master bedroom enjoys two closets, private bath and access to the outdoors • 3 bedrooms, 2 baths, 1-car garage • Crawl space or slab foundation, please specify when ordering

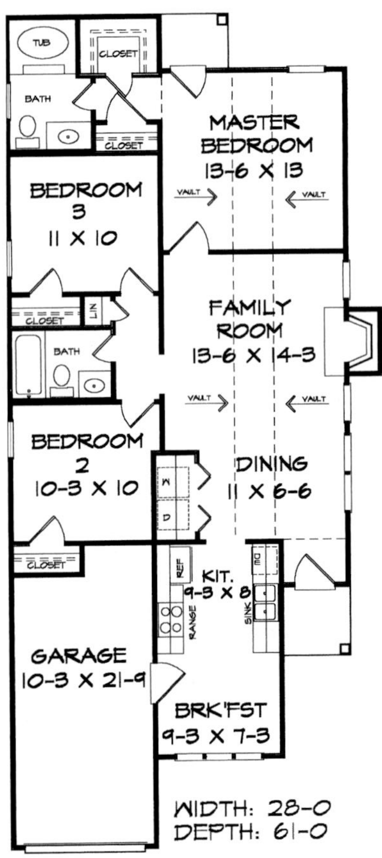

Atrium Living For Views On A Narrow Lot

Plan #582-007D-0103

Price Code A

Special Features • 1,231 total square feet of living area • Dutch gables and stone accents provide an enchanting appearance • The spacious living room offers a masonry fireplace, atrium with window wall and is open to a dining area with bay window • Kitchen has a breakfast counter, lots of cabinet space and glass sliding doors to a balcony • 380 square feet of optional living area on the lower level • 2 bedrooms, 2 baths, 1-car drive-under garage • Walk-out basement foundation

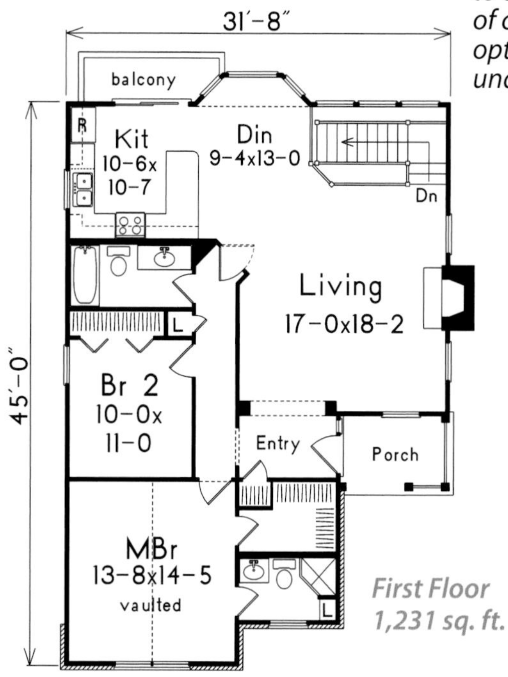

First Floor
1,231 sq. ft.

Optional Lower Level

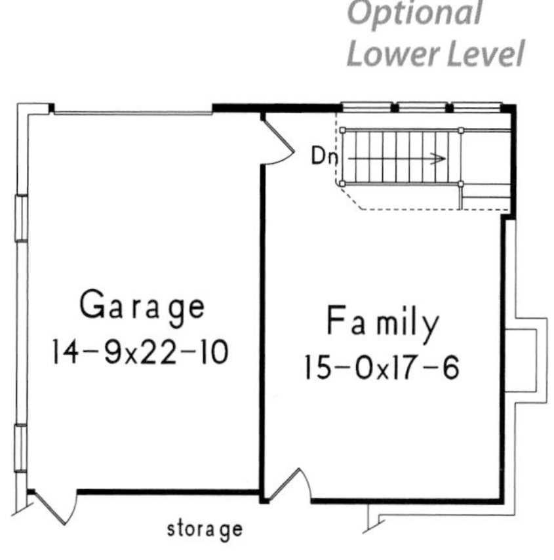

Plan #582-015D-0023

Price Code B

Special Features • 1,649 total square feet of living area • Energy efficient home with 2" x 6" exterior walls • Ideal design for a narrow lot • Country kitchen includes an island and eating bar • Master bedroom has 12' vaulted ceiling and a charming arched window • 4 bedrooms, 2 1/2 baths, 2-car side entry garage • Basement or crawl space foundation, please specify when ordering

Width: 30'-0"
Depth: 52'-0"

Second Floor
791 sq. ft.

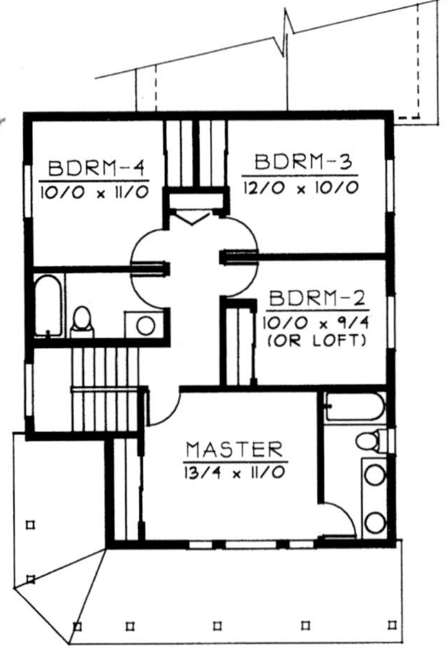

First Floor
858 sq. ft.

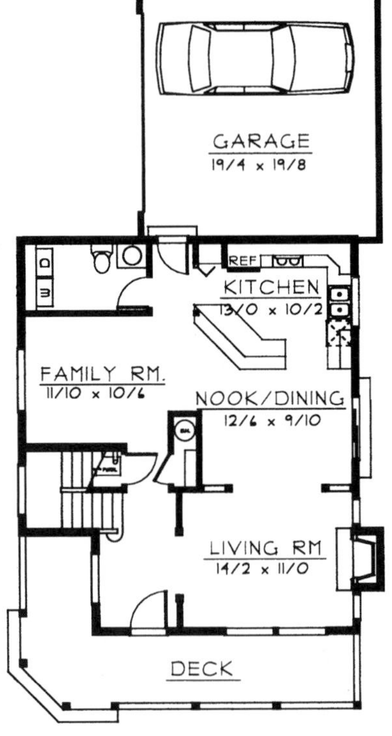

Sportsman's Paradise Cabin

Plan #582-055D-0063

Price Code A

Special Features • 1,397 total square feet of living area • Den with rock hearth fireplace opens to dining area and kitchen • Kitchen and dining area have an eat-in bar with access to a rear grilling porch • Second floor bedrooms have unique ceilings and lots of closet space • 3 bedrooms, 2 baths • Crawl space or slab foundation, please specify when ordering

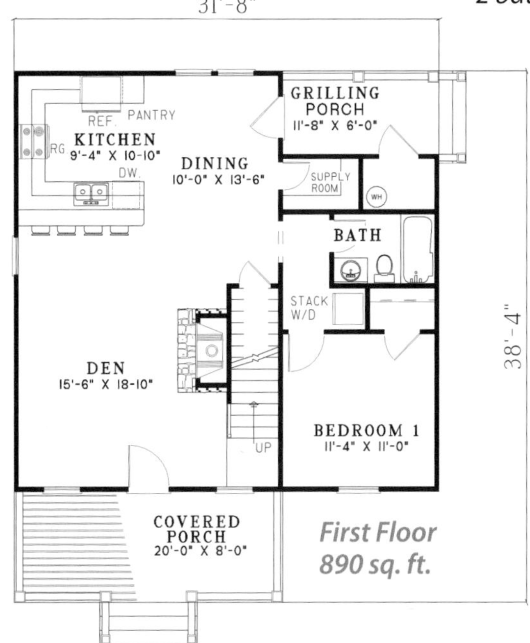

First Floor
890 sq. ft.

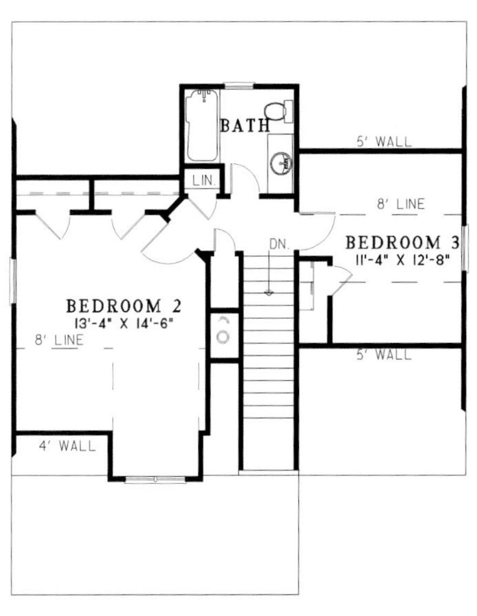

Second Floor
507 sq. ft.

Broad Porch And Gabled Entry Add Character To Home

Plan #582-078D-0004

Price Code D

Special Features • *1,425 total square feet of living area* • *Double-door vestibule entrance features a large closet and window seat* • *The living and dining rooms boast vaulted ceilings for added volume and drama* • *The kitchen is equipped with a pantry, laundry alcove and French doors opening to a deck* • *3 bedrooms, 2 baths* • *Basement or crawl space foundation, please specify when ordering*

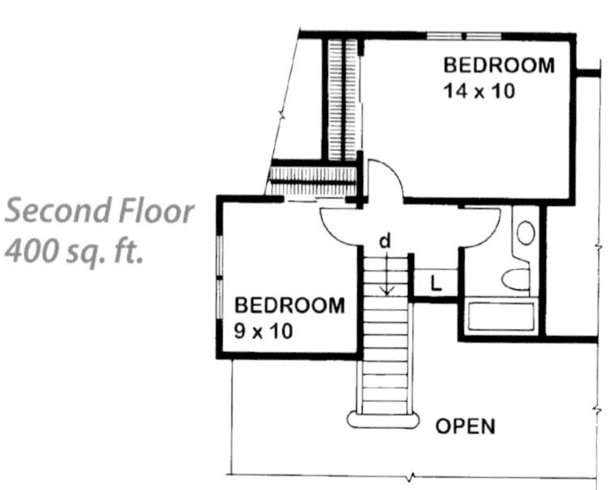

Second Floor
400 sq. ft.

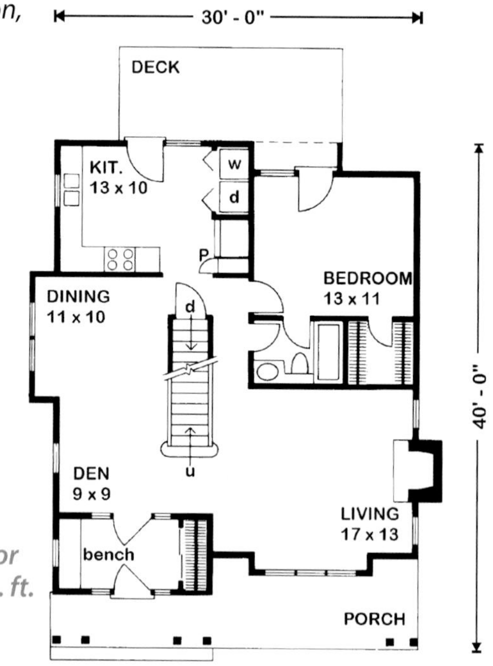

First Floor
1,025 sq. ft.

Plan #582-008D-0150

Price Code B

Special Features • 1,680 total square feet of living area • Highly functional lower level includes a wet hall with storage, laundry area, workshop and cozy ski lounge with an enormous fireplace • First floor is warmed by a large fireplace in living/dining area which features a spacious wrap-around deck • Lots of sleeping space for guests or a large family • 5 bedrooms, 2 1/2 baths • Basement foundation

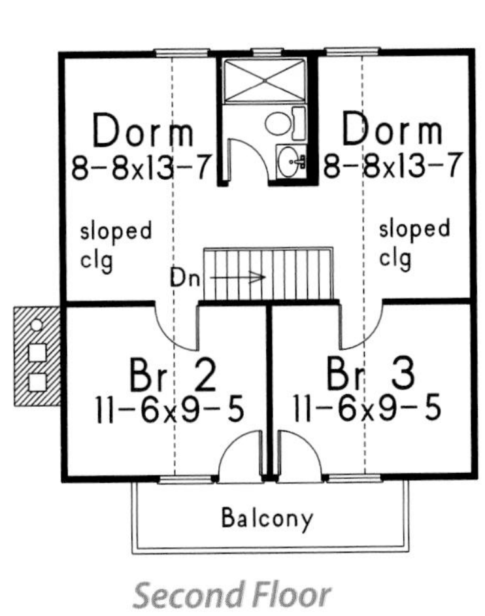

Second Floor
528 sq. ft.

26'-8"
Br 1
9-4x10-3
R
Kit
8-1x
9-1
Dn
Up
24'-0"
Living/Dining
23-4x12-9
Deck

First Floor
576 sq. ft.

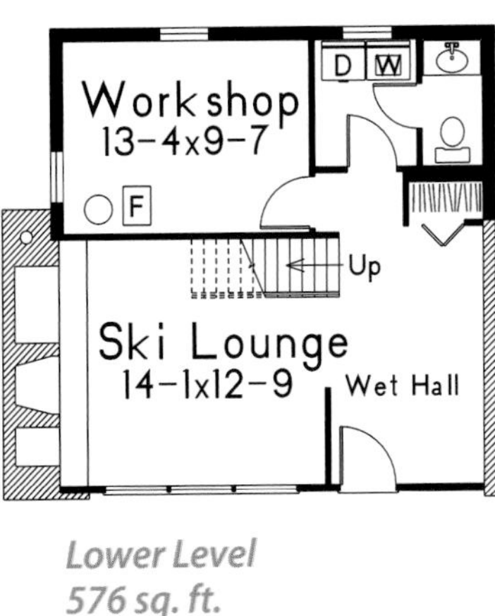

Lower Level
576 sq. ft.

Plan #582-078D-0022

Price Code D

Special Features • 1,465 total square feet of living area • Spacious living room is warmed by a hearth fireplace flanked by windows • First floor bedroom enjoys a private entry to a bath • Study on the second floor is brightened by six Craftsman/Prairie Style windows • A convenient coat closet is located at the entrance • 3 bedrooms, 2 baths • Basement or crawl space foundation, please specify when ordering

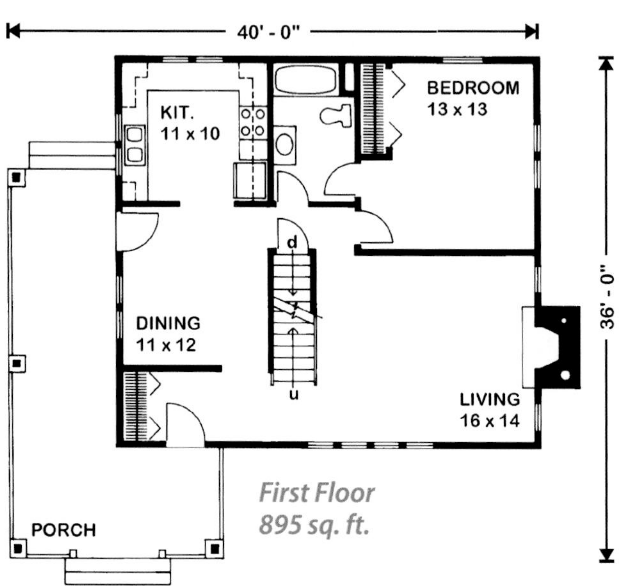

First Floor
895 sq. ft.

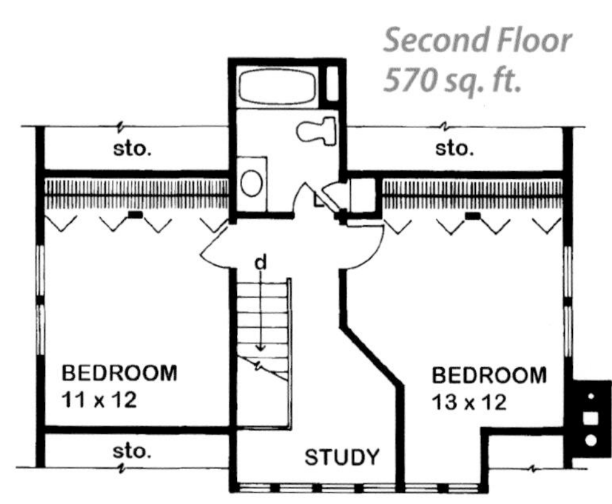

Second Floor
570 sq. ft.

Delightful Victorian

Plan #582-013D-0020

Price Code C

Special Features • 1,985 total square feet of living area • Cozy family room features a fireplace and double French doors opening onto the porch • The open kitchen includes a convenient island • Extraordinary master bedroom has a tray ceiling and a large walk-in closet • Lovely bayed breakfast area has easy access to the deck • 3 bedrooms, 2 1/2 baths • Basement or crawl space foundation, please specify when ordering

First Floor
1,009 sq. ft.

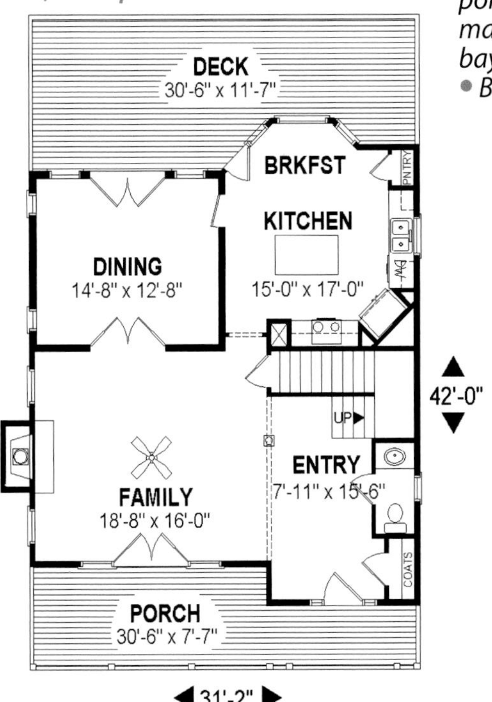

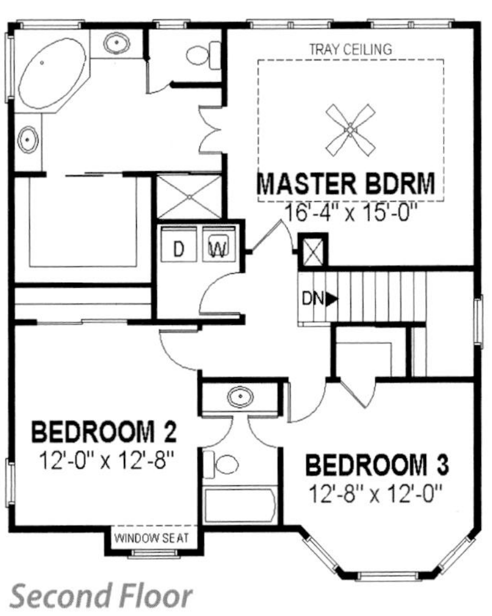

Second Floor
976 sq. ft.

Plan #582-007D-0039

Price Code B

Rear View

Special Features • 1,563 total square feet of living area • Enjoyable wrap-around porch and lower sundeck • Vaulted entry is adorned with a palladian window, plant shelves, stone floor and fireplace • Huge vaulted great room has magnificent views through a two-story atrium window wall • 2 bedrooms, 1 1/2 baths • Basement foundation

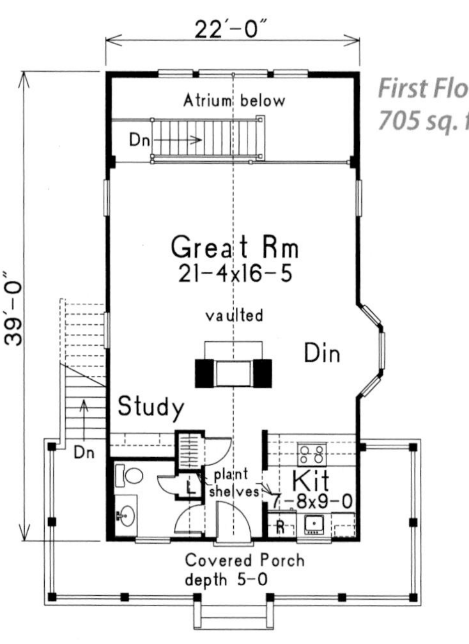

First Floor
705 sq. ft.

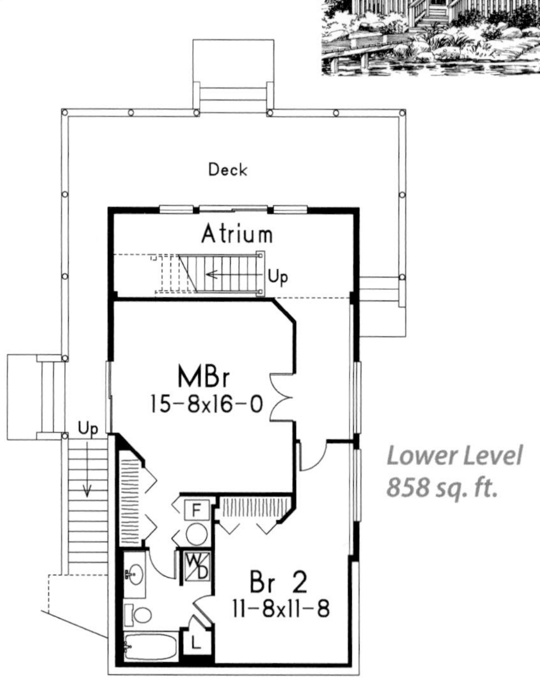

Lower Level
858 sq. ft.

Traditional Home For A Small Lot

Plan #582-016D-0029

Price Code C

Special Features • 1,635 total square feet of living area • Large wrap-around front porch • Open living and dining rooms are separated only by columns for added openness • Kitchen includes a large work island and snack bar • Master bedroom with tray ceiling has three closets • 3 bedrooms, 2 1/2 baths, 2-car garage • Basement, crawl space or slab foundation, please specify when ordering

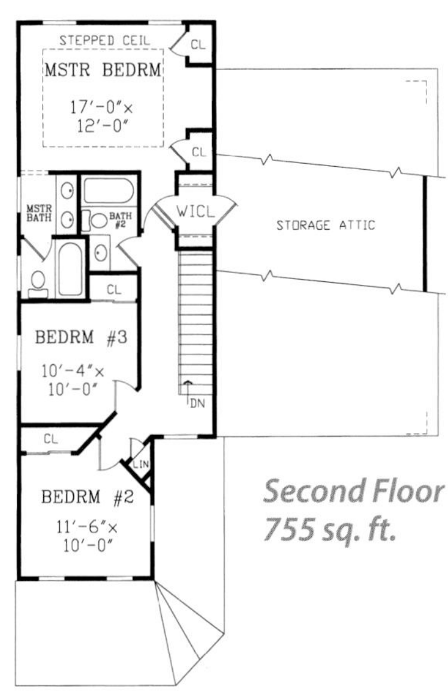

Second Floor
755 sq. ft.

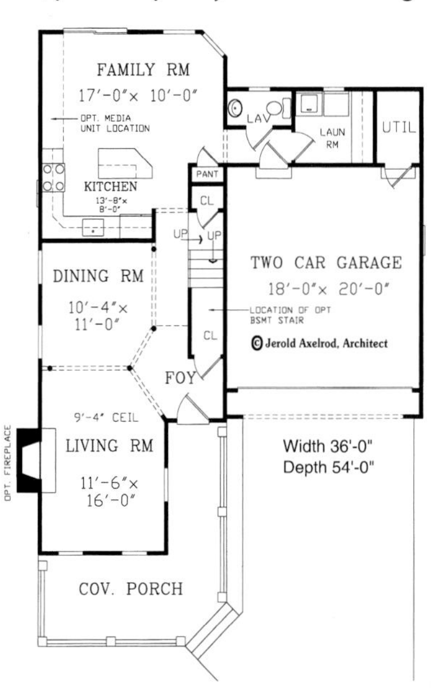

Width 36'-0"
Depth 54'-0"

First Floor
880 sq. ft.

Distinguished Styling For A Small Lot

Plan #582-007D-0060 Price Code B

Special Features • 1,268 total square feet of living area • Multiple gables, a large porch and arched windows create a classy exterior • Innovative design provides openness in great room, kitchen and breakfast room • Secondary bedrooms have a private hall with bath • 3 bedrooms, 2 baths, 2-car garage • Basement foundation, drawings also include crawl space and slab foundations

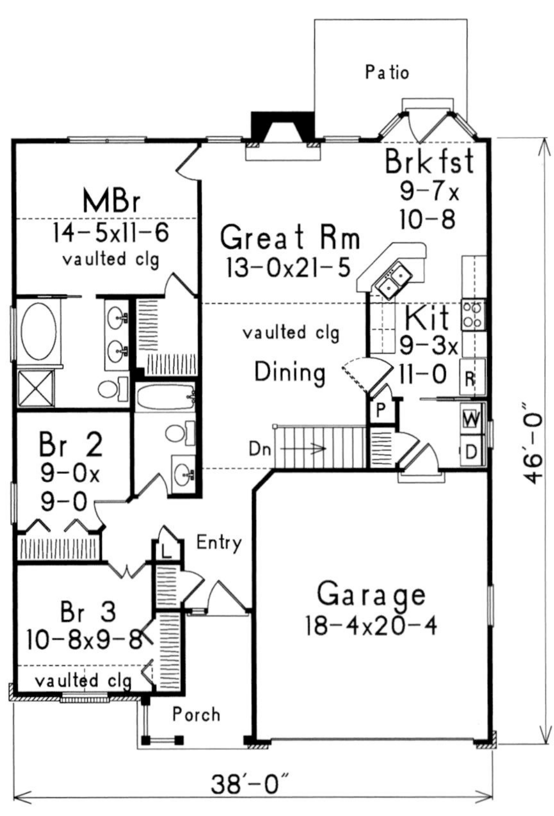

Country Feel With All The Comforts

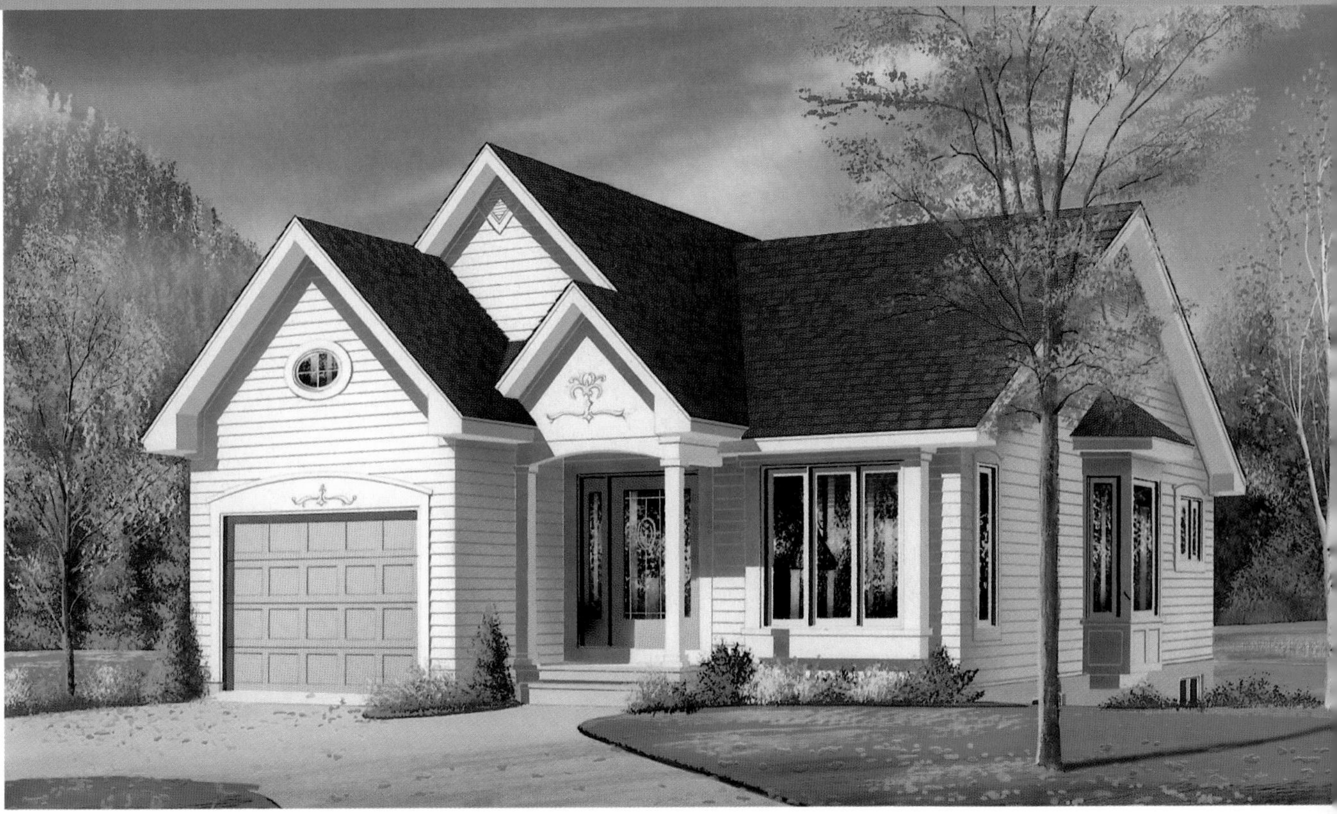

Plan #582-032D-0011 **Price Code AA**

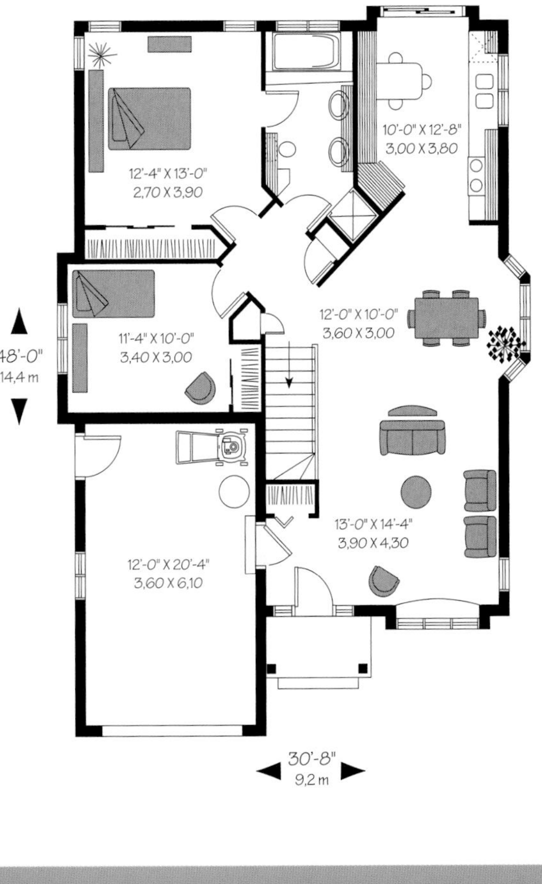

12'-4" X 13'-0"
2,70 X 3,90
10'-0" X 12'-8"
3,00 X 3,80
12'-0" X 10'-0"
3,60 X 3,00
11'-4" X 10'-0"
3,40 X 3,00
48'-0"
14,4 m
12'-0" X 20'-4"
3,60 X 6,10
13'-0" X 14'-4"
3,90 X 4,30
30'-8"
9,2 m

Special Features • 1,103 total square feet of living area • Energy efficient home with 2" x 6" exterior walls • All bedrooms in one area of the house for privacy • Bay window enhances dining area • Living and dining areas combine for a spacious feeling • Lots of storage throughout • 2 bedrooms, 1 bath, 1-car garage • Basement foundation

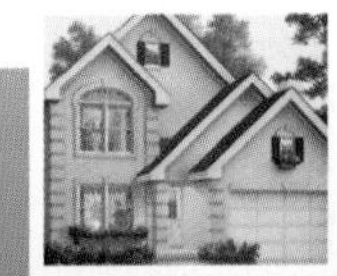

Plan #582-011D-0019

Price Code E

Special Features • 1,978 total square feet of living area • Designed for a sloping lot, this multi-level home intrigues the eye • Sunlight filters into the grand two-story foyer and living room from tall windows • Master suite has elegant front-facing windows and a private bath • 3 bedrooms, 2 1/2 baths, 2-car drive under garage • Walk-out basement foundation

Lower Level

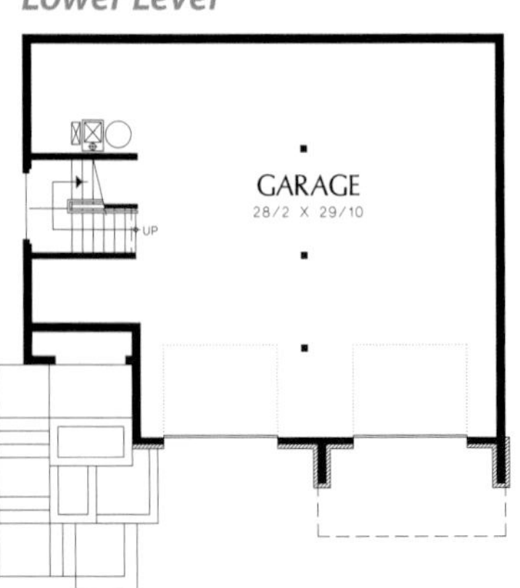

First Floor
1,106 sq. ft.

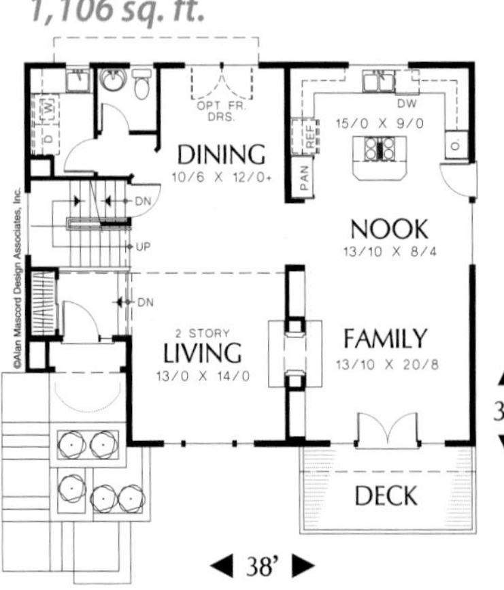

Second Floor
872 sq. ft.

Porch Creates A Welcoming Facade

Plan #582-078D-0020

Price Code D

Special Features • 1,700 total square feet of living area • The family and living rooms provide both formal and informal gathering areas • U-shaped kitchen serves the adjoining dining room and breakfast nook with ease • Bedrooms are located on the second floor for privacy • 3 bedrooms, 2 1/2 baths • Basement or crawl space foundation, please specify when ordering

First Floor
990 sq. ft.

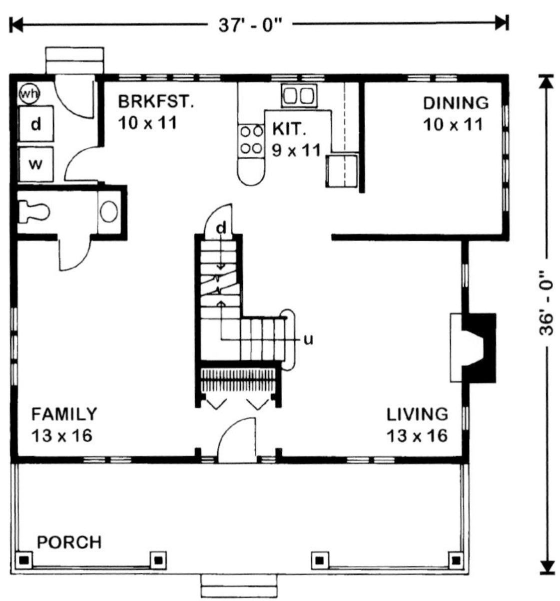

Second Floor
710 sq. ft.

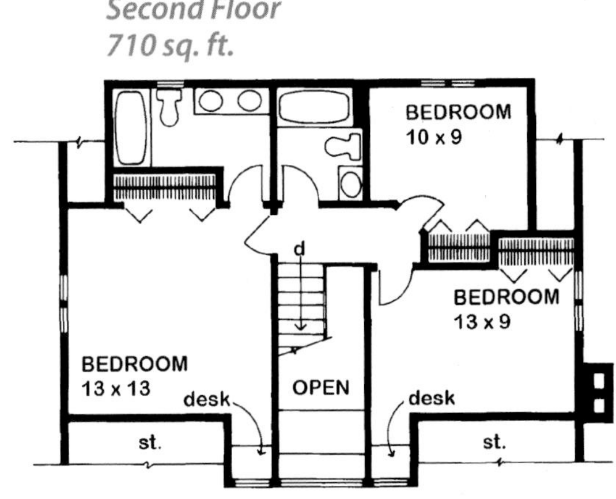

www.houseplansandmore.com

Covered Porch Adds Appeal

Plan #582-032D-0040

Price Code A

Special Features • 1,480 total square feet of living area • Energy efficient home with 2" x 6" exterior walls • Cathedral ceilings in family and dining rooms • Master bedroom has a walk-in closet and access to bath • 2 bedrooms, 2 baths • Basement foundation

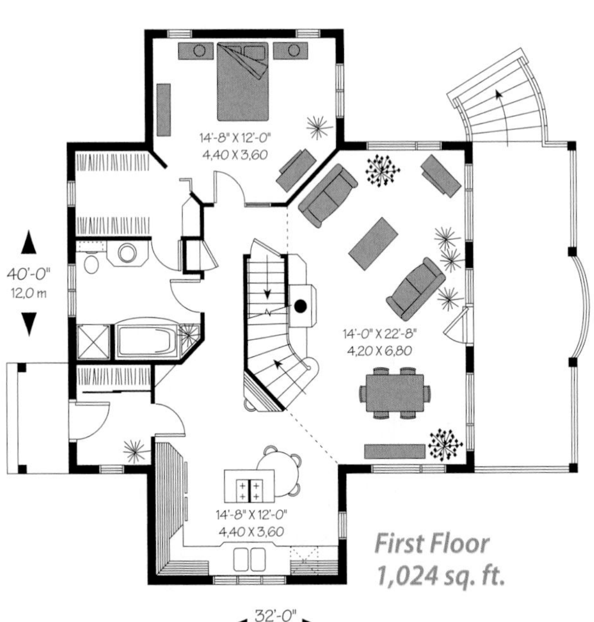

First Floor
1,024 sq. ft.

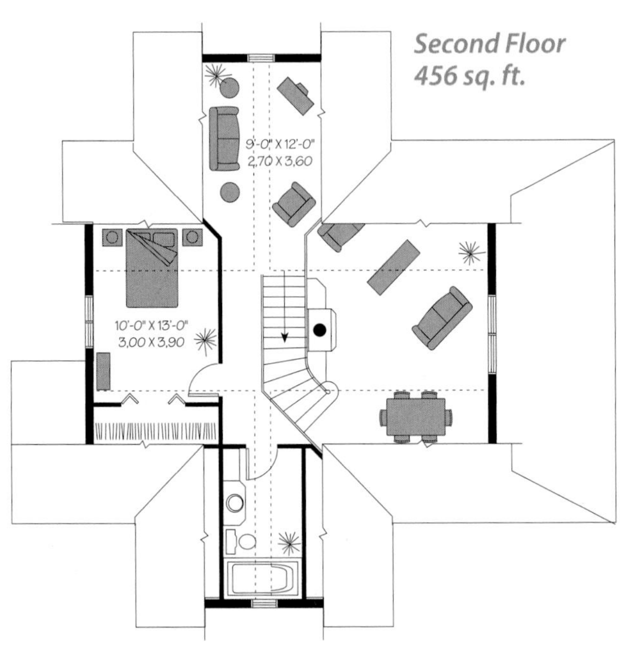

Second Floor
456 sq. ft.

Plan #582-058D-0010 **Price Code AAA**

Special Features • 676 total square feet of living area • See-through fireplace between bedroom and living area adds character • Combined dining and living areas create an open feeling • Full-length front covered porch is perfect for enjoying the outdoors • Additional storage available in utility room • 1 bedroom, 1 bath • Crawl space foundation

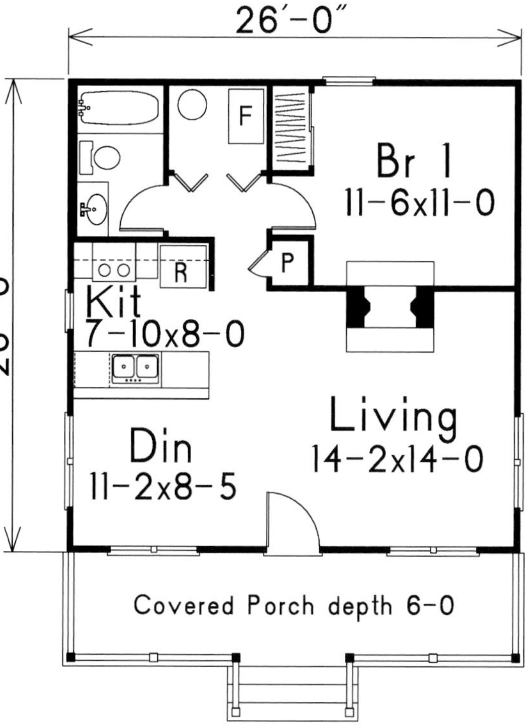

26'-0"
26'-0"
F
Br 1
11-6x11-0
P
R
Kit
7-10x8-0
Living
14-2x14-0
Din
11-2x8-5
Covered Porch depth 6-0

Country Appeal For A Small Lot

Plan #582-007D-0088

Price Code A

Special Features • *1,299 total square feet of living area* • *Large porch for enjoying relaxing evenings* • *First floor master bedroom has a bay window, walk-in closet and roomy bath* • *Two generous bedrooms with lots of closet space, a hall bath, linen closet and balcony overlook comprise second floor* • *3 bedrooms, 2 1/2 baths* • *Basement foundation*

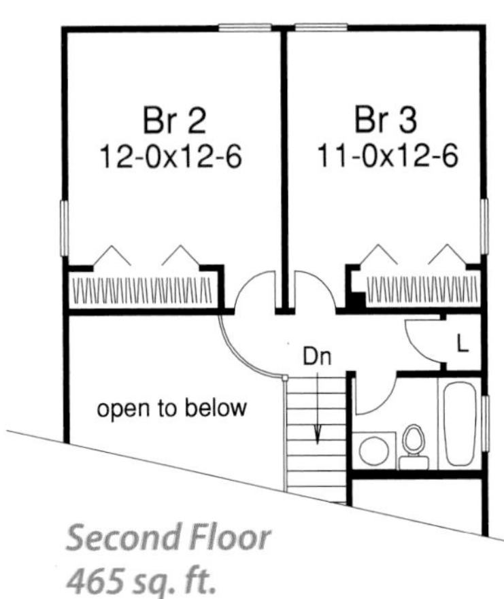

Second Floor
465 sq. ft.

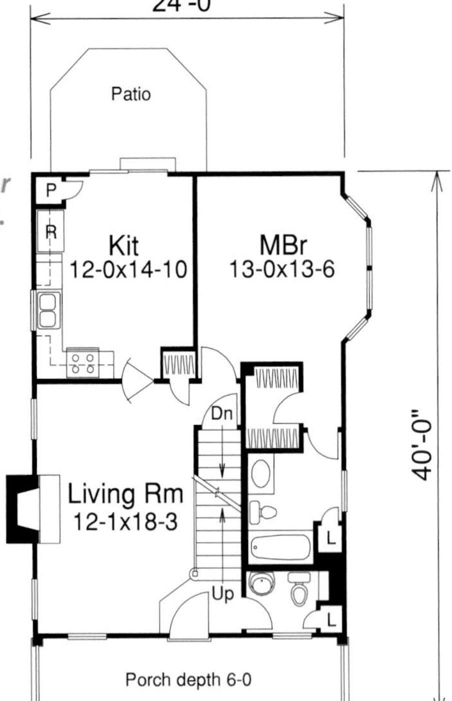

First Floor
834 sq. ft.

Plan #582-062D-0058

Price Code AA

Special Features • 1,108 total square feet of living area • Master bedroom offers a walk-in closet, a full bath and a box-bay window • Vaulted ceilings in kitchen, living and dining rooms make this home appear larger than its actual size • Compact, but efficient kitchen is U-shaped so everything is within reach • Optional lower level has an additional 1,108 square feet of living area • 3 bedrooms, 2 baths • Basement or crawl space foundation, please specify when ordering

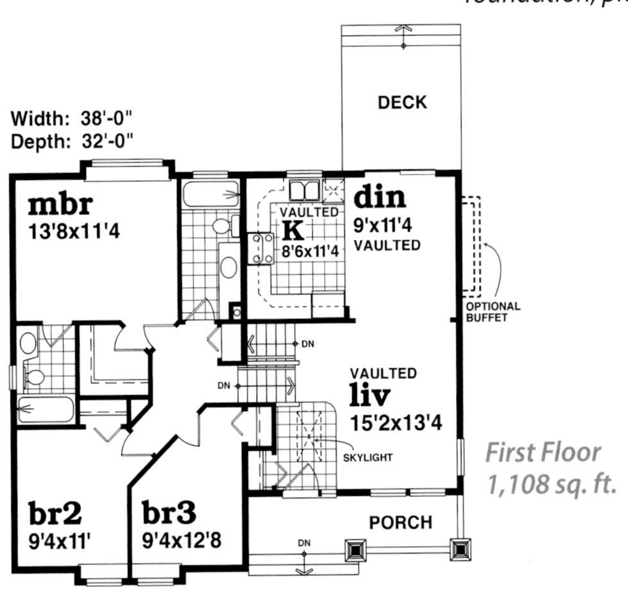

First Floor
1,108 sq. ft.

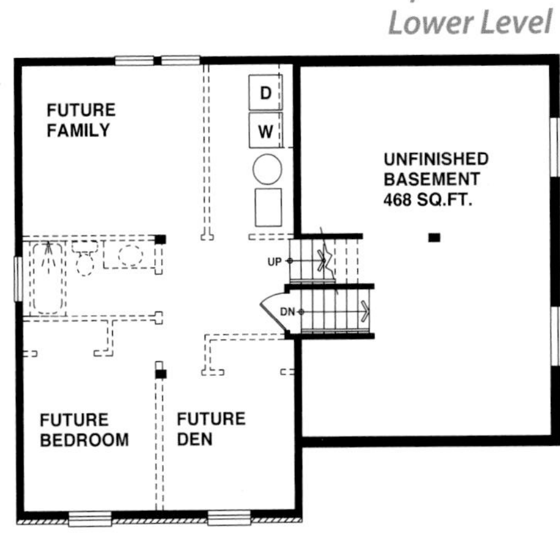

Optional Lower Level

Plan #582-055D-0099

Price Code C

Special Features • 1,897 total square feet of living area • Kitchen has counter for dining that overlooks into the great room • Dining area directly accesses covered porch • Second floor porch connects to master suite creating a quiet outdoor escape • 3 bedrooms, 3 baths • Crawl space or slab foundation, please specify when ordering

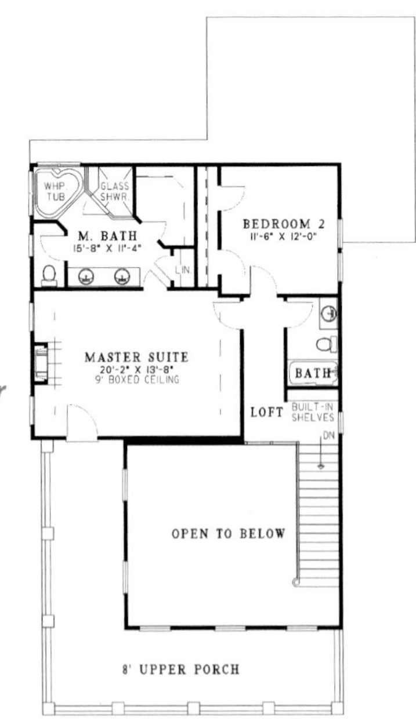

Second Floor
793 sq. ft.

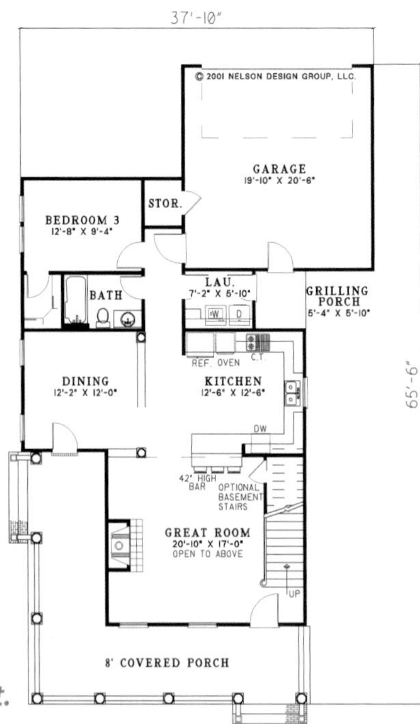

First Floor
1,104 sq. ft.

Ideal Home For Lake, Mountain Or Seaside

Rear View

Plan #582-007D-0028

Price Code B

Special Features • *1,711 total square feet of living area • Entry leads to a vaulted great room with exposed beams, two-story window wall, fireplace, wet bar and balcony • Bayed breakfast room shares the fireplace and joins a sun-drenched kitchen and deck • Vaulted first floor master bedroom features a double-door entry, two closets and bookshelves • Spiral stairs and a balcony dramatize the loft that doubles as a spacious second bedroom • 2 bedrooms, 2 1/2 baths • Basement foundation*

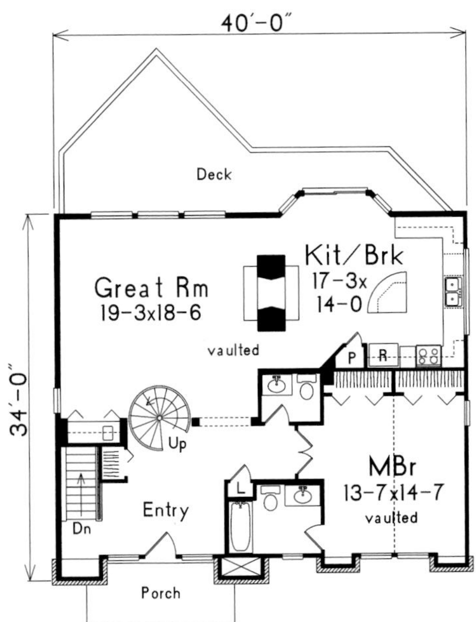

First Floor
1,314 sq. ft.

Second Floor
397 sq. ft.

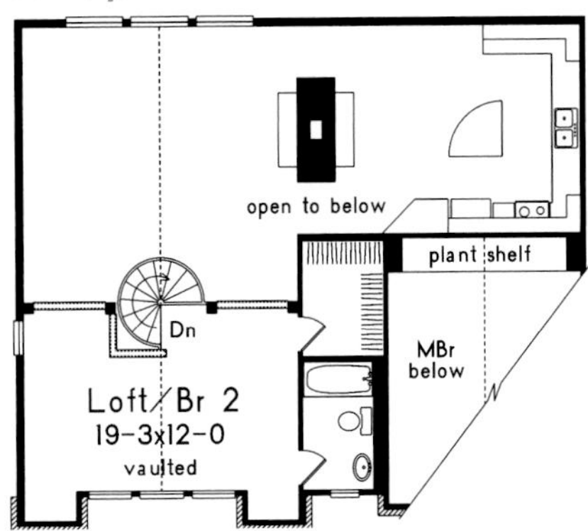

www.houseplansandmore.com

Uncomparable Country Cottage

Plan #582-078D-0013 **Price Code D**

Special Features • 1,175 total square feet of living area • The two-story living room is brightened by multiple levels of double-hung windows and creates a dramatic impression • The compact kitchen is logically laid out for maximum efficiency • Both bedrooms enjoy privacy and walk-in closets • The second floor loft area provides a magnificent view of the first floor living space • 2 bedrooms, 2 baths • Basement or crawl space foundation, please specify when ordering

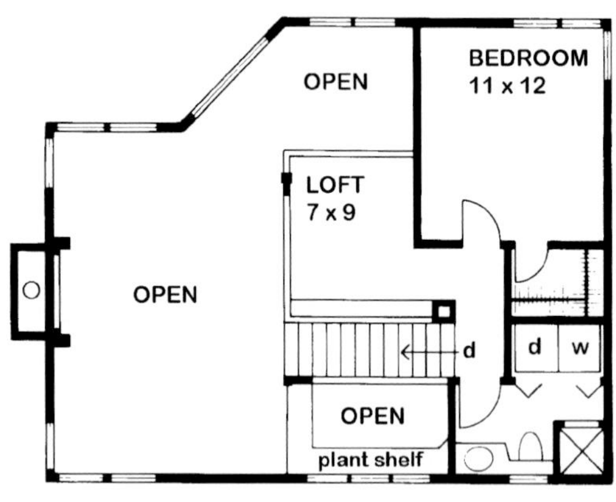

Second Floor
375 sq. ft.

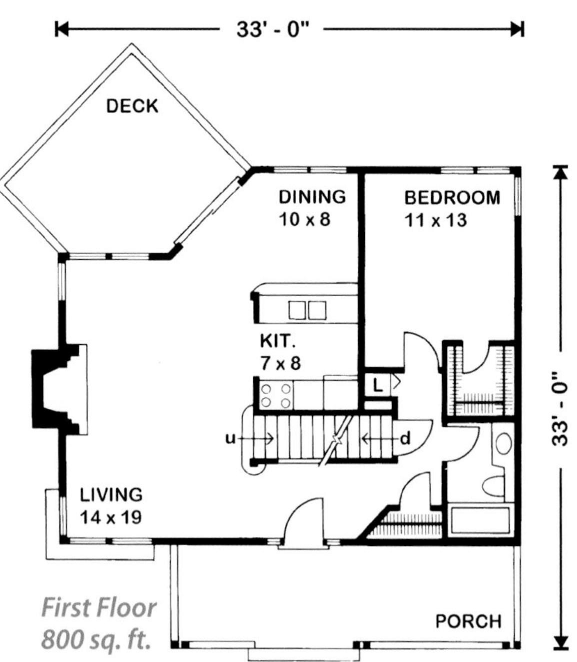

First Floor
800 sq. ft.

Plan #582-007D-0110 Price Code AA

Special Features • 1,169 total square feet of living area • Front facade features a distinctive country appeal • Living room enjoys a wood-burning fireplace and pass-through to kitchen • A stylish U-shaped kitchen offers an abundance of cabinet and counterspace with view to living room • A large walk-in closet, access to rear patio and private bath are many features of the master bedroom • 3 bedrooms, 2 baths, 1-car garage • Basement foundation

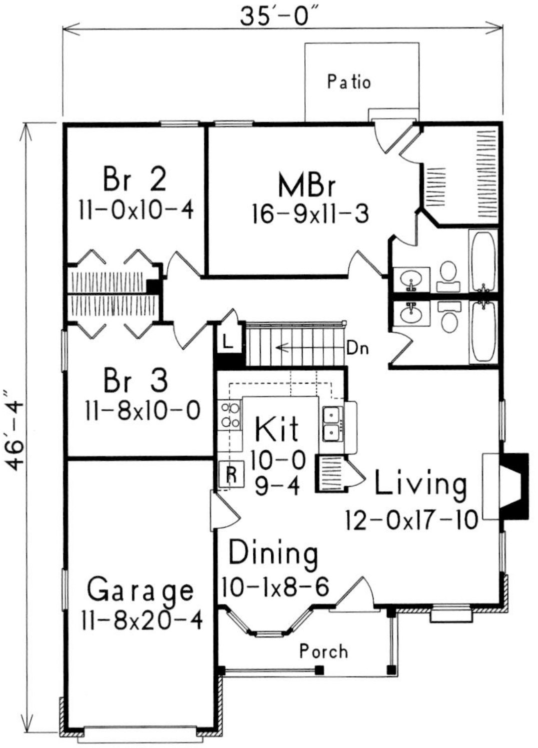

35′-0″
46′-4″
Patio
Br 2 11-0x10-4
MBr 16-9x11-3
Dn
Br 3 11-8x10-0
Kit 10-0 9-4
Living 12-0x17-10
Dining 10-1x8-6
Garage 11-8x20-4
Porch

www.houseplansandmore.com

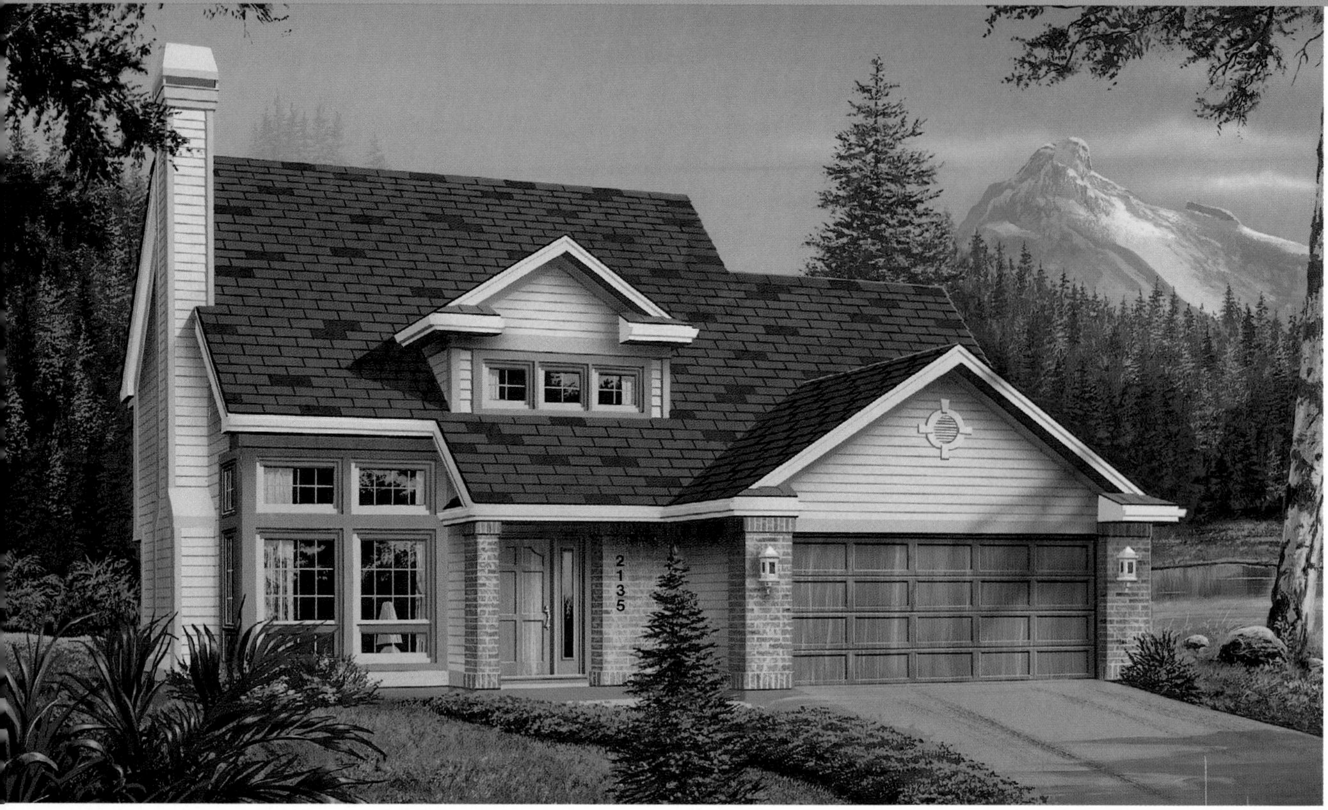

Plan #582-011D-0016

Price Code D

Special Features • 1,902 total square feet of living area • A two-story great room is stunning with a fireplace and many windows • Breakfast nook and kitchen combine creating a warm and inviting place to dine • Second floor hall overlooks to great room below • Bonus room on the second floor is included in the square footage • 3 bedrooms, 2 1/2 baths, 2-car garage • Crawl space foundation

Second Floor
672 sq. ft.

First Floor
1,230 sq. ft.

1-800-DREAM HOME (373-2646)

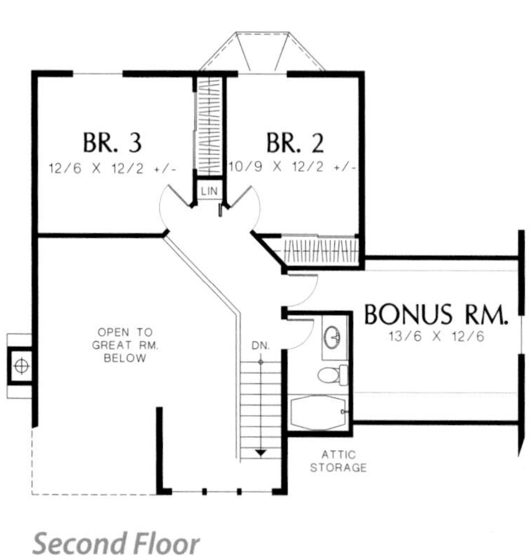

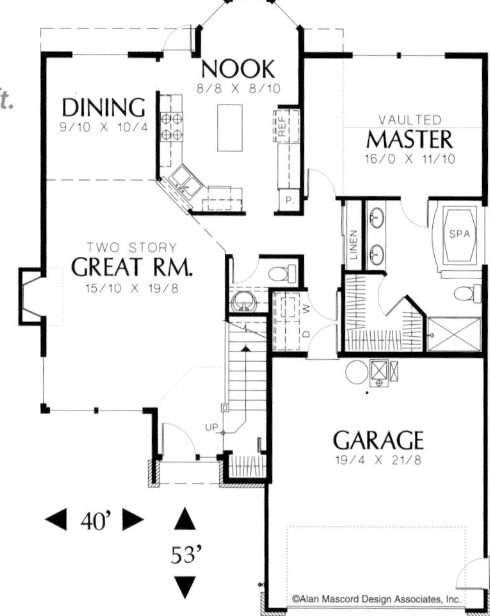

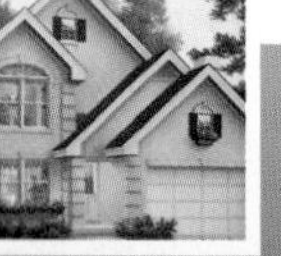

Plan #582-007D-0013

Price Code A

Special Features • *1,492 total square feet of living area* • *Cleverly angled entry spills into the living and dining rooms which share warmth from the fireplace flanked by arched windows* • *Master bedroom includes a double-door entry, huge walk-in closet, shower and bath with picture window* • *Stucco and dutch hipped roofs add warmth and charm to facade* • *3 bedrooms, 2 1/2 baths, 2-car garage* • *Basement foundation*

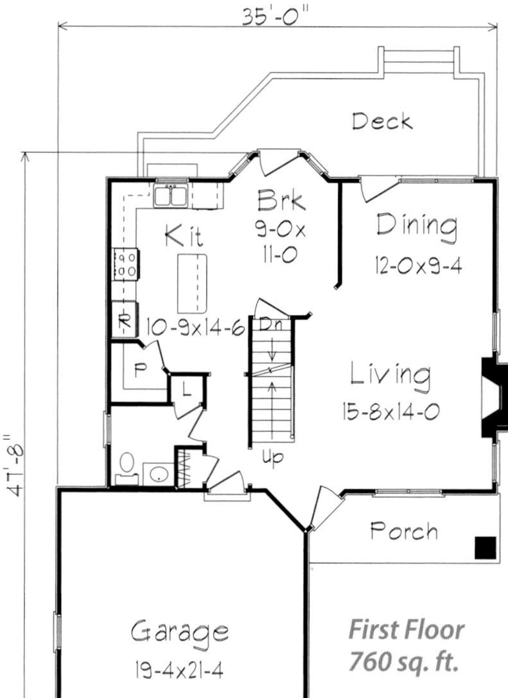

35'-0"
47'-8"
Deck
Brk 9-0x11-0
Kit 10-9x14-6
Dining 12-0x9-4
Living 15-8x14-0
Dn
Up
P
L
Porch
Garage 19-4x21-4

First Floor 760 sq. ft.

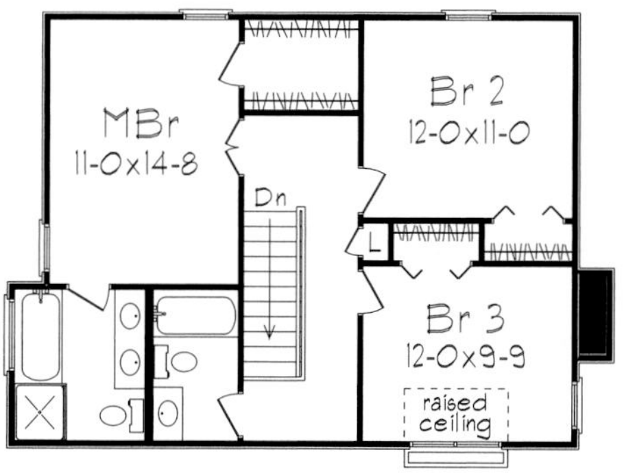

Second Floor 732 sq. ft.

www.houseplansandmore.com

Plan #582-022D-0014 **Price Code B**

Special Features • 1,556 total square feet of living area • A compact home with all the amenities • Country kitchen combines practicality with access to other areas for eating and entertaining • Two-way fireplace joins the dining and living areas • Plant shelf and vaulted ceiling highlight the master bedroom • 3 bedrooms, 2 1/2 baths, 2-car garage • Basement foundation

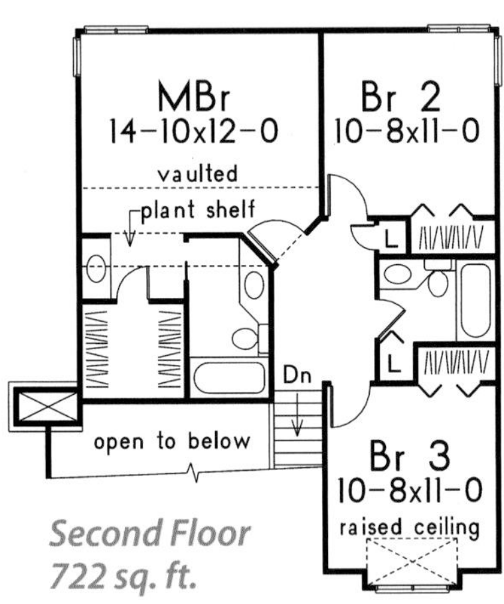

Second Floor
722 sq. ft.

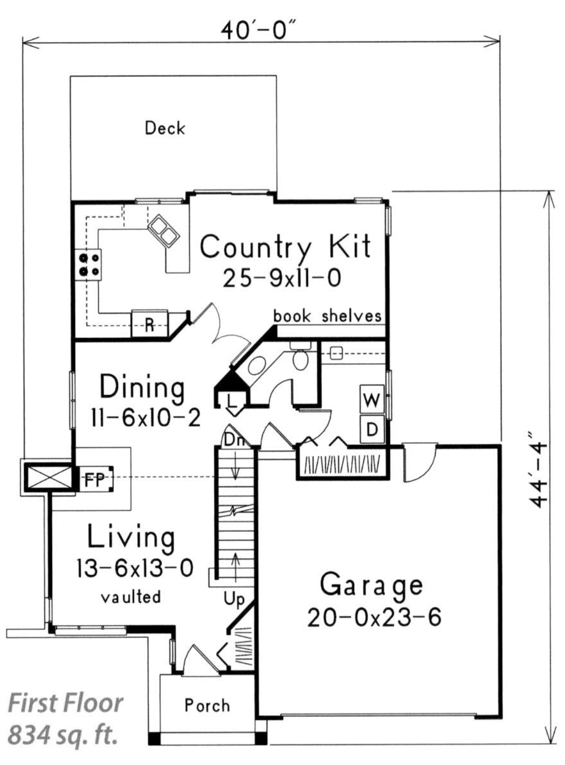

First Floor
834 sq. ft.

Spacious Vaulted Great Room

Plan #582-041D-0006

Price Code AA

Special Features • 1,189 total square feet of living area • All bedrooms are located on the second floor • Dining room and kitchen both have views of the patio • Convenient half bath is located near the kitchen • Master bedroom has a private bath • 3 bedrooms, 2 1/2 baths, 2-car garage • Basement foundation

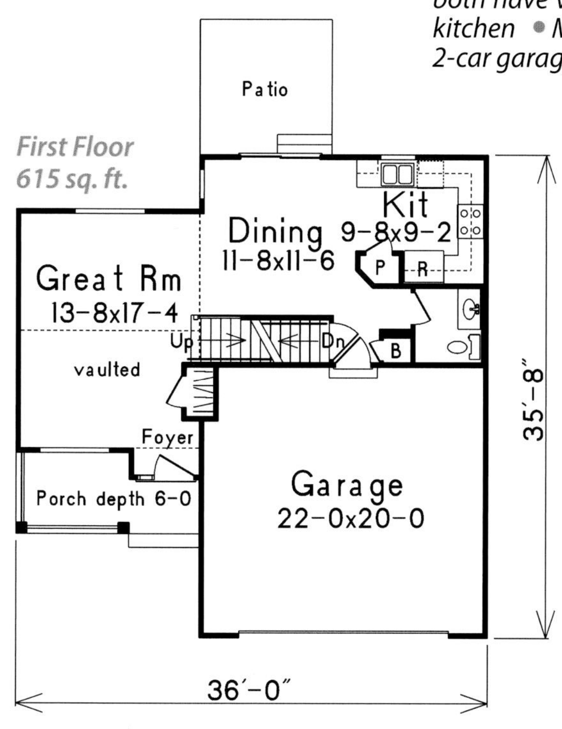

First Floor
615 sq. ft.

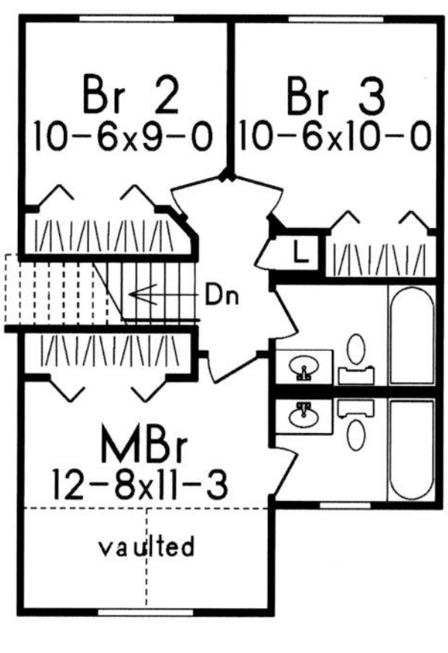

Second Floor
574 sq. ft.

Plan #582-001D-0077 — Price Code B

Special Features • 1,769 total square feet of living area • Living room boasts an elegant cathedral ceiling and fireplace • U-shaped kitchen and dining area combine for easy living • Secondary bedrooms include double closets • Secluded master bedroom features a sloped ceiling, large walk-in closet and private bath • 3 bedrooms, 2 baths • Basement foundation, drawings also include crawl space and slab foundations

Second Floor
463 sq. ft.

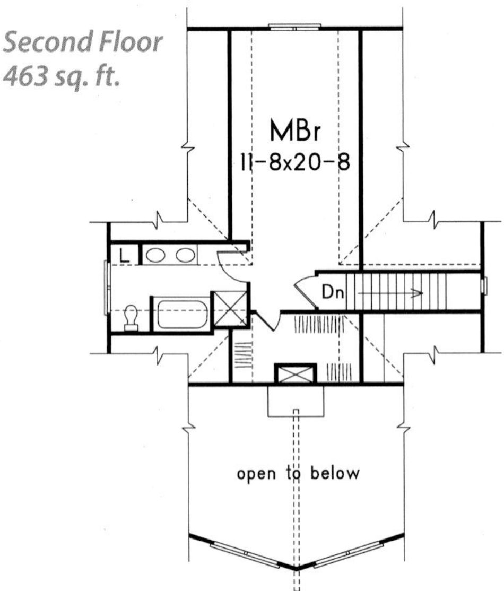

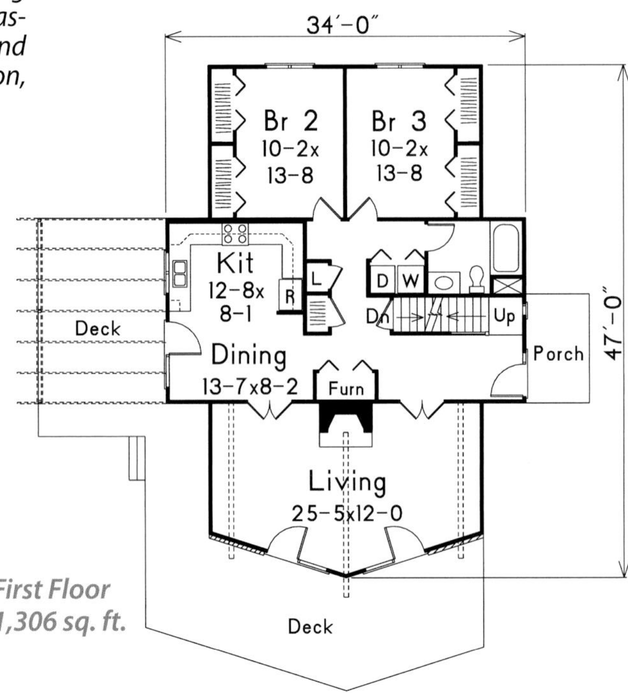

First Floor
1,306 sq. ft.

Expansive Glass Wall In Living Areas

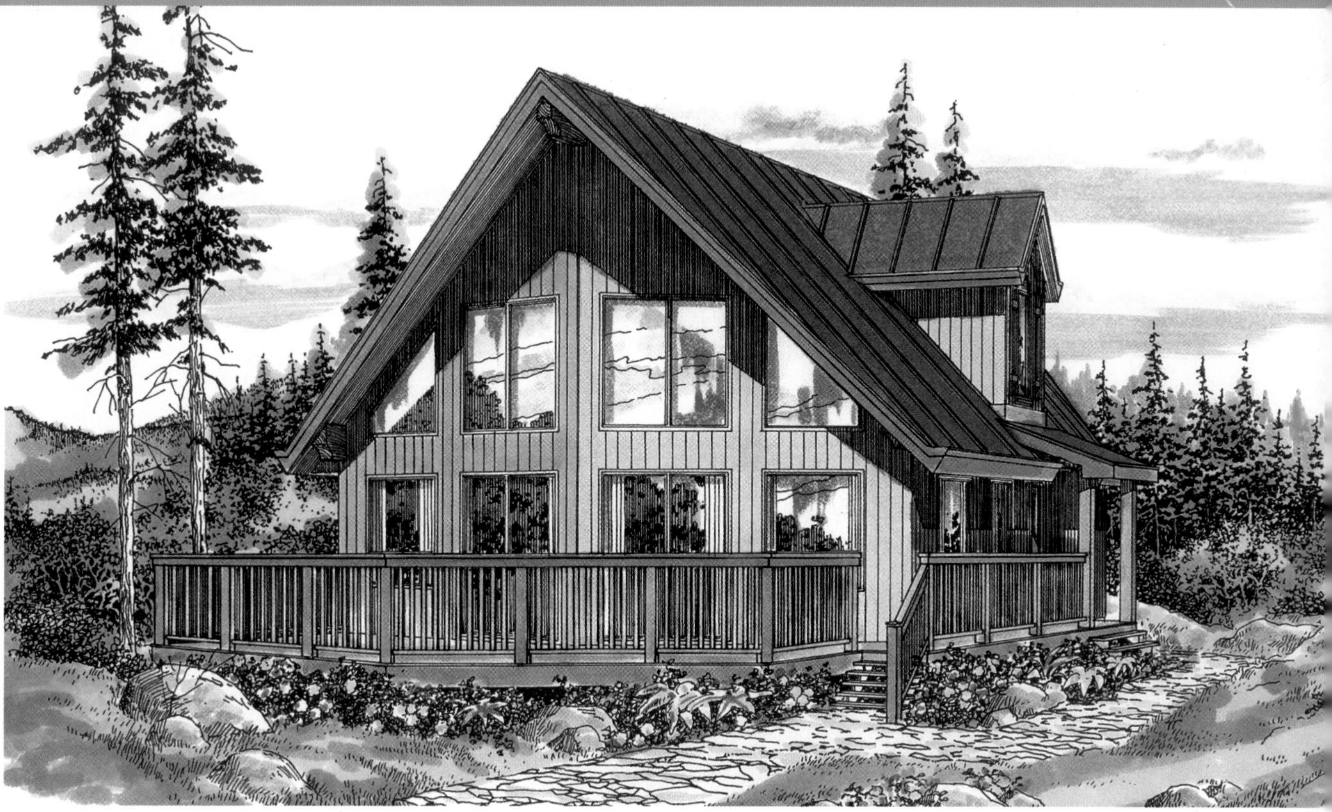

Plan #582-062D-0048

Price Code B

Special Features • 1,543 total square feet of living area • Enormous sundeck makes this a popular vacation style • A woodstove warms the vaulted living and dining rooms • A vaulted kitchen has a prep island and breakfast bar • Second floor vaulted master bedroom has private bath and walk-in closet • 3 bedrooms, 2 baths • Crawl space foundation

Width: 28'-0"
Depth: 39'-9"

First Floor
1,061 sq. ft.

Second Floor
482 sq. ft.

www.houseplansandmore.com

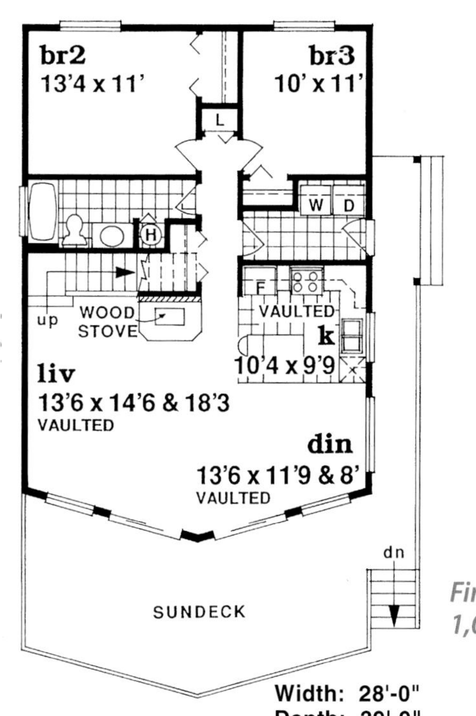

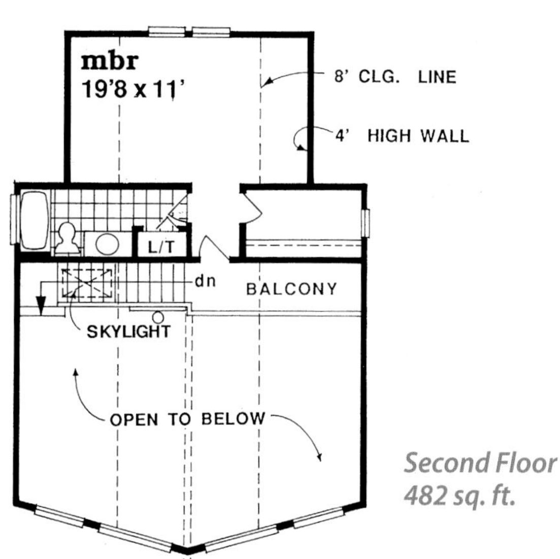

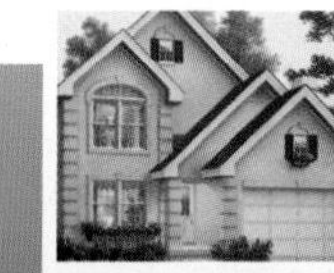

Recessed Stone Entry Provides A Unique Accent

Plan #582-037D-0018 **Price Code AAA**

Special Features • 717 total square feet of living area • Incline ladder leads up to cozy loft area • Living room features plenty of windows and vaulted ceiling • U-shaped kitchen includes a small bay window at the sink • 1 bedroom, 1 bath • Slab foundation

First Floor
627 sq. ft.

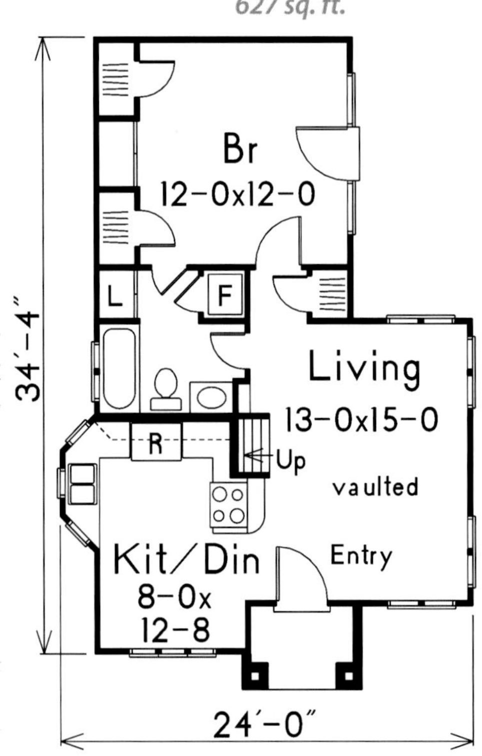

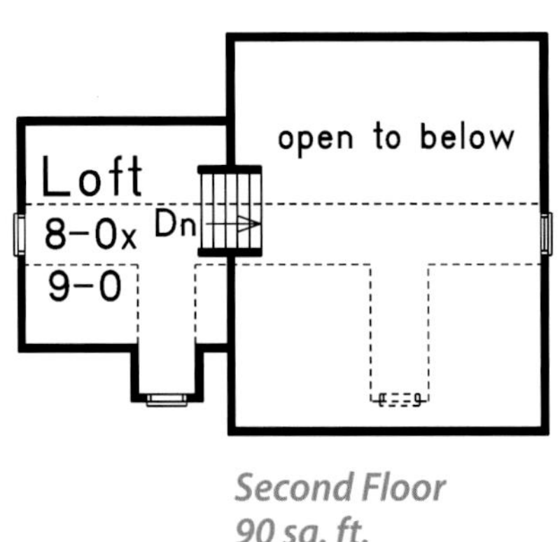

Second Floor
90 sq. ft.

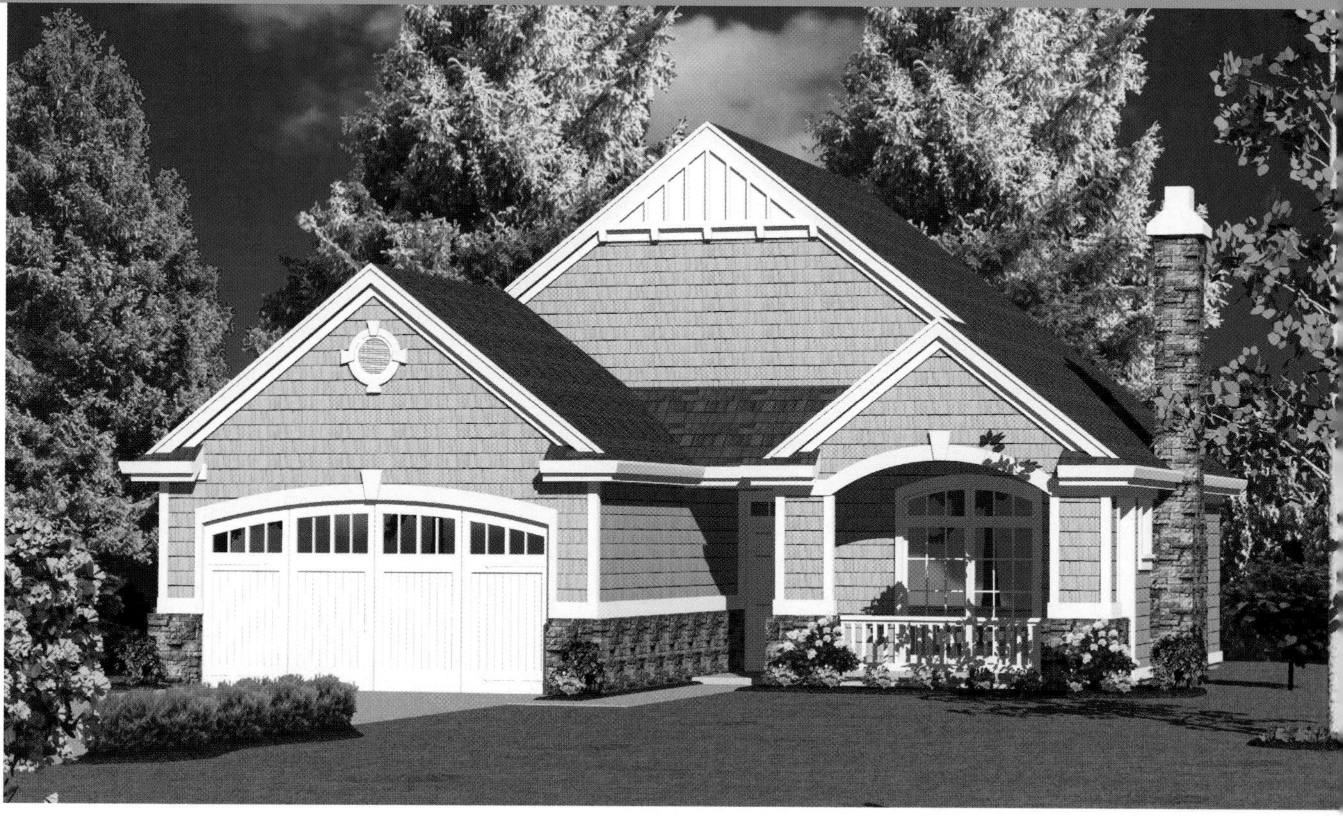

Plan #582-011D-0001

Price Code C

Special Features • 1,275 total square feet of living area • The kitchen expands into the dining area with the help of a center island • Decorative columns keep the living area open to other areas • Covered front porch adds charm to the entry • 3 bedrooms, 2 baths, 2-car garage • Crawl space foundation

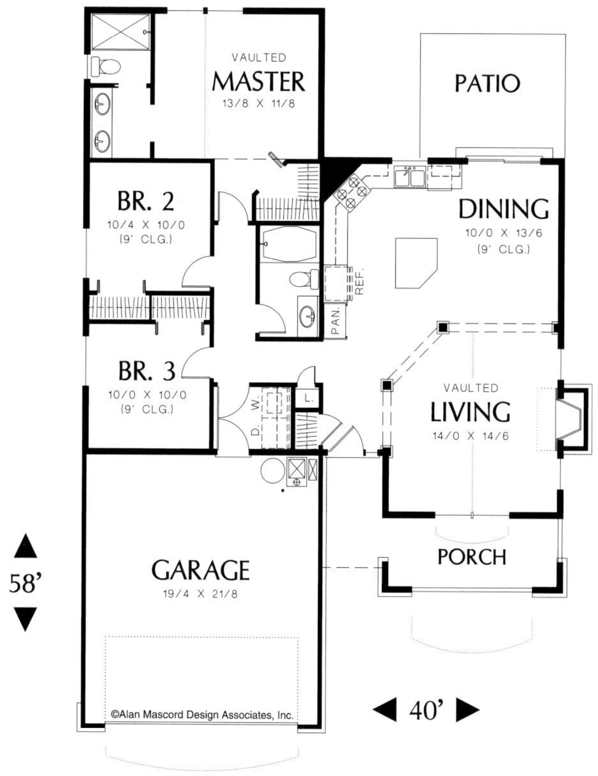
VAULTED
MASTER
13/8 X 11/8
PATIO
BR. 2
10/4 X 10/0
(9' CLG.)
DINING
10/0 X 13/6
(9' CLG.)
REF.
PAN.
BR. 3
10/0 X 10/0
(9' CLG.)
VAULTED
LIVING
14/0 X 14/6
W.
D.
L.
PORCH
GARAGE
19/4 X 21/8
58'
40'
©Alan Mascord Design Associates, Inc.

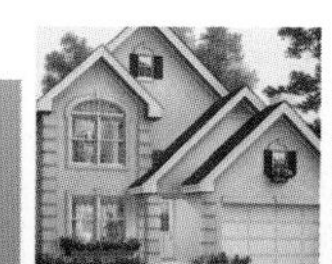

Quaint Exterior, Full Front Porch

Plan #582-053D-0030

Price Code B

Special Features • *1,657 total square feet of living area* • *Stylish pass-through between living and dining areas* • *Master bedroom is secluded from living area for privacy* • *Large windows in breakfast and dining areas* • *3 bedrooms, 2 1/2 baths, 2-car drive under garage* • *Basement foundation*

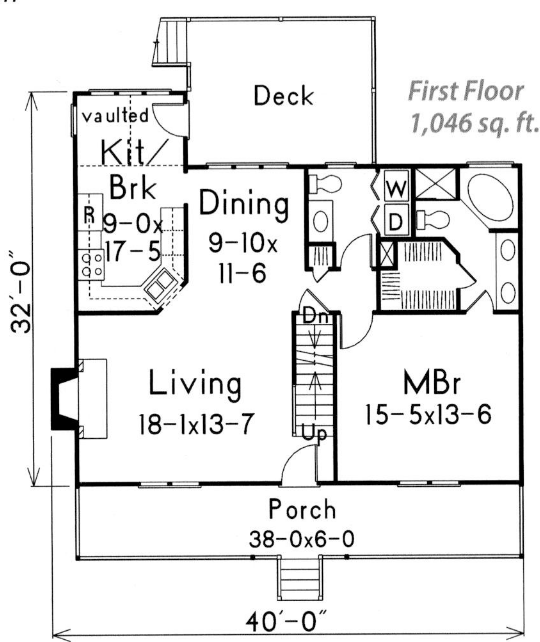

First Floor
1,046 sq. ft.

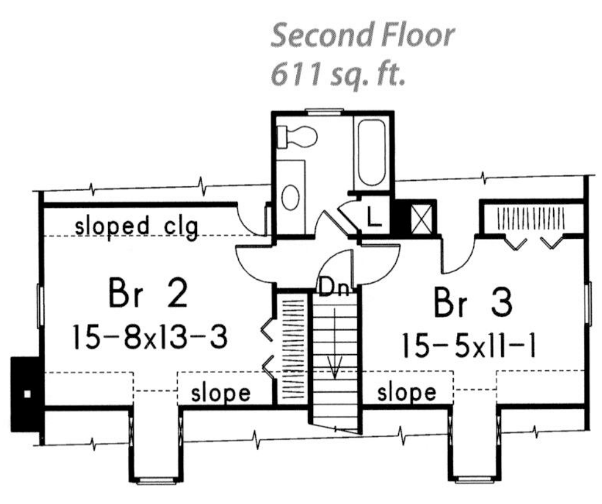

Second Floor
611 sq. ft.

Terrific Design Loaded With Extras

Plan #582-008D-0162

Price Code AAA

Special Features • 865 total square feet of living area • Central living area provides an enormous amount of space for gathering around the fireplace • Outdoor ladder on wrap-around deck connects top deck with main deck • Kitchen is bright and cheerful with lots of windows and access to deck • 2 bedrooms, 1 bath • Pier foundation

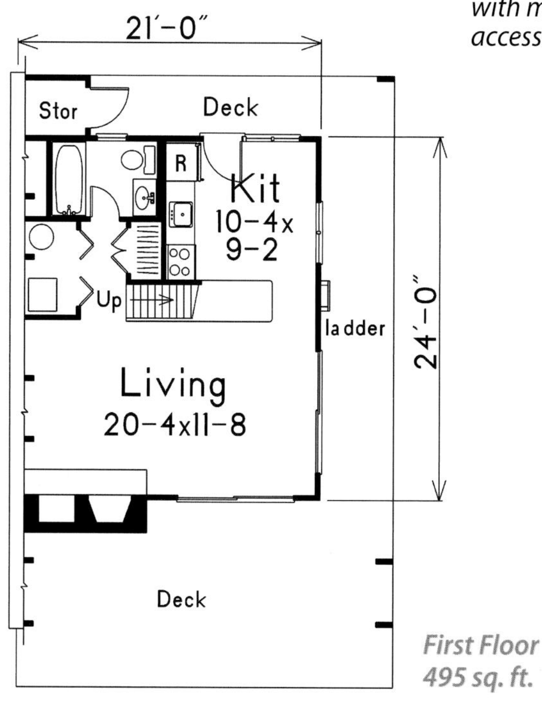

First Floor
495 sq. ft.

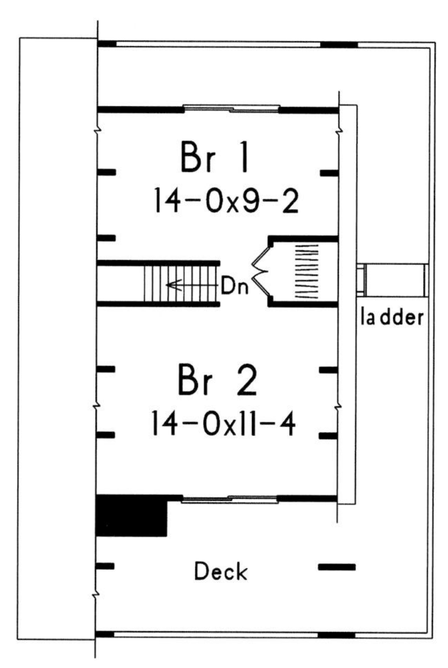

Second Floor
370 sq. ft.

Floor-To-Ceiling Window Expands Compact Two-Story

Plan #582-022D-0002

Price Code A

Special Features • 1,246 total square feet of living area • Corner living room window adds openness and light • Out-of-the-way kitchen with dining area accesses the outdoors • Private first floor master bedroom has a corner window • Large walk-in closet is located in bedroom #3 • Easily built perimeter allows economical construction • 3 bedrooms, 2 baths, 2-car garage • Basement foundation

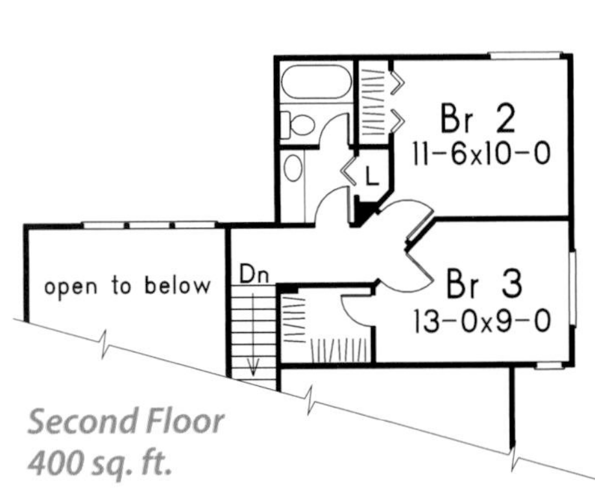

Second Floor
400 sq. ft.

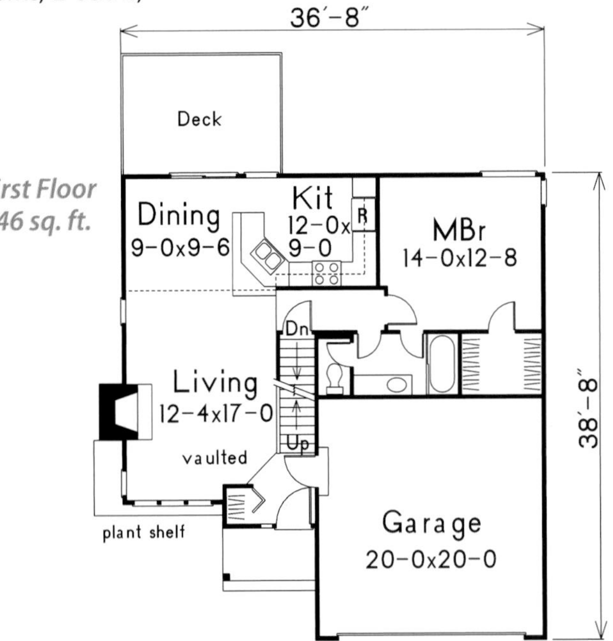

First Floor
846 sq. ft.

Plan #582-078D-0025

Price Code D

Special Features • *1,015 total square feet of living area* • *A massive fieldstone fireplace separates the living and dining spaces, both of which feature beamed and vaulted ceilings* • *The master bedroom enjoys a walk-in closet, private entry to bath and French doors to access the porch* • *The cozy kitchen is fully equipped and is conveniently adjacent to a well-planned utility room* • *2 bedrooms, 1 bath* • *Basement or crawl space foundation, please specify when ordering*

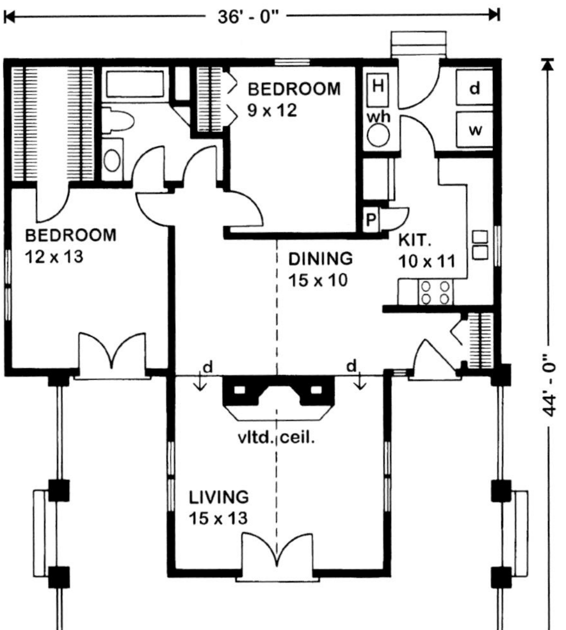

Cabin Cottage With French Door Entry

Plan #582-055D-0064

Price Code B

Special Features • 1,544 total square feet of living area • Great room has a vaulted ceiling and fireplace • 32' x 8' grilling porch in rear • Kitchen features a center island • 3 bedrooms, 2 baths • Crawl space or slab foundation, please specify when ordering

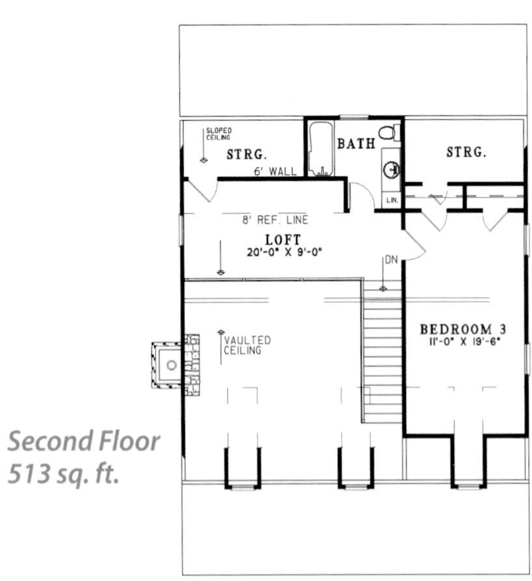

Second Floor
513 sq. ft.

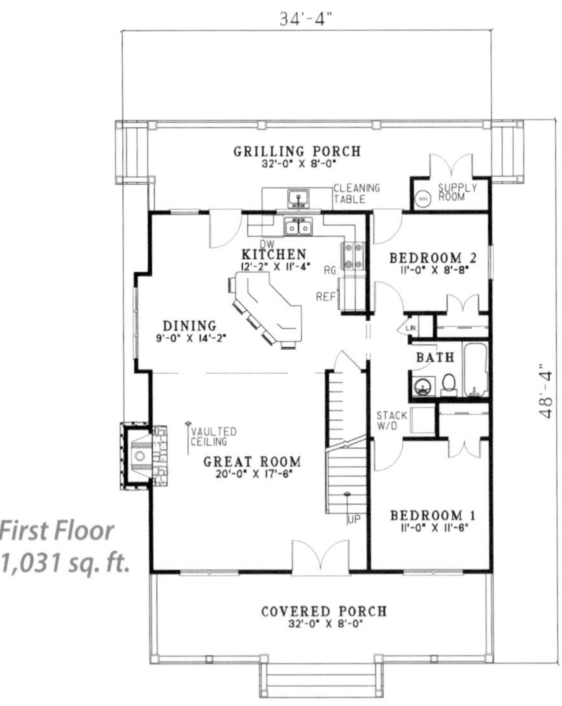

First Floor
1,031 sq. ft.

Plan #582-011D-0021

Price Code C

Special Features • *1,464 total square feet of living area* • *Contemporary styled home has a breathtaking two-story foyer and a lovely open staircase* • *U-shaped kitchen is designed for efficiency* • *Elegant great room has a cozy fireplace* • *3 bedrooms, 2 1/2 baths, 2-car garage* • *Crawl space foundation*

Second Floor
809 sq. ft.

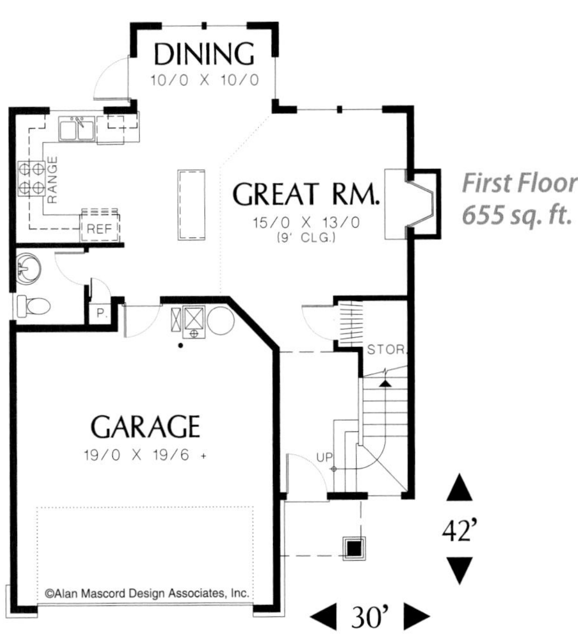

First Floor
655 sq. ft.

www.houseplansandmore.com

Plan #582-078D-0011

Price Code D

Special Features • 950 total square feet of living area • Two porches provide relaxing atmospheres • The combined living and dining areas are warmed by a large hearth fireplace and brightened by Palladian windows • Wrap-around kitchen offers a pantry, laundry area, and plant window beyond sink • A spectacular loft overlooking the living and dining areas provides an additional 270 square feet of living area • 2 bedrooms, 1 bath • Crawl space foundation

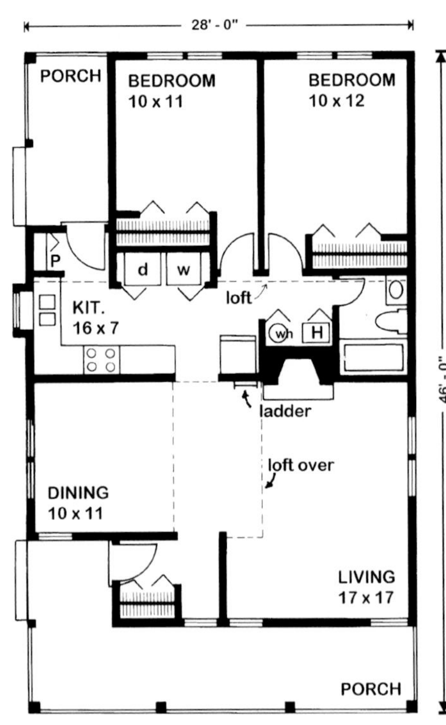

Nostalgic Porch And Charming Interior

Plan #582-016D-0055

Price Code B

Special Features • 1,040 total square feet of living area • Affordable home has the ability to accommodate a small or large family • An island in the kitchen greatly simplifies your food preparation efforts • A wide archway joins the formal living room to the dramatic angled kitchen and dining room • Optional second floor has an additional 597 square feet of living area • 4 bedrooms, 2 baths • Basement, crawl space or slab foundation, please specify when ordering

First Floor
1,040 sq. ft.

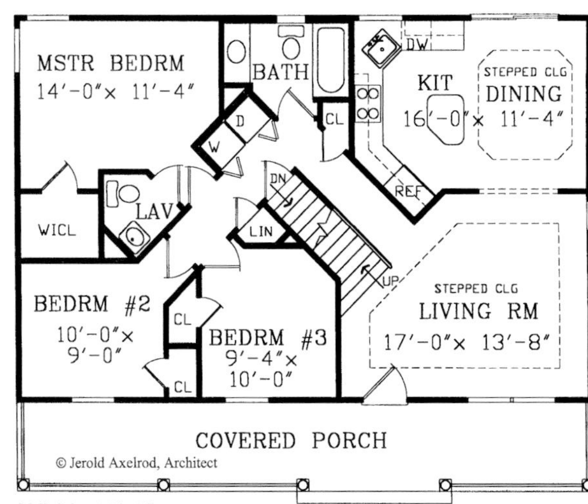

Width 40'-0"
Depth 32'-0"

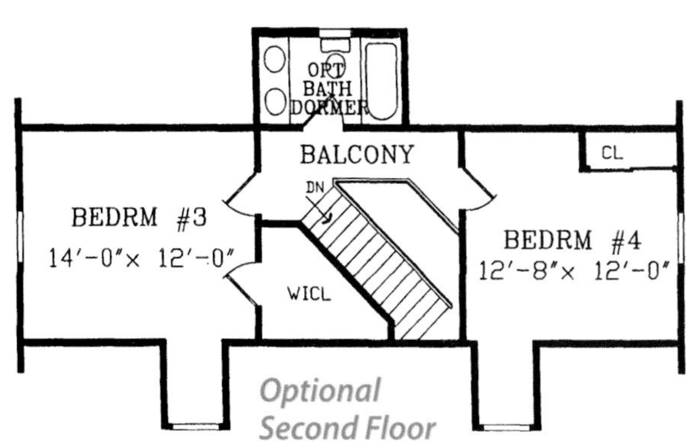

Optional
Second Floor

Plan #582-026D-0161

Price Code A

Special Features • 1,375 total square feet of living area • Den can easily convert to a second bedroom • A center island in the kitchen allows extra space for organizing and food preparation • Centrally located laundry room • 1 bedroom, 2 baths, 2-car rear entry garage • Basement foundation

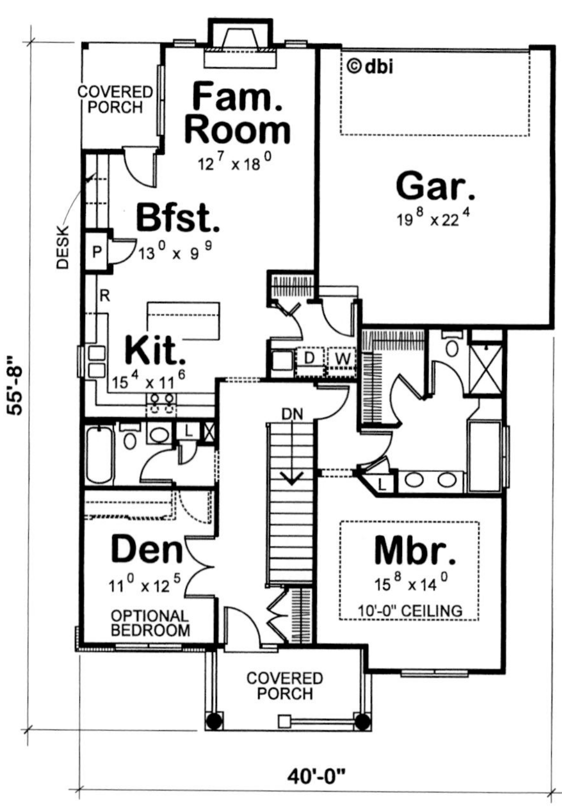

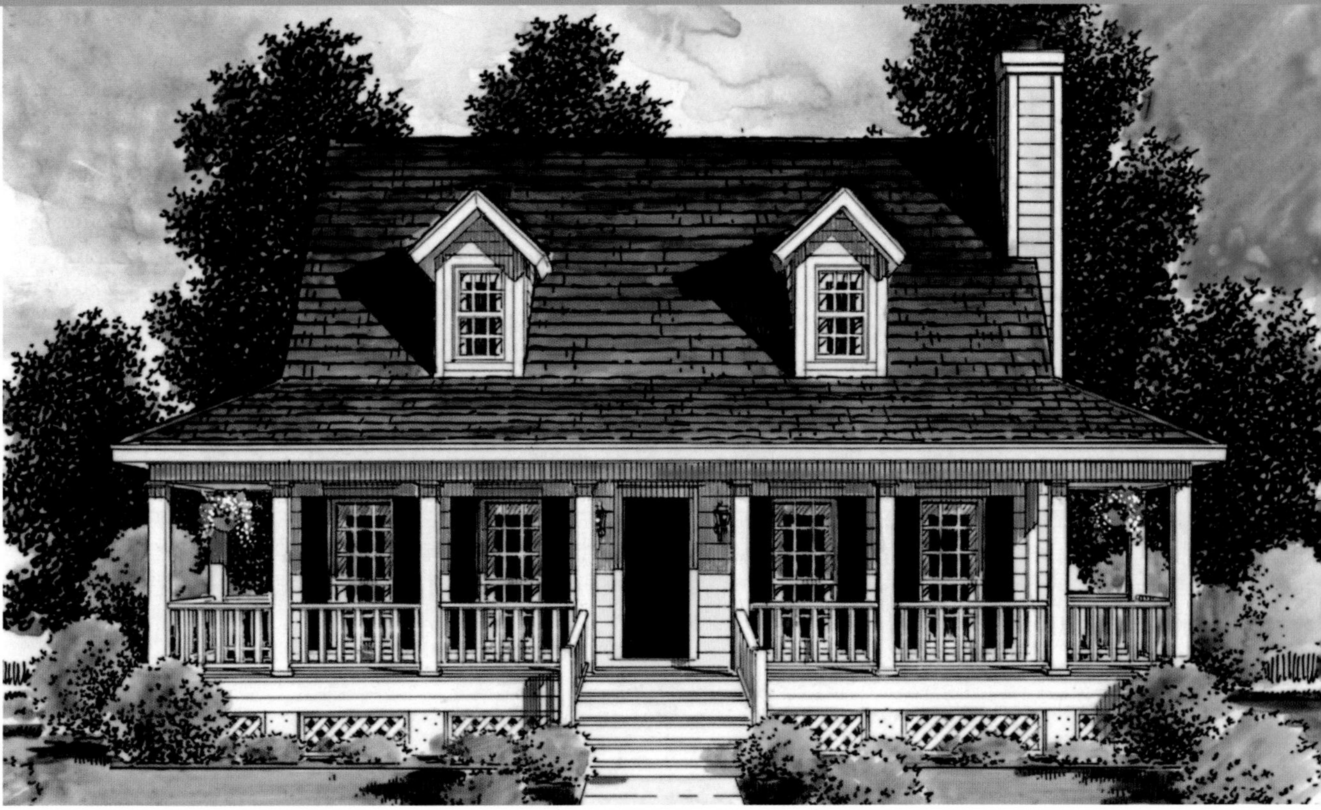

Plan #582-024D-0006

Price Code C

Special Features • *1,618 total square feet of living area • Secondary bedrooms with walk-in closets are located on the second floor and share a bath • Utility room is tucked away in kitchen for convenience but is out-of-sight • Dining area is brightened by a large bay window • 3 bedrooms, 2 1/2 baths • Slab or crawl space foundation, please specify when ordering*

Second Floor
572 sq. ft.

First Floor
1,046 sq. ft.

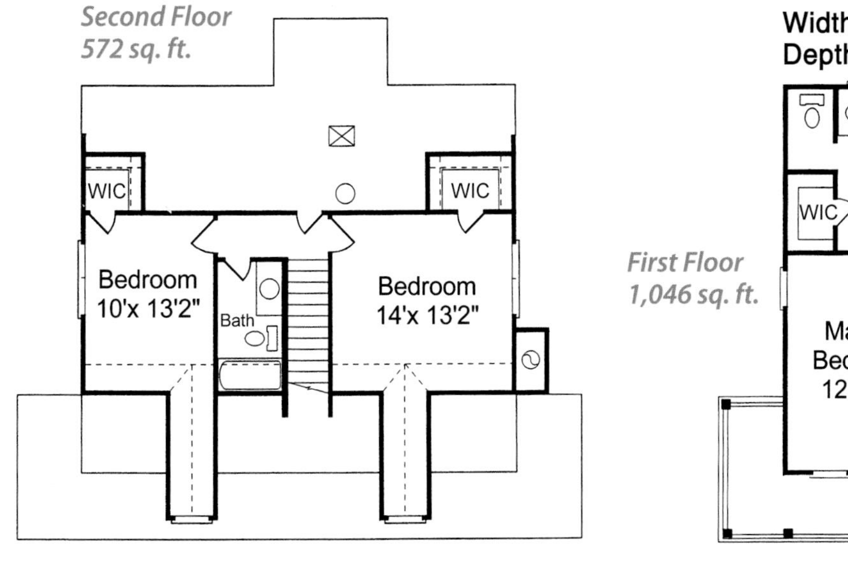

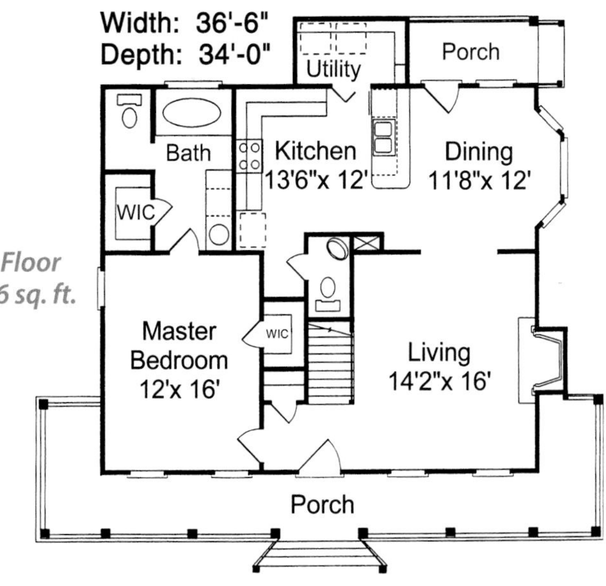

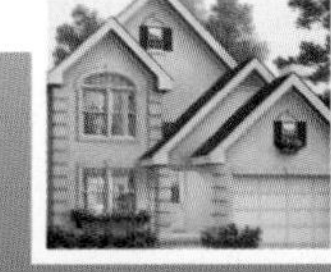

Three-Car Apartment Garage With Country Flair

Plan #582-007D-0070 Price Code AA

Special Features • 929 total square feet of living area • Spacious living room with dining area has access to 8' x 12' deck through glass sliding doors • Splendid U-shaped kitchen features a breakfast bar, oval window above sink and impressive cabinet storage • Master bedroom enjoys a walk-in closet and large elliptical feature window • Laundry, storage closet and mechanical space are located off first floor garage • 2 bedrooms, 1 bath, 3-car side entry garage • Slab foundation

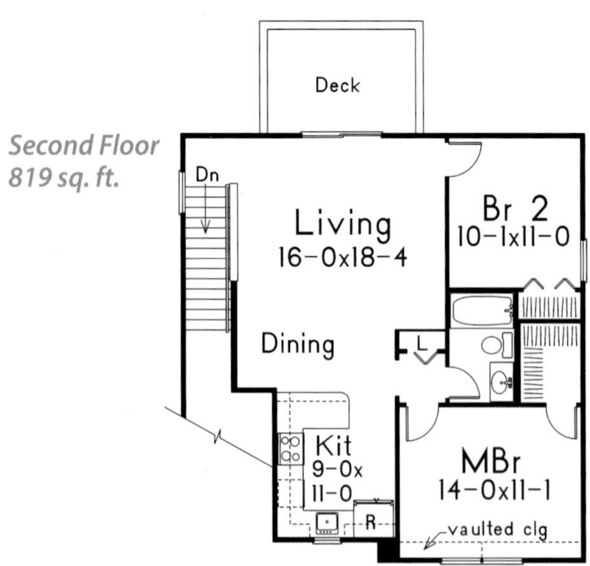

Second Floor
819 sq. ft.

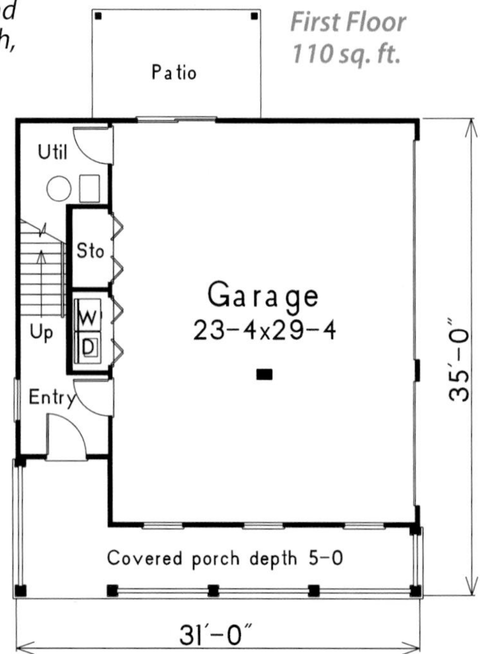

First Floor
110 sq. ft.

Dramatic Cathedral Ceiling In Living Area

Plan #582-032D-0015

Price Code B

Special Features • 1,556 total square feet of living area • Energy efficient home with 2" x 6" exterior walls • Master bedroom has walk-in closet • Separate entry with closet is a unique feature • 3 bedrooms, 2 baths • Basement foundation

First Floor
952 sq. ft.

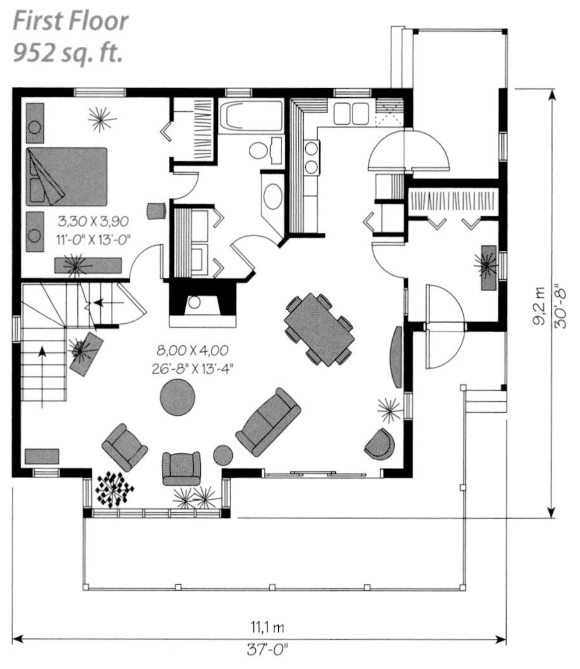

Second Floor
604 sq. ft.

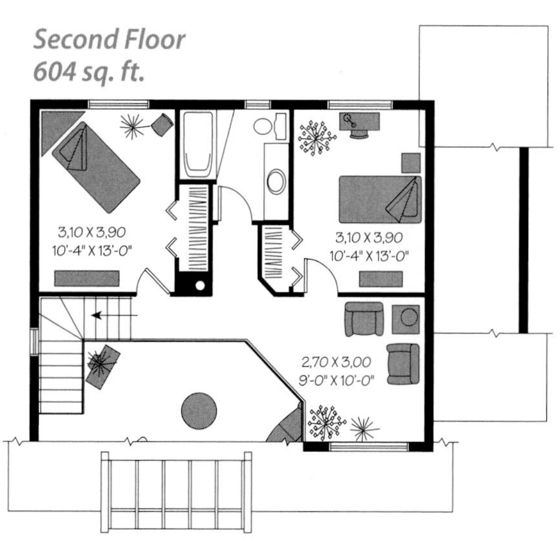

Comfortable Living In This Narrow Lot Home

Plan #582-055D-0116   Price Code A

Special Features • 1,462 total square feet of living area • U-shaped kitchen has everything within reach • All bedrooms have access to their own bath • Master bath has double vanity, shower and a whirlpool tub with glass block window • 3 bedrooms, 3 baths, 2-car rear entry garage • Crawl space or slab foundation, please specify when ordering

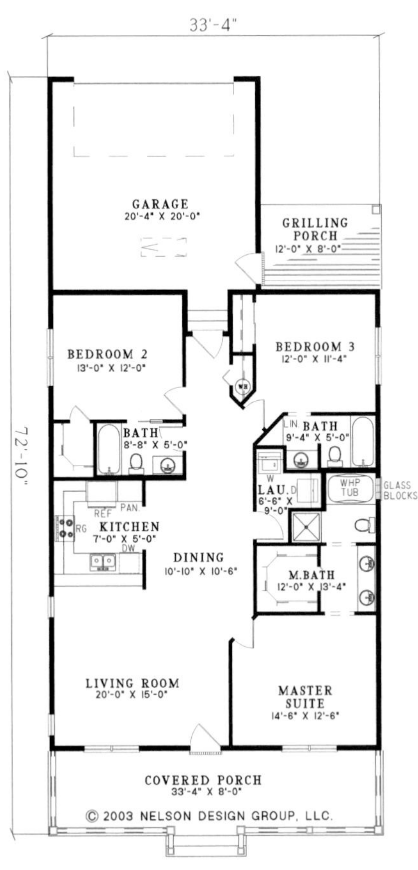

Country Accents Make This Home

Plan #582-062D-0059

Price Code B

Special Features • 1,568 total square feet of living area • Master bedroom is located on first floor for convenience • Cozy great room has fireplace • Dining room has access to both the front and rear porches • Two secondary bedrooms and a bath complete the second floor • 3 bedrooms, 2 1/2 baths • Basement or crawl space foundation, please specify when ordering

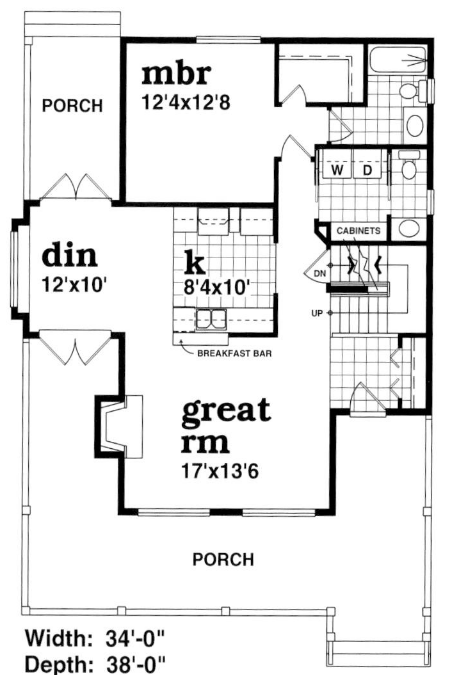

Width: 34'-0"
Depth: 38'-0"

First Floor
1,012 sq. ft.

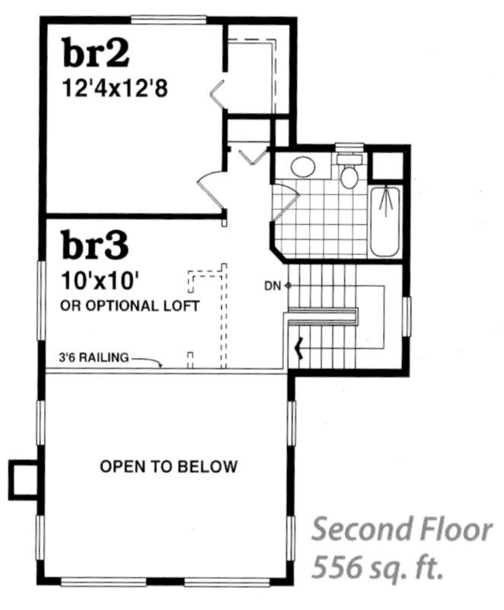

Second Floor
556 sq. ft.

Four Bedroom Home For A Narrow Lot

Plan #582-007D-0102

Price Code A

Special Features • 1,452 total square feet of living area • Large living room features cozy corner fireplace, bayed dining area and access from entry with guest closet • Forward master bedroom enjoys having its own bath and linen closet • Three additional bedrooms share a bath with double-bowl vanity • 4 bedrooms, 2 baths • Basement foundation

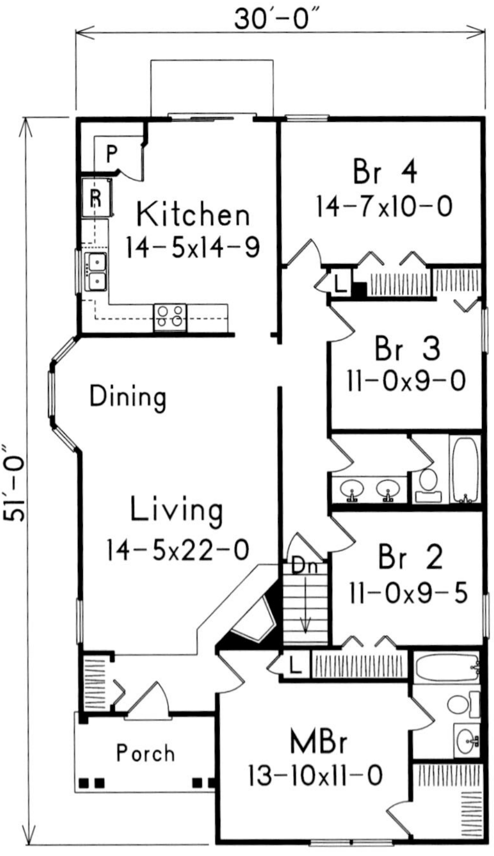

Chalet Cottage

Plan #582-062D-0031

Price Code AA

Special Features • 1,073 total square feet of living area • The front-facing deck and covered balcony add to outdoor living areas • The fireplace is the main focus in the living room, separating the living room from the dining room • Three large storage areas are found on the second floor • 3 bedrooms, 1 1/2 baths • Basement or crawl space foundation, please specify when ordering

Width: 24'-0"
Depth: 36'-0"

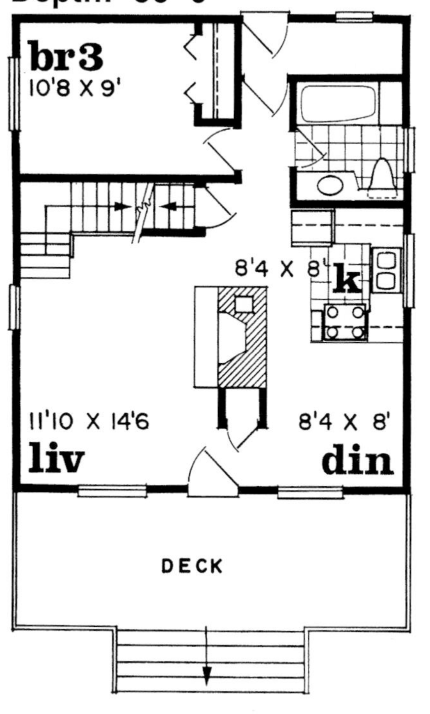

First Floor
672 sq. ft.

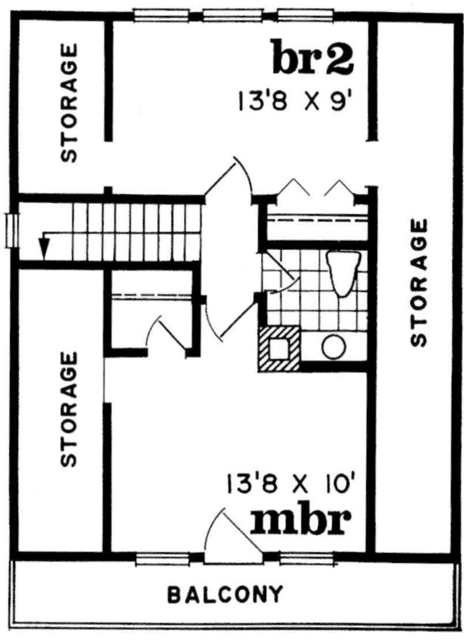

Second Floor
401 sq. ft.

Trendsetting Appeal For A Narrow Lot

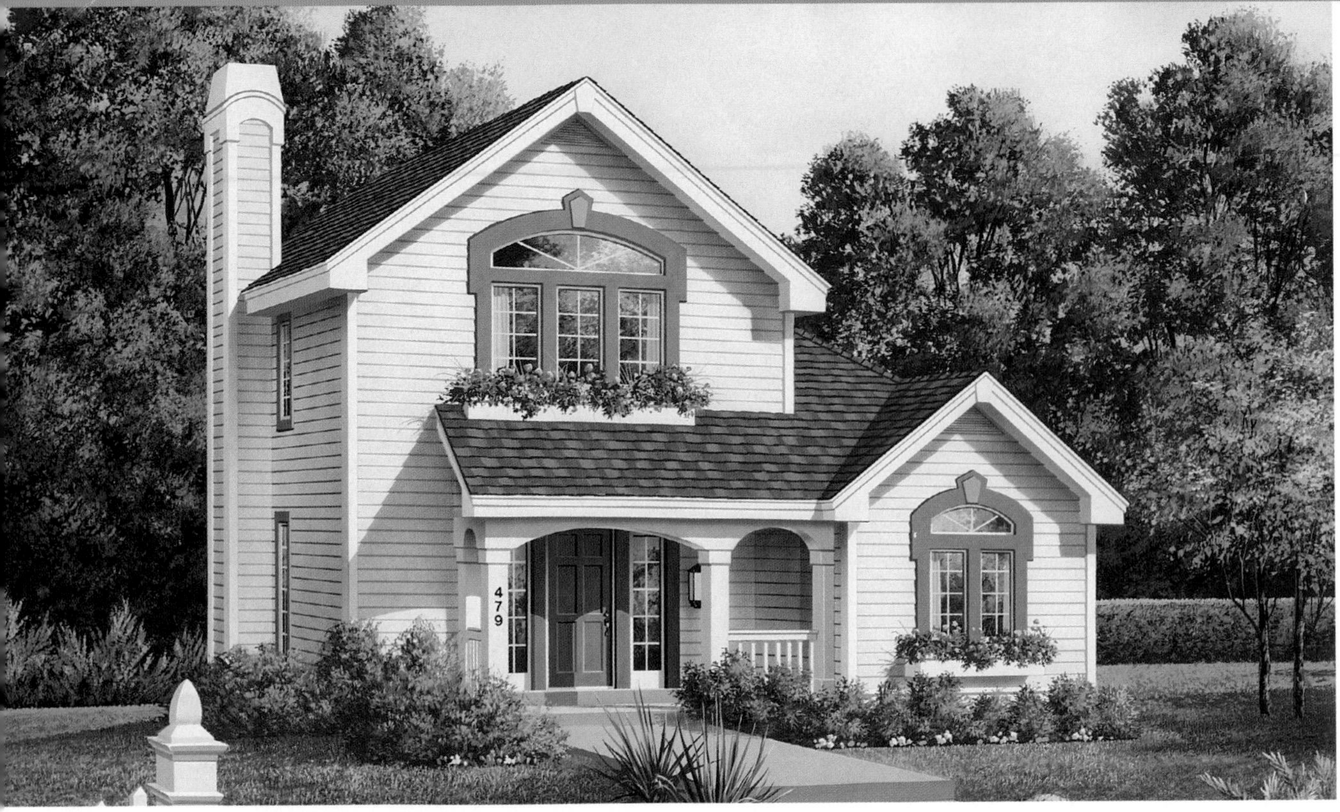

Plan #582-007D-0032

Price Code A

Special Features • 1,294 total square feet of living area • Great room features a fireplace and large bay with windows and patio doors • Enjoy a laundry room immersed in light with large windows, arched transom and attractive planter box • Vaulted master bedroom features a bay window and two walk-in closets • Bedroom #2 boasts a vaulted ceiling, plant shelf and half bath, perfect for a studio • 2 bedrooms, 1 full bath, 2 half baths, 1-car rear entry garage • Basement foundation

Second Floor
576 sq. ft.

First Floor
718 sq. ft.

1-800-DREAM HOME (373-2646)

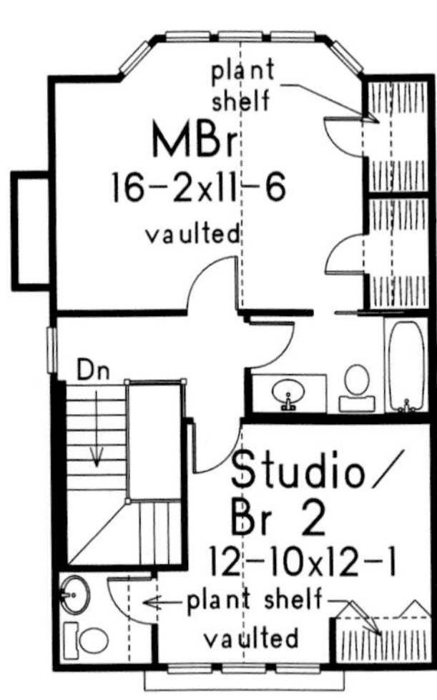

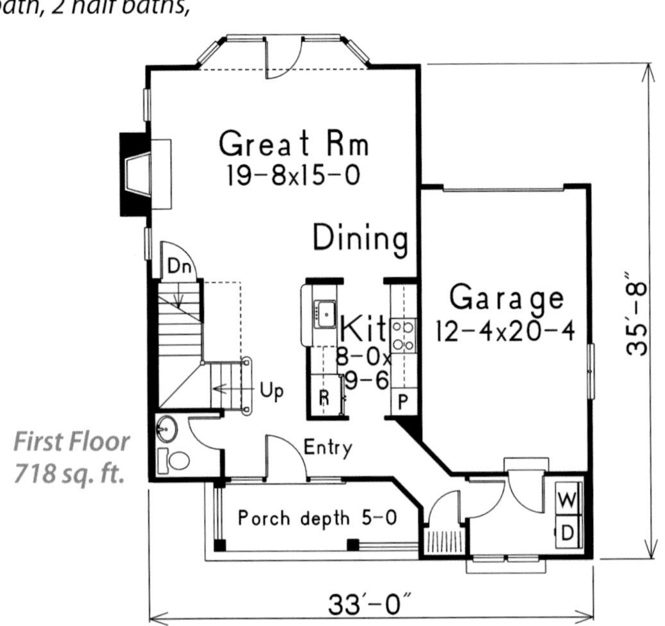

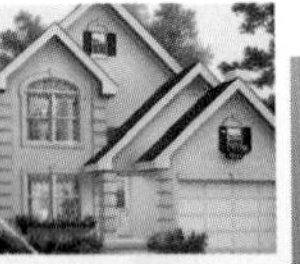

Plan #582-013D-0001 Price Code AA

Special Features • 1,050 total square feet of living area • Master bedroom has its own private bath and access to the outdoors onto a private patio • Vaulted ceilings in the living and dining areas create a feeling of spaciousness • Laundry closet is convenient to all bedrooms • Efficient U-shaped kitchen • 3 bedrooms, 2 baths, 1-car garage • Basement or slab foundation, please specify when ordering

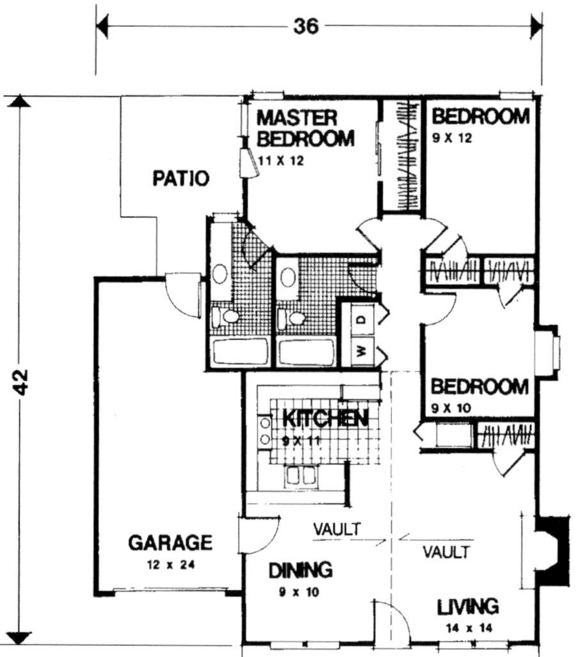

36

42

MASTER BEDROOM 11 X 12

BEDROOM 9 X 12

PATIO

W D

BEDROOM 9 X 10

KITCHEN 9 X 11

VAULT

VAULT

GARAGE 12 x 24

DINING 9 x 10

LIVING 14 x 14

Plan #582-078D-0036

Price Code D

Special Features • 1,035 total square feet of living area • Spacious living room is warmed by a stone fireplace and features a bay window with window seat • Country kitchen opens to the dining room and includes sliding glass doors leading to the patio • On the second floor, two bedrooms complete the design and share a full bath • 2 bedrooms, 1 1/2 baths • Basement and crawl space foundation, please specify when ordering

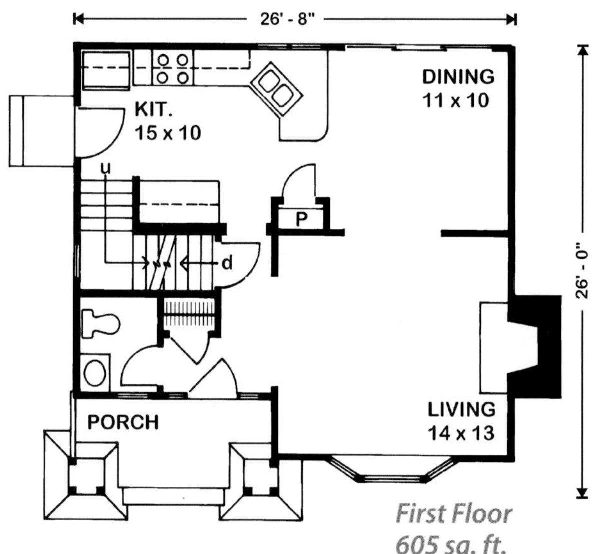

First Floor
605 sq. ft.

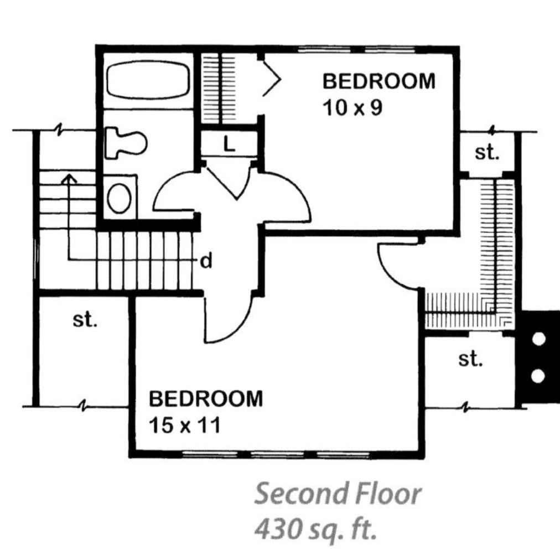

Second Floor
430 sq. ft.

Plan #582-025D-0001

Price Code AA

Special Features • 1,123 total square feet of living area • Eating bar in kitchen extends dining area • Dining area and great room flow together creating a sense of spaciousness • Master suite has privacy from other bedrooms as well as a private bath • Utility room is conveniently located near kitchen • 3 bedrooms, 2 baths • Crawl space or slab foundation, please specify when ordering

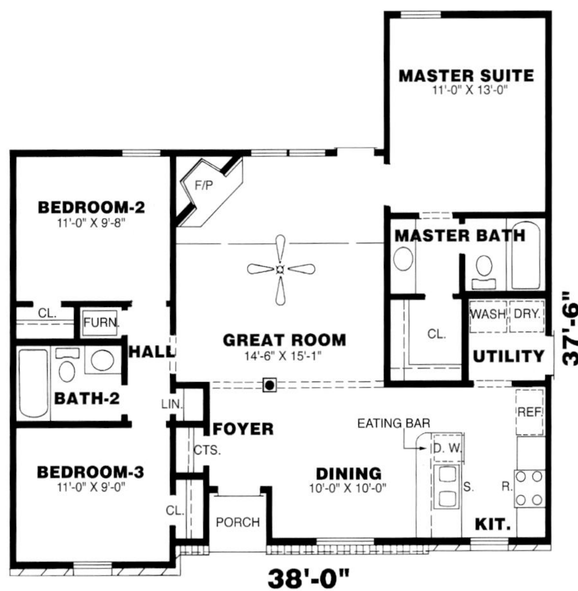

Beautiful Views Of Terrace From Dining Area

Plan #582-032D-0009 **Price Code AA**

Special Features • *1,199 total square feet of living area* • *Energy efficient home with 2" x 6" exterior walls* • *Open living spaces are ideal for entertaining* • *Spacious kitchen has lots of extra counterspace* • *Nice-sized bedrooms are separated by bath* • *2 bedrooms, 1 bath* • *Basement foundation*

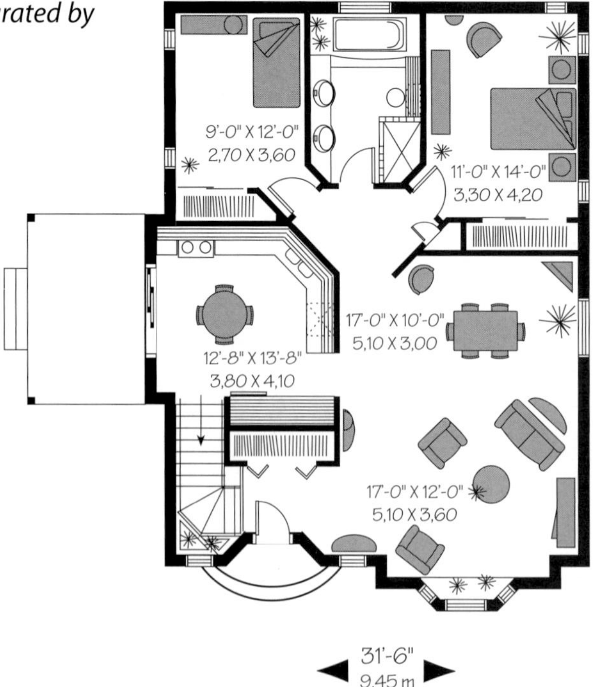

38'-8"
11,6 m

31'-6"
9,45 m

Expansive Deck Enhances Outdoor Living Areas

Plan #582-062D-0052

Price Code B

Special Features • 1,795 total square feet of living area • Window wall in living and dining areas brings the outdoors in • Master bedroom has a full bath and walk-in closet • Vaulted loft on second floor is a unique feature • 3 bedrooms, 2 1/2 baths • Basement or crawl space foundation, please specify when ordering

First Floor
1,157 sq. ft.

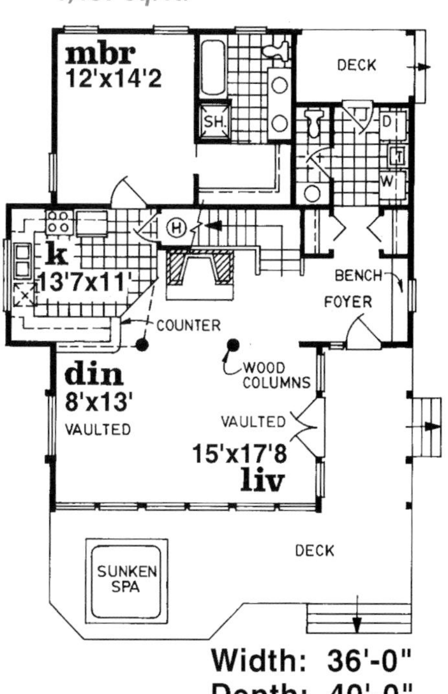

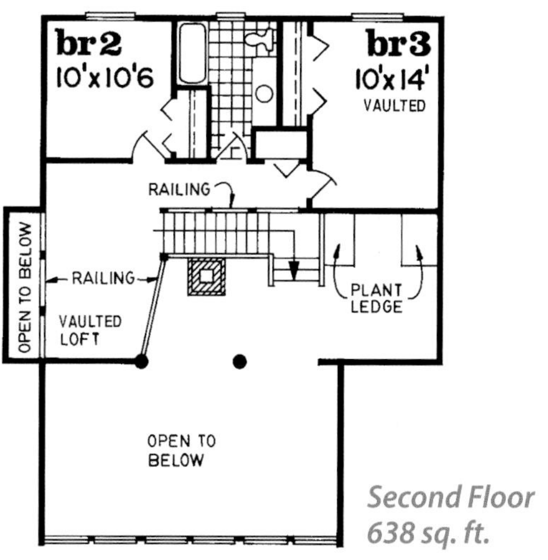

Second Floor
638 sq. ft.

Plan #582-078D-0018

Price Code D

Special Features • 900 total square feet of living area • Decorative exterior includes welcoming front porch and authentic gingerbread ornamentation • The double-door entry leads into the expansive living room • The kitchen has ample counterspace and a handy washer/dryer alcove • 2 bedrooms, 1 1/2 baths • Crawl space foundation

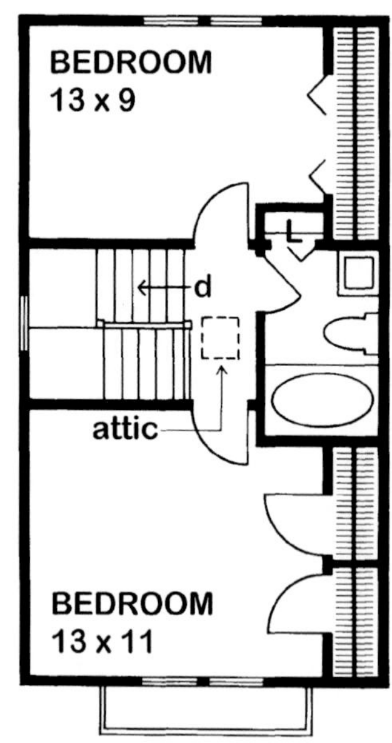

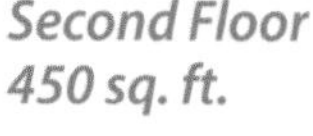
Second Floor
450 sq. ft.

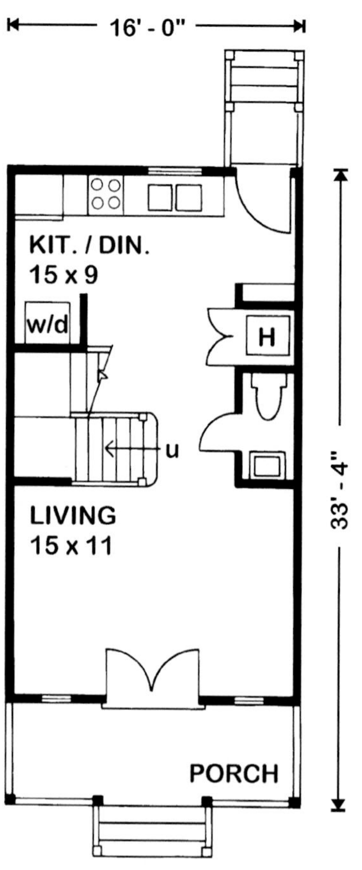

First Floor
450 sq. ft.

Plan #582-032D-0051

Price Code A

Special Features • 1,442 total square feet of living area • Energy efficient home with 2" x 6" exterior walls • Kitchen accesses bayed area and porch which provide a cozy atmosphere • Open living area makes relaxing a breeze • 3 bedrooms, 2 baths • Basement foundation

First Floor
922 sq. ft.

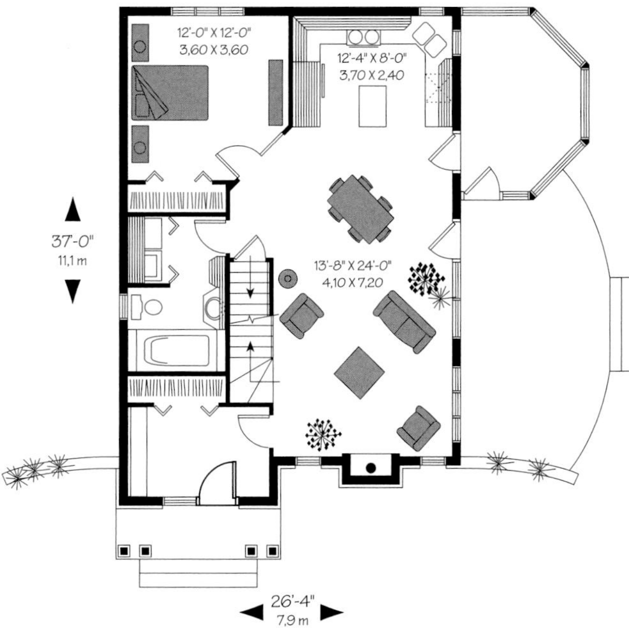

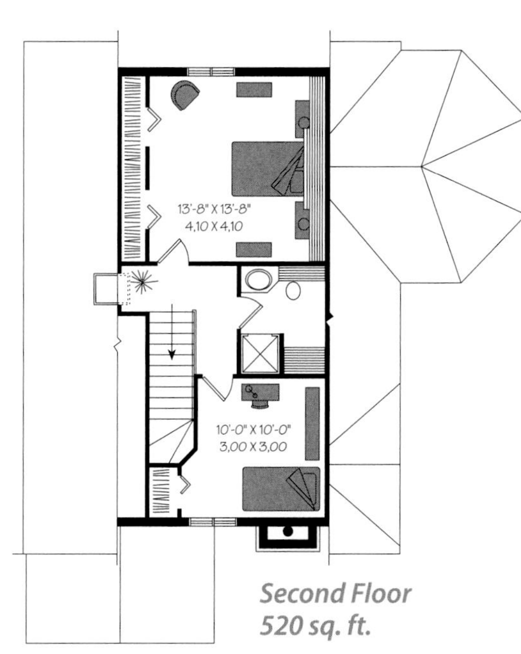

Second Floor
520 sq. ft.

Stylish Retreat For A Narrow Lot

Plan #582-007D-0105 Price Code AA

Special Features • *1,084 total square feet of living area • Delightful country porch for quiet evenings • The living room offers a front feature window which invites the sun and includes a fireplace and dining area with private patio • The U-shaped kitchen features lots of cabinets and bayed breakfast room with built-in pantry • Both bedrooms have walk-in closets and access to their own bath • 2 bedrooms, 2 baths • Basement foundation*

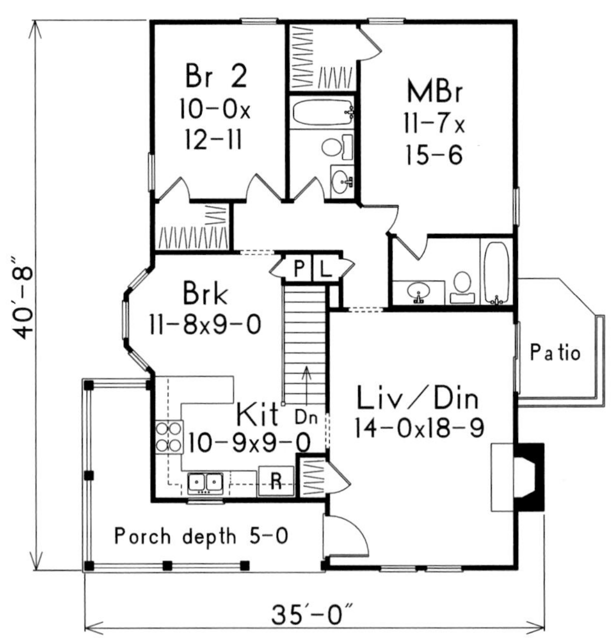

Large Front Porch Adds Welcoming Appeal

Plan #582-037D-0017

Price Code AAA

Special Features • 829 total square feet of living area • U-shaped kitchen opens into living area by a 42" high counter • Oversized bay window and French door accent dining room • Gathering space is created by the large living room • Convenient utility room and linen closet • 1 bedroom, 1 bath • Slab foundation

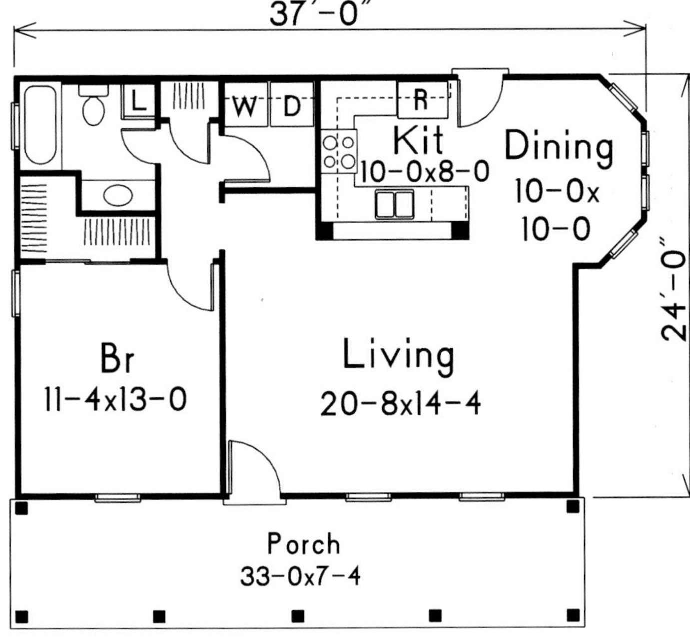

Great Room's Symmetry Steals The Show

Plan #582-007D-0014

Price Code C

Special Features • 1,985 total square feet of living area • Charming design for a narrow lot • Dramatic sunken great room features vaulted ceiling, large double-hung windows and transomed patio doors • Grand master bedroom includes a double-door entry, large closet, elegant bath and patio access • 4 bedrooms, 3 1/2 baths, 2-car garage • Basement foundation

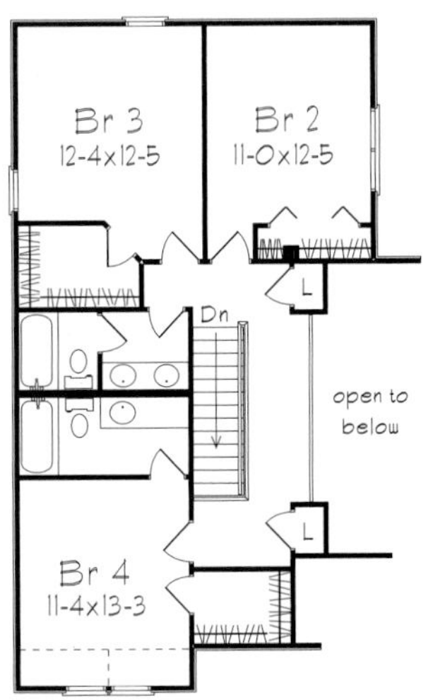

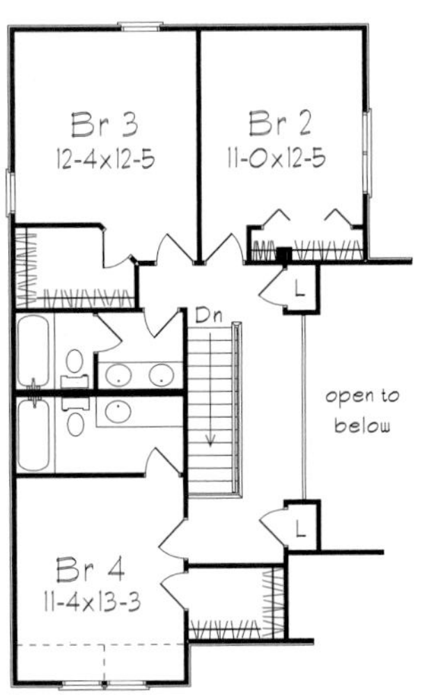

Second Floor
871 sq. ft.

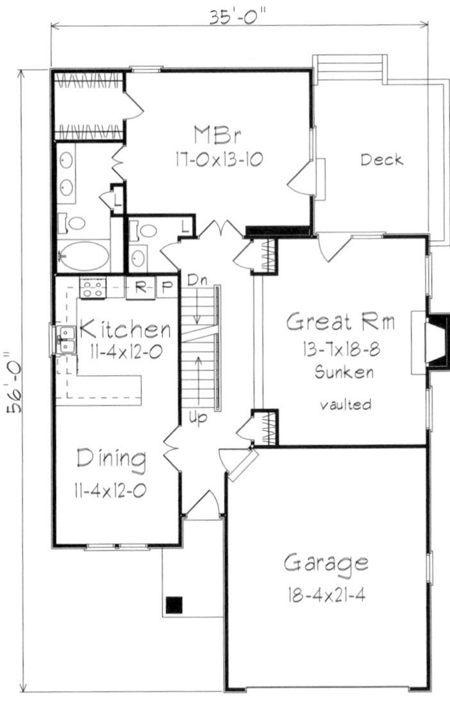

First Floor
1,114 sq. ft.

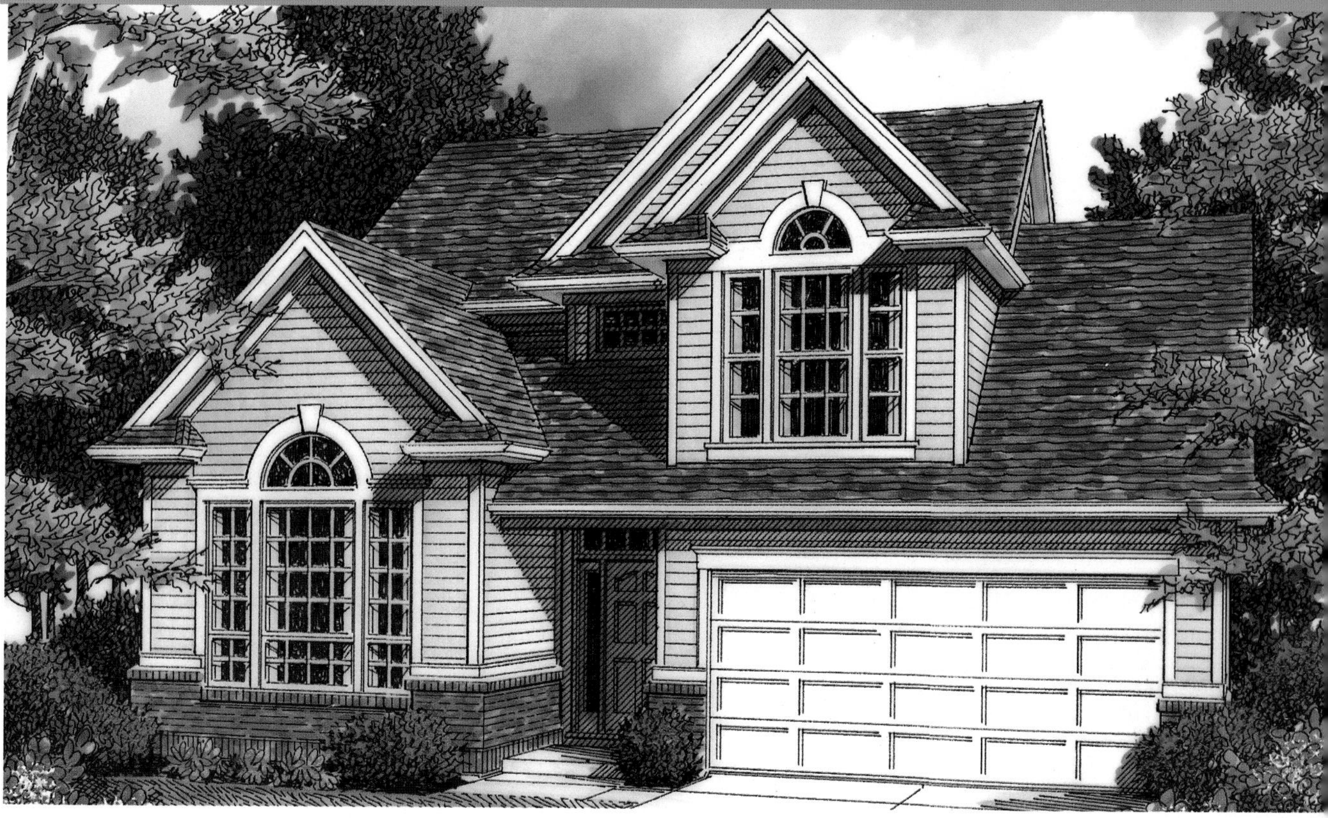

Plan #582-011D-0022

Price Code D

Special Features • 1,994 total square feet of living area • Breakfast nook overlooks kitchen and great room creating an airy feeling • A double-door entry off the family room leads to a cozy den ideal for a home office • Master suite has a walk-in closet and private bath • 3 bedrooms, 2 1/2 baths, 2-car garage • Crawl space foundation

First Floor
1,112 sq. ft.

Second Floor
882 sq. ft.

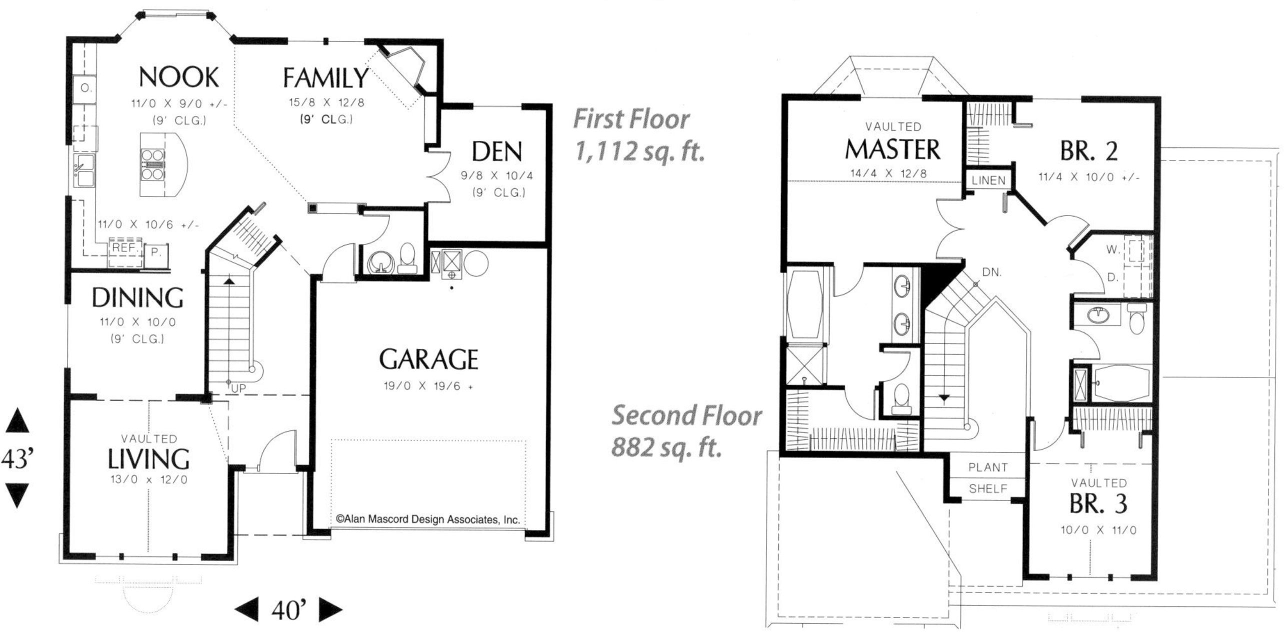

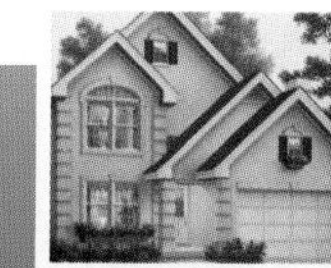

Three Bedroom Luxury In A Small Home

Plan #582-007D-0107 **Price Code AA**

Special Features • 1,161 total square feet of living area • Brickwork and feature window add elegance to home for a narrow lot • Living room enjoys a vaulted ceiling, fireplace and opens to kitchen • U-shaped kitchen offers a breakfast area with bay window, snack bar and built-in pantry • 3 bedrooms, 2 baths • Basement foundation

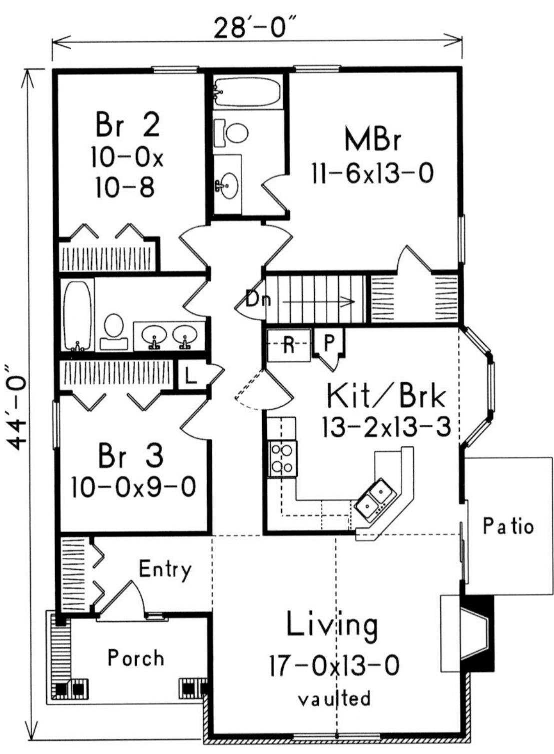

Double Dormers Add Curb Appeal

Plan #582-024D-0011

Price Code C

Special Features • *1,819 total square feet of living area* • *Unique bath layout on the second floor allows for both bedrooms to have their own private sink area while connecting to main bath* • *Window wall in dining area floods area with sunlight* • *Walk-in closets in every bedroom* • *3 bedrooms, 2 1/2 baths* • *Crawl space or slab foundation, please specify when ordering*

First Floor
1,242 sq. ft.

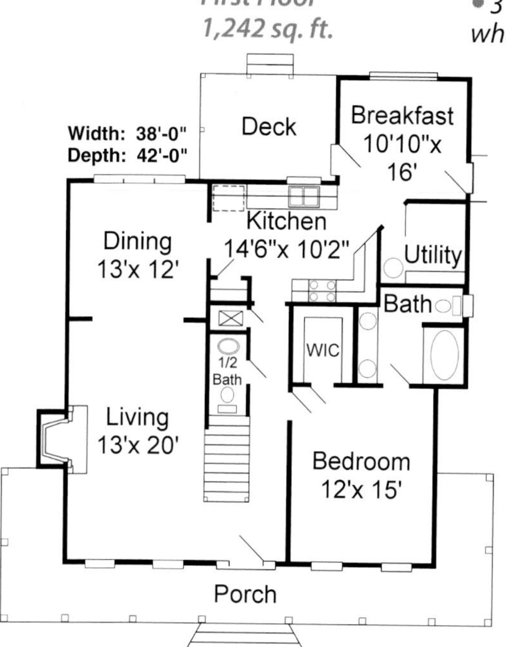

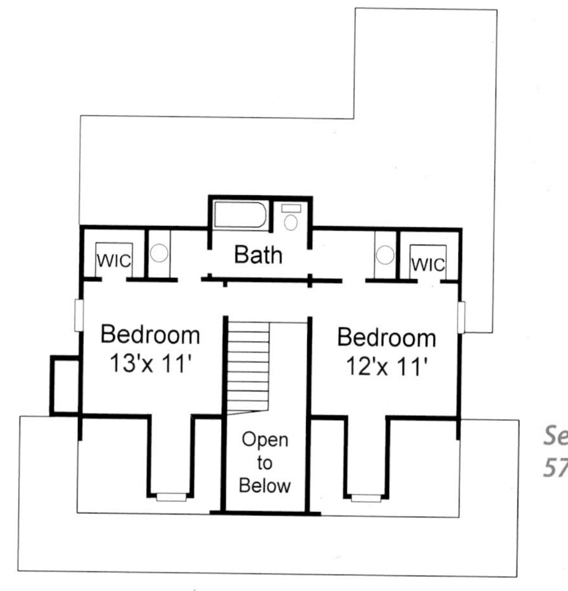

Second Floor
577 sq. ft.

Side Entrance Makes Home Ideal For A Narrow Lot

Plan #582-076D-0017 Price Code B

Special Features • 1,123 total square feet of living area • Spacious kitchen and breakfast area feature vaulted ceilings and patio access • Fireplace warms the adjoining family and dining rooms • Secondary bedrooms are secluded and share a bath • 3 bedrooms, 2 baths, 1-car garage • Crawl space or slab foundation, please specify when ordering

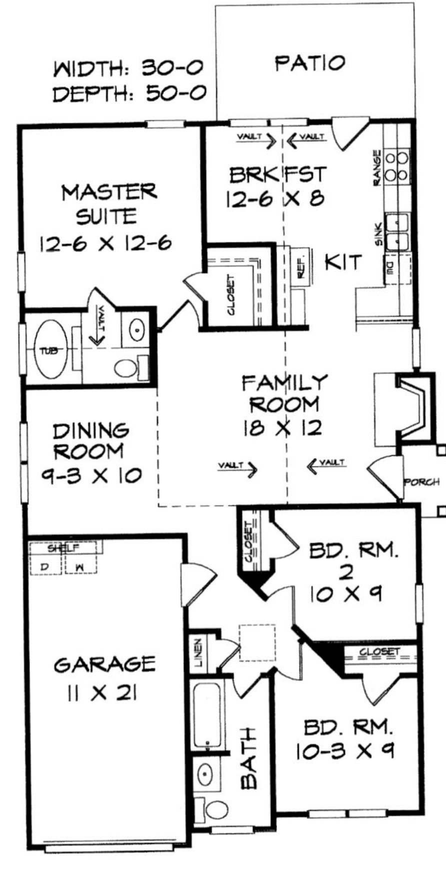

Unique Angled Entry

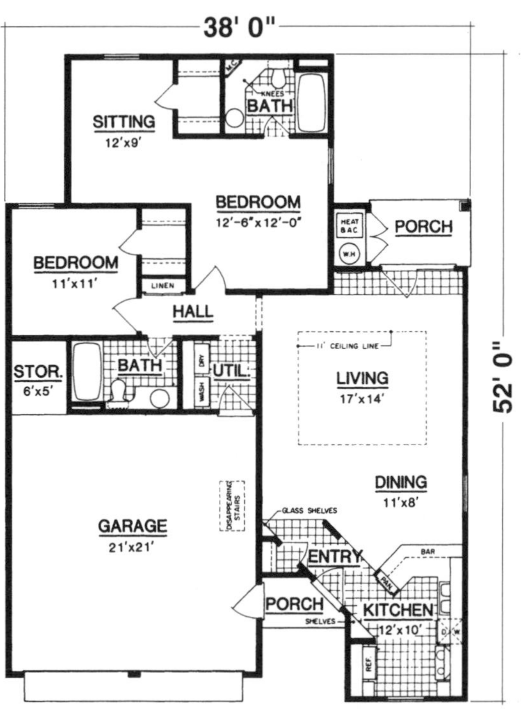

Plan #582-020D-0014

Price Code AA

Special Features • 1,150 total square feet of living area • Bedroom with attached sitting area would make a nice master bedroom • Living and dining rooms have 11' high box ceilings • Ornate trimwork accents the wood sided exterior • 2 bedrooms, 2 baths, 2-car garage • Slab foundation, drawings also include crawl space foundation

Graciously Designed Refuge

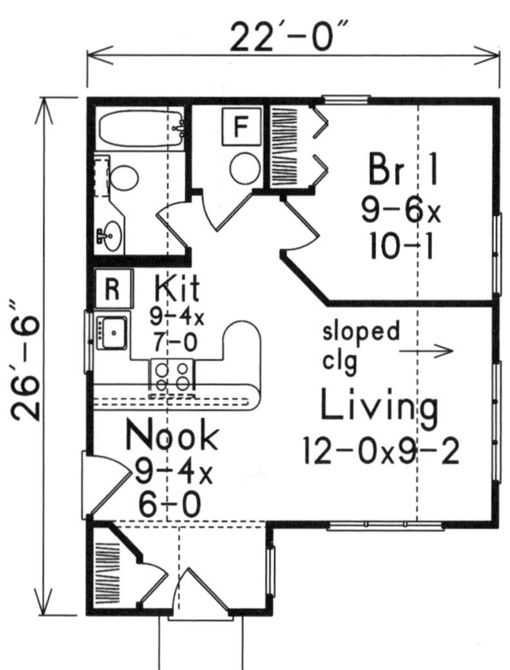

Plan #582-008D-0154

Price Code AAA

Special Features • 527 total square feet of living area • Cleverly arranged home has it all • Foyer spills into the dining nook with access to side views • An excellent kitchen offers a long breakfast bar and borders the living room with free-standing fireplace • A cozy bedroom has a full bath just across the hall • 1 bedroom, 1 bath • Crawl space foundation

Plan #582-022D-0001

Price Code AA

Special Features • 1,039 total square feet of living area • Cathedral construction provides the maximum in living area openness • Expansive glass viewing walls • Two decks, front and back • Charming second story loft arrangement • Simple, low-maintenance construction • 2 bedrooms, 1 1/2 baths • Crawl space foundation

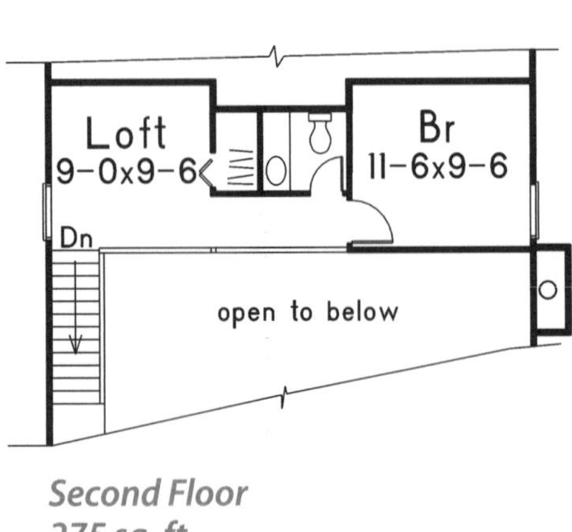

Second Floor
275 sq. ft.

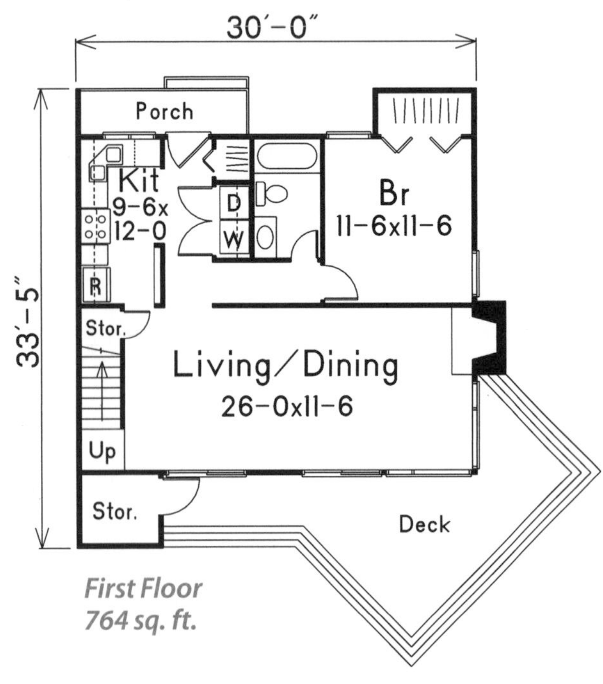

First Floor
764 sq. ft.

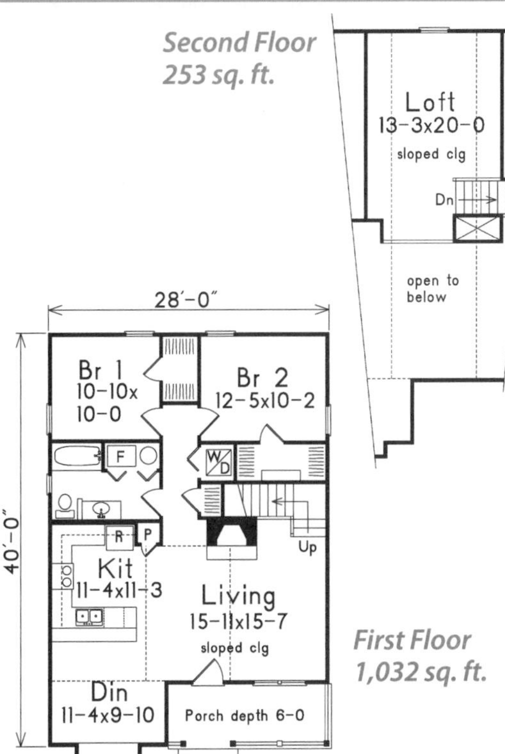

Plan #582-058D-0008 **Price Code A**

Special Features • 1,285 total square feet of living area • Dining nook creates warm feeling with sunny box-bay window • Second floor loft is perfect for a recreation space or office hideaway • Bedrooms include walk-in closets allowing extra storage space • Kitchen, dining and living areas combine making a perfect gathering place • 2 bedrooms, 1 bath • Crawl space foundation

Charming Home With Entry Porches

Plan #582-045D-0016 **Price Code AA**

Special Features • 1,107 total square feet of living area • L-shaped kitchen has serving bar overlooking the dining/living room • Second floor bedrooms share a bath with linen closet • Front porch opens into foyer with convenient coat closet • 3 bedrooms, 2 baths • Basement foundation

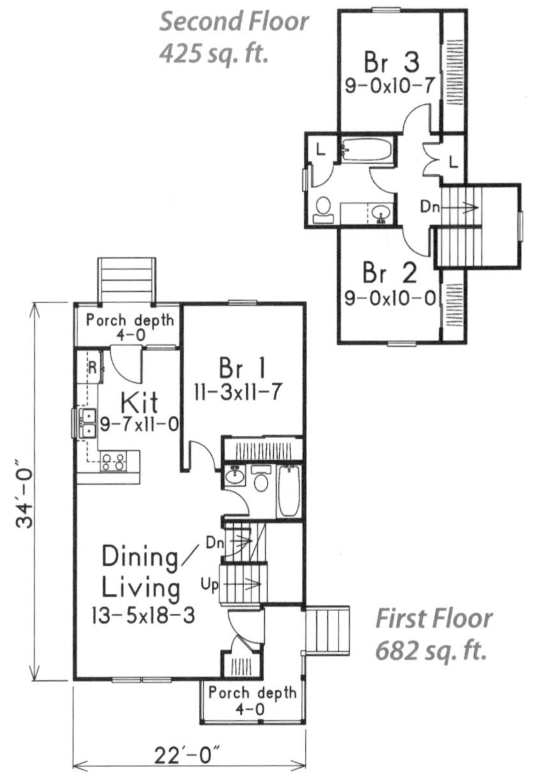

Plan #582-008D-0147

Price Code A

Special Features • 1,316 total square feet of living area • Massive vaulted family/living room is accented with a fireplace and views to the outdoors through sliding glass doors • Galley-style kitchen is centrally located • Unique separate shower room near bath doubles as a convenient mud room • 3 bedrooms, 1 bath • Crawl space foundation

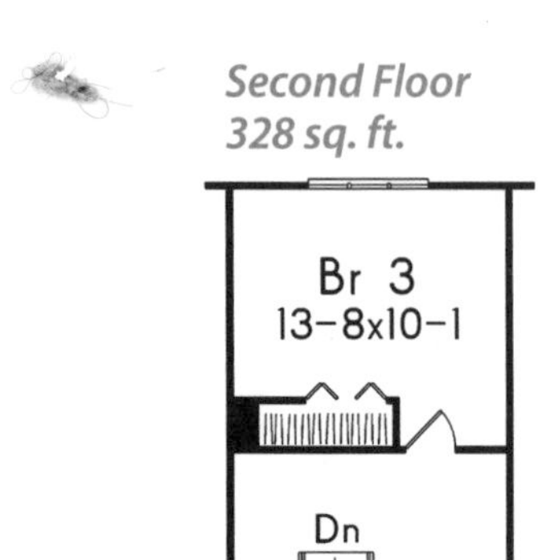

Second Floor
328 sq. ft.

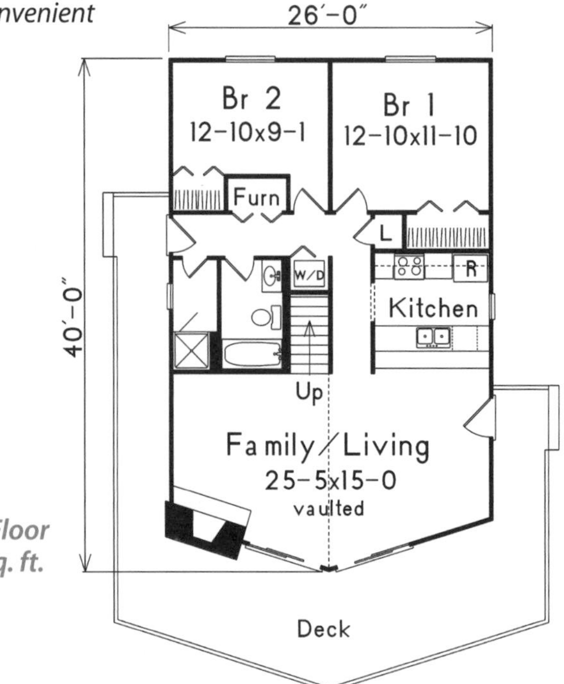

First Floor
988 sq. ft.

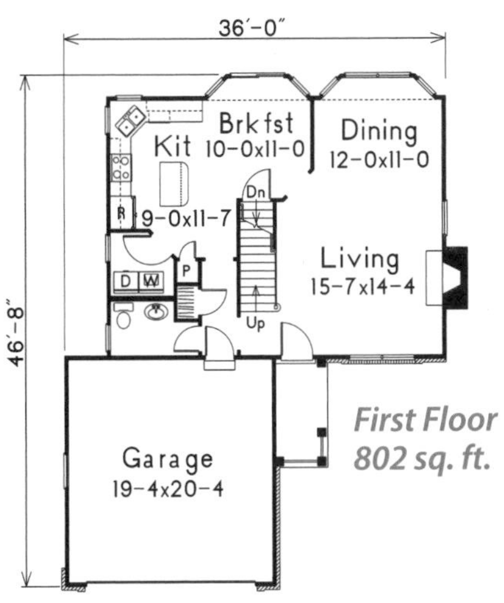

First Floor
802 sq. ft.

Second Floor
773 sq. ft.

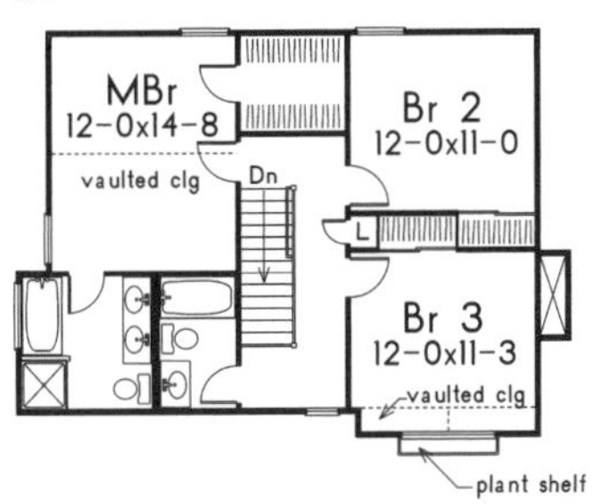

Plan #582-007D-0054

Price Code B

Special Features • 1,575 total square feet of living area • Inviting porch leads to spacious living and dining rooms • Kitchen with corner windows features an island snack bar, attractive breakfast room bay, convenient laundry and built-in pantry • A luxury bath and walk-in closet adorn the master bedroom suite • 3 bedrooms, 2 1/2 baths, 2-car garage • Basement foundation, drawings also include crawl space and slab foundation

Corner Windows Grace Library

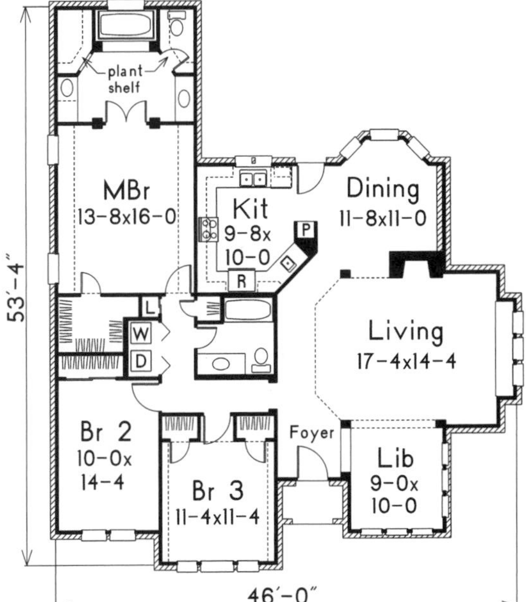

Plan #582-037D-0026

Price Code C

Special Features • 1,824 total square feet of living area • Living room features 10' ceiling, fireplace and media center • Dining room includes bay window and convenient kitchen access • Master bedroom features a large walk-in closet and luxurious bath with a double-door entry • Modified U-shaped kitchen features pantry and bar • 3 bedrooms, 2 baths, 2-car detached garage • Slab foundation

Plan #582-024D-0038

Price Code B

Special Features • 1,743 total square feet of living area • 9' ceilings on first floor • Covered porch off living area is spacious enough for entertaining • Private study on second floor is ideal for a computer area or office • 3 bedrooms, 3 baths, 2-car drive under carport • Pier foundation

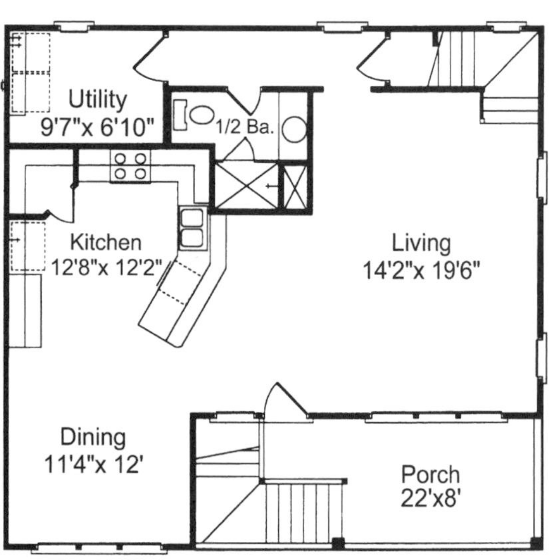

First Floor
912 sq. ft.

Width: 34'-0"
Depth: 32'-0"

Second Floor
831 sq. ft.

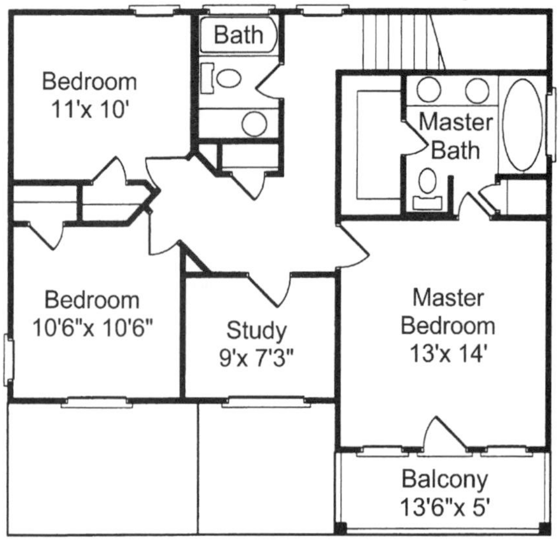

Bath
Bedroom
11'x 10'
Master
Bath
Bedroom
10'6"x 10'6"
Study
9'x 7'3"
Master
Bedroom
13'x 14'
Balcony
13'6"x 5'

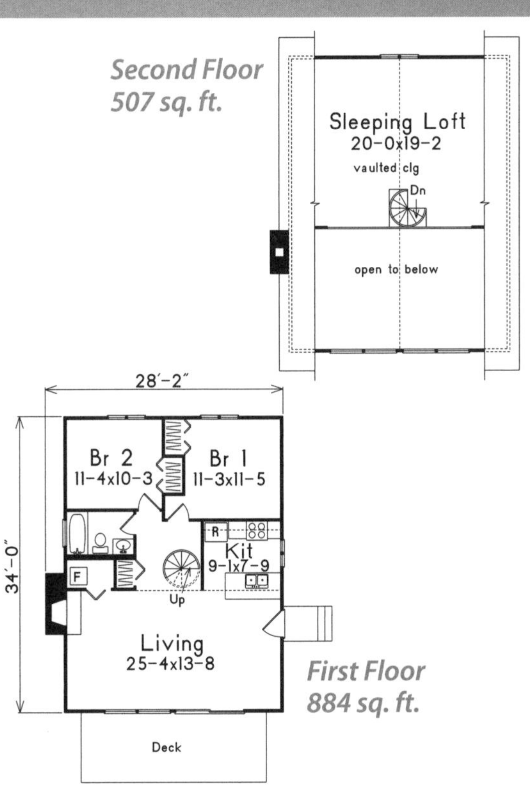

Plan #582-008D-0140

Price Code A

Special Features • 1,391 total square feet of living area • Large living room with masonry fireplace features a soaring vaulted ceiling • A spiral staircase in the hall leads to a huge loft area overlooking living room below • Two first floor bedrooms share a full bath • 2 bedrooms, 1 bath • Pier foundation, drawings also include crawl space foundation

Country Charm For A Narrow Lot

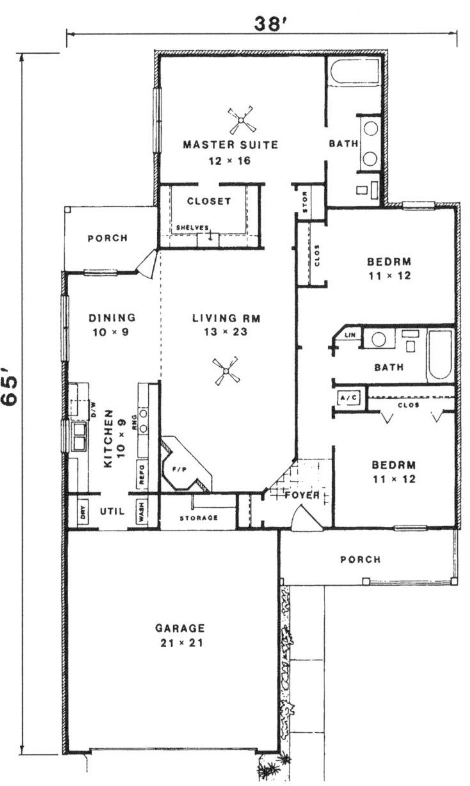

Plan #582-069D-0007

Price Code A

Special Features • 1,372 total square feet of living area • Cozy living room with large corner fireplace • Master suite has a very spacious closet and a private bath • The secondary bedrooms are located in their own hall and away from other living areas • 3 bedrooms, 2 baths, 2-car garage • Slab or crawl space foundation, please specify when ordering

Country Cottage Offers Large Vaulted Living Space

Plan #582-058D-0004

Price Code AA

Special Features • 962 total square feet of living area • Both the kitchen and family room share warmth from the fireplace • Charming facade features covered porch on one side, screened porch on the other and attractive planter boxes • L-shaped kitchen boasts convenient pantry • 2 bedrooms, 1 bath • Crawl space foundation

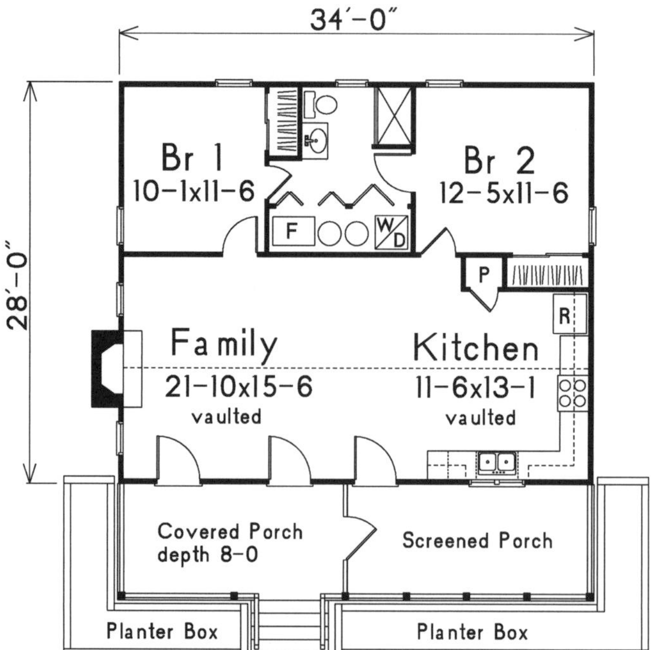

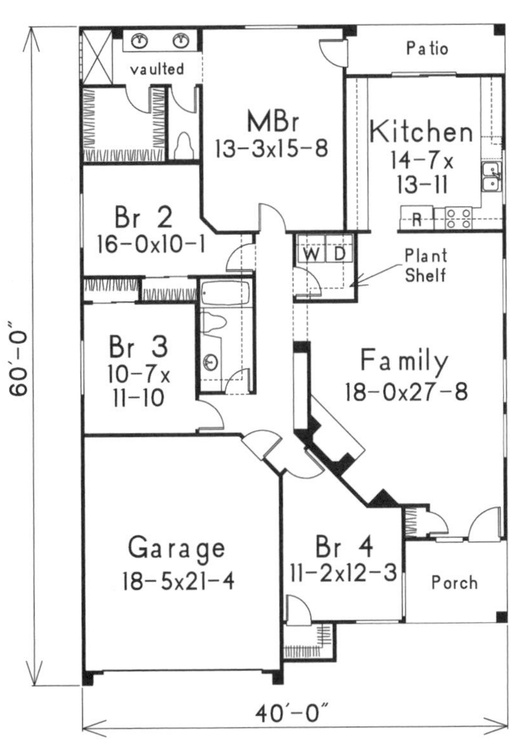

Plan #582-061D-0001

Price Code B

Special Features • 1,747 total square feet of living area • Entry opens into large family room with coat closet, angled fireplace and attractive plant shelf • Kitchen and master bedroom access covered patio • Functional kitchen includes ample workspace • 4 bedrooms, 2 baths, 2-car garage • Slab foundation

Second Floor
415 sq. ft.

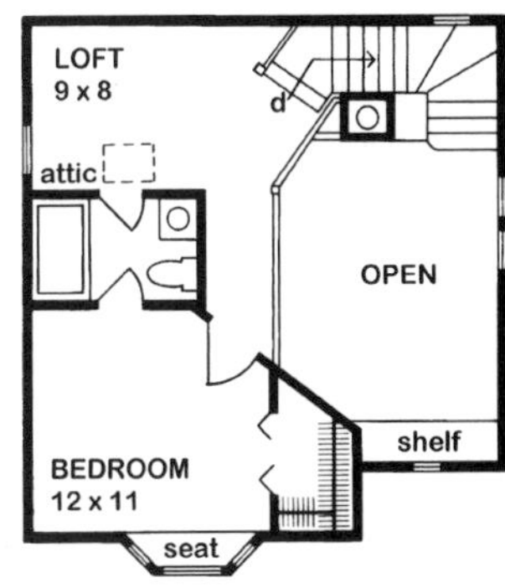

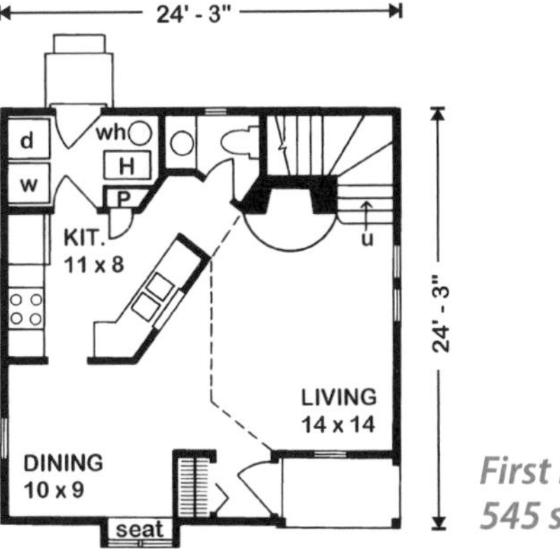

First Floor
545 sq. ft.

Plan #582-078D-0024

Price Code D

Special Features • 960 total square feet of living area • Two-story living room dominates the first floor • The dining room features a cozy window seat and is easily served by the pass-through kitchen • Open sleeping loft has the option of being enclosed to serve as a second bedroom • 1 bedroom, 1 1/2 baths • Crawl space foundation

Plan #582-008D-0141

Price Code A

Special Features • 1,211 total square feet of living area • Extraordinary views are enjoyed from the vaulted family room through sliding doors • Functional kitchen features a snack bar and laundry closet • Bedroom and bunk room complete first floor while a large bedroom with two storage areas and balcony complete the second floor • Additional plan for second floor creates 223 square feet of additional bedroom space • 3 bedrooms, 1 bath • Crawl space foundation, drawings also include basement foundation

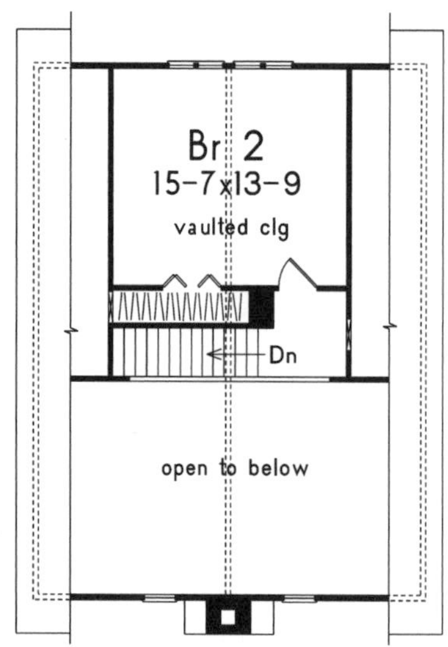
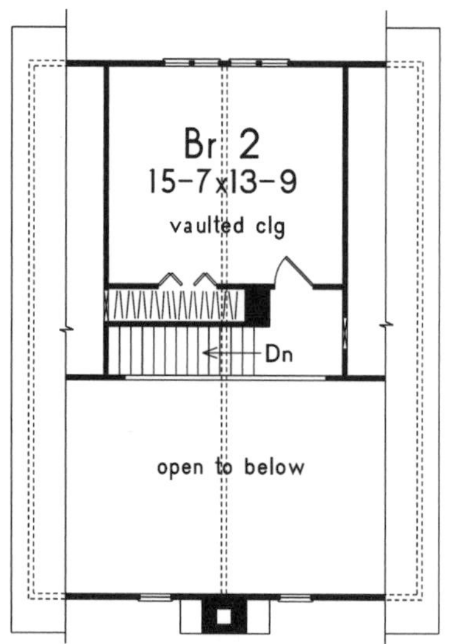

Second Floor
327 sq. ft.

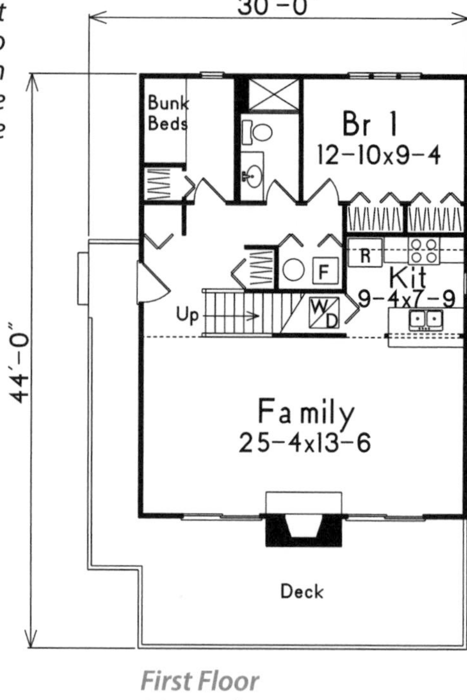

First Floor
884 sq. ft.

Quaint Cottage With Inviting Front Porch

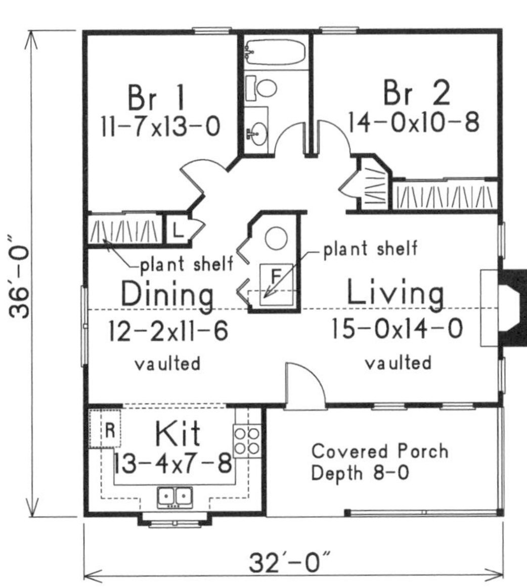

Plan #582-058D-0003 **Price Code AA**

Special Features • 1,020 total square feet of living area • Living room is warmed by a fireplace • Dining and living rooms are enhanced by vaulted ceilings and plant shelves • U-shaped kitchen with large window over the sink • 2 bedrooms, 1 bath • Slab foundation

Ideal Design For A Narrow Lot

Plan #582-047D-0010 **Price Code B**

Special Features • 1,576 total square feet of living area • Cozy family room has access to the patio through glass sliding doors and is near to the sunny dining area • Angled wall in breakfast nook is a unique design feature • Upon entering the master bedroom guests will notice the solarium garden • 3 bedrooms, 2 baths, 2-car garage • Slab foundation

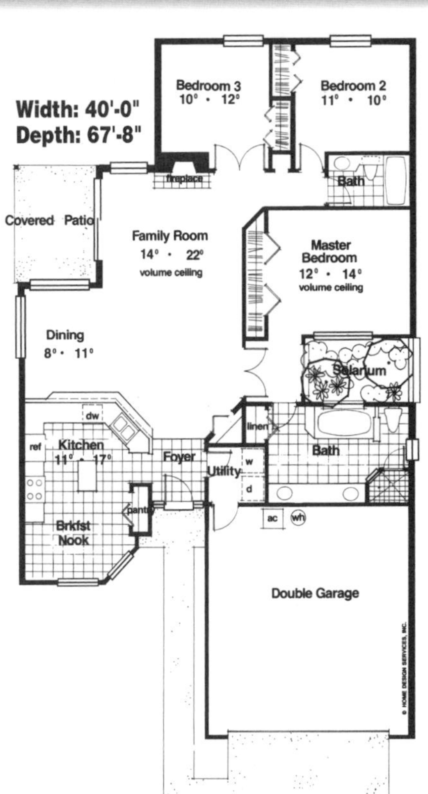

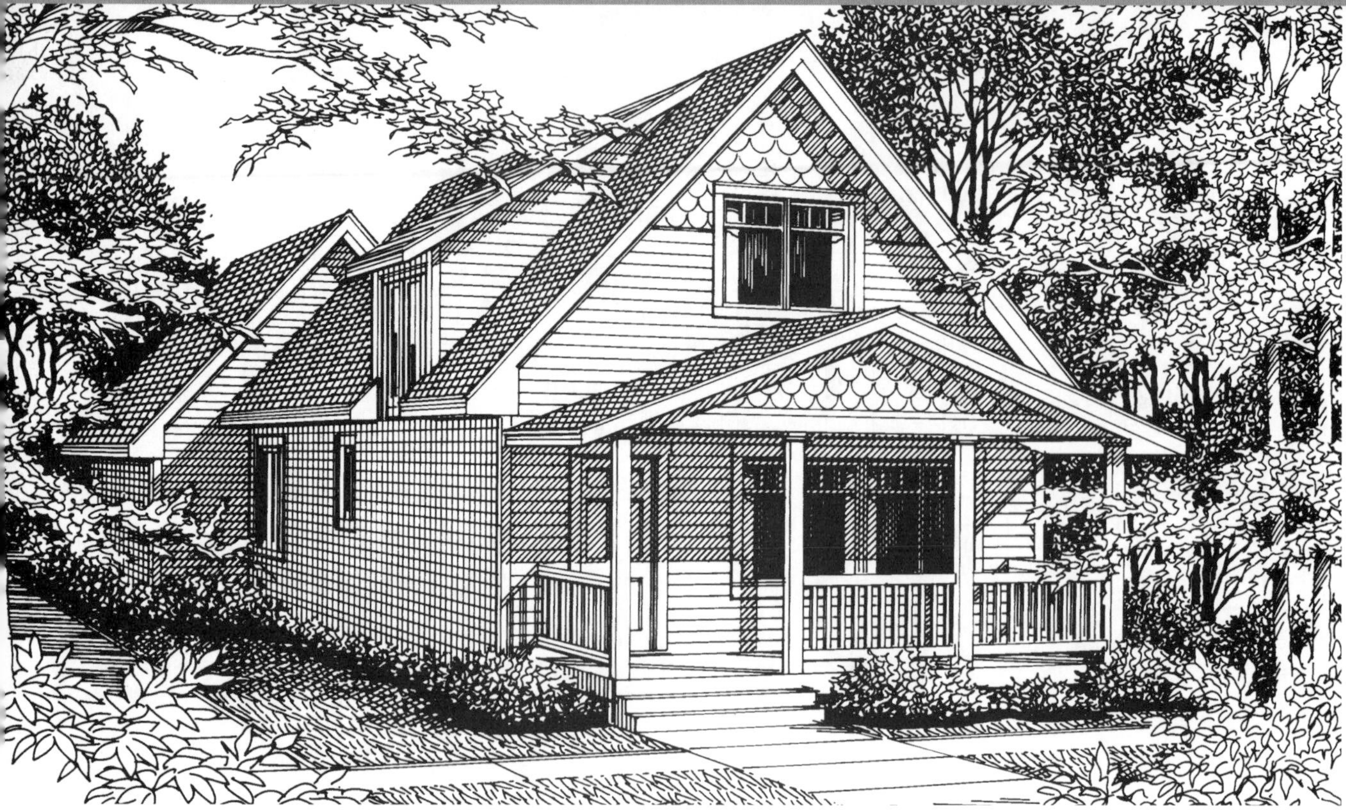

Plan #582-015D-0020

Price Code A

Special Features • 1,251 total square feet of living area • Open living areas make this home feel larger • Utility closet is located on the second floor for convenience • The kitchen includes an abundance of counterspace • 3 bedrooms, 2 baths, 2-car rear entry garage • Crawl space foundation

Width: 27'-0"
Depth: 62'-0"

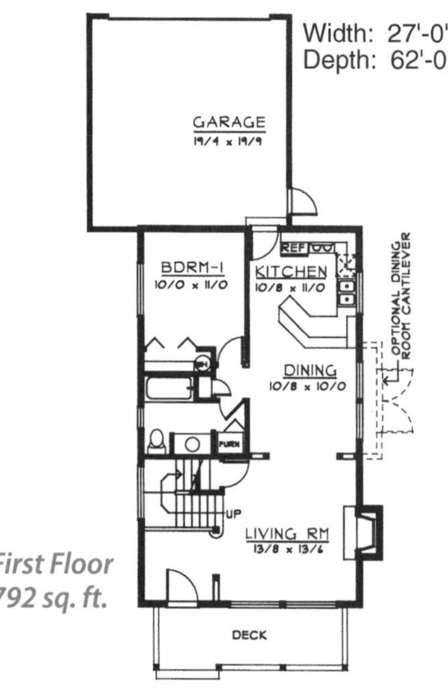

First Floor
792 sq. ft.

Second Floor
459 sq. ft.

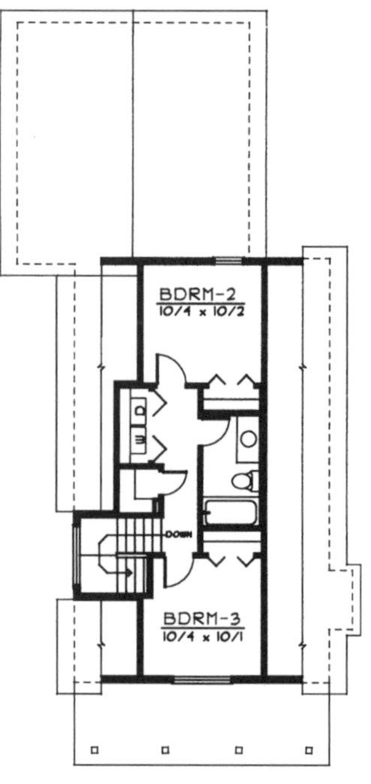

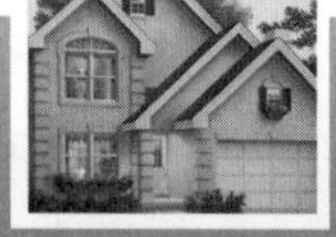

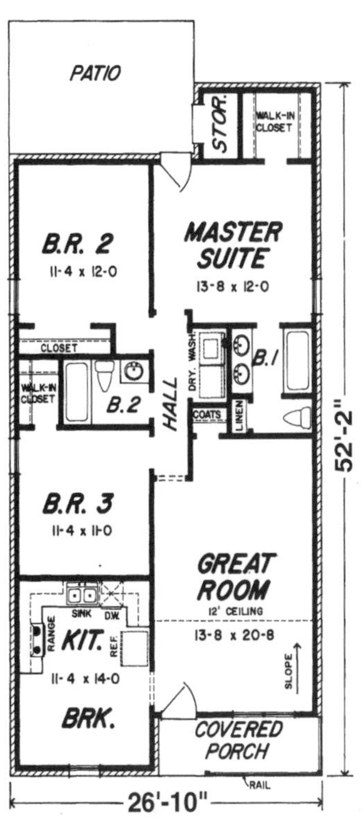

Plan #582-060D-0017

Price Code A

Special Features • 1,253 total square feet of living area • Compact kitchen with convenient breakfast room nearby • 12' ceiling in great room adds a spacious feel • Two secondary bedrooms share a hall bath • Laundry closet is located near all the bedrooms • 3 bedrooms, 2 baths • Slab foundation

Two-Story Home Perfect Fit For Small Lot

Plan #582-045D-0018

Price Code AAA

Special Features • 858 total square feet of living area • Stackable washer/dryer is located in the kitchen • Large covered porch graces this exterior • Both bedrooms have walk-in closets • 2 bedrooms, 1 bath • Crawl space foundation

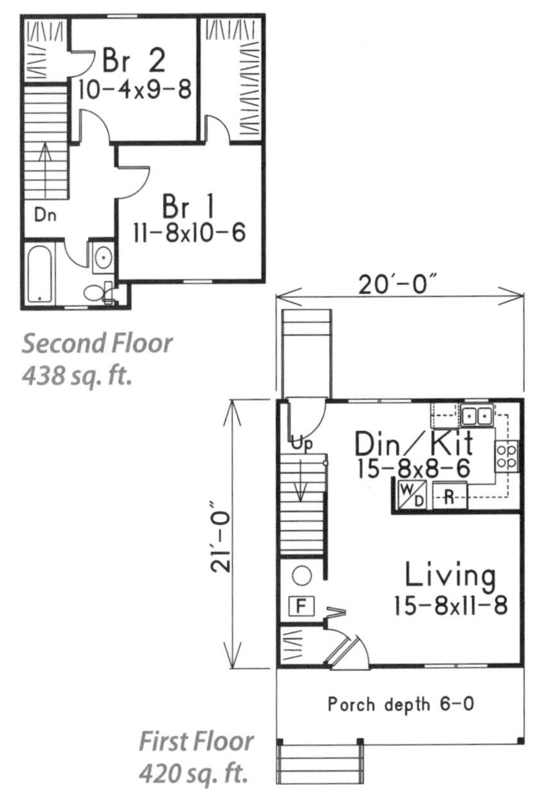

Second Floor
438 sq. ft.

First Floor
420 sq. ft.

Plan #582-058D-0006

Price Code A

Special Features • 1,339 total square feet of living area • Full-length covered porch enhances front facade • Vaulted ceiling and stone fireplace add drama to the family room • Walk-in closets in bedrooms provide ample storage space • Combined kitchen/dining area adjoins the family room for the perfect entertaining space • 3 bedrooms, 2 1/2 baths • Crawl space foundation

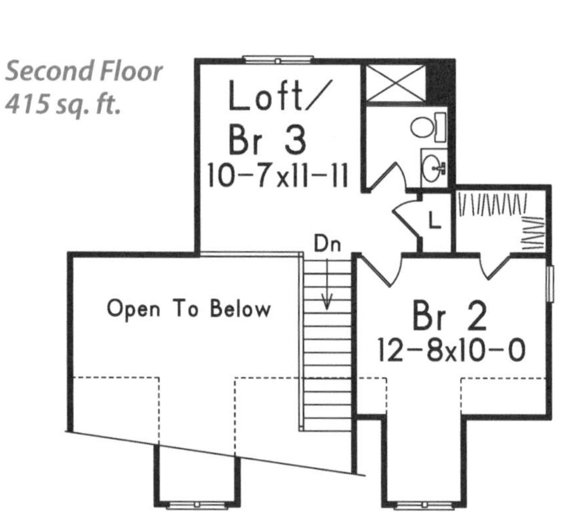

Second Floor
415 sq. ft.

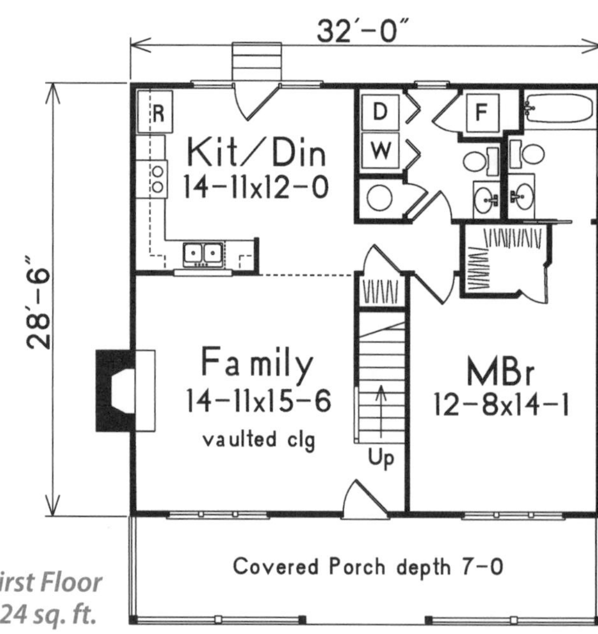

First Floor
924 sq. ft.

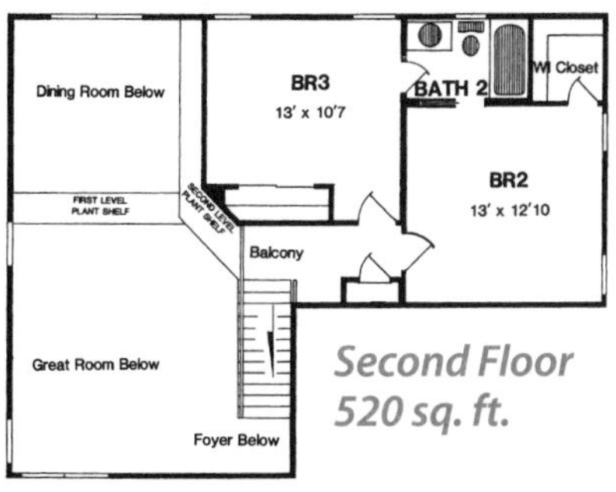

Second Floor
520 sq. ft.

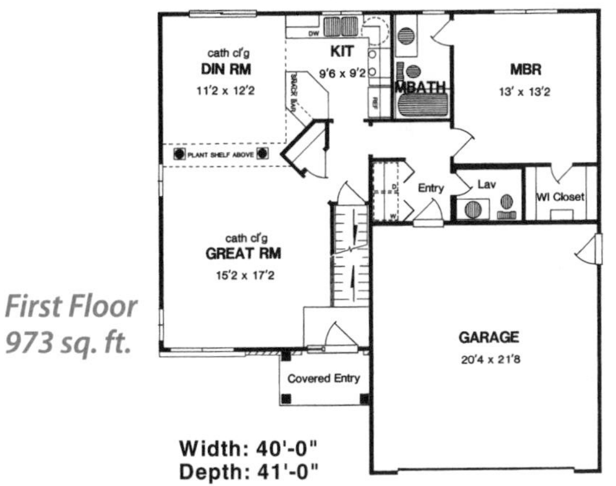

First Floor
973 sq. ft.

Plan #582-034D-0013

Price Code A

Special Features • 1,493 total square feet of living area • First floor master bedroom maintains privacy • Dining and great rooms have a feeling of spaciousness with two-story high ceilings • Utilities are conveniently located near garage entrance • 3 bedrooms, 2 1/2 baths, 2-car garage • Basement foundation

Charming Home For Narrow Lot

Plan #582-076D-0003

Price Code B

Special Features • 1,344 total square feet of living area • Kitchen, bayed breakfast area and spacious family room combine for an easy flow of family activities • The private secondary bedrooms are generously sized and share a bath • The master suite features a walk-in closet, whirlpool tub and a double-bowl vanity • 3 bedrooms, 2 baths, 2-car garage • Slab foundation

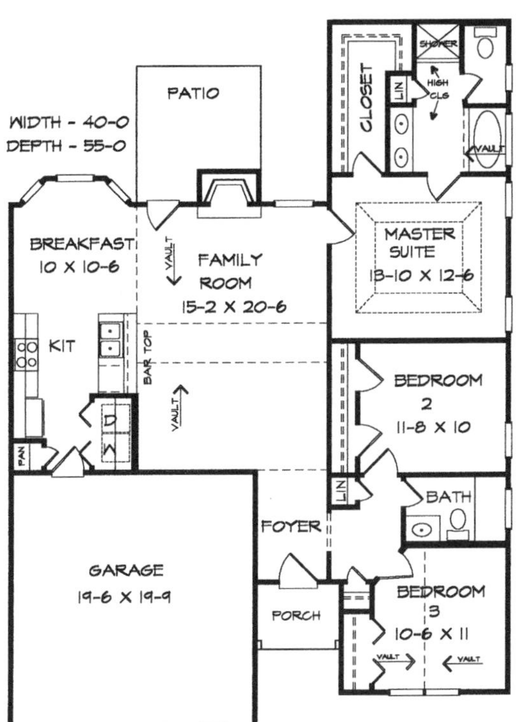

Plan #582-058D-0012 Price Code AA

Special Features • *1,143 total square feet of living area* • *Enormous stone fireplace in family room adds warmth and character* • *Spacious kitchen with breakfast bar overlooks family room* • *Separate dining area is great for entertaining* • *Vaulted family room and kitchen create an open atmosphere* • *2 bedrooms, 1 bath* • *Crawl space foundation*

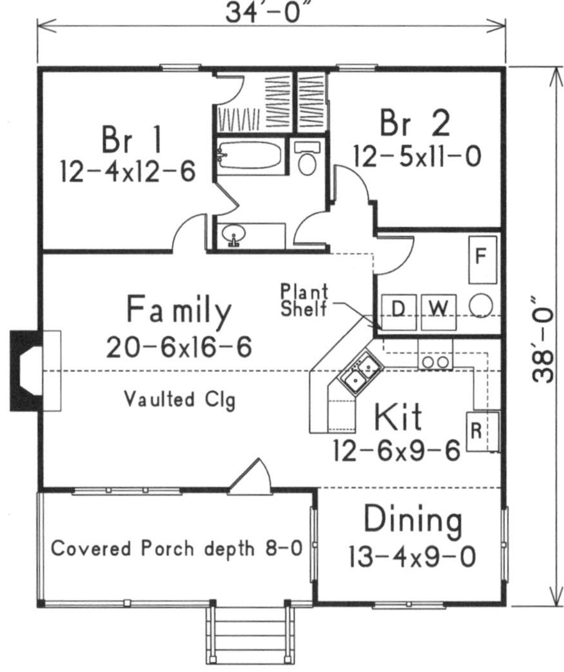

Cozy Cottage Attracts Attention

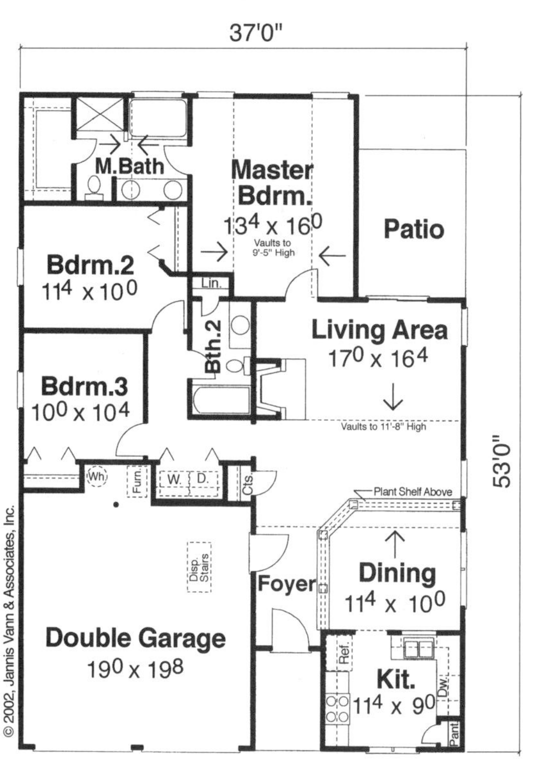

Plan #582-052D-0012

Price Code A

Special Features • 1,365 total square feet of living area • Plant shelf above the dining area creates interest to the interior • Direct access from the master bedroom into the living area • Vaulted living area focuses on a centered fireplace • 3 bedrooms, 2 baths, 2-car garage • Basement or slab foundation, please specify when ordering

Decorative Accents Highlight Facade

Plan #582-047D-0022

Price Code B

Special Features • 1,768 total square feet of living area • Uniquely designed vaulted living and dining rooms combine making great use of space • Informal family room has a vaulted ceiling, plant shelf accents and kitchen overlook • Sunny breakfast area conveniently accesses kitchen • 3 bedrooms, 2 baths, 2-car garage • Slab foundation

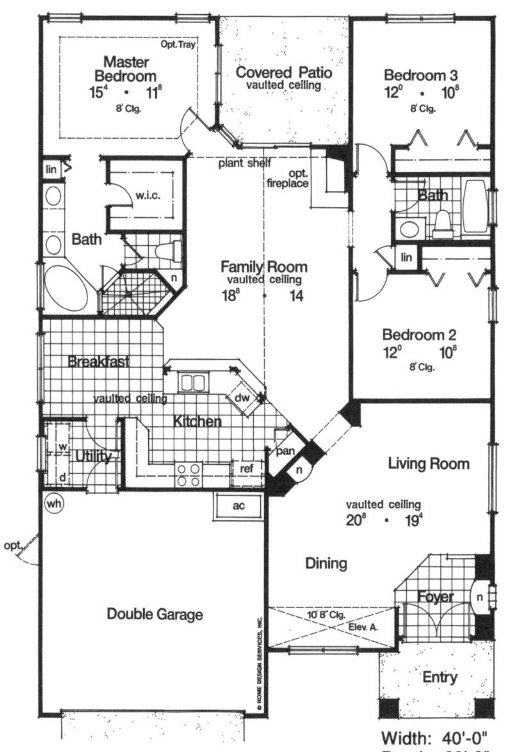

Plan #582-058D-0031

Price Code AA

Special Features • 990 total square feet of living area • Covered front porch adds charming feel • Vaulted ceilings in kitchen, family and dining rooms create a spacious feel • Large linen, pantry and storage closets throughout • 2 bedrooms, 1 bath • Crawl space foundation

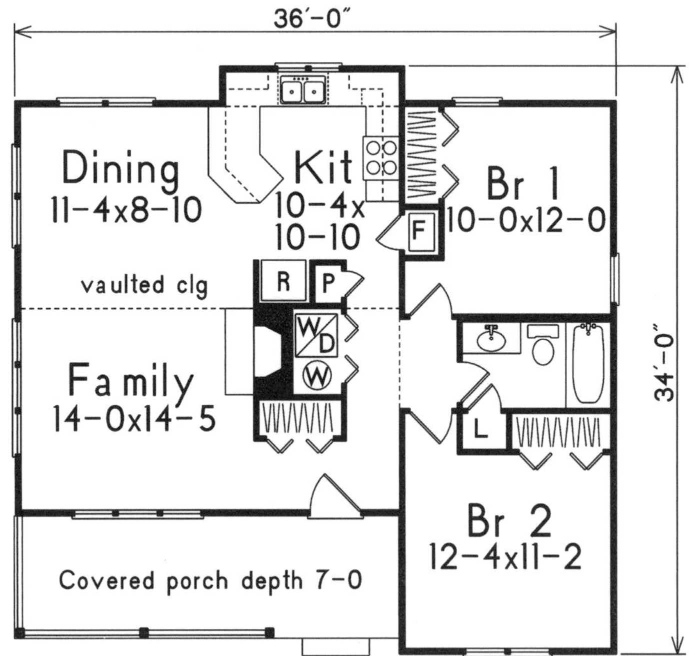

A Chalet For Lakeside Living

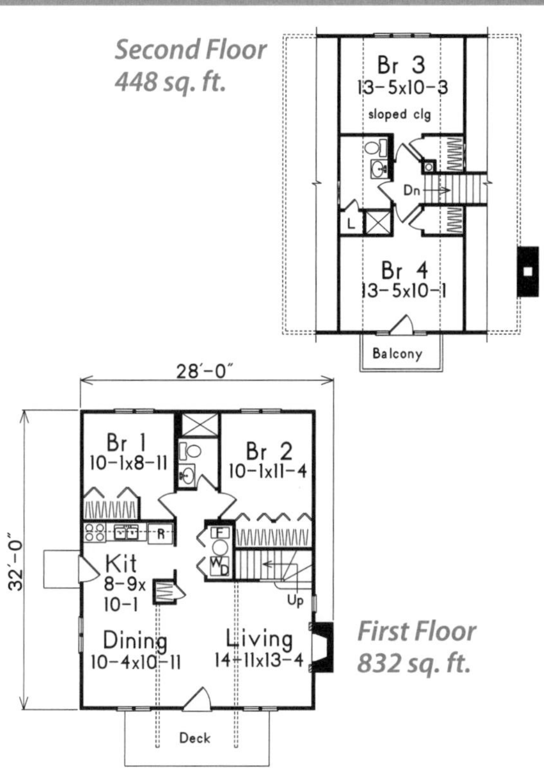

Plan #582-008D-0138

Price Code A

Special Features • 1,280 total square feet of living area • Attention to architectural detail has created the look of an authentic Swiss cottage • Spacious living room, adjacent kitchenette and dining area all enjoy views to the front deck • Hall bath shared by two sizable bedrooms is included on the first and second floors • 4 bedrooms, 2 baths • Crawl space foundation, drawings also include basement and slab foundations

Compact Home, Perfect Fit For Narrow Lot

Plan #582-045D-0013

Price Code AA

Special Features • 1,085 total square feet of living area • Rear porch provides a handy access through the kitchen • Convenient hall linen closet is located on the second floor • Breakfast bar in the kitchen offers additional counterspace • Living and dining rooms combine for open living • 3 bedrooms, 2 baths • Basement foundation

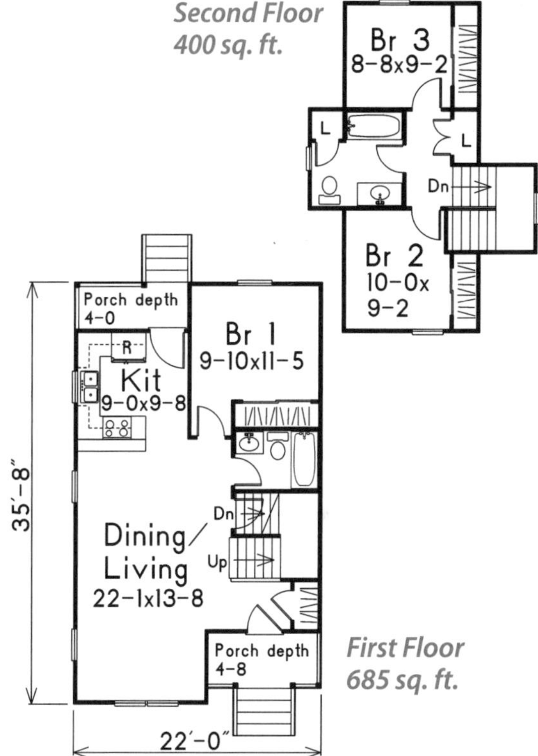

Plan #582-008D-0163

Price Code A

Special Features • *1,280 total square feet of living area • A front porch deck, ornate porch roof, massive stone fireplace and Old-English windows all generate inviting appeal • Large living room accesses kitchen with spacious dining area • Two spacious bedrooms with ample closet space comprise second floor • 4 bedrooms, 2 baths • Basement foundation, drawings also include slab and crawl space foundations*

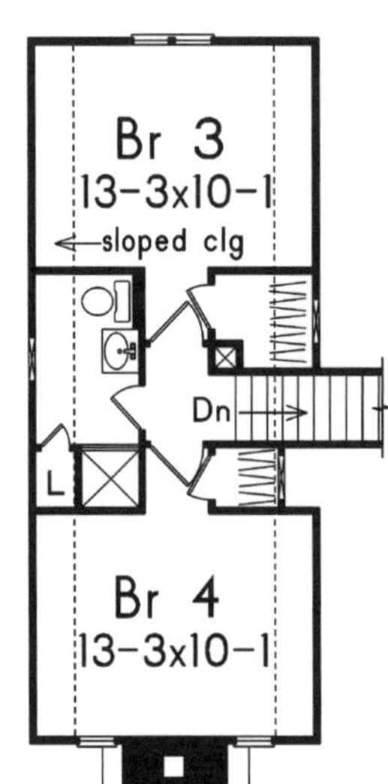

Second Floor
448 sq. ft.

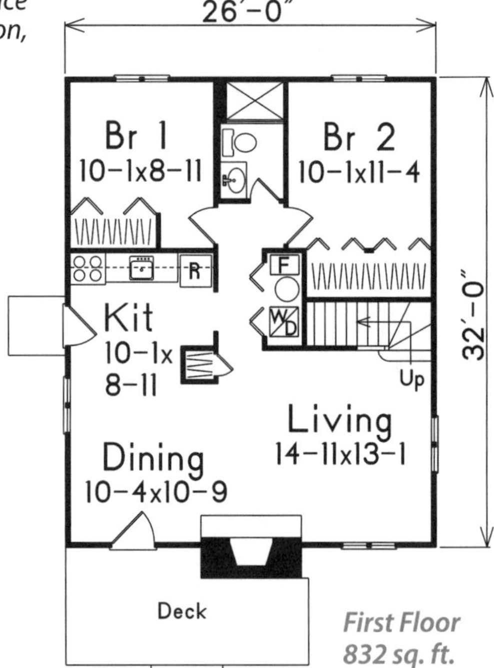

First Floor
832 sq. ft.

Compact Home With Functional Design

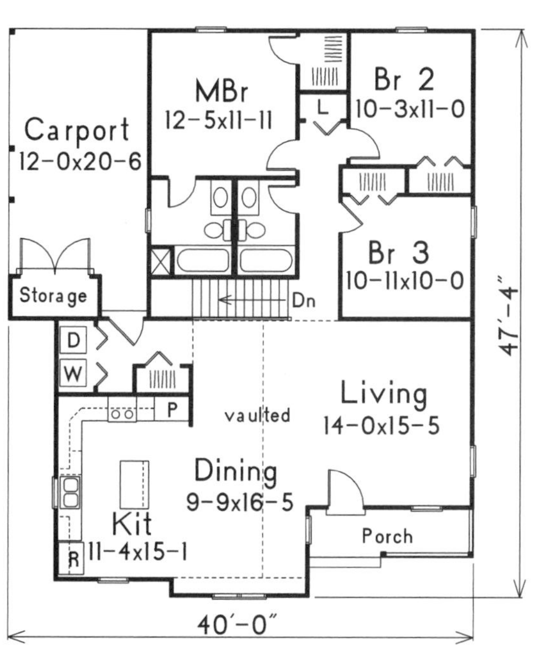

Plan #582-001D-0035 **Price Code A**

Special Features • 1,396 total square feet of living area • Gabled front adds interest to facade • Living and dining rooms share a vaulted ceiling • Master bedroom features a walk-in closet and private bath • Functional kitchen boasts a center work island and convenient pantry • 3 bedrooms, 2 baths, 1-car carport • Basement foundation, drawings also include crawl space foundation

Vaulted Living Area With Corner Fireplace

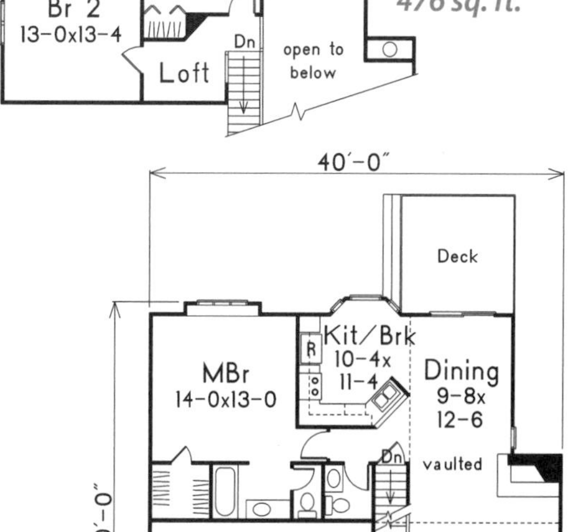

Plan #582-022D-0017 **Price Code A**

Special Features • 1,448 total square feet of living area • Dining room conveniently adjoins kitchen and accesses rear deck • Private first floor master bedroom • Secondary bedrooms share a bath and cozy loft area • 3 bedrooms, 2 1/2 baths, 2-car garage • Basement foundation

Plan #582-008D-0136

Price Code AA

Special Features • 1,106 total square feet of living area • Delightful A-frame provides exciting vacation-style living all year long • Deck accesses a large living room with an open soaring ceiling • Enormous sleeping area is provided on the second floor with balcony overlook to living room below • 2 bedrooms, 1 bath • Pier foundation

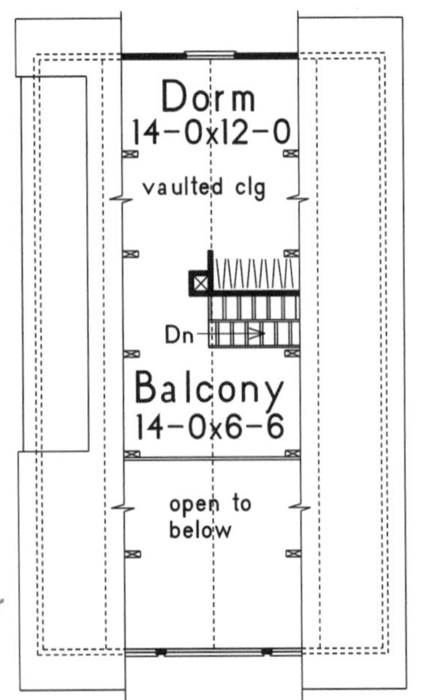

Second Floor
314 sq. ft.

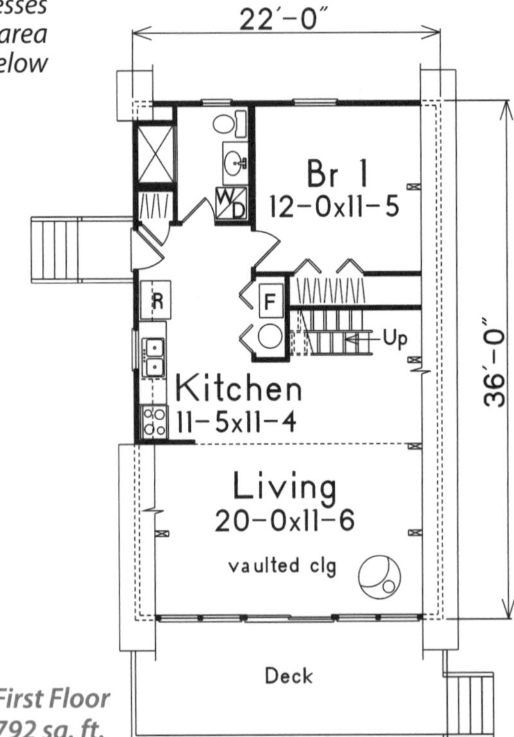

First Floor
792 sq. ft.

Open Living Space Creates Comfortable Atmosphere

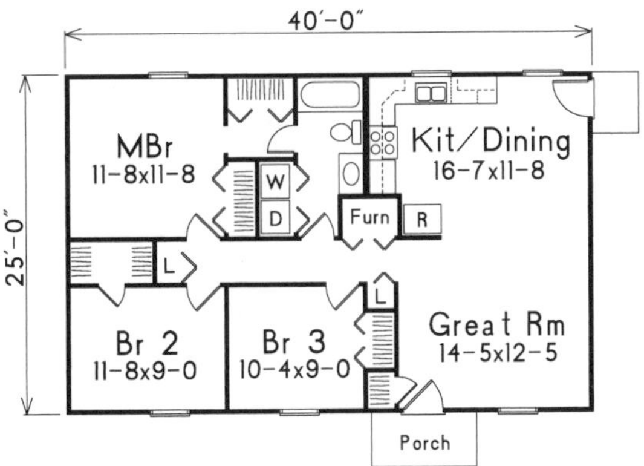

Plan #582-001D-0041 **Price Code AA**

Special Features • *1,000 total square feet of living area* • *Bath includes convenient closeted laundry area* • *Master bedroom includes double closets and private access to bath* • *Foyer features handy coat closet* • *L-shaped kitchen provides easy access outdoors* • *3 bedrooms, 1 bath* • *Crawl space foundation, drawings also include basement and slab foundations*

Innovative Design For That Narrow Lot

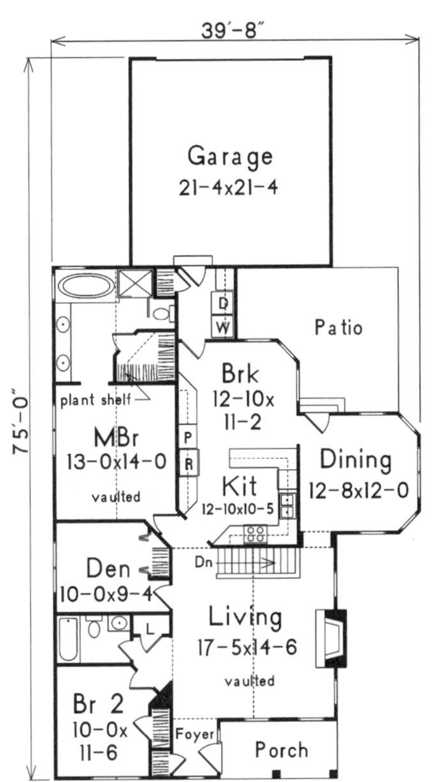

Plan #582-045D-0010 **Price Code B**

Special Features • *1,558 total square feet of living area* • *Illuminated spaces are created by visual access to the outdoor living areas* • *Vaulted master bedroom features a bath with whirlpool tub, separate shower and large walk-in closet* • *Convenient laundry area has garage access* • *Practical den or third bedroom* • *U-shaped kitchen is adjacent to sunny breakfast area* • *2 bedrooms, 2 baths, 2-car rear entry garage* • *Basement foundation*

Plan #582-007D-0073

Price Code AA

Special Features • 902 total square feet of living area • Vaulted entry with laundry room leads to a spacious second floor apartment • The large living room features an entry coat closet, L-shaped kitchen with pantry and dining area/balcony overlooking atrium window wall • Roomy bedroom with walk-in closet is convenient to hall bath • 1 bedroom, 1 bath, 2-car side entry garage • Slab foundation

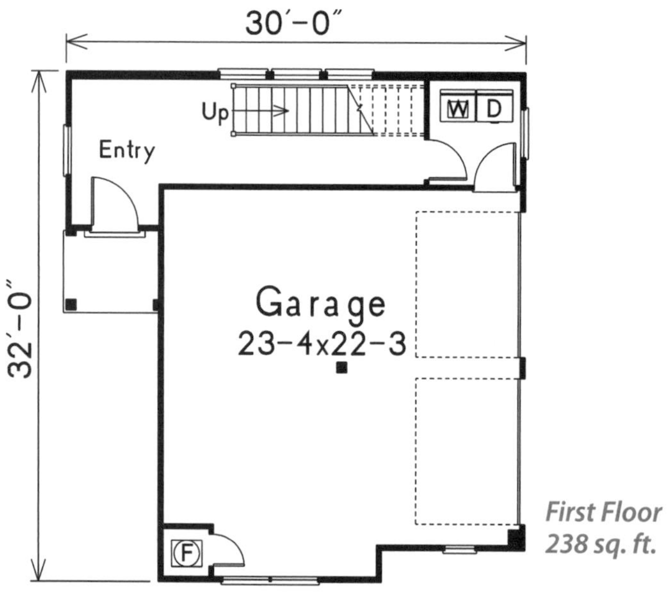

First Floor
238 sq. ft.

Second Floor
664 sq. ft.

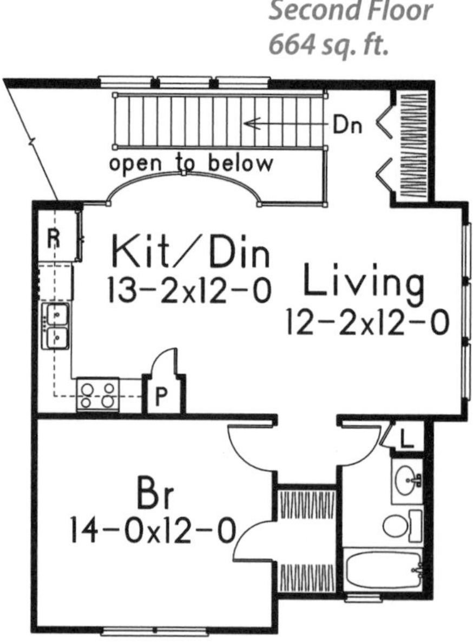

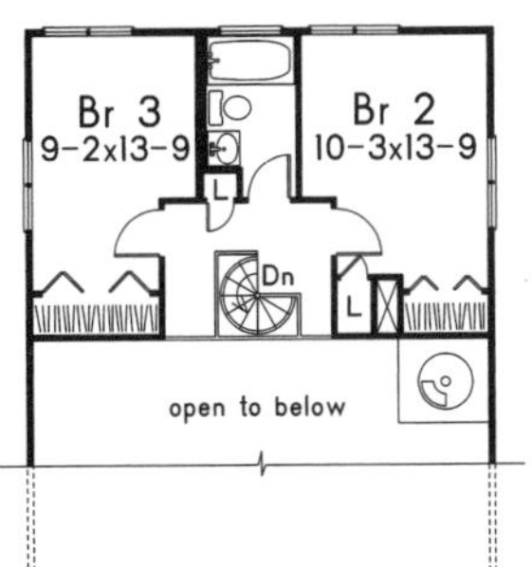

Second Floor
429 sq. ft.

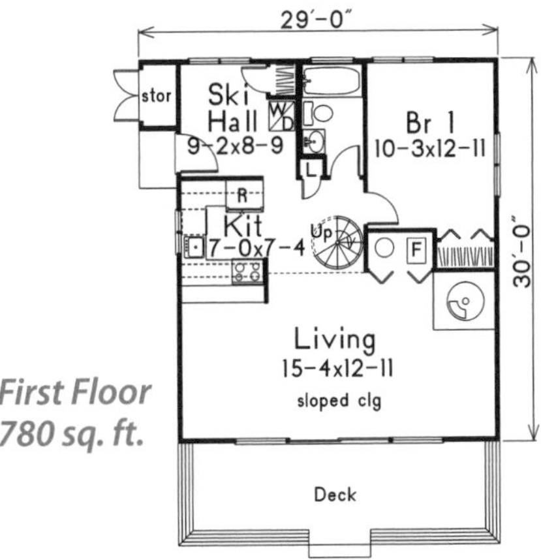

First Floor
780 sq. ft.

Plan #582-008D-0132

Price Code A

Special Features • 1,209 total square feet of living area • Bracketed shed roof and ski storage add charm to vacation home • Living and dining rooms enjoy a sloped ceiling, second floor balcony overlook and view to a large deck • Kitchen features snack bar and access to second floor via circular stair • 3 bedrooms, 2 baths • Crawl space foundation

Warm And Inviting

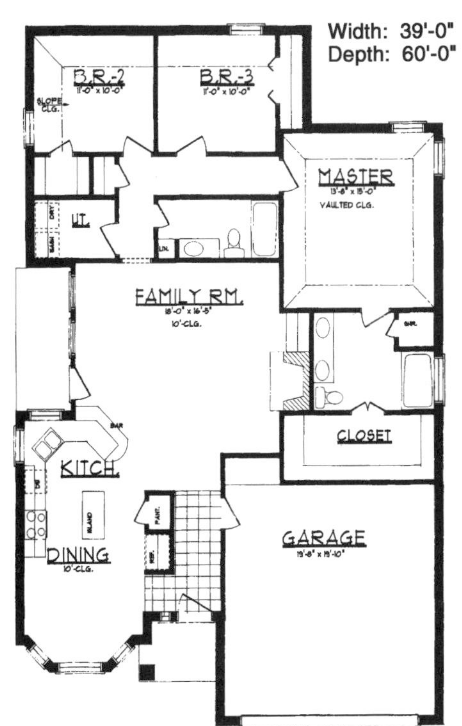

Plan #582-031D-0002

Price Code B

Special Features • 1,605 total square feet of living area • Large family room with fireplace and built-in bookshelves is perfect for gathering • The laundry room is located near the bedrooms for convenience • Bedrooms are secluded for privacy • 3 bedrooms, 2 baths, 2-car garage • Slab foundation

Plan #582-078D-0029

Price Code D

Special Features • *1,400 total square feet of living area* • *Large front porch with stone piers accent facade* • *The expansive living room is brightened by a multitude of windows and warmed by a grand fireplace* • *A breakfast bar connects the kitchen and dining area* • *The spacious utility room includes an alternate entrance to home* • *2 bedrooms, 2 baths* • *Basement or crawl space foundation, please specify when ordering*

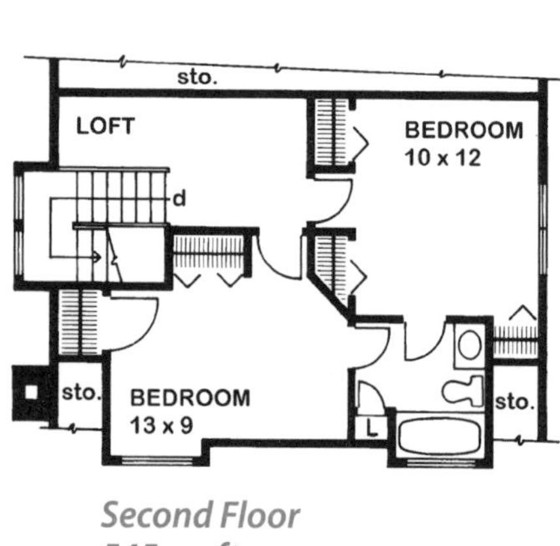

Second Floor
545 sq. ft.

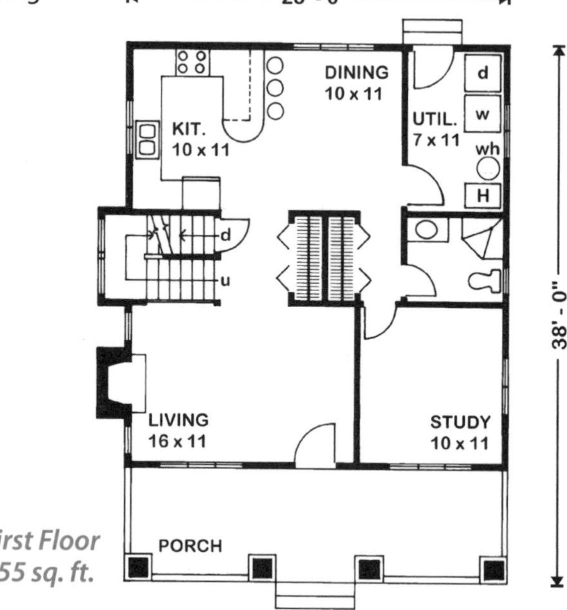

First Floor
855 sq. ft.

Charming Exterior And Cozy Interior

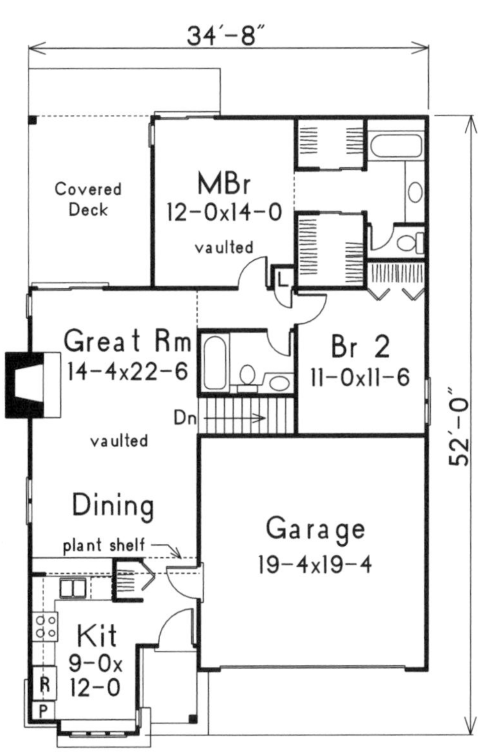

Plan #582-022D-0024 **Price Code AA**

Special Features • 1,127 total square feet of living area • Plant shelf joins kitchen and dining room • Vaulted master bedroom has double walk-in closets, deck access and private bath • Great room features vaulted ceiling, fireplace and sliding doors to covered deck • Ideal home for a narrow lot • 2 bedrooms, 2 baths, 2-car garage • Basement foundation

Special Planning In This Compact Home

Plan #582-045D-0015 **Price Code A**

Special Features • 977 total square feet of living area • Comfortable living room features a vaulted ceiling, fireplace, plant shelf and coat closet • Both bedrooms are located on the second floor and share a bath with double-bowl vanity and linen closet • Sliding glass doors in the dining room provide access to the deck • 2 bedrooms, 1 1/2 baths, 1-car garage • Basement foundation

Second Floor
432 sq. ft.

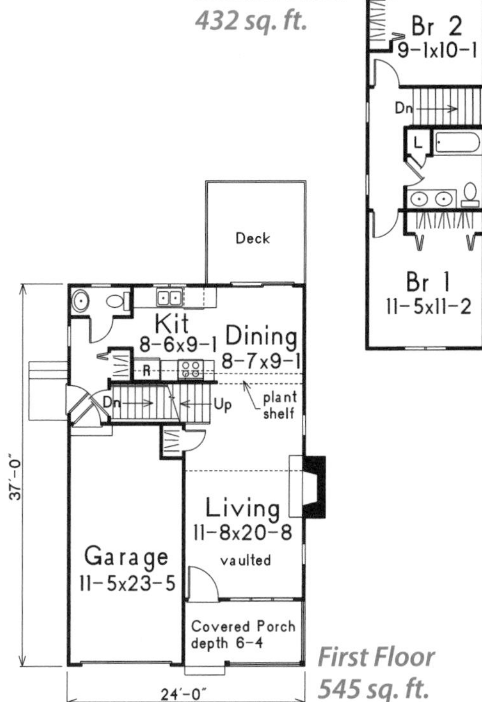

First Floor
545 sq. ft.

Plan #582-022D-0021

Price Code AA

Special Features • 1,020 total square feet of living area • Kitchen features open stairs, pass-through to great room, pantry and deck access • Master bedroom features private entrance to bath, large walk-in closet and sliding doors to deck • Informal entrance into home through the garage • Great room has a vaulted ceiling and fireplace • 2 bedrooms, 1 bath, 2-car garage • Basement foundation

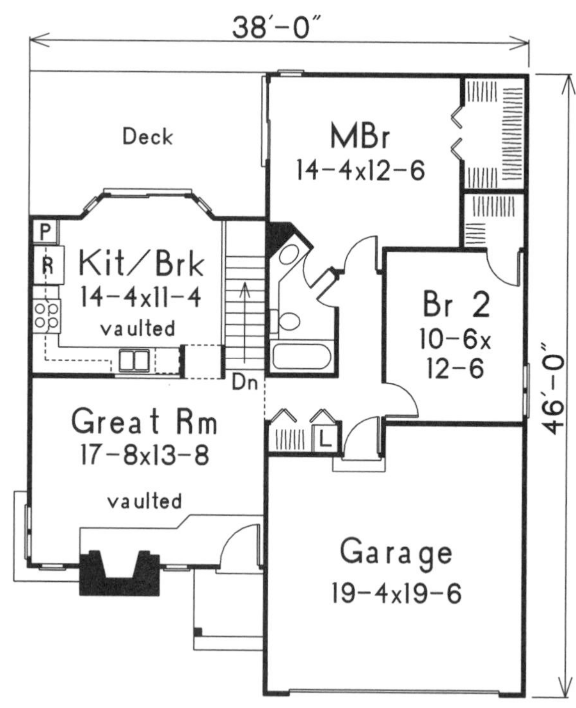

Covered Porch Adds To Perfect Outdoor Getaway

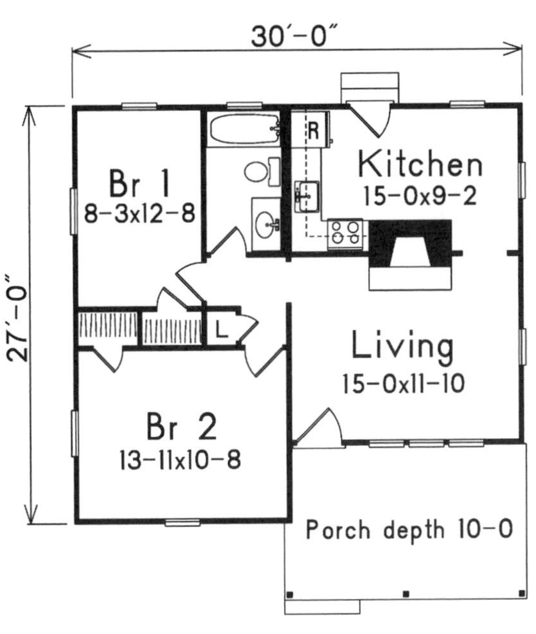

Plan #582-008D-0159 **Price Code AAA**

Special Features • 733 total square feet of living area • Bedrooms are separate from kitchen and living area for privacy • Lots of closet space throughout this home • Centrally located bath is easily accessible • Kitchen features a door accessing the outdoors and a door separating it from the rest of the home • 2 bedrooms, 1 bath • Pier foundation

Quaint Country Home Is Ideal

Plan #582-040D-0029 **Price Code AA**

Special Features • 1,028 total square feet of living area • Well-designed bath contains laundry facilities • L-shaped kitchen has a handy pantry • Tall windows flank family room fireplace • Cozy covered porch provides unique angled entry into home • 3 bedrooms, 1 bath • Crawl space foundation

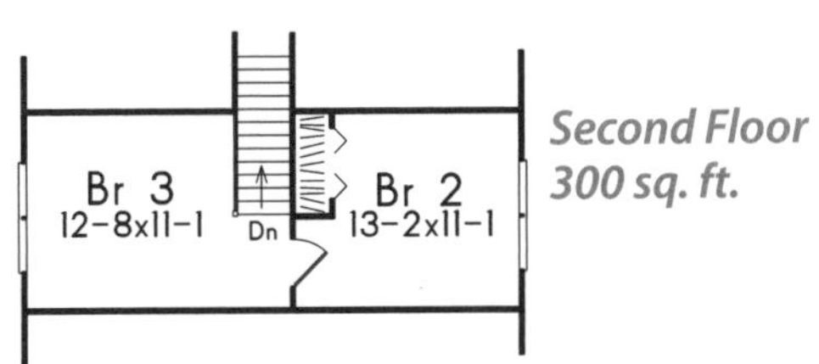

Second Floor
300 sq. ft.

First Floor
728 sq. ft.

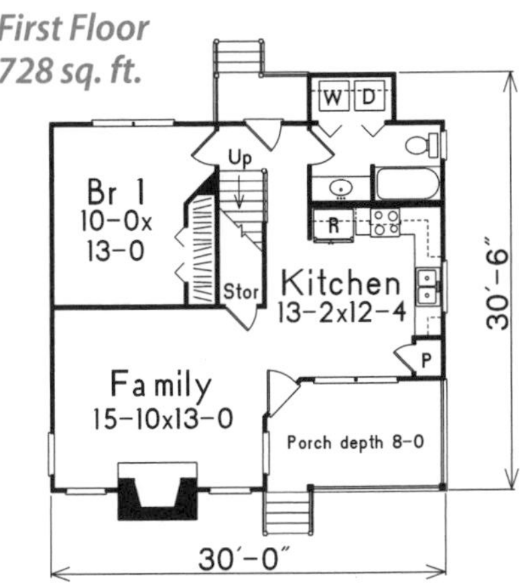

Double Dormers Accent This Cozy Vacation Retreat

Plan #582-037D-0019

Price Code AAA

Special Features • *581 total square feet of living area* • *Kitchen/living room features area for dining and spiral steps leading to the loft area* • *Large loft space can easily be converted to a bedroom or home office* • *Entry space has a unique built-in display niche* • *1 bedroom, 1 bath* • *Slab foundation*

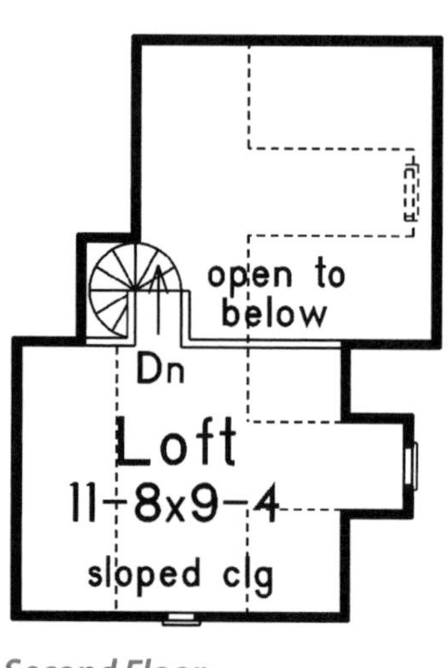

Second Floor
132 sq. ft.

First Floor
449 sq. ft.

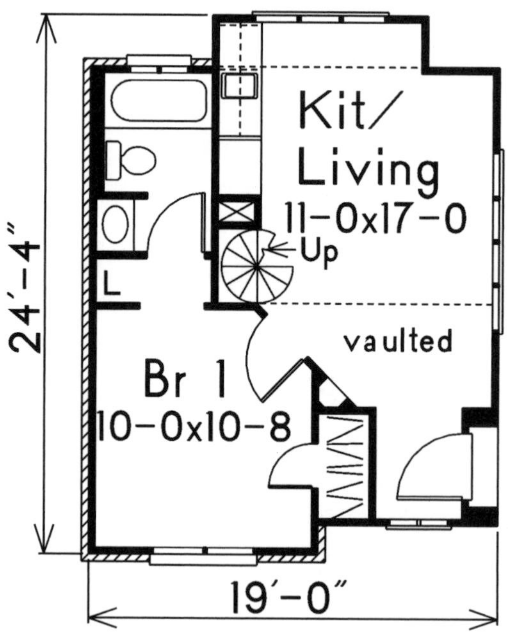

Cottage With Atrium

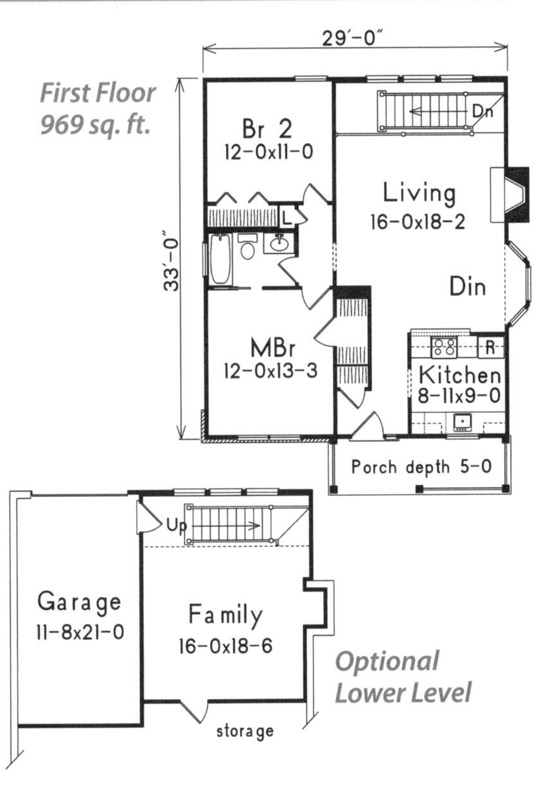

Plan #582-007D-0104 **Price Code AA**

Special Features • 969 total square feet of living area • Eye-pleasing facade enjoys stone accents with country porch for quiet evenings • A cozy fireplace and atrium with sunny two-story windows grace the living room • Step-saver kitchen includes a pass-through snack bar • 325 square feet of optional living area on the lower level • 2 bedrooms, 1 bath, 1-car rear entry garage • Walk-out basement foundation

Excellent For Weekend Entertaining

36'-0"
W/D
Kit/ Dining 13-4x13-8
R
F
P
Br 1 11-1x10-9
L
36'-0"
vaulted clg
Family 13-4x13-8
Porch vaulted clg
L
Br 2 10-10x 10-10
Screened Porch 16-0x8-0

Plan #582-058D-0011 **Price Code AA**

Special Features • 924 total square feet of living area • Box-bay window seats brighten interior while enhancing front facade • Spacious kitchen with lots of cabinet space and large pantry • T-shaped covered porch is screened for added enjoyment • Plenty of closet space throughout with linen closets in both bedrooms • 2 bedrooms, 1 bath • Slab foundation

Seaside Style With Open Interior

Plan #582-047D-0015

Price Code B

Special Features • 1,679 total square feet of living area • Enormous deck surrounds the home with space for outdoor living • Spiral staircase leads to the master bedroom which includes a private balcony, bath with step-up tub and lots of closet space • Neatly designed kitchen has access to screened deck for entertaining • 3 bedrooms, 2 baths, 3-car drive under garage • Pier foundation

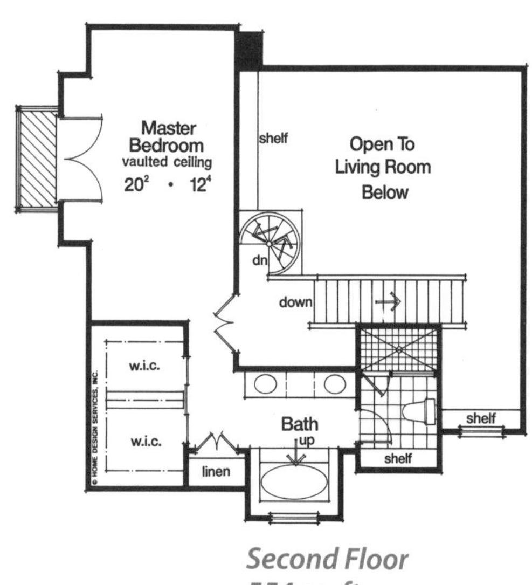

Second Floor
554 sq. ft.

First Floor
1,125 sq. ft.

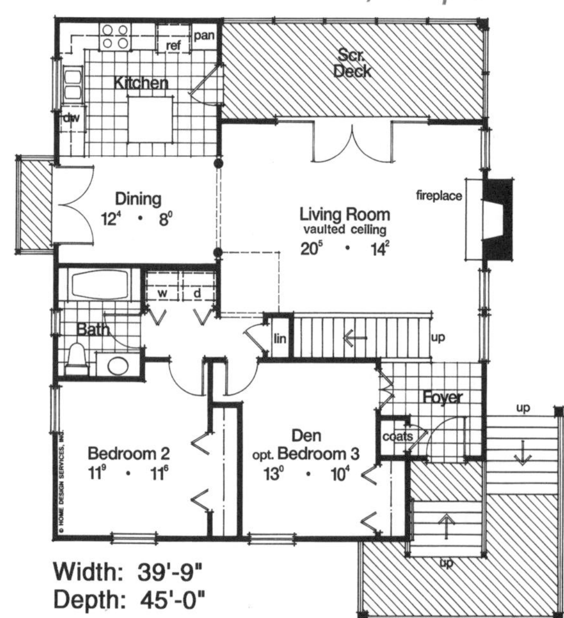

Width: 39'-9"
Depth: 45'-0"

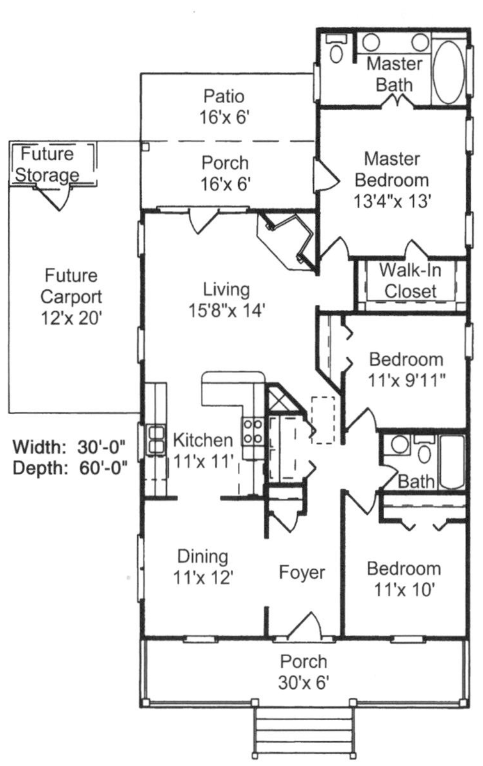

Plan #582-024D-0001

Price Code A

Special Features • 1,363 total square feet of living area • Formal dining area is conveniently located next to kitchen • Master bedroom has private bath and walk-in closet • Covered porch has patio which allows enough space for entertaining • 3 bedrooms, 2 baths, optional 1-car carport • Slab foundation

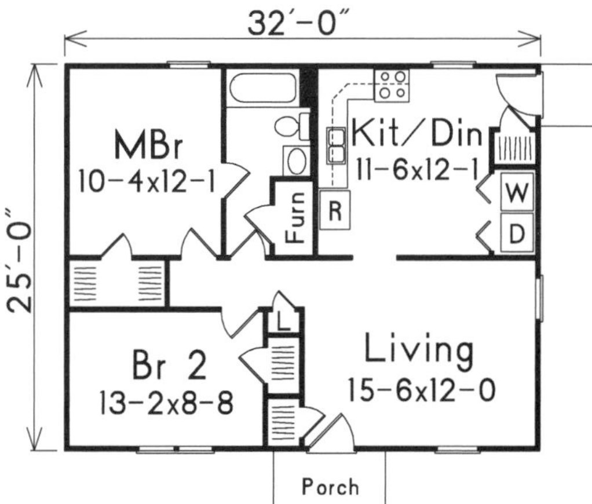

Plan #582-001D-0088

Price Code AAA

Special Features • 800 total square feet of living area • Master bedroom has walk-in closet and private access to bath • Large living room features handy coat closet • Kitchen includes side entrance, closet and convenient laundry area • 2 bedrooms, 1 bath • Crawl space foundation, drawings also include basement foundation

Plan #582-058D-0007

Price Code AA

Special Features • 1,013 total square feet of living area • Vaulted ceilings in both the family room and kitchen with dining area just beyond breakfast bar • Plant shelf above kitchen is a special feature • Oversized utility room has space for full-size washer and dryer • Hall bath is centrally located with easy access from both bedrooms • 2 bedrooms, 1 bath • Slab foundation

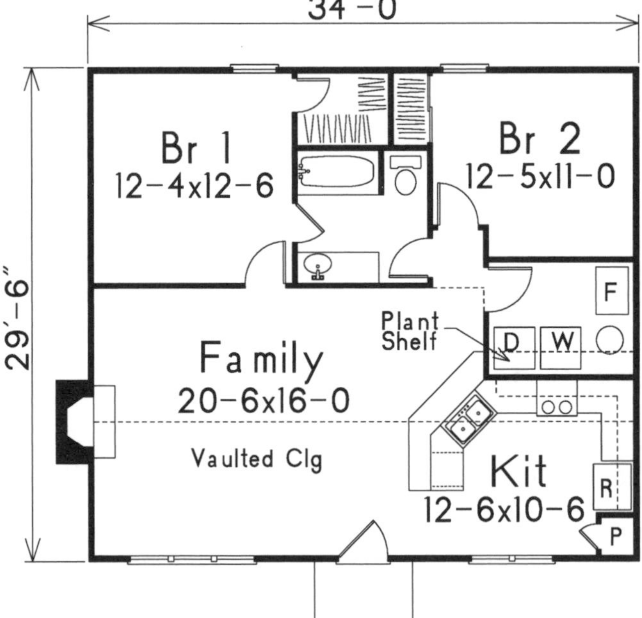

Dormer And Covered Porch Add To Country Charm

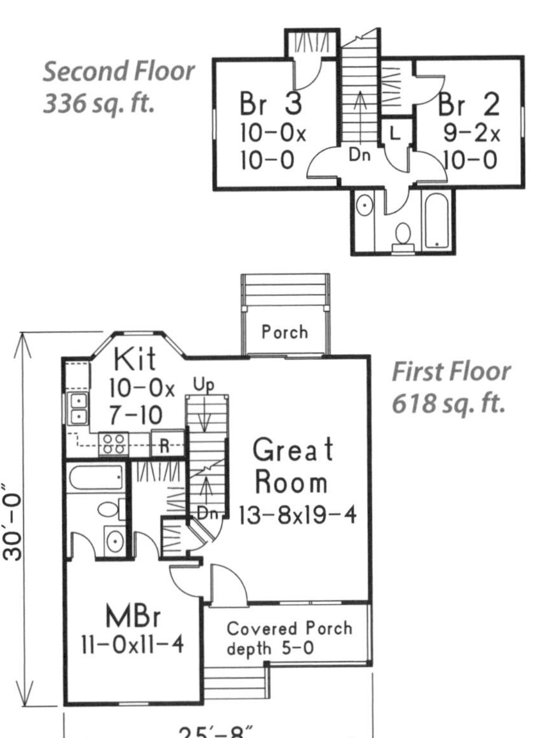

Plan #582-045D-0017 — Price Code AA

Special Features • 954 total square feet of living area • Kitchen has cozy bayed eating area • Master bedroom has a walk-in closet and private bath • Large great room has access to the back porch • Convenient coat closet near front entry • 3 bedrooms, 2 baths • Basement foundation

Inviting Victorian Details

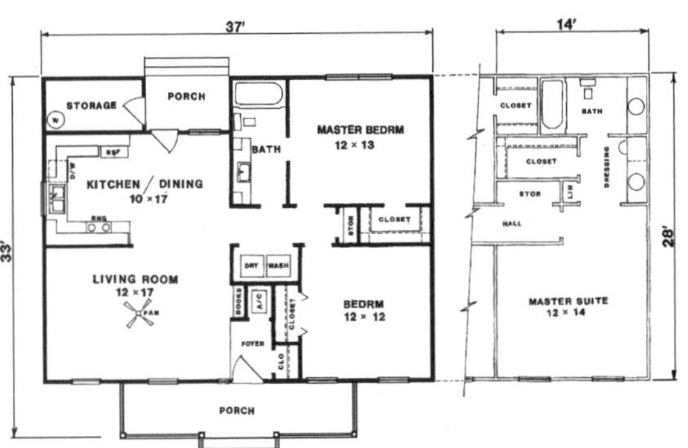

Plan #582-069D-0001 — Price Code AA

Special Features • 947 total square feet of living area • Efficiently designed kitchen/dining area accesses the outdoors onto a rear porch • Future expansion plans included which allow the home to become 392 square feet larger with 3 bedrooms and 2 baths • 2 bedrooms, 1 bath • Crawl space or slab foundation, please specify when ordering

Cozy Traditional Ranch Home

Plan #582-076D-0016

Price Code B

Special Features • *1,126 total square feet of living area* • *Fireplace warms the adjoining kitchen, dining and family rooms* • *Relaxing master bedroom enjoys a walk-in closet and vaulted bath* • *Laundry area is located in the garage* • *3 bedrooms, 2 baths, 2-car garage* • *Slab foundation*

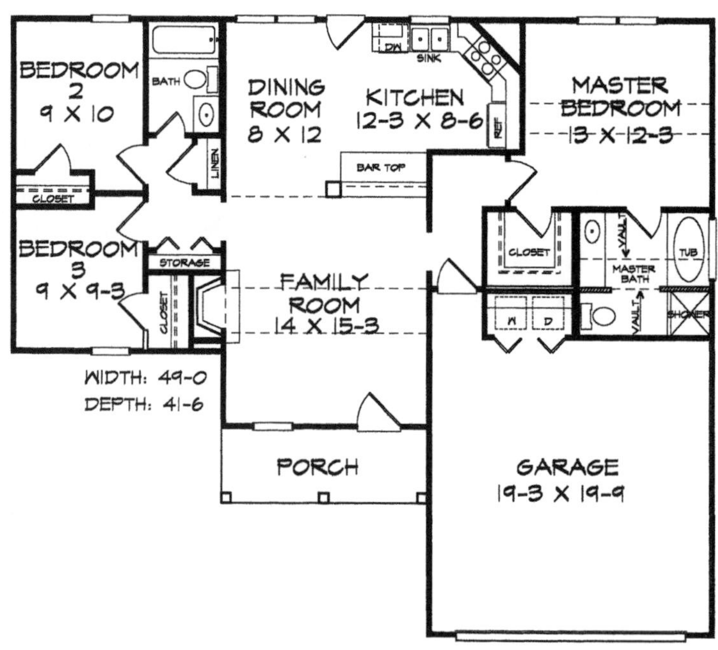

Innovative Ranch Has Cozy Corner Patio

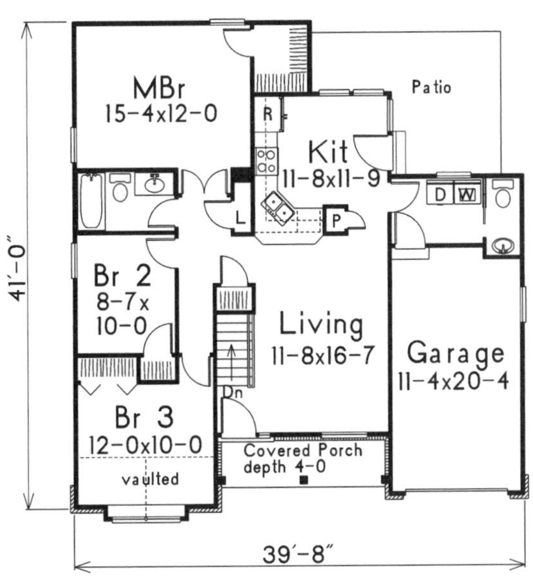

Plan #582-007D-0031

Price Code AA

Special Features • 1,092 total square feet of living area • Box window and inviting porch with dormers create a charming facade • Eat-in kitchen offers a pass-through breakfast bar, corner window wall to patio, pantry and convenient laundry with half bath • Master bedroom features a double-door entry and walk-in closet • 3 bedrooms, 1 1/2 baths, 1-car garage • Basement foundation

Ideal Home For A Narrow Lot

Plan #582-060D-0013

Price Code AA

Special Features • 1,053 total square feet of living area • Handy utility closet off breakfast room • Sloped ceiling in great room adds a dramatic touch • Organized kitchen has everything close by for easy preparation • 3 bedrooms, 2 baths • Slab or crawl space foundation, please specify when ordering

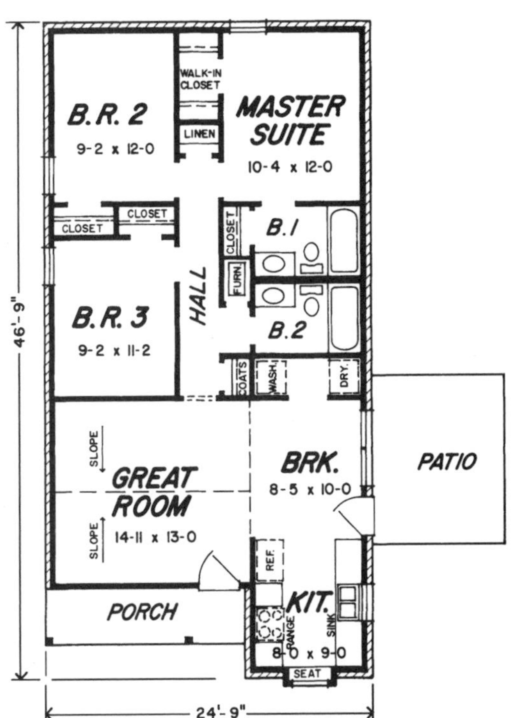

Great Home With Side Entry

Plan #582-036D-0056

Price Code B

Special Features • 1,604 total square feet of living area • Ideal design for a narrow lot • Living and dining areas combine for a spacious feel • Secluded study has a double-door entrance for privacy • Master bedroom has a spacious private bath • 3 bedrooms, 2 baths, 2-car garage • Slab foundation

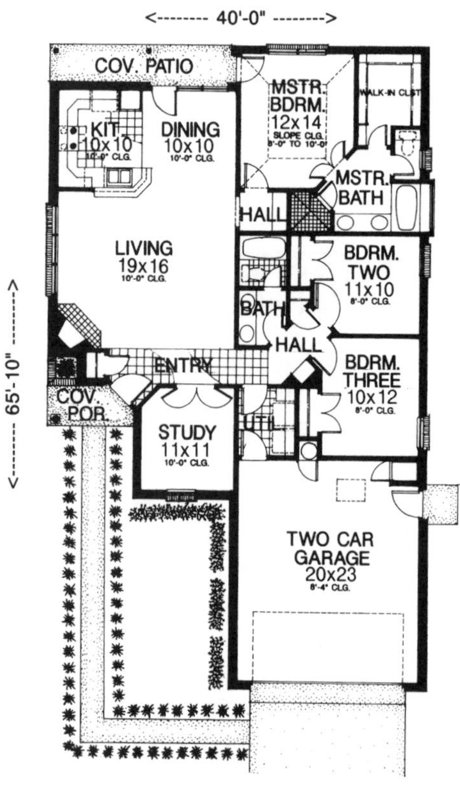

Leisure Living With Interior Surprise

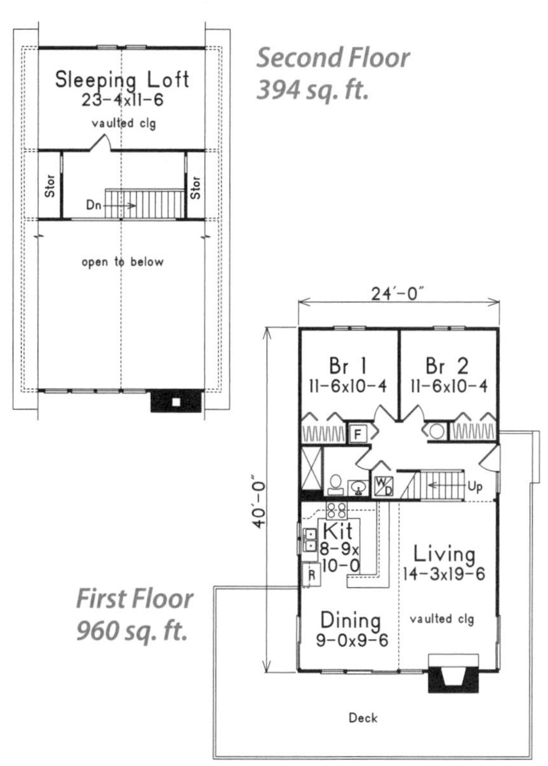

Second Floor
394 sq. ft.

First Floor
960 sq. ft.

Plan #582-008D-0160 **Price Code A**

Special Features • 1,354 total square feet of living area • Soaring ceilings highlight the kitchen, living and dining areas creating dramatic excitement • A spectacular large deck surrounds the front and both sides of the home • An impressive U-shaped kitchen has a wrap-around breakfast bar and shares fantastic views with both the first and second floors through an awesome wall of glass • 2 bedrooms, 1 bath • Crawl space foundation

Contemporary Design For Open Family Living

Plan #582-022D-0007 **Price Code B**

Special Features • 1,516 total square feet of living area • All living and dining areas are interconnected for a spacious look and easy movement • Covered entrance leads into sunken great room with a rugged corner fireplace • Family kitchen combines practicality with access to other areas • Second floor loft opens to rooms below and can convert to a third bedroom • Dormer in bedroom #2 adds interest • 2 bedrooms, 2 1/2 baths, 2-car garage • Basement foundation

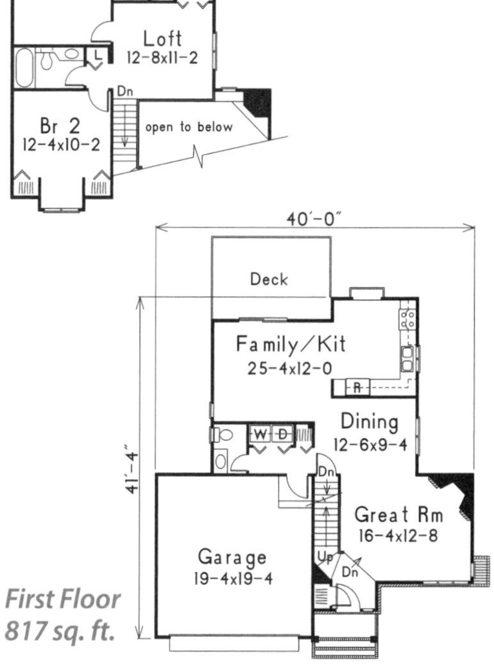

Second Floor
699 sq. ft.

First Floor
817 sq. ft.

Interesting Plan With Decorative Dormer

Plan #582-007D-0044 Price Code B

Special Features • 1,516 total square feet of living area • Spacious great room is open to dining area with a bay and unique stair location • Attractive and well-planned kitchen offers breakfast bar and built-in pantry • Smartly designed master bedroom enjoys patio views • 3 bedrooms, 2 baths, 2-car garage • Basement foundation

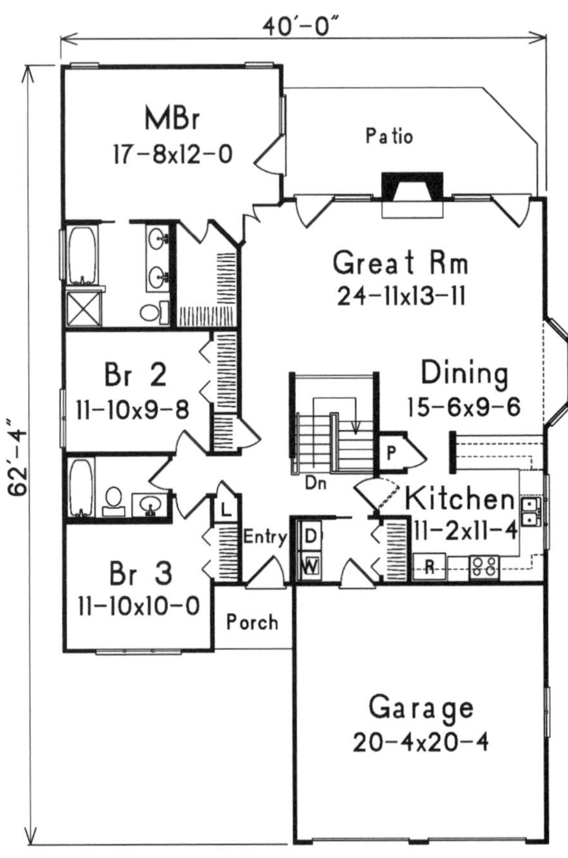

Fantastic A-Frame Get-Away

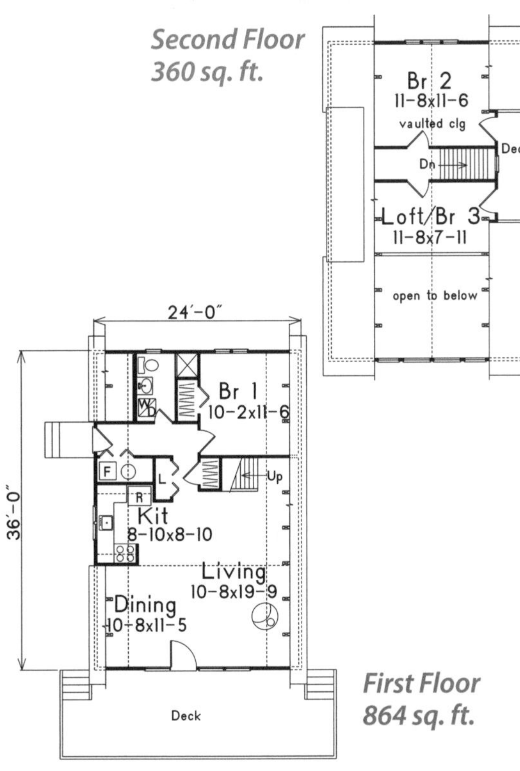

Second Floor
360 sq. ft.

First Floor
864 sq. ft.

Plan #582-008D-0142 — Price Code A

Special Features • 1,224 total square feet of living area • Get away to this cozy A-frame featuring three bedrooms • Living and dining rooms with free-standing fireplace walk out onto a large deck • U-shaped kitchen has a unique built-in table at the end of the counter for intimate gatherings • Both second floor bedrooms enjoy their own private balcony • 3 bedrooms, 1 bath • Crawl space foundation

Perfect Home For A Small Family

Plan #582-001D-0040 — Price Code AAA

Special Features • 864 total square feet of living area • L-shaped kitchen with convenient pantry is adjacent to dining area • Easy access to laundry area, linen closet and storage closet • Both bedrooms include ample closet space • 2 bedrooms, 1 bath • Crawl space foundation, drawings also include basement and slab foundations

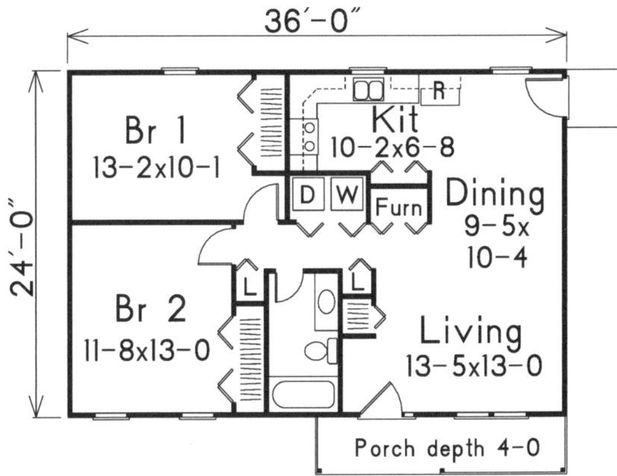

Large Loft Area Offers Endless Possibilities

Plan #582-014D-0016

Price Code A

Special Features • 1,426 total square feet of living area • Large front deck invites outdoor relaxation • Expansive windows, skylights, vaulted ceiling and fireplace enhance the living and dining room combination • Nook, adjacent to the living room, has a cozy window seat • Kitchen is open to the living and dining rooms • 1 bedroom, 1 bath • Crawl space foundation

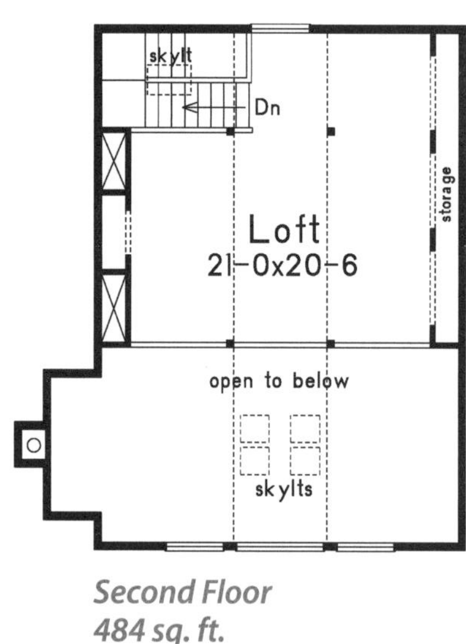

Second Floor
484 sq. ft.

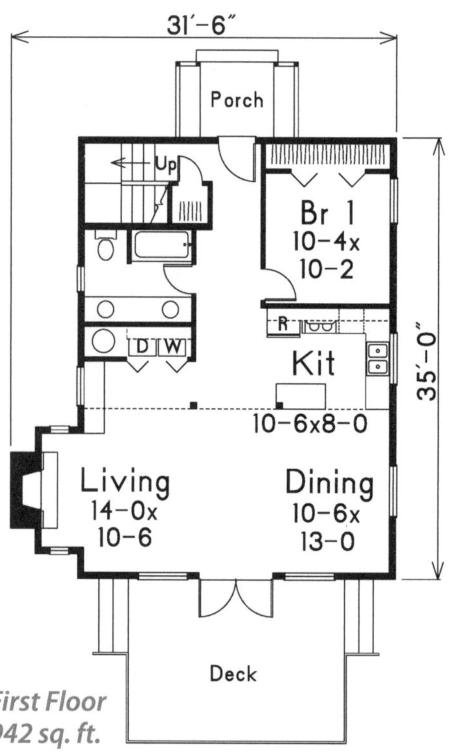

First Floor
942 sq. ft.

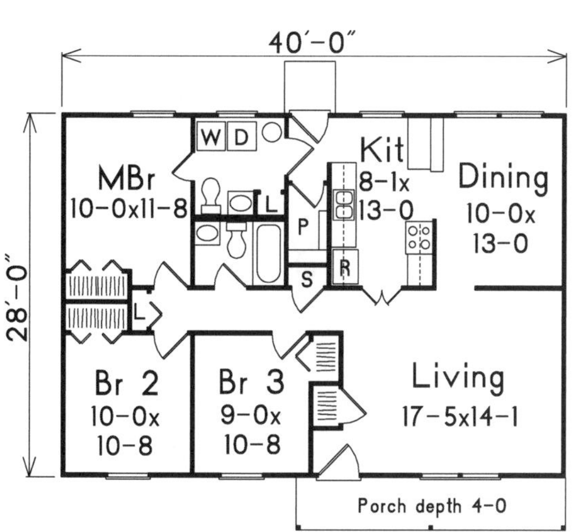

Plan #582-001D-0093 **Price Code AA**

Special Features • 1,120 total square feet of living area • Master bedroom includes a half bath with laundry area, linen closet and kitchen access • Kitchen has charming double-door entry, breakfast bar and a convenient walk-in pantry • Welcoming front porch opens to large living room with coat closet • 3 bedrooms, 1 1/2 baths • Crawl space foundation, drawings also include basement and slab foundations

Open Layout Ensures Easy Living

Plan #582-045D-0012 **Price Code AA**

Special Features • 976 total square feet of living area • Cozy front porch opens into large living room • Convenient half bath is located on first floor • All bedrooms are located on second floor for privacy • Dining room has access to the outdoors • 3 bedrooms, 1 1/2 baths • Basement foundation

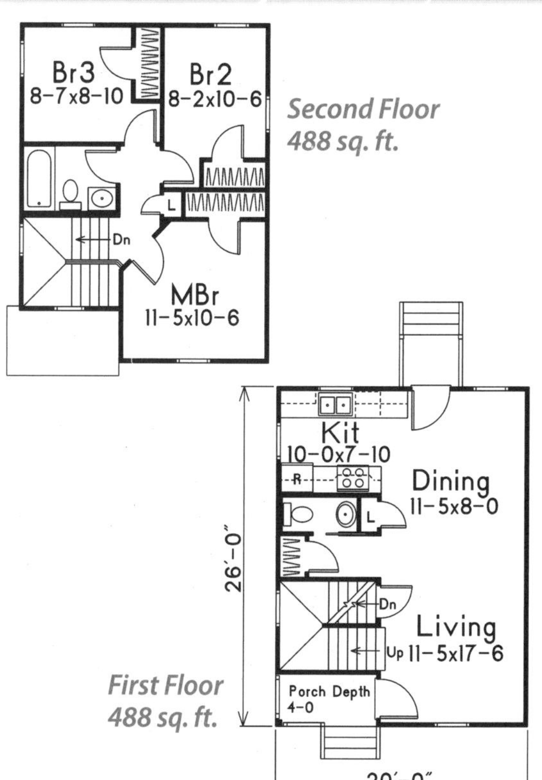

Plan #582-008D-0072

Price Code A

Special Features • 1,200 total square feet of living area • Enjoy lazy summer evenings on this magnificent porch • Activity area has fireplace and ascending stair from cozy loft • Kitchen features built-in pantry • Master bedroom enjoys large bath, walk-in closet and cozy loft overlooking room below • 2 bedrooms, 2 baths • Crawl space foundation

Second Floor
416 sq. ft.

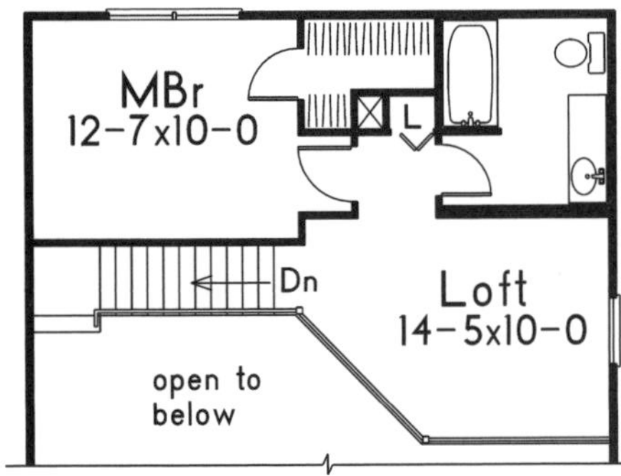

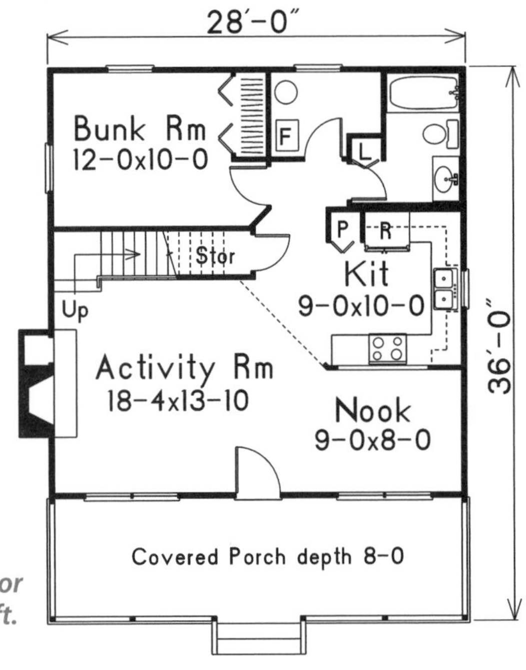

First Floor
784 sq. ft.

Elegance In A Starter Or Retirement Home

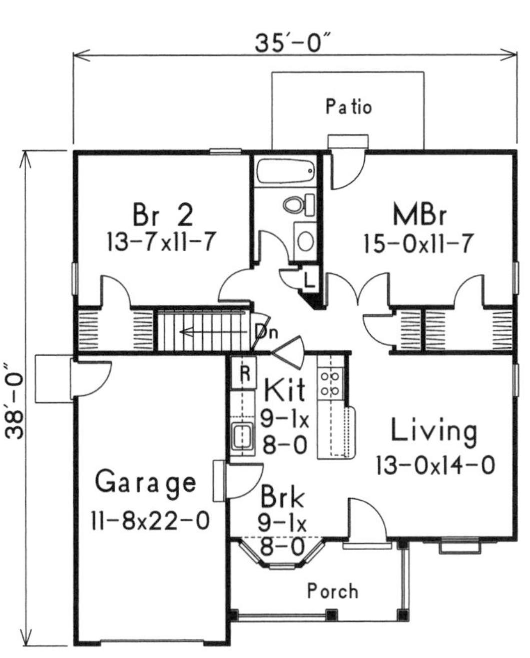

Plan #582-007D-0109

Price Code AAA

Special Features • 888 total square feet of living area • Home features an eye-catching exterior and has a spacious porch • The breakfast room with bay window is open to the living room and adjoins the kitchen with pass-through snack bar • The bedrooms are quite roomy and feature walk-in closets • The master bedroom has a double-door entry and access to the rear patio • 2 bedrooms, 1 bath, 1-car garage • Basement foundation

Efficient Layout In This Multi-Level Home

Plan #582-010D-0004

Price Code B

Special Features • 1,617 total square feet of living area • Kitchen and breakfast area overlook great room with fireplace • Formal dining room features a vaulted ceiling and an elegant circle-top window • All bedrooms are located on the second floor for privacy • 3 bedrooms, 2 1/2 baths, 2-car garage • Partial crawl space/slab foundation

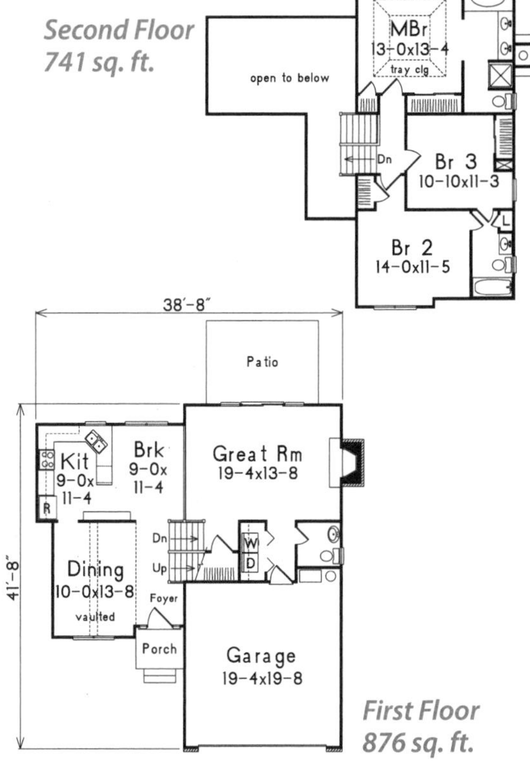

Plan #582-015D-0021

Price Code B

Special Features • 1,584 total square feet of living area • Kitchen overlooks family room creating a natural gathering place • Double vanity in master bath • Dining room flows into living room • 3 bedrooms, 2 1/2 baths, 2-car rear entry garage • Crawl space foundation

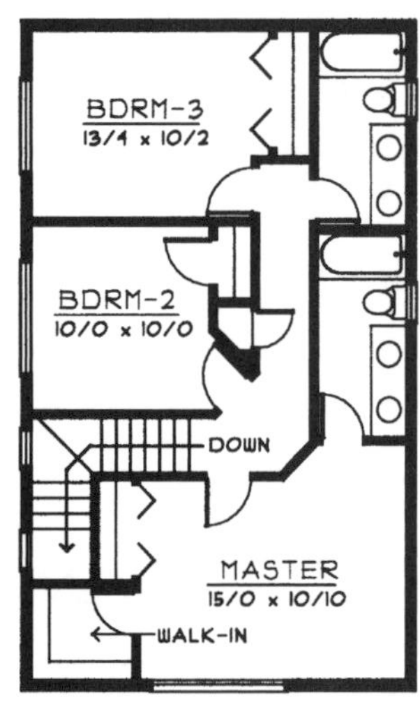

Second Floor
792 sq. ft.

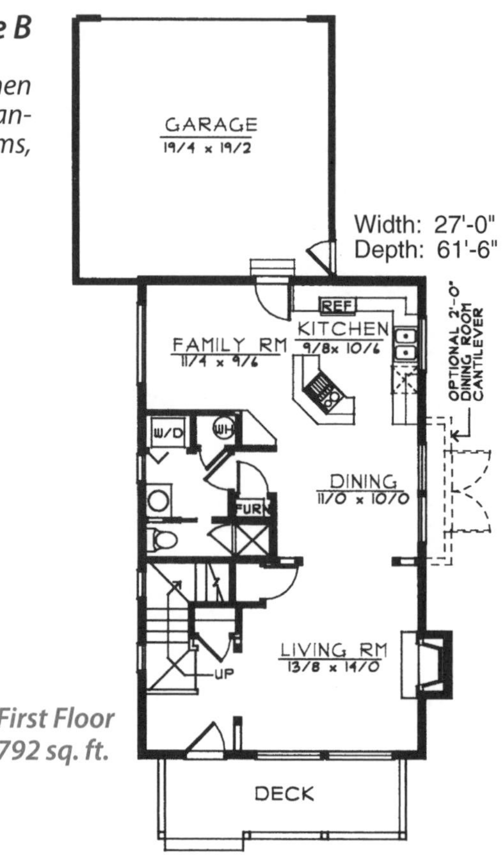

First Floor
792 sq. ft.

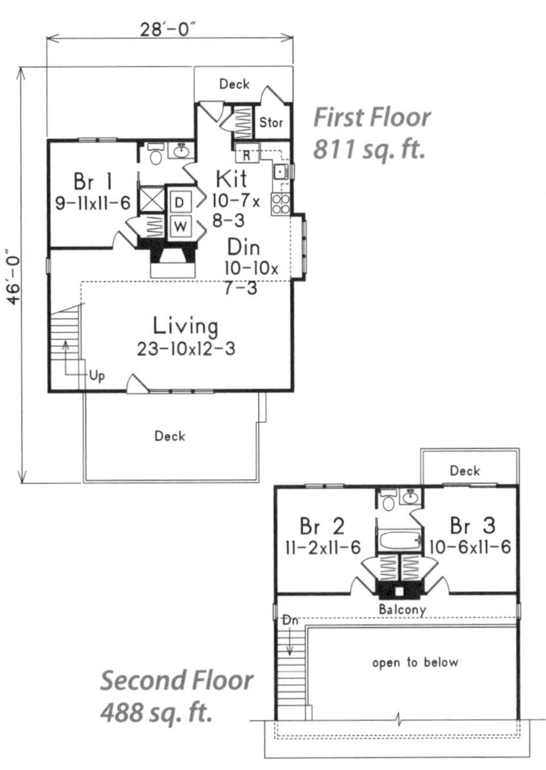

First Floor
811 sq. ft.

Deck
Br 2
11-2x11-6
Br 3
10-6x11-6
Balcony
Dn
open to below

Second Floor
488 sq. ft.

Plan #582-008D-0143

Price Code A

Special Features • 1,299 total square feet of living area • Convenient storage for skis, etc. is located outside the front entrance • Kitchen and dining room receive light from box-bay window • Large vaulted living room features a cozy fireplace and overlook from second floor balcony • Two second floor bedrooms share a Jack and Jill bath • 3 bedrooms, 2 baths • Crawl space foundation, drawings also include slab foundation

Gabled Front Porch Adds Charm And Value

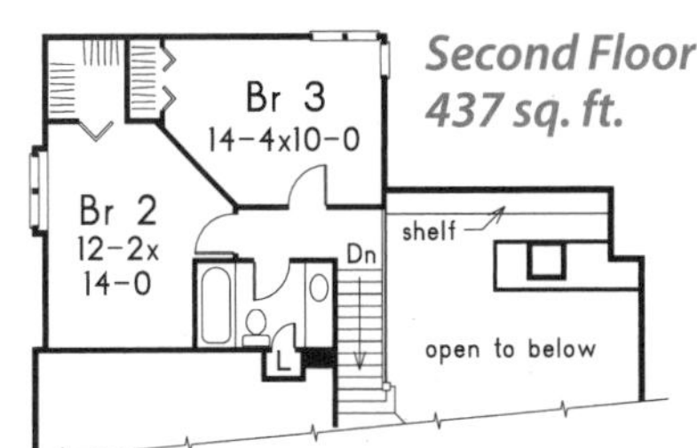

Second Floor
437 sq. ft.

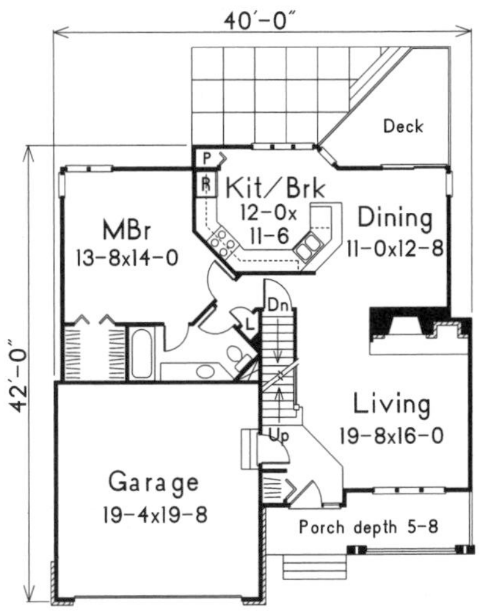

First Floor
1,006 sq. ft.

Plan #582-022D-0006

Price Code A

Special Features • 1,443 total square feet of living area • Raised foyer and cathedral ceiling in living room • Impressive tall-wall fireplace between living and dining rooms • Open U-shaped kitchen with breakfast bay • Angular side deck accentuates patio and garden • First floor master bedroom has a walk-in closet and a corner window • 3 bedrooms, 2 baths, 2-car garage • Basement foundation

Plan #582-001D-0086

Price Code AA

Special Features • 1,154 total square feet of living area • U-shaped kitchen features a large breakfast bar and handy laundry area • Private second floor bedrooms share half bath • Large living/dining area opens to deck • 3 bedrooms, 1 1/2 baths • Crawl space foundation, drawings also include slab foundation

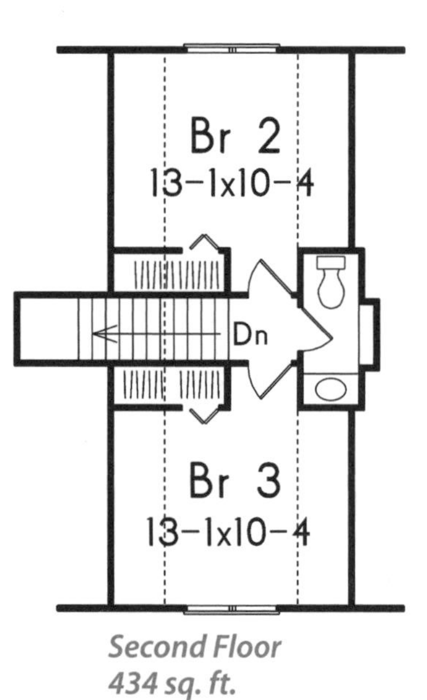

Second Floor
434 sq. ft.

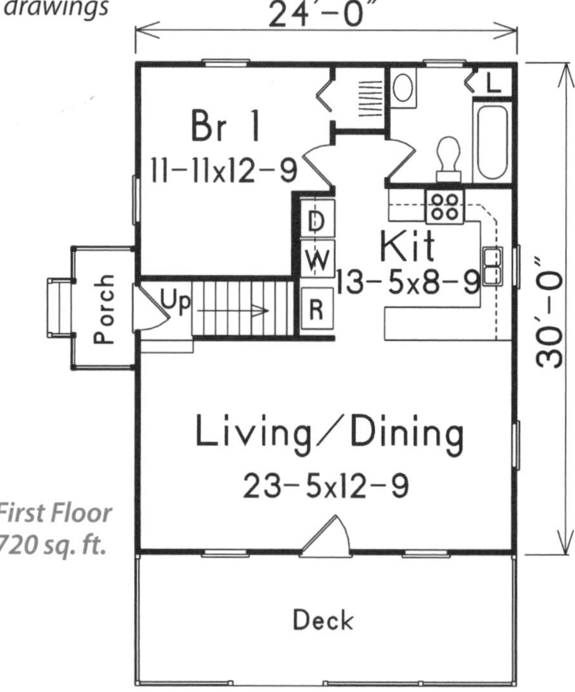

First Floor
720 sq. ft.

Roughing It In Luxury

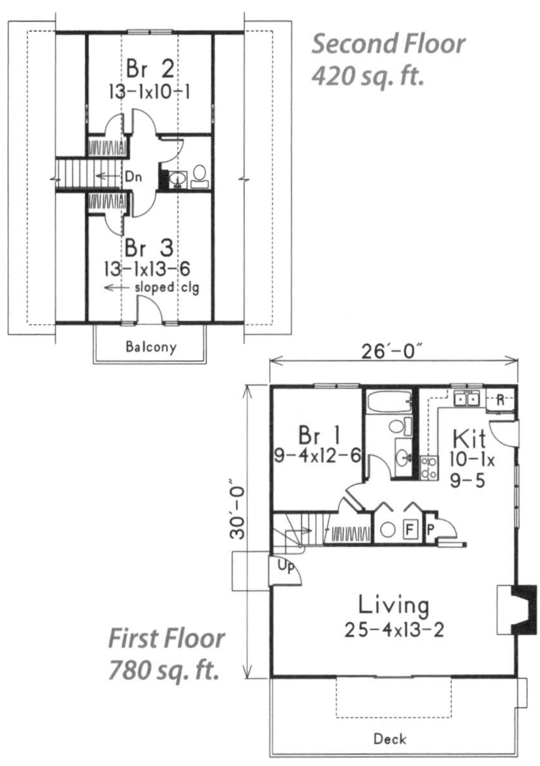

Second Floor
420 sq. ft.

First Floor
780 sq. ft.

Plan #582-008D-0155 **Price Code A**

Special Features • 1,200 total square feet of living area • Ornate ranch-style railing enhances exterior while the stone fireplace provides a visual anchor • Spectacular living room features inviting fireplace and adjoins a charming kitchen with dining area • Two second floor bedrooms share a full bath • 3 bedrooms, 1 1/2 baths • Crawl space foundation, drawings also include slab foundation

Ideal Ranch With Side Entry Garage

Plan #582-001D-0033 **Price Code B**

Special Features • 1,624 total square feet of living area • Master bedroom has a private entry from the outdoors • Garage is adjacent to the utility room with convenient storage closet • Large family and dining areas feature a fireplace and porch access • Pass-through kitchen opens directly to cozy breakfast area • 3 bedrooms, 2 baths, 2-car side entry garage • Basement foundation, drawings also include crawl space and slab foundations

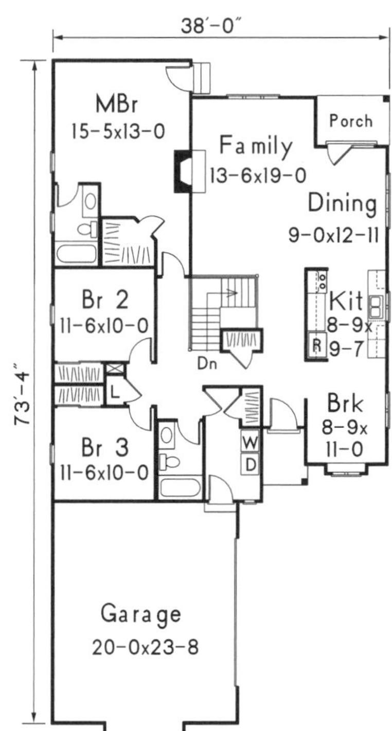

Dramatic Look For Quiet Hideaway

Plan #582-008D-0145

Price Code B

Special Features • 1,750 total square feet of living area • Family room is brightened by floor-to-ceiling windows and sliding doors providing access to the large deck • Second floor sitting area is perfect for a game room or entertaining • Kitchen includes eat-in dining area plus outdoor dining patio as a bonus • Plenty of closet and storage space throughout • 3 bedrooms, 2 baths • Basement foundation, drawings also include crawl space and slab foundations

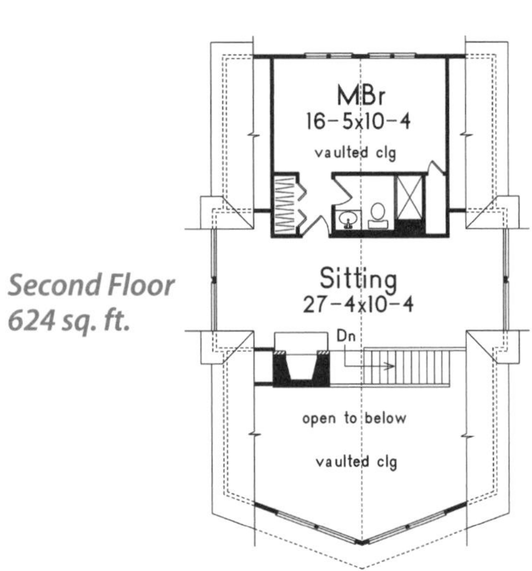

Second Floor
624 sq. ft.

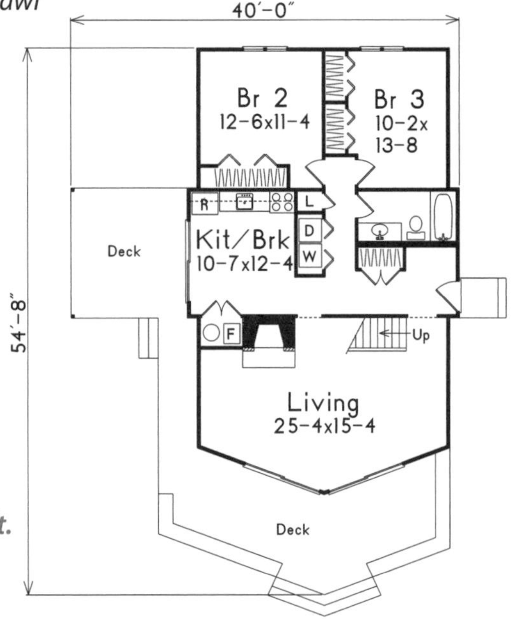

First Floor
1,126 sq. ft.

Compact Home Maximizes Space

Plan #582-045D-0014 **Price Code AA**

Special Features • 987 total square feet of living area • Galley kitchen opens into cozy breakfast room • Convenient coat closets are located by both entrances • Dining/living room offers an expansive open area • Breakfast room has access to the outdoors • Front porch is great for enjoying outdoor living • 3 bedrooms, 1 bath • Basement foundation

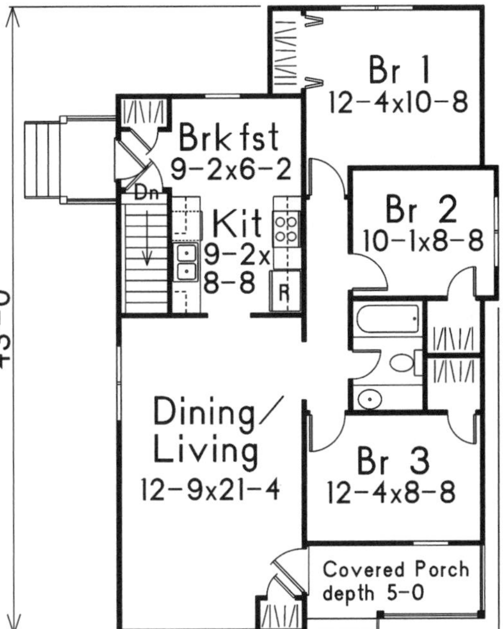

Br 1
12-4x10-8
Brkfst
9-2x6-2
Dn
Kit
9-2x
8-8
R
Br 2
10-1x8-8
Dining/
Living
12-9x21-4
Br 3
12-4x8-8
Covered Porch
depth 5-0
43'-0"
27'-0"

Plan #582-028D-0001

Price Code AAA

Special Features • 864 total square feet of living area • Large laundry area accesses the outdoors as well as the kitchen • Front covered porch creates an ideal outdoor living area • Snack bar in kitchen creates a quick and easy dining area • 2 bedrooms, 1 bath • Crawl space or slab foundation, please specify when ordering

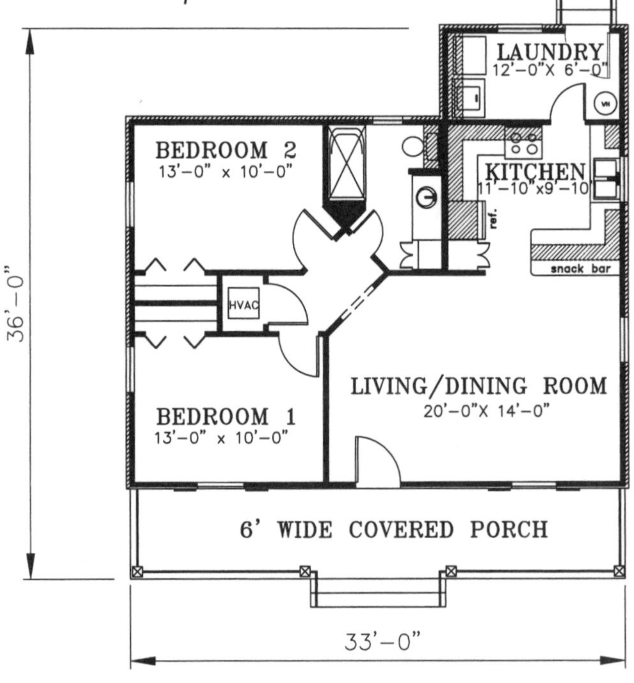

Beautiful Entry Enhances This Home

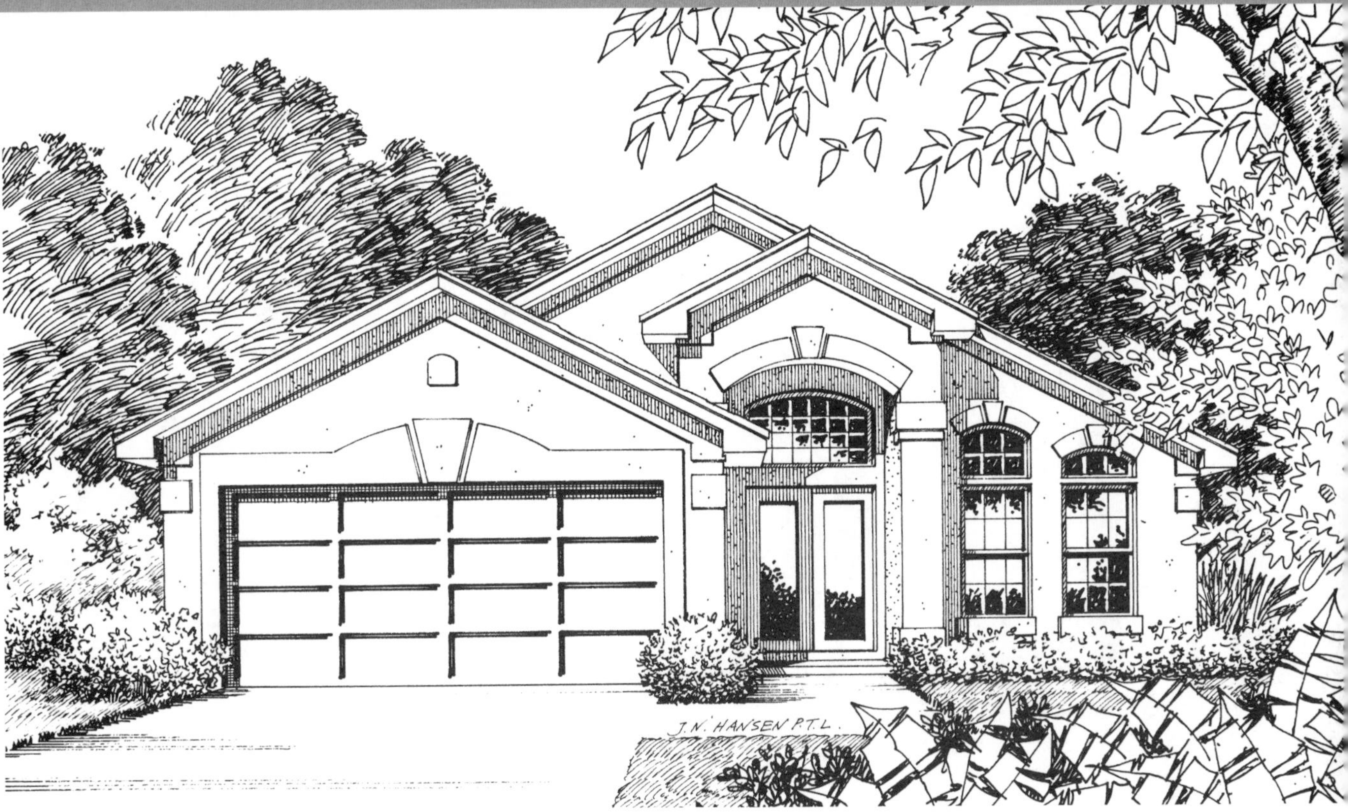

Plan #582-047D-0009 | Price Code B

Special Features • 1,565 total square feet of living area • Master bedroom has an enormous luxury bath with corner step-up tub and double sinks • Majestic living and dining rooms are open and airy • Vaulted ceilings are highlighted throughout this home • 3 bedrooms, 2 baths, 2-car garage • Slab foundation

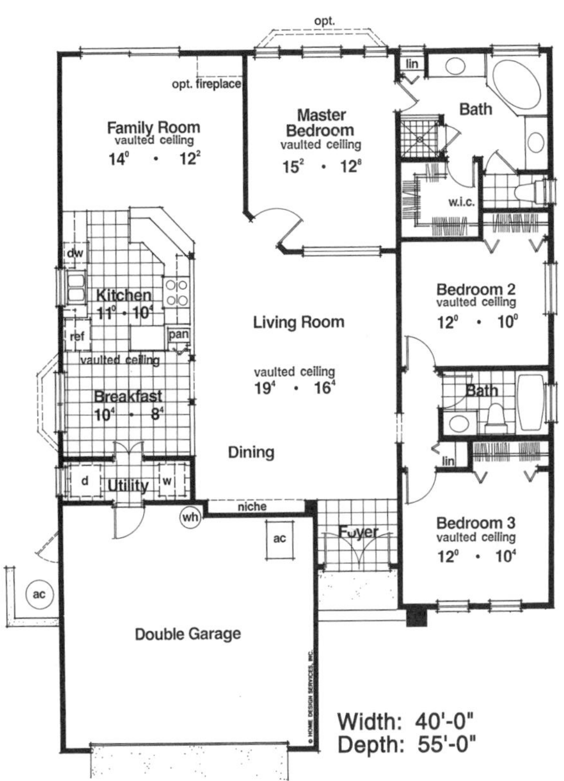

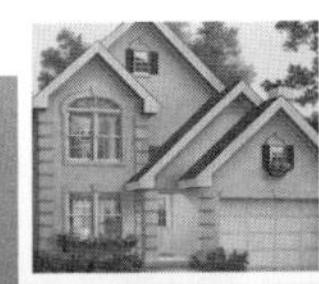

Front Dormers Add Light, Space And Appeal

Plan #582-001D-0056

Price Code B

Special Features • *1,705 total square feet of living area* • *Cozy design includes two bedrooms on first floor and two bedrooms on second floor for added privacy* • *L-shaped kitchen provides easy access to the dining room and the outdoors* • *Convenient first floor laundry area* • *4 bedrooms, 2 baths* • *Crawl space foundation, drawings also include basement and slab foundations*

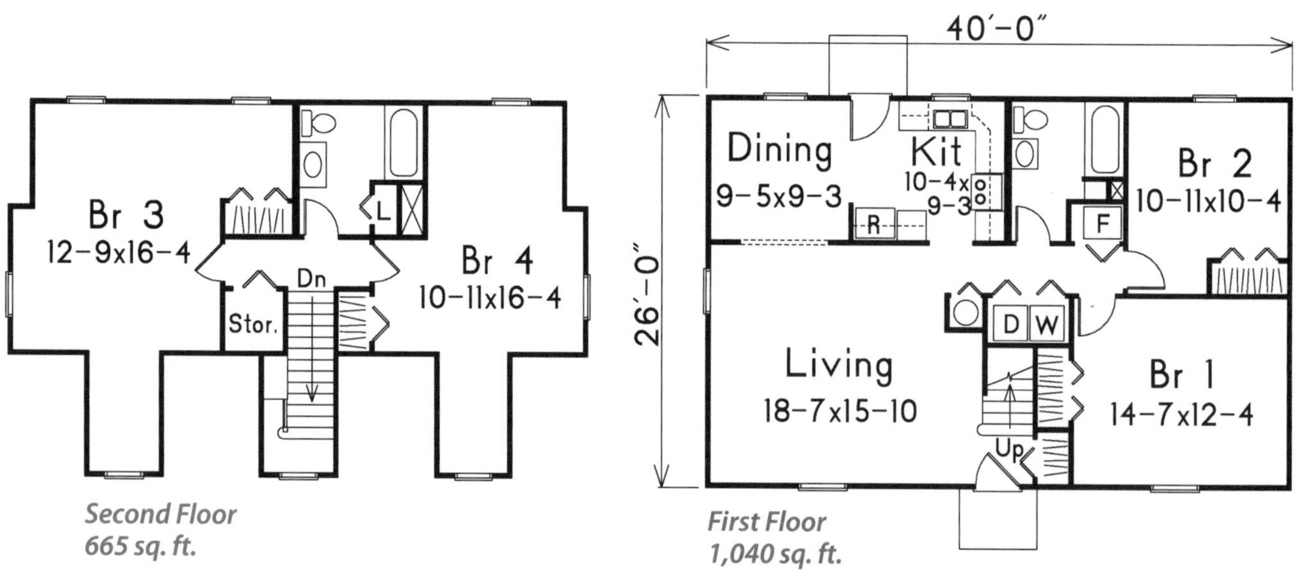

Second Floor
665 sq. ft.

First Floor
1,040 sq. ft.

Compact, Convenient And Charming

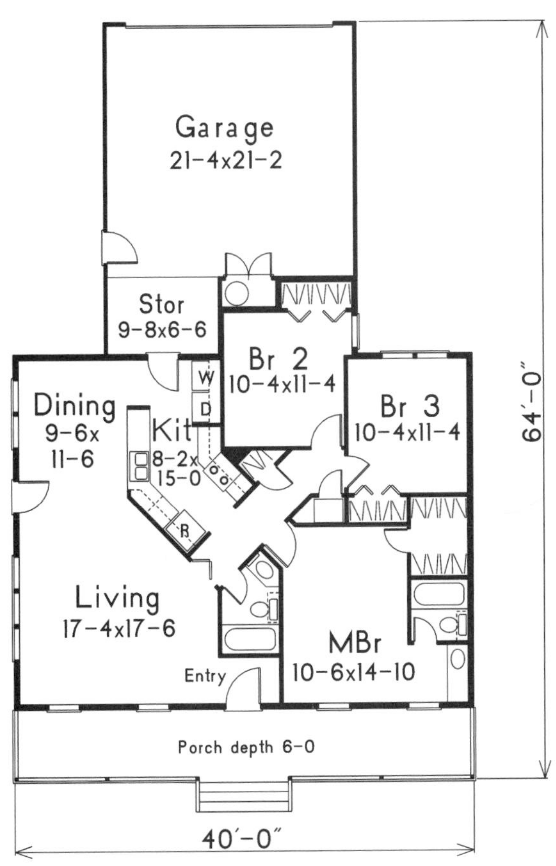

Plan #582-021D-0008

Price Code A

Special Features • 1,266 total square feet of living area • Narrow frontage is perfect for small lots • Energy efficient home with 2" x 6" exterior walls • Prominent central hall provides a convenient connection for all main rooms • Design incorporates full-size master bedroom complete with dressing room, bath and walk-in closet • Angled kitchen includes handy laundry facilities and is adjacent to an oversized storage area • 3 bedrooms, 2 baths, 2-car rear entry garage • Crawl space foundation, drawings also include slab foundation

Contemporary Escape

Plan #582-008D-0135

Price Code C

Special Features • 1,836 total square feet of living area • Foyer sparkles with spiral stair, sloped ceilings and celestial windows • Living room enjoys fireplace with bookshelves and views to outdoors • U-shaped kitchen includes eat-in breakfast area and dining nearby • Master bedroom revels in having a balcony overlooking the living room, a large walk-in closet and private bath • 3 bedrooms, 2 1/2 baths • Crawl space foundation, drawings also include slab foundation

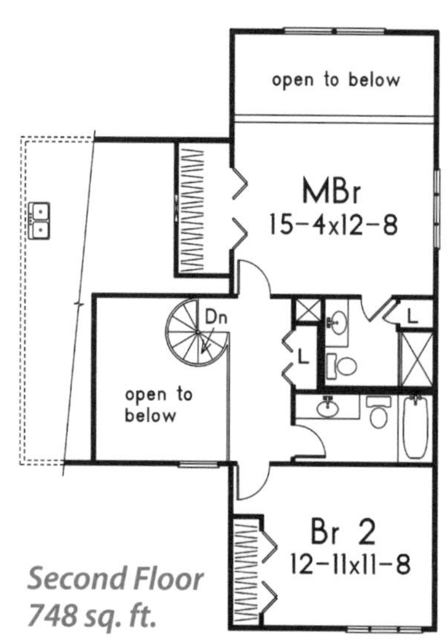

Second Floor
748 sq. ft.

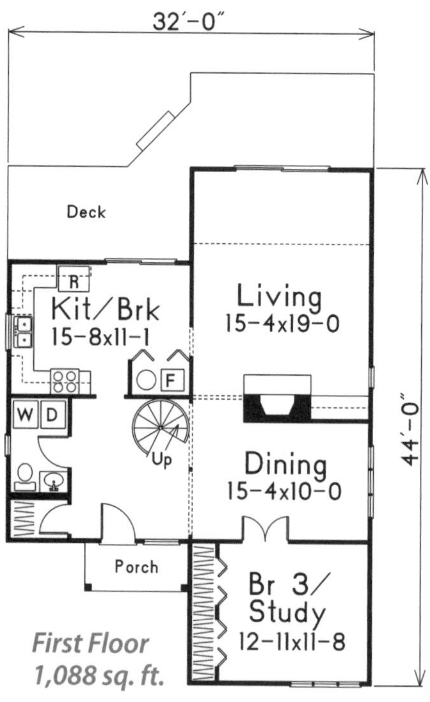

First Floor
1,088 sq. ft.

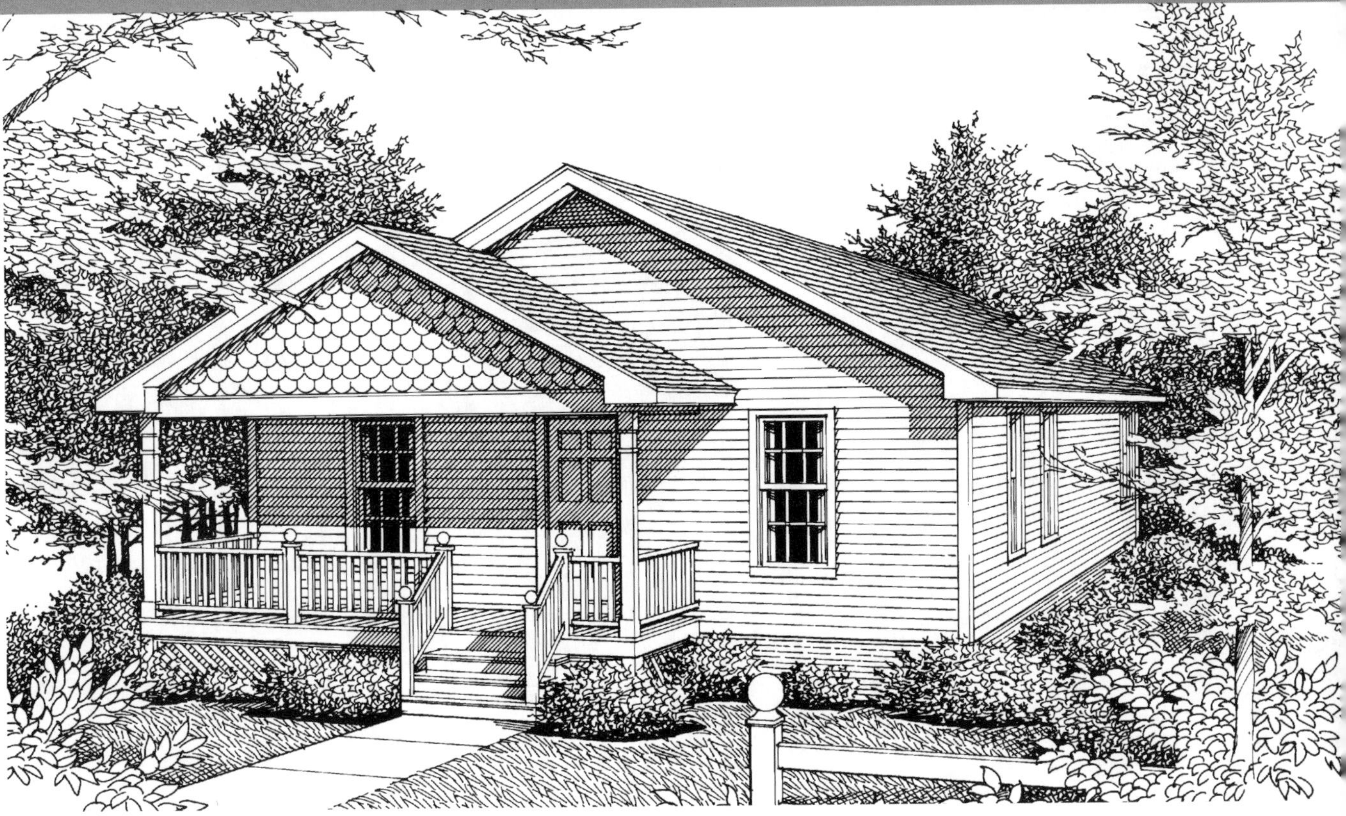

Gabled, Covered Front Porch

Plan #582-001D-0036

Price Code A

Special Features • *1,320 total square feet of living area* • *Functional U-shaped kitchen features pantry* • *Large living and dining areas join to create an open atmosphere* • *Secluded master bedroom includes private full bath* • *Covered front porch opens into large living area with convenient coat closet* • *Utility/laundry room is located near the kitchen* • *3 bedrooms, 2 baths* • *Crawl space foundation*

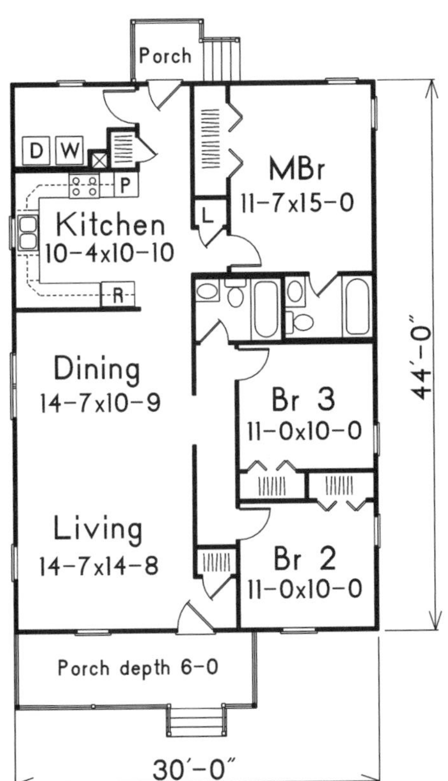

Master Bedroom Is Spacious And Private

Plan #582-008D-0149

Price Code AA

Special Features • 1,160 total square feet of living area • Kitchen/dining area combines with the laundry area creating a functional and organized area • Spacious vaulted living area has large fireplace and is brightened by glass doors accessing large deck • Ascend to second floor loft by spiral stairs and find a cozy hideaway • Master bedroom is brightened by many windows and includes a private bath and double closets • 1 bedroom, 1 bath • Crawl space foundation

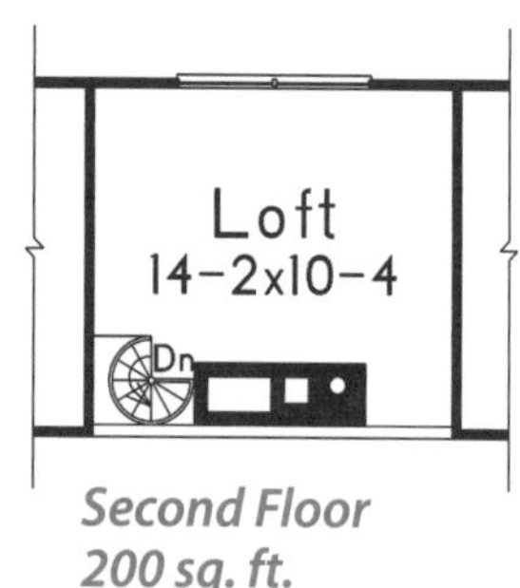

Second Floor
200 sq. ft.

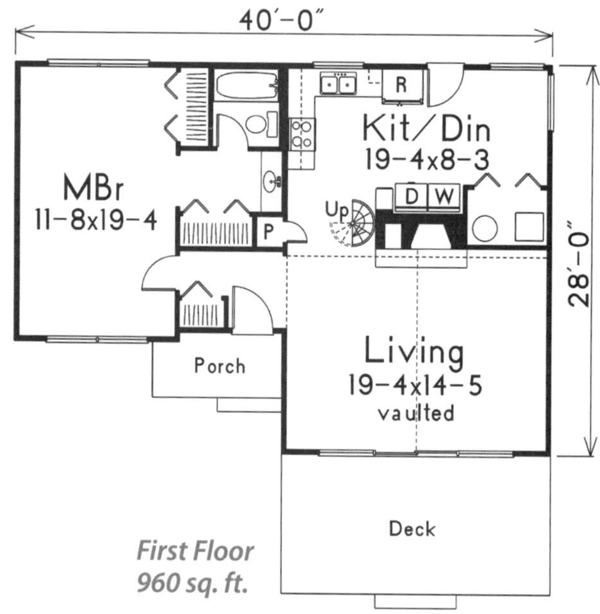

First Floor
960 sq. ft.

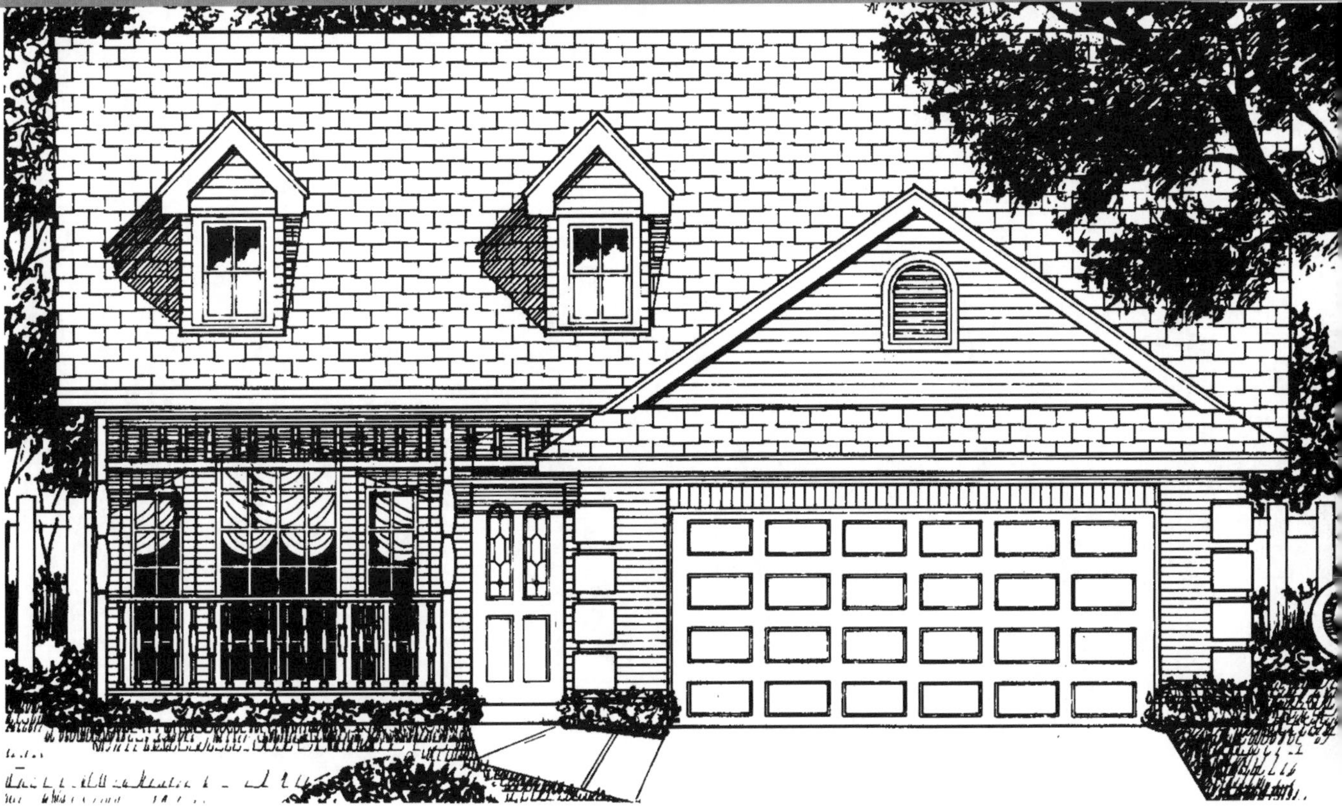

Plan #582-031D-0004

Price Code B

Special Features • 1,710 total square feet of living area • Bedrooms have plenty of closet space • Laundry area located near bedrooms for efficiency • Corner fireplace warms large family room with 10' ceiling • 4 bedrooms, 2 baths, 2-car garage • Slab foundation

Width: 39'-0"
Depth: 60'-0"

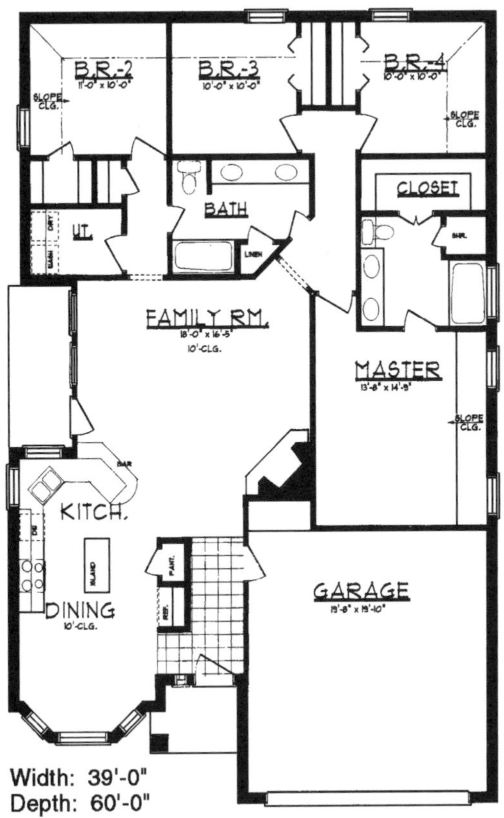

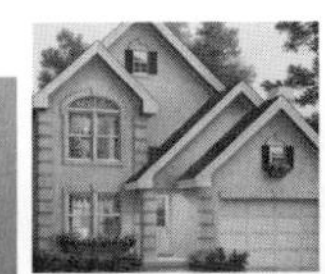

Plan #582-015D-0026

Price Code B

Special Features • 1,770 total square feet of living area • Private master bedroom on second floor has balcony, bath and large walk-in closet • Oversized laundry room has extra storage and counterspace • Dining room is adjacent to kitchen making entertaining easy • 2 bedrooms, 2 baths • Basement or walk-out basement foundation, please specify when ordering

Second Floor
677 sq. ft.

First Floor
1,093 sq. ft.

Width: 28'-0"
Depth: 40'-9"

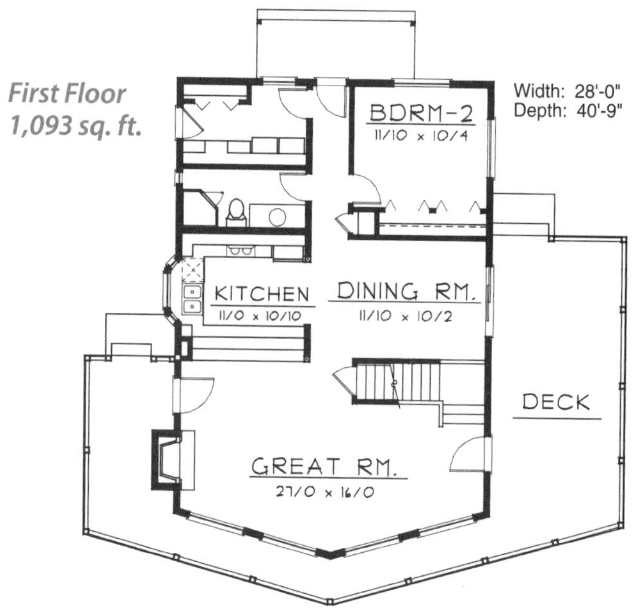

Compact Two-Story With All The Conveniences

Plan #582-001D-0092

Price Code B

Special Features • *1,664 total square feet of living area* • *Master bedroom includes private bath, dressing area and walk-in closet* • *Spacious rooms throughout* • *Kitchen features handy side entrance, adjacent laundry room and coat closet* • *3 bedrooms, 2 1/2 baths* • *Crawl space foundation, drawings also include basement and slab foundations*

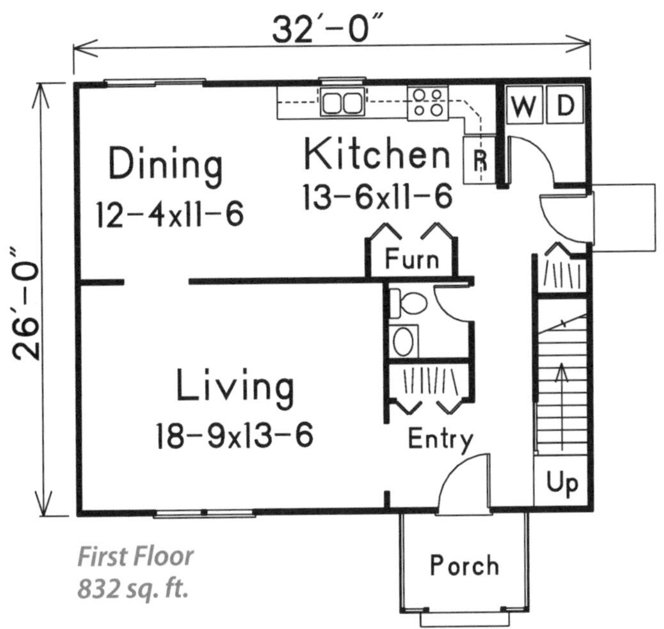

First Floor
832 sq. ft.

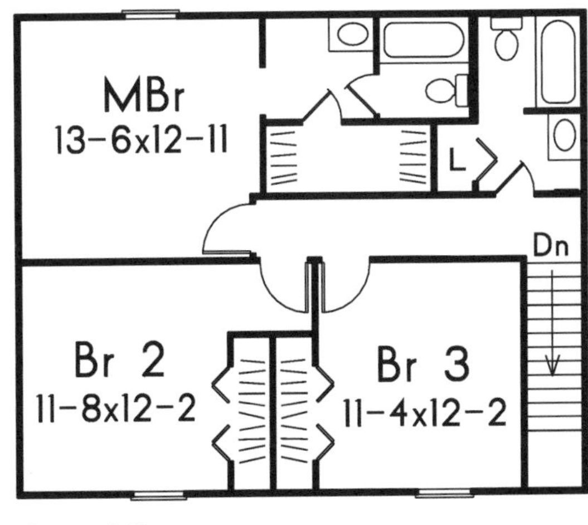

Second Floor
832 sq. ft.

Plan #582-049D-0001

Price Code B

Special Features • 1,700 total square feet of living area • 9' ceilings on first floor • Both living and family rooms have a fireplace for coziness • Efficient kitchen with snack bar and nearby dining room • Two full baths add privacy if housing guests • 2 bedrooms, 2 baths • Basement foundation

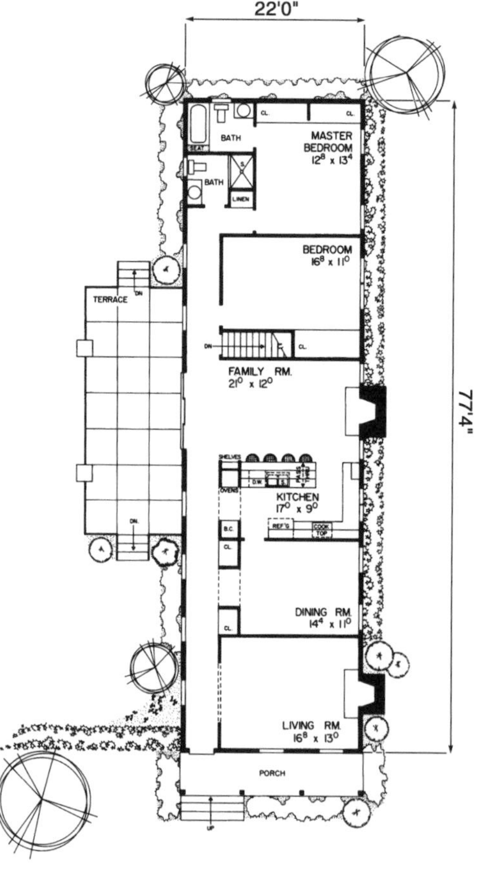

1-800-DREAM HOME (373-2646)

Exciting Living For A Narrow Sloping Lot

Plan #582-007D-0106

Price Code A

Special Features *• 1,200 total square feet of living area • Entry leads to a large dining area which opens to kitchen and sun-drenched living room • An expansive window wall in the two-story atrium lends space and light to living room with fireplace • The large kitchen features a breakfast bar, built-in pantry and storage galore • 697 square feet of optional living area on the lower level includes a family room, bedroom #3 and a bath • 2 bedrooms, 1 bath • Walk-out basement foundation*

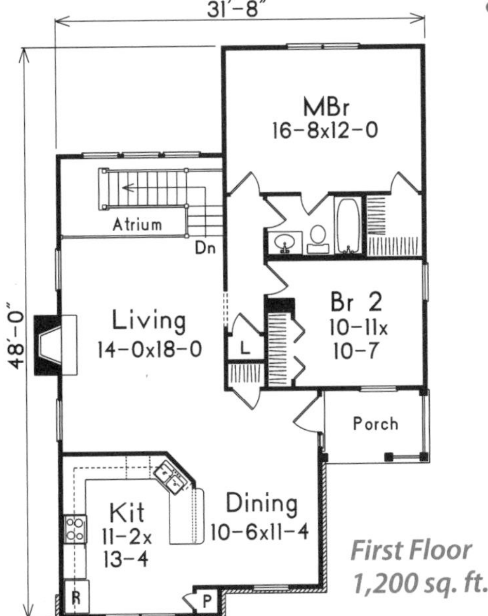

First Floor
1,200 sq. ft.

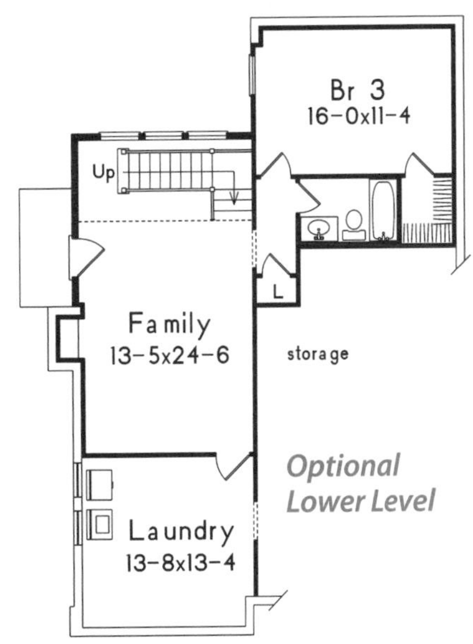

Optional
Lower Level

Plan #582-001D-0087

Price Code A

Special Features • *1,230 total square feet of living area* • *Spacious living room accesses huge deck* • *Bedroom #3 features a balcony overlooking the deck* • *Kitchen with dining area accesses the outdoors* • *Washer and dryer tucked under stairs* • *3 bedrooms, 1 bath* • *Crawl space foundation, drawings also include slab foundation*

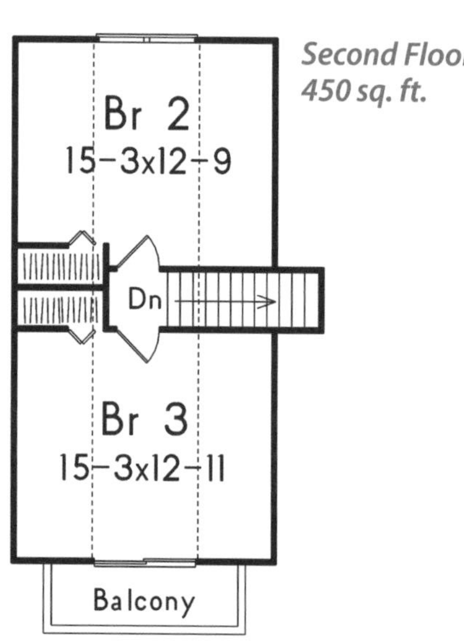

Second Floor
450 sq. ft.

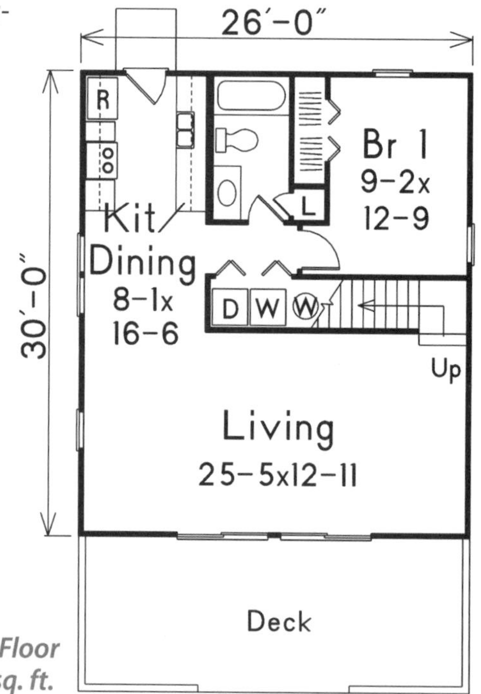

First Floor
780 sq. ft.

Plan #582-060D-0014

Price Code AA

Special Features • *1,021 total square feet of living area* • *11' ceiling in great room expands living area* • *Kitchen and breakfast room combine allowing easier preparation and cleanup* • *Master suite features private bath and an oversized walk-in closet* • *3 bedrooms, 2 baths, optional 2-car garage* • *Slab or crawl space foundation, please specify when ordering*

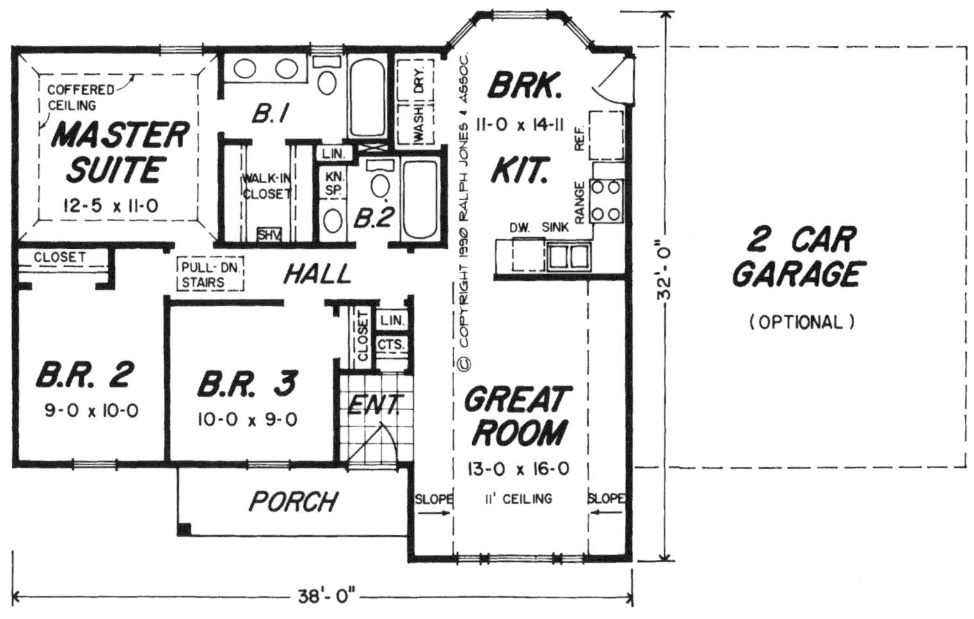

Plan #582-022D-0022

Price Code A

Special Features • 1,270 total square feet of living area • Spacious living area features angled stairs, vaulted ceiling, exciting fireplace and deck access • Master bedroom includes a walk-in closet and private bath • Dining and living rooms join to create an open atmosphere • Eat-in kitchen has a convenient pass-through to dining room • 3 bedrooms, 2 baths, 2-car garage • Basement foundation

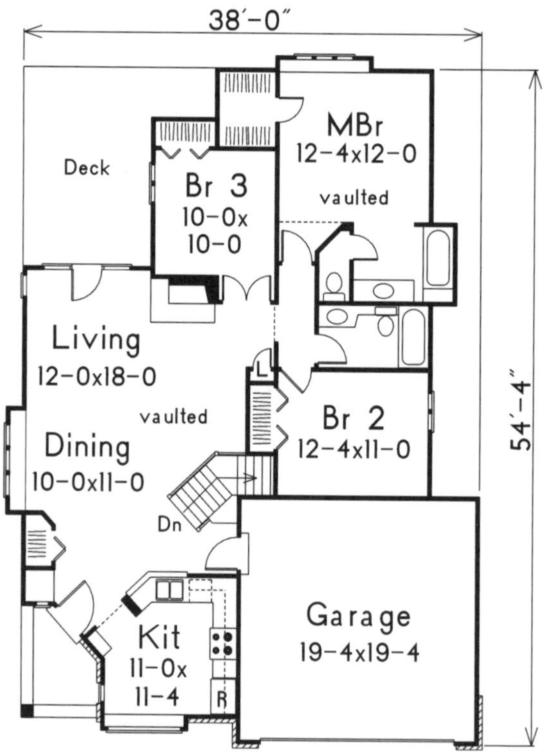

Unique A-Frame Detailing Has Appeal

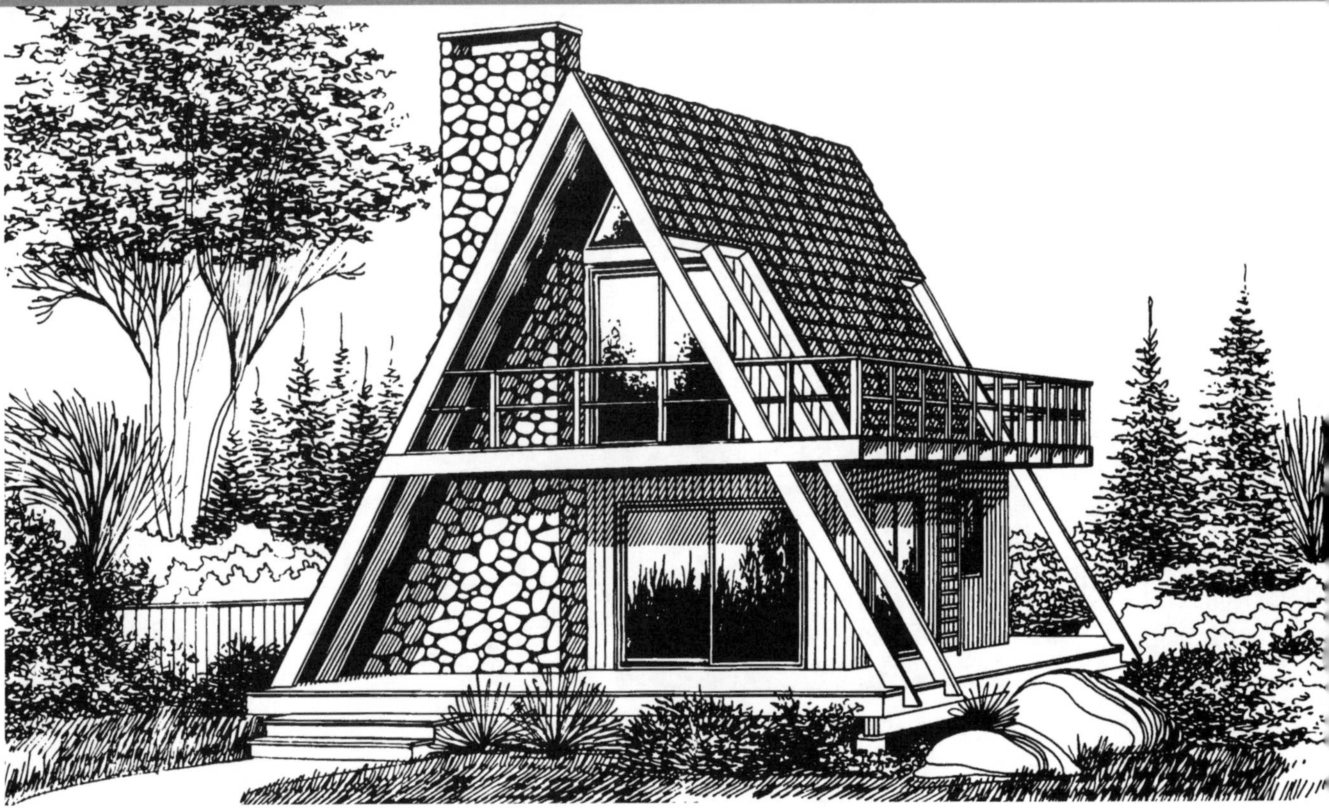

Plan #582-008D-0139

Price Code A

Special Features • 1,272 total square feet of living area • Stone fireplace accents living room • Spacious kitchen includes snack bar overlooking living room • First floor bedroom is roomy and secluded • Plenty of closet space for second floor bedrooms plus a generous balcony which wraps around second floor • 3 bedrooms, 1 1/2 baths • Crawl space foundation

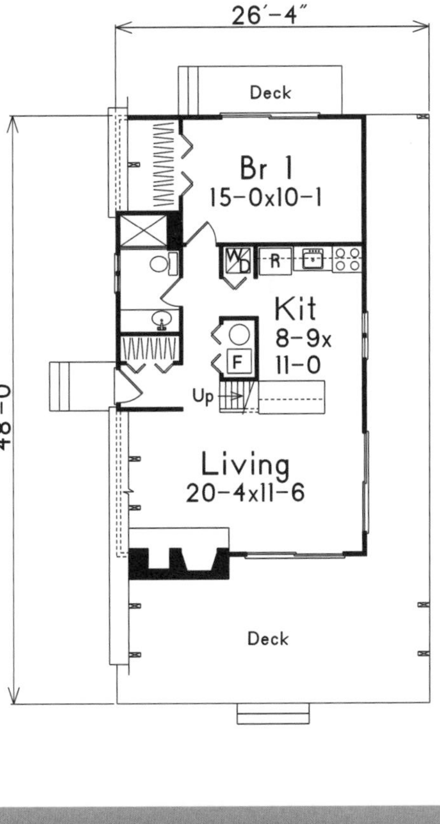

26'-4"
48'-0"
Deck
Br 1
15-0x10-1
W D
R
Kit
8-9x
11-0
F
Up
Living
20-4x11-6
Deck

First Floor
792 sq. ft.

Br 2
14-6x9-7
Dn
Br 3
14-6x11-5
sloped clg
Balcony

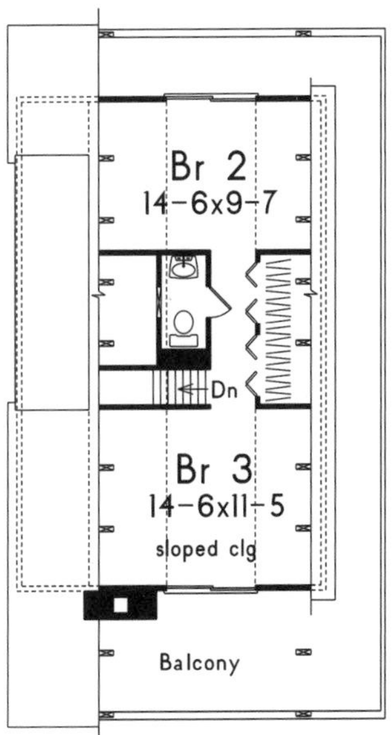

Second Floor
480 sq. ft.

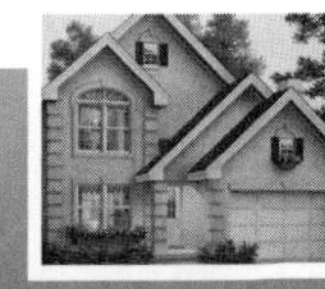

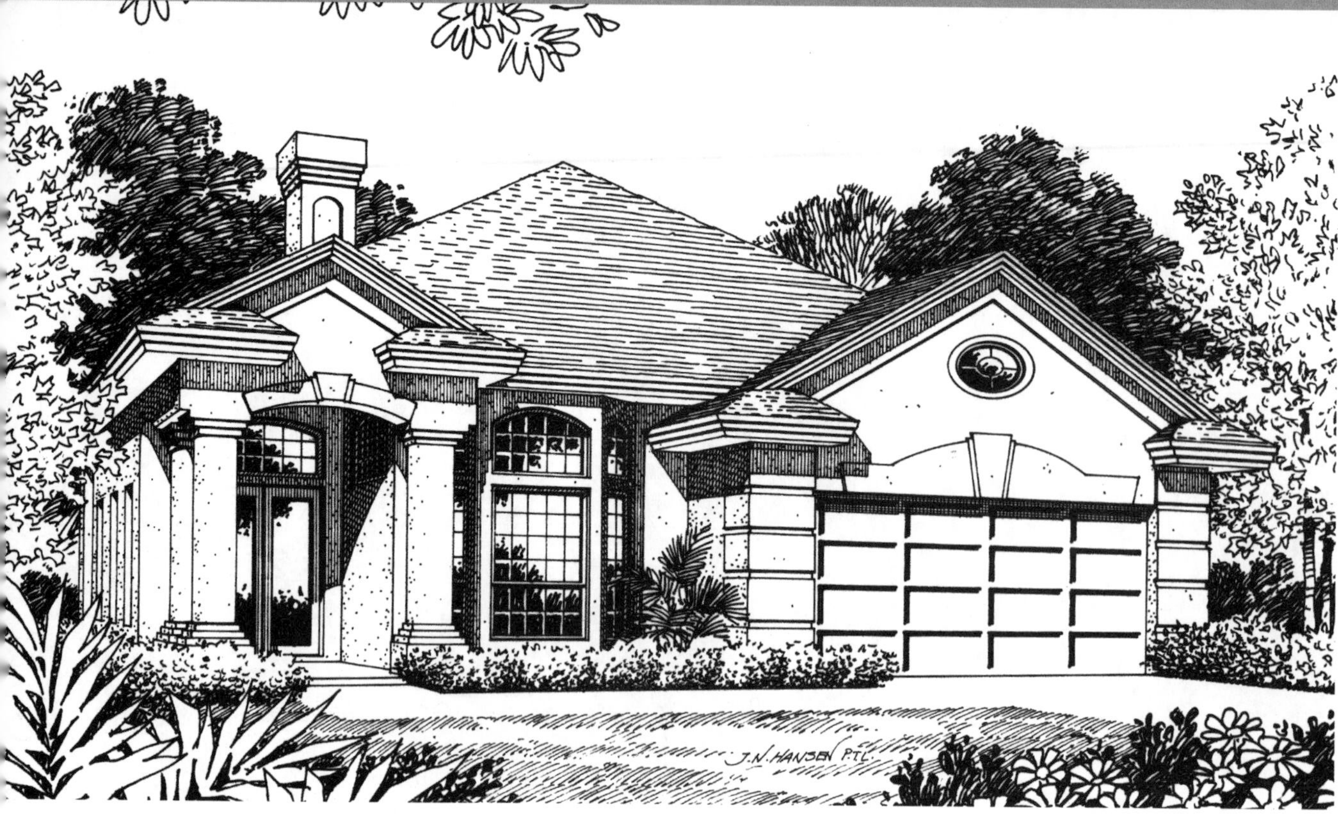

Plan #582-047D-0021

Price Code B

Special Features • 1,787 total square feet of living area • See-through fireplace between dining and family rooms adds warmth and charm • Luxurious master bedroom has a private bath and an entrance onto the covered patio • Convenient kitchen has pass-through into spacious dining area • 3 bedrooms, 2 baths, 2-car garage • Slab foundation

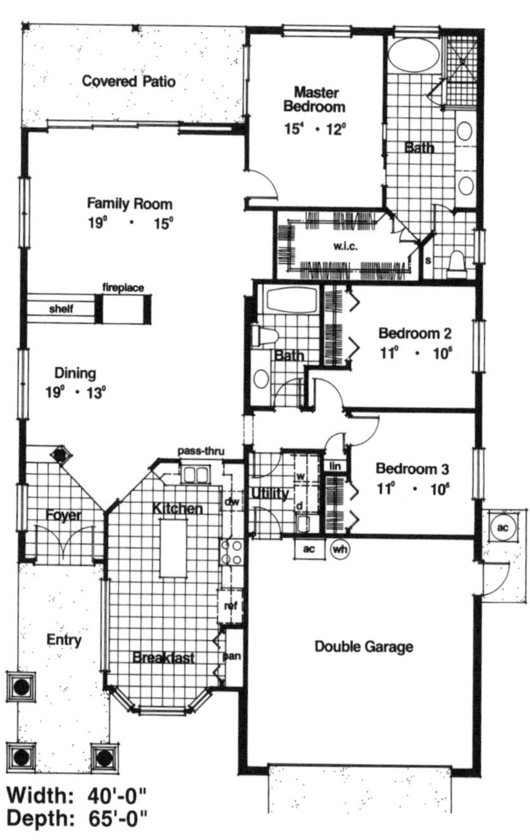

Distinctive Home For Sloping Terrain

Plan #582-007D-0061

Price Code A

Special Features • 1,340 total square feet of living area • Grand-sized vaulted living and dining rooms offer fireplace, wet bar and breakfast counter open to spacious kitchen • Vaulted master bedroom features a double-door entry, walk-in closet and an elegant bath • Basement includes a huge two-car garage and space for a bedroom/bath expansion • 3 bedrooms, 2 baths, 2-car drive under garage with storage area • Basement foundation

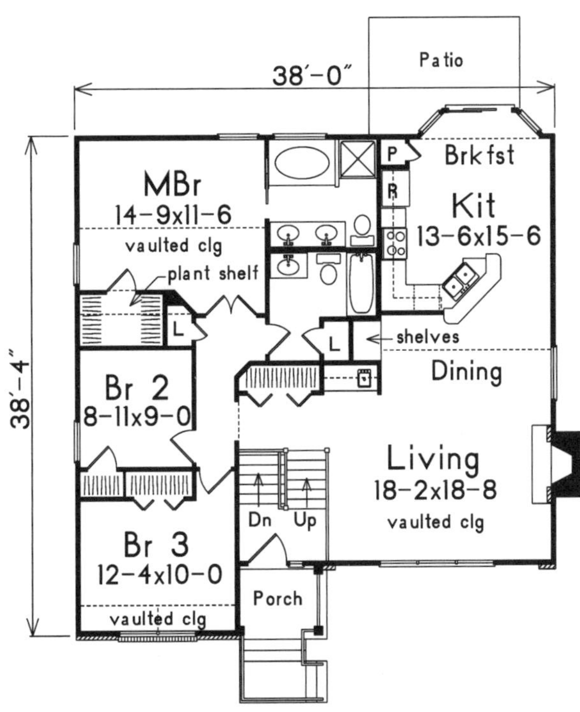

Plan #582-001D-0089

Price Code AA

Special Features • 1,000 total square feet of living area • Master bedroom has double closets and an adjacent bath • L-shaped kitchen includes side entrance, closet and convenient laundry area • Living room features handy coat closet • 3 bedrooms, 1 bath • Crawl space foundation, drawings also include basement and slab foundations

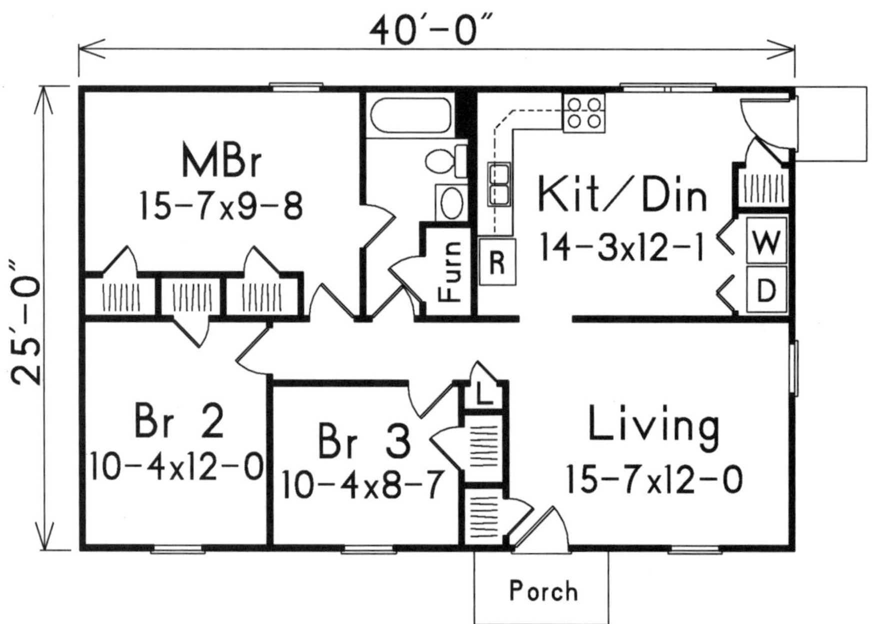

Great Relaxed-Styled Plan

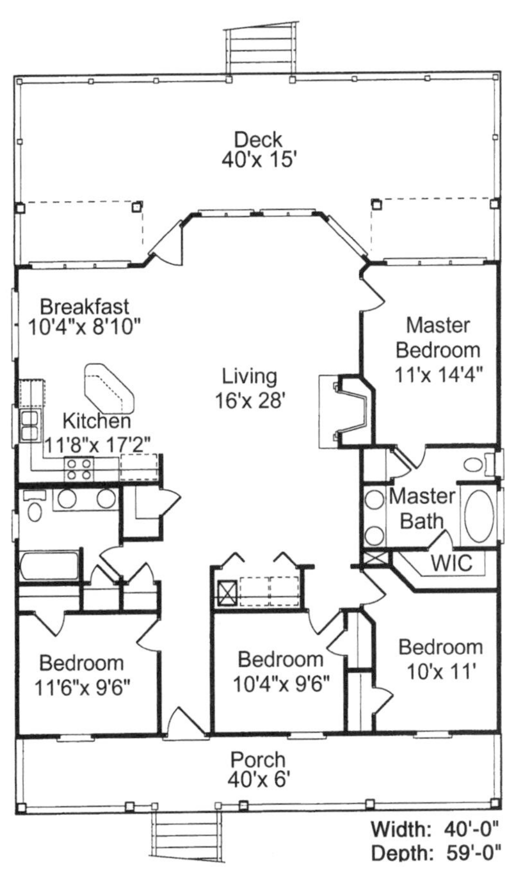

Plan #582-024D-0003 **Price Code B**

Special Features • *1,520 total square feet of living area* • *9' ceilings throughout this home* • *Living room has a fireplace and a large bay window that connects to an oversized deck* • *Master bedroom has a wall of windows allowing terrific views to the outdoors* • *4 bedrooms, 2 baths* • *Pier foundation*

Dining With A View

Plan #582-007D-0038

Price Code B

Special Features *• 1,524 total square feet of living area • Delightful balcony overlooks two-story entry illuminated by oval window • Roomy first floor master bedroom offers quiet privacy • All bedrooms feature one or more walk-in closets • 3 bedrooms, 2 1/2 baths, 2-car garage • Basement foundation, drawings also include crawl space and slab foundations*

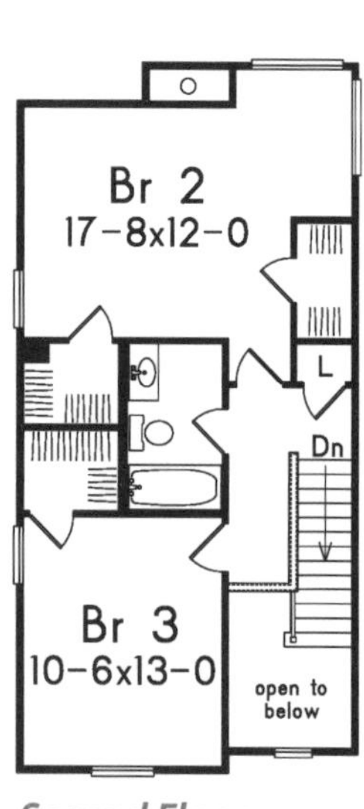

Second Floor
573 sq. ft.

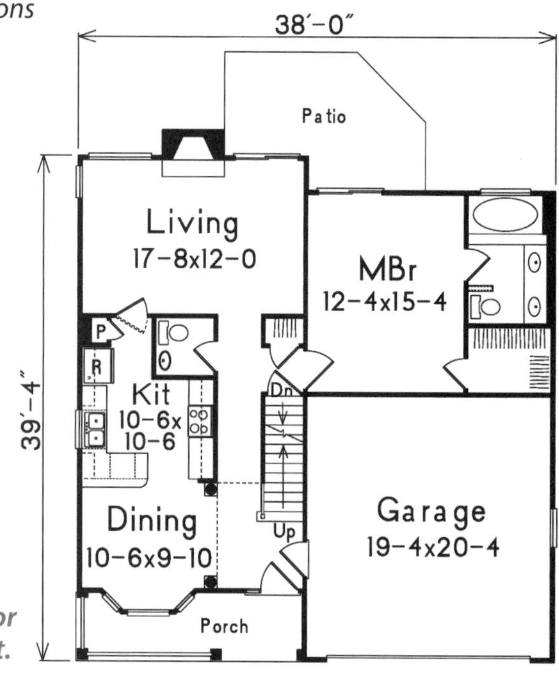

First Floor
951 sq. ft.

1-800-DREAM HOME (373-2646)

Rustic Haven

Plan #582-008D-0134

Price Code A

Special Features • 1,275 total square feet of living area • Wall shingles and stone veneer fireplace all fashion an irresistible rustic appeal • Living area features fireplace and opens to an efficient kitchen • Two bedrooms on second floor • 4 bedrooms, 2 baths • Basement foundation, drawings also include crawl space and slab foundations

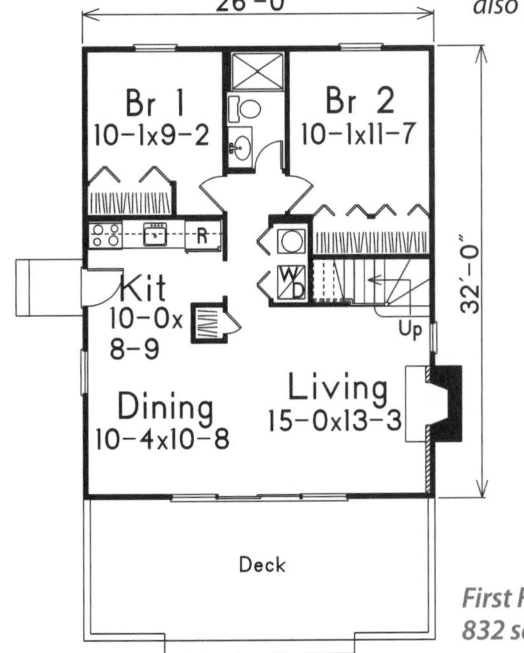

First Floor
832 sq. ft.

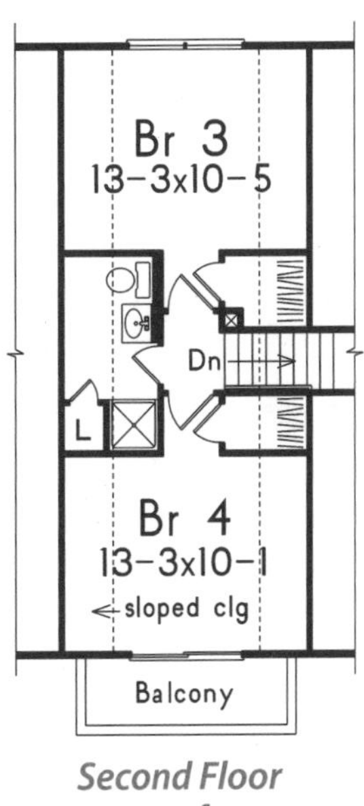

Second Floor
443 sq. ft.

Apartment Garage With Surprising Interior

Plan #582-007D-0040

Price Code AAA

Special Features • 632 total square feet of living area • Porch leads to vaulted entry and stair with feature window, coat closet and access to garage/laundry • Cozy living room offers vaulted ceiling, fireplace, large palladian window and pass-through to kitchen • A garden tub with arched window is part of a very roomy bath • 1 bedroom, 1 bath, 2-car garage • Slab foundation

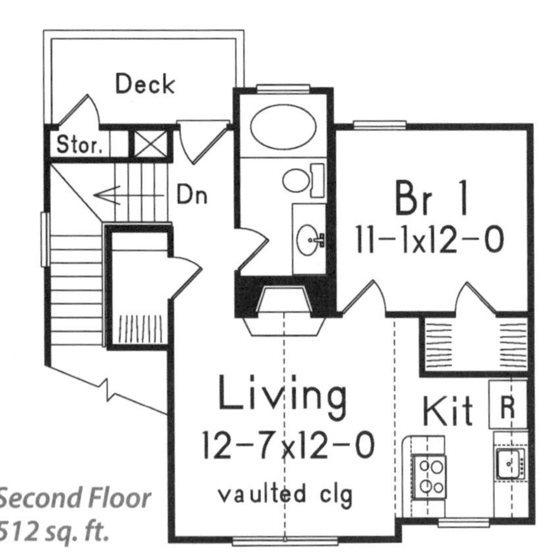

Second Floor
512 sq. ft.

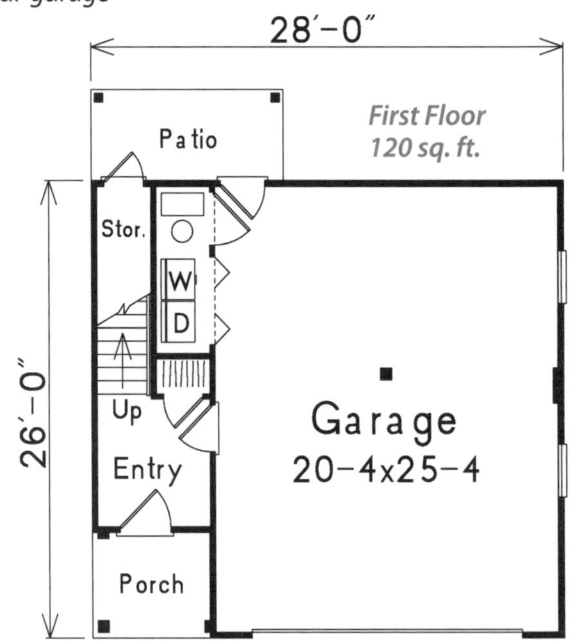

First Floor
120 sq. ft.

Quality plans for building your future, with extras that provide unsurpassed value, ensure good construction and long-term enjoyment.

A quality home - one that looks good, functions well, and provides years of enjoyment - is a product of many things - design, materials, craftsmanship.

But it's also the result of outstanding blueprints - the actual plans and specifications that tell the builder exactly how to build your home.

And with our BLUEPRINT PACKAGES you get the absolute best. A complete set of blueprints is available for every design in this book. These "working drawings," are highly detailed, resulting in two key benefits:

- *Better understanding by the contractor of how to build your home and...*
- *More accurate construction estimates.*

When you purchase one of our designs, you'll receive all of the BLUEPRINT components shown here - elevations, foundation plan, floor plans, sections, and/or details. Other helpful building aids are also available to help make your dream home a reality.

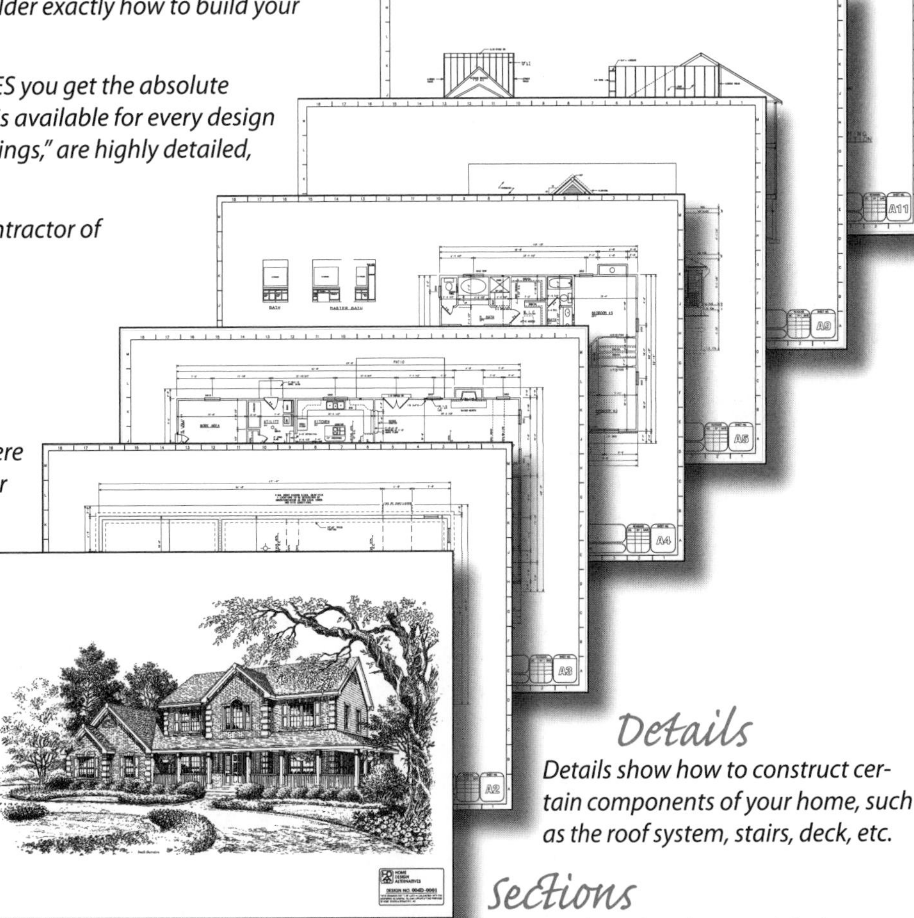

Cover Sheet

The cover sheet is the artist's rendering of the exterior of the home. It will give you an idea of how your home will look when completed and landscaped.

Interior Elevations

Interior elevations provide views of special interior elements such as fireplaces, kitchen cabinets, built-in units and other features of the home.

Foundation Plan

The foundation plan shows the layout of the basement, crawl space, slab or pier foundation. All necessary notations and dimensions are included. See plan page for the foundation types included. If the home plan you choose does not have your desired foundation type, our Customer Service Representatives can advise you on how to customize your foundation to suit your specific needs or site conditions.

Details

Details show how to construct certain components of your home, such as the roof system, stairs, deck, etc.

Sections

Sections show detail views of the home or portions of the home as if it were sliced from the roof to the foundation. This sheet shows important areas such as load-bearing walls, stairs, joists, trusses and other structural elements, which are critical for proper construction.

Floor Plans

The floor plans show the placement of walls, doors, closets, plumbing fixtures, electrical outlets, columns and beams for each level of the home.

Exterior Elevations

Exterior elevations illustrate the front, rear and both sides of the house, with all details of exterior materials and the required dimensions.

Plan #	Square Feet	Price Code	Page	Material List	Right Reading Reverse	Use Canada Shipping
582-021D-0010	1,444	A	212	•		
582-021D-0011	1,800	D	24	•		
582-021D-0012	1,672	C	237	•		
582-021D-0016	1,600	B	290	•		
582-022D-0001	1,039	AA	402	•		
582-022D-0002	1,246	A	370	•		
582-022D-0003	1,351	A	323	•		
582-022D-0004	1,359	A	241	•		
582-022D-0005	1,360	A	69	•		
582-022D-0006	1,443	A	447	•		
582-022D-0007	1,516	B	439	•		
582-022D-0008	1,565	B	306	•		
582-022D-0012	1,550	B	267	•		
582-022D-0014	1,556	B	362	•		
582-022D-0016	1,835	C	55	•		
582-022D-0017	1,448	A	421	•		
582-022D-0018	1,368	A	9	•		
582-022D-0019	1,283	A	213	•		
582-022D-0021	1,020	AA	428	•		
582-022D-0022	1,270	A	466	•		
582-022D-0023	950	AA	135	•		
582-022D-0024	1,127	AA	427	•		
582-023D-0016	1,609	B	84	•		
582-023D-0017	1,596	B	114	•		
582-023D-0018	1,556	B	155	•		
582-023D-0019	1,539	B	329	•		
582-024D-0001	1,363	A	433			
582-024D-0003	1,520	B	471			
582-024D-0004	1,500	B	31			
582-024D-0006	1,618	C	377			
582-024D-0009	1,704	B	186			
582-024D-0011	1,819	C	399			
582-024D-0038	1,743	B	406			
582-025D-0001	1,123	AA	387			
582-025D-0003	1,379	A	308			
582-025D-0005	1,429	A	43			
582-025D-0006	1,612	B	229			
582-025D-0010	1,677	B	204			
582-025D-0012	1,634	B	112			
582-025D-0013	1,686	B	19			
582-026D-0040	1,347	A	72	•		
582-026D-0096	1,341	A	137	•		
582-026D-0123	1,998	C	29	•		
582-026D-0137	1,758	B	321	•	•	
582-026D-0141	1,814	C	269	•	•	
582-026D-0154	1,392	A	49	•	•	
582-026D-0155	1,691	B	227	•		
582-026D-0161	1,375	A	376	•	•	
582-026D-0162	1,575	B	247			
582-028D-0001	864	AAA	452		•	
582-028D-0002	1,377	A	16		•	
582-028D-0003	1,716	B	202		•	
582-028D-0004	1,785	B	192		•	
582-028D-0006	1,700	B	272		•	
582-029D-0002	1,619	B	13	•		
582-030D-0001	1,374	A	110			
582-030D-0002	1,429	A	74			
582-030D-0004	1,791	B	139			
582-030D-0005	1,815	C	285			
582-030D-0006	1,896	C	318			
582-031D-0002	1,605	B	425			
582-031D-0004	1,710	B	459			
582-031D-0005	1,735	B	249			
582-031D-0009	1,960	C	153			
582-032D-0009	1,199	AA	388	•	•	•
582-032D-0011	1,103	AA	349	•	•	•
582-032D-0015	1,556	B	379	•	•	•
582-032D-0019	1,995	C	210	•	•	•
582-032D-0022	1,760	B	4	•	•	•
582-032D-0040	1,480	A	352	•	•	•
582-032D-0051	1,442	A	393	•	•	•
582-033D-0002	1,859	D	188	•		
582-033D-0005	1,954	D	78	•		
582-033D-0009	1,711	C	108	•		
582-033D-0012	1,546	C	28	•		
582-033D-0013	1,813	D	316	•		
582-034D-0002	1,456	A	255			
582-034D-0013	1,493	A	415			
582-034D-0014	1,792	B	107			
582-034D-0015	1,868	C	80			
582-034D-0016	1,873	C	259			
582-034D-0019	1,992	C	312			
582-035D-0005	1,281	A	244	•		
582-035D-0011	1,945	C	141	•		
582-035D-0021	1,978	C	301	•		
582-035D-0026	1,845	C	101	•		
582-035D-0028	1,779	B	75	•		
582-035D-0032	1,856	C	298	•		
582-035D-0038	1,862	C	261	•		
582-035D-0046	1,080	AA	283	•		
582-035D-0047	1,818	C	122	•		
582-035D-0048	1,915	C	273	•		
582-035D-0050	1,342	A	83	•		
582-035D-0051	1,491	A	98	•		
582-035D-0053	1,467	A	265	•		
582-035D-0055	1,583	B	309	•		
582-035D-0060	1,290	A	151	•		
582-036D-0045	1,577	B	85			
582-036D-0047	1,702	B	280			
582-036D-0048	1,830	C	70			
582-036D-0056	1,604	B	438			
582-036D-0060	1,760	B	121			
582-037D-0002	1,816	C	161	•		
582-037D-0006	1,772	C	246	•		
582-037D-0008	1,707	C	123	•		
582-037D-0010	1,770	B	332	•		
582-037D-0011	1,846	C	221	•		
582-037D-0012	1,661	B	115	•		
582-037D-0017	829	AAA	395	•		
582-037D-0018	717	AAA	366	•		
582-037D-0019	581	AAA	430	•		
582-037D-0020	1,994	D	171	•		
582-037D-0022	1,539	B	293	•		
582-037D-0026	1,824	C	405	•		
582-038D-0007	1,907	C	27	•		
582-038D-0009	1,893	B	174	•		
582-038D-0032	1,554	B	214	•		
582-038D-0034	1,625	B	163	•		
582-038D-0036	1,470	A	142	•		
582-038D-0039	1,771	B	42	•		
582-038D-0040	1,642	B	46	•		
582-038D-0044	1,982	C	143	•		
582-039D-0001	1,253	A	90	•		
582-039D-0002	1,333	A	125	•		
582-039D-0004	1,406	A	231	•		
582-039D-0011	1,780	B	304	•		
582-039D-0012	1,815	C	315	•		
582-039D-0015	1,855	C	270	•		
582-040D-0001	1,814	D	166	•		
582-040D-0002	1,958	D	106	•		
582-040D-0003	1,475	B	176	•		
582-040D-0006	1,759	B	252	•		
582-040D-0010	1,496	A	127	•		
582-040D-0014	1,595	B	275	•		
582-040D-0015	1,655	B	52	•		
582-040D-0024	1,874	C	310	•		
582-040D-0026	1,393	B	10	•		
582-040D-0027	1,597	C	182	•		
582-040D-0029	1,028	AA	429	•		
582-040D-0031	1,687	B	97	•		
582-040D-0032	1,808	C	325	•		
582-040D-0033	1,829	C	257	•		
582-041D-0004	1,195	AA	129	•		
582-041D-0005	1,239	A	61	•		
582-041D-0006	1,189	AA	363	•		
582-043D-0003	1,890	C	131			
582-043D-0005	1,734	B	124			
582-043D-0008	1,496	A	240			
582-043D-0009	1,751	B	276			
582-045D-0009	1,684	B	266	•		
582-045D-0010	1,558	B	423	•		
582-045D-0012	976	AA	443	•		
582-045D-0013	1,085	AA	419	•		
582-045D-0014	987	AA	451	•		
582-045D-0015	977	A	427	•		
582-045D-0016	1,107	AA	403	•		
582-045D-0017	954	AA	435	•		
582-045D-0018	858	AAA	413	•		
582-045D-0019	1,134	AA	133	•		
582-047D-0009	1,565	B	453			
582-047D-0010	1,576	B	411			
582-047D-0012	1,627	B	79			
582-047D-0015	1,679	B	432			
582-047D-0016	1,703	B	100			
582-047D-0018	1,750	B	281			
582-047D-0020	1,783	B	159			
582-047D-0021	1,787	B	468			
582-047D-0022	1,768	B	417			
582-047D-0026	1,817	C	314			
582-048D-0001	1,865	D	67	•		
582-048D-0011	1,550	B	181	•		
582-049D-0001	1,700	B	462	•		
582-049D-0004	1,997	C	73	•		
582-049D-0006	1,771	B	307	•		
582-049D-0008	1,937	C	233	•		
582-049D-0009	1,673	B	317	•		
582-049D-0010	1,669	B	87			
582-049D-0011	1,974	C	156	•		

Home Plans Index

Plan #	Square Feet	Price Code	Page	Material List	Right Reading Reverse	Use Canada Shipping
582-051D-0022	1,451	A	82			
582-051D-0037	1,536	B	135			
582-051D-0040	1,495	A	148			
582-051D-0053	1,461	A	242			
582-051D-0058	1,462	A	330			
582-051D-0060	1,591	B	228			
582-051D-0062	1,342	A	109			
582-052D-0002	1,208	A	15			
582-052D-0003	1,208	A	165			
582-052D-0007	1,273	A	54			
582-052D-0011	1,325	A	126	•		
582-052D-0012	1,365	A	417			
582-052D-0013	1,379	A	326			
582-052D-0031	1,735	B	189	•		
582-052D-0038	1,787	B	223			
582-053D-0001	1,582	B	137	•		
582-053D-0002	1,668	C	187	•		
582-053D-0003	1,992	C	209	•		
582-053D-0029	1,220	A	33	•		
582-053D-0030	1,657	B	368	•		
582-053D-0032	1,404	A	278	•		
582-053D-0035	1,527	B	324	•		
582-053D-0037	1,408	A	250	•		
582-053D-0040	1,407	A	238	•		
582-053D-0042	1,458	A	284	•		
582-053D-0043	1,732	B	157	•		
582-053D-0044	1,340	A	92	•		
582-053D-0047	1,438	A	88	•		
582-053D-0049	1,261	A	66	•		
582-053D-0053	1,609	B	95	•		
582-053D-0055	1,803	C	145	•		
582-053D-0056	1,880	C	152	•		
582-053D-0058	1,818	C	263	•		
582-055D-0026	1,538	B	203	•	•	
582-055D-0044	1,797	B	139	•	•	
582-055D-0046	1,934	C	178	•	•	
582-055D-0051	1,848	C	391	•	•	
582-055D-0063	1,397	A	341	•	•	
582-055D-0064	1,544	B	372	•	•	
582-055D-0067	1,472	A	22	•	•	
582-055D-0099	1,897	C	356	•	•	
582-055D-0100	1,294	A	219	•	•	
582-055D-0116	1,462	A	380	•	•	
582-056D-0001	1,624	E	175			
582-056D-0007	1,985	G	17			
582-056D-0008	1,821	E	217			
582-056D-0009	1,606	B	149			
582-056D-0013	1,404	E	185			
582-056D-0022	1,817	C	230			
582-056D-0023	1,277	E	193			
582-058D-0003	1,020	AA	411	•		
582-058D-0004	962	AA	408	•		
582-058D-0006	1,339	A	414	•		
582-058D-0007	1,013	AA	434	•		
582-058D-0008	1,285	A	403	•		
582-058D-0010	676	AAA	353	•		
582-058D-0011	924	AA	431	•		
582-058D-0012	1,143	AA	416	•		
582-058D-0013	1,073	AA	62	•		
582-058D-0016	1,558	B	25	•		
582-058D-0020	1,428	A	36	•		
582-058D-0021	1,477	A	258	•		
582-058D-0022	1,578	B	300	•		
582-058D-0024	1,598	B	268	•		
582-058D-0029	1,000	AA	134	•		
582-058D-0030	990	AA	147	•		
582-058D-0031	990	AA	418	•		
582-058D-0032	1,879	C	77	•		
582-058D-0033	1,440	A	113	•		
582-058D-0038	1,680	B	245	•		
582-058D-0043	1,277	A	319	•		
582-060D-0006	1,945	C	141			
582-060D-0013	1,053	AA	437			
582-060D-0014	1,021	AA	465			
582-060D-0015	1,192	AA	253			
582-060D-0016	1,214	A	299			
582-060D-0017	1,253	A	413			
582-060D-0018	1,398	A	322			
582-060D-0021	1,475	A	104			
582-060D-0022	1,436	A	91			
582-060D-0026	1,497	A	277			
582-060D-0027	1,628	B	303			
582-061D-0001	1,747	B	409	•		
582-061D-0002	1,950	C	138	•		
582-062D-0029	1,670	B	60			
582-062D-0031	1,073	AA	383	•	•	•
582-062D-0048	1,543	B	365	•		•
582-062D-0050	1,408	A	20	•	•	•
582-062D-0052	1,795	B	389	•	•	•
582-062D-0053	1,405	A	169	•		•
582-062D-0058	1,108	AA	355	•		•
582-062D-0059	1,568	B	381	•	•	•
582-065D-0010	1,508	B	143	•		
582-065D-0027	1,595	B	34			
582-065D-0034	1,509	B	153			
582-065D-0035	1,798	B	177			
582-065D-0038	1,663	B	197			
582-065D-0040	1,874	C	195			
582-067D-0002	1,627	B	103			
582-067D-0004	1,698	B	155			
582-067D-0005	1,698	B	94			
582-067D-0006	1,840	C	38			
582-068D-0003	1,784	B	119	•		
582-068D-0004	1,969	C	64	•		
582-068D-0005	1,433	A	128	•		
582-068D-0006	1,399	A	145	•		
582-068D-0010	1,849	C	239	•		
582-069D-0001	947	AA	435	•		
582-069D-0005	1,267	A	333	•		
582-069D-0006	1,277	A	18			
582-069D-0007	1,372	A	407			
582-069D-0010	1,458	A	234	•		
582-069D-0012	1,594	B	154	•		
582-069D-0017	1,926	C	56	•		
582-070D-0001	1,300	A	211			
582-070D-0002	1,700	B	147			
582-070D-0004	1,791	B	198			
582-070D-0006	1,841	C	218			
582-070D-0007	1,974	B	39			
582-076D-0001	1,352	B	149		•	
582-076D-0003	1,344	B	415		•	
582-076D-0004	1,335	B	96		•	
582-076D-0005	1,322	B	170		•	
582-076D-0006	1,277	B	311		•	
582-076D-0009	1,251	B	262			
582-076D-0010	1,236	B	279		•	
582-076D-0013	1,177	B	32			
582-076D-0014	1,163	B	289			
582-076D-0016	1,126	B	436		•	
582-076D-0017	1,123	B	400		•	
582-076D-0018	1,116	B	338		•	
582-076D-0019	1,083	B	99		•	
582-076D-0020	1,072	B	292		•	
582-076D-0021	1,053	B	295		•	
582-076D-0022	1,342	B	297		•	
582-076D-0023	1,318	B	291		•	
582-077D-0001	1,638	C	179	•		
582-077D-0002	1,855	D	199	•		
582-077D-0003	1,896	D	40			
582-078D-0001	1,695	D	58	•		
582-078D-0002	1,925	D	151	•		
582-078D-0004	1,425	D	342	•		
582-078D-0005	1,525	D	205	•		
582-078D-0008	1,450	D	48	•		
582-078D-0011	950	D	374	•		
582-078D-0012	1,575	D	173	•		
582-078D-0013	1,175	D	358	•		
582-078D-0016	1,655	D	207	•		
582-078D-0018	900	D	390	•		
582-078D-0019	1,895	D	215	•		
582-078D-0020	1,700	D	351	•		
582-078D-0022	1,465	D	344	•		
582-078D-0024	960	D	409	•		
582-078D-0025	1,015	D	371	•		
582-078D-0029	1,400	D	426	•		
582-078D-0035	1,635	D	190	•		
582-078D-0036	1,035	D	386	•		
582-078D-0040	1,905	D	130	•		

NOTE

Technical Specifications - *At the time the construction drawings were prepared, every effort was made to ensure that these plans and specifications meet nationally recognized building codes (BOCA, Southern Building Code Congress and others). Because national building codes change or vary from area to area some drawing modifications may be necessary to comply with your local codes or to accommodate specific building site conditions. We advise you to consult with your local building official for information regarding codes governing your area.*

Once you find the home plan you've been looking for, here are some suggestions on how to make your Dream Home a reality. To get started, order the type of plans that fit your particular situation.

Your Choices:

The 1-set package - *We offer a 1-set plan package so you can study your home in detail. This one set is considered a study set and is marked "not for construction." It is a copyright violation to reproduce blueprints.*

The Minimum 5-set package - *If you're ready to start the construction process, this 5-set package is the minimum number of blueprint sets you will need. It will require keeping close track of each set so they can be used by multiple subcontractors and tradespeople.*

The Standard 8-set package - *For best results in terms of cost, schedule and quality of construction, we recommend you order eight (or more) sets of blueprints. Besides one set for yourself, additional sets of blueprints will be required by your mortgage lender, local building department, general contractor and all subcontractors working on foundation, electrical, plumbing, heating/air conditioning, carpentry work, etc.*

Reproducible Masters - *If you wish to make some minor design changes, you'll want to order reproducible masters. These drawings contain the same information as the blueprints but are printed on erasable and reproducible paper which clearly indicates your right to copy or reproduce. This will allow your builder or a local design professional to make the necessary drawing changes without the major expense of redrawing the plans. This package also allows you to print copies of the modified plans as needed. The right of building only one structure from these plans is licensed exclusively to the buyer. You may not use this design to build a second or multiple dwelling(s) without purchasing another blueprint. Each violation of the Copyright Law is punishable in a fine.*

Mirror Reverse Sets - *Plans can be printed in mirror reverse. These plans are useful when the house would fit your site better if all the rooms were on the opposite side than shown. They are simply a mirror image of the original drawings causing the lettering and dimensions to read backwards. Therefore, when ordering mirror reverse drawings, you must purchase at least one set of right-reading plans. Some of our plans are offered mirror reverse right-reading. This means the plan, lettering and dimensions are flipped but read correctly. See the Home Plans Index on pages 476-478 for availability.*

Other Great Products...

BUILDING A HOME?

It sounds like lots of fun and just might be the biggest purchase you will ever make. But the process of building a home can be a tricky one. This program walks you through the process step-by-step. Compiled by consumers who have built new homes and learned the hard way. This is not a "how-to" video, but a visual checklist to open your eyes to issues you would never think about until you have lived in your home for years. *Available in VHS or DVD.*

$19.97 VHS **$26.97** DVD

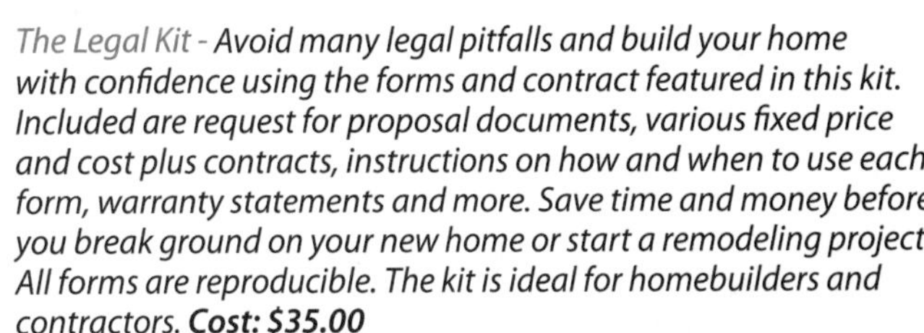

The Legal Kit - *Avoid many legal pitfalls and build your home with confidence using the forms and contract featured in this kit. Included are request for proposal documents, various fixed price and cost plus contracts, instructions on how and when to use each form, warranty statements and more. Save time and money before you break ground on your new home or start a remodeling project. All forms are reproducible. The kit is ideal for homebuilders and contractors.* ***Cost: $35.00***

Detail Plan Packages - *Three separate packages offer homebuilders details for constructing various foundations; numerous floor, wall and roof framing techniques; simple to complex residential wiring; sump and water softener hookups; plumbing connection methods; installation of septic systems, and more. Each package includes three-dimensional illustrations and a glossary of terms. Purchase one or all three. Note: These drawings do not pertain to a specific home plan.* ***Cost: $20.00 each or all three for $40.00***

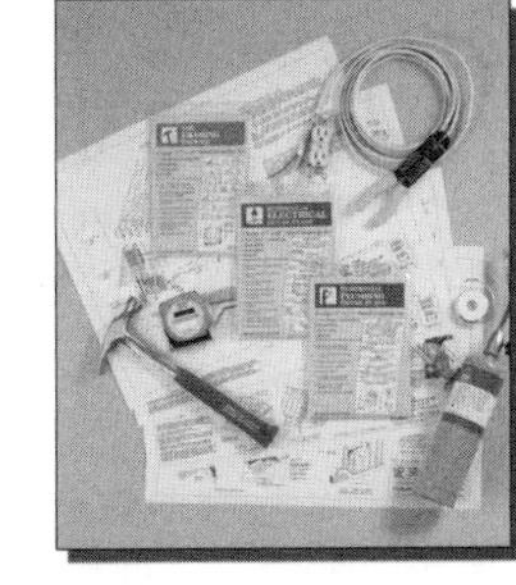

More Helpful Building Aids...

Your Blueprint Package contains the necessary construction information to build your home. We also offer the following products and services to save you time and money in the building process.

Express Delivery - *Most orders are processed within 24 hours of receipt. Please allow 7-10 business days for delivery. If you need to place a rush order, please call us by 11:00 a.m. Monday-Friday CST and ask for express service (allow 1-2 business days).*

Technical Assistance - *If you have questions, please call our technical support line at 1-314-770-2228 between 8:00 a.m. and 5:00 p.m. Monday-Friday CST. Whether it involves design modifications or field assistance, our designers are extremely familiar with all of our designs and will be happy to help you. We want your home to be everything you expect it to be.*

Material List - *Material lists are available for many of the plans in this magazine. Each list gives you the quantity, dimensions and description of the building materials necessary to construct your home. You'll get faster and more accurate bids from your contractor while saving money by paying for only the materials you need. See the Home Plans Index on pages 476-478 for availability.* ***Cost: $125***

How To Order

For fastest service, Call Toll-Free
1-800-DREAM HOME (1-800-373-2646) day or night

Three Easy Ways To Order

1. CALL toll free 1-800-373-2646 for credit card orders. MasterCard, Visa, Discover and American Express are accepted.
2. FAX your order to 1-314-770-2226.
3. MAIL the Order Form to: HDA, Inc.
   944 Anglum Road
   St. Louis, MO 63042

Order Form

Please send me -

PLAN NUMBER 582-____________

PRICE CODE______ (see index on pages 476-478)

Specify Foundation Type (see plan page for availability) ______

☐ Slab ☐ Crawl space ☐ Pier
☐ Basement ☐ Walk-out basement

☐ Reproducible Masters $ ______
☐ Eight-Set Plan Package $ ______
☐ Five-Set Plan Package $ ______
☐ One-Set Study Package (no mirror reverse) $ ______

Additional Plan Sets*
☐ ____ (Qty.) at $45.00 each $ ______

Mirror Reverse*
☐ Right-reading $150 one-time charge
(see index on pages 476-478 for availability) $ ______
☐ Print in Mirror Reverse (where right-reading is not available)
____ (Qty.) at $15.00 each $ ______

☐ Material List* $125 (see index for availability) $ ______
☐ Legal Kit (see page 479) $ ______

Detail Plan Packages: (see page 479)
☐ Framing ☐ Electrical ☐ Plumbing $ ______

Building Smart: (see page 479)
☐ VHS $19.97 #FP00001 ☐ DVD $26.97 #FP00002 $ ______

SUBTOTAL $ ______
Sales Tax (MO residents add 6%) $ ______
☐ Shipping / Handling (see chart at right) $ ______
TOTAL (US funds only - sorry no CODs) $ ______

I hereby authorize HDA, Inc. to charge this purchase to my credit card account (check one):

☐ MasterCard ☐ VISA ☐ Discover Novus ☐ American Express Cards

Credit Card number ____________

Expiration date ____________

Signature ____________

Name ____________
(Please print or type)

Street Address ____________
(Please **do not** use a PO Box)

City ____________

State ____________

Zip ____________

Daytime phone number (_____) - ________

E-mail address ____________

I'm a ☐ Builder/Contractor ☐ Homeowner ☐ Renter
I ☐ have ☐ have not selected my general contractor

Thank you for your order!

Before You Order

Exchange Policies - Since blueprints are printed in response to your order, we cannot honor requests for refunds. However, if for some reason you find that the plan you have purchased does not meet your requirements, you may exchange that plan for another plan in our collection within 90 days of purchase. At the time of the exchange, you will be charged a processing fee of 25% of your original plan package price, plus the difference in price between the plan packages (if applicable) and the cost to ship the new plans to you.

Please note: Reproducible drawings can only be exchanged if the package is unopened.

Building Codes & Requirements - At the time the construction drawings were prepared, every effort was made to ensure that these plans and specifications meet nationally recognized codes. Our plans conform to most national building codes. Because building codes vary from area to area, some drawing modifications and/or the assistance of a professional designer or architect may be necessary to comply with your local codes or to accommodate specific building site conditions. We advise you to consult with your local building official for information regarding codes governing your area.

Questions? Call Our Customer Service Number
1-314-770-2228

Blueprint Price Schedule

Price Code	1-Set	SAVE $110 5-Sets	SAVE $200 8 Sets	BEST VALUE Reproducible Masters
AAA	$225	$295	$340	$440
AA	$325	$395	$440	$540
A	$385	$455	$500	$600
B	$445	$515	$560	$660
C	$500	$570	$615	$715
D	$560	$630	$675	$775
E	$620	$690	$735	$835
F	$675	$745	$790	$890
G	$765	$835	$880	$980
H	$890	$960	$1005	$1105

Plan prices guaranteed through January 1, 2006.
Please note that plans are not refundable.

Additional Sets* - Additional sets of the plan ordered are available for an additional cost (see order form at left). Five-set, eight-set, and reproducible packages offer considerable savings.

Mirror Reverse Plans* - Available for an additional $15.00 per set, these plans are simply a mirror image of the original drawings causing the dimensions and lettering to read backwards. Therefore, when ordering mirror reverse plans, you must purchase at least one set of right-reading plans. Some of our plans are offered mirror reverse right-reading. This means the plan, lettering and dimensions are flipped but read correctly. To purchase a mirror reverse right-reading set, the cost is an additional $150.00. See the Home Plans Index on pages 476-478 for availability.

One-Set Study Package - We offer a one-set plan package so you can study your home in detail. This one set is considered a study set and is marked "not for construction." It is a copyright violation to reproduce blueprints.

**Available only within 90 days after purchase of plan package or reproducible masters of same plan.*

Shipping & Handling Charges

U.S. Shipping	1-4 Sets	5-7 Sets	8 Sets or Reproducibles
Regular (allow 7-10 business days)	$15.00	$17.50	$25.00
Priority (allow 3-5 business days)	$25.00	$30.00	$35.00
Express* (allow 1-2 business days)	$35.00	$40.00	$45.00
Canada Shipping (to/from) - Plans with suffix 032D & 062D - see index			
Standard (allow 8-12 business days)	$25.00	$30.00	$35.00
Express* (allow 3-5 business days)	$40.00	$40.00	$45.00

* For express delivery please call us by 11:00 a.m. Monday-Friday CST

Overseas Shipping/International - Call, fax, or e-mail (plans@hdainc.com) for shipping costs.